THE NUREMBERG MILITARY TRIBUNALS AND THE ORIGINS OF INTERNATIONAL CRIMINAL LAW

The Nuremberg Military Tribunals and the Origins of International Criminal Law

KEVIN JON HELLER

OXFORD
UNIVERSITY PRESS

OXFORD

UNIVERSITY PRESS

Great Clarendon Street, Oxford OX2 6DP

Oxford University Press is a department of the University of Oxford.
It furthers the University's objective of excellence in research, scholarship,
and education by publishing worldwide in

Oxford New York

Auckland Cape Town Dar es Salaam Hong Kong Karachi
Kuala Lumpur Madrid Melbourne Mexico City Nairobi
New Delhi Shanghai Taipei Toronto

With offices in

Argentina Austria Brazil Chile Czech Republic France Greece
Guatemala Hungary Italy Japan Poland Portugal Singapore
South Korea Switzerland Thailand Turkey Ukraine Vietnam

Oxford is a registered trade mark of Oxford University Press
in the UK and in certain other countries

Published in the United States
by Oxford University Press Inc., New York

British Library Cataloguing in Publication Data

Data available

Library of Congress Cataloging in Publication Data

Data available

Typeset by SPI Publisher Services, Pondicherry, India
Printed in Great Britain
on acid-free paper by
CPI Antony Rowe, Chippenham, Wiltshire

ISBN 978–0–19–955431–7

1 3 5 7 9 10 8 6 4 2

To my father,
For bringing me into the world

To Stuart,
For teaching me how to live in it

To my mother,
For everything

Acknowledgments

Writing a book is a solitary endeavor, so I am profoundly grateful to the many people who have relieved the isolation over the past three years. At the University of Georgia, where the project began, I want to thank Dan Bodansky, Peter Spiro, Paul Heald, and Jessica Lawrence—especially Jess, for so many reasons. I also want to thank the law school for funding my initial research into the tribunals.

At the University of Auckland, thanks are due to Scott Optican, Paul Rishworth, the late Mike Taggart, An Hertogen, and John Ip. My many conversations with John about the project were particularly invaluable; he has earned his free copy of the book. I also want to thank the two Auckland students who provided me with such valuable research assistance, Zyanya Hill and Zöe Hamill. And, of course, I need to thank Golriz Ghahraman, who has been my finest student and one of my dearest friends for the past four years.

At the University of Melbourne, my gratitude goes to Gerry Simpson, Adrienne Stone, Anne Orford, Tim McCormack, Sarah Finnin, and Carrie McDougall, friends and brilliant colleagues all. And I owe an immense debt to Edwina Myer, Jordina Rust, and Robyn Curnow for their research assistance. Important parts of the book would not exist without them.

I also want to thank the countless other scholars who have so generously given me their time during this project, from discussing ideas to reading draft chapters. They include—and I apologize for any omissions—Donald Bloxham, Rob Cryer, Roger Clark, Marko Milanovic, John Q. Barrett, Steve Vladeck, Claus Kress, Dave Glazier, David Luban, Bill Schabas, Jens Ohlin, Mark Osiel, Gideon Boas, Kai Ambos, Carsten Stahn, Diane Amann, Frederic Megret, Alex Zahar, Dapo Akande, Greg Gordon, Chris Jenks, Edwin Bikundo, John Dehn, and Michael Salter. And, of course, thanks go to all of my colleagues at *Opinio Juris*, who have both supported me and kindly indulged my self-promotory blogging.

I would be remiss if I did not extend my appreciation to the wonderful librarians in the law library at Columbia University, who helped me navigate Telford Taylor's papers, and to the librarians at the National Archives in Baltimore. Jonathan Bush was also kind enough to share with me his knowledge of the archives in both locations.

In terms of producing the book, I want to thank Merel Alstein, OUP's anonymous reviewers, and the Estate of Ben Shahn for allowing me to use "The Red Stairway" on the cover.

Finally, I need to single out three individuals for my most heartfelt appreciation. The first is John Louth, who gave a young, untested scholar the opportunity to write a book for the world's leading academic press and then supported him in so many different ways during the writing process. I am forever in your debt, John; all scholars should be fortunate enough to have an editor like you. The second is Mark

Drumbl, who has been my mentor and my friend since my first year in academia. He is a remarkable scholar and an even more remarkable person. Thank you, Mark, for your boundless generosity. The third, first by being last, is Bianca Dillon, who has been my friend, my constant companion, and my strongest supporter for the past two years. My debt to you, Bianca, is incalculable; without you, this book could quite literally not have been written.

Contents

List of Abbreviations

CCS	Combined Chiefs of Staff
EDC	European Defense Community
FIAT	Field Information Agencies Technical
IMT	International Military Tribunal
JCE	joint criminal enterprise
JCS	Joint Chiefs of Staff
NMT	Nuremberg Military Tribunals
OCC	Office, Chief of Counsel of War Crimes
OCCPAC	Office of the United States Chief of Counsel for Prosecution of Axis Criminality
OMGUS	Office of Military Government, United States
OSS	Office of Strategic Services
POW	prisoner of war
SHAEF	Supreme Headquarters Allied Expeditionary Force
SPD	Subsequent Proceedings Division
TCP	taking a consenting part
UNWCC	United Nations War Crimes Commission
URP	Uniform Rules of Procedure
USFET	United States Forces European Theater
WJC	World Jewish Congress

Bibliographic Abbreviations

Telford Taylor Papers, Columbia Law School: TTP – Series# – Subseries# – Box# – Folders#

The National Archives at College Park: NA – Record Group# – Box# – Folders# – Document#

Table of Cases

Table of Instruments

Introduction

On 9 December 1946, 23 defendants sat in the main courtroom of Nuremberg's Palace of Justice. Most were doctors, such as Karl Brandt, Hitler's personal physician, and Waldemar Hoven, the chief doctor at Buchenwald. Some had been high-ranking Nazi officials, like Viktor Brack, the Chief Administrative Officer in the Reich Chancellery. All stood accused of horrific crimes, as Brigadier General Telford Taylor, the chief prosecutor, explained to the three-judge bench:

The defendants in this case are charged with murders, tortures, and other atrocities committed in the name of medical science. The victims of these crimes are numbered in the hundreds of thousands. A handful only are still alive; a few of the survivors will appear in this courtroom. But most of these miserable victims were slaughtered outright or died in the course of the tortures to which they were subjected.

. . .

The charges against these defendants are brought in the name of the United States of America. They are being tried by a court of American judges. The responsibilities thus imposed upon the representatives of the United States, prosecutors and judges alike, are grave and unusual. They are owed not only to the victims, and to the parents and children of the victims, that just punishment be imposed on the guilty, and not only to the defendants, that they be accorded a fair hearing and decision. Such responsibilities are the ordinary burden of any tribunal. Far wider are the duties which we must fulfill here.

These larger obligations run to the peoples and races on whom the scourge of these crimes was laid. The mere punishment of the defendants, or even of thousands of others equally guilty, can never redress the terrible injuries which the Nazis visited on these unfortunate peoples. For them it is far more important that these incredible events be established by clear and public proof, so that no one can ever doubt that they were fact and not fable, and that this Court, as the agent of the United States and as the voice of humanity, stamp these acts, and the ideas which engendered them, as barbarous and criminal.[1]

Thus began the *Medical* case, the first of 12 trials held by the United States in the Palace of Justice, many in the same courtroom that had witnessed the IMT trial. Over the next 28 months, the Nuremberg Military Tribunals[2] (NMTs) tried 177

---

[1] *Medical*, Prosecution Opening Argument, I *Trials of War Criminals Before the Nuernberg Military Tribunals Under Control Council Law No. 10*, 27 (1949) (hereinafter "TWC").

[2] Although the trials are often referred to as the "Subsequent Proceedings," the "American Military Tribunals," or the "United States Military Tribunals," I have chosen to refer to them as the "Nuremberg Military Tribunals," because that is the name used both by Telford Taylor, and by the Green Set, the 15-volume official record of the trial. See Telford Taylor, *Final Report to the Secretary of the Army on*

defendants representing "all the important segments of the Third Reich"[3]: Nazi judges and prosecutors; SS officers; military leaders; German industrialists and financiers; members of mobile killing squads; Nazi ministers and diplomats. 142 of those defendants were convicted; 25 were sentenced to death; dozens of others were sentenced to life imprisonment or lengthy prison terms. Very few who escaped the gallows, however, ever served even a fraction of their sentences. The last NMT defendant walked out of Germany's Landsberg Prison a free man in 1958.

* * *

In his final report on the NMT trials, submitted to the Secretary of the Army in August 1949, Telford Taylor predicted that "there will be no lack of books and articles in the years to come" about "the actual outcome of the trials, the legal reasoning of the judgments, the historical revelations of the documents and testimony, [and] the immediate and long-term significance of the trials in world affairs."[4] Six decades later, it is clear that Taylor was a better prosecutor than prognosticator. Very few books and articles on the trials exist—and the vast majority of those were written by the judges,[5] prosecutors,[6] and defense attorneys[7] who participated in them. The scholarly literature, in turn, has focused almost without exception[8] on individual trials[9] and specific legal issues.[10] Indeed, only two general studies of the trials have ever been written: Telford Taylor's *Nuremberg Trials: War Crimes and International Law*, published by the Carnegie Endowment for International Peace in 1949; and August von Knieriem's *The Nuremberg Trials*, published in 1959.[11] Neither book is scholarly, and both are anything but comprehensive. Taylor's short book simply provides a basic history of the tribunals, summarizes the trials, and comments on a few of what he saw as the trials' most important legal issues. Von Knieriem's much longer study is a sustained attack on the fairness of the trials—which is not surprising, given that he was I.G. Farben's chief lawyer and had been prosecuted (unsuccessfully) in *Farben*.

The lack of academic interest in the trials is difficult to explain. Scholars have produced literally dozens of books and hundreds of articles about the IMT trial, yet

---

the Nuernberg War Crimes Trials Under Control Council Law No. 10, 36 (1949); I TWC 4. I have, however, changed their spelling from the old-fashioned "Nuernberg" to the more modern "Nuremberg."

[3] Memo from Taylor to Jackson, 30 Oct. 1946, NA-153-1018-8-84-1, at 1.

[4] Taylor, *Final Report*, vii.

[5] See, e.g., Paul M. Hebert, "The Nurnberg Subsequent Trials," 16 *Ins. Counsel J.* 226 (1949).

[6] See, e.g., Josiah DuBois, *The Devil's Chemists: 24 Conspirators of the International Farben Cartel Who Manufacture Wars* (1952).

[7] See, e.g., Otto Kranzbuehler, "Nuremberg Eighteen Years Afterwards," 14 *Depaul L. Rev.* 333 (1964–65).

[8] Matthew Lippman's historical work is the primary exception. See, e.g., Matthew Lippman, "The Other Nuremberg: American Prosecutions of Nazi War Criminals in Occupied Germany," 3 *Ind. Int'l & Comp. L. Rev.* 1 (1992).

[9] See, e.g., Hilary Earl, *The Nuremberg SS-Einsatzgruppen Trial, 1945–1958* (2010).

[10] See, e.g., Allison M. Danner, "The Nuremberg Industrialist Prosecutions and Aggressive War," 46 *Va. J. Int'l L.* 651 (2006).

[11] August von Knieriem, *The Nuremberg Trials* (1959).

a strong case can be made that the NMT trials are of far greater jurisprudential importance than their more famous predecessor. The IMT is justly celebrated for establishing that "[c]rimes against international law are committed by men, not by abstract entities, and only by punishing individuals who commit such crimes can the provisions of international law be enforced."[12] The tribunal also gave birth— perhaps through immaculate conception[13]—to crimes against peace, crimes against humanity, and the crime of criminal membership. But there is remarkably little criminal law in the IMT judgment: nothing on evidence and procedure; almost nothing on modes of participation, defenses, or sentencing. Even the discussion of the crimes themselves is relatively cursory and unsystematic.

The NMTs, by contrast, addressed all of those areas in detail. In some cases, their approach to international criminal law was misguided; particularly striking examples include the *Einsatzgruppen* tribunal's conclusion that international law permitted the morale bombings of civilians, even with atomic weapons, and the *Hostage* tribunal's holding that, under certain conditions, it was permissible to execute innocent civilians in reprisal. More often, though, the tribunals' jurisprudence was very progressive: requiring witnesses to be informed of their right not to incriminate themselves (*Medical*) and refusing to convict defendants solely on the basis of hearsay (*Ministries*); extending crimes against peace to include both aggressive wars and bloodless invasions (*Ministries*); insisting on the strict separation of the *jus ad bellum* and the *jus in bello* (*Hostage*); concluding that international law prohibited peacetime crimes against humanity that were not connected to aggressive war (*Einsatzgruppen*) and convicting defendants of genocide (*Justice*); adopting a finely-grained version of enterprise liability that distinguished between creators and executors (*Pohl*); and insisting that international humanitarian law limits military necessity "even if it results in the loss of a battle or even a war" (*Hostage*).

The NMTs are also of great historical interest. Robert Kempner, one of Telford Taylor's chief deputies, referred to the trials as "the greatest history seminar ever held,"[14] a description that applies equally to the courtroom proceedings and to the judgments. The tribunals generated a massive documentary record of Nazi criminality, one that dwarfs the IMT's: the transcripts of the twelve trials run 132,855 legal-size pages and include the testimony of more than 1,300 witnesses and the contents of more than 30,000 separate documents.[15] The twelve judgments, in turn—which total 3,828 pages—reflect the factual density of the trials, describing at great length everything from Hitler's transformation of the German courts into a "nationally organized system of injustice and persecution" (*Justice*) to the role that German industrialists played in financing Hitler's rise to power and equipping the

---

[12] *Judgment of the International Military Tribunal for the Trial of German War Criminals* 41 (1946).

[13] See, e.g., F.B. Schick, "The Nuremberg Trial and the International Law of the Future," 41 *Am. J. Int'l L.* 770 (1947).

[14] Quoted in Lawrence Douglas, "History and Memory in the Courtroom: Reflections on Perpetrator Trials," in *The Nuremberg Trials: International Criminal Law Since 1945*, 95 (Herbert R. Reginbogin & Cristoph J. Safferling eds., 2006).

[15] OCCWC, Statistics of the Nurnberg Trials, 15 Mar. 1949, TTP-5-1-1-25, at 4–6.

Nazi war machine (*Flick, Farben, Krupp*) to how the Reich planned its various invasions and wars of aggression (*Ministries*).

The NMT trials are particularly important, however, because they foregrounded the Holocaust in a way that the IMT did not. As Lawrence Douglas has noted, although the IMT "has been hailed in many tributes as a path-breaking proceeding about the Holocaust," crimes against Jews actually "played a largely ancillary role in the trial."[16] Indeed, Justice Jackson rejected a joint request by the World Jewish Congress and the American Jewish Congress to focus at least one count in the indictment specifically on the Holocaust,[17] because he was more interested in using the trial to establish the criminality of aggressive war[18] and was concerned that emphasizing the Holocaust would lead "other victimized groups [to] demand comparable status."[19] Because of Jackson's aggression-centered approach to the IMT trial, the tribunal's judgment devotes a mere 12 paragraphs to the Nazis' systematic murder of the Jews.

The NMT trials could not have been more different. "For students of the Holocaust, these cases, perhaps more than the first Nuremberg trial, the Auschwitz cases in Poland and West Germany, or even Eichmann, represent an attempt at full judicial scrutiny of Nazi genocide."[20] The prosecution actively sought that scrutiny: although Telford Taylor rejected including a "Jewish case" in the NMT trials,[21] he emphasized the extermination and persecution of Jews in nearly all of his opening arguments and included such crimes in all 12 indictments. His office also made a deliberate decision—supported by the Departments of State and War—to attempt to establish genocide as a crime against humanity, even though it was not mentioned in Control Council Law No. 10, the tribunals' enabling statute.[22] As a result of these efforts, the judgments are replete with detailed narratives of various aspects of the Holocaust: the creation and administration of the concentration camps in *Pohl*; the construction of Auschwitz III-Monowitz in *Farben*; the "resettlement" of Jews in occupied territory and the systematic theft of their property in *RuSHA*; the extermination of Jews in the Soviet Union in *Einsatzgruppen*; the use of Jewish slave labor by German industry in *Krupp*; the implementation of the Nuremberg Laws in *Ministries*.

* * *

There is, in short, a significant need for a comprehensive jurisprudential and historical analysis of the NMT trials. This book attempts to provide that analysis. First, in terms of jurisprudence, it seeks to explain how the tribunals as a whole

---

[16] Douglas, *History and Memory*, in *Nuremberg Trials*, 96.

[17] Robert Wolfe, "Flaws in the Nuremberg Legacy," 12 *Holocaust & Genocide Studies* 434, 440 (1998).

[18] John Hagan, *Justice in the Balkans* 25 (2003).

[19] Wolfe, 440.

[20] Jonathan A. Bush, "Soldiers Find Wars: A Life of Telford Taylor," 37 *Colum. J. Transnat'l L.* 675, 681–2 (1999).

[21] See Chapter 3.

[22] Genocide is discussed in Chapter 10.

dealt with specific legal issues. Agreement was far more common than disagreement, and the tribunals routinely cited the conclusions of their predecessors in support of their own. But it is important to recognize that the tribunals did not speak with one voice, because a number of modern courts and tribunals have cited minority positions as if they were representative of the "NMT" as a whole. In *Presbyterian Church of Sudan v. Talisman Energy*, for example, the U.S. Court of Appeals for the Second Circuit relied solely on the *Ministries* tribunal's acquittal of Karl Rasche, the head of the Dresdner Bank, for the proposition that "international law at the time of the Nuremberg trials recognized aiding and abetting liability only for purposeful conduct."[23] In fact, Rasche was the *only* defendant in any of the trials held to a purposive standard: not only did every other tribunal apply a knowledge standard for aiding and abetting, the *Ministries* tribunal *itself* applied a knowledge standard to other defendants.[24] Regardless, the purposive standard is now the Second Circuit's official position, sounding what one scholar has described as the "death knell for most corporate liability claims under the Alien Tort Statute."[25] If this study had existed a few years ago, the court might have reached a very different conclusion.

The second goal of the book is to place the trials in their historical context. While the trials were being planned, Churchill gave his "Iron Curtain" speech, the United States conducted atomic tests Able and Baker, and the French landed in Indochina. The trials themselves witnessed Truman's announcement of his famous doctrine, Czechoslovakia's fall to the Soviets, and the beginning of the Berlin Blockade. And after the trials were over, the fate of the convicted defendants was determined alongside the emergence of the Soviet Union as the world's second atomic power, the rise of McCarthyism, the beginning of the Korean War, and the formation of the Warsaw Pact.

The history of the trials, in short, is the (early) history of the Cold War. Cold War pressures affected every aspect of the trials, from the initial decision to hold zonal trials instead of a second IMT to the release of the last convicted defendant in 1958. Sometimes those pressures were indirect, coloring the ways in which the judges viewed the trials. The presiding judge in *High Command*, for example, admitted to his sons that his hatred of the Soviets and fear of a Soviet invasion of Nuremberg were so profound that the defendants' crimes no longer seemed "so bad" to him. More often, though, the pressures were all too direct, such as when Republicans claimed on the floor of the House of Representatives that Taylor's staff was overrun by communists, or when the director of the War Department's War Crimes Division told the lead prosecutor in *Farben* that the Department was concerned that a successful prosecution of German industrialists for aggression might undermine the willingness of American industrialists to support U.S. foreign policy. It is

---

[23] 582 F.3d 244, 259 (2nd Cir. 2009).

[24] See the discussion in Chapter 12.

[25] Roger Alford, "Second Circuit Adopts Purpose Test for ATS Corporate Liability," *Opinio Juris*, 2 Oct. 2009, <http://opiniojuris.org/2009/10/02/second-circuit-adopts-purpose-test-for-ats-corporate-liability/> (accessed 12 January 2011).

impossible, of course, to draw a straight line between the Cold War and specific decisions by the tribunals and by American war-crimes officials. But there is little question that, in the absence of such indirect and direct pressures, the defendants would have been convicted of additional crimes and would have served far longer sentences. As Fritz ter Meer, one of the defendants convicted in *Farben*, noted to reporters when he was released for "good conduct" in 1950, two years into his seven-year sentence: "Now they have Korea on their hands, the Americans are a lot more friendly."[26]

* * *

The book is divided into five sections. The first focuses on the origins of the NMT trials. Chapter 1 explores the Allied decision to forego a second IMT in favor of zonal trials, Telford Taylor's appointment as the chief prosecutor of those trials, and the logistical problems that initially limited the ability of Taylor's office—first called the Subsequent Proceedings Division (SPD), later re-named the Office, Chief of Counsel for War Crimes (OCC)—to create a comprehensive trial program. Chapter 2 examines the structure of the OCC and discusses the operation of the tribunals themselves: where they sat, how individual tribunals were formed, and the role of their administrative wing, the Central Secretariat. Chapter 3 explains how the OCC selected defendants for prosecution and traces the evolution of the OCC's trial program, which Taylor originally expected to consist of at least 36 trials. Finally, Chapter 4, which serves as a reference for the rest of book, provides a synopsis of each of the 12 trials that were actually held—the counts in the indictment, biographical information about the judges, the verdicts and sentences, and noteworthy aspects of each trial.

The second section of the book turns to the law and rules governing the tribunals. Chapter 5 explores four difficult questions concerning the legal character and jurisdiction of the NMTs: whether they were international tribunals, domestic courts, or something else; whether they applied international law or domestic law; whether they had personal jurisdiction over the German defendants; and whether the law they applied violated the principle of non-retroactivity. Chapter 6 focuses on the rules of evidence applied by the NMTs, particularly the rules permitting the use of hearsay. Chapter 7 then discusses the tribunals' procedural regime, asking whether the rules adequately protected the defendants' right to a fair trial and ensured equality of arms between the prosecution and defense.

The three chapters in the third section of the book examine the "special part" of Law No. 10: crimes against peace, war crimes, and crimes against humanity, respectively. Chapter 8 focuses on the tribunals' criminalization of invasions, their insistence that only leaders could commit a crime against peace, and their careful delineation of the *actus reus* and *mens rea* of the crime. Chapter 9 catalogs the war crimes recognized by the tribunals—against POWs, against civilians, against property—and explains their approach to controversial issues such as the

---

[26] Diarmuid Jeffreys, *Hell's Cartel: IG Farben and the Making of Hitler's War Machine* 347 (2008).

definition of "occupation," whether partisans could qualify as lawful combatants, and whether unlawful combatants could be summarily executed. Chapter 10 discusses how the tribunals distinguished crimes against humanity from war crimes and explores the divide among the tribunals over the criminality of peacetime atrocities and persecutions that were not committed in connection with crimes against peace.

Section four of the book then turns to the "general part" of criminal law. Chapter 11 explains how the tribunals defined the various modes of participation in Law No. 10, such as ordering, command responsibility, and taking a "consenting part" in a crime—a mode of participation unique to the trials. It also refutes the common claim that the trials serve as precedent for holding corporations criminally responsible for international crimes. Chapter 12 explores the tribunals' rich jurisprudence concerning enterprise liability, comparing and contrasting that mode of participation with the substantive crimes of conspiracy and criminal membership. And Chapter 13 discusses the various defenses recognized by the tribunals, with particular emphasis on their treatment of superior orders, duress/necessity, mistake, and military necessity.

Section five, which bookends the first section, focuses on the fate of the convicted defendants and the long-term impact of the NMTs. Chapter 14 discusses the sentences imposed by the tribunals, asking whether they were consistent within and between cases. Chapter 15 then recounts the collapse of the American war-crimes program after the NMTs shut down, showing how Cold War pressures—particularly the perceived need to rearm Germany as part of the struggle against communism—ultimately led the overwhelming majority of the convicted defendants to be released long before their sentences expired. Finally, Chapter 16 explores the significant influence, both positive and negative, that the NMT judgments have had on international criminal law.

1

From the IMT to the Zonal Trials

Introduction

On 1 November 1943, Britain, the United States, and the Soviet Union published the "Declaration on German Atrocities in Occupied Europe"—the Moscow Declaration—to "give full warning" to the Nazis that, when the war ended, the Allies intended to "pursue them to the uttermost ends of the earth . . . in order that justice may be done." The final paragraph of the Moscow Declaration provided that "[t]he above declaration is without prejudice to the case of the major criminals whose offences have no particular geographical location and who will be punished by a joint decision of the Governments of the Allies." That reservation ultimately led the Allies to create the IMT and to authorize the United States to hold the NMT trials.[1]

This chapter explains the Allied decision to forego a second IMT trial in favor of zonal trials. Section I discusses the approval of JCS 1023/10, the directive issued by the Joint Chiefs of Staff in July 1945 that first authorized the U.S. military to conduct trials in the American zone of occupation. Section II addresses the Allied Control Council's enactment of Control Council Law No. 10, the U.S. decision to create the NMTs, and Telford Taylor's appointment as the head of the Subsequent Proceedings Division, the forerunner of the OCC. Section III examines the early logistical issues that limited the SPD's ability to create a comprehensive prosecutorial program, the most important of which was the prospect of a second IMT trial.

I. JCS 1023/10

As Valerie Hébert has shown, U.S. war-crimes policy proceeded on two separate but oft-intersecting tracks in the wake of the Moscow Declaration. The first, led by the War Department, involved planning for the IMT. The second, led by the Joint Chiefs of Staff and culminating in JCS 1023/10 and Control Council Law No. 10, involved determining what to do with lower-ranking Nazi war criminals who would not be tried internationally.[2]

---

[1] Taylor, *Final Report*, 7.
[2] Valerie Hébert, *Hitler's Generals on Trial* 25 (2010).

Initially, the first track overshadowed the second. The U.S. Army did not begin drafting the directive that would ultimately become JCS 1023/10 until August 1944, nine months after the Moscow Declaration was issued. The third version of that directive—JCS 1023/3—was approved by the Joint Chiefs of Staff on 1 October 1944 and forwarded to the Combined Chiefs of Staff a few weeks later. The Combined Chiefs never acted on JCS 1023/3, however, because the U.S. government soon became preoccupied with the fate of the highest-ranking Nazi war criminals.[3]

Those contentious negotiations ultimately culminated in the Yalta Memorandum, sent to President Roosevelt on 22 January 1945 by the Attorney General and the Secretaries of War and State. The Yalta Memorandum recommended a dual war-crimes program in which the "prime" Nazi leaders would be tried before an international tribunal (as opposed to being summarily executed), while less important Nazis would be tried "in occupation courts; or in the national courts of the country concerned or in their own military courts; or, if desired, by international military courts."[4]

The war-crimes program contemplated by JCS 1023/3 differed "in several important respects" from the recommendations of the Yalta Memorandum. The Joint Chiefs of Staff thus advised the Combined Chiefs of Staff in April 1945 not to approve the directive.[5] No further progress on the directive would be made for the next three months.

On 26 April 1945, President Truman—who had succeeded to the presidency two weeks earlier, following Roosevelt's death—approved JCS 1067/6, the basic directive regarding military government in Germany. Paragraph 8 of the directive, entitled "Suspected War Criminals and Security Arrests," authorized the apprehension and detention of a vast number of war criminals, from Adolf Hitler to all of the members of the Gestapo, the SD, and the SS. A week later, President Truman appointed Justice Jackson as Chief of Counsel for the Prosecution of Axis Criminality.[6]

Germany surrendered unconditionally to the Allies on May 8, and less than a month later Justice Jackson submitted an interim report to President Truman in which he sketched the general outlines of the U.S. war-crimes program.[7] The report began by noting that his authority as Chief of Counsel extended—pursuant to the Moscow Declaration—only to those "major criminals whose offenses have no particular geographical localization." That limitation, according to Jackson, excluded offences against American military personnel, which would be tried by the U.S. military; "localized offenses or atrocities against persons or property," which would be prosecuted by national authorities; and treason, which would also be prosecuted nationally.[8]

---

[3] Taylor, *Final Report*, 3.
[4] Memo to President Roosevelt from the Secretaries of State and War and the Attorney General, 22 Jan. 1945, sec. VI.
[5] Taylor, *Final Report*, 3.
[6] Executive Order No. 9547, 2 May 1945.
[7] Report to the President by Mr. Justice Jackson, 6 June 1945 ("Jackson Interim Report").
[8] Ibid., sec. I.

Jackson then turned to how he proposed to deal with the major war criminals, the most controversial section of his report.[9] He believed that the IMT—which was still being negotiated by the Allies—should have jurisdiction over three categories of crimes: "atrocities and offences against persons or property constituting violations of…the laws, rules, and customs of land and naval warfare," such as mistreating prisoners of war; "atrocities and offences, including atrocities and persecutions on racial or religious grounds, committed since 1933"; and "[i]nvasions of other countries and initiation of wars of aggression in violation of International Law or treaties." Individuals would be criminally responsible if they were involved "in the formulation or execution of a criminal plan involving multiple crimes," if they "incited, ordered, procured, or counselled the commission" of such crimes, or if they took what the Moscow Declaration had described as "a consenting part" therein. Head-of-state immunity would not be recognized, but the tribunal would have the discretion to decide whether to recognize the defense of superior orders.[10]

Criminal liability, however, would not be limited to individuals. Jackson also intended to prove the "criminal character of several voluntary organizations which have played a cruel and controlling part in subjugating first the German people and then their neighbors," such as the SS and the Gestapo. If the IMT deemed an organization criminal, members of that organization other than those tried by the tribunal would then be prosecuted "before regular military tribunals"—an early indication of Jackson's preference for zonal instead of international trials. The criminal nature of the convicted organization would be binding during such subsequent proceedings; the individual member would be limited to pleading "personal defenses or extenuating circumstances, such as that he joined under duress," and would bear the burden of proof for those defenses and circumstances.[11]

Jackson's interim report accelerated the war-crimes program. On 19 June 1945, the Combined Chiefs of Staff (CCS) lifted previous restrictions—imposed at the end of 1944—that limited military trials to offenses involving "the security or the successful carrying out of the military operations or occupation."[12] According to the new regulations, theater commanders were empowered to try suspected war criminals other than those "who held high political, civil or military positions," whose prosecution was to be deferred until the CCS decided whether they were to be tried by an international tribunal.[13] The Theater Judge Advocate in Germany quickly began to prepare the military tribunals that would prosecute the atrocities committed in various concentration camps later in 1945.[14]

Jackson's report also encouraged the Joint Chiefs of Staff to renew work on JCS 1023, the general war-crimes directive, and on July 15 they approved a new draft, JCS 1023/10, entitled "Directive on the Identification and Apprehension of

---

[9] See Taylor, *Final Report*, 131 (Appendix B).   [10] Jackson Interim Report, sec. III(5).
[11] Ibid., sec. III(3).   [12] Quoted in Taylor, *Final Report*, 3 n. 15.
[13] Ibid., 3.   [14] See, e.g., Hébert, *Hitler's Generals*, 26.

Persons Suspected of War Crimes or Other Offenses and Trial of Certain Offenders." JCS 1023/10 closely tracked Jackson's report, instructing the commander-in-chief of the U.S. occupation forces, General Eisenhower, to detain all persons suspected of committing one of the crimes mentioned in the report: war crimes, crimes against peace, and crimes against humanity.[15] The directive then divided those suspects into two categories: "[p]ersons who have held high political, civil or military position in Germany or in one of its allies, co-belligerents, or satellites," who were to be detained until the Control Council decided whether to try them before an international tribunal; and less-important suspects, who were to be either delivered to one of the United Nations for trial[16] or tried by the United States in "appropriate military courts."[17] Finally, the directive instructed General Eisenhower to "urge" the other occupying powers to adopt the same policies.[18]

II. Law No. 10 and the Subsequent Proceedings Division

In September 1945, General Eisenhower appointed Brigadier General Edward C. Betts, the Theater Judge Advocate, to oversee the "effective application" of JCS 1023/10.[19] Betts responded by instructing the head of the American Legal Division of the Allied Control Council, Charles H. Fahy—Roosevelt's Solicitor General during the war—to draft a law that would permit the Allies to prosecute suspected war criminals in zonal trials.[20] Jackson strongly believed that zonal trials were a better option than subsequent quadripartite trials, particularly in light of the tensions that had already begun to emerge between the Americans and Soviets involved in IMT preparations. The London Charter was also set to expire in August 1946, making a law sanctioning the prosecution of major war criminals other than those prosecuted by the IMT a practical necessity.[21]

Fahy's team proved more than equal to the task. On November 1, after weeks of intensive work, the Control Council's Coordinating Committee approved a draft of Law No. 10.[22] A slightly revised version of Law No. 10 was then enacted by the Control Council itself on 20 December 1945.[23]

In the interim, Betts turned his attention to the massive logistical problems created by JCS 1023/10. The directive had resulted in the detention of nearly 100,000 Germans,[24] only a fraction of whom would be prosecuted by the IMT and in the concentration-camp trials. On October 19, Betts suggested to Justice Jackson that his organization, the Office of the United States Chief of Counsel for Prosecution of Axis Criminality (OCCPAC), take responsibility for organizing the post-IMT trials

---

[15] JCS 1023/10, para. 5(a), reprinted in Taylor, *Final Report*, 245 (Appendix C).
[16] Ibid., para. 6.
[17] Ibid., para. 7.
[18] Ibid., para. 1.
[19] Taylor, *Final Report*, 5.
[20] Ibid., 6.
[21] Memo from Jackson to OCCPAC, 7 Feb. 1946, TTP-20-1-3-34.
[22] Taylor, *Final Report*, 6.   [23] Ibid.   [24] Earl, 26.

that would be held in the American zone. He also expressed his hope that Justice Jackson would continue as Chief of Counsel, although he acknowledged the possibility that Jackson would appoint one of his subordinates at OCCPAC instead.[25]

As Betts suspected, Jackson had no intention of remaining in Nuremberg after the IMT trial concluded. He wanted to return to Washington as soon as possible to resume his position on the Supreme Court, and he admitted that the prospect of dealing with the nearly 100,000 Germans in U.S. custody "frightened" him.[26] Nevertheless, because Jackson recognized that it "would discredit the whole effort" if the United States did not prosecute the other war criminals in its custody, he encouraged Betts to pursue zonal trials and promised to help plan them while he was still in Nuremberg. He warned the General, however, that OCCPAC would need considerable staff and funding if it was to fulfill JCE 1023/10's mandate.[27]

Over the next six weeks, as the IMT trial got underway, Betts continued to discuss the logistics of implementing JCS 1023/10 with a number of U.S. officials, including Jackson and Telford Taylor. All agreed that, given the large number of potential defendants, preparations for zonal trials could not wait until the IMT trial was concluded.[28] Finally, on December 3, Betts' group issued the following written recommendations:

(a) The Theater Judge Advocate would continue to be responsible for the trial of cases involving war crimes against United States nationals and atrocities committed in concentration camps overrun by United States troops;

(b) Mr. Justice Jackson's Nuernberg organization, the Office, Chief of Counsel for the Prosecution of Axis Criminality, would constitute the "parent organization" in preparing for trials under Law No. 10;

(c) Mr. Justice Jackson would proceed to appoint a Deputy Chief of Counsel to "organize and plan" for such trials.[29]

While President Truman considered the recommendations—he would ultimately approve them on 16 January 1946[30]—Betts, Fahy, and Jackson focused on finding Jackson's successor. They first approached Frank Shea, an IMT prosecutor who was overseeing the economic aspects of the case—slave labor, plunder, preparations for aggressive war—to see if he was interested. After some initial reluctance, Shea said he would accept the position if he received a presidential appointment, passage to Nuremberg for his wife, and guaranteed support from the Army. He quickly backtracked, however, when Jackson told him that taking over the subsequent proceedings would likely limit his ability to participate in the IMT trial.[31] Shea then suggested to Betts and Fahy that they should approach General William "Wild

[25] Letter from Betts to Jackson, 19 Oct. 1945, cited in Hébert, *Hitler's Generals*, 231.
[26] Draft of letter from Jackson to Betts, 24 Oct. 1945, cited in ibid.
[27] Ibid.
[28] Earl, 30.
[29] Taylor, *Final Report*, 10.
[30] Executive Order 9679, 16 Jan. 1946, reprinted in ibid. at 267 (Appendix G).
[31] Telford Taylor, *The Anatomy of the Nuremberg Trials: A Personal Memoir* 273 (1992).

Bill" Donovan—the legendary head of the Office of Strategic Services (OSS), who was also serving as one of Jackson's deputies—instead.[32]

When contacted by Betts on October 22, General Donovan said that he would succeed Jackson as long as "it [was] cleared up and down the line."[33] Nevertheless, after talking to General Clay, the head of the Office of Military Government, United States (OMGUS), Fahy told Shea that Clay would "much prefer" him to Donovan. Fahy also told Shea that he would make a concerted effort to meet all of his conditions for accepting the position. Fahy's entreaties went nowhere, however, because Jackson reiterated on October 25 that his successor would be unable to "carry any substantial part of the actual labor of the major trial."[34] Indeed, that same day, Jackson reorganized the IMT staff in a way that antagonized Shea, leading him to leave Nuremberg for good less than two weeks later. That left Donovan, but his relationship with Jackson was also deteriorating, and he followed Shea back to the United States not long thereafter.[35]

In his post-war account of the Nuremberg trial, Telford Taylor speculated that Jackson's interest in Shea and Donovan was little more than a pretext to remove them from the IMT staff. As Taylor notes, Jackson and Donovan had already fought over the indictment at the first trial, and Jackson was aware that other prosecutors on his staff, particularly John Amen and Robert Storey, were very critical of Shea's "economic case."[36] Indeed, Amen had said that OCCPAC's job was to convict war criminals, not "reform European economies," and Storey believed that the economic case would "make us all look silly."[37]

Whatever the explanation, Fahy then turned to Taylor, a 37-year-old Colonel who had been serving as one of Jackson's senior deputies in OCCPAC. Taylor had spent much of the war at Bletchley Park, where he had served as a liasion between American and British officials and had been responsible for securely distributing decoded German war plans—Magic and Ultra—to American field commanders. Because Taylor's experience in military intelligence was unique among Jackson's IMT staff, he had been assigned to prosecute the General Staff and High Command of the German Armed Forces (OKW) as a criminal organization.[38]

Taylor was interested in the position, but made it clear to Fahy that he did not want to give up his role in the IMT trial, which was about to begin.[39] Fahy did not object, and neither did Jackson—further evidence that Jackson's uncompromising position with Shea was a pretext for getting rid of him. Taylor then conditionally accepted, insisting that his appointment not be publicly announced until a number of issues—two personal, two logistical—had been resolved.[40]

The personal issues were minor obstacles. To begin with, Taylor insisted that his wife be allowed to join him in Nuremberg. Jackson had always taken the position that service in OCCPAC was a temporary assignment that did not justify

---

[32] Ibid.   [33] Ibid.   [34] Ibid., 274.   [35] Ibid.
[36] Mark Turley, *From Nuremberg to Nineveh* 103 (2008).
[37] Ibid.
[38] Bush, *Soldiers Find Wars*, 679.
[39] Taylor, *Anatomy*, 274.   [40] Ibid.

the presence of wives; indeed, he had rejected a number of requests from his staff similar to Taylor's.[41] Taylor remained firm, however, recognizing that overseeing the zonal trials might require him to remain in Nuremberg for a number of years.[42] Finally, after OMGUS changed its regulations to permit civilians and soldiers stationed in Germany to be accompanied by their wives, Taylor got his wish.[43]

Taylor also believed that it would be inappropriate for a mere Colonel to prosecute German generals or represent the United States in international negotiations over the war-crimes program. He thus wrote to Jackson in early 1946 that "[i]f it is decided that I should undertake the assignment, I feel that I should be given the rank which the appointment needs. This should be done not in my interest, but in the interest of the assignment and so that the United States may be more effectively represented in international negotiations on war crimes matters."[44] Jackson was more favorably disposed to this request and Taylor was quickly promoted to Brigadier General.[45]

The logistical issues were far more serious. The first stemmed from Article II of Law No. 10, which gave the zonal trials jurisdiction over the crime of "[m]embership in categories of a criminal group or organization declared criminal by the International Military Tribunal." Depending on how the organizational charges fared at the IMT, Article II meant that more than 100,000 Germans could potentially be subject to prosecution.[46] That number "could not possibly be dealt with ... without hundreds of courts and years of hearings,"[47] even if the judges at the IMT accepted Jackson's position that members of organizations deemed criminal would bear the burden of proving "personal defenses or extenuating circumstances, such as that he joined under duress." Worse still, by the time Law No. 10 had been approved by the Control Council, it had become clear that the IMT judges were likely to further restrict criminal responsibility for criminal membership,[48] which would make individual trials even more complicated and time-consuming.[49]

Taylor considered the criminal-membership issue so serious that he considered refusing to assume responsibility for the zonal trials. Fortunately, in mid-January 1946, Fahy sent him a copy of a Draft Report produced by the Denazification Policy Board, which had been established by the United States in November 1945 with Fahy as its chair. The Draft Report was based on the assumption that the zonal trials would "not be able to prosecute more than a few hundred, or at the outside, a few thousand major and sub-major war criminals." It thus recommended "that the

[41] Memo from Jackson to Peterson, 14 Mar. 1946, TTP-20-1-3-34, at 1–2.
[42] Taylor, *Anatomy*, 290.
[43] Ibid., 291.
[44] Memo from Taylor to Jackson and Fahy, 6 Feb. 1946, TTP-20-1-3-34, at 2.
[45] Taylor, *Anatomy*, 292.
[46] Ibid., 273.   [47] Ibid., 278.   [48] Ibid., 277–8.   [49] Ibid., 278.

vast majority of the so-called 'organization cases' . . . be handled under the denazification program rather than separately."[50]

Taylor was more than satisfied with this division of labor, which he believed
would "bring the task of the Office of Chief of Counsel, after the present proceedings, into manageable proportions." Indeed, with the criminal-membership issue
solved, he was able to send Jackson a memo on 30 January 1946 that offered his
"best guess at the shape of things to come" for the U.S. war-crimes program:

(a) One more international trial, at which the list of defendants will include a heavy
    concentration of industrialists and financiers.

(b) Several or a series of trials of other major criminals to be tried in American courts in
    the American zone. The defendants in these trials will consist of those major war
    criminals not included in the international trials, and who can not appropriately be
    tried in the courts of the occupied countries or by one of the other allied powers.

(c) A continuation of the trials of local criminals being conducted by the American
    Theater Judge Advocate.

(d) Trials of other major war criminals in the courts of the occupied countries or by one
    of the other allied powers.

(e) Treatment of the general run of organizational cases under the denazification
    program.[51]

The second logistical issue was the lack of qualified lawyers who were interested in
remaining in Nuremberg for the zonal trials, which at this early stage Taylor
anticipated would involve "in the neighborhood" of 100 defendants.[52] According
to Taylor, no more than six to eight members of the IMT staff were willing to work
on the zonal trials, none of whom he felt comfortable leaving in charge of the
SPD while he returned to the United States to recruit new staff.[53] Taylor thus
recommended to Jackson in the January 30 memo that "the United States enter
into no commitments whatsoever for any further trials of war criminals until we can
ascertain that staff will be available to handle same."[54] He also reiterated his request
that he not be announced as Jackson's successor until the staffing problem had been
addressed.[55]

On February 7, Taylor left Nuremberg for Washington. Jackson had given him a
letter for Robert Patterson, the Secretary of War, in which Jackson sought Patterson's assurance that the War Department would facilitate recruiting and guarantee
adequate funds for the zonal trials.[56] Taylor presented the letter to Patterson, who
introduced Taylor to the head of the War Department's Civil Affairs Division,

---

[50] Taylor, *Anatomy*, 279. On 5 March 1946, the Draft was published by the Länderrat as the "Law
for Liberation from National Socialism and Militarism."

[51] Memo from Taylor to Jackson, 30 Jan. 1946, NA-260-183a1-2-13, at 1.

[52] Memo from Taylor to Jackson, 5 Feb. 1946, TTP-20-1-3-34, at 2.

[53] Memo from Taylor to Jackson, 30 Jan. 1946, at 2–3.

[54] Ibid.

[55] Taylor, *Anatomy*, 287.

[56] Letter from Jackson to Patterson, 7 Feb. 1946, TTP-20-1-1-34, at 1.

Major General John K. Hildring. Hildring, in turn, referred Taylor to his subordinate in charge of war crimes, Colonel Mickey Marcus.[57]

Although Taylor's friends in New York had begun recruiting for him even before he arrived in D.C., Marcus' efforts proved the most fruitful. By the end of March, Taylor had been able to recruit 35 attorneys[58] and dozens of administrators, court reporters, translators, stenographers, and typists.[59] The first recruits, a group of 27 attorneys, arrived in Nuremberg the second week of May,[60] and the others soon followed.[61]

In the interim, on 29 March 1946—after the bulk of the recruiting had been completed—Jackson publicly announced that he was naming Taylor his Deputy Chief of Counsel and placing him in charge of the Subsequent Proceedings Division, which had been formally created in January after President Truman approved Betts' recommendations.[62] The SPD would remain part of OCCPAC until Jackson resigned and Taylor became Chief of Counsel for War Crimes. At that point, the SPD would be placed under the auspices of OMGUS.[63]

III. The Prospect of a Second International Trial

Taylor returned to Nuremberg on April 26 and assumed control of the SPD.[64] He and his staff were immediately faced with what Taylor called a "rather special problem," one anticipated in his January 30 memo to Jackson: the prospect of a second IMT trial. The uncertainty surrounding that issue made it almost impossible for the SPD to plan the zonal trials, because the IMT judgment "was certain to be an extremely weighty precedent... [that] would determine or comment upon numerous basic legal questions which would also arise before the Law No. 10 tribunals."[65]

Taylor was deeply involved in the negotiations over a second IMT at the time, and the Allies did not conclusively abandon the idea until November 1946. As a result, for the first six months of its existence, the SPD "occupied a very inconspicuous place in the scheme of things at Nuernberg."[66]

The question of a second IMT, however, arose long before the SPD was created. The London Charter clearly contemplated the possibility of multiple IMT trials: Article 22 provided that "[t]he first trial shall be held at Nuremberg, and any subsequent trials shall be held at such places as the tribunal may decide"; Article 23 permitted "[o]ne or more of the Chief Prosecutors" to "take part in the prosecution at each Trial"; and Article 30 referred to the obligation of the signatories to meet "[t]he expenses of the Tribunal and of the Trials." That possibility became much

---

[57] Taylor, *Anatomy*, 289.   [58] Taylor, *Final Report*, 11.
[59] Taylor, *Anatomy*, 291.
[60] Letter from Taylor to Peterson, 22 May 1946, NA-153–1018-8-84-1, at 4.
[61] Taylor, *Final Report*, 14.
[62] See OCC General Memo No. 15, 29 Mar. 1946, TTP-20-1-3-34.
[63] Ibid.   [64] Taylor, *Anatomy*, 292.
[65] Taylor, *Final Report*, 21.   [66] Ibid.

less abstract two weeks before the IMT trial, when Gustav Krupp's counsel filed a motion with the tribunal requesting that the proceedings against him be deferred on the ground that he was too mentally and physically unsound to be tried—a request that was supported by the tribunal's own medical commission.[67] Krupp was the only German industrialist indicted by the IMT prosecutors, even though all of the Allies had agreed that it was important to include private economic actors in the trial.[68] If Krupp's case was severed, no representative of German industry would stand trial at the IMT.

With the exception of the Soviets, all of the Allies filed briefs opposing Krupp's severance motion. Jackson's brief reaffirmed the U.S. government's view that "the great industrialists of Germany were guilty of the crimes charged in this Indictment quite as much as its politicians, diplomats, and soldiers" and argued that if Gustav Krupp was not fit for trial, he should be tried *in absentia*, which was permitted by the London Charter.[69] The brief also suggested that, in the alternative, the tribunal should replace Gustav with his son, Alfried Krupp.[70] The Americans had always favored prosecuting Alfried instead of Gustav, because the younger Krupp had played a critical role in the company as early as 1941 and had assumed formal control of the company—blessed by Hitler himself in the *Lex Krupp*—in November 1943. Unfortunately, because of a mix-up between the prosecutors, the Americans did not realize until it was too late that the other Allies favored prosecuting Gustav instead.[71]

The British also favored trying Gustav *in absentia*, insisted that his critical role in the Nazi conspiracy to wage aggressive war justified trying him even if he was not able to understand the charges against him. Their motion was silent, however, concerning the possibility of replacing Gustav with his son Alfried.[72]

The French motion echoed Jackson's, arguing that the tribunal should either try Gustav *in absentia* or replace him—now its preferred choice—with Alfried. The motion also foreshadowed the debates to come by justifying its opposition to eliminating the Krupp concern from the trial on the ground that "the other prosecutors do not contemplate the possibility of preparing at this time a second trial directed against the big German industrialists."[73]

The Allies' arguments fell on deaf ears. On 15 November 1945, the IMT granted Gustav Krupp's motion "in accordance with justice" and severed him from the trial. The following day it also denied the Allies' motion—which by then had been joined by the Soviets—to substitute Alfried for Gustav.[74] The tribunal did not, however, completely rule out the possibility of Gustav eventually standing trial. On the contrary, it ordered "that the charges in the indictment against Gustav Krupp von Bohlen shall be retained upon the docket of the tribunal for trial hereafter, if the physical and mental condition of the defendant should permit"—a clear reference to the possibility of a second trial. That order led Jackson

---

[67] Taylor, *Anatomy*, 153.   [68] Ibid., 90.
[69] London Charter, Art. 12.
[70] Taylor, *Anatomy*, 154.
[71] Ibid., 92.   [72] Ibid., 154.   [73] Ibid., 155.   [74] Ibid., 158.

to immediately file a memorandum reminding the tribunal and the other Allies that "the United States has not been, and is not by this order, committed to participate in any subsequent Four Power trial. It reserves freedom to determine that question after the capacity to handle one trial under difficult conditions has been tested."[75]

Jackson's reluctance to endorse a second IMT trial was not surprising, because he had already concluded that zonal trials might be preferable to holding even the *first* IMT trial. On July 23, frustrated by the slow pace of preparations for the trial, he had informed the other Allies that "the United States might well withdraw from this matter and turn our prisoners over to the European powers to try, or else agree on separate trials, or something of that sort."[76] He had offered similar sentiments the following week during a phone conversation with Samuel Rosenman, who had been Special Counsel to President Roosevelt and was now a legal advisor to President Truman; according to Rosenman, Jackson told him that, unless the Soviets were willing to defer to the United States in terms of the definitions of crimes and certain other matters, he would "take the course of having each nation try the criminals in its respective jurisdiction."[77] Those concerns applied even more strongly to the prospect of a second IMT trial, particularly as Jackson was convinced that the Soviets would insist that any such trial be held in their zone of occupation with a Soviet presiding judge.[78]

The French and British response to Krupp's severance, however, made it much more likely that the Allies would hold a second IMT trial despite Jackson's reluctance. France was particularly aggrieved by the decision, not only because many French nationals had been forced to work in Krupp factories during the war,[79] but also because it hoped that an international conviction of an industrialist would facilitate domestic prosecutions of French industrialists who had collaborated with the Nazis.[80] The British were not as enthusiastic about a second trial involving industrialists, but agreed to support a second trial because of French lobbying and its own embarrassing refusal to support replacing Gustav Krupp with Alfried.[81] France and Britain thus published a joint declaration on 20 November 1945—the day the IMT trial began—indicating that their delegations were "now engaged in the examination of the cases of other leading German industrialists... with a view to their attachment with Alfried Krupp, in an indictment to be presented at a subsequent trial."[82]

Formal discussions among the prosecutors about the possibility of a second IMT trial resumed the following April. In the interim, though, the French and British found a new ally: Telford Taylor. Taylor shared Jackson's concerns about the Soviets regarding the location of the second trial and the nationality of the presiding judge, and he was generally skeptical of quadripartite trials, because he disliked

---

[75] Quoted in Taylor, *Final Report*, 23.
[76] Telford Taylor, "The Nuremberg Trials," in *Perspectives on the Nuremberg Trial* 372, 384 (Guénaël Mettraux ed., 2008).
[77] Taylor, *Anatomy*, 72.
[78] Earl, 33.
[79] Taylor, *Final Report*, 23.
[80] Donald Bloxham, *Genocide on Trial* 24 (2001).
[81] Ibid., 24–5.   [82] Taylor, *Final Report*, 23.

"continental and Soviet law principles unfamiliar to the American public."[83] Nevertheless, he believed that a second trial focused primarily, if not exclusively, on a small number of private economic actors would be both cheaper and more legally straightforward than the first trial.[84] He also thought that it was an open question whether industrialists "could be as broadly charged or as effectively tried" in zonal trials.[85]

Sir Hartley Shawcross, the British Attorney General, brought the issue of the second IMT trial up at the 4 April 1946 meeting of the Committee of Chief Prosecutors. He was ambivalent, but noted that "preparations must be started now" if a second trial was to be held. General Rudenko said that the Soviets were interested in holding a second trial, but wanted to defer a final decision until after the first trial concluded. Auguste Champetier de Ribes, the French prosecutor, reiterated his government's desire to hold a second trial. Jackson insisted that the United States would not commit itself to a second trial until he knew the results of the first one. Instead of reaching a final decision, therefore, the Committee decided to appoint a small working group to begin identifying potential economic defendants for a second IMT.[86]

Jackson reported the results of the meeting to Patterson at the War Department four days later, taking the position that although he was still opposed to a second trial, he believed that the SPD should prepare for the possibility that one would nevertheless be held.[87] Patterson responded on April 24, approving Jackson's recommendation but agreeing with him that a second trial would be "highly undesirable."[88] Patterson and Jackson's opposition, however, was not indicative of the U.S. government as a whole. In particular, Rosenman continued to believe that a second trial was necessary—and that failing to cooperate with the other Allies would undermine the United States' credibility with the international community.[89]

When Taylor returned to Nuremberg from his recruiting trip at the end of April, Jackson appointed him his representative on the working group established by the Committee of Chief Prosecutors.[90] Nevertheless, Jackson continued to make his opposition to a second IMT trial known. On May 13 he sent a long memorandum to President Truman summarizing his reasons for preferring zonal trials. Some were logistical, such as the inevitable length and expense of a quadripartite trial.[91] But Jackson also had substantive reasons for opposing a second IMT. To begin with, he believed that one of the primary goals of the war-crimes program—establishing "the responsibility of Germany for starting the war, and . . . proving high planning of atrocities and war crimes"—had already been accomplished through the use of

[83] Quoted in Paul Weindling, "From International to Zonal Trials: The Origins of the Nuremberg Medical Trial," 14 *Holocaust & Genocide Studies* 367, 369 (2000).
[84] Memo from Taylor to Jackson, 30 Jan. 1946, TTP-20-1-3-34, at 1.
[85] Memo from Taylor to Cohen, 18 Jun. 1946, reprinted in Taylor, *Final Report*, 281 (Appendix F).
[86] Taylor, *Final Report*, 24.
[87] Ibid.   [88] Ibid.
[89] Letter from Rosenman to Truman, 27 May 1946, cited in Hébert, *Hitler's Generals*, 234.
[90] Taylor, *Final Report*, 24.
[91] Jackson to Truman, 13 May 1946, 3–4.

captured documents at the first trial. A second trial would thus add little to the historical record "except subsidiary detail."[92]

Jackson also believed that the case against industrialists and financiers prosecuted at a subsequent IMT trial would be no stronger than the case against Schacht, which he considered to be "one of the weakest in the present trial."[93] A second trial would thus likely end in disaster—and "with an American presiding officer, with nearly all the evidence ours, with most of the prisoners ours, and with the lead in the prosecution ours," the blame would almost certainly fall on the United States.[94]

Finally, and most notably, Jackson had undergone a complete *volte-face* concerning the very desirability of prosecuting industrialists and financiers. In his report to President Truman in June 1945, he had emphasized the need to prosecute individuals "in the financial, industrial, and economic life of Germany who ... are provable to be common criminals."[95] Now, despite acknowledging the absence of such individuals from the first trial, he was convinced that prosecuting industrialists and financiers would be counterproductive to the coming struggle against the Soviets, whom he believed were committed to overthrowing the capitalist system[96]:

I also have some misgivings as to whether a long public attack concentrated on private industry would not tend to discourage industrial cooperation with our Government in maintaining its defenses in the future while not at all weakening the Soviet position, since they do not rely upon private enterprise.[97]

Despite Jackson's objections, the representatives of the Committee of Chief Prosecutors met three times between May 15 and July 2 to select potential defendants for a second IMT trial. All of the representatives agreed that a second trial should not involve more than eight defendants and that Alfried Krupp should be one of the eight. They then settled on four more industrialists and financiers: Kurt von Schroeder, a German banker who had raised a significant amount of money for the Nazis as a member of Himmler's notorious Circle of Friends, proposed by the British; Hermann Roechling, the coal and steel magnate who had played a significant role in Germany's rearmament, proposed by the French; and Hermann Schmitz and Georg von Schnitzler, two high-ranking officials in the I.G. Farben chemical combine, whose use of slave labor and involvement in German rearmament was being documented by Taylor's SPD.[98] The representatives also addressed the location of a second trial, with the British and French favoring Nuremberg for continuity reasons, the Soviets unsurprisingly preferring Berlin, and Taylor reserving judgment until a later date.[99]

On July 25, a few weeks after the group disbanded to report back to their respective Chief Prosecutors, Attorney General Shawcross wrote a letter to Jackson

[92] Ibid., 5. [93] Ibid., 2. [94] Ibid., 5. [95] Taylor, *Anatomy*, 91.
[96] Tom Bower, *Blind Eye to Murder* 343 (1981).
[97] Memorandum for the President on American Participation in Further International Trials of Nazi War Criminals, 13 May 1946, NA-549–2236-1, at 3.
[98] Taylor, *Final Report*, 25. The Russians did not offer any names, but reserved the right to do so at a later date. According to Taylor, they never did. Ibid.
[99] Earl, 36.

suggesting that they "make as early a declaration as possible that we are prepared to participate in a second trial involving the five defendants whose names have been agreed." He also indicated that he "felt little doubt the British government will adopt this view."[100] Sir Hartley not only underestimated Jackson's aversion to a second trial, he also overestimated his government's support for one. Unbeknownst to him, Ernest Bevin, the Foreign Secretary, and Orme Sargent, the Permanent Under-Secretary in the Foreign Office, had already decided to ask James Byrnes, the U.S. Secretary of State, to enter into an agreement with the Foreign Office to oppose a second trial.[101] Sargent was particularly opposed to prosecuting industrialists, suggesting that a second trial would devolve into a "wrangle between the capitalist and communist ideologies" and that "[t]he Russians might exploit the proceedings to discuss irrelevancies such as . . . our attitude to German rearmament."[102] Byrnes readily agreed to the deal, in large part because the American business community was strongly opposed to prosecuting industrialists.[103]

Shawcross was never told about the deal between the Secretary of State and the Foreign Office, and he did not learn that the Foreign Office was opposed to a second trial until 31 July 1946. By that time, Taylor had submitted a long memorandum to the Secretary of War, Patterson, expressing his support for a second IMT trial.[104] A number of considerations, Taylor believed, militated in favor of deferring to the other Allies' wishes. To begin with, Taylor pointed out that, in light of Article 14 of the London Charter—which gave any two Chief Prosecutors the right "to settle the final designation of major war criminals to be tried by the Tribunal"—the United States could only refuse to participate in a second IMT trial by giving notice of its intent to terminate the Charter. "In that event, the entire responsibility for terminating the international machinery [would] fall on the United States," causing significant harm to the U.S.'s international reputation.[105]

Taylor also believed that any U.S.-initiated effort to terminate the London Charter would "be most unfortunate from the standpoint of general international jurisprudence." The future importance of the legal principles embodied in the Charter would be determined by the willingness of the international community to adhere to them, and terminating the Charter before its time would simply undermine "the prospects for [their] universal acceptance."[106]

Finally, Taylor feared that terminating the London Charter would undermine the legal basis of the zonal trials that his office was currently preparing:

It is probable, though not absolutely clear, that a termination of the London Agreement is a complete termination for all purposes, so that Articles 10 and 11, relating to zonal trials of members of organizations, would be terminated. Furthermore, the Article (6) which specifies the three categories of crimes, would probably likewise disappear. Although

---

[100] Letter from Shawcross to Jackson, 25 July 1946, NA-153–1018-8-1-54-2, at 1.
[101] Bower, 345.
[102] Bloxham, 30.
[103] Bower, 346.
[104] Memorandum for the Secretary of War, 29 July 1946, para. 5, reprinted in Taylor, *Final Report*, 272 (Appendix J).
[105] Ibid., Memorandum, para. 7.   [106] Ibid., Memorandum, para. 9.

I have not fully examined the question, I believe that those consequences would be harmful to our zonal trials under Control Council Law No. 10.[107]

The memo concluded by addressing the logistical issues raised by a second IMT trial. The number of defendants would not exceed eight, with the United States assuming responsibility for the case against Alfried Krupp and the Farben defendants, Schmitz and von Schnitzler.[108] The charges would involve not only traditional war crimes, but also crimes against peace, because the defendants had "joined with German leaders in other walks of life in assisting Hitler's rise to power, waging aggressive war."[109] The trial would last no more than three months and "would run simultaneously with our 'zonal' trials in which SS leaders, militarists, government officials, and other diverse types will be defendants."[110]

Jackson was so disturbed by Taylor's endorsement of a second IMT that he returned to the United States at the end of the July to discuss the issue in person with Byrne and Patterson.[111] Both agreed with him that another trial was undesirable—but they took no official position, mindful of Rosenman's belief that it would be better to acquiesce to the other Allies than risk being seen as backtracking on the U.S. commitment to prosecuting Nazi war criminals. Jackson, Byrnes, and Patterson also agreed that, if a second IMT trial was not held, the industrialists and financiers being investigated by Taylor's SPD would be prosecuted in zonal trials.[112]

The issue of a second trial flared up again after the IMT delivered its judgment on 1 October 1946. Schacht was acquitted, leading many at Nuremberg to speculate that the British had engineered his acquittal in order to protect German industrialists and financiers. That theory was not completely without merit: Francis Biddle, the American judge at the IMT, disclosed that Sir Geoffrey Lawrence, the British judge, had described Schacht as a "man of character" far removed from the "ruffians" that otherwise filled the dock.[113]

Six days later, as part of his final report to President Truman on the IMT, Jackson submitted his resignation as Chief of Counsel. His final report noted that "[t]here are many industrialists, militarists, politicians, diplomats, and police officials whose guilt does not differ from those who have been convicted except that their parts were at lower levels and have been less conspicuous."[114] The question was whether the most important of those war criminals should be tried by a second IMT or in zonal trials. As he had so many times before, he made clear his strong preference for the latter:

The most expeditious method of trial and the one that will cost the United States the least in money and in manpower is that each of the occupying powers assume responsibility for the trial within its own zone [and] with the prisoners in its own custody. Most of these defendants can be charged with single and specific crimes which will not involve a repetition

[107] Ibid., Memorandum, para. 8.   [108] Ibid., 273, Memorandum, para. 13.
[109] Ibid., Memorandum, para. 17.   [110] Ibid., Memorandum, para. 15.
[111] Taylor, *Final Report*, 25–6.   [112] Ibid., 26.   [113] Bower, 347.
[114] Robert Jackson, Final Report to the President Concerning the Nurnberg War Crimes Trial, reprinted in 20 *Temp. L. Q.* 338, 340 (1946).

of the whole history of the Nazi conspiracy. The trials can be conducted in two languages instead of four, and since all of the judges in any one trial would be of a single legal system no time would be lost adjusting [to] different systems of procedure.[115]

Jackson did not reiterate his belief that a second IMT trial involving industrialists and financiers would be a propaganda coup for the Soviets. By the time he submitted his report, however, many officials in the U.S. government had come to the same conclusion.[116]

On October 17, Jackson's resignation became official. The following day, OMGUS promulgated Military Government Ordinance No. 7, which formally established the zonal trials. On October 24, General Joseph McNarney, the Military Governor, disbanded the SPD and reconstituted it as the Office, Chief of Counsel for War Crimes, a division of OMGUS. He then appointed Taylor the new Chief of Counsel of the OCC.[117]

President Truman decided that the United States would not participate in a second IMT trial in late October or early November,[118] but he did not inform the other Allies of his decision until January, 1947. In the interim, two other events conspired to make a second IMT trial less likely. First, the newly christened OCC relied on Article IV of Law No. 10 to ask Britain to extradite nine suspects for prosecution in the zonal trials: six industrialists, including Alfried Krupp; Field Marshal Erhard Milch; and two Ministers in the Nazi government, Friedrich Gaus and Otto Thierack.[119] The British happily acceded to the request, with Patrick Dean, an advisor to the Foreign Office, noting with satisfaction that "[i]f any of the trials do go wrong and the industrialists escape, the primary political criticism will rest on American shoulders and not ours."[120] Second, as explored in more detail in Chapter 3, the first two NMT trials got underway. The *Medical* trial began on December 9 and the *Milch* trial began on 2 January 1947. Those trials did not rule out a second IMT, but they sent a powerful message that the United States was prepared to assume primary responsibility for prosecuting the high-ranking war-crimes suspects—industrialist, financier, and otherwise—that the IMT had left unpunished.

Despite those developments, the United States would have preferred to let the second IMT trial die a slow, quiet death. Unfortunately, France circulated a diplomatic note in late December 1946 suggesting that the Committee of Chief Prosecutors "should reconvene as soon as possible" to discuss the second trial. The note forced the Americans' hand, and on 22 January 1947 the United States officially informed the British, French, and Soviet Foreign Offices that "[i]t is the view of this Government that further trials of German war criminals can be more expeditiously held in national or occupation courts and that additional proceedings before the International Military Tribunal itself are not required."[121] According to Taylor, the U.S. message put the issue of a second trial to rest once and for all.[122]

---

[115] Ibid.   [116] Earl, 37–8.   [117] Taylor, *Final Report*, 13.
[118] Earl, 38.   [119] Bloxham, 32.   [120] Bower, 346.
[121] Taylor, *Final Report*, 27.   [122] Ibid.

2

The OCC and the Tribunals

Introduction

The previous chapter discussed the United States' decision to forego a second IMT in favor of zonal trials. This chapter discusses the structure of the Nuremberg Military Tribunals, which conducted those trials. Section I examines Ordinance No. 7, the military directive that established the NMTs and specified their evidentiary and procedural rules. Section II explores the structure and funding of the tribunals' prosecutorial wing, Telford Taylor's OCC. Section III focuses on the Military Tribunals themselves—their location; the structure and function of their administrative section, the Central Secretariat; and the selection of judges.

I. Ordinance No. 7

Article III of Law No. 10 authorized each zone commander, within his zone of occupation, to "cause all persons...arrested and charged" with violating Law No. 10 "to be brought to trial before an appropriate tribunal."[1] Article III was silent, however, concerning what constituted "an appropriate tribunal." The U.S. answer came in the form of Ordinance No. 7, which was enacted on 18 October 1946 by General Clay in his role as Military Governor and commander of the U.S. zone. Ordinance No. 7's stated purpose was "to provide for the establishment of military tribunals which shall have the power to try and punish persons charged with offenses recognized as crimes in Article II of Control Council Law No. 10."[2]

The first draft of Ordinance No. 7 was written in July 1946 by Bessie Margolin, who had been seconded to the OCC by the Department of Labor, for whom she worked as an Assistant Solicitor. That draft was then reviewed and revised in August by Telford Taylor, other senior prosecutors in the OCC, and lawyers in OMGUS's Legal Division.[3] The final draft could have been completed sooner than October 18, but Taylor and the others believed that it was important to wait for the IMT to issue its judgment, in case any of the tribunal's rulings affected the Ordinance.[4]

---

[1] Law No. 10, Art. III(1)(d). [2] Ordinance No. 7, Art. I.
[3] Taylor, *Final Report*, 28 n. 73. [4] Ibid., 28.

It is reasonable to suggest that it was inappropriate for the OCC to play such a critical role in drafting the evidentiary and procedural rules that governed its prosecutions. Modern tribunals normally entrust that responsibility to the judges, who—at least in theory—have no vested interest in the outcome of the trials over which they preside.[5] Indeed, Taylor acknowledged in his Final Report that there was "a certain amount of criticism of the set-up on the ground that the prosecution was in too powerful a position from an administrative standpoint" and that he would not recommend such an arrangement for future tribunals.[6] As he pointed out, however, it would have been difficult to exclude the OCC from the drafting of Ordinance No. 7—at the time the ordinance was drafted, no judges had been appointed and the Central Secretariat did not yet exist.[7]

II. The OCC

The OCC was divided into two basic sections, what Taylor called the "professional segment" and the "service segment," respectively.[8] The professional segment was responsible for preparing cases for trial and presenting them in court; the service segment was responsible for the day-to-day administration of the OCC and for providing logistical support to the professional segment. Both sections were ulti-mately responsible to Taylor.

A. Structure

1. The Professional Segment

For the first few months of the OCC's existence, Taylor's Deputy to the Chief Counsel, Josiah M. DuBois, Jr., was in charge of the professional segment. In 1944, Dubois had written the famous "Report to the Secretary on the Acquiescence of This Government in the Murder of the Jews," which had led Henry Morgenthau, Jr., the Secretary of the Treasury, to establish the War Refugee Board. DuBois joined the OCC as Deputy to the Chief Counsel in January 1947[9] and briefly functioned, in Taylor's absence, as Acting Chief of Counsel in April 1948.[10]

In early 1947, Taylor eliminated the Deputy to the Chief Counsel position[11] and assigned DuBois to be Deputy Chief Counsel—the title given to the individual in charge of a particular trial—in *Farben* (Case No. 6),[12] an experience that would ultimately lead DuBois to write *The Devil's Chemists*, the seminal account of that trial. From that point on, the heads of the various divisions and trial teams in the

---

[5] See, e.g., ICTY Statute, Art. 15; STL Statute, Art. 28.
[6] Taylor, *Final Report*, 106.
[7] Ibid., 38.
[8] Ibid., 39.
[9] Ibid., 3.
[10] OCCWC General Order No. 6, 12 April 1948, NA-238-145-2-6.
[11] Taylor, *Final Report*, 39.
[12] Background Information for Correspondents, 3.

professional segment reported directly to Taylor, although a new position, "Executive Counsel," was created to coordinate their work and to oversee the assignment of personnel to them.[13] Four different individuals served as Executive Counsel during the life of the OCC, the most notable of whom was Benjamin B. Ferencz. Ferencz was one of the youngest members of OCC; he was only 23 when he served as the Chief Prosecutor in *Einsatzgruppen* (Case No. 9).[14]

The professional segment of the OCC initially consisted of seven different groups. Four were legal divisions: the Military Division, the Ministries Division, the SS Division, and the Economics Division. Their mission was "to secure, analyze, and prepare evidence to be used in the prosecution of major war criminals in certain related fields, usually constituting more than one case."[15] Two were trial teams, one responsible for preparing *Farben*, the other responsible for preparing *Flick*. Finally, an Evidence Division located suspects and witnesses and managed the evidence used by the legal divisions and the trial teams.[16]

a. Military Division

Taylor distributed an organizational memo to his staff on 17 May 1946 indicating that "[t]hree groups will concern themselves with the analysis and preparation of evidence against potential war criminals *other* than industrialists and financiers."[17] The first group, the Military Division, had a dual mandate: preparing the "organizational cases"—those involving members of the organizations, such as the Gestapo, then being prosecuted by the IMT[18]—and developing "evidence concerning military and naval war criminals."[19]

The Military Division spent the summer of 1946 interviewing IMT defendants, including Hermann Goering and Albert Speer, about other war-crimes suspects.[20] The Military Division then prepared both *Milch* (Case No. 2) and the *Hostage* case (Case No. 7), presenting the former in its entirety and presenting the latter until late 1947, when its chief was forced to resign because of illness. The Military Division then merged with the SS Division, and the resulting "Military & SS Division" completed the *Hostage* case and prepared and presented *High Command* (Case No. 12).[21]

b. Ministries Division

The Ministries Division was primarily concerned with preparing cases against "leading officials of the German Foreign Office,"[22] although it was also involved

---

[13] Taylor, *Final Report*, 39.
[14] Ibid.
[15] OCCWC Organizational Memo, undated, NA-260-183a1-1-1, at 8.
[16] Taylor, *Final Report*, 39–40.
[17] OCCWC Organizational Memo No. 1, 17 May 1946, NA-153–1018-1-85-2, at 2 (emphasis added).
[18] John Q. Barrett, "Henry T. King, Jr., at Case, and on the Nuremberg Case," 60 *Case W. Res. L. Rev.* 1, 5 (2010).
[19] Organizational Memo No. 1, at 2.
[20] Barrett, 5.
[21] Taylor, *Final Report*, 39–40.　　[22] Organizational Memo No. 1, at 2.

in investigating officials in a number of economic ministries.[23] The Division went through three different Directors, the most important—and to many Germans, the most infamous[24]—of whom was Robert M.W. Kempner, appointed in February 1947.[25] Kempner was a German Jew who had held a number of positions in the Prussian government before 1933, including serving as Chief Legal Advisor to the State Police Administration,[26] prior to being expelled from Germany because of his opposition to National Socialism.[27] Kempner had emigrated to America in 1940 where, as a member of the Justice Department, he had been involved in preparing trials against German agents involved in espionage, propaganda, and sabotage within the continental United States.[28] His extensive knowledge of German law and politics had led Justice Jackson to appoint him to the IMT staff after the war ended; in addition to being heavily involved in interrogations, he had presented the prosecution's case against Frick, the "Protector" of Bohemia and Moravia.[29]

The Ministries Division prepared and presented the *Justice* case (Case No. 3), which ran from March to October 1947. The Division was then redesignated the "Political Ministries Division" and its personnel who were investigating the economic ministries were reassigned, along with the personnel of the Dresdner Bank Trial Team (discussed below), to a new "Economic Ministries Division."[30] The two divisions joined forces in 1948 to present the *Ministries* case.[31]

c. SS Division

The SS Division was responsible for preparing cases involving "the leaders of the SS and the leaders of the German health and medical service."[32] The SS Division was the most active of the divisions, preparing and presenting the *Medical* case, *Pohl* (Case No. 4), *RuSHA* (Case No. 8), and *Einsatzgruppen*.[33] The SS Division was also involved, as noted above, in presenting *High Command* after it merged with the Military Division.

d. Economics Division

The Economics Division was responsible for preparing cases "against Nazi economic leaders involved in preparations for aggressive war, slave labor, and spoliation of property in occupied countries."[34] Its Director was Drexel Sprecher, who had spent the war in the Army and working for the OSS.[35] Sprecher had

---

[23] Taylor, *Final Report*, 40.
[24] Peter Maguire, *Law and War: An American Story* 149 (2001).
[25] OCCWC General Order No. 6, 25 Feb. 1947, NA-238-145-2-6.
[26] Background Information for Correspondents, 3.
[27] Maguire, 149.
[28] Background Information for Correspondents, 3.
[29] Ibid.
[30] Taylor, *Final Report*, 40.
[31] Undated Organizational Memo, 8.
[32] Organizational Memo No. 1, at 2.
[33] Taylor, *Final Report*, 39–40.
[34] OCCWC Memo, Economics Division, NA-238-165-7-7.
[35] Du Bois, 53.

joined the IMT in June 1945 and had helped present the cases against Schirach, the Nazi Youth Leader, and Fritzsche, the head of the Reich Propaganda Ministry's Radio Division.[36] He had also moonlighted with the SPD from February 1946 on, "concentrating on a future case against Nazi industrialists" at Taylor's direction.[37]

The Economics Division began work by sending teams throughout the European Theater to collect documents and conduct interrogations.[38] Based on its investigations, the Division decided to supplement the *Flick* and *Farben* cases—which had been planned from the inception of the OCC—with cases against the leading officials of the Krupp combine and the Dresdner Bank.[39] The Economics Division was then dissolved in May 1947, with its personnel distributed among the existing Flick and Farben teams and the newly created Krupp and Dresdner Bank teams.[40]

e. Trial Teams

As noted, Taylor created the Farben and Flick trial teams when the OCC began work. The Krupp team was not created until May 1947, even though the Americans had been committed to prosecuting Alfried Krupp since the Gustav/Alfried fiasco at the IMT. The OCC had nevertheless targeted the younger Krupp from the beginning: the Farben trial team had additionally been given responsibility for undertaking "the analysis and preparation for use of material concerning Alfried Krupp."[41]

The Dresdner Bank team was also created in May 1947. The team was consistently plagued by staffing problems: the Economics Division had initially assigned only a "skeleton force" to the case in mid-December 1946,[42] and although those numbers had improved when the Economics Division dissolved—six attorneys and 14 research analysts spread out between Nuremberg and Berlin—most of the lawyers "had little experience and, excluding service in the armed forces, [were] fresh from the law schools," while the research analysts were "with certain exceptions a mediocre group."[43] All in all, "the Dresdner Bank team [was] much worse off than the other economic case teams."[44]

f. Evidence Division

The Evidence Division, which was first established as part of the SPD,[45] was responsible for supporting the work of the legal divisions and the trial teams. The Division was divided into three branches. The most important was the Interrogation Branch, created in June 1946, which conducted interrogations of both

[36] Background Information for Correspondents, 4.
[37] Memorandum from Sprecher to Jackson, 14 Feb. 1946, TTP-20-1-3-34, at 1.
[38] OCCWC Memo, Economics Division, 1.
[39] Undated Organizational Memo, 8.
[40] OCCWC Memo, Dissolution of the Economics Division, 6 May 1947, NA-238-145-2-6.
[41] Organizational Memo No. 1, at 1.
[42] Memo from Ragland to Taylor, 15 Aug. 1947, TTP-5-1-2-20, at 2.
[43] Ibid., 3.
[44] Ibid.
[45] OCCWC, Interrogation Branch, Evidence Division, TTP-5-1-3-39, at 1.

witnesses and defendants.[46] Seventeen interrogators worked full-time in the Interrogation Branch in October 1946; that number grew to 24 by June 1947 and then decreased to 12 by June 1948, as the final NMT trial, *High Command*, was winding down.[47] All of the interrogators were highly skilled—requirements for the position included extensive interrogation experience; fluency in speaking, reading, and writing both German and English; a "broad background" in German social, economic, and political conditions at the time; and a "sound grounding" in the structure and activities of the Nazi government.[48] The Interrogation Branch conducted a staggering number of interrogations during its existence, 9,456 in all.[49] Indeed, from October 1946 to December 1947, the Branch averaged 370 interrogations per interrogator.[50]

The Evidence Division also included an Apprehension and Locator Branch, which—as its name indicates—was initially responsible for locating individuals being investigated by the OCC. It was later charged with ensuring that witnesses and defendants were apprehended, detained, and either transferred or (when located in a different occupation zone) extradited to Nuremberg for use by the prosecution.[51]

The third branch of the Evidence Division was Document Control, which had two primary responsibilities: protecting and registering all of the documentary evidence brought to Nuremberg, and assembling that evidence into "document books" that the prosecutors could introduce at trial.[52]

g. Special Projects Division

During the course of the NMT trials, German prosecutors frequently asked the OCC for evidence in its possession relating to defendants undergoing denazification. In response to those requests, Tayor created—at Ben Ferencz's urging[53]—a fifth division of the professional segment, Special Projects, in June 1947.[54] The Special Projects Division had a straightforward mission: "the delivery of evidence collected in Nurnberg to German Prosecution agencies."[55] Despite its small size—a Director, a Deputy Director, a research analyst, an administrative assistant, and a secretary[56]—the Division was extremely successful: it not only "procured all requested evidence and screened and collected evidence on every individual which passed the Nurnberg jail,"[57] it transferred approximately 300 cases to German and Allied agencies and provided information in approximately 200 other cases to various U.S. agencies, such as the War Crimes Branch of OMGUS, the Decartelization Branch, and the Restitution Branch.[58]

---

[46] Taylor, *Final Report*, 40.
[47] OCCWC, Interrogation Branch, Evidence Division, 1.
[48] Ibid.
[49] Ibid.
[50] Taylor, *Final Report*, 45.
[51] Undated Organizational Memo, 3.
[52] Taylor, *Final Report*, 41.
[53] Lang Memo on History of Special Projects Division, 31 Aug. 1948, NA-260-186a1-99-14, at 1.
[54] Ibid.   [55] Ibid., 1.   [56] Ibid., 2.   [57] Ibid., 3.   [58] Ibid.

2. The Service Segment

The service segment of the OCC, which was overseen by an Executive Officer, initially consisted of four divisions: the Adminstrative Division, the Reproduction Division, the Signal Division, and the Language Division. A fifth, the Publications Division, was created in 1948 as the OCC neared deactivation.

a. Administrative Division

The Administrative Division provided basic administrative services to the OCC. It consisted of five branches: an Adjutant and Military Personnel Branch, which maintained personnel records for OCC employees who were in the military; a Finance Branch; a Civilian Personnel Branch, which maintained personnel records for civilian OCC employees; a Fiscal, Budget, and Personnel Control Branch, which prepared budgets for OMGUS; and a Liaison Branch, which dealt with all requests to the Nuremberg Military Post—the post office—for accommodations, transportation, and supplies.[59] The Director of the Administrative Division also oversaw the activities of a branch office in Frankfurt and a Liasion Officer in Berlin.[60]

b. Reproduction Division

The Reproduction Division was responsible for photostating and mimeographing documents used by the OCC, including trial transcripts and documents offered into evidence. It also prepared the various maps, charts, and displays the prosecutors used at trial.[61] Not including the *Ministries* case, the Reproduction Division produced 2,296,958 photostats, 640,000 offset prints, and 950,000 stencils during its lifetime—a stack that, by the Public Information Office's estimate, would have reached 13.4 miles high.[62]

c. Signal Division

The Signal Division maintained the OCC's communications equipment and installed the simultaneous-translation system that the tribunals used in the various courtrooms.[63]

d. Language Division

The Language Division, the largest in the service segment, had what Taylor described as a "truly formidable" task: "the translation into German of all English documents and into English of all German documents... and the furnishing of all court interpreting services and of court reporting in both English and German."[64] Given the complexity of the trials, translators were divided into groups and asked to translate related documents, allowing them to develop expertise with specific

---

[59] Taylor, *Final Report*, 42.   [60] Undated Organizational Memo, 4.
[61] Taylor, *Final Report*, 41–2.   [62] OCCWC, Statistics of the Nurnberg Trials, 7.
[63] Taylor, *Final Report*, 42.   [64] Ibid.

military, legal, and medical terminologies.[65] Although the Language Division reported to the Executive Officer on administrative matters, it reported directly to Taylor regarding all policy matters.[66]

e. Publications Division

In late summer 1948, as the final trials were winding down, Taylor created a Publications Division. That division was responsible for preparing the indictments, important trial records, and judgments for later publication in English and German.[67] Publication issues are dealt with at greater length in Chapter 16.

3. Public Information Office

In addition to the professional and service segments of the OCC, a Public Information Office was directly responsible to Taylor. The Public Information Office, which had a staff of six, provided journalists covering the NMTs with documents and evidentiary material and otherwise helped journalists understand the legal issues involved in the trials.[68]

4. Satellite Branches

Although most of its work was conducted out of its office at Nuremberg, the OCC maintained four satellite branches in other cities. The primary satellite, established in summer 1946, was located in Berlin. The Berlin Branch was created to process the vast number of captured German documents located in Berlin and to liaise with OMGUS headquarters.[69] Another satellite branch was located in Frankfort; it analyzed the locally-kept records of I.G. Farben. Finally, OCC representatives were stationed in Paris to liaise with the Supreme Headquarters of the Allied Expeditionary Forces (SHAEF) and in Washington to deal with documents held in the Pentagon's German Military Documents Section.[70]

B. Staffing

1. Prosecutors

The OCC employed 94 prosecutors during its existence—less than 20 percent of its total staff. One prosecutor worked on eight cases, eight prosecutors worked on three cases, and 19 prosecutors worked on two cases.[71] The number of prosecutors varied significantly by trial. Thirty-four attorneys were involved in *Ministries*, by far the largest staff. Only five attorneys, by contrast, were involved in the

---

[65] Taylor, *Final Report*, 42.   [66] Ibid.   [67] Ibid., 41.   [68] Ibid., 43.
[69] John Mendelsohn, *Trial by Document: The Use of Seized Records in the United States Proceedings at Nurnberg* 58 (1988).
[70] Ibid.
[71] Background Information for Correspondents, 1.

Justice case. After *Ministries*, the largest staffs were involved in the industrialist cases: 11 in *Flick*, 13 in *Farben*, and 12 in *Krupp*.[72] Notably, other than Taylor, all of the prosecutors were civilians during the trials.[73]

Taylor never publicly discussed whether he was satisfied with the prosecutors that worked in his office. On the eve of the OCC's creation, however, he wrote to Howard C. Petersen, the Assistant Secretary of War, to express his disappointment with the attorneys recruited by OMGUS's War Crimes Branch. Taylor didn't pull any punches. What he needed, he said, were "a lot of bright young boys and . . . two or three really outstanding trial men." Instead, with a few notable exceptions, the War Crimes Branch had given him either "utterly vacuous political hacks" or "the middle-aged in-between variety who cannot be given dirty work and are not good enough to trust with solo flights."[74]

2. Foreign Delegations

A number of countries sent delegations to Nuremberg to assist the OCC. Delegations from France, Poland, Czechoslovakia, and the Netherlands remained in Nuremberg throughout the trials; delegations from Norway, Greece, Yugoslavia, and Belgium watched one or more trials. The delegations varied significantly in size: France sent 72 people, while Czechoslovakia, the Netherlands, and Greece each sent eight.[75] According to Taylor, "[b]oth the permanent and the temporary foreign delegations were of great assistance to the prosecution in ascertaining the facts concerning crimes and atrocities alleged to have been committed in countries which they represented and in procuring documents and witnesses for the court proceedings."[76]

In addition to sending the largest delegation, France was also the most interested in becoming formally involved in the trials. In October 1946, the Ministry of Justice asked the OCC to permit it to designate two French attorneys to join the prosecution staff in the *Medical* case. Although there is no evidence that the French attorneys ever participated in that trial, Charles Gerthoffer, who had been France's assistant prosecutor at the IMT, later addressed the tribunal and questioned a witness in *Ministries*.[77]

Britain also briefly sent a delegation to the OCC. In an attempt to spur British interest in the NMT trials, Taylor had originally proposed having a British prosecutor participate in *Krupp*, perhaps alongside a French and Soviet prosecutor. The Foreign Office was lukewarm about the idea; instead, as a "palliative to OMGUS," it dispatched an official observer, Gordon Hilton, to the OCC for a renewable period of three months.[78] Hilton was "dubious about the utility of his own position, and equivocal about the trials themselves"; less than two weeks after

---

[72] Ibid., 2.   [73] Taylor, *Final Report*, 43.
[74] Letter from Taylor to Petersen, 30 Sept. 1946, TTP-20-1-3-34, at 3.
[75] Bloxham, 41.   [76] Taylor, *Final Report*, 46.
[77] Ibid., 29 n. 80.   [78] Bloxham, 40.

his arrival, he said he would rather return to Britain on unpaid leave than remain in Nuremberg.[79] Nevertheless, he did not leave the OCC until he had witnessed the three industrialist trials.[80]

3. Female Prosecutors

Taylor was clearly ahead of his time when it came to recruiting female prosecutors. No woman ever spoke at the IMT, either for the United States or for one of the other Allies. By contrast, Taylor's prosecution staff included nearly a dozen women, and most of those women appeared as counsel in one of the trials.[81] Indeed, only five trials—*Pohl, Flick, Hostage, Einstazgruppen,* and *High Command*—did not include a female prosecutor. Esther J. Johnson appeared at the *Medical* trial and in *RuSHA*; Dorothy M. Hunt appeared in *Milch*; Sadie B. Arbuthnot appeared in the *Justice* case; Mary Kaufman, who had worked for the National Labor Relations Board, and Belle Mayer, who had represented the Treasury Department at the London Conference, appeared in *Farben*; Cecelia H. Goetz appeared in the *Krupp* trial; and Dorothea G. Minskoff appeared in *Ministries*. Women also dominated the Economics Division, which figured prominently in the OCC's early planning: when the division was dissolved and its personnel reassigned, three of the four attorneys—Sadi Mase, Mary Bakshian, and Cecelia Goetz—and five of the 14 research analysts were women.[82]

Cecelia Goetz's role in the OCC was particularly notable. Goetz had stellar credentials: she had graduated second in her class from NYU Law School, had been Editor-in-Chief of the law review—a first in American legal education, at least among the major law reviews—and had worked during the war as an attorney in the Civil Division of the Department of Justice.[83] The War Department had initially resisted Taylor's desire to hire her as a prosecutor, a senior-level position in the OCC, but Taylor had ultimately prevailed—as he did on a number of occasions when he wanted to hire female prosecutors.[84] Goetz turned down a supervisory role in the Justice Department to join Taylor's staff, which would have been the first such role ever offered to a woman.[85] Her gamble paid off: she not only appeared regularly in the *Krupp* trial, she was an Associate Counsel, a position that placed her above six male prosecutors.

---

[79] Bloxham, 41.

[80] Ibid.

[81] Drexel A. Sprecher, "The Central Role of Telford Taylor as U.S. Chief of Counsel in The Subsequent Proceedings," 37 *Colum. J. Transnat'l L.* 673, 674 (1999).

[82] OCCWC Memo, Dissolution of the Economics Division.

[83] Diane Marie Amann, "Portraits of Women at Nuremberg," in *Proceedings of the Third International Humanitarian Law Dialogs* 31, 44 (Elizabeth Andersen & David M. Crane eds, 2010).

[84] Cecelia Goetz, "Impressions of Telford Taylor at Nuremberg," 37 *Colum. J. Transnat'l L.* 669, 669 (1999).

[85] Amann, 44.

4. Jews and Communists

The presence of female prosecutors was not the only aspect of the OCC's staff that caused controversy. Many of Taylor's prosecutors were Jewish, and many of those, such as Robert Kempner, were German-speaking refugees.[86] As fear of the Soviets undermined U.S. support for the NMT trials—particularly those involving the industrialists—it became increasingly common to explain the trials as being primarily motivated by Jewish "vindictiveness."[87] The following statement by Congressman John Rankin, a Democrat from Mississippi, on the floor of the House in November 1947, was typical:

What is taking place in Nuremberg, Germany, is a disgrace to the United States. Every other country has now washed its hands and withdrawn from this Saturnalia of persecution. But a racial minority, two and half years after the war closed, are in Nuremberg not only hanging German soldiers but trying German businessmen in the name of the United States.[88]

Similar sentiments were expressed in December 1948 by two Representatives who believed that rebuilding the German economy was being hindered by the industrialist trials. According to John Taber, a Republican from New York, "the trouble is that they"—OMGUS—"have too many of these people who are not American citizens mixed up in those trials, and they are very hostile to the Germans." Harold Knutson, a Republican from Minnesota (who, ironically, had emigrated to the United States from Norway), agreed and suggested, "[i]s it not just possible that these aliens who are employed by the Government to prosecute these cases do not want to let go of a good thing?"[89] "There is no question about that," Taber responded. "On top of that, they do not have the right kind of disposition to create good will and get rid of the attitude that some of these people have had."[90]

Not even General Clay, otherwise a strong supporter of the American war-crimes program, was immune from believing that the supposed excesses of the program were attributable to Jews' desire for revenge against the Nazis. As he said years later:

The British and French didn't have the same feelings towards the Nazis that we did. Neither one had a huge Jewish population that had developed a hatred you could well understand, which was true in this country. I'm not critical of it at all because I can understand how it developed ... Well, they went too far in their demands for denazification.[91]

Another common—and related—criticism of the OCC was that it had been infiltrated by Communists. On 9 July 1947, for example, Congressman George A. Dondero, a Republican from Michigan, attacked John Patterson, the Secretary

---

[86] Hagan, 27; Maguire, 172.

[87] That allegation, it should be pointed out, was not directed only at the Jewish prosecutors. During the *Farben* trial, Drexel Sprecher was accused of being "anti-German" by an assistant to one of the judges. Bower, 358.

[88] Quoted in ibid., 351.

[89] Maguire, 174.   [90] Ibid.

[91] Quoted in Maguire, 172. During the *Farben* trial, one of the judges also reportedly complained that "[t]here are too many Jews on the prosecution." Josiah E. DuBois, *Generals in Grey Suits* 182 (1953).

of War, for failing to prevent "Communist sympathizers" from infiltrating the Army.[92] Dondero specifically alleged that ten members of the prosecution staff in the *Farben* trial were such sympathizers, including Belle Mayer and Josiah DuBois, the latter of whom he described as "a known left-winger from the Treasury Department who had been a close student of the Communist party line."[93] Incensed, DuBois publicly challenged Dondero to repeat the accusation outside of the House of Representatives, where he would not be immune from a libel claim. Not surprisingly, Dondero refused.[94]

C. Funding

Very little information exists about the OCC's budget. It is clear, however, that funding problems caused serious harm to the OCC's overall planning. Indeed, one of Taylor's prosecutors, Abraham Pomerantz—a "prize catch" for the OCC, because he was an experienced litigator who had sued German shipping companies as a commercial litigator before the war[95]—eventually quit because he had become convinced, with ample justification, that OMGUS was intentionally underfunding the organization.[96]

Budget discussions first took place in February 1946 at a meeting between Taylor and fiscal officers of the United States Forces European Theater (USFET). The budget proposed at that meeting called for the OCC—then still the SPD—to employ a total of 491 personnel at an overall cost of $2,953,797. This figure, according to Taylor, did not include the costs of any personnel involved in the IMT trial, which had started a few months earlier, nor did it include the payment of judges, their staff, or employees of the Central Secretariat.[97]

Taylor then traveled to Washington to discuss the OCC's budget with the Assistant Secretary of War and the head of the War Department's Civil Affairs Division. The three men agreed that the NMT trials should involve 200–400 defendants and that the trials should begin as soon as possible after the IMT ended using as many zonal courts as necessary. They also determined that the OCC would require a "very substantial increase" in the 491 personnel previously discussed with USFET.[98]

After returning to Nuremberg, Taylor submitted a request to USFET to fund 982 positions in the OCC. USFET not only refused to allocate the requested amount, it did not even allocate sufficient funds for the originally contemplated 491 positions. Instead, in late August, it arbitrarily set the OCC's budget for fiscal 1947 at $1,000,000.[99] Even worse, contrary to Taylor's initial agreement with

---

[92] Jeffreys, 318.　　[93] Quoted in Bower, 351.

[94] Jeffreys, 318.

[95] Jonathan A. Bush, "The Prehistory of Corporations and Conspiracy in International Criminal Law: What Nuremberg Really Said," 109 *Colum. L. Rev.* 1094, 1149 (2009).

[96] Ibid., 1171–2.

[97] Memo from Taylor to Deputy Military Governor, 27 Aug. 1946, NA-260-183a1-2-11, at 3.

[98] Ibid., 4.　　[99] Ibid.

USFET, that budget was required to cover the more than 200 IMT personnel who were expected to continue working on the IMT case well into the new fiscal year, costs that Taylor estimated at a minimum of $100,000 per quarter.[100]

Taylor immediately fired off an angry memo to Frank Keating, the Deputy Military Governor of OMGUS. Noting that the $1,000,000 was "far out of line" with what had been discussed previously, Taylor observed that "[t]he result of the budget is that the zonal trial program as outlined in this memorandum, and as generally approved by the War Department, will be delayed unless steps are taken to obtain additional appropriations."[101] He thus asked OMGUS to approve a revised appropriation of $3,222,275—the amount the OCC estimated it needed to finance the six trials it planned to begin in 1947 and to cover the remaining expenses of the IMT trial.[102]

To some extent, the War Department was sympathetic to Taylor and the OCC's plight. General Clay wrote to Taylor on September 13 to inform him that the War Department was submitting a request for $3,500,000 "to cover all war crimes trials with major portions for Germany" and was making immediately available to the OCC an additional $1,000,000, bringing its allocation at the time to $2,000,000. The latter figure, Clay asserted, "will permit you to instigate immediate action to carry out your program for balance of fiscal year 1947 as submitted to this office."[103]

Although the $3,500,000 was a considerable improvement over USFET's initial $1,000,000, it still fell far short of the OCC's needs. Taylor's budget request covered only fiscal 1947; he had also requested an additional $2,200,000 to cover the first six months of fiscal 1948—funds that he believed the OCC would require following the planned completion of the trials by 31 December 1947.[104] The OCC never received the 1948 funds: in mid-1947, Keating told Taylor in no uncertain terms that no additional funding would be forthcoming.[105] The resulting budgetary shortfall, combined with the shortage of available judges and the fact that the trials were progressing much more slowly than anticipated—seven would carry over into 1948, and *Ministries* would not end until November 18—forced Taylor to scale back the OCC's trial schedule considerably, reducing the number of defendants from his initial estimate of "at least 266" to 185 and the number of trials from 36 to 12.

There is little question that—as Pomerantz insisted—the War Department deliberately underfunded the OCC. Keating later admitted to Clay that he had told Taylor there would be "no exceptions" made to the existing budget because Taylor's trial schedule was "getting a bit out of hand."[106] Clay clearly agreed with

---

[100] Ibid., 5.   [101] Ibid.
[102] Ibid.
[103] Memo from Clay to Office of U.S. Chief of Counsel, War Crimes Commission, 13 Sept. 1946, NA-260-183a1-2-11, at 1.
[104] Memo from Taylor to Deputy Military Governor, 27 Aug. 1946, 3.
[105] Bloxham, 50.   [106] Ibid.

Keating's assessment: having described Taylor's manpower requests as "excessive" as early as September 1946,[107] Clay never pressed the War Department for additional funds for the OCC. According to Bloxham, their reluctance to support Taylor's more ambitious program came from a familiar source: "the dictates of the Cold War."[108]

III. The Military Tribunals

A. The Court

Ordinance No. 7 was silent concerning the location of the tribunals. The NMTs ultimately replaced the IMT in the Palace of Justice in Nuremberg, but that decision was not made until late 1946, when it became clear that a second IMT would not be held. Prior to that time, "[c]onsiderable time and energy" was spent considering alternative locations in Nuremberg and other cities in the American zone, such as Regensberg, Straubing, and Lendshut.[109]

Once the decision was made, the Palace of Justice had to be renovated to accommodate the possibility that six tribunals—Taylor's initial estimate—would function simultaneously. The IMT courtroom was left untouched, and five new courtrooms were constructed: one that held 24 defendants, like the IMT courtroom, and four that each held 14 defendants.[110] IBM then installed the same kind of simultaneous-interpretation equipment in the new courtrooms that had proven so successful in the IMT trial.[111]

B. The Secretariat

Article XII of Ordinance No. 7 provided that "[a] Central Secretariat to assist the tribunals to be appointed hereunder shall be established as soon as practicable." The Secretary General was selected by and administratively subordinate to OMGUS,[112] but it was "subject to the supervision of the members of the tribunals," instead of to General Clay.[113] OMGUS formally created the Central Secretariat on 25 October 1946.

Like the Registry at a modern tribunal, the Central Secretariat served as the "administrative and executive arm of the tribunals."[114] Pursuant to Article XIV of Ordinance No. 7, it was responsible for receiving documents submitted by the prosecution and defense, preparing records of the trial proceedings, and providing clerical services to the tribunals. It was also tasked with providing a range of services

---

[107] Letter from Clay to Heubner, 9 Sept. 1946, quoted in Mark E. Spicka, "The Devil's Chemists on Trial," 61 *The Historian* 865, 873 (1999).

[108] Bloxham, 51.

[109] Memo from OCCWC to War Dept., 17 Aug. 1946, NA-153–1018-5-85-1, at 1.

[110] Taylor, *Final Report*, 77. The effect the size of the courtrooms had on the OCC's case planning is discussed in Chapter 3.

[111] Ibid., 20.   [112] Ibid., 33.   [113] Ordinance No. 7, Art. XIII.

[114] Taylor, *Final Report*, 31.

to defense counsel through the Defense Information Center, which the Secretary General created not long after his appointment.[115] The Defense Center—as it was renamed in early 1947—served as a liaison between the prosecution and the defense; procured defense witnesses and documents; provided the defense with the prosecution's evidence and motions; arranged for offices, equipment, billeting, and food; and issued travel order for defense counsel to travel throughout the German occupied zone.[116]

By the time OMGUS created the Central Secretariat, the OCC had been in existence for nearly 10 months. As a result, the OCC "was obliged to undertake numerous functions which, under other circumstances, might more logically have been discharged by the Central Secretariat."[117] Those functions included procuring court reporters and interpreters, reproducing and distributing documents, and handling the tribunal's day-to-day administrative matters.

C. The Tribunals

Article II(b) of Ordinance No. 7 provided that each tribunal "shall consist of three or more members to be designated by the Military Governor. One alternate member may be designated to any tribunal if deemed advisable by the Military Governor." Assigning judges to a specific tribunal was actually the second step in the appointment process; the judges themselves were selected by the President in his role as Commander-in-Chief.[118] The tribunals were administratively subordinate to OMGUS, but remained "independent and responsible only to themselves in their judicial actions."[119]

The OCC had no official role in the selection or designation of judges. Taylor later admitted, however, that General Clay would consult with him when he decided whether to renew a judge's appointment—a not infrequent occurrence, given that eight of the 32 judges who served on the NMT heard more than one case.[120] In fact, the one judge who served on three cases, Michael Musmanno, actually met with Taylor to address Taylor's concerns about his "extravagant and often ill-advised displays of feeling" on the bench. According to Taylor, Judge Musmanno "did, indeed, confess error and promised to keep better control of himself. It was on this basis that he remained in Nuremberg; the entire *Milch* tribunal remained on the *Pohl* case, and thereafter Musmanno stayed on as presiding judge in the *Einsatzgruppen* case."[121] There is no question that Musmanno was a colorful figure—as described in Chapter 4—and Taylor's concerns might well have been warranted. But it should go without saying that conditioning

---

[115] Final Report of the Defense Center, XV TWC 187.
[116] Ibid., 188.
[117] Taylor, *Final Report*, 38.
[118] Letter from Young to Sutton, 31 Dec. 1947, NA-153–1018-8-86-2-1.
[119] Taylor, *Final Report*, 33.
[120] See OCCWC Background Information, Judges of the Six Military Tribunals, undated, TTP-5-1-1-10 ("Background Information on Judges").
[121] Letter from Taylor to Irving, 9 Mar. 1972, TTP-14-6-10–13, at 3.

a judge's appointment on the Chief of Counsel's approval is irreconcilable with judicial independence.

Although the tribunals were military, all of the judges except Musmanno, who was a Naval officer, were civilians. According to Taylor, a number of factors counseled making use of civilian lawyers instead of lay military officers—a decision that separated the NMTs from other American military tribunals, such as those hearing cases at Dachau:

Firstly, while the usual type of issues under the laws and customs of war (such as military courts martial are accustomed to deal with) would undoubtedly arise, the trials under Law No. 10 would also involve numerous other complicated issues of law and fact which could best be dealt with by professional jurists. Secondly, in trials of the scope and importance such as those under Law No. 10, it seemed to me desirable that the reasons for the Tribunals' decisions should be fully set forth in judicial opinions; military courts martial do not customarily render opinions. Thirdly, excellent as the work of military courts-martial usually is, it seemed to me that judgments by professional, civilian judges would command more prestige both within Germany and abroad, in the legal profession and with the general public alike. Fourthly, in any event it would have been extremely difficult to procure enough senior military officers to furnish the necessary number of judges for the Nuernberg tribunal.[122]

Taylor's preference for civilian judges was reflected in Article II(b) of Ordinance No. 7, which provided that "all members and alternates shall be lawyers who have been admitted to practice, for at least five years, in the highest courts of one of the United States or its territories or of the District of Columbia, or who have been admitted to practice in the United States Supreme Court."

The decision to staff the NMTs with civilian judges has always been criticized. In May 1948, for example, Bishop Theophil Wurm, the chairman of Germany's Protestant Church Council—and one of the most strident and persistent critics of the war-crimes program, as discussed in Chapter 15—wrote to General Clay to complain that the NMT was "to-day, after the other victor nations have withdrawn, a purely American Tribunal which no longer possesses the prerequisites of a Military Tribunal. By the appointment of civilians as judges for a trial of prisoners of war of officer's rank the Nürnberg Tribunal has departed from the up to now customary practice laid down in the statutes of international law."[123] Wurm's view was echoed nearly 40 years later by Hans Laternser, Field Marshal List's primary attorney in the *Hostage* case, who wrote that "[t]hese courts did not at all fulfil the characteristics of a military court. A court does not become a military court by being so called; a court becomes a military court only by its staffing with officers whose ranks correspond to that of the defendants."[124] Neither critic, however, provided

[122] Taylor, *Final Report*, 28–9.
[123] Letter from Bishop Wurm to Clay, 20 May 1948, in Theophil Wurm et al., *Memorandum by the Evangelical Church in Germany on the Question of War Crimes Trials Before American Military Courts* 25 (1949), NA-238-213-4 ("Wurm Memorandum").
[124] Dr. Hans Laternser, "Looking Back at the Nuremberg Trials with Special Consideration of the Processes Against Military Leaders," in Mettraux, 483.

any legal support for the claim that a military tribunal had to use military officers as judges. Nor could they—after all, the IMT had itself made use of civilian judges, as General Clay reminded Bishop Wurm in his response to his letter.[125]

Once OMGUS decided to use civilian judges, it had to recruit them. As noted above, Ordinance No. 7 required only five years of practice; no judicial experience was required. Taylor, the War Department, and OMGUS all agreed, however, that it was critically important for the NMT judges to be of the same "standing and prestige"[126] as the judges who served at the IMT, because the "calibre of this tribunal and the history of this trial would lose some of its significance for the future if... individuals in somewhat comparable positions were conducted before tribunals significantly less competent or less carefully selected."[127] They also believed that the very best judges should be assigned to the industrialist cases, given their complexity and notoriety.[128]

The War Department's initial planning reflected this desire to recruit prominent judges, but implicitly acknowledged that it would be difficult to do so. A 7 August 1946 memo stated that the War Department wanted to recruit judges in the mold of Jerome Frank, Learned Hand, and Roscoe Pound.[129] It nevertheless suggested that they staff the tribunals not only with federal trial and appellate judges, but also with "[p]ersons of high standing in the recognized law schools"; state court judges, "including retired judges"; and "members of the Bar of high standing." Regarding the latter, the memo emphasized that no tribunal should consist solely of practicing attorneys—at a minimum, the presiding judge needed to have judicial experience.[130]

A number of federal judges expressed interest in serving at Nuremberg, including William Denman, a judge on the Ninth Circuit who had been a professor at Hastings College of Law, and Lloyld L. Black, a judge in the Eastern District of Washington who had presided over the trial of Gordon K. Hirabayashi, a Japanese-American who had defied a removal order.[131] In early November, however, the Chief Justice of the Supreme Court, Fred Vinson, refused to make federal judges available to the NMTs. The problem was not that a federal judge could not sit on a military tribunal: Francis Biddle, the Attorney General, had already upheld the legality of Jackson and John J. Parker, a Fourth Circuit judge, serving on the IMT.[132] Instead, Vinson simply believed that the federal judiciary's increasing backlog of cases in federal court made it impossible to spare any judges.[133]

The War Department was thus left with state judges and members of state bar associations. Recruitment was initially slowed by OMGUS's policy of not permit-

[125] Letter from Clay to Bishop Wurm, 19 June 1948, in Wurm Memorandum, 33.
[126] Memo from Bontecou to Gunn, 7 Aug. 1946, NA-153–1018-8-84-1, at 1.
[127] Memo from Fahy to Secretary of State, 24 July 1946, NA-153–1018-8-84-1, at 3.
[128] Letter from Taylor to Petersen, 30 Sept. 1946, 2.
[129] Memo from Bontecou to Gunn, 7 Aug. 1946, 2.
[130] Ibid., 1.
[131] Cable from WDSCA to OCCWC, 8 Oct. 1946, NA-153–1018-13-87-2.
[132] Letter from Gunn to Hall, 10 Oct. 1946, NA-153–1018-8-84-1.
[133] Letter from Gunn to Denman, 15 Nov. 1946, NA-153–1018-8-84-1.

ting wives to accompany their husbands to Nuremberg—just as it had delayed Taylor's acceptance of the Chief of Counsel position—but accelerated when the policy was reversed. Thirty-two judges were ultimately recruited, the first of whom, Walter Beals, a Justice of the Supreme Court of Washington, was appointed by the President on 24 October 1946. Twenty-five of the 32 were state court judges, including 11 who, like Beals, sat on their state's highest court. The other seven included a law school dean and practicing attorneys.

The first 24 judges that arrived in Nuremberg were divided into six tribunals, designated Tribunals I–VI. Each consisted of three members and an alternate. Only one alternate judge ever replaced a member of a tribunal: after Carrington T. Marshall, the former Chief Justice of the Ohio Supreme Court, was forced to resign from the *Justice* case because of illness, Justin W. Harding took over from him.[134] The initial six tribunals, which were created between 25 October 1946 and 8 August 1947, heard the first seven NMT cases. Tribunals I–V then heard the final five cases, although they were staffed either solely with new judges or with a combination of old and new judges.

Article XIII of Ordinance No. 7 permitted the tribunals to create a Committee of Presiding Judges "when at least three tribunals [were] functioning." That Committee—which was responsible for overseeing the Central Secretariat and the day-to-day functioning of the tribunals—was created on 17 February 1947 after Tribunal III was formed to try the *Justice* case. The Committee reached its peak strength between November 1947 and February 1948, when seven tribunals were functioning at once,[135] and held its final meeting on 11 August 1948 after Tribunal II filed its supplemental judgment in *Pohl* and disbanded, reducing the number of active tribunals to two.[136]

Chapter 4, which contains synopses of the 12 NMT trials, provides information on the judges themselves. It is clear from their overall profile, though, that the War Department failed to recruit judges equivalent to those that served on the IMT. As Sprecher later recalled: "Some of them were very good . . . On the other hand, there were some judges that weren't. The War Department didn't have any real means of checking them out . . . It was difficult to recruit top level judges, the Nuremberg Trials were not front page stuff after the first trial."[137]

---

[134] XV TWC 1040.   [135] Ibid., 1049.
[136] Ibid., 1062.   [137] Quoted in Maguire, 153.

3

The Evolution of the Trial Program

Introduction

As noted in the previous chapter, although Taylor's initial forecast called for at least 36 trials involving at least 266 defendants, the OCC ultimately managed to hold only 12 trials involving 185 defendants. This chapter explains that dramatic reduction. Section I focuses on the OCC's early planning, describing how the OCC determined which of the nearly 100,000 war-crimes suspects detained pursuant to JCS 1023/10 were eligible to be prosecuted in the zonal trials and then examining the general principles the OCC used to group those potential defendants into particular cases. Section II traces the gradual evolution of the OCC's actual trial program, explaining how the OCC selected the 12 trials and explaining why, for various reasons, it decided to abandon a number of other cases.

I. Principles of Selection

A. Early Planning

The OCC—then still known as the SPD—began to determine who would be tried in the zonal trials in May 1946, not long after Taylor returned from his recruiting trip to Washington.[1] Some progress had already been made: as Acting Chief of Counsel in Taylor's absence, Drexel Sprecher had created a section within the SPD dedicated to examining the evidence against industrialists and financiers.[2] Nevertheless, the SPD was still faced with the daunting task of finding a way to examine the individual criminal responsibility of the nearly 100,000 Germans who had been detained in the American zone as suspected war criminals pursuant to JCS 1023/10.

Taylor began by establishing a working group "for the purpose of making an over-all study of Germany's political, military, economic, and social organization so that the principal channels of responsibility and authority in the Reich government and industry could be determined, and the most responsible individuals in each field of enterprise or government activity identified."[3] The group, which was overseen by Werner Peiser, a German scholar who had been dismissed from the

---

[1] Taylor, *Final Report*, 159.   [2] Earl, 42.   [3] Taylor, *Final Report*, 55.

Prussian civil service in 1933 and who had served as an interrogator for the IMT, had to work quickly: pressure was mounting on OMGUS to release the civilian detainees, and Clay thought that, in terms of stabilizing Germany, it was psychologically important for there to be no delay between the end of the IMT trial and the beginning of the NMT trials.[4] Indeed, although he knew that the timeline was optimistic, Clay wanted all of the trials to be concluded by the end of 1947.[5]

By August 1946, Peiser's group had identified approximately 2,500 "major war criminals."[6] The SPD then began the even more difficult process of reducing the 2,500 to a number it could actually prosecute. Despite his concerns about the SPD's budget, Taylor's initial planning was extremely ambitious. In his August 27 memo to Keating requesting additional funding, Taylor stated that "it is planned to select from this group 200 to 400 of the worst offenders," leaving the others to be prosecuted by the denazification tribunals.[7] Those 200 to 400 suspects would be tried in six zonal courts, each of which Taylor expected would be able to conduct at least six trials per year—a total of 36 trials. The number of defendants at each trial would vary, but the SPD was assuming an average of seven defendants for planning purposes. 252 defendants could thus be tried each year.[8]

Taylor's timetable for completing the SPD's work was equally ambitious. He anticipated that two zonal courts would begin trials in November 1946, two would begin in December 1946, and the final two would begin in January 1947. If all went according to plan, Taylor believed that his office would be able to meet Clay's 31 December 1947 deadline.[9]

B. Selecting Defendants

Narrowing the list of 2,500 suspects to 200–400 required the OCC—as it soon became—to further refine its selection criteria. Sprecher, now the Director of the Economics Division, had already drafted a list of criteria for industrialists and financiers. That list identified a number of activities that were indicative of criminality, such as making "substantial financial contributions" to the Nazis and profiting from plunder or slave labor.[10] The Ministries Division adopted similar criteria, including "participation in the Nazi regime" and "preparation for aggressive war."[11]

Once a Division settled on selection criteria, it then determined which suspects it would actually indict. The basic requirement for indictment, according

---

[4] Cable from Clay to War Department, 4 Sept. 1946, NA-153–1018-5-85-1, at 1.

[5] Ibid.

[6] Memo from Taylor to Deputy Military Governor, 27 Aug. 1946, 2. In his Final Report, Taylor put the number at just less than 5,000. See Taylor, *Final Report*, 55. It is unclear which figure is correct.

[7] Ibid.   [8] Ibid.   [9] Ibid.

[10] OCCWC, Points of Information and Evidence Relevant to the Investigation of Leading German Industrialists, 3 June 1946, NA-238-159-4-12, at 1–2.

[11] Ministries Group, Criteria of Criminality for Prospective Defendants, undated, NA-238–20401-7, at 1–2.

to Taylor, was narrowly legal: whether "there appeared to be substantial evidence of criminal conduct under accepted principles of international penal law."[12] Indeed, Taylor later insisted—with justification—that the NMT trials were "carried out for the punishment of crime, not for the punishment of political or other beliefs, however mistaken or vicious."[13]

To be sure, it was easier for the OCC to articulate the "substantial evidence" requirement than to apply it. Taylor openly acknowledged that he and his staff could not simply select defendants on the basis of "what the evidence showed," because the available evidence "was infinitely vast and varied, and we could not possibly scan more than a small fraction of it."[14] Two questions are thus critically important: how reliable was the limited evidence that was available to the OCC, and how reliable was the process that the OCC used to determine whether the evidence against a suspect qualified as substantial?

1. Evidence

There are significant questions about the reliability of the evidence that the OCC used to select defendants. For example, although interrogations were a critical source of inculpatory evidence, Taylor himself admitted that those conducted prior to the establishment of the Interrogation Branch by IMT interrogators—a significant percentage of the total number of interrogations—were almost always worthless, because very few of the interrogators spoke German.[15] The Interrogation Branch's procedures were far better, as discussed above, yet the quality of its interrogations was still uneven.[16]

Captured German documents, the OCC's primary source of evidence, also posed difficulties. Nearly 90 percent of the documents introduced at the NMT trials had not been used by the IMT and thus had to be screened and analyzed by the OCC.[17] Most of the OCC's research analysts were highly qualified; the Ministries Division, for example, required not only fluency in German and knowledge of French, but also knowledge of Nazi history, "legal experience plus a knowledge of international law," and "acquaintance with criminal investigation techniques."[18] Those qualifications, however, could only partially offset the fact that the OCC had neither the time nor the resources to thoroughly screen the mass of captured documents.[19] As Ferencz noted in a September 1946 memo to Taylor, the Berlin Branch's investigations were undermined by its "shortage of skilled personnel."[20] Only five analysts from the Ministries Division were analyzing documents from the

---

[12] Preliminary Report to the Secretary of the Army by the Chief of Counsel for War Crimes, 12 May 1948, reprinted in Taylor, *Final Report*, 114 (Appendix A).
[13] Ibid., 2.
[14] Taylor, *Final Report*, 75.   [15] Ibid., 60.
[16] Frank M. Buscher, *The U.S. War Crimes Trial Program in Germany, 1946–1955*, 354 (1989).
[17] Mendelsohn, 61.
[18] Ibid., 88.   [19] Ibid.
[20] Memo from Ferencz to Taylor, 21 Sept. 1946, NA-238-159-4-28, at 1.

Ministry of Foreign Affairs, even though "the size of the job to be done is overwhelming."[21] The SS Division had nine analysts, but the group was faced with "an almost inexhaustible amount of material."[22] And the Economics Division was making good progress, but did not have the capacity to investigate any newly identified defendants and needed a replacement for one of its analysts who had been loaned to the Ministries Division.[23]

2. Analysis

There is also reason to believe that the OCC's lack of time and resources negatively affected its ability to apply its "substantial evidence" criterion, leading it to indict suspects against whom the evidence was weak and to ignore suspects potentially more deserving of prosecution. That is Michael Marrus's explanation, for example, of the *Medical* case's "haphazard, hastily improvised character"[24]:

As Taylor later admitted, he and his colleagues were swamped with evidence, and had real difficulty digesting what had been gathered for them. One result was that important perpetrators slipped through the Americans' net (the most notorious of whom was Josef Mengele, the "Angel of Death" of Auschwitz), while others were charged on the basis of insufficient evidence. Evidence of overly hasty prosecution abounds in the cases of the seven accused who were acquitted—the average number of acquittals in the subsequent proceedings being three.[25]

Cecelia Goetz's personal experience with the OCC suggests that such problems were not unique to the *Medical* case. When she arrived in Nuremberg, she was struck by "what appeared to be a lack of systematic organization."[26] After being assigned to work on *Flick*, for example, she was told to collect evidence "[w]ithout any guidance" whatsoever. Even worse, when she complained about the "vagueness" of her assignment, she was quickly transferred to *Krupp*.[27]

Ben Ferencz's September 1946 memo to Taylor concerning the Berlin Branch is equally troubling. Ferencz noted that none of the analysts were gathering evidence against members of the Gestapo or officials in the Ministries of Propaganda, Education, and Finance, even though "[a]ll of these are at least as worthy of prosecution as some of the objectives now being pursued."[28] The problem, according to Ferencz, was that "no attorney in Nurnberg is assigned to the preparation of the prosecution, and hence there has been no 'push' from Nurnberg on these matters . . . the analysts here are already busy with the problems at hand, and [do not have] time to search for evidence against persons in whom no interest has been expressed."[29]

---

[21] Memo from Ferencz to Taylor, 3.   [22] Ibid., 6.   [23] Ibid., 8.   [24] Ibid.
[25] Michael R. Marrus, "The Nuremberg Doctors' Trial in Historical Context," 73 *Bull. Hist. Med.* 106, 110–1 (1999).
[26] Goetz, 670.   [27] Ibid.
[28] Memo from Ferencz to Taylor, 21 Sept. 1946, 1.   [29] Ibid., 2.

C. Trial Groups

As the selection of defendants progressed, it became increasingly obvious that the number of suspects who satisfied the OCC's selection criteria far exceeded the number of suspects the OCC could realistically indict.[30] The question thus arose "as to how the defendants should be grouped for purposes of trial."[31]

Taylor's solution was to group defendants into cases "according to the sphere of activity in which they were primarily engaged": suspects who had conducted medical experiments would be tried together; suspects who were involved in a particular branch of the SS would be prosecuted in a case limited to that branch's activities; industrialists and financiers who had supported the Nazis would be tried in a case that focused on the particular combine or bank with which they were associated; and so on.[32] Such an approach, Taylor believed, would not only "narrow the factual scope of the trials,"[33] it would also create a "balanced program, covering representatives of all the important segments of the Third Reich."[34] The "balanced program" was considered particularly important, because the prosecution staff believed that it would dispel the illusion "now being zealously fostered in Germany and elsewhere that the Third Reich was solely a tyranny of Hitler and his personal henchmen."[35]

In retrospect, it might have been a mistake for the OCC to construct cases solely on the basis of the defendants' occupations. Consider, for example, the OCC's lack of success at obtaining convictions for crimes against peace: although four different trials involved such crimes—*Farben*, *Krupp*, *Ministries*, and *High Command*—only five defendants in *Ministries* were ever convicted,[36] and two of those defendants later had their convictions set aside.[37] As we will see in Chapter 8, the charges failed against the military defendants in *High Command* because the prosecution was unable to prove that the defendants had been in a position to influence Hitler's plans for aggressive war, while the charges against the industrialist defendants in *Krupp* and *Farben* failed because the prosecutors failed to prove that the defendants had knowledge of those plans. It seems reasonable to suggest that the evidence might have been much stronger if, instead of relegating those charges to four trials involving a variety of different crimes, the OCC had dedicated a case to crimes against peace and included all of the most important defendants within it. An aggression-specific trial—one that centralized all of the evidence of aggression that was introduced piecemeal at the four trials—would have greatly increased the

---

[30] Taylor, *Final Report*, 73. Indeed, Taylor would later claim that, with sufficient time and resources, the OCC could have convicted between 2,000 and 20,000 defendants. Bower, 352–3.

[31] Taylor, *Final Report*, at 76.

[32] Ibid., 76–7.   [33] Ibid., 160.

[34] Memo from Taylor to Jackson, 30 Oct. 1946, NA-153–1018-8-1-54-2, at 1.

[35] Transcript of Radio Recording, Elwyn Jones, "The American Trials at Nuremberg," 20 Oct. 1947, TTP-14-3-1-17, at 3.

[36] Taylor, *Final Report*, 214.   [37] See Chapter 8.

OCC's ability to explain Hitler's aggressive plans and the defendants' various roles within them. Such a trial would also have made logistical sense, given that the complexity of the crimes against peace charges required Taylor to largely defer trials involving them until later in the OCC's program—*Krupp*, *Ministries*, and *High Command* were Cases 10, 11, and 12, respectively.

Interestingly, on 22 August 1946, Abe Pomerantz, the OCC prosecutor who had sued German shipping companies before the war, sent a long memo to Taylor urging him to consider joining all of the industrialist defendants suspected of committing crimes against peace into one case. Such a trial, Pomerantz argued, was "[i]n the interest of painting a whole picture" of the role the industrialists had played in supporting the Nazis' wars of aggression.[38] Sprecher rejected Pomerantz's suggestion, contending that a trial involving industrialists from a number of different corporations would be too complex and time-consuming.[39] That was a surprising response, given that just three months later, on November 30, Sprecher suggested to Taylor that the industrialist cases should be followed up by "one big case of from 12 to 24 of the leaders in the slave labor program" and by other thematic cases, such as one that focused on plunder.[40] Taylor never acted on Sprecher's proposal.

Wise or not, having decided on occupation-centered cases, the OCC then had to determine which suspects within the targeted occupations it would include in them. That decision involved three steps. The OCC began by determining a minimum level of responsibility for inclusion in a particular case. It then identified in which of the Palace of Justice's six courtrooms the trial would be held. Finally, it indicted as many suspects who satisfied the responsibility criterion that could be accommodated in the selected courtroom.[41]

According to Taylor, courtroom size played a role in the construction of "several" cases.[42] One of those was *Ministries*—as discussed in more detail below, Taylor specifically refused a request from the World Jewish Congress to expand the trial on the ground that no additional space was available. The others appear to be *Flick*, *Farben*, *RuSHA*, *Einsatzgruppen*, and *High Command*. An OCC memo concerning arrestees indicates that Joseph Gebhardt, Chief of Tax Control in the Reich Ministry of Finance, was not included in *Flick* solely for space reasons.[43] *Farben* and *Einsatzgruppen* each involved 24 defendants—the maximum the two largest courtrooms could hold—but the OCC's first trial program identified 35 suspects in the former[44] and 27 in the latter.[45] There were 14 defendants in *RuSHA* and *High*

---

[38] Memo from Pomerantz to Taylor, 22 Aug. 1946, NA-238-202-6-4, at 8.

[39] Cited in Bush, *Conspiracy*, 1156 n. 215.

[40] Memorandum from Sprecher to Taylor, 30 Nov. 1946, Gantt Collection in Towson University Archives, Box OO.

[41] Ibid.   [42] Ibid.

[43] Arrests by Request of OCCWC, undated, TTP-5-1-3-41, at 2.

[44] Memo from Taylor to Clay, 14 Mar. 1947, NA-153–1018-13–87-0-1, at 14 ("First Trial Program").

[45] Ibid., 8.

Command—the maximum the four smaller courtrooms could comfortably accommodate—but *RuSHA* included 23 defendants in the OCC's second trial program[46] and there were 25 suspects in *High Command* in its first.[47] The arrestee memo, moreover, indicates that General Johannes Friessner, who had commanded Army Group North and Army Group Southeast, was not included in *High Command* because the dock was already full.[48]

II. Creation of the Trial Program

As noted earlier, Taylor initially anticipated that the OCC would hold 36 trials. Three trial programs later—dated 14 March, 20 May, and 4 September 1947— that number had been reluctantly reduced to 12. This section traces the gradual erosion of the OCC's ambitions, explaining why some trials were included in the final trial program while others were abandoned.

A. The Initial Cases

Taylor's earliest attempt to forecast the OCC's trial program came in a memo to Petersen, then the Secretary of War, on 30 September 1946,[49] not long after Werner Peiser's group had completed its overall study. At this point, the OCC had begun planning seven of the 36 trials that Taylor envisioned. The first trial, which was slated to begin in late 1946, would involve "a large group of defendants (between 20 and 24) who are responsible for initiating and guiding the German program of medical experimentation on human beings."[50] The *Medical* case would then be followed by cases centered on Oswald Pohl, the Chief of the SS Economic and Administrative Main Office (WVHA), and Otto Thierack, the Nazi Minster of Justice—the *Justice* case.[51]

Taylor hoped to begin the *Medical*, *Pohl*, and *Justice* cases by the end of 1946. The OCC would then initiate in mid-January 1947 its ambitious slate of four industrialist cases, involving Krupp, Farben, Dresdner Bank, and a combination of the Flick Concern and the Vereinigte Stahlwerke, a coal, iron and steel conglomerate whose chairman was Fritz Thyssen. Taylor believed that the first three would "probably" be *Krupp*, *Farben*, and *Dresdner Bank*, although he noted that *Flick-Vereinigte Stahlwerke* might be moved up, because planning for the case was "progressing very well."[52]

Around this time, the OCC also decided to drop one of the cases it had been planning. On October 4, William Caming, one of Taylor's prosecutors, informed

---

[46] Memo from Taylor to Clay, 20 May 1947, NA-260-183a1-2-17, at 5 ("Second Trial Program").
[47] First Trial Program, 14.
[48] Arrests by Request of OCCWC, 2.
[49] Letter from Taylor to Petersen, 30 Sept. 1946, 2.
[50] Ibid.   [51] Ibid.   [52] Ibid.

an analyst in the Berlin Branch that "the decision has been made to suspend the case against members of the Ministry for Church Affairs," which meant that "further investigation of documents pertaining to Dr. Herman Muhs, Ludwig Müller, and Dr. Friedrich Werner [wa]s not required."[53] Werner had been the president of the German Protestant Church; Müller had been the Reich Bishop and an advisor to Hitler on Protestant affairs; and Muhs had succeeded Hans Kerrl as the head of the Ministry. Interestingly, Muhs would not be ruled out as a potential defendant until Taylor's second trial program; as discussed below, the March 14 program lists Muhs as a potential defendant in what was initially called the *Propaganda and Education* case.[54]

1. *The* Medical *Case (Case No. 1)*

As Taylor anticipated, the *Medical* case became the first NMT trial. The indictment was filed on 25 October 1946, one day after the SPD formally became the OCC, and the trial began on December 9.

Despite its early start, the OCC did not begin to plan the *Medical* trial until June 1946.[55] Much of what the Allies knew at the time about the Nazis' medical experiments had been uncovered by British, French, and American FIAT (Field Information Agencies Technical) groups, which had spent the second half of 1945 interrogating leading German doctors about the experiments.[56] On 11 May 1946, OMGUS contacted the War Department to suggest that it convene a meeting "to examine evidence collected by FIAT and discuss possible international action re scientific and medical experiments on live human being[s]."[57] Four days later, 15 FIAT officers—four American, nine British, and two French—met to consider how to proceed. The OCC declined to participate in the meeting, which Weindling interprets as a "lack of interest in medical war crimes at the time."[58]

Despite the OCC's absence, the FIAT officers debated whether medical experiments should be prosecuted in quadripartite or zonal trials.[59] Colonel Clio Straight, a member of the U.S. War Crimes Office's Legal Branch, suggested that "under agreement between war crimes agencies of the various nations, each country might take up one case, follow it up and arrange for a trial in the zone of the country concerned."[60] As Weindling notes, "[t]he meeting indicates that the U.S. was now committed to a zonal trials program."[61]

In late June, the OCC began to consider whether one or more of the NMT trials should focus on the Nazis' medical experiments. According to Andrew Ivy, a University of Illinois physiology professor who would later give perjured testimony for the prosecution in the *Medical* trial—a story told in the next chapter—"a plan of responsibility, procedure, and strategy for the Medical trials was discussed" at the

---

[53] Letter from Caming to Flechtheim, 4 Oct. 1946, NA-238-204-1-7.
[54] First Trial Program, 20.   [55] Weindling, *Zonal Trials*, 376.
[56] Ibid., 373.   [57] Ibid., 374.   [58] Ibid., 375.
[59] Ibid.   [60] Ibid., 375–6.   [61] Ibid.

meeting, and it was "tentatively suggested that General Taylor's group would try the medical cases."[62]

At that point, the OCC began to identify potential defendants. Alexander Hardy, one of the OCC's prosecutors, instructed the Berlin Branch to investigate Karl Brandt, Hitler's personal physician and the Reich Commissioner for Health and Sanitation, who was "by far the highest-placed of the medical suspects."[63] Around the same time, Taylor convinced the British to allow the OCC to prosecute the so-called "Hohenlychen Group," a group of seven doctors and nurses associated with the SS's Hohenlychen sanitarium who were believed to be responsible for the appalling medical experiments conducted on women prisoners in the Ravensbrueck concentration camp.[64]

On September 2, Taylor announced that 15 suspects had been identified. The most important were Brandt; Karl Gebhardt, Himmler's personal physician and the director of the Hohenlychen sanitarium; Wolfram Sievers, the managing director of the *Ahnenerbe*-SS who had been involved in the murder of 112 Jews in Auschwitz "for the purpose of completing a skeleton collection for the Reich University of Strasbourg"[65]; Victor Brack, the Chief Administrative Officer in the Chancellery of the Fuhrer, who had organized the T4 euthanasia program; and Field Marshal Milch, whom the OCC believed was connected to the high-altitude and freezing experiments conducted at Dachau. Eight of those 15 would eventually be named as defendants in the *Medical* case.[66]

A week later, Taylor released a revised list of 23 suspects. The September 9 list differed considerably from the September 2 list, indicating how quickly the OCC was working. Six of the 15 suspects on the original list had been removed, most notably Milch.[67] A number of others had been added, including Siegfried Handloser, the Chief of the Medical Services of the Armed Forces, and Gerhard Rose, a Brigadier General in the Luftwaffe Medical Service who had personally conducted typhus and malaria experiments at Dachau and Buchenwald. As Weindling points out, the revised list indicates "that the prosecution's strategy was to demonstrate the links among the medical vivisectors in the camps, the SS administration, and the bureaucracy involved in the campaign of 'euthanasia'."[68]

A number of scholars have argued that Taylor decided to open the NMT trials with the *Medical* case instead of *Krupp* or *Farben* because the U.S. government was ambivalent about prosecuting industrialists and financiers. Weindling, for example, claims that "[b]y August 1946 the requirement was for a U.S. military trial in Nuremberg to prosecute a group *other* than financiers and industrialists. The U.S. war-crimes department postponed the pending Flick/Krupp trial as politically

---

[62] Ibid., 376.   [63] Ibid., 378.

[64] Ulf Schmidt, "'The Scars of Ravensbrück': Medical Experiments and British War Crimes Policy, 1945–1950," 23 *German Hist.* 20, 21 (2005).

[65] *Medical*, Indictment, para. 7, I TWC 14.

[66] Karl Brandt, Sievers, Mrugowsky, Brack, Rudolf Brandt, Gebhardt, Fischer, and Oberheuser.

[67] The others were Oberhauser, Treite, Rosenthal, Haagen, and Bouhler.

[68] Weindling, *Zonal Trials*, 381.

too sensitive, and looked for an alternative trial that could rapidly and conclusively demonstrate Nazi guilt for atrocities."[69]

It is true that, by mid-1946, the U.S. government had begun to doubt the wisdom of prosecuting industrialists.[70] Nevertheless, it is highly unlikely that Taylor decided to begin with the *Medical* case for political, not legal, reasons. Most importantly, that idea is inconsistent with Taylor's own explanation of his decision: that the *Medical* case was simply far easier to prepare than any of the industrialist cases. As Taylor told Petersen in his September 30 memo, although "[d]ocumentary evidence for the [*Medical*] case is very plentiful and quite sensational in spots," making it "a rather easy case to try and to decide, and therefore I think a good one to start with," the industrialist cases were "far more difficult to prepare" and could not realistically begin before the middle of January 1947.[71] Moreover, Taylor later specifically insisted that "neither General Clay nor Washington gave me any instructions, or at any time got in touch with me about when to begin the trials."[72]

It is also clear that Taylor himself was committed to prosecuting industrialists and financiers as early as possible. When Taylor realized that the United States intended to hold zonal trials instead of a second IMT trial focused on economic defendants, he immediately wrote Jackson to insist that it "be made absolutely clear that the zonal trial program will include industrialists and financiers," because "an announcement that there will be no international trial is likely to be taken as an indication that we will not try" them.[73] That insistence is difficult to reconcile with the idea that Taylor wanted to avoid beginning with one of the industrialist cases because they were "politically too sensitive."

To be sure, it is possible that—as Weindling implies—OMGUS simply ordered Taylor to open the NMTs with a case that was not politically sensitive. Such an order, however, would have directly contradicted Article III(a) of Ordinance No. 7, which gave Taylor complete prosecutorial discretion to "determine the persons to be tried by the tribunals." Taylor openly admitted in his Final Report that, despite Article III(a), General Clay had refused to allow him to include Field Marshals von Rundstedt, von Manstein, and von Brauchitsch in *High Command*[74]—a story told in more detail below. It thus seems unlikely that he would have failed to mention a similar order not to begin with one of the industrialist cases.

Scholars who defend the political interpretation often point out that Sprecher began to research industrialists in February 1946, nearly five months before the OCC decided to hold a medical trial, and that the SS Division, which was in charge of preparing the case, "had no special medical expertise" and made use of "only one full-time medical consultant."[75] The implication is that the *Medical* trial's

---

[69] Ibid., 370 (emphasis in original).
[70] See Chapter 1.
[71] Letter from Taylor to Petersen, 30 Sept. 1946, 2.
[72] Letter from Taylor to Irving, 22 Nov. 1971, TTP-14-6-10–13, at 1.
[73] Letter from Taylor to Jackson, 30 Oct. 1946, at 1
[74] Taylor, *Final Report*, 82–3.
[75] Marrus, 110.

"haphazard, hastily improvised character" reflected the fact that it was originally intended to begin *after* the industrialist trials.

There are a number of problems with that argument. To begin with, although Sprecher did begin investigating industrialists as early as February, there is little evidence that substantial progress had been made by mid-May, when the first cadre of attorneys arrived from the United States and Taylor divided the OCC into divisions and trial teams. Sprecher himself acknowledged that he had not yet been formally assigned to the SPD in February and thus was still devoting most of his attention to the IMT.[76] By the time Taylor decided to open the trials with the *Medical* case, therefore, the industrialists had only been investigated for an additional six weeks.

Had the industrialist cases and the *Medical* case been equally difficult to prepare, those six weeks might indicate that the decision to begin with the *Medical* case was political. But that was not the situation. First, the *Medical* case was less factually complicated than *Flick*, *Farben*, or *Krupp*. The Nazis' medical experiments might have involved numerous doctors working in a variety of institutions, but the industrialist cases involved massive corporations accused of a wide variety of different crimes—everything from slave labor to Aryanization to extermination. The *Medical* case also did not involve crimes against peace, which were scheduled to be included in all of the industrialist cases.[77] That was a critical difference, because Taylor believed that the *mens rea* requirement of such crimes—that the defendant acted with the "guilty intent to initiate an aggressive war"[78]—meant that cases involving crimes against peace "took much longer to prepare than those solely concerned with war crimes and atrocities."[79] Sprecher, the head of the Economics Division, agreed.[80]

Second, the industrialist cases were much more legally complicated. The primary issues in the *Medical* case were factual, not legal—whether the OCC could prove that the defendants either personally committed the experiments or were in a position to stop them and did nothing. The industrialist cases, by contrast, raised a number of exceptionally difficult legal questions: whether the corporations should be charged as juristic persons or the charges should be limited to individual corporate directors; whether the indictments should allege conspiracies to commit crimes against peace, crimes against humanity, and war crimes or simply the underlying substantive crimes; and so on.[81] The OCC debated those questions well into December 1946, as Jonathan Bush has shown,[82] making it nearly impossible for Taylor to open the NMTs with an industrialist trial.

---

[76] Letter from Sprecher to Jackson, 14 Feb. 1946, TTP-20-1-3-34, at 1.
[77] The OCC ultimately decided not to bring crimes against peace charges in *Flick*.
[78] Chapter 8 discusses the elements of crimes against peace.
[79] Taylor, *Final Report*, 67.
[80] Memo from Sprecher to Mercer, undated, TTP-5-1-2-22, at 1.
[81] See generally Bush, *Conspiracy*, 1130–73.
[82] Ibid., 1170–2.

2. Milch *(Case No. 2)*

The Military Division prepared and presented the *Milch* case.[83] The indictment was filed on 13 November 1946, and the trial began on 2 January 1947. *Milch* was the only case that did not involve multiple defendants.

As noted above, Milch was originally scheduled to be tried in the *Medical* case, because the OCC believed that he had been involved in the Dachau high-altitude and freezing experiments. The OCC never abandoned that belief, but it became increasingly clear to the prosecutors investigating Milch that it would be very difficult, if not impossible, to prove that he was criminally responsible for those experiments. Henry King, one of the prosecutors assigned the Military Division, identified four major evidentiary problems in a 5 September 1946 memo to Clark Denney, the director of the division. First, Milch was not "a medical man" and the "human experiments, at best constituted a comparatively minor phase" of his career in the Luftwaffe. Second, there was little evidence connecting Milch to Sigmund Rascher, the SS doctor who had conducted the experiments (and who was now dead, having been executed by the SS at Dachau shortly before liberation). Third, although Erich Hippke, the Luftwaffe's Chief Medical Officer, could potentially tie Milch to Rascher, Hippke had yet to be apprehended. Finally, although Milch had made a number of damaging statements concerning his involvement in the use of slave labor while being interrogated, "he ... denied absolutely any knowledge of human experiments."[84]

Henry Heymann, a research analyst, seconded King in a memo to James Conway, one of the prosecutors, written around the same time. Heymann pointed out that the only evidence against Milch regarding the Dachau experiments were letters that he had signed authorizing the experiments but now denied ever reading. That defense could not "be lightly brushed aside," according to Heymann, because "[i]n a large organization, it frequently happens that letters (even of great importance) are prepared by subordinates, and are signed by executives who do not know their contents."[85] Heymann thus bluntly concluded that "[t]his phase of the Milch case, at the present stage of preparation, is such that a verdict of not guilty must result."[86]

Because of their concerns, both King and Heymann urged Taylor to sever Milch from the *Medical* case. King was particularly insistent, because he believed that including Milch "would necessarily relegate the 'forced labour' and 'aggressive war' phases of the *Milch* case to a secondary position," thereby depriving the OCC of "the opportunity to write a broad historical record of a particularly criminal phase of the German economic war effort, as well as of a vital phase of Germany's preparations for aggressive war."[87]

---

[83] Taylor, *Final Report*, 39–40.
[84] Memo from King to Denney, 5 Sept. 1946, NA-238-188-1-1, at 1.
[85] Memo from Heymann to Conway, undated, 3.
[86] Ibid., 2.
[87] Memo from King to Denney, 5 Sept. 1947, at 1–2.

King prevailed on the severance issue, but Taylor ultimately decided not to charge Milch with crimes against peace, even though he believed that "there was substantial evidence at hand on the basis of which the charge of war-making could properly have been made"[88]—a decision he later regretted.[89] According to Taylor, given that *Milch* was scheduled to become Case No. 2, there simply was not enough time to prepare the crimes against peace charges.[90]

That explanation, however, begs an important question. If the evidence against Milch for crimes against peace was strong, and if King was right that those charges would have helped the OCC document Nazi aggression, why not simply delay the trial until the necessary preparations had been completed—perhaps including Milch, who was a Field Marshal, in the *High Command* case, which was slated to include crimes against peace?

Taylor would have preferred to do exactly that, because he believed that "there was no legal necessity for trying Milch by himself." The problem was that Tribunal II had just arrived in Nuremberg "and no other case was far enough advanced for trial at that time (December 1946)."[91] Taylor thus decided to begin Milch "a little sooner than anticipated," because "it seemed unwise" for the tribunal "to be sitting around with nothing to do."[92]

3. The Justice Case (Case No. 3)

As noted earlier, the *Justice* case was one of the eight cases that Taylor identified in his September 30 memo to Petersen. The case was planned by a trial team that had been created in mid-1946 within the Ministries Division under the direction of Charles H. LaFollette,[93] who had served two terms as a Republican congressman from Indiana and had been offered a position as an NMT judge[94] before joining the OCC in 1946.[95] Sixteen defendants were indicted on 4 January 1947, but Carl Westphal, a Ministerial Counsellor in the Reich Ministry of Justice, committed suicide after being served the indictment.[96] When trial began on March 5, therefore, there were only 15 defendants in the dock.

The *Justice* case is one of the best-known NMT trials, because it inspired the 1961 movie *Judgment at Nuremberg*, which won numerous Academy Awards. At the time, however, the *Justice* case "received scant attention in the press or professional literature."[97] The problem, according to Taylor, was that the three members of the Nazi government who should have been the principal defendants

[88] Taylor, *Final Report*, 67.   [89] Ibid.   [90] Ibid.
[91] Ibid., 78. Note that the statement reinforces the conclusion that Taylor did not open the trials with one of the industrialist cases for legal, not political reasons.
[92] Letter from Taylor to Irving, 22 Nov. 1971, 2.
[93] OCCWC General Order No. 6, 25 Feb. 1947.
[94] Memo from Marcus to McCabe, 18 Nov. 1946, NA-153–1018-8-84.
[95] Background Information for Correspondents, 3.
[96] First Trial Program, 18.
[97] Taylor, *Final Report*, 169.

in the case were all dead: Franz Guertner, the Reich Minister of Justice from 1933–41, had died in early 1941; his successor, Otto Georg Thierack, had committed suicide in a British internment camp in October 1946 after hearing that his trial was imminent; and Roland Frieser, who was the President of the infamous "People's Court" and had represented the Justice Ministry at the Wannsee Conference, had been killed in an air raid near the end of the war.[98] The OCC was thus left to indict lower-level (though certainly important) suspects such as Schlegelberger, Rothaug, and Herbert Klemm, the State Secretary in the Ministry of Justice.

In his memo to Petersen, Taylor predicted that the "*Thierack* case"—Thierack was still alive when Taylor wrote the memo—would be "one of the most interesting and constructive of all."[99] He made a similar comment in his Final Report, describing the case as "to jurists possibly the most interesting of all the Nuremberg trials."[100] To some extent, however, Taylor's later enthusiasm appears to have been designed for public consumption: according to Robert King, one of the prosecutors involved in the *Justice* case, Taylor lost interest in the trial after Thierack committed suicide.[101]

4. Pohl *(Case No. 4)*

Pohl was prepared and presented by the SS Division. Taylor, who believed that the case would be "easy and probably effective," hoped that the OCC would be able to begin the trial by the end of 1946.[102] In fact, the indictment was not filed until 13 January 1947 and the trial did not begin until April 8.

The 18 defendants that stood trial in *Pohl* were all officials in the WVHA. The OCC originally intended to include three additional high-ranking WVHA officials: Fritz Lechler, the manager of TexLed, an SS garment factory; Wilhelm Burger, an SS Colonel who had overseen the provision of supplies to the concentration camps, including Auschwitz and Dachau; and Gerhard Maurer, also an SS Colonel, who had been responsible for allocating prisoner labor to German industry. Unfortunately, Lechler injured himself too severely in a suicide attempt to stand trial, and Burger and Maurer were not apprehended until after the other defendants were arraigned.[103] (Burger was actually arrested while watching the arraignment from the gallery![104]) The OCC thus recommended that they should be detained pending the outcome of the *Pohl* trial and that, thereafter, "suitable machinery should be developed for their trial on similar charges."[105] No subsequent trial ever materi-

---

[98] Taylor, *Final Report*, 168–9.
[99] Letter from Taylor to Petersen, 30 Sept. 1946, 2.
[100] Taylor, *Final Report*, 169.
[101] Bruce M. Stave et al., *Witnesses to Nuremberg: An Oral History of American Participants at the War Crimes Trials* 163 (1998).
[102] Letter from Taylor to Petersen, 30 Sept. 1946, 2.
[103] First Trial Program, 6.
[104] OCCWC, Press Review No. 99, 20 Mar. 1947, Gantt Collection in Towson University Archives, Box GG.
[105] Ibid.

alized, although Maurer was later executed by Poland in 1953 and Burger was sentenced to eight years' imprisonment by a German court in 1966 for supplying Zyklon-B to the concentration camps.

The most interesting absence from *Pohl* was Karl Wolff, Himmler's Chief of Staff until 1943 and then the Supreme SS and Police Leader in Italy. The French and Soviet prosecutors had wanted to include Wolff in the IMT trial, but Jackson (with British support) vetoed the suggestion at the request of the OSS's Allen Dulles, who had promised to protect Wolff from prosecution because of the critical role he had played in Operation Sunrise, the secret March 1945 negotiations between the Nazis and the Allies that had led to the surrender of German forces in Italy.[106] Wolff had led the negotiations on behalf of the surrendering forces.

Wolff's near-miss at the IMT meant that he would almost certainly be prosecuted by the OCC, especially as he was in U.S. custody when the OCC was created. Indeed, Taylor acknowledged in 1978 that when he replaced Jackson, he was "under the impression that we would surely indict him in one of our 'subsequent' trials,"[107] *Pohl* being the most obvious choice. The OCC even requested information from Army intelligence in July 1946 concerning "Wolff or forced labor program or anti-partisan activities by Germans in Italy."[108]

Despite the OCC's apparent interest, Taylor never indicted Wolff. His rationale was the same one that had led Jackson to oppose including Wolff in the IMT trial: Dulles had promised him immunity from prosecution. As Taylor later wrote to David Irving, he believed—correctly, as we now know—that "there was some basis" for Wolff's claim that the promise existed.[109]

Taylor was under no legal obligation, of course, to honor Dulles' promise. But it is clear that he felt informal pressure to do so. At some point in late 1947—when the OCC was finalizing its last two cases—Dulles' senior aide, Gerd von Gavernitz, wrote to Robert Kempner, who had worked with the OSS during the war, to ask him to intervene with Taylor on Wolff's behalf. Gavernitz specifically cited the "outstanding support" that Wolff had rendered during Operation Sunrise "at great personal risk."[110] Kempner inquired about Taylor's plans for Wolff and informed Gavernitz of what he learned.[111] Not long thereafter, the British War Crimes Executive asked the OCC to extradite Wolff to Britain. Taylor agreed in November 1947—and later admitted that, given the complicated politics that had surrounded Wolff from the beginning, he was "not a bit sorry" to see him go.[112]

---

[106] Michael Salter, *Nazi War Crimes, U.S. Intelligence and Selective Prosecution at Nuremberg* 128 (2007).

[107] Letter from Taylor to Smith, 1 June 1978, TTP-14-6-15–325, at 1.

[108] Salter, 132.

[109] Letter from Taylor to Irving, 9 Mar. 1972, TTP-14-6-10–13, at 2.

[110] Quoted in Salter, 133.

[111] Ibid.

[112] Letter from Taylor to Smith, 1 June 1978.

5. Flick *(Case No. 5)*

Flick, the first of the industrialist cases, was prepared and presented by the Flick Trial Team, one of the OCC's six original divisions. The initial indictment was filed on 8 February 1947; an amended indictment was filed on March 17.[113] Trial began on April 19.

Only six defendants stood trial in *Flick*, making it—after *Milch*—the second smallest of the 12 trials. A January 17 memorandum written by Charles Lyon indicates that the Flick team considered four different approaches to selecting defendants, each more expansive than the last.[114] The first was the "hard punch" approach, which involved indicting only the two suspects whose convictions were, according to Lyons, "100% assured": Friedrich Flick himself and Otto Steinbrinck, Flick's principal assistant until 1940 and then a leading official in Vereinigte Stahlwerke. The second was the "ownership and front office" approach, which expanded the list to include four of Flick's "chief lieutenants" who had served on the *Aufsichstrat* (Supervisory Board) of numerous companies affiliated with the Flick Concern, such as Odilo Burkhart, who had been in charge of Flick's steel and soft coal enterprises, and Konrad Kaletsch, who had handled all of Flick's financial matters. The third was the "total concern" approach, which added seven leading officials in the various Flick companies who had been responsible for the use of slave labor. And the fourth was the "bad man" approach, which included four additional "lesser officials" who had been connected to Flick's slave-labor program.[115]

The February 8 indictment adopted the "ownership and front office" approach, bringing charges against Flick, Steinbrinck, Burkhart, and Kaletsch.[116] The list would also have included Otto Ernst, Flick's son and minority partner, but Lyon had concluded that indicting multiple members of the Flick family might be seen as "jungle justice."[117] Hermann Terberger, a leading official in Eisenwerk Gesellschaft Maxhimilianshuette, a Flick company, was indicted instead.[118] The March 17 indictment was substantially the same, but added Burkhart—who, after being protected by the Russians, was "suddenly and inexplicably" found in the French zone and turned over to the OCC.[119]

As noted earlier, the *Flick* trial was originally scheduled to include officials from Vereinigte Stahlwerke as well as from the Krupp Concern. In the end, the OCC indicted only Otto Steinbrinck, who had spent most of his career with Flick. The most surprising omission—at least to the reporters covering the trial—was Fritz

---

[113] The amended indictment was repeatedly revised at the request of the prosecution during trial. Those changes are discussed in Chapter 6.

[114] Memo from Lyon to Ervin, 17 Jan. 1947, Gantt Collection in Towson University Archives, Box FF.

[115] Ibid.

[116] Bush, *Conspiracy*, 1194.

[117] Memo from Lyon to Ervin, 17 Jan. 1947.

[118] Ibid.   [119] Bush, *Conspiracy*, 1194.

Thyssen, the Chairman of Vereinigte Stahlwerke, who had played a major role in Hitler's rise to power. In fact, Taylor had always been ambivalent about prosecuting Thyssen, who had fled Germany when war broke out, had voted (by telegraph) against war with Poland as a member of the Reichstag, and who had spent a number of years in a concentration camp after being arrested in France.[120] Taylor informed OMGUS in May 1946 that he did not have enough information about Thyssen to justify a decision,[121] and he later became convinced that the evidence against Thyssen was so weak that "his indictment would have been a serious mistake, and his selection as a defendant from among others against whom the evidence was far stronger, a preposterous error."[122]

That said, Taylor did regret the limited number of defendants in the case and its narrow focus on the Flick Concern. In his view, "a much more telling and significant proceeding would have resulted had the more important defendants in the 'Flick' and 'Krupp' cases been grouped in a single case, together with other Ruhr iron-masters from the largest of the combines (such as Ernst Poensgen of the Vereinigte Stahlwerke) and other large concerns (such as Gutehoffnungshuette and Mannesmann)."[123]

Taylor decided against a larger case for two reasons. First, the location of the Ruhr meant that a trial involving industrialists based there would have been more properly tried in the British occupation zone. When the *Flick* case was prepared— in late 1946 and early 1947—it was still possible that the British would prosecute Krupp and other Ruhr industrialists itself or would participate with the OCC in such a trial. Taylor thus thought it inadvisable to pre-empt that possibility by expanding the case beyond the Flick Concern and the one Vereinigte Stahlwerke official who had been Flick's personal assistant.[124]

Second, a larger trial would simply have taken too long to prepare. Once again, crimes against peace were the culprit: although the OCC had decided not to bring such charges against the Flick officials because the necessary records were scattered across Germany and too difficult to obtain,[125] there was no question that crimes against peace were going to be at the heart of *Krupp* trial. A combined trial would thus have substantially delayed the first industrialist case.[126]

B. The March 14 Program

Taylor submitted his first complete trial program to OMGUS on 14 March 1946. At that point, the *Medical*, *Milch*, and *Justice* trials were underway and indictments had been filed in *Pohl* and *Flick*. Erich Hippke, the Luftwaffe's Chief

[120] Taylor, *Final Report*, 83.
[121] Summary of OCC-OMGUS Meeting, 28 May 1946, NA-238-159-1-2, at 2.
[122] Taylor, *Final Report*, 83.
[123] Ibid., 79.   [124] Ibid.
[125] Economics Division Press Release, U.S. Will Try Nazi Capitalists, undated, NA-238-202-3-1, at 2.
[126] Taylor, *Final Report*, 79.

Medical Officer—and the ostensible link between Milch and Rascher—had been apprehended since the beginning of the *Medical* trial; he and other important Nazi doctors were being detained for possible prosecution in a second medical case.[127]

Taylor's trial program now called for 18 trials, including the five that were already underway. Taylor considered 10 of the 13 pending trials "practically necessary, if the Nurnberg war crimes program is to achieve its announced purposes," while the other three were "perhaps less necessary and could be sacrificed if considerations of time and economy so require."[128] Holding all 18 trials would result in 225 total defendants; holding only the necessary 15 would result in 180.[129] Either way, Taylor believed that all of the trials would be substantially completed by the end of 1947.[130]

1. The Necessary Ten

a. RuSHA
The *RuSHA* case focused on the SS Main Race and Resettlement Office, which had conducted racial examinations for a number of SS offices involved in the Germanization program. The primary defendant was intended to be Richard Hildebrandt, the head of RuSHA from April 1943 until the end of the war. Hildebrandt was in Polish custody at the time, but the Poles had agreed to extradite him to the American zone to stand trial.[131]

In addition to ten additional defendants from RuSHA itself—including Herbert Heubner, the head of RuSHA's office in Poland—the March 14 program also identified five certain defendants from "other divisions of the SS which dealt primarily with the execution of Nazi racial theories." The Lebensborn Society, which the prosecution believed had been involved in kidnapping Polish children for Germanization, would be represented by Max Sollman, the Chief of the Lebensborn, and Guenther Tesch, the head of its Main Legal Department. The Main Staff Office of the Reich Commissioner for the Strengthening of Germanism (RKFDV), which had overseen the Germanization program, would be represented by Ulrich Greifelt, the head of the RKFDV, and Rudolf Creutz, his chief deputy. Finally, the Main Office for Repatriation of Racial Germans (VoMI), which had been responsible for transferring "racial Germans" from their native countries into Germany, would be represented by Werner Lorenz, VoMI's Chief.[132]

b. Prisoner of War
The *Prisoner of War* case included nine defendants from the SS and Wehrmacht who were involved in POW affairs. The lead defendants were slated to be Gottlob Berger, the Chief of the SS's Central Office; General Adolf Westhoff, the Wehrmacht's Inspector General for POW Affairs; and General Hermann Reinecke, the head of the Wehrmacht's General Office.[133]

---

[127] First Trial Program, 9.   [128] Ibid., 1.   [129] Ibid., 5.
[130] Ibid.   [131] Ibid., 7.   [132] Ibid.   [133] Ibid., 10.

c. *Field Commander*

The *Field Commander* case, which later became the *Hostage* case, focused on war crimes committed by German field commanders in the Balkans, Norway, and Greece. The March 14 program identified three primary defendants: Field Marshal Wilhelm List, the Commander-in-Chief of the 12th Army in Greece and Yugoslavia and then the Commander-in-Chief of Army Group A; Field Marshal Maximilian von Weichs, the Commander-in-Chief of the 2nd Army during the Balkans Campaign and later the Supreme Commander Southeast; and General Lothar Rendulic, the Commander-in-Chief of the 2nd Panzer Army in Yugoslavia and then Commander-in-Chief of the 20th Mountain Army in Norway. The program also mentioned 11 possible defendants, such as General Franz Boehme, Rendulic's successor in Norway.[134]

d. *Principal Military*

The *Principal Military* case, which eventually became *High Command*, included military leaders "selected so as to represent not only the Army (OKH) but also the Navy, Air Force, and the Supreme Command of the Wehrmacht (OKW)."[135] The charges against most of the defendants were intended to parallel the war-crimes charges against Jodl and Keitel at the IMT: "to wit, the preparation, distribution, and enforcement of criminal orders, such as the order for the murder of all Commandoes [sic] even after they had surrendered."[136] Some of the defendants would also be charged with crimes against peace.[137] Interestingly, despite Doenitz's conviction at the IMT for waging aggressive war,[138] Taylor did not intend to bring crimes against peace charges against defendants who "merely participated in carrying out the attack, but against whom there is no evidence of advance planning or instigation."[139]

The March 14 program identified 25 possible defendants, although Taylor made it clear that "[f]urther examination of documents and other evidence... will be necessary before a final list of the defendants can be made."[140] The list included the three Field Marshals—Walter von Brauchitsch, Erich von Manstein, and Gerd von Rundstedt—whom Clay would later order Taylor not to prosecute.

e. *Farben*

The March 14 program identified 35 possible defendants from the Farben corporation, including Carl Krauch, the Chairman of the Aufsichtsrat; Hermann Schmitz, the Chairman of the Vorstand, whom Jackson had wanted to try at the IMT[141]; and Georg von Schnitzler, a member of the Vorstand's Central Committee and the chief of the committee that oversaw Farben's domestic and foreign sales.

---

[134] Ibid., 11.   [135] Ibid., 3.   [136] Ibid.   [137] Ibid.
[138] See IMT Judgment, 107–8.
[139] First Trial Program, 3.
[140] Ibid., 12.
[141] Bush, *Conspiracy*, 1113. Jackson later wanted to include Schmitz in the potential second IMT trial. Ibid., 1116.

Taylor estimated that the indictment would include between 20 and 24 of the defendants and would be filed within three weeks.[142]

f. *Krupp*

Not surprisingly, the March 14 program listed Alfried Krupp as the primary defendant in the *Krupp* case. It also identified five other certain defendants, including Erich Mueller, a member of Krupp's Vorstand and Direktorium who had been the head of armament production, and Friedrich von Buelow, a deputy member of the Vorstand who had been Krupp's counter-intelligence chief. Finally, the program mentioned six other possible defendants, from which "one or two" might be selected.[143] That list included Karl Eberhardt, the head of Krupp's war materials department, and Hans Kupke, the head of Krupp's camps for foreign workers.

g. *Dresdner Bank*

Although the *Dresdner Bank* case had been planned from the beginning, the March 14 program exhibited increasing uncertainty about its prospects. Taylor stated that "[i]n all probability, the case will comprise eight or a dozen defendants" drawn from a list of bank officials that included Carl Goetz, the Chairman of the Aufsichtsrat, and Karl Rasche, a leading member of the Vorstand. The most interesting potential defendant in *Dresdner Bank* was, in fact, not on the March 14 list: Kurt von Schroeder, the German banker who had raised a significant amount of money for the Nazis as a member of Himmler's notorious Circle of Friends. The OCC had considered indicting von Schroeder in *Flick*, but Foster Adams felt that *Dresdner Bank* was a more appropriate home. That appears to have been the dominant sentiment among the prosecutors, although it is important to note that Sprecher—who was, as Jonathan Bush has pointed out, "usually not a voice of caution"[144]—questioned whether the available evidence justified including von Schroeder in *Dresdner Bank*.

The OCC also faced an additional problem regarding von Schroeder: he was in British custody, and by early 1947 the British had lost all interest in prosecuting or extraditing him, even though they had originally proposed that he be included in a second IMT trial.[145] That seemed to end the matter—until the OCC requested von Schroeder to testify for the prosecution in *Flick*. Adams suggested that "the Americans should let Schroeder come to Nuremberg, while working behind the scenes to add Schroeder as a defendant" in *Dresdner Bank*. "If the addition could be made, prosecutors might persuade or embarrass the British into allowing his status to change from witness to defendant."[146] It was a bold if somewhat underhanded plan, but it never came to fruition. In fact, von Schroeder ultimately testified for the defense in *Flick* and the prosecution in *Krupp*.

[142] First Trial Program, 14.   [143] Ibid., 15.
[144] Bush, *Conspiracy*, 1192 n. 362.
[145] Ibid., 1190–1.   [146] Ibid., 1191–2.

h. *Food and Agriculture-Hermann Goering Works*

According to the March 14 program, "[t]he common denominator of the defendants in this case is that they are all leading government officials in the economic
field."[147] The program mentioned 12 certain defendants, including Walther Darre
and Herbert Backe, successive Ministers of Food and Agriculture; Paul Koerner,
Goering's Deputy in the Four-Year Plan; and Wilhelm Keppler, Secretary of State
and one of Hitler's economic advisors. It also identified seven other suspects
"from whom a few defendants might be selected." They included Emil Puhl,
Vice-President of the Reichsbank.[148]

In addition to the government officials, Taylor proposed to include officials of
the Hermann Goering Works (HGW) in the case, because the company, "was
primarily governmental rather than private in character."[149] Potential defendants
included Paul Pleiger, the head of HGW,[150] who had been included on Jackson's
list of defendants for a second IMT trial.[151]

i. *Government Administration*

The *Government Administration* case focused on "Hans Lammers, Otto Meissner,
and other principal officials who constituted Hitler's immediate entourage in
his capacity as Reichschancellor."[152] Lammers had been the head of the Reich
Chancellery; Meissner had been chief of the Presidential Chancellery. The March
14 program also considered seven other suspects to be "certain" defendants,
including Friedrich Kritzinger, the Reich Chancellery's State Secretary, and
Wilhelm Stuckart, the Undersecretary of the Interior.[153]

j. *Foreign Office*

The *Foreign Office* case, which would later become *Ministries*, was originally
limited—as the name implied—to officials from the Reich Foreign Office. The
two leading defendants, according to the March 14 program, would be Baron
Gustav Steengracht von Moyland, Ernst von Weizsaecker's successor as Secretary of
State, and Ernst Bohle, the chief of the *Ausland*, the Foreign Organization. Other
defendants would be selected from a list of 17 suspects, including von Weizsaecker
himself; Franz Six, the head of the Cultural Division; and Ernst Woermann, the
Ambassador to China.[154]

2. The Optional Three

a. *SD-Gestapo-RSHA*

The March 14 program's first "optional" case—which eventually became *Einsatzgruppen*—focused on "Otto Ohlendorf and other principal officials of the Sicher-
heitsdienst, the Gestapo, and the Main Security Office (RSHA) of the SS."[155]
Ohlendorf had testified at the IMT that Einsatzgruppe D, which he had commanded,

---

[147] First Trial Program, 17. [148] Ibid. [149] Ibid., 4. [150] Ibid., 17.
[151] Bush, *Conspiracy*, 1116. [152] First Trial Program, 4.
[153] Ibid., 18. [154] Ibid., 19. [155] Ibid., 2.

had killed more than 90,000 Jews in the Crimea and Southern Ukraine during the war. Indeed, his testimony—which was both extensive and remarkably forthright[156]—was the primary reason that Taylor thought the case was optional: "[t]he evidence against Ohlendorf and the other defendants who would be involved in such a case was so thoroughly developed by the International Military Tribunal that it may be unnecessary for the Office of Chief of Counsel to handle this case, provided that other suitable judicial machinery is available or can be created."[157]

Taylor insisted, however, on the latter condition. In his view, denazification was an unacceptable option for the other potential defendants, "inasmuch as ten years' imprisonment is the maximum sentence which can be imposed by the Spruch-kammers."[158] Taylor's position was sound—a number of the suspects identified in the March 14 program as potential defendants would ultimately be sentenced to death in the *Einsatzgruppen* trial, such as Walter Blume, the commanding officer of Einsatzgruppe B's Sonderkommando 7a, and Willy Seibert, Ohlendorf's Deputy Chief in Einsatzgruppe D.

b. *Warsaw Destruction*

The second "optional" case was scheduled to include "the military and SS leaders who were responsible for the destruction of Warsaw, and other atrocities com-mitted there."[159] The March 14 program identified two principal defendants: Colonel-General Heinz Guderian, who had commanded the XIX Corps during the invasion of Poland, and General Nikolaus von Vormann, the commander of the 9th Army during the Warsaw Uprising. It also listed 12 possible defendants, including Oskar Dirlewanger, an SS *Obersturmführer* whose vicious—even by Nazi standards—"Dirlewanger Brigade," which was composed entirely of convicted German criminals, had killed more than 40,000 civilians during the Warsaw Uprising. Taylor believed that the case was important, but he acknowledged in the memo that "[i]n view of the primarily Polish interest in the case, it may well be unnecessary for the Office of Chief of Counsel to handle it."[160]

c. *Propaganda and Education*

The final "optional" case was intended to include "Otto Dietrich, Max Amann, Arthur Axmann, and other leading officials in the field of propaganda and educa-tion."[161] Dietrich had been Chief of the Press Division in the Reich Ministry of Propaganda; Amann had been President of the Reich Press Chamber; and Axmann had succeeded von Schirach as Reich Youth Leader. Other potential defendants included Gustav School, Reich Leader of Students and Lecturers; Bernard Rust, Minister of Education; and Carl Schmitt, "University professor and propagandist."[162]

Taylor insisted that the *Propaganda and Education* case was important "from the standpoint of the purposes of the Office of Chief of Counsel."[163] Nevertheless, he acknowledged in the memo that the IMT judgment made it unclear whether the case would succeed. The IMT had convicted both Streicher, the publisher of *Der*

---

[156] Earl, 72–3.   [157] First Trial Program, 2.   [158] Ibid.
[159] Ibid., 3.   [160] Ibid.   [161] Ibid., 5.   [162] Ibid.   [163] Ibid., 5.

Sturmer, and von Schirach, the *Gauleiter* of Vienna,[164] which Taylor thought was "distinctly helpful."[165] But it had acquitted Fritzsche, the head of the Propaganda Ministry's Radio Division, because the prosecution had failed to prove that he had intended "to incite the German peoples to commit atrocities on conquered peoples."[166] His acquittal, Taylor believed, "somewhat obstructed" the case.[167]

C. Cases 6 and 7

Taylor submitted his second trial program to OMGUS on 20 May 1947. In the interim, the OCC had filed indictments in two cases: *Farben* and *Hostage*.

1. Farben *(Case No. 6)*

Farben was prepared and presented by the Farben Trial Team, one of the OCC's original divisions. The indictment was filed on 3 May 1947, although the trial did not begin until August 27, nearly four months later.

From the beginning, the Farben team found it extremely difficult to prepare the case. The most significant problem was that the documentary evidence needed for trial was so vast and so scattered that it took nearly two years to collect and analyze.[168] All three of the OCC's satellite offices—in Berlin, Frankfurt, and Washington—were involved in processing evidence against Farben,[169] and the Farben team had to send field teams into a number of countries, including France, Poland, Yugoslavia, and Belgium, in order to obtain critical documents.[170] Even worse, much of the documentary evidence was in far from usable form. When two representatives of OMGUS's Cartels Section arrived in Frankfurt in April 1945, for example, they discovered that "four hundred tons of IG's documents which had been carefully filed over the years were being unceremoniously tipped out of the windows and burnt in the courtyard," because a SHAEF commander needed the building "cleared of refuse" so they could use it as their headquarters. Liberated slave laborers were using the rest for bedding.[171]

The trial team also had to deal with Farben's repeated attempts to destroy documents that it knew were inculpatory:

Huge bonfires of IG documents had been burning for some days before the Americans captured Frankfurt. Other documents had been hidden in forests, mines and farmyard barns, stored in cupboards and even sewn into clothes. IG had rented a monastery's refectory to store "personal effects of bombed out employees." The sixty-eight packing cases were crammed with agreements between IG and French, British, and American companies.[172]

---

[164] IMT Judgment, 101–2, 113–4.   [165] First Trial Program, 5.
[166] IMT Judgment, 127–8.   [167] First Trial Program, 5.
[168] Bower, 311.   [169] Undated Organizational Memo, 6.
[170] Ibid.   [171] Bower, 310–1.   [172] Ibid., 312.

Other key documents were found in a bathroom cupboard, where they had been hidden by the defendant Otto Ambros, a member of the Farben Vorstand who had managed Farben's plant at Auschwitz. "Ambros had methodically destroyed bundles of incriminating files, but had hidden just a handful whose destruction even he could not contemplate. It was a fatal, but isolated, mistake. Their discovery, as in most cases, resulted from chance information from an informer."[173]

As Taylor anticipated, 24 Farben officials ultimately stood trial, including Krauch, Schmitz, von Schnitzler, and Ambros. Other important defendants included August von Knieriem, Farben's Chief Counsel; Fritz ter Meer, a member of the Vorstand's Central Committee and the chief of the committee that planned and directed all of Farben's production; and Walter Duerrfeld, who had been the director and construction manager of Farben's Auschwitz and Monowitz plants.

2. The Hostage Case *(Case No. 7)*

The *Hostage* case was prepared by the Military Division. The indictment was filed on 10 May 1947 and trial began on July 15. The final list of defendants was nearly the same as the March 14 list; the most important difference was the removal of Franz Boehme, who had committed suicide prior to arraignment.

Hostage's relatively early placement in the trial program was the product of two factors. The first was evidentiary: "documentary proof" that the systematic murder of hostages in Yugoslavia, Albania, and Greece was "carried out pursuant to orders emanating from the highest levels of the Wehrmacht came readily to hand."[174] The second was logistical: the three primary defendants in the case—List, von Weichs, and Rendulic—were already in U.S. custody.[175]

D. The May 20 Program

Taylor described his 20 May 1946 memo to OMGUS as a "more precise schedule of war crimes cases."[176] The new program called for 16 trials instead of 18, involving approximately 220 defendants[177]—only five fewer than the 225 Taylor had estimated would be tried in all 18 cases. Taylor hoped that the OCC would file the remaining nine indictments within two months, and he still believed that the "bulk" of the trials would be completed prior to 1 January 1948, as General Clay had requested. He acknowledged, though, that "several trials will still be in process at the end of 1947 which may continue two or three months into 1948."[178] Clay approved the May 20 program on June 9.[179]

With the exception of *Dresdner Bank*, all of the remaining cases had evolved since the March 14 program. The May 20 program's elimination of two cases, however, was obviously the most significant development in the trial schedule.

---

[173] Bower, 353.   [174] Taylor, *Final Report*, 80.   [175] Ibid.
[176] Second Trial Program, 2.   [177] Ibid.   [178] Ibid.
[179] Memo from Taylor to Deputy Military Governor, 4 Sept. 1947, NA-549–2236-1, summary, para. 3 ("Third Trial Program").

Moreover, between the two programs, the OCC had also decided not to pursue cases against a variety of industrial and financial defendants, including the Deutsche Bank.

1. Cases Eliminated from the March 14 Program

The first casualty was the *Warsaw Destruction* case, which Taylor decided would be more appropriately prosecuted by the Polish government. That might have been a mistake: it appears that the Poles prosecuted only one of the suspects on the March 14 list—Paul Otto Geibel, the head of the SS and police in Warsaw during the Uprising, who was sentenced to life imprisonment in 1954. Neither General Guderian nor General von Vormann ever stood trial for their crimes, although Guderian remained in U.S. custody until June 1948. Dirlewanger also avoided trial, though for a more understandable reason: it was later learned that he had been beaten to death by Polish prison guards in June 1945.

Taylor eliminated a second case by combining *Government Administration* and *Propaganda and Education* into a more general case that included "the principal ministerial officials in departments other than the Foreign Office and the Economic Department."[180] Hans Lammers, Arthur Axmann, and Otto Dietrich remained principal defendants, but the May 20 program demoted Max Amann, the President of the Reich Press Chamber, and Otto Meissner, the chief of the Presidental Chancellery, to the list of possible defendants. That six-person list included two previously identified defendants, Gustav School and Friedrich Kritzinger.[181]

Combining the two cases resulted in a net loss of ten defendants, although Wilhelm Stuckart was later tried in *Ministries*. The most notable absence from the new list was Carl Schmitt. After Schmitt joined the Nazi Party in 1933, he had been appointed the director of the University Teachers Group of the National Socialist League of German Jurists and had written a number of pro-Nazi and anti-Semitic articles for the self-published *German Jurists' Newspaper*. Schmitt had resigned his position as Reich Professional Group Leader after a falling-out with the SS in 1937, but he had been able to keep his professorship at the University of Berlin because Goering protected him.[182]

Taylor never explained why Schmitt was included on the March 14 list of defendants but was left off the May 20 list. Joseph Bendersky has convincingly argued, however, that although the OCC considered Schmitt to be National Socialism's *Kronjurist*, Robert Kempner's four "amateurish and ill-prepared"[183] interrogations of Schmitt simply failed to uncover anything particularly incriminating.[184] By contrast, Helmut Quaritsch has claimed that Kempner interrogated Schmitt multiple times not because he thought Schmitt was a war criminal, but

---

[180] Ibid., 15.   [181] Ibid., 18.

[182] Joseph W. Bendersky, "The Expendable Kronjurist: Carl Schmitt and National Socialism, 1933–1936," 14 *J. Contemp. Hist.* 309, 323 (1979).

[183] Joseph W. Bendersky, "Carl Schmitt's Path to Nuremberg: A Sixty-Year Reassessment," 139 *Telos* 6, 8 (2007).

[184] Ibid., 30.

because he wanted Schmitt to testify for the prosecution in the *Ministries* case.[185] That is something of an overstatement, given Schmitt's inclusion as a possible defendant in *Propaganda and Education*. Moreover, Bendersky's account of the interrogations makes clear that, at least at first, Kempner genuinely believed Schmitt could be prosecuted for his role as the "theorist" of Nazi aggression.

That said, the OCC clearly did view Schmitt as a potential witness in *Ministries*, although he never actually testified at the trial and was released less than three months after he was detained. During the third interrogation, Kempner asked Schmitt to write an essay for the OCC about the role of the Reich Chancellery in a totalitarian state.[186] (Schmitt obliged.) Even more revealingly, a confidential OCC memo written no earlier than August 1948 notes that the Ministries Division had ordered Schmitt's arrest on 23 March 1947 because he was considered a "material witness for the Ministries Case."[187] That description is important, because the memo lists a number of suspects whom the OCC considered "potential defendants"—including potential defendants in *Ministries*.

2. Other Eliminated Cases

In addition to eliminating two cases from the March 14 schedule, May 20's "more precise" trial program also marked the end of OCC efforts to pursue charges against a number of other industrialists and financiers. The OCC had spent much of 1946 identifying potential defendants, efforts that had culminated in an August 1 list of 72 "leading industrialists, financiers, and economic figures in Nazi Germany who may be subject to prosecution under Control Council No. 10"[188] and a proposal by Sprecher in late July to ask the British to extradite Otto Steinbrinck of Vereinigte Stahlwerke and the heads of Mannesmann, the Deutsche Bank, and Degussa.[189] There were a number of notable absences from the list, such as any of Daimler-Benz's officials other than Max Wolf.[190] Daimler-Benz had committed numerous crimes during the war, ranging from the use of slave labor to forcing women to work in company-run brothels.[191]

In the end, though, the August 1 list's lack of comprehensiveness proved academic. On 3 June 1947, Sprecher informed the Chief of the OCC's Apprehension and Locator Branch that the prosecutors no longer required a number of individuals whose apprehension had been requested by the former Economics Division.[192] In addition to Fritz Thyssen and Koppenberg, the list included the banker Karl Blessing; Hermann Roechling, the Saar industrialist who would later be convicted by the French of deportation and plunder; Hermann von Siemens, a

---

[185] Ibid., 8.

[186] Ibid., 31–2.   [187] Arrests by Request of OCCWC, 3.

[188] List of Leading Industrialists, Financiers, and Economic Figures in Nazi Germany Who May Be Subject to Prosecution Under Control Council No. 10, 1 Aug. 1946, Gantt Collection in Towson University Archives, Box OO.

[189] Bush, *Conspiracy*, 1131.

[190] Ibid., 1133.   [191] Ibid., 1132.

[192] Memo from Sprecher to Martin, 3 June 1947, NA-238-165-1-8, at 1.

director of Siemens, which had made liberal use of slave labor at Auschwitz[193]; and Rudolf Walz, the managing technical director of Bosch, whom Taylor had specifically told Clay he hoped to prosecute.[194]

The OCC's most difficult decision involved a possible case against the Deutsche Bank, the largest in Germany, whose clients included numerous companies that had utilized slave labor, including Siemens, Mannesmann, BMW, and Farben. The Deutsche Bank had experienced "sudden and phenomenal growth" during the war, largely as a result of its acquisition of Jewish-owned German banks and companies through Aryanization and its plunder of banks in occupied countries, such as Creditanstalt Wiener Bankverein, one of Austria's largest.[195] The OCC was particularly interested in Hermann Abs, a member of the Vorstand who had sat on Farben's Aufsichtsrat and whom Elwyn-Jones had targeted for prosecution in a second IMT.[196]

In early May, Taylor called a special OCC meeting to determine whether to bring charges against the bank. A 324-page report prepared by OMGUS's Finance Division on both the Deutsche Bank and the Dresdner Bank had concluded that there was enough evidence to convict Abs and other members of the Deutsche Bank's Vorstand. According to Bowers, however, "Sprecher and Taylor had to disagree. All the report proved was how well the bank's directors had concealed their own activities." Taylor thus "reluctantly" decided not to indict anyone associated with the bank.[197]

3. RuSHA

The May 20 program added seven defendants to the *RuSHA* case. The RuSHA list now included Otto Hofmann, Hildebrandt's predecessor, and Fritz Schwalm, Hofmann's Chief of Staff. The Lebensborn list now included Inge Viermetz, Sollman's deputy, and Gregor Ebner, the head of the Health Department. The RKFDV list now included Konrad Meyer-Hetling and Otto Schwarzenberger, the Chief of the Planning Office and the Chief of Finance, respectively. And the VoMI list now included Heinz Brueckner, one of the office heads. The additions brought the total number of defendants to 23.[198]

4. SD-Gestapo-RSHA

The most significant change in the *SD-Gestapo-RSHA* case was that its increasing focus on the activities of the Einsatzgruppen—discussed below—meant that Taylor no longer considered it to be optional. The March 14 list had identified Ohlendorf and 26 "tentative" defendants; the May 20 list contained 31. New additions included Otto Rasch, the commander of Einsatzgruppe C, which had killed more than 118,000 civilians in the Ukraine, and three of Rasch's subcommanders: Erwin Schulz, Paul Blobel, and Ernst Biberstein.[199]

---

[193] Bower, 17.   [194] Ibid., 355.   [195] Ibid., 16.   [196] Ibid., 346.
[197] Ibid., 354–5.   [198] Second Trial Program, 5   [199] Ibid., 6.

5. Prisoner of War

The only change to the *Prisoner of War* case was the addition of one potential defendant whose name, unfortunately, is not readable on the May 20 program.[200]

6. Principal Military

The May 20 program reduced the number of potential defendants in the *Principal Military* case from 25 to six, although Taylor reiterated that the list could not be finalized until additional documents had been analyzed. Three of the defendants were Field Marshals: Georg von Kuechler, who had commanded Army Group North during the siege of Leningrad; Wilhelm von Leeb, von Kuechler's predecessor with Army Group North; and Hugo Sperrle, the head of the Luftwaffe. One was a General Admiral in the *Kriegsmarine*, Otto Schniewind. And two were Generals: Georg-Hans Reinhardt, von Kuechler's successor with Army Group North; and Walter Warlimont, Deputy Chief of the Wehrmacht's Operations Staff.[201] Field Marshals von Brauchitsch, von Manstein, and von Rundstedt were no longer included in the list, reflecting Taylor's growing recognition that it was unlikely he would be able to prosecute them.

7. Krupp

The only change in *Krupp* was that the OCC had decided to "probably" prosecute all six of the potential defendants in the March 14 program, instead of simply "one or two." The May 20 program, therefore, included 12 likely defendants.[202]

8. Food and Agriculture-Hermann Goering Works

The May 20 program removed two certain defendants and one possible defendant from the March 14 list.[203] Franz Seldte, who had been Reich Minister of Labor, was removed because he had died of natural causes on April 1. Herbert Backe was removed because he had committed suicide five days after Seldte's death. And Hans Riecke, Backe's Deputy in the Four-Year Plan, had been denazified after the OCC determined that he was not sufficiently important to prosecute.

9. Foreign Office

The only change in the *Foreign Office* case was that Paul Schmidt, the head of the Foreign Office's news and press division, had been dropped as a suspect.[204] Schmidt would later testify for the prosecution in the *Ministries* trial.

---

[200] Second Trial Program, 7.   [201] Ibid., 10.
[202] Ibid., 12.   [203] Ibid., 13.   [204] Ibid., 14.

E. Cases 8–10

Taylor submitted his final trial program to OMGUS on 4 September 1947. In the interim, the OCC had filed indictments in three cases—*RuSHA, Einsatzgruppen,* and *Krupp*—and had decided to abandon the possibility of holding a second medical trial.

1. RuSHA *(Case No. 8)*

The *RuSHA* case was prepared and presented by the SS Division. According to Sprecher, the case was one of the easiest to prepare—requiring less than six months—because "the groundwork had been laid in the preparation and trial of other cases."[205] The indictment was filed on 7 July 1947 and the trial began on October 20.

Fourteen people were ultimately indicted. All of the defendants added by the May 20 program were included in the final trial, as were all of the March 14 defendants from the Lebensborn, RKFDV, and VoMI. Of the 11 original RuSHA defendants, however, only Richard Hildebrandt and Herbert Huebner were indicted. Dropped defendants included Kurt Mayer, the head of the Reich Office for Genealogy Research, and Herbert Aust, one of RuSHA's leading—and most eugenics-oriented—racial examiners. The OCC wanted to include Fritz Bartels, the head of the Reich Central Office of Health Leadership, in the trial, but he was not apprehended and transferred to Nuremberg until after the indictment had already been filed.[206]

2. Einsatzgruppen *(Case No. 9)*

Einsatzgruppen, which was also planned and prepared by the SS Division, was one of the last cases to be approved for trial. Taylor had not initially anticipated prosecuting Ohlendorf with other Einsatzgruppen leaders; as indicated by the March 14 program, he intended to include Ohlendorf in a more general SS case.[207] Indeed, a number of OCC investigators were initially opposed to an Einsatzgruppen-centered trial, because—notwithstanding Ohlendorf's testimony at the IMT—they did not yet fully grasp the enormity of the crimes committed by the mobile killing squads.[208]

Two developments reoriented the OCC's planning. To begin with, although most of the high-ranking SD, Gestapo, and RSHA officials that the OCC wanted to prosecute were either missing (most notably Eichmann[209]) or known to be

---

[205] Memo from Sprecher to Mercer, undated, 1.
[206] Arrests by Request of OCCWC, 1.
[207] First Trial Program, 2.
[208] Earl, 73.
[209] At the time, military authorities wrongly believed that Eichmann had committed suicide. Ibid., 48.

dead,[210] the Apprehension and Locator Branch had been able to find a number of Einsatzgruppen commanders and subordinate officers.[211] Availability alone thus dictated limiting the case to the Einstazgruppen. More importantly, though, the Berlin Branch had begun to analyze the Einsatzgruppen Reports, a massive collection of eight to nine million documents that detailed the Einsatzgruppen's crimes with chilling precision.[212] The reports had been seized by the Allies in September 1945, but the Berlin Branch did not "discover" them until March 1947 because of its limited invetigative resources.[213]

Once the OCC prosecutor in charge of the Berlin Branch, Ben Ferencz, recognized the importance of the Einsatzgruppen Reports, he returned to Nuremberg to lobby Taylor to dedicate a case to Ohlendorf and the other leaders of the Einsatzgruppen.[214] That was a significant request, given that Taylor not only expected the case to be much broader, but considered even the broader case to be "optional"—and indeed Taylor initially rejected it, insisting that the OCC simply lacked the time and resources to try another case.[215] Nevertheless, at some point between the May 20 program and July 3, when the initial indictment was filed, Taylor changed his mind.[216]

Ferencz, whom Taylor named chief prosecutor of the *Einsatzgruppen* case,[217] then began to prepare for trial. The first issue he faced was how to deal with the Soviets, on whose soil many of the worst atrocities had been committed. Ferencz sent Frederic Burin, one of the Berlin Branch's research analysts, to discuss the possibility of a joint prosecution of the Einsatzgruppen commanders with the Soviet Military Administration. The Soviet representative was initially "intrigued" by the idea, but later in the meeting took the position that the Soviets would want to prosecute the suspects in their custody on their own. That was the last time the OCC communicated with the Soviets about the case.[218]

Once Ferencz realized that the OCC was on its own, his team—which included an alcoholic prosecutor named James Heath and two "cast-offs" from other prosecution teams[219]—began identifying which of the 2,000–3,000 members of the Einsatzgruppen to indict. At least one of the team's key suspects, Heinz Schubert, Ohlendorf's adjutant in Einsatzgruppe D, had been released from confinement for lack of evidence that he had committed or witnessed the commission of any war crimes.[220] He was detained again and included in the trial. Another suspect, Franz Six, was scheduled to be tried as part of the *Foreign Office* case because he had been the head of the Foreign Office's Cultural Division before being

[210] Tayor, *Final Report*, 203 n. 80.   [211] Ibid., 80.   [212] Earl, 77–9.
[213] Ibid., 77.   [214] Ibid., 79.   [215] Ibid.
[216] Earl claims that Taylor made this decision in late March, but the May 20 program, which continued to list the broader case, indicates that the final decision was actually made considerably later.
[217] Memorandum from Walton to Sachs, 22 Mar. 1947, cited in Earl, 79.
[218] Ibid., 80–1.
[219] Ibid., 204. Heath would ultimately be listed only as a "consultant" in the *Einsatzgruppen* case. Ibid., 204 n. 115.
[220] Ibid., 78.

appointed commander of Einsatzgruppe B's Vorkommando Moscow. Taylor decided to transfer Six to *Einsatzgruppen*.

The OCC filed the first indictment in the case on 3 July 1947. That indictment contained 18 names, all but one of whom—Erich Naumann, the commander of Einsatzgruppe B—had been included on the May 20 list. The July 3 indictment was then amended on July 29 to include six additional defendants. Four of those had been on the May 20 list,[221] but two had been identified subsequent to the second trial program: Waldemar Klingelhoefer, Six's successor as commander of Vorkommando Moscow; and Waldemar von Radetzky, Deputy Chief of Sonderkommando 4a of Einsatzgruppe C. Trial began on September 29 with 23 defendants instead of 24, because Emil Haussmann, an officer in Einsatzkommando 12 of Einsatzgruppe D, had committed suicide two days after being arraigned.[222]

3. Krupp *(Case No. 10)*

Krupp—which would be the last of the industrialist cases—was prepared and presented by the Krupp Trial Team, which was established when the Economics Division was dissolved. The indictment was filed on 16 August 1947 and trial began on December 8.

The 12 defendants at the *Krupp* trial included Alfried Krupp and all of the defendants that both the March 14 and May 20 programs had considered "certain."[223] It also included two of the defendants identified as "possible" by the two programs, Eberhardt and Kupke, as well as four members of Krupp's Vorstand that had not been previously identified: Eduard Houdremont, Karl Pfirsch, Heinrich Korschan, and Ewald Loeser. Loeser's inclusion incensed the British, who insisted that he had been cleared of wrongdoing by their intelligence services and had only been extradited to the United States by mistake. Britain also insisted—providing still more evidence that it had no interest in punishing industrialists—that the charges against him be dropped on the ground that he was "an essential man in the administration of the North German Iron and Steel Control, and in the economic rehabilitation of the British Zone."[224]

4. *The Second Medical Case*

As noted earlier, because Erich Hippke, the Chief Medical Officer of the Luftwaffe, had been captured too late to be included in the first medical trial, the March 14 program had recommended that he "and certain others in the same category should be retained in confinement until the conclusion of the case and thereafter should be tried in some appropriate proceeding."[225] Those others had been identified in an August 15 memo from Alexander Hardy to Taylor; the list of 15 suspects

[221] Braune, Haensch, Steimle, and Strauch. Second Trial Program, 6.
[222] *Einsatzgruppen*, IV TWC 411.
[223] Mueller, Janssen, Ihn, von Buelow, and Lehmann.
[224] Quoted in Bush, *Conspiracy*, 1192.   [225] Second Trial Program, 8.

included Karl Clauberg, "the most reprehensible of all the remaining medical men not tried," who had been involved in the Auschwitz sterilization experiments; Otto Bickenbach, who had been involved in the phosgene gas experiments at Fort Ney in France; and Eugen Gildemeister, who had conducted typhus experiments at Buchenwald.[226]

Toward the end of August, Taylor finally abandoned the possibility of a second Medical case. The OCC's limited resources and the rapidly approaching end of the war-crimes program were almost certainly the most important factors. It is likely, though, that two other considerations played a role in Taylor's decision. First, Milch had been acquitted on the medical experimentation charge, which made it unlikely that any of the suspects on Hardy's list who had not been personally involved in the experiments—such as Karl Gutzeit, who had been aware of the experiments connected to the racial hygiene program as a member of Handloser's staff[227]—could be successfully prosecuted.[228] Second, most of the most important suspects on the list were either still at large (such as Clauberg), rumored to be dead (such as Gildemeister), or scheduled to be tried by another Ally (such as Bickenbach, who was in French custody).

F. The September 4 Program

By the time Taylor submitted his final trial program on 4 September 1946, the OCC had initiated 10 of the 16 cases that Clay had approved. Two had been completed: *Medical* and *Milch*. Taylor estimated that six of the eight cases that were still in progress would be completed by the end of 1947, while *Krupp* and *Farben* would continue until April or May 1948.[229]

The remaining six cases were more problematic. Taylor reiterated in the September 4 memo that "the program recommended on 14 March, amended on 20 May, and approved as amended on 9 June, is sufficiently comprehensive and well-balanced ... that it should be executed appropriately as it stands."[230] He acknowledged, however, that funding, time, and personnel problems meant that the program had to be scaled back.[231]

Funding
Taylor pointed out that the budget approved by OMGUS provided trial-related expenses only through the end of fiscal year 1947. As a result, the budget simply did not allow the OCC to prosecute all six of the remaining cases. Taylor remained confident, however, that the budget did not require more than "moderate curtailment" of the May 20 program.[232]

[226] Memo from Hardy to Taylor, 15 Aug. 1947, NA-260-186a1-102-11, at 1–2.
[227] Ibid., 2.   [228] Weindling, 383.   [229] Third Trial Program, 1–2.
[230] Ibid., 2.   [231] Ibid., 3.   [232] Ibid.

Time

When General Clay approved the May 20 program on June 9, he insisted that no trial should begin after 1947 and that all trials should end by June 1948.[233] According to Taylor, although the remaining cases were "in a fairly advanced state of preparation," it would not be possible to prosecute all six within those parameters. The OCC would have to run all of the trials simultaneously to meet Clay's deadline, and it simply lacked sufficient clerical staff to "cope with so many cases at once."[234]

The problem, according to Taylor, was that the earlier cases had taken much longer to begin and to complete than he had expected. One reason was simply logistical: Tribunals V and VI had arrived late in Nuremberg, delaying the start of the *Hostage* and *Farben* trials. Another reflected the OCC's poor planning: in a number of cases, the OCC had simply filed indictments that, in retrospect, appeared "unnecessarily broad"—an error for which Taylor was "quite prepared to take the blame."[235]

Taylor's other reasons are particularly interesting. First, Taylor observed that it was particularly difficult to prove the guilt of high-ranking military, governmental, and economic officials. The NMT trials were not like the Dachau trials, in which "most of the defendants [could] be shown to have committed murders or other atrocities with their own hands."[236] On the contrary, the OCC could only convict its defendants by introducing "extensive documentation and testimony showing that they were responsible for the acts of subordinates, that they know of those acts, and that they approved, planned, or encouraged" them.[237]

Second, Taylor argued that the German defense counsel availed themselves of every opportunity to slow down the trials, because they had realized that "delaying tactics, if successful, [would] tend to work a contraction of the overall scope of the program." The OCC was doing everything in its power to avoid such delays, but the "substantial shift in the attitude toward the trials on the part of the public . . . and the judges" meant that their protests were increasingly falling on deaf ears.[238]

Third, Taylor noted that it simply took a very long time to prosecute large groups of defendants who were facing the possibility of a death sentence. The *Medical* case was an example: although the case lasted 139 trial days, which "superficially appears like a very long time," that averaged out to only six trial days per defendant.[239] Moreover, most of those days were dedicated to the defense's case-in-chief, because the judges had "quite properly insisted that the defense be given every possible opportunity to deny or explain away the crimes."[240] Indeed, in two trials—*Medical* and *Pohl*—the defense had taken more than four times as long as the prosecution to present its case.[241]

---

[233] Ibid.   [234] Ibid.   [235] Ibid., 4.   [236] Ibid.   [237] Ibid.
[238] Ibid.   [239] Ibid., 5.   [240] Ibid., 4.   [241] Ibid., 5.

Personnel

Although the funding and time limitations were important, "the single most serious limitation on the execution of the remainder of the war crimes program" was the absence of judges to hear the remaining cases.[242] Only two or three of the current judges intended to remain in Nuremberg after their trials concluded, and they would be needed for the *Krupp* trial. The OCC's ability to begin the six remaining trials on the May 20 program thus depended on the War Department's ability to recruit new judges with the "utmost expedition"[243]—and Taylor was fully aware that recruiting 18 new judges in time to meet the July 1948 deadline was "clearly beyond the realm of actual possibility."[244]

The question, then, was not *whether* the May 20 program should be curtailed, but by *how much*. Taylor considered three options: abandoning the remaining six cases; eliminating one or more cases; or consolidating the six cases into four or less.

1. Abandonment

Taylor was adamantly opposed to abandoning the remainder of the war-crimes program, because he believed that failing to prosecute so many high-ranking Nazi officials would—despite eroding support for the trials—"distort and amputate the program to a point where serious criticism might be aroused within Germany, the United States, and within the countries formerly occupied by the Germans."[245] Taylor pointed to three shortcomings in the 10 cases that had been initiated to date. First, and most importantly, only the *Justice* case had focused on "the field of government and politics"—and that case, though "exceptionally interesting legally," was not "a major case within the framework of the Third Reich as a whole."[246] Government defendants in the remaining cases were far more important, such as Walther Darre, Hans Lammers, and Otto Dietrich.[247]

Second, only the *Hostage* case was primarily concerned with the German military, and it was "relatively narrow" in scope.[248] The *Principal Military* case was thus particularly important, because it included numerous high-ranking officers, such as von Rundstedt, von Manstein, and von Brauchitsch—whom Taylor obviously had still not completely abandoned as possible defendants—as well as Field Marshals von Leeb and von Kuchler.[249]

Third, none of the ten cases focused on financiers. The *Dresdner Bank* case was intended to fill that gap.[250]

2. Elimination

Taylor was ambivalent about this option. He acknowledged that *Prisoner of War* and *Food and Agriculture-Hermann Goering Works* could be dropped from the trial program "without serious damage," although he insisted that Darre, the principal

---

[242] Third Trial Program, 1–2.   [243] Ibid.   [244] Ibid., 3.   [245] Ibid., 6.
[246] Ibid., 5.   [247] Ibid., 5–6.   [248] Ibid., 6.   [249] Ibid.   [250] Ibid.

defendant in the latter, would have to be included in one of the remaining cases.[251] But he drew the line at eliminating any of the other four, which he considered "so important that their complete abandonment is out of the question."[252]

3. Contraction

Taylor's preferred option, therefore, was to consolidate the six remaining cases into four or less. He pointed out that he had already instructed his staff to consolidate *Prisoner of War* with *Principal Military*, trying the two most important defendants in the former—Gottlob Berger and General Reinecke—together with the military defendants in the latter. An additional case could be eliminated, he believed, by consolidating *Foreign Office* with the (already consolidated) *Government Administration-Propaganda and Education* case.[253] That would mean four cases would be left to try: *Prisoner of War-Principal Military*; *Foreign Office-Government Administration-Propaganda and Education*; *Food and Agriculture-Hermann Goering Works*; and *Dresdner Bank*.

Taylor was optimistic that the OCC's budget and personnel would be sufficient to complete the four cases by the end of June 1948. He recognized, though, that the War Department might find it "extremely difficult" to recruit the 12 new judges that the four cases would require. He thus suggested, as a fall-back position, even more significant consolidation, reducing the number of defendants in *Foreign Office-Government Administration-Propaganda and Education* and adding the most important defendants from *Dresdner Bank* and/or *Food and Agriculture-Hermann Goering Works*: Carl Goetz and Karl Rasche from the former; Walther Darre, Paul Koerner, and Paul Pleiger from the latter. Taylor's preference was to not include the *Dresdner Bank* defendants, because although "the merger of Pleiger, Koerner, and Darre with the other ministers can be defended with some show of logic . . . the merger of Rasche and Goetz has only a tenuous logical basis, and should not be resorted to except as a last extremity."[254]

G. Final Planning

General Clay's response to the September 4 program—reflected in a memo to Kenneth Royall, then the Secretary of War, on September 8—was generally positive. He continued to maintain that it was essential for all of the NMT trials to be concluded by the end of fiscal year 1947, but he also recognized that the success of the war-crimes program depended on completing as many of the six remaining cases as possible. In his view, three were particularly important: *Principal Military*, *Foreign Office*, and *Dresdner Bank*.[255] Indeed, he believed that those cases were more important than *RuSHA*, *Einsatzgruppen*, and *Krupp*—although he knew

---

[251] Ibid., 7.   [252] Ibid.
[253] Ibid.   [254] Ibid., 8.
[255] Cable from Clay to AGWAR, 8 Sept. 1947, NA-153–1018-1-84-1, at 2.

that it was too late to drop the indictments in those cases.[256] Clay thus asked Secretary Royall to obtain nine new judges for the OCC.

Four days later, Royall informed Clay that the War Department would only be able to obtain six new judges. Royall agreed with Clay that the *Principal Military* and *Foreign Office* cases were essential, but he questioned the desirability of trying *Dresdner Bank*.[257] Clay replied on September 19 that two new tribunals would be "sufficient to complete the Nurnberg War Crimes program," which would then encompass 12 trials.[258] *Prisoner of War* and *Principal Military* would be (and already had been) consolidated into one case; *Foreign Office* would be combined with *Government Administration-Propaganda and Education*; *Food and Agriculture-Hermann Goering Works* and *Dresdner Bank* would be dropped entirely. Taylor would decide later whether to include defendants from the dropped cases in *Foreign Office*.[259]

On October 13, despite a "flurry of memos" from OCC personnel defending the cases,[260] Taylor informed the War Department that—as expected—it had decided to abandon *Food and Agriculture-Hermann Goering Works* and *Dresdner Bank*. Four defendants in those cases would be moved to *Foreign Office*: Paul Koerner, Paul Pleiger, and Emil Puhl from the former; Karl Rasche from the latter.[261] Including Puhl and Rasche, Taylor pointed out, would "increase Banking representation" in the overall war-crimes program.[262]

Taylor regretted dropping *Dresdner Bank*. Rawlings Ragland—by then the Chief of the Dresdner Bank trial team—had concluded in mid-August that "[t]he work done to date suggests that on the basis of really adequate preparation a fairly persuasive case of criminal activity on the part of leading Dresdner Bank officials could be made out,"[263] particularly in terms of their knowing support for the SS's use of slave labor and acts of plunder.[264] Rawlings had also reminded Taylor that, in light of OMGUS's well-publicized report on the Dresdner Bank's activities, it might "prove difficult or embarrassing to drop the case."[265]

The problem, once again, was time. By mid-August, Ragland had "serious doubts" that "any really adequate indictment could be drawn up before the first of next year" and was convinced that "adequate preparation for trial could not be completed until a somewhat later date."[266] The decision to pursue the Dresdner Bank had been motivated, in large part, by the OMGUS report: the OCC had assumed that "preparation of a case charging Dresdner Bank officials with war crimes would consist largely of supplementing and buttressing materials already

---

[256] Cable from Clay to AGWAR, 2–3.
[257] Cable from AGWAR to Clay, 12 Sept. 1947, NA-153–1018-1-84-1.
[258] Cable from Clay to AGWAR, 19 Sept. 1947, NA-153–1018-1-84-1, at 1.
[259] Ibid.
[260] Bush, *Conspiracy*, 1217.
[261] Cable from OCCWC to Army War Crimes Branch, 13 Oct. 1947, NA-153-1-84-1, at 1.
[262] Ibid.
[263] Memo from Ragland to Taylor, 15 Aug. 1947, 3.
[264] Ibid., 11.   [265] Ibid.   [266] Ibid., 19.

gathered together in preparation of the Report."[267] In fact, the report was of "little aid" to the case—"the real job not only of screening the documentary materials, but also of locating much of the material, remains to be done."[268] That additional work, Rawlings knew, was simply far beyond the resources of the understaffed and underskilled Dresdner Bank team.[269]

H. Cases 11 and 12

1. Ministries *(Case No. 11)*

The Ministries Division prepared the *Foreign Office-Government Administration-Propaganda and Education* case, which was now being called simply *Ministries*. In late 1947, after Taylor finalized the trial program, the Ministries Division was renamed the "Political Ministries Division" and a new division, "Economic Ministries," was formed by combining the members of the now-defunct Dresdner Bank team with the members of the Ministries Division who were investigating the economic ministries.[270]

The *Ministries* indictment was filed on November 18, and the trial began on 6 January 1948. No case had evolved as much over time. Only five of the 18 suspects in the original *Foreign Office* case ultimately stood trial in *Ministries*: Gustav Steengracht von Moyland, Ernst Bohle, Karl Ritter, Ernst von Weizsaecker, and Ernst Woermann. Twelve others had been identifed as major war criminals by the March 14 program. Six came from the original *Food and Agriculture-Hermann Goering Works* case: Walther Darre, Paul Koerner, Paul Pleiger, Hans Kehrl, Wilhelm Keppler, and Emil Puhl. Three came from the original *Government Administration* case: Hans Lammers, Otto Meissner, and Wilhelm Stuckart. Otto Dietrich came from the original *Propaganda and Education* case. Gottlob Berger came from the original *Prisoner of War* case. And Karl Rasche came from the original *Dresdner Bank* case.

Four of the 21 final defendants in *Ministries*, by contrast, had never previously been identified as suspects by the OCC. They were added between October 13, when Taylor finalized the trial program, and November 18, when the indictment was filed. Otto von Erdsmannsdorff had been the Minister to Hungary until 1941 and then Woermann's deputy in the Foreign Office's Political Division. Edmund Veesenmayer had been the Reich's Plenipotentiary in Hungary. Walter Schellenberg had been the head of the SS's foreign intelligence division and had personally staged the "Velo Incident" that had provided the pretext for Hitler's invasion of the Netherlands. And Lutz Schwering von Krosigk had been the Reich Minister of Finance until 1945 and Reich Minister for Foreign Affairs thereafter.

Ministries could have been even larger. On 19 November 1947, the World Jewish Congress (WJC) sent a memorandum to Royall—now the Secretary of the Army, the War Department having been abolished—urging him to include six additional

---

[267] Ibid., 2.   [268] Ibid., 1.   [269] Ibid., 3.   [270] Taylor, *Final Report*, 40.

defendants in the case.[271] Four had been involved in the infamous Wannsee Conference, during which the Nazis planned the "final solution of the Jewish question": Erich Neumann, an Undersecretary in the Four-Year Plan; Georg Leibbrandt, the head of the Political Department in the Ministry for the Eastern Occupied Territories; Otto Hofmann, the head of RuSHA; and Friedrich Kritzinger, the Reich Chancellery's State Secretary. The final two, Hermann Krumey and Ernst Girzik, were high-ranking SS officers who had worked closely with Heinrich Muller, the head of the Gestapo, and Adolf Eichmann.[272]

As the memo made clear, the WJC would have preferred the OCC to hold a "special Jewish trial" involving (at least) those six suspects. In its view, the NMT trials had simply not focused enough on the architects of Holocaust:

Trials by American military courts on the basis of [Law No. 10] have brought to justice a number of Germans responsible for crimes against Jews … none of those trials, because of the persons involved and the character of the cases prosecuted, concerned those who were at the top of the Nazi hierarchy, who actually planned the destruction of the European Jewish communities, and under whose direction and supervision the extirpation of these millions was carried out.[273]

The WJC recognized that it was likely too late for the OCC to hold another trial. But it argued that there was "no legal or practical impediment" to including the suspects in *Ministries*. Indeed, the WJC claimed that doing so was necessary to fulfill the "sacred duty of the Allies, who have repeatedly and solemnly proclaimed that the crimes against the Jewish people will not be condoned, to do their utmost to bring the culprits to justice."[274]

A week later, on November 26, Taylor informed the Army that he did not intend to include any of the WJC's suggested defendants in the *Ministries* case. Hoffman was being tried in *RuSHA*. Kritzinger, who had been scheduled to be a defendant in *Government Administration*, had recently died. Krumey was not in U.S. custody. That left Neumann, Liebbrandt, and Girzik, all of whom were currently in Nuremberg. Taylor acknowledged that a "prima facie case" existed against Neumann and Liebbrandt, but insisted—implicitly blaming Clay for his inability to accommodate the WJC's request—that he could not indict them "because of acceleration in war crimes program and desire to terminate by July 1948."[275] Preparing their cases would simply take too long.[276]

Taylor's rejection of the WJC's plea to expand *Ministries*—which he did not communicate to the WJC itself for another month, "an eternity for so punctual a

[271] Letter from Wise to Royall, 19 Dec. 1947, NA-153–1018-8-84-1.
[272] Memo from World Jewish Congress, 19 Nov. 1947, NA-153–1018-8-84-1, at 3.
[273] Ibid., 3.
[274] Ibid., 4.
[275] Teleconference with Taylor, 26 Nov. 1947, NA-153–1018-8-84-1.
[276] Taylor also cited the size of the courtroom, but he could have included three additional defendants without exceeding the maximum number—24—that the larger courtrooms could accommodate.

correspondent"[277]—was not the first time that he had failed to act on a request to focus the NMT trials more directly on the Holocaust. On 6 February 1947, Taylor had informed Tom Ervin, his close friend and then Executive Counsel, that someone (it is not clear who) had suggested to him that "it would be desirable to have an entire case which would concern itself *only* with the charge that the Nazis exterminated approximately 6,000,000 Jews," because the Holocaust was "by far the most important and sinister item in the entire Nazi history."[278] Taylor told Ervin that he had "come to no conclusion on the wisdom of this proposal," but asked him to consider it. Taylor also noted that he believed it would be difficult to select defendants for a Holocaust-centered trial, because the OCC was prosecuting "central planners and organizers," not "people in the concentration camp or camp commandant level," and "most of the people who played an important role in ordering and planning the Jewish extermination probably committed many other crimes as well."[279]

Although it is unwise to read too much into a single memo, Taylor's gut reaction to the possibility of a trial focused solely on the Holocaust is troubling. First, the suggestion predated even the March 14 trial program, so Taylor's later rationale for not expanding *Ministries*—that there was not enough time—did not yet apply. There *was* time to create a Holocaust-centered trial in February 1947.

Second, although aspects of the Holocaust played an important role in a number of the OCC's cases—slave labor in *Krupp* and *Farben*; the concentration camps in *Pohl*; Germanization in *RuSHA*; deportation in *Ministries*—none of them were functionally equivalent to a Holocaust-centered trial. Indeed, the February suggestion came long before Taylor approved transforming *SD-Gestapo-RSHA* into *Einsatzgruppen*, the trial that focused most specifically on the extermination of the Jews. It is thus difficult to argue that a Holocaust-centered trial was somehow duplicative or unnecessary.

Finally, Taylor's suggestion that "most of the people who played an important role in ordering and planning the Jewish extermination probably committed many other crimes as well" seems to misunderstand why the WJC and others wanted a trial focused specifically on the Holocaust. The February request did not deny that the architects of the Holocaust had committed atrocities against non-Jews; it claimed that the atrocities committed against Jews were of a magnitude and gravity that justified at least one trial dedicated to them. It is thus difficult to avoid the conclusion that Taylor's response trivialized the crimes committed against the Jews—implying that the "many other crimes" were just as important, if not more so.

---

[277] Bush, *Conspiracy*, 1187.
[278] Memorandum from Taylor to Ervin, 6 Feb. 1947, Gantt Collection in Towson University Archives, Box FF, at 1.
[279] Ibid.

2. High Command *(Case No. 12)*

The *High Command* case was prepared and presented by the Military & SS Division, which had been created in late 1947 after illness forced Clark Denney to resign as the head of the Ministries Division. Ten of the 14 defendants in the *High Command* trial had been identified in the March 14 program. The other four were General Reinecke, the only defendant in *Prisoner of War* who had been moved to *High Command* after Taylor's decision to combine the two; General Karl von Roques, who had commanded the rear areas of Army Group South and Army Group A; General Otto Woehler, who had been the Commander in Chief of the 8th Army and Army Group South; and Rudolf Lehmann, who had been the Chief of the Wehrmacht's Legal Division. The latter three also did not appear in either the May 20 or September 4 programs, indicating that they were last-minute additions to the trial.

Conspicuously missing from the dock were, of course, Field Marshals von Brauchitsch, von Manstein, and von Rundstedt. Unlike the other defendants, the three men were in British custody when the OCC was making final decisions about whom to indict.[280] Taylor originally proposed prosecuting all of the high-ranking military officers in a joint U.S.-British tribunal, as permitted by Article II(c) of Ordinance No. 7. The British, however, preferred to simply extradite von Brauchitsch, von Manstein, and von Rundstedt to the United States.[281] Taylor then decided to include the Field Marshals in the *Principal Military* case, as reflected by the March 14 trial program.

Despite Article III of Ordinance No. 7, which provided that "[t]he Chief of Counsel for War Crimes shall determine the persons to be tried by the tribunals," General Clay refused to allow Taylor to ask the British to extradite von Brauchitsch, von Manstein, and von Rundstedt. Instead, Clay ordered Taylor "to try only the field marshals and other officers already in American custody, and to transmit (in August 1947) the evidence which appeared to incriminate Rundstedt, Mannstein [sic], and Brauchitsch to the British authorities."[282] Taylor complied, informing his staff on November 17, ten days before the *High Command* indictment was filed, to drop further research on the Field Marshals.[283]

This was, according to Taylor, "the only occasion upon which my plans as to the inclusion of particular defendants were disapproved by General Clay."[284] But it was a particularly bitter occasion. As reflected in an OCC memo dated 13 October 1947, captured German documents indicated that von Brauchitsch, von Manstein, and von Rundstedt were clearly responsible for the widespread killing of hostages, for supporting and protecting the Einsatzgruppen, and for participating in the

---

[280] Memo from OCCWC to Army War Crimes Branch, 13 Oct. 1947, 2.
[281] Bloxham, 44.
[282] Taylor, *Final Report*, 82–3.
[283] Cable from Taylor to Young & Olbeter, 17 Nov. 1947, NA-153–1018-8-84-1.
[284] Taylor, *Final Report*, 82.

slave-labor program.[285] Taylor was also convinced that the OCC would have little trouble convicting the three Field Marshals. The October 13 memo stated that the "[c]ases against Rundstedt and Mannstein [sic] are strongest of all and evidence assembled in Washington is overwhelming" and claimed that von Brauchitsch's conviction was "as certain as the outcome of a lawsuit ever can be."[286]

Finally, Taylor believed that the legitimacy of the *High Command* trial depended, at least in part, on the inclusion of the three Field Marshals. The October 13 memo noted that the "very nature" of the evidence in the case was "such that trial of Leeb and Kuechler without Rundstedt and others held in England will certainly raise pointed inquiries as to why they were not made defendants."[287] The comparison with von Leeb was particularly apt: unlike von Brauchitsch, von Manstein, and von Rundstedt, who were in active service throughout the war, von Leeb had resigned as the commander of Army Group north in January 1942 and never saw active duty again.[288] Indeed, at least one scholar has suggested that von Leeb was the primary defendant in *High Command* not because he was more culpable than than his co-defendants—he clearly wasn't—but because the absence of von Brauchitsch, von Manstein, and von Rundstedt meant that he was the best known of the Field Marshals available for trial.[289]

---

[285] Memo from OCCWC to War Crimes Washington, 13 Oct. 1947, 3.

[286] Ibid., 3–4.

[287] Ibid., 4.

[288] John J. Douglass, "High Command Case: A Study in Staff and Command Responsibility," 6 *Int'l Lawyer* 686, 690 (1972).

[289] Ibid. Bloxham also notes that Taylor considered von Rundstedt and von Brauchitsch to be of "far greater significance to the German people" than the other defendants. Bloxham, 43.

4

The Trials

Introduction

The previous chapter explained the evolution of the 12 NMT trials. This chapter concludes that discussion by providing a brief synopsis of those trials. Each synopsis has three primary sections: (1) the counts in the indictment; (2) biographical information about the judges who heard the case; and (3) the verdicts and sentences. A number of synopses also contain a fourth section on noteworthy aspects of the trial, such as its historical context, evidence of bias on the part of the judges, or misconduct by one of the parties.

I. The *Medical* Case

A. The Indictment

Twenty-three defendants ultimately stood trial. Twenty-one had been included on Taylor's September 9 list. The other two had been added prior to trial: Bertha Oberhauser, a doctor at Ravensbrueck who had been a member of the Hohenly-chen Group; and Waldemar Hoven, the chief doctor at Buchenwald.

The indictment contained four counts. Count One alleged that all of the defendants had engaged in a "common design or conspiracy" to commit war crimes and crimes against humanity. Count Two, the war-crimes count, alleged that the defendants were responsible for a variety of medical experiments conducted "without the subjects' consent, upon civilians and members of the armed forces of nations then at war with the German Reich," including high-altitude, freezing, malaria, and sea-water experiments at Dachau; spotted fever, poison, and incendiary experiments at Buchenwald; and sterilization experiments at Auschwitz and Ravensbrueck. The count also alleged that Rudolf Brandt and Sievers were responsible for the Strasbourg skeleton-collection murders and that Karl Brandt, Blome, Brack, and Hoven were responsible for participating in the Reich's euthanasia program.[1] Count Three, the crimes against humanity count, alleged that the same experiments and murders constituted crimes against humanity when conducted "upon German civilians and nationals of other countries."[2] Finally, Count 4

---

[1] *Medical*, Indictment, paras 8–9, I TWC 15.   [2] Ibid., 16, para. 11.

alleged that ten of the defendants were guilty of criminal membership because they had been members of the SS during the war.

B. The Tribunal

The *Medical* case was heard by Tribunal I, which consisted of Walter B. Beals (presiding), Harold L. Sebring, and Johnson Tal Crawford, with Victor C. Swearingen serving as the alternate. Beals, the first judge to be invited by the War Department to serve on a tribunal, was a Justice of the Supreme Court of Washington and had served, as a Major in the Army, on an American military tribunal in France during World War I. Sebring was a Justice of the Supreme Court of Florida who had been decorated during World War I by both the U.S. and France for valor in combat. Crawford was a justice of the Oklahoma District Court and had also served during World War I. Swearingen, a former Special Assistant to the Attorney General of the United States, had been a Lt. Colonel in the Army during World War II and served after the war as chief of the Operations Section of the War Department's War Crimes Office.[3]

C. Noteworthy Aspects

The *Medical* trial involved two notable instances of misconduct by witnesses. In the first, a prosecution witness, Karl Hoellenrainer, tried to attack Beiglboeck after being asked to identify the defendant as the man who conducted salt-water experiments on him. The tribunal held Hoellenrainer in contempt pursuant to Article VI of Ordinance No. 7, which permitted tribunals to "deal summarily with any contumacy," and sentenced him to 90 days in the Nuremberg Prison. It released him three weeks later after Hoellenrainer apologized for his actions.[4]

The more serious misconduct involved Andrew Ivy, the head of the University of Illinois at Chicago's Medical College, who was the prosecution's star expert witness at trial. Prior to his testimony, Ivy was present during the cross-examination of another prosecution witness, Walter Leibrandt, a professor of medical history at the University of Erlangen, who had testified that experimentation on humans was unethical even if the subjects consented and the experiments had medical value. On cross-examination, Leibrandt admitted that the standard he endorsed condemned not only the defendants' experiments, but also American malaria experiments conducted on inmates at Stateville Prison in Illinois during the war. Concerned by Leibrandt's testimony, Ivy decided to defend the Stateville experiments by testifying that they had been overseen and approved by a public ethics committee. There was just one problem: no such committee had existed, much less one that had approved the experiments.

Undaunted, Ivy returned to the United States and convinced the Governor of Illinois, Dwight Green, to form an ad hoc committee—the Green Committee—to

---

[3] Background Information on Judges, 1–2.
[4] See *Medical*, Further Order of the Tribunal, 21 July 1947, XV TWC 967–70.

advise him on the ethics of medical experimentation involving human subjects. Ivy did not tell the Governor that he intended to testify when he returned to Nuremberg, the committee never met, and the committee's "report" was authored by Ivy himself. Ivy nevertheless not only claimed at the *Medical* trial that the Green Committee had approved the Stateville experiments, he responded to a defense question about whether "the formation of the committee had anything to do with the fact that this trial is going on" by testifying that no such connection existed.[5] It is unlikely that the prosecution was aware of the true facts—but it is beyond question that Ivy blatantly perjured himself.

D. Outcome

Tribunal I announced the verdicts on 19 August 1947 and imposed sentence the next day. Seven defendants were acquitted: Blome, Pokorny, Romberg, Rostock, Ruff, Schaefer, and Weltz. The highest-ranking acquittees were Rostock, who had been Chief of the Office for Medical Science and Research under Karl Brandt, and Kurt Blome, who had been the Deputy Health Leader of the Reich under Leo Conti. The remaining acquittees were less important—officials involved in aviation medicine (Ruff and Weltz) or staff doctors in various Reich medical institutes (Pokorny, Schaefer, and Romberg).

The other 16 defendants were each convicted on both Count Two (war crimes) and Count Three (crimes against humanity). Nine were also convicted of membership in the SS. No defendant was convicted on Count One because—as discussed in Chapter 12—the tribunals held, following a joint session, that conspiring to commit war crimes or crimes against humanity was not criminal under Law No. 10. Sentences ranged dramatically. Seven defendants were sentenced to death; five were sentenced to life imprisonment, and the other six received sentences ranging from a high of 20 years to a low of 10 years. Oberhauser, the only female defendant convicted in any of the trials,[6] received a 20-year sentence.

II. *Milch*

A. The Indictment

Field Marshal Milch was indicted on three counts. Counts One and Two involved war crimes. Count One alleged that Milch was responsible for slave labor and deportation to slave labor because, in his capacity as a member of the Central Planning Board from 1942–45, he had helped create the Nazis' slave labor program, which had resulted in the deportation of at least 5,000,000 workers to Germany.[7] Count Two alleged that Milch was responsible for the high-altitude and

---

[5] Horst H. Freyhofer, *The Nuremberg Medical Trial: The Holocaust and the Origin of the Nuremberg Medical Code* 102–3 (2004).

[6] Inge Viermetz, the only other female defendant, was acquitted in *RuSHA*.

[7] *Milch*, Indictment, para. 4, II TWC 361.

freezing experiments conducted at Dachau[8]—although, revealingly, the count provided no factual allegations connecting Milch to the experiments. Finally, Count Three alleged that the acts in Counts One and Two constituted crimes against humanity insofar as they involved German nationals and nationals of other countries.

B. The Tribunal

Milch was heard by Tribunal II, which consisted of Robert M. Toms (presiding), Donald F. Phillips, Michael A. Musmanno, and an alternate, John L. Speight. Toms was a Circuit Court judge in Michigan and a former prosecutor whom Clarence Darrow had described—after facing off against him in the famous Sweet Trials in 1925—as "one of the fairest and most humane prosecutors that I ever met."[9] Phillips was a judge of the Superior Court of North Carolina who had been decorated by the French for his service as a 1st Lt. in World War I. Speight was a lawyer who had served as a Special Attorney in the Justice Department during World War II.[10]

Musmanno was one of the most interesting judges at Nuremberg—and the only judge to hear three different cases (*Milch, Pohl,* and *Einsatzgruppen*). He was exceptionally well-educated, holding six degrees, including a PhD from the University of Rome. Prior to the war he had worked as a defense attorney in Pennsylvania, been elected to the Pennsylvania legislature, and served as a judge in the state's Court of Common Pleas. He had defended Sacco and Vanzetti in 1927 and was so devastated by their executions that he came to believe that the death penalty was little more than state-legislated murder.[11] During the war he had served as a Navy liaison officer to the Fifth Army in the Italian Campaign, being wounded twice in combat. After the Allies liberated Sorrento, he had been appointed Military Governor of the peninsula.[12]

As noted in the previous chapter, Musmanno was the only non-civilian to serve on one of the tribunals—he finished the war as a Commander in the Navy. Taylor had expressed concern to OMGUS and the War Department about the idea of a Commander "sitting on a tribunal which may be called upon to try field marshals and high ranking generals,"[13] but relented in the face of positive recommendations from General Clark and Mickey Marcus. The Navy nevertheless promoted Musmanno to Captain after he was formally appointed to Tribunal II to at least partially equalize the disparity.[14]

---

[8] *Milch*, Indictment, 362–3, paras 8–9.
[9] <http://www.encyclopedia.com/doc/1G2-3498200150.html> (accessed 12 January 2011).
[10] Background Information on Judges, 2–3.
[11] Earl, 232–4.
[12] Ibid., 235.
[13] Memo from Taylor to Petersen and Clay, 21 Nov. 1946, NA-153–1018-5-85-1, at 1.
[14] Earl, 238–9.

C. Outcome

Trial began on 2 January 1947 and ended with sentencing on April 17. The prosecution's case-in-chief lasted only eight days and involved the live testimony of only three witnesses.[15] The verdict was a split decision. The tribunal acquitted Milch on Count Two, concluding—as the OCC expected—that the prosecution had failed to prove Milch's connection to the medical experiments beyond a reasonable doubt.[16] But it convicted him on Counts One and Three, finding that he knew about the slave-labor program and "himself urged more stringent and coercive means to supplement the dwindling supply of labor in the Luftwaffe."[17] The tribunal sentenced Milch to life imprisonment.

III. The *Justice* Case

A. The Indictment

The 15 defendants in the case were all accused of participating in what the *Justice* tribunal described as "a nationwide government-organized system of cruelty and injustice ... perpetrated in the name of law by the authority of the Ministry of Justice, and through the instrumentality of the courts."[18] Most of the defendants were officials in the Ministry of Justice, such as Schlegelberger and Klemm. The others were judges and prosecutors affiliated with the Nazis' notorious People's Court and Special Courts, including Rothaug, Oeschey, and Lautz.

The indictment contained four counts. Count One charged all of the defendants with conspiring to commit war crimes and crimes against humanity. Counts Two and Three then detailed the specific war crimes and crimes against humanity that formed the objects of the conspiracy. Count Two, the war-crimes count, emphasized the Nazis' barbaric Night and Fog program, "whereby civilians of occupied territories who had been accused of crimes of resistance against occupying forces were spirited away for secret trial by certain Special Courts of the Justice Ministry within the Reich."[19] Count Three, the crimes against humanity count, focused on the fate of German civilians under the Nazis. It alleged that, following the invasion of Poland in September 1939, the Ministry of Justice had used the People's Court and Special Courts to create "a reign of terror to suppress political opposition to the German Reich" and to further the extermination of German Jews by applying discriminatory laws to them in legal proceedings that lacked "all semblance of judicial process."[20] Finally, Count Four alleged that seven defendants were guilty of criminal membership in the SS, SD, or Leadership Corps of the Nazi Party.

---

[15] John Alan Appleman, *Military Tribunals and International Crimes* 152 (1954).
[16] *Milch*, II TWC 778.　　[17] Ibid., 787.　　[18] *Justice*, III TWC 985.
[19] *Justice*, Indictment, para. 13, III TWC 21.　　[20] Ibid., 23, para. 21.

B. The Tribunal

The *Justice* case was heard by Tribunal III, which consisted of Carrington T. Marshall, James T. Brand, Mallory B. Blair, and an alternate, Justin W. Harding. Judge Marshall, who was the Chief Justice of the Ohio Supreme Court, was the first presiding judge, but health issues forced him to resign his position toward the end of the prosecution's case-in-chief. Judge Brand replaced him as the presiding judge and Judge Harding joined the tribunal. Brand was a Justice of the Supreme Court of Oregon. Blair was an Associate Justice of the Court of Civil Appeals in Texas. Harding, who had served as a Major in the Army during World War I and as a JAG Colonel during World War II, was a lawyer who had been a federal judge in Alaska from 1929 to 1933—the only federal judge to sit on any of the tribunals.[21]

C. Outcome

Trial began on 5 March 1947 and ended on December 4. Four defendants were acquitted: Barnickel, Cuhorst, Nebelung, and Petersen. Cuhorst was the Chief Justice of the Special Court in Stuttgart; the others were either judges or prosecutors with the People's Court. Seven of the 10 defendants were convicted on both Count Two (war crimes) and Count Three (crimes against humanity); Rothaug was convicted solely on Count Three. Four defendants were acquitted on Count Four (membership), while three were convicted. Alstoetter was convicted solely of criminal membership in the SS. Four defendants were sentenced to life (Schlegelberger, Klemm, Oeschey, and Rothaug); four were sentenced to ten years' imprisonment (von Ammon, Mettgenberg, Lautz, and Joel); one was sentenced to seven years (Rothenberger); and one was sentenced to five years (Alstoetter).

IV. *Pohl*

A. The Indictment

The 18 defendants in the *Pohl* case were all officials in the WVHA, one of 12 main SS offices. The WVHA had been responsible for the administrative needs of the entire SS, including overseeing the concentration camps, and had "managed and controlled a vast number of economic enterprises" that were "operated almost entirely by the use of concentration camp labor."[22] Pohl had been the chief of the WVHA; Frank and Loerner had been his deputies. The other defendants had either directed one of the five departments in the WVHA, known as *Amtsgruppe*, or had run one of the offices within a department. For example, Heinz Fanslau had been the chief of Amtsgruppe A, which was the supreme authority for the finance

---

[21] Background Information on Judges, 3.   [22] *Pohl*, V TWC 966.

and administration of the SS as a whole, while Josef Vogt had been the head of the auditing office within Amtsgruppe A.

The *Pohl* indictment followed the pattern established in the *Medical* case. Count One charged all of the defendants with conspiring to commit war crimes and crimes against humanity. In particular, it alleged that the defendants had conspired to establish and maintain concentration camps in Germany and other countries; to supply concentration-camp inmates to various public and private "industries, enterprises, and undertakings"; to provide subjects for medical experiments; to exterminate the Jews; and to plunder the private property of civilians deported to Germany.[23] Count Two, the war-crimes count, provided additional detail about the WVHA's operations in occupied territory, particularly concerning the murder and mistreatment of civilians and POWs in the concentration camps. Count Three alleged that the acts in the previous counts constituted crimes against humanity insofar as they involved German nationals and nationals of other countries. And Count Four alleged that all of the defendants except Hohberg, the executive officer of the Amtsgruppe that managed the SS's economic enterprises, were guilty of criminal membership in the SS.

B. The Tribunal

The *Pohl* case was heard by Tribunal II—Toms, Phillips, and Musmanno. Toms was once again the presiding judge.

C. Outcome

Trial began on 8 April 1947 and ended on November 3. Three of the defendants were acquitted: Vogt because of his relative unimportance in Amstgruppe A[24]; Rudolf Scheide, the Chief of Amtsgruppe B's Office V, because the only evidence of his guilt was his official WVHA title[25]; and Horst Klein because his office in Amstgruppe W, which dealt with social and cultural affairs, had not been connected to the concentration-camp system.[26] All of the other defendants were convicted on both Count Two and Count Three, and all but Volk were convicted on Count Four. Four were sentenced to death (Pohl, Eirenshmalz, Sommer, and Loerner); three were sentenced to life (Frank, Mummenthey, and Kiefer); and nine were sentenced to between 10 and 25 years' imprisonment.

The convicted defendants in *Pohl*, like convicted defendants in all of the cases, filed petitions with General Clay asking for sentence reductions.[27] Unlike the other cases, though, the judges of Tribunal II asked Clay to reconvene the tribunal so that they could consider revising the defendant's sentences.[28] Their request, which Clay granted, was based on the claim of two defendants that the tribunal had considered briefs that the prosecution had submitted in support of its closing argument, even

---

[23] *Pohl*, Indictment, para. 3, V TWC 202.   [24] Ibid., 1002.
[25] Ibid., 1017.   [26] Ibid., 1060.
[27] General Clay's sentence reviews are discussed in Chapter 15.   [28] Appleman, 166–7.

though it had expressly instructed both the prosecution and defense at trial not to submit such briefs. The tribunal did not state whether it had, in fact, considered the prosecution's briefs. Nevertheless, "[i]n conformity with the policy of the Tribunal to afford defense counsel every possible opportunity to present full and complete arguments in behalf of the defense," it gave the defendants permission to submit their own closing briefs.[29]

All 15 defendants submitted such briefs. In response, Tribunal II reduced Loerner's death sentence to life imprisonment, Kiefer's life sentence to 20 years, Fanslau's 25-year sentence to 20 years, and Bobermin's 20-year sentence to 15 years.

V. *Flick*

A. The Indictment

The indictment contained five counts. Count One alleged that the six defendants had committed war crimes and crimes against humanity by making use of "tens of thousands of slave laborers and prisoners of war ... in the industrial enterprises and establishments owned, controlled, or influenced by them" and by subjecting those workers to "inhumane conditions with respect to their personal liberty, shelter, food, pay, hours of work, and health."[30] Count Two alleged that all of the defendants other than Terberger had committed war crimes and crimes against humanity by systematically plundering public and private industrial property in France and the "Occupied East."[31] Count Three alleged that between January 1936 and April 1945 Flick, Steinbrinck, and Kaletsch had committed crimes against humanity by participating in "persecutions on racial, religious, and political grounds, including particularly the 'Aryanization' of properties belonging in whole or in part to Jews" who lived in Germany, Czechoslovakia, and other countries.[32] Count Four alleged that between January 1933 and April 1945 Flick and Steinbrinck had committed war crimes and crimes against humanity by financing the SS's many atrocities against the Jews. Finally, Count Five alleged that Steinbrinck was guilty of criminal membership in the SS.

B. The Tribunal

Flick was heard by Tribunal IV, which consisted of Charles B. Sears (presiding), Frank N. Richman, William C. Christianson, and an alternate, Richard D. Dixon. Sears was the Official Referee of New York's Court of Appeals, having spent the previous 23 years as a judge on the New York Supreme Court. Richman was a former Judge of the Supreme Court of Indiana. Christianson was an Associate

---

[29] *Pohl*, Order Permitting Defendants to File Additional Briefs, 14 July 1948, V TWC 1166.
[30] *Flick*, Indictment, para. 6, VI TWC 15.
[31] Ibid., 18–9, para. 10.   [32] Ibid., 21, para. 13.

Justice of the Supreme Court of Minnesota. Dixon was a former Judge of the Supreme Court of North Carolina[33] and had originally been recruited by OMGUS to serve as the Deputy Secretary General of the NMTs.[34]

C. Outcome

Trial began on 21 April 1947 and ended on December 22. Burkhart, Kaletsch, and Terberger were acquitted, the tribunal concluding that all three were entitled to a defense of necessity on the slave-labor count (Count One) and that Burkhart and Kaletsch had played only minor roles in the plunder of the Rombach plant in France—the only act of plunder it considered criminal. No defendant was convicted on Count Three, the Aryanization count, because the tribunal held that Law No. 10 did not criminalize pre-war crimes against humanity that were not connected to war crimes or crimes against peace. Friedrich Flick and Weiss were convicted of slave labor in connection with the company's use of slave labor at its Linke-Hoffman Works; Flick was also convicted of plundering the Rombach plant (Count Two) and cooperating with the SS, a crime that the tribunal considered functionally equivalent to membership in the SS.[35] Steinbrinck was convicted only of criminal membership (Count Five). Flick was sentenced to seven years' imprisonment; Steinbrinck, five years; and Weiss, 2½ years.

VI. *Farben*

A. The Indictment

The 24 defendants who stood trial in *Farben* divided into three categories. Nineteen were members of the Vorstand, including Schmitz, von Schnitzler, and Ambros. One, Krauch, was the Chairman of the Aufsichtsrat. Four directed various plants and department within Farben, such as Duerrfeld. Because of health reasons, Max Brueggemann was dismissed from the trial in September 1947 at the joint request of the prosecution and defense.[36]

The indictment, at 51 pages the longest in the trials, contained five counts. Count One alleged that all of the defendants, "acting through the instrumentality of Farben and otherwise," had committed crimes against peace by participating in the Nazis' numerous acts of aggression, from the invasion of Austria in March 1938 to the war against the United States in December 1941. The count traced the long history of the relationship between Farben and the Nazis, emphasizing Farben's financing of Hitler's regime, the "tremendous expansion of Farben's manufacturing facilities far in excess of the needs of a peacetime economy," and the company's awareness that Hitler intended to use its arms to wage aggressive war.[37] Count Two

---

[33] Background Information on Judges, 4.   [34] Earl, 217–8.
[35] *Flick*, VI TWC 1216.   [36] *Farben*, VIII TWC 1362.
[37] *Farben*, Indictment, para. 18, VII TWC 19.

alleged that all of the defendants had committed war crimes and crimes against humanity by systematically plundering the occupied territories. Count Three alleged that all of the defendants had committed war crimes and crimes against humanity by using hundreds of thousands of slaves in Farben's various plants and factories. The count particularly emphasized Farben's construction of the infamous buna plant at Auschwitz, Auschwitz III-Monowitz.[38] Count Four charged Schneider, Buetefisch, and von der Heyde with criminal membership in the SS. And Count Five alleged that all of the defendants had conspired to commit the crimes against peace identified in Count One.

B. The Tribunal

Farben was heard by Tribunal VI, which consisted of Curtis G. Shake (presiding), James Morris, Paul M. Hebert, and an alternate, Clarence F. Merrell. Shake was the former Chief Justice of the Indiana Supreme Court. Morris was a Justice and former Chief Justice of the Supreme Court of North Dakota. Hebert was the Dean of the Louisiana State University School of Law; during the war he had served as Chief of the Industrial Law Branch in the Judge Advocate General's Office in Washington, D.C. Merrell was a lawyer in North Dakota and Indiana.[39]

C. Outcome

Trial began on 27 August 1947 and ended on 30 July 1948. The Associated Press released a number of the verdicts before they were announced by the tribunal, provoking considerable outrage at the journalist, Tom Reedy, who was responsible for the mix-up.[40] Ten of the 23 defendants were acquitted, including Hoerlein, a Nobel Prize-winning chemist, and von Knieriem. One defendant, Fritz ter Meer, was convicted of both plunder (Count Two) and slave labor (Count Three). Ambros, Duerrfeld, and Buetefisch were convicted solely on Count Three, while nine others—most notably Krauch—were convicted solely of plunder. All of the defendants were acquitted of the crimes against peace charges (Counts One and Five), and the three defendants accused of membership in the SS (Count Four) were acquitted of that charge, as well. Sentences ranged from eight years for Ambros and Duerrfeld to 1½ years for Jaehne and Kugler.

D. Noteworthy Aspects

The prosecution was appalled by the verdicts and sentences. Josiah DuBois, Taylor's deputy at the trial, described the judgment as "the fantastic foundation of an Auschwitz that never was, and then the tower of straw built up over it."[41]

[38] *Farben*, Indictment, 54–8, paras 132–43.
[39] Background Information on Judges, 5–6.
[40] Letter from Deane to Taylor, 3 July 1987, TTP-14-7-22–489, at 3.
[41] DuBois, *Devil's Chemists*, 340.

Judge Hebert, who issued a passionate dissent on the slave-labor charges, agreed with DuBois, telling him not long after the trial that "[w]hen I first read the indictment, it was difficult to believe that all of this had happened. By the time we reached the end, I felt that practically every sentence of the indictment had been proved many times over."[42]

The problem was that Judge Hebert's colleagues appear to have been predisposed toward the defendants from the beginning. Drexel Sprecher, the chief of the Farben Trial Team, later claimed that one of the judges' assistants attacked him in the bar of the Grand Hotel as "anti-German."[43] Tom Bowers describes Judge Morris as "outspokenly prejudiced" against the prosecution and notes that his wife "often invited the wives of IG Farben directors on trial for drinks, especially Baroness von Schnitzler."[44] And the German press reported at the time that Judge Shake often hosted the defendants' German lawyers at the Grand Hotel, despite the fact that Germans were not normally allowed inside it.[45]

The majority's hostility toward the prosecution was also evident at trial. As discussed in Chapter 6, the *Farben* tribunal restricted the prosecution's cross-examination of defendants and defense witnesses to 20 percent of the time required for direct examination, even though it did not impose a similar time limit on the cross-examination of prosecution witnesses. Indeed, Judge Shake consistently chided the prosecution for being too slow, at one point asking a prosecutor how much longer cross-examination would take and then responding, when the prosecutor said that he had just finished, "Sorry I didn't speak sooner."[46] Even worse, when the prosecution introduced compelling evidence that Wolfgang Alt, a Farben employee who had been serving as an "assistant defense counsel" for the defendant Ambros, had instructed officials at Farben's Ludwigshafen plant to hide a large number of documents concerning Auschwitz from American officials and had personally hidden documents in his home, the tribunal refused to cite Alt for contempt, found that he had done nothing wrong, and actually admonished the prosecution—based on an inaccurate assessment of the situation—for "taking matters into their own hands by threatening potential witnesses with arrest and participating in an unwarranted violation of the privacy of the home of a member of the staff of defense counsel."[47]

Such evident bias, of course, requires explanation. The answer seems to be twofold. To begin with, Judge Morris simply rejected the idea that private economic actors, driven by the profit motive instead of by ideology, could commit serious international crimes. As he told a journalist after his retirement, he believed "some people were tried [at Nuremberg] who should not have been—they were a bunch of eager selfish big businessmen like you would find in any country."[48]

The judges in the majority also apparently believed that prosecuting German industrialists was a bad idea in light of the growing Soviet threat, because it might

---

[42] Jeffreys, 339. [43] Bower, 358. [44] Ibid. [45] Ibid.
[46] Appleman, 183. [47] *Farben*, Order, 8 Mar. 1948, XV TWC 1039.
[48] Quoted in Alberto L. Zuppi, "Slave Labor in Nuremberg's I.G. Farben Case: The Lonely Voice of Paul M. Hebert," 66 *La. L. Rev.* 495, 523 (2006).

deter American industrialists from providing the U.S. government with the resources it needed to fight the Cold War. That theme emerges clearly in a series of exchanges between Judge Morris and DuBois. On the very first day of trial, Morris told DuBois that "[w]e have to worry about the Russians now; it wouldn't surprise me if they overran the courtroom before we get through."[49] DuBois recounted that statement in his book *The Devil's Chemists*, leading Morris to write him the following year. Instead of denying the statement, however, Morris expressed satisfaction that DuBois' book "recognizes my appreciation of the Russian menace," adding that he "had already become alarmed over the Moscow influence that was then so visibly present in Nurnberg." He also pointed out that, given that the last Farben defendant was released by 1951, "[i]t would seem that the tribunal was entirely in step with the progress of history and that we were wise in not creating dangerous precedents which would have been an impediment to the future foreign policy of our country."[50] DuBois wrote back that judges were supposed to ignore such extra-legal concerns and that he believed "the fear of Russia and communism weighed so heavily on your mind that you grossly misinterpreted, in good faith, many incidents."[51]

Judge Morris was not alone, of course, in his belief that convictions in *Farben* might undermine the war against communism. The U.S. government agreed: as DuBois noted in his book *The Generals in Grey Suits*, Mickey Marcus, the head of the War Department's war-crimes division, told him before the trial that the Department's attitude toward the case against Farben was determined by two things, "Russia and the atom," and that it believed a prosecution—particularly for crimes against peace—would discourage both German and American industrialists from working with the U.S. government.[52]

VII. The *Hostage* Case

A. The Indictment

The indictment contained four counts, all of which alleged the commission of both war crimes and crimes against humanity. Count One alleged that the defendants had ordered the execution of thousands of civilian hostages in occupied territory in reprisal for attacks on German troops. The count emphasized that the hostages had been executed "without benefit of investigation or trial," pursuant to "arbitrarily established ratios varying from 50 to 100 for each German soldier killed and 25 to 50 for each German soldier wounded."[53] Count Two alleged that the defendants had plundered public and private property, wantonly destroyed cities and towns, and murdered civilians in occupied Norway, Greece, Yugoslavia, and Albania.

---

[49] Bower, 358.
[50] Letter from Morris to DuBois, 26 Mar. 1953, TTP-4-1-LC2-9.
[51] Letter from DuBois to Morris, 9 Apr. 1953, TTP-4-1-LC2-9, at 1–2.
[52] DuBois, *Generals*, 20–1.
[53] *Hostage*, Indictment, para. 1, XI TWC 766.

Count Three alleged that the defendants had illegally ordered their subordinates to deny POW status to and summarily execute captured members of "the military forces of nations at war with Germany."[54] Count Four alleged that the defendants had terrorized, imprisoned in concentration camps, and deported to slave labor the civilian populations of Greece, Yugoslavia, and Albania.

B. The Tribunal

The *Hostage* case was heard by the second iteration of Tribunal V, now consisting of Charles F. Wennerstrum (presiding), Edward F. Carter, and George J. Burke. Wennerstrum—who would provoke significant controversy shortly after the trial, as discussed below—was a Justice of the Iowa Supreme Court. Carter was a Justice of the Supreme Court of Nebraska. Burke had been Chief Counsel for the Office of Price Administration in D.C. during the war.[55]

C. Outcome

Trial began on 15 July 1947 and ended on 19 February 1948. Von Weichs was dismissed from the trial during the defense case because of ill health. Two defendants were acquitted: Hermann Foertsch and Kurt Ritter von Geitner, both of whom were chiefs of staff to higher-ranking defendants.[56] Seven of the other eight defendants were convicted on Count One (execution of hostages); only von Leyser, Rendulic's subordinate, was acquitted on that count. Felmy, the Commander Southern Greece, was the only defendant convicted on Count Two (plunder). Five of the eight defendants, including List and Rendulic, were convicted on Count Three (execution of POWs). List and Kuntze were both sentenced to life imprisonment; Rendulic and Speidel were sentenced to 20 years; and the remaining defendants were sentenced to between seven and 15 years.

D. Noteworthy Aspects

On February 20, one day after the verdicts were announced and literally hours before departing Nuremberg, Judge Wennerstrum conducted a private interview with Hal Foust, a correspondent for the conservative *Chicago Tribune*. Wennerstrum condemned the *Hostage* trial as "victor's justice," accused the prosecution staff of failing "to maintain objectivity aloof from vindictiveness, aloof from personal ambitions for convictions," and said that he "never would have come" to Nuremberg if he had known the true nature of the trials.[57] On February 23 the *Tribune* ran a story about the interview entitled "Presiding Judge at Nuremberg

---

[54] Ibid., 772, para. 11.
[55] Background Information on Judges, 6.
[56] The criminal responsibility of chiefs of staff for ordering and command responsibility is discussed in Chapter 11.
[57] "Presiding Judge at Nuremberg Disillusioned," *Chicago Tribune*, 23 Feb. 1948, 5.

Disillusioned"; the interview was picked up by Reuters and published in all of the major U.S. papers, including the *New York Times* and *Washington Post.*[58]

Judge Wennerstrum's criticisms were rejected by his fellow judges. The other members of Tribunal V, Judges Carter and Burke, stated that they believed the trial had been "well thought out" and "tried fairly."[59] Similarly, Judge Brand, who had heard the *Justice* case, described Wennerstrum's interview as "a libel upon our most revered institution, and a slur upon every one of the 35 judges who participated in the trials."[60]

Taylor also responded to Wennerstrum—and inadvertently triggered one of the most controversial episodes in the trials. His response appeared in the *Chicago Tribune* the same day as Wennerstrum's interview was published,[61] making it clear that he had received advance notice of the interview. The timing led Hal Foust to complain to the Army that Taylor had instructed a member of his staff to intercept the interview.[62] In fact, as the Inspector General found after an extensive investigation, Taylor had obtained the interview by accident. He had first learned about it from one of his prosecutors, who had seen Foust and Wennerstrum talking in the Palace of Justice and then heard the Judge boasting that he had given an interview to the *Chicago Tribune* that would "blast the trials."[63] The next day, in response to a request for an earlier Foust dispatch, a press employee in Frankfurt had inadvertently given the OCC both the earlier dispatch and the Wennerstrum interview.[64] Taylor had then used the interview to write and distribute his response.

VIII. *RuSHA*

A. The Indictment

The indictment contained three counts. Count One alleged that the defendants had committed crimes against humanity by taking part in "a systematic program of genocide, aimed at the destruction of foreign nations and ethnic groups, in part by murderous extermination, and in part by elimination and suppression of national characteristics." That program, according to the count, involved a variety of acts, including preventing the reproduction of enemy nationals, forced Germanization, slave labor, and the persecution and extermination of Jews.[65] Count Two alleged that the defendants had committed a variety of war crimes, such as plunder, murder, deportation, and enslavement. Count Three alleged that all of the defendants except Viermetz, the female defendant, had been members of the SS.

---

[58] Hébert, *Hitler's Generals*, 238–9 n. 24.   [59] Ibid.

[60] Letter from Brand to Young, 18 Oct. 1948, NA-153–1018-15–89-1, at 3–4.

[61] "U.S. Prosecutor Blasts Attack on Nazi Trial," *Chicago Tribune*, 23 Feb. 1948, 5.

[62] Memo from Huebner to CSUSA Washington, 23 Apr. 1948, NA-153–1018-1-85-1, at 1.

[63] Letter from Deane to Taylor, 3 July 1987, 3–4.

[64] Ibid., 4.

[65] *RuSHA*, Indictment, para. 2, IV TWC 609–10.

B. The Tribunal

RuSHA was heard by the second iteration of Tribunal I, which now consisted of Lee B. Wyatt (presiding), Daniel T. O'Connell, and Johnson Tal Crawford, the sole holdover from the original Tribunal I. Wyatt was an Associate Justice of the Supreme Court of Georgia. O'Connell was an Associate Justice of the Superior Court of Massachusetts and had served in World War I.[66]

C. Outcome

Trial began on 20 October and ended on 10 March 1948. Vermietz, the female defendant, was acquitted without discussion. Five of the defendants were convicted solely of criminal membership: Meyer-Hetling, Ebner, Schwarzenberger, Sollman, and Tesch. All were sentenced to time served—less than three years in each case. The other eight defendants were convicted on all three counts. Greifelt, the head of the RKFDV, was sentenced to life imprisonment. Hoffman and Hildebrandt, the successive heads of RuSHA, were sentenced to 25 years each. The other five received sentences of between 10 and 20 years.

IX. *Einsatzgruppen*

A. The Indictment

The amended indictment in *Einsatzgruppen* was modeled on the *RuSHA* indictment. Count One, a crimes against humanity count, alleged that the defendants had used the Einsatzgruppen to carry out "a systematic program of genocide."[67] Count Two alleged that the defendants had committed a variety of war crimes, including the murder of POWs and civilians in occupied territory and wanton destruction not justified by military necessity. Count Three alleged that all of the defendants had been members of the SS and that some of the defendants had also been members of the SD or Gestapo.

B. The Tribunal

Einsatzgruppen was heard by the third iteration of Tribunal II: Michael Musmanno; John J. Speight, the alternate in *Milch*; and Richard Dixon, the alternate in *Flick*. According to Earl, Dixon was considered a capable judge, while Speight was viewed by his colleagues as "ineffective" and a "cipher."[68] Musmanno, now presiding, requested the Navy to promote him "one more notch" to Commodore in order to

---

[66] Background Information on Judges, 6–7.
[67] *Einsatzgruppen*, Indictment, para. 2, IV TWC 15. [68] Earl, 219.

reduce the "incongruity" between his rank (Captain) and the rank of the four defendants who were Generals in the SS. The Navy rejected his request.[69]

C. Outcome

Trial began on 29 September 1947 and ended on 9 April 1948. No defendant was acquitted, although Otto Rasch, the commanding officer of Einsatzgruppe C, was severed from the case during trial for health reasons.[70] Twenty of the 22 remaining defendants were convicted on all three counts; Ruehl and Graf were convicted only of criminal membership. Fifteen defendants, including Ohlendorf and five of the six defendants added to the case in the amended indictment, were sentenced to death. (Von Radetzky was sentenced to 20 years.) The other defendants received sentences ranging from life (Nosske and Jost) to time served (Graf). Ohlendorf bowed his head to the judges when he learned of his death sentence,[71] anticipating Eichmann's similar action 13 years later.

D. Noteworthy Aspects

The decision to impose the death penalty was very difficult for Musmanno, even though he had already sentenced defendants to death in *Pohl*. As noted earlier, he was personally opposed to the death penalty. Moreover, he admitted in an early draft of his 1961 account of the trial, *The Eichmann Kommandos*, that he had come to see the defendants not as "beasts" but as "personable individuals."[72] After the trial, in fact, Musmanno had spent a number of weeks at a Cistercian monastery contemplating the defendants' fates.[73]

X. *Krupp*

A. The Indictment

The *Krupp* indictment was modeled on the indictment in *Farben*. Count One alleged that the defendants had committed crimes against peace by financing the Nazis' rise to power and then "fully and willingly cooperating in the rearmament of Germany for foreign aggression."[74] Count Two alleged that all of the defendants other than Lehmann and Kupke had committed war crimes and crimes against humanity by systematically plundering public and private property, particularly industrial property, in countries occupied by the Nazis. Count Three alleged that all of the defendants had committed war crimes and crimes against humanity by

---

[69] Earl, 239.
[70] *Einsatzgruppen*, IV TWC 411.
[71] Earl, 264.
[72] Ibid., 262. Musmanno eliminated those comments from the published version of the book.
[73] Ibid.
[74] *Krupp*, Indictment, para. 15, IX TWC 15.

participating in the "enslavement and deportation of foreign and German nationals, including concentration camp inmates," and by forcing POWs to engage in the manufacture and transport of armament in munitions.[75] Finally, Count Four alleged that the defendants had conspired to commit the crimes against peace detailed in Count One.

B. The Tribunal

Krupp was heard by the second iteration of Tribunal III, which now consisted of Hu C. Anderson (presiding), Edward J. Daly, and William J. Wilkins. Anderson was the presiding judge of the Tennessee Court of Appeals and had served in World War I. Daly was a judge of the Superior Court of Connecticut and the state's former Attorney General. Wilkins was a judge of the Superior Court of Washington and had served as Judge Advocate for the Second Air Force in Colorado during the war. He had been awarded a Silver Star for his service during World War I.[76]

C. Outcome

Trial began on 8 December 1947 and ended on 31 July 1948. One defendant, Pfirsch, was acquitted. No defendant was convicted on Count One or Count Four, because the tribunal granted a defense motion to dismiss the crimes against peace charges on the ground that the prosecution's evidence was insufficient as a matter of law. Four defendants were convicted of both plunder (Count Two) and slave labor (Count Three), most notably Alfried Krupp. Two defendants, Eberhardt and Loeser, were convicted solely of plunder, while four defendants, including von Buelow, were convicted solely of slave labor. Krupp, Mueller, and von Buelow were each sentenced to 12 years; the other defendants were sentenced to between time served and 10 years. Krupp was also ordered to forfeit all of his real and personal property.

D. Noteworthy Aspects

Two events in February 1948 had a major impact on the *Krupp* trial: the Soviets overthrew the Czechoslovakian government, and the Military Governor in the Soviet zone issued an order preventing access to Berlin.[77] The possibility that the Soviets would move further west so unsettled the judges still in Nuremberg that John Young, the presiding judge in *High Command*, asked General Clay whether OMGUS had made plans to evacuate the judges and their families in case of a Soviet attack. Although Clay assured him that it had, a number of Americans left Nuremberg, including Judge Daly's wife and daughter.[78]

---

[75] Ibid., 29, para. 46.
[76] Background Information on Judges, 7.
[77] Maguire, 167.
[78] William John Wilkins, *The Sword and the Gavel* 194 (1981).

The intensification of the Cold War also affected the trial—as well as the ongoing *Ministries* and *High Command* trials—more directly. After the events of February 1948, visiting American politicians began to overtly pressure the OCC and the tribunals to end the trials as quickly as possible.[79] One of the prosecutors in *Ministries*, for example, reported that it was "bluntly asserted to the prosecution staff and to the judges in private conversations . . . that the real enemy, Russia, was growing stronger and the trials were further weakening efforts to restore Germany to the necessary economic viability that would permit her to serve as a bulwark against communism."[80]

Such pressure obviously did not prevent the *Krupp* tribunal from convicting the defendants of slave labor and plunder. There is also no evidence that the tribunal's rejection of the crimes against peace charges was motivated by the concerns expressed by Judge Morris in *Farben*. What is clear, however, is that the *Chicago Daily Tribune* spoke for many conservative elements in the United States when it later claimed that although the trials were "designed to give the maximum aid possible to Communist penetration of Germany," the "partial acquittals offer some hope that the administration and its military representatives in Germany are backing away from the insane policy of destroying the German people, really in vengeance."[81]

Krupp also witnessed the NMT trials' most dramatic confrontation between judges and defense attorneys. On January 16, all ten of the attorneys attending the morning court session stormed out of the courtroom to protest a ruling by the judges concerning the use of commissioners.[82] The tribunal continued with the trial without the attorneys until lunch—an unwise decision, as Taylor later noted[83]—and then, when they failed to appear for the afternoon session, held six of the attorneys in contempt and ordered their arrest. Five of the imprisoned attorneys later apologized to the tribunal and were permitted to continue with the case, but one—Guenter Geisseler—refused to apologize and was prohibited from continuing to represent Alfried Krupp.[84]

XI. *Ministries*

A. The Indictment

The 50-page indictment, the second longest in the trials, contained eight counts. Count One alleged that most of the defendants had committed crimes against peace by participating, in various ways, in the Nazis' wars of aggressions and invasions. Count Two alleged that the same defendants had conspired to commit

---

[79] Maguire, 184.   [80] Quoted in ibid.   [81] Quoted in Danner, 672.

[82] The role of commissioners in the trials is discussed in Chapter 6.

[83] Telford Taylor, "The Krupp Trial: Fact v. Fiction," 53 *Colum. L. Rev.* 197, 206 (1953).

[84] *Krupp*, Ruling of Tribunal III in Matters Relating to Contempt of Court, 21 Jan. 1948, XV TWC 1012.

crimes against peace. Count Three, a war crimes count, alleged that a number of the defendants were responsible for the murder of POWs because they had participated in the issuance and execution of the "lynch law" for Allied flyers and the Commando Order. Count Four, a crimes against humanity count, alleged that between January 1933 and September 1939 a number of the defendants had participated in the murder, mistreatment, and persecution of German Jews. Count Five alleged that most of the defendants had committed war crimes and crimes against humanity by participating in the Nazis' "systematic program of genocide."[85] Count Six alleged that a number of the defendants had committed war crimes and crimes against humanity by plundering public and private property, both real and personal, in occupied territory. Count Seven alleged that most of the defendants had committed war crimes and crimes against humanity by enslaving and deporting civilians in occupied territory on a massive scale. Finally, Count Eight alleged that a number of the defendants had been members of the SS, SD, or Leadership Corps.

B. The Tribunal

Ministries was heard by the second iteration of Tribunal IV, consisting of William C. Christianson (presiding), who had been part of Tribunal IV in *Flick*, Robert T. Maguire, and Leon W. Powers. Maguire, who had been recommended by Judge Brand—OMGUS had asked Brand to remain in Nuremberg after the *Justice* case, but he had declined—was a lawyer in Oregon and a Standing Master in Chancery for the U.S. District Court of Oregon.[86] The historian Peter Maguire, Judge Maguire's grandson, described him as "a conservative Republican" who was nevertheless "sympathetic to the views of the War Department."[87] Powers was a former Justice of the Iowa Supreme Court.[88]

C. Outcome

Trial began on 6 January 1948 and ended on 13 April 1949. The tribunal dismissed Count Four during trial, having concluded that Law No. 10 did not criminalize peacetime crimes against humanity that were not connected to war crimes or crimes against peace.[89] Two defendants were acquitted: von Erdmannsdorff, Woermann's deputy in the Foreign Office; and Meissner, the head of the Presidential Chancellory. Five defendants were convicted of crimes against peace—the first and only such convictions in the trials: Lammers, Koerner, Keppler, von Weizsaecker, and Woermann. The other defendants were convicted on various

---

[85] *Ministries*, Indictment, para. 39, XII TWC 44.
[86] Background Information on Judges, 7–8.
[87] Maguire, 177.
[88] Background Information on Judges, 7–8.
[89] That issue is discussed in Chapter 10.

permutations of the non-dismissed counts. Berger received the longest sentence, 25 years. Stuckart received the shortest sentence, time served.

A week before the end of trial, the *Ministries* tribunal issued an order permitting the defendants to file motions alleging errors of fact or law in the forthcoming judgment. Nineteen defendants did so. The tribunal dismissed most of the defendants' claims as meritless, but set aside Steengracht von Moyland's conviction for the murder of POWs (Count Three) and von Weizsaecker and Woermann's convictions for crimes against peace (Count One).[90] The tribunal also reduced the sentences of the three defendants from seven to five years.[91] Judge Christianson dissented on both the dismissed charges and the sentence reductions.[92]

XII. *High Command*

A. The Indictment

The indictment contained four counts. Like the *Farben* and *Krupp* indictments, Counts One and Four alleged that the defendants had committed crimes against peace and had conspired to commit crimes against peace, respectively. Notably, the count emphasized the defendants' participation in planning the various wars of aggression and invasions; their waging of those wars and invasions was secondary.[93] Count Two alleged that the defendants had committed war crimes and crimes against peace against by participating in the issuance and execution of the Commissar and Commando Orders, by murdering and mistreating POWs, and by forcing POWs to engage in work directly connected to war operations. Count Three alleged that the defendants had committed war crimes and crimes against peace in occupied territory by deporting and enslaving civilians, plundering private and public property, and engaging in wanton destruction not justified by military necessity.

B. The Tribunal

High Command was heard by the second iteration of Tribunal V, now consisting of John C. Young (presiding), Winfield B. Hale, and Justin W. Harding, who had been the alternate in the *Justice* case. Young was the former Chief Justice of the Supreme Court of Colorado. Hale was Judge Anderson's colleague on the Tennessee Court of Appeals.[94]

---

[90] The crimes against peace dismissals are discussed in Chapter 8.

[91] *Ministries*, XIV TWC 946.

[92] Ibid., 960–7, Order and Memorandum of the Tribunal and Separate Memorandum of Presiding Judge Christianson, 12 Dec. 1949.

[93] See, e.g., *High Command*, Indictment, para. 10, X TWC 17.

[94] Background Information on Judges, 8.

C. Outcome

Trial began on 5 February 1948 and ended on October 28. On the first day of trial, General Blaskowitz committed suicide by throwing himself down a staircase in the Nuremberg prison.[95] According to Hans Laternser, von Leeb's attorney, one of the prosecutors told him the same day that "Blaskowitz did not need to do that as he would certainly have been acquitted"—a statement that led Laternser to wonder why, if that was true, the OCC had bothered to indict him.[96]

Two of the 13 remaining defendants were acquitted: Hugo Sperrle and Otto Schniewind. None of the defendants were convicted of crimes against peace, because the tribunal held that they did not satisfy the crime's leadership requirement.[97] All of the defendants other than von Leeb were convicted on both Count Two and Count Three; von Leeb was convicted only on Count Three. Warlimont and Reinecke were sentenced to life imprisonment. The other defendants were sentenced to between time served (von Leeb) and 22 years (von Roques).

D. Noteworthy Aspects

Like Judge Morris, Judge Young—the judges' delegate to General Clay in the aftermath of Czechoslovakia and the Berlin Blockade—was deeply afraid of the Russians. He considered communism "a hellish thing... like cancer," viewed the Americans in Nuremberg as "a bunch of sitting ducks," and constantly stated that he "never wanted to get away from anything so bad in my life."[98] That fear directly affected his view of the trial: in a letter written in late June 1948, he admitted to his sons that "most of the things were done to the Russians and I am getting so that doesn't seem so bad to me" and complained regarding the crimes against peace charges that "[i]t is certainly a peculiar situation to be trying men for aggressive war against a nation whose aggressive tactics have the world now in a state of turmoil and alarm. Just like trying one gangster for killing another gangster from a gang that is on a rampage while the trial is going on."[99] Judge Young also grew increasingly desensitized to the atrocities that the defendants had committed, at one point telling his sons that "it is getting like the story Johnny likes—'Along came a locust and took another grain of corn'—only it is 'Along came an SD and killed another bunch of Jews'."[100]

---

[95] Statement by Deane, 5 Feb. 1948, TTP-5-1-4-63.
[96] Laternser, in Mettraux, 475.
[97] That requirement is discussed in Chapter 8.
[98] Quoted in Hébert, *Hitler's Generals*, 136.
[99] Quoted in ibid., 129.   [100] Quoted in ibid., 128.

5

Jurisdiction and Legal Character
of the Tribunals

Introduction

This chapter explores the jurisdiction and legal character of the NMTs. Section I discusses the tribunals' subject-matter jurisdiction, with a particular emphasis on the ways in which Law No. 10 went beyond the substantive provisions of the London Charter. Section II examines the vexing issue of whether the tribunals were American courts, as the defendants insisted, or international courts, as the tribunals themselves insisted. It concludes that, in fact, they were neither—they were interallied special tribunals created by the Control Council pursuant to its sovereign legislative authority in Germany. Section III explains why, even though they were not international courts, the tribunals nevertheless applied international law. Section IV addresses the issue of whether the law applied by the tribunals violated the principle of non-retroactivity, particularly the provisions of Law No. 10 that went beyond the London Charter. Finally, Section V focuses on the personal jurisdiction of the tribunals, demonstrating that their ability to prosecute the defendants was based on an amalgam of passive-personality, protective, and universal jurisdiction.

I. Subject-Matter Jurisdiction

Ordinance No. 7 provided that the NMTs had the power "to try and punish persons charged with offenses recognized as crimes in Article II of Control Council Law No. 10." Article II recognized four crimes: crimes against peace, war crimes, crimes against humanity, and membership in a criminal organization. All four crimes were modeled on the parallel provisions of the London Charter, but all four differed from the Charter in important ways.

A. Crimes Against Peace

The London Charter's definition of crimes against peace differed from Law No. 10's definition in two respects. First, whereas the Charter restricted the modes of participation in crimes against peace to planning, preparing, initiating, and waging,

Law No. 10's list was illustrative—"including, but not limited to." Despite the broader language of Law No. 10, however, no tribunal ever suggested that other modes of participation were possible. Second, Law No. 10 criminalized "invasions" as well as aggressive wars. That extension of the Charter, which would play an important role in the tribunals' subsequent jurisprudence, reflected JCS 1023/10, which defined crimes against peace for purposes of apprehending suspected war criminals as "initiation of invasions of other countries and wars of aggression."[1]

B. War Crimes

There were two differences between the war-crimes provisions in the London Charter and Law No. 10, neither of which was ever discussed by the tribunals. First, Article II(1)(b) of Law No. 10 addressed the mistreatment of "civilian population *from* occupied territory," while Article 6(b) of the Charter addressed the mistreatment of "civilian population *of or in* occupied territory." Second, whereas Article 6(b) referred to "violations of the laws or customs of war," Article II(1)(b) referred to "[a]trocities or offenses against persons or property constituting violations of the laws or customs of war."

C. Crimes Against Humanity

The most significant differences between the London Charter and Law No. 10 concerned crimes against humanity. First, Article II(1)(c) of Law No. 10 did not include Article 6(c)'s "before or during the war" language. Although that omission seemed to limit crimes against humanity to acts committed during the war, Article II(5) made clear that Law No. 10 also applied to pre-war acts by expressly providing that "[i]n any trial or prosecution for a crime herein referred to, the accused shall not be entitled to the benefits of any statute of limitation in respect to the period from 30 January 1933 to 1 July 1945." Second, Article 6(c) did not contain a statute-of-limitations provision equivalent to Article II(5) of Law No. 10. Third, Article II(1)(c) eliminated Article 6(c)'s requirement that crimes against peace be committed "in execution of or in connection with any crime within the jurisdiction of the Tribunal"—the so-called "nexus" requirement. As we will see in Chapter 10, the OCC relied heavily on those three differences when it argued—unsuccessfully—that Article II(1)(c) criminalized pre-war crimes against humanity that had no connection to either war crimes or crimes against peace.

D. Criminal Membership

Articles 9 and 10 of the London Charter permitted the IMT to declare that certain groups and organizations associated with the Nazis were "criminal organizations" and provided that a "competent national authority" could prosecute individual

---

[1] JCS 1023/10, para. 2(b).

members of convicted groups and organizations for the crime of criminal membership. Article II(1)(d) of Law No. 10 recognized "[m]embership in categories of a criminal group or organization declared criminal by the International Military Tribunal" as a criminal act, thereby creating the substantive offence that the drafters of the London Charter had anticipated.

E. Conspiracy

Although the IMT limited conspiracy to crimes against peace,[2] Article 6(c) of the London Charter provided that "[l]eaders, organizers, instigators and accomplices participating in the formulation or execution of a common plan or conspiracy to commit any of the foregoing crimes are responsible for all acts performed by any persons in execution of such plan." Law No. 10 did not contain a similar provision; Article II(2)(d) limited criminal responsibility to individuals "connected with plans or enterprises" involving the commission of a war crime, crime against humanity, or crime against peace. By contrast, Article I of Ordinance No. 7 specifically authorized the NMTs to prosecute any of the offenses in Article II of Law No. 10, "including conspiracies to commit any such crimes."

F. Modes of Participation

Other than providing that "participating in the formulation or execution of a common plan or conspiracy" was criminal, the London Charter was silent concerning the possible modes of participation in war crimes and crimes against humanity. By contrast, as discussed in Chapters 11 and 12, Article II(2) of Law No. 10 provided a comprehensive list of the ways in which an individual could be responsible for a crime.

II. The Character of the Tribunals

As noted earlier, Ordinance No. 7 relied on Law No. 10 to establish "Military Tribunals" for the prosecution of individuals charged with violating the substantive provisions of Law No. 10. That designation, however, raises an important—and complicated—question: what was the legal character of the NMTs? Were they international tribunals, like the IMT? American courts? Or were they something else entirely?

The tribunals themselves generally took the first position. In the *Justice* case, for example, Tribunal III held that "[t]he tribunals authorized by Ordinance No. 7 are dependent upon the substantive jurisdictional provisions of C. C. Law 10 and are thus based upon international authority and retain international characteristics."[3] Similarly, in *Ministries*, Tribunal IV held that "[t]his is not a tribunal of the United

---

[2] IMT Judgment, 44.   [3] *Justice*, III TWC 958.

States of America, but is an International Military Tribunal, established and exercising jurisdiction pursuant to authority given for such establishment and jurisdiction by Control Council Law No. 10."[4]

NMT critics, by contrast, insisted the tribunals were American courts. Von Knieriem claimed it was "incontestable" that "[t]he Nuremberg Tribunals were not international but American tribunals."[5] And Bishop Wurm argued in a letter to Clay that "[t]he Nürnberg Military Tribunal is to-day, after the other victor nations have withdrawn, a purely American Tribunal which no longer possesses the prerequisites of a Military Tribunal."[6] Their position was by no means frivolous: at various times both the tribunals and the OCC made statements implying that the tribunals were American, not international. In *Farben*, Judge Curtis Shake observed from the bench that "this Tribunal is an American Court constituted under American Law."[7] And in his opening statement in the *Justice* case, Telford Taylor told Tribunal III that "[a]lthough this Tribunal is internationally constituted, it is an American court. The obligations which derive from these proceedings are, therefore, particularly binding on the United States."[8]

A. What Makes a Tribunal International?

To determine the legal character of the NMTs, we must first identify what distinguishes an international tribunal from a domestic court. Perhaps surprisingly, that issue has been largely ignored by scholars. The primary exception is Robert Woetzel, whose 1962 book *The Nuremberg Trials in International Law*[9] dedicated an entire chapter to explaining why the IMT qualified as a genuinely international tribunal—a conclusion that most scholars, though certainly not all, accept.[10] If Woetzel's explanation of the IMT's legal character is correct, it is not possible to maintain that the NMTs were international tribunals.

Woetzel identified four possible theories of what makes a court international. The first is that "a court can be regarded as international if it applies international law." Woetzel rightly dismissed that theory as "spurious," pointing out that "many national, civil, and military tribunals apply international law in certain cases and judge international crimes."[11] The second is that "an international court is one that is based on powers of occupation under international law." That theory is flawed, according to Woetzel, because the rules of belligerent occupation impose significant

---

[4] *Ministries*, Order, 29 Dec. 1947, XV TWC 325.
[5] Von Knieriem, 100.
[6] Letter from Wurm to Clay, 20 May 1948, in Wurm Memorandum, 25.
[7] Quoted in von Knieriem, 97.
[8] Quoted in ibid.
[9] Robert K. Woetzel, *The Nuremberg Trials in International Law* (1962).
[10] Georg Schwarzenberger, for example, considered the IMT to be a "municipal tribunal of extraordinary jurisdiction which the four Contracting Powers share in common." Georg Schwarzenberger, "The Judgment of Nuremberg," in Mettraux, 171.
[11] Woetzel, 42.

limitations on the occupier,[12] the most important of which is the obligation to respect the occupied state's laws "unless absolutely prevented."[13]

The third theory is that "a tribunal can be regarded as international if its basis is a treaty or an international agreement, instead of it being the organ of a single state." Woetzel took this theory more seriously, because it indicates that the IMT was international. He pointed out, though, that a tribunal created pursuant to a multi-state agreement would be international only in the literal sense, because "a tribunal set up under such an agreement would only be entitled to the combined powers of jurisdiction of the contracting parties, but no more."[14] Differently put, such a tribunal would "be indisputably international only in so far as the contracting members are affected by it, within their respective spheres of jurisdiction."[15] Viewed in this light, the IMT would have qualified as international with regard to the Allies, but would not have been international with regard to Germany, which never signed the London Charter or consented to the IMT's jurisdiction over Germans.[16]

The final theory, which Woetzel ultimately endorsed, is that a tribunal is international if it is "instituted by one or a group of nations with the consent and approval of the international community."[17] That approval, according to Woetzel, cannot simply be assumed by the nations that create a tribunal; the international community must offer its "clear endorsement" of the tribunal's internationality. The best endorsement would be by an organization empowered to speak on behalf of the international community, such as the United Nations.[18] Alternatively, if such an organization was "paralysed in its activity due to unforeseen circumstances or non-existent," the requisite endorsement could be given by a "combination of states that represent the 'quasi-totality of civilised nations'."[19]

Judged according to this theory, the IMT was clearly an international tribunal. Although the UN General Assembly had not yet met when the IMT trial began in November 1945, the 17 members of the United Nations War Crime Commission (UNWCC) represented "the quasi-totality of civilised nations" and 15 of the 17 members, along with six other nations, including the United Kingdom and the Soviet Union, adhered to the London Charter. Moreover, once the trial was concluded, the 51 members of the General Assembly specifically and unanimously recognized the internationality of the IMT in Resolution 95(1). Those actions, according to Woetzel, indicate "that the IMT clearly had the sanction of the international community and can be considered an international court."[20]

---

[12] Ibid.
[13] Hague Convention (IV) Respecting the Laws and Customs of War on Land and Its Annex, 18 Oct. 1907, Art. 43 ("Hague Convention 1907").
[14] Woetzel, 42–3.
[15] Ibid., 43.
[16] Ibid. The issue of the Allies consenting on behalf of Germany is discussed in the personal jurisdiction section below.
[17] Ibid., 49.   [18] Ibid., 52.   [19] Ibid., 53.   [20] Ibid., 56–7.

B. Were the NMTs International Tribunals?

If the defining feature of an international tribunal is that it is created with the consent and approval of the international community, the NMTs cannot be considered international. The tribunals generally applied the substantive law of the London Charter, but the tribunals were authorized by Law No. 10, not by the Charter.[21] That is a critical difference: although the London Charter clearly enjoyed the consent and approval of the international community, Law No. 10 "was a multi-national agreement that was never directly confirmed by the United Nations or any other international body, nor were the conclusions of the twelve subsequent Nuremberg trials endorsed by the quasi-totality of states acting through an international organisation."[22]

Indeed, the argument used by the tribunals themselves to justify their internationality—that they were "dependent upon the substantive jurisdictional provisions" of Law No. 10 (*Justice*) or were "established by the International Control Council, the high legislative branch of the four Allied Powers" (*Flick*)—leads to absurd results. Law No. 10 did not simply authorize the Allies to create zonal courts; it also authorized the German government, with the consent of the occupying authorities, to create German courts with jurisdiction over "crimes committed by persons of German citizenship or nationality against other persons of German citizenship or nationality, or stateless persons."[23] As Freyhofer points out, Law No. 10 "became part of the German legal system and led to the indictment and conviction of many more perpetrators in later years."[24] The tribunals' view of internationality would thus lead to the conclusion that all of the German courts created pursuant to Law No. 10 were also international tribunals, which cannot be correct.

C. Were the NMTs American Courts or Tribunals?

The tribunals' failure to qualify as international does not mean, however, that they were American. The NMTs were clearly not Article III courts, because only Congress has the authority to "ordain and establish" inferior federal courts[25] and the tribunals were created not by Congress but by General Clay in his dual role as Military Governor and Commander of the American Zone.[26] For similar reasons, they cannot be considered "tribunals of the United States" whose decisions

---

[21] Article I of Law No. 10, in fact, specifically provided that "[a]dherence to the provisions of the London Agreement by any of the United Nations . . . shall not entitle such Nations to participate or interfere in the operation of this Law within the Control Council area of authority in Germany."

[22] Woetzel, 243 n. 49.

[23] Law No. 10, Art. III(d).

[24] Freyhofer, 89.

[25] U.S. Constitution, Art. III, sec. 1.

[26] Ordinance No. 7, Art. II(a).

were reviewable by federal courts. The United States Court of Appeals for the D.C. Circuit specifically rejected that argument in *Flick v. Johnson*:

> [Military Tribunal IV's] power and jurisdiction arose out of the joint sovereignty of the Four victorious Powers. The exercise of their supreme authority became vested in the Control Council. That body enacted Law No. 10, for the prosecution of war crimes... Pursuant to that power, and agreeably to rules duly promulgated by Ordinance No. 7, the Zone Commander constituted Military Tribunal IV, under whose judgment Flick is now confined. Thus the power and jurisdiction of that Tribunal stemmed directly from the Control Council, the supreme governing body of Germany, exercising its authority in behalf of the Four Allied Powers... Accordingly, we are led to the final conclusion that the tribunal which tried and sentenced Flick was not a tribunal of the United States.[27]

Although scholars at the time questioned the fairness of the D.C. Circuit's decision, they did not question whether it was legally correct.[28] Indeed, *Flick* was consistent with *Hirota v. MacArthur*, in which the Supreme Court had held that the IMTFE was not an American tribunal because it had been created "by General MacArthur as the agent of the Allied Powers."[29] The NMTs might not have qualified as international courts, distinguishing them from the IMTFE, but there is no doubt General Clay created the tribunals in his capacity as an agent of the Control Council.

D. The NMTs as Inter-Allied Special Tribunals

This analysis, of course, raises an important question: if the NMTs were neither international tribunals nor American courts, what were they? The best answer is that they were inter-allied special tribunals created pursuant to Law No. 10, a multilateral agreement enacted by the Allied Control Council as the supreme legislative authority in Germany. That description of the NMTs relies upon three interrelated propositions: (1) by virtue of debellatio, the Allies possessed absolute sovereignty over Germany; (2) the Allies jointly exercised their sovereignty as a condominium via the Control Council; and (3) the Control Council had the right to authorize the creation of inter-allied special tribunals through Law No. 10, because the Allies had the right to do collectively what each could have done singly.

1. Debellatio

The Allied Control Council enacted Law No. 10 to establish "a uniform legal basis in Germany for the prosecution of war criminals." As its number indicates, Law No. 10 was one of many fundamental changes the Control Council imposed on Germany in the aftermath of the war, many of which directly affected Germany's judicial system. Law No. 1 repealed discriminatory Nazi laws. Law No. 4 reorganized

---

[27] *Flick v. Johnson*, 174 F.2d 983, 986 (D.C. Cir. 1949). Tribunal IV had specifically held in *Flick* that "[t]he Tribunal is not a court of the United States as that term is used in the Constitution of the United States."

[28] "Review of International Criminal Convictions," 59 *Yale L.J.* 997, 1004–5 (1950).

[29] 338 U.S. 197, 198 (1948).

Germany's court system and precluded German courts from prosecuting Nazi crimes. And Law No. 11 repealed various provisions of the German Penal Code, including the crime of treason.

The Control Council's authority to enact Law No. 10 was first referenced in Judge Musmanno's concurring opinion in *Milch*. According to Musmanno, because Germany lacked a government of its own following surrender, "the very circumstances of Germany's present political situation not only justifies but demands that the Control Council establish government in its three fundamental phases; namely, the judiciary, the executive, and the legislative."[30] A divided Tribunal III then specifically held in the *Justice* case that the dissolution of the German government and the High Command's unconditional surrender authorized Law No. 10:

> The unconditional surrender of Germany took place on 8 May 1945. The surrender was preceded by the complete disintegration of the central government and was followed by the complete occupation of all of Germany. There were no opposing German forces in the field; the officials who during the war had exercised the powers of the Reich Government were either dead, in prison, or in hiding ... It is this fact of the complete disintegration of the government in Germany, followed by unconditional surrender and by occupation of the territory, which explains and justifies the assumption and exercise of supreme governmental power by the Allies.[31]

Scholars use the term "debellatio" to refer to a situation in which victorious powers are entitled to assume absolute sovereignty over a state because its government, as a result of total military defeat, has ceased to exist.[32] As we will see below, the Allies relied on debellatio to avoid being bound by the rules of belligerent occupation, which would likely have prevented the Control Council from enacting Law No. 10. The question, then, is whether the Allies were, in fact, entitled to invoke the doctrine in the context of Germany's unconditional surrender.

Benvenisti, perhaps the leading contemporary scholar of the law of occupation, has convincingly argued that debellatio "has no place in contemporary international law," because it is based on "an archaic conception that assimilated state into government" and was implicitly rejected by the 1949 Geneva Conventions, whose limits on belligerent occupation make no exception for situations involving unconditional surrender.[33] He acknowledges, however, that the doctrine applied in the post-World War II era and that "it was generally accepted that the conditions for debellatio had been met with respect to Germany and hence the four occupying powers had acquired sovereign title over it."[34] Indeed, the majority in the *Justice* case specifically referenced two scholars, Hans Kelsen and Alwyn Freeman, in defense of its conclusion that debellatio justified the Control Council's absolute sovereignty over Germany. Kelsen cited the High Command's unconditional surrender in the Berlin Declaration as evidence "that a so-called debellatio of

---

[30] *Milch*, Musmanno Concurrence, II TWC 848.
[31] *Justice*, III TWC 959–60.
[32] Eyal Benvenisti, *The International Law of Occupation* 92 (2004).
[33] Ibid., 94–5.   [34] Ibid., 93.

Germany has taken place, which is the essential condition of 'assuming supreme authority with respect to Germany including all the powers possessed by the German Government'."[35] Similarly, Freeman argued that "a distinction is clearly warranted between measures taken by the Allies prior to the destruction of the German government and those taken thereafter," because in the latter period the German government's absence meant that the Allies were "entitled to exercise all the attributes of sovereignty over the area."[36] Many other scholars writing in the aftermath of the war agreed, including John H.E. Fried, who had served as the legal advisor to the NMT defendants; Quincy Wright, who had been Jackson's legal advisor at the IMT, and Georg Schwarzenberger.[37]

The idea that debellatio justified the Control Council's absolute sovereignty over Germany was not, however, universally accepted. Most notably, Judge Blair dissented from the majority's invocation of debellatio in the *Justice* case, insisting that "there is no rule which would, because of the unconditional surrender of the German armed forces, transfer the sovereignty of Germany to the Allied occupants, or to either of them, in their respective zones of occupation."[38] Indeed, in his view, the Allies had made "no act or declaration . . . either before or since their occupation of Germany under the terms of the unconditional surrender, which could possibly be construed as showing that they intend by the subjugation and occupation of Germany to transfer her sovereignty to themselves."[39]

Judge Blair's rejection of debellatio relied on Rule 275 of the U.S. Army's Rules of Land Warfare, which provided that a military occupation did not result in a transfer of sovereignty to the U.S. unless it involved "subjugation or conquest." Implicit in his argument was the idea the Berlin Declaration had not resulted in such "subjugation or conquest" because it specifically provided that the Allies' assumption of sovereign authority did not "affect the annexation of Germany."[40] Other scholars who rejected debellatio—mostly German—relied on the absence of annexation more explicitly. Kurt von Laun, for example, argued that the Allies' failure to annex Germany meant that the German state continued to exist even after its complete military defeat, because "the opinion that Germany has ceased to exist as a state can only be based on the assumption that she has been annexed. From the point of view of law, not military conquest but the declaration of the annexation is decisive."[41]

---

[35] Hans Kelsen, "The Legal Status of Germany According to the Declaration of Berlin," 39 *Am. J. Int'l L.* 518, 520 (1945).

[36] Alwyn V. Freeman, "War Crimes by Enemy Nationals Administering Justice in Occupied Territory," 41 *Am. J. Int'l L.* 579, 605 (1947).

[37] John H.E. Fried, "Transfer of Civilian Manpower From Occupied Territory," 40 *Am. J. Int'l L.* 303, 327–8 (1946); Quincy Wright, "The Law of the Nuremberg Trial," in Mettraux, 331–2; Schwarzenberger, in Mettraux, 174.

[38] *Justice*, Blair Separate Opinion, III TWC 1180–1. Note that Judge Blair concurred in the final judgment; he dissented on specific points of law in his separate opinion.

[39] Ibid., 1182.

[40] Allied Declaration Regarding the Defeat of Germany, 5 June 1945, Preamble.

[41] Kurt von Laun, "The Legal Status of Germany," 45 *Am. J. Int'l L.* 267, 270 (1951); see also Woetzel, 80.

Scholars who based the Control Council's authority on debellatio were aware of the annexation issue, but uniformly rejected the idea that the transfer of sovereignty to the Allies required annexation. Wright, for example, argued that "if a state or states are in a position to annex a territory they have the right to declare the lesser policy of exercising sovereignty temporarily for specified purposes with the intention of eventually transferring the sovereignty to someone else."[42] Kelsen's position was similar—and he noted that, because Germany had ceased to exist as a state, rejecting debellatio would have meant that no state was in control of Germany's territory.[43] Their position is clearly the superior one: the law of occupation is designed to ensure that occupation is temporary, a goal that would be undermined by requiring annexation as a condition precedent to a victorious power assuming sovereignty over a state whose government has ceased to exist.[44]

2. Condominium

In most situations involving debellatio, sovereignty over a defeated state that has ceased to exist transfers to a single power. That was obviously not the case in Germany: the Berlin Declaration provided that the four Allies jointly assumed "supreme authority with respect to Germany, including all the powers possessed by the German Government, the High Command and any state, municipal, or local government or authority." Most scholars referred to this joint assumption of sovereignty as a "condominium." Kelsen, for example, wrote that "[t]he sovereignty under which the German territory, together with its population has been placed is the joined sovereignty of the occupant powers. If two or more states exercise jointly their sovereignty over a certain territory, we speak of a condominium."[45]

Scholars who rejected the existence of debellatio also rejected the idea that the Allies possessed sovereignty over Germany as a condominium. Von Laun argued that "[i]f Germany has not been annexed, she cannot have been a condominium."[46] And Woetzel claimed that "it would be wrong . . . to speak of a condominium of the Allied Powers, since this would mean annexation which the Allies had specifically ruled out."[47] Once again, however, defenders of debellatio insisted that the greater power to annex included the lesser power to assume sovereignty temporarily through a condominium. Kelsen, Wright, Schwarzenberger, and Max Rheinstein all took that position,[48] although Rheinstein preferred to describe the Allies' joint sovereignty as a "co-imperium," which he believed reflected the absence of

---

[42] Wright, *Law of the Nuremberg Trial*, in Mettraux, 332.
[43] Kelsen, *Legal Status*, 521.
[44] Benvenisti, 5.
[45] Kelsen, *Legal Status*, 524.
[46] Von Laun, 270.
[47] Woetzel, 81.
[48] Kelsen, *Legal Status*, 524; Wright, *Law of the Nuremberg Trial*, in Mettraux, 331; Schwarzenberger, in Mettraux, 174; Max Rheinstein, "The Legal Status of Occupied Germany," 47 *Mich. L. Rev.* 23, 37 (1948).

annexation. Rheinstein cited Anglo-Egyptian Sudan and the New Hebrides as historical precedent for the Allied condominium/co-imperium.[49]

3. Inter-Allied Special Tribunals

As is well known, the IMT justified its creation by pointing out that "[t]he making of the Charter was the exercise of the sovereign legislative power by the countries to which the German Reich unconditionally surrendered... In doing so, they have done together what one any of them might have done singly; for it is not to be doubted that any nation has the right thus to set up special courts to administer law."[50] That is a questionable justification, because the IMT was not actually created by the "sovereign legislative power" in Germany—the Control Council. On the contrary, as Leo Gross has pointed out, the IMT was created by an executive agreement between the Allies, despite U.S. suggestions that relying on the Control Council was the preferable method.[51]

The "sovereign legislative power" rationale works quite well for the NMTs, however, because they *were* created by the Control Council—through Law No. 10. Indeed, the tribunals specifically relied on that rationale to justify their existence. In the *Justice* case, for example, Tribunal III emphasized that the Control Council's status as the *de facto* government of Germany justified Law No. 10: "by virtue of the situation at the time of unconditional surrender, the Allied Powers were provisionally in the exercise of supreme authority, valid and effective until such time as, by treaty or otherwise, Germany shall be permitted to exercise the full powers of sovereignty. We hold that the legal right of the four Powers to enact C. C. Law 10 is established."[52] Similarly, in *Einsatzgruppen*, Tribunal II justified the creation of the NMTs by emphasizing that the Control Council was entitled to apply the pooled jurisdiction of the Allies: "[t]here is no authority which denies any belligerent nation jurisdiction over individuals in its actual custody charged with violation of international law. And if a single nation may legally take jurisdiction in such instances, with what more reason may a number of nations agree, in the interest of justice, to try alleged violations of the international code of war?"[53] Even Judge Blair, otherwise critical of the majority's analysis in the *Justice* case, accepted that, because a state of war officially still existed, "the Allied Powers, or either of them, have the right to try and punish individual defendants in this case."[54]

Scholarly opinion at the time supported the idea that the NMTs were inter-allied special tribunals. Kelsen, for example, argued that "[t]he Control Council established by the Declaration of Berlin in its capacity as the main agency of the condominium over the former German territory is the proper authority to prosecute the German war criminals." Indeed, he even claimed that because international law

---

[49] Rheinstein, 37.   [50] IMT Judgment, 38.

[51] Leo Gross, *Selected Essays on International Law and Organization* 158–9 (1993).

[52] *Justice*, III TWC 963.

[53] *Einsatzgruppen*, IV TWC 460.

[54] *Justice*, Blair Separate Opinion, III TWC 1194.

obligated states to punish war crimes committed by their nationals, the Control Council's authorization of military tribunals "fulfill[ed] an obligation imposed on it in its capacity as successor of the German government."[55] Many other scholars agreed, including Wright; Schwarzenberger; Sheldon Glueck, a professor at Harvard Law School; and Willard B. Cowles, who had served in the Judge Advocate General's office during the war.[56] Cowles additionally noted that an inter-allied special tribunal like the NMTs was not unprecedented, because such a tribunal was used at Archangel in the aftermath of World War I.[57]

4. Why Not German Courts?

It is also possible, of course, to view the NMTs as German courts instead of as inter-allied special tribunals. The argument is essentially the same: the Allies were the supreme legislative authority in Germany as a result of debellatio; the Allies exercised that authority as a condominium via the Control Council; the Control Council used its authority to create German courts to prosecute war criminals. There is nothing inherently wrong with that view, as long as we recognize that those courts applied international law, not the law of occupation or German law—issues addressed in the next section. Nevertheless, "inter-allied special tribunal" is still the more accurate description. First, it is clear that the Control Council itself did not believe that the tribunals authorized by Article III(1)(d) of Law No. 10 were German courts, because that provision specifically distinguished between Allied "tribunals," which had jurisdiction over all of the crimes in Article II, and "German courts," which had to be authorized by the occupying powers and could only prosecute acts committed by Germans against other Germans. Second, Article III(2) specifically authorized each Ally to determine the "rules and procedure" of the tribunals it created pursuant to Law No. 10, thus leaving open the possibility that those tribunals would prosecute the same substantive crimes via very different procedures. Indeed, that is exactly what happened, as illustrated by the fact that the NMTs did not provide defendants with any kind of appellate review, while the tribunal France used to prosecute Hermann Roechling and his four co-defendants permitted the defendants to appeal their convictions to the Superior Military Government Court.[58] The "German court" interpretation, therefore, means that the Control Council deliberately authorized the creation of German courts with the same subject-matter jurisdiction but very different procedural regimes. That seems like a strained interpretation of the Control Council's intentions, particularly in light of the distinction it drew in Article III(1)(d) between Allied tribunals and German courts.

[55] Kelsen, *Legal Status*, 524–5.
[56] Wright, *Law of the Nuremberg Trial*, in Mettraux, 330–1; Schwarzenberger, in Mettraux, 174; Sheldon Glueck, "By What Tribunal Shall War Offenders Be Tried?," 56 *Harv. L. Rev.* 1059, 1083 (1943); Willard B. Cowles, "Trials of War Criminals (Non-Nuremberg)," 42 *Am. J. Int'l L.* 299, 318 (1948).
[57] Cowles, 318.   [58] XV TWC 1143.

III. What Kind of Law Did the NMTs Apply?

Properly understood, in short, the NMTs were inter-allied special tribunals created by the Control Council as the sovereign legislative authority in Germany. But what kind of law did they apply? NMT critics argued at various times that the tribunals applied the law of occupation, American law, or German law. The tribunals themselves, by contrast, uniformly concluded that they applied international law. This section explains why the tribunals were correct.

A. The Law of Occupation

NMT critics often claimed that the tribunals applied the law of occupation, by which they meant that the Hague Regulations concerning belligerent occupation limited the Control Council's legislative authority over Germany. Von Knieriem, for example, argued that Law No. 10 was "a uniform law established by the occupying powers for the whole of Germany, that is to say, that it is occupation law."[59] Von Laun agreed, adding that the applicability of the Hague Regulations was not affected by "the type of occupation, by conditions in Germany, or by the questions whether a state of war exists or whether hostilities continue." In his view, the Hague Regulations would have ceased to apply only if the Allies evacuated Germany or formally annexed it.[60] The defendants in *Ministries* made a similar argument.[61]

It is not difficult to understand why the critics argued that the tribunals applied occupation law. Article 43 of the Hague Regulations provides that "[t]he authority of the legitimate power having in fact passed into the hands of the occupant, the latter shall take all the measures in his power to restore, and ensure, as far as possible, public order and safety, while respecting, unless absolutely prevented, the laws in force in the country." Although there is a non-frivolous argument that the Control Council's radical restructuring of the German judicial system could have been justified by Article 43's "absolutely prevented" exception,[62] most scholars believe that—as Woetzel put it—"it is doubtful that [such] summary action could have been justified according to international law."[63] Indeed, the *Justice* tribunal cited an article by George Zinn, the Minister of Justice in Hessen, in which Zinn claimed that if the Allies were belligerently occupying Germany, "then all legal and constitutional changes brought about since 7 May 1945 would cease to be valid once the Allied troops were withdrawn and all Nazi laws would again and automatically become the law of Germany." The tribunal described that outcome as "a consummation devoutly to be avoided."[64]

The tribunals, however, uniformly rejected the Hague Regulations argument. Their rationale was familiar: debellatio. According to the *Ministries* tribunal, the

---

[59] Von Knieriem, 25.   [60] Von Laun, 274–5.
[61] *Ministries*, XIV TWC 690.   [62] Benvenisti, 91 n. 135 (collecting cites).
[63] Woetzel, 85.   [64] *Justice*, III TWC 962.

High Command's unconditional surrender meant that the Allies were not belligerently occupying Germany and thus Article 43 did not apply to the actions of the Control Council:

There is a great difference between the rights and powers of the Allied governments in the Reich today, and the rights and powers of the Reich in the territories that it belligerently occupied, following its invasions and through the war years. The Allied occupation of Germany following her unconditional surrender and the disbanding of her armies, and the subsequent Allied exaction of reparations to restore and rehabilitate in a measure the territories devastated and despoiled by Germany do not make a situation falling within the contemplation of the provisions of the Hague Convention applicable to belligerent occupancy.[65]

The *Justice* tribunal agreed, pointing out that the existence of debellatio "distinguishes the present occupation of Germany from the type of occupation which occurs when, in the course of actual warfare, an invading army enters and occupies the territory of another state, whose government is still in existence and is in receipt of international recognition, and whose armies, with those of its allies, are still in the field." In its view, the Hague Regulations applied only to the latter *occupation bellica*.[66]

The *Justice* tribunal claimed that its interpretation of the Control Council's authority was "supported by modern scholars of high standing in the field of international law," and indeed it was. The tribunal itself cited Freeman, Fried, Kelsen, and Lord Wright, the head of the UNWCC.[67] Other scholars who believed that debellatio ended the Allies' belligerent occupation of Germany included Friedmann and Schwarzenberger.[68] British courts had also reached the same conclusion by the time the tribunal released its judgment[69]—and French, Dutch, and even German courts would later agree.[70]

Finally, although the tribunals' reliance on debellatio appears sound, it is worth noting that Judge Blair believed that they should have avoided determining whether the Control Council was bound by the Hague Regulations. In his view, that issue was irrelevant to the tribunals' authority to apply the substantive provisions of Law No. 10, because "[n]o authority or jurisdiction to determine the question of the present status of belligerency of the occupation of Germany has been given" to the tribunals. In other words, the tribunals were required to apply Law No. 10 as written; they had no right to question the legitimacy of the law itself.[71]

---

[65] *Ministries*, XIV TWC 690.

[66] *Justice*, III TWC 960.

[67] See the citations in ibid., 961–2.

[68] W. Friedmann, "The Legal and Constitutional Position of Germany Under Allied Military Government," 3 *Res Judicatae* 133, 136 (1947); Schwarzenberger, in Mettraux, 174.

[69] See, e.g., *Grahame v. Director of Prosecutions* [1947] AD Case No. 103.

[70] France: *In re Bauerle* [1949] AD Case No. 93; Netherlands: *In re Flesche* [1949] AD Case No. 87; Germany: Recidivist (American Military Tribunal) Case, 1951 ILR 617.

[71] *Justice*, Blair Separate Opinion, III TWC 1178.

B. American Law

In addition to arguing that the tribunals were American courts, NMT critics also claimed that the tribunals applied American criminal law and were thus bound by the U.S. Constitution. Von Knieriem, for example, argued that "[i]f... the Nuremberg Tribunals were American courts"—as he believed they were—"they could not apply any legal rules other than those which American legislation allowed them to apply."[72] The tribunals, however, were no less hostile to the idea that they applied American law and were bound by the U.S. Constitution than they were to the idea that they were American courts. The *Flick* tribunal, for example, stated unequivocally that "[t]he Tribunal administers international law. It is not bound by the general statutes of the United States or even by those parts of its Constitution which relate to courts of the United States."[73] The *Krupp* tribunal reached the same conclusion, pointing out that the tribunals recognized "certain safeguards for persons charged with crimes" as binding "not... because of their inclusion in the Constitution and statutes of the United States, but because they are understood as principles of a fair trial."[74] Similar statements can be found in both *Ministries* and the *Justice* case.[75]

This position is clearly correct. If the tribunals did not qualify as American courts, it is difficult to see how they could have applied American law. Moreover— and even more important in this context—the tribunals were created pursuant to Law No. 10, which was enacted by the Control Council, a condominium of the four Allies that possessed supreme legislative authority over Germany. As Tribunal III pointed out in the *Justice* case, given the quadripartite foundation of Law No. 10, "it follows of necessity that there is no national constitution of any one state which could be invoked to invalidate the substantive provisions of such international legislation."[76] Indeed, the Control Council enacted Law No. 10 precisely "to establish a uniform legal basis in Germany for the prosecution of war criminals and other similar offenders."[77]

C. German Law

Finally, a number of NMT defendants claimed that the tribunals applied German law. That was the defendants' argument, for example, in the *Justice* case. Their motivation was obvious: if the tribunals applied German law—which was certainly plausible, given that the Control Council was acting as the *de facto* German government—they could not be convicted for actions that were legal under German law at the time they were committed.[78]

Interestingly, both the OCC and various American war-crimes officials also occasionally claimed that the tribunals applied German law. Their motivation,

---

[72] Von Knieriem, 87.   [73] *Flick*, VI TWC 1188.   [74] *Krupp*, IX TWC 1331.
[75] *Ministries*, Order, 29 Dec. 1947, XV TWC 325; *Justice*, III TWC 984.
[76] *Justice*, III TWC 965.   [77] Law No. 10, Preamble.   [78] Woetzel, 60.

however, was quite different: they believed that if the tribunals applied German law, they would be able to prosecute crimes in Law No. 10 that were not necessarily criminal under international law, particularly crimes against humanity committed against German Jews that were not connected to the Nazis' wars of aggression. In early 1947, for example, Taylor asked Damon Gunn, an official in the Theater Judge Advocate's Office, whether such crimes violated international law and were thus punishable under the London Charter. Gunn replied that "the answer is in the negative, if considered as stated, under International Law," but he insisted that "this appears to be immaterial because these persons can be punished by these Courts, under provisions of Control Council Law No. 10 which is the German Law."[79] Taylor later made precisely that argument in *Flick*.[80]

Both the defendants and the Americans would ultimately be disappointed, because the tribunals unequivocally rejected the idea that they applied German law. As Tribunal III said in the *Justice* case:

The Nuernberg Tribunals are not German courts. They are not enforcing German law. The charges are not based on violation by the defendants of German law. On the contrary, the jurisdiction of this Tribunal rests on international authority. It enforces the law as declared by the IMT Charter and C. C. Law 10, and within the limitations on the power conferred, it enforces international law as superior in authority to any German statute or decree.[81]

This argument is sound. There is no question that the Control Council often relied on its supreme legislative authority in Germany to create German law; Law No. 11, which rewrote the German Penal Code, is an example. But Law No. 10 was not intended to create German law—it was designed to apply the international law of the London Charter to German war criminals via the procedural mechanism of zonal trials. Law No. 10, in other words, was the law *in* Germany, but it was not the law *of* Germany.

D. International Law

The tribunals' insistence that they did not apply either American or German law was based on the same idea: that they were international courts that applied international law. We have already seen that the first assumption is untenable. But what about the second? Could the tribunals have applied international law if they were inter-allied special tribunals, not international courts?

At first glance, the answer to that question seems obvious. National courts prosecuted violations of international law long before the NMTs—particularly violations of the laws of war—so there is no reason that the tribunals, which were based on the pooled jurisdiction of the individual Allies, could not have prosecuted violations of international law. That answer, however, assumes that the substantive law the tribunals applied—Article II of Law No. 10—genuinely

---

[79] Memo from Gunn to Assistant Secretary of War, 7 Mar. 1947, NA-153–1018-8, at 1.
[80] IX *Law Reports of Trials of War Criminals* 45 n. 1 (1949) (hereinafter "LRTWC").
[81] *Justice*, III TWC 984.

qualified as international. To paraphrase Woetzel's question about the IMT, were the crimes listed in Law No. 10 "really international crimes based on international law"?[82]

Without exception, the tribunals insisted that they were. First, they argued that the crimes in Law No. 10 were international crimes because they were based on the London Charter, which the international community had ratified as international law. Second, they claimed that regardless of the international community's ratification of the London Charter, the crimes in Law No. 10 reflected pre-existing rules of international law.

1. International Ratification

Two tribunals relied on the international community's ratification of the London Charter to justify the internationality of Law No. 10. In *Einsatzgruppen*, Tribunal II held that Law No. 10's crimes against humanity provision qualified as international law because it was based on Article 6(c) of the London Charter, to which 19 states had adhered "[f]ollowing the London Agreement of 8 August 1945 between the four Allied powers."[83] Tribunal III reached a similar conclusion in the *Justice* case, adding that Law No. 10's incorporation of the London Charter guaranteed its internationality not only because "23 states, including all of the great powers" adhered to the Charter, but also because "the IMT Charter must be deemed declaratory of the principles of international law in view of its recognition as such by the General Assembly of the United Nations."[84]

This explanation of Law No. 10's internationality depends, of course, on the idea that the London Charter actually qualified as international law. Most scholars, both past and present, have relied on the adherence rationale, arguing that the Charter declared international law because it was enacted by the Allies on behalf of the international community. Quincy Wright, for example, took the position that "[w]hile such an assumption of competence would theoretically be a novelty in international law, it would accord with the practice established during the nineteenth century under which leading powers exercised a predominant influence in initiating new rules of international law."[85] Lord Wright argued that the Charter "should be regarded as a declaration of international law because, though it was an agreement to which the original parties were only the four Great Powers, it was acceded to by practically all the Allies."[86] Schwelb and Schwarzenberger took similar positions,[87] as did Woetzel and Bassiouni more recently.[88]

---

[82] Woetzel, 241.

[83] *Einsatzgruppen*, IV TWC 498.

[84] *Justice*, III TWC 698.

[85] Wright, *Law of the Nuremberg Trial*, in Mettraux, 333.

[86] Lord Wright, "The Killing of Hostages as a War Crime," 25 *Brit. Y.B. Int'l L.* 296, 304 (1948).

[87] Egon Schwelb, "Crimes Against Humanity," in Mettraux, 152–3; Schwarzenberger, in Mettraux, 174.

[88] Woetzel, 54; M. Cherif Bassiouni, *Crimes Against Humanity in International Criminal Law* 83 (2nd rev. edn., 1999).

Woetzel also endorsed the idea that the UN's subsequent ratification of the London Charter and the IMT judgment meant that the Charter was declaratory of international law. In his view, General Assembly Resolution 95(1) is "of special importance" to the internationality of the Charter, because the IMT, unlike the Permanent Court of International Justice, did not directly apply general international law but was bound by the terms of the Charter. Resolution 95(1) thus provides "further tangible evidence for assuming that the principles of the Charter...were valid principles of international law," not simply special occupation law enacted by the Allies as the supreme legislative authority in Germany.[89]

2. Pre-Existing International Law

Most of the tribunals, by contrast, claimed that they applied international law not because the London Charter had been approved by the international community, but because Law No. 10 reflected pre-existing rules of international law, both customary and conventional. In the *Hostage* case, for example, Tribunal V held that "[t]he crimes defined in Control Council Law No. 10...were crimes under pre-existing rules of international law," because "the practices and usages of war which gradually ripened into recognized customs with which belligerents were bound to comply recognized the crimes specified herein as crimes subject to punishment."[90] Similarly, in *High Command*, Tribunal V claimed—quoting the IMT—that "[t]he Charter, supplemented by Control Council Law No. 10, is not an arbitrary exercise of power, but...is the expression of international law existing at the time of its creation."[91] Statements to the same effect can be found in *Flick* and *Krupp*.[92]

The two tribunals that relied on the ratification rationale, it is worth noting, also relied on the pre-existing law rationale—likely because of the retroactivity problems inherent in the former, which are discussed in the next section. In the *Justice* case, Tribunal III claimed that, with a few exceptions, Law No. 10 was not "original substantive legislation," but simply provided "procedural means previously lacking for the enforcement within Germany of certain rules of international law which exist throughout the civilized world independently of any new substantive legislation."[93] More succinctly, the *Einsatzgruppen* tribunal held that "while the Tribunal derives its existence" from the London Charter, "its jurisdiction over the subject matter results from international law valid long prior to World War II."[94]

IV. Retroactivity

The ratification and custom rationales each raise important questions about whether Law No. 10 violated the principle of non-retroactivity. The ratification rationale is obviously difficult to reconcile with that principle: the crimes that the IMT and

---

[89] Woetzel, 57.   [90] *Hostage*, XI TWC 1239.   [91] *High Command*, XI TWC 476.
[92] *Flick*, VI TWC 1189; *Krupp*, IX TWC 1331.
[93] *Justice*, III TWC 966.   [94] *Einsatzgruppen*, IV TWC 154.

NMTs prosecuted were committed long before the Charter was drafted, much less adhered to or retrospectively approved. The custom rationale does not have the same weakness, but it nevertheless depends on the empirical claim—contested by NMT critics—that the crimes in Article II of Law No. 10 were, in fact, criminal under international law prior to World War II.

A. Does the Principle of Non-Retroactivity Apply?

Both rationales, of course, presume that the tribunals could not prosecute acts that were not criminal under international law at the time they were committed. The IMT had wavered on that issue. At one point in the judgment, the tribunal said that "[t]he law of the Charter is decisive, and binding,"[95] implying that it had no authority to question the customary status of the crimes in the Charter. But it still entertained the defendants' *ex post facto* challenge, treating the principle of non-retroactivity as a "principle of justice" that was satisfied as long as the defendants had known that their actions were wrong when they engaged in them.[96]

Tribunal III exhibited similar ambivalence in the *Justice* case. In response to defense claims that the crimes in Law No. 10 violated the principle of non-retroactivity, it insisted that it had no authority to question whether those crimes reflected pre-existing rules of international law. According to the tribunal, because Law No. 10 was "the legislative product of the only body in existence having and exercising general lawmaking power throughout the Reich," it could not "go behind the statute" and "declare invalid the act to which it owes its existence."[97] It then immediately stated, however, that although it was entitled to treat Law No. 10 as "a binding rule regardless of the righteousness of its provisions," the better course was to determine whether the law was consistent with the principle of non-retroactivity.[98]

Like the IMT, the *Justice* tribunal considered non-retroactivity to be a "principle of justice and fair play," not a limit on the Control Council's sovereignty.[99] But it did not adopt the IMT's view that the principle required no more than generalized knowledge of wrongfulness. On the contrary, it made the IMT test both easier and more difficult to satisfy. It made it easier to satisfy by holding that the principle of non-retroactivity was satisfied as long as the defendant "knew or should have known" that his actions were wrongful—a negligence standard instead of a knowledge standard. But it made it more difficult to satisfy by holding that the defendant must have known or had reason to know both that his actions were wrongful ("shocking to the moral sense of mankind") and that "he would be subject to punishment if caught."[100]

---

[95] IMT Judgment, 38.

[96] Ibid., 39. A number of scholars supported that interpretation of non-retroactivity, most notably Kelsen and Stefan Glaser. Hans Kelsen, "Will the Judgment in the Nuremberg Trial Constitute a Precedent in International Law?," in Mettraux, 283; Stefan Glaser, "The Charter of the Nuremberg Tribunal and New Principles of International Law," in Mettraux, 64.

[97] *Justice*, III TWC 964–5. [98] Ibid., 963. [99] Ibid., 977. [100] Ibid., 978.

The *Justice* tribunal was the only tribunal that considered the principle of non-retroactivity to be a principle of justice instead of a limit on sovereignty. All of the other tribunals that considered the issue concluded that the principle prohibited them from punishing defendants for acts that were not criminal under international law at the time they were committed—a significant development in international criminal law. The *Farben* tribunal, for example, held that Law No. 10 "cannot be made the basis of a determination of guilt for acts or conduct that would not have been criminal under the law as it existed at the time of the rendition of the judgment by the IMT."[101] Similarly, in the *Hostage* case, Tribunal V described "[t]he rule that one may not be charged with crime for committing an act which was not a crime at the time of its commission" as a "fundamental right" and held that the right prohibited "retroactive pronouncements."[102] The *Flick* and *Krupp* tribunals reached the same conclusion.[103]

B. Did Law No. 10 Violate the Principle of Non-Retroactivity?

Although the tribunals occasionally rejected specific charges against defendants on the ground that they exceeded pre-existing rules of international law, they consistently rejected claims that the substantive provisions of Law No. 10 violated the principle of non-retroactivity. Some of the tribunals made sweeping claims to that effect. In *Flick*, for example, Tribunal IV simply claimed that "[t]he Tribunal is giving no *ex post facto* application to Control Council Law No. 10. It is administering that law as a statement of international law which previously was at least partly uncodified... No act is adjudged criminal by the Tribunal which was not criminal under international law as it existed when the act was committed."[104] Other tribunals, by contrast, addressed the retroactivity of war crimes, crimes against peace, and crimes against humanity individually.

1. War Crimes

The tribunals had little trouble concluding that international law criminalized the war crimes in Law No. 10. Article II(1)(b) essentially replicated Article 6(b) of the London Charter, and the IMT had held that the Charter's crimes "were already recognized" via the Hague Convention IV of 1907 and the Geneva Convention of 1929, both of which had achieved customary status.[105] The tribunals followed the IMT. In *Einsatzgruppen*, for example, Tribunal II held that the war crimes in Law No. 10 "have been international law for decades if not centuries."[106] The *Hostage* and *High Command* tribunals reached similar conclusions.[107]

---

[101] *Farben*, VIII TWC 1098.   [102] *Hostage*, XI TWC 1241.
[103] *Flick*, VI TWC 1189; *Krupp*, IX TWC 1331.
[104] *Flick*, VI TWC 1189.
[105] IMT Judgment, 64–5.
[106] *Einsatzgruppen*, IV TWC 458.
[107] *Hostage*, XI TWC 1240; *High Command*, XI TWC 534.

2. Crimes Against Peace

Two tribunals held that Law No. 10's definition of crimes against peace was consistent with international law. In *High Command*, Tribunal V examined two questions: whether aggressive war was criminal, and who could be convicted of participating in a crime against peace. Its affirmative answer to the first question was relatively cursory: echoing the IMT,[108] the tribunal simply pointed out that the 1928 Kellogg-Briand Pact, which had "renounced war as an instrument of national policy," had been signed (at the time) by Germany and 62 other states.[109] Its analysis of the second question—which the IMT had not addressed—was more searching, but strangely devoid of any reference to history. The tribunal simply held that international law limited criminal responsibility for aggressive war to "policy makers" who had the power "to shape or influence" the plans for war; it refused to find that, "at the present stage of development, international law declares as criminals those below that level who, in the execution of this war policy, act as the instruments of the policy makers."[110]

Tribunal IV went even further in *Ministries*. With regard to individual criminal responsibility, it rejected as "fallacious" the defendants' claim that "heads of states and officials thereof cannot be held personally responsible for initiating or waging aggressive wars and invasions because no penalty had been previously prescribed for such acts."[111] It provided two examples of such penalties: Frederick the Great being summoned to Regensburg to explain, under threat of exile, why he had invaded Saxony; and Napoleon's banishment to St. Helena for sailing from Elba to try to regain his crown. The tribunal also made clear, however, that that it would have had "no hesitation" in upholding individual responsibility for participating in aggressive war "even if history furnished no examples" of it.[112]

The most important difference between *Ministries* and *High Command* centered on the criminality of invasions, which Law No. 10 criminalized but the London Charter did not. Although the *Ministries* tribunal also relied on the Kellogg-Briand Pact, it specifically held that international law condemned *both* invasions and aggressive wars: "[t]he initiation of wars and invasions with their attendant horror and suffering has for centuries been universally recognized by all civilized nations as wrong, to be resorted to only as a last resort to remedy wrongs already or imminently to be inflicted."[113] From a retroactivity standpoint, that was a critical conclusion. The *Ministries* tribunal ultimately convicted two defendants—Wilhelm Keppler and Hans Lammers—for participating in the invasions of Austria and Czechoslovakia,[114] which the IMT had held were aggressive acts but not aggressive wars. Their convictions would thus have violated the principle of non-retroactivity had the *Ministries* tribunal not held that customary international law was broader than the law of the London Charter.

---

[108] IMT Judgment, 39.   [109] *High Command*, XI TWC 490.
[110] Ibid., 489.   [111] *Ministries*, XIV TWC 321.
[112] Ibid.   [113] Ibid., 319.
[114] Keppler was convicted of participating in the invasions of both Austria and Czechoslovakia. Lammers was convicted of participating in the invasion of Czechoslovakia.

Judge Powers, it is important to note, angrily rejected the tribunal's insistence that invasions were criminal under customary international law:

[N]either in the Kellogg-Briand Pact, nor any other treaty, so far as I am aware, is there any treaty or agreement affecting the countries here involved with reference to mere invasions— at least not invasions accomplished under the circumstances under which Austria and Czechoslovakia were invaded. The thing which is prohibited by all of these treaties is war. If we start with the premise that what was intended was to describe crimes which were already crimes under international law, we will have to exclude invasions, because there was no possible basis for claiming that a mere invasion was contrary to international law, prior to the enactment of Law 10.[115]

Judge Powers would seem to have the better of the argument. As Law No. 10 recognized, invasions and wars of aggression are different acts: unlike a war of aggression, which involves actual violence, an invasion is "the implementation of the national policy of the invading state by force even though the invaded state, due to fear or a sense of the futility of resistance in the face of superior force, adopts a policy of nonresistance."[116] Numerous scholars have rejected the IMT's conclusion that aggressive wars were criminal under international law prior to World War II,[117] but at least the IMT could point to the Kellogg-Briand Pact. The majority in *Ministries* could not even rely on the Pact to justify the criminality of invasions, because—as Judge Powers pointed out—it was silent concerning them.

3. Crimes Against Humanity

The IMT divided crimes against humanity into two categories: "war crimes… committed on a vast scale" during the war in occupied territory; and "inhumane acts" that took place either before the war or during the war outside of occupied territory, but were committed "in execution of, or in connection with, any crime within the jurisdiction of the Tribunal."[118] The IMT never specifically discussed the customary status of either category, which no doubt explains why so many scholars claim that crimes against humanity represented a new kind of international crime.[119]

Both categories, however, were at least arguably defensible. When committed in occupied territory, crimes against humanity in the first category were simply aggravated versions of war crimes and thus posed no retroactivity problems. The more difficult situation involved the second category: acts that did not qualify as war crimes either for geographic or for temporal reasons. The IMT's decision to criminalize such acts no doubt represented "a progressive historical development"

---

[115] *Ministries*, Powers Dissent, XIV TWC 881.
[116] *High Command*, XI TWC 485.
[117] See, e.g., F.B. Schick, "Crimes Against Peace," 38 *J. Crim. L. & Criminology* 770 (1947–48).
[118] IMT Judgment, 65.
[119] See, e.g., Kranzbuehler, 343.

in the evolution of crimes against humanity.[120] But that does not mean that the IMT thereby violated the principle of non-retroactivity. As Bassiouni has pointed out, the IMT's recognition of the second category of crimes against humanity did not criminalize any underlying acts that were not previously criminal; all of those acts would have qualified as war crimes had they been committed during the war in occupied territory. Indeed, such crimes against humanity were "based on the same moral and legal principles" as traditional war crimes: namely, the "laws of humanity" mentioned in the Preambles to the Hague Conventions of 1899 and 1907 that had long existed and that had always underpinned the "norms and rules of the humanization and regulation of armed conflict."[121] Bassiouni thus rightly argues that it would have "empt[ied] international law of its value content" to insist that the principle of non-retroactivity prohibited the IMT from punishing crimes against humanity that fell into the second category: because such crimes had to have been committed "in execution of, or in connection with, the war"—the nexus requirement—their commission no less transgressed the values underlying the Hague Regulations than the commission of traditional war crimes.[122] Indeed, the *Ministries* tribunal specifically relied upon the freedom of religion protected by the Hague Regulations to justify its conclusion that the Nazis' systematic "persecution of churches and clergy" during the war in Germany (and in other Axis countries) was a crime against humanity.[123]

That rationale not only justifies the IMT's second category of crimes against humanity, it also explains why the IMT felt that the nexus requirement was so important. As Bassiouni notes, "[t]he result of limiting the scope of Article 6(c) was the exclusion of all Nazi crimes against the Jews before 1939. But that trade-off was intended to strengthen the validity of the crime in light of the requirements of the 'principles of legality'."[124] More specifically, although inhumane acts unconnected to the war were undoubtedly reprehensible no matter where or when they were committed, they only transgressed the "moral and legal principles" underlying traditional war crimes, thus justifying their punishment, if the nexus was satisfied.

Law No. 10 complicated the tribunals' analysis of crimes against humanity, because it eliminated the nexus requirement. Three tribunals considered the customary status of atrocities and persecutions committed prior to the war that did not satisfy the requirement: *Ministries*, *Justice*, and *Einsatzgruppen*. In *Ministries*, Tribunal IV read the nexus requirement into Law No. 10 on the ground that it was required by customary international law[125]: "the crimes here defined as crimes against humanity and as perpetrated against German nationals were not, when committed, crimes against international law, there being no claim that such

[120] Bassiouni, 70.   [121] Ibid., 77.
[122] Ibid., 75.   [123] *Ministries*, XIV TWC 522.
[124] Bassiouni, 29.
[125] As discussed in Chapter 10, the *Flick* tribunal also held that the nexus was required. It did so, however, by analyzing the relationship between Law No. 10 and the London Charter, not by examining customary international law.

crimes were perpetrated in connection with crimes against peace or war crimes." To hold otherwise, the tribunal insisted, "would be to disregard the well-established principle of justice that no act is to be declared a crime which was not a crime under law existing at the time when the act was committed."[126]

By contrast, the *Einsatzgruppen* and *Justice* tribunals held that international law prohibited pre-war crimes against humanity that did not satisfy the nexus requirement. In *Einsatzgruppen*, Tribunal II acknowledged that Law No. 10's elimination of the nexus requirement was "an innovation in the empire of law," but denied that the innovation violated the principle of non-retroactivity. On the contrary, the tribunal insisted—echoing but expanding the IMT's emphasis on the mass nature of crimes against humanity—that crimes against humanity were simply "wholesale and systematic" versions of acts that were "long known and understood" as criminal "under the general principles of criminal law." Law No. 10 thus did not create new law by criminalizing even peacetime crimes against humanity; it simply provided a forum in which to prosecute such violations of "the common heritage of civilized peoples."[127]

Tribunal III's rejection of the nexus requirement in the *Justice* case also emphasized the scale of crimes against humanity. The tribunal acknowledged that Law No. 10 only criminalized "the type of criminal activity which prior to 1939 was and still is a matter of international concern." But it rejected the argument, made by the defendants, that "violations of the laws and customs of war [were] the only offenses recognized by common international law." In its view, regardless of whether the Nazis' pre-war acts constituted "technical violations of laws and customs of war," they were "acts of such scope and malevolence, and they so clearly imperiled the peace of the world, that they must be deemed to have become violations of international law."[128] Genocide was a "prime illustration": as evidenced by the General Assembly's recent resolution, genocide had been "recognized as a violation of common international law" on account of "its magnitude and its international repercussions."[129]

The *Justice* tribunal provided a number of historical examples in support of the idea that there had long been "an international interest and concern in relation to what was previously regarded as belonging exclusively to the domestic affairs of the individual state,"[130] such as President van Buren's intervention in Turkey in 1840 to protect Jews and France's use of force in 1861 to prevent religious atrocities in Lebanon. The tribunal additionally cited the Commission on Responsibility of Authors of the War, which had concluded in the aftermath of World War I that "[a]ll persons belonging to enemy countries...who have been guilty of offences against the laws and customs of war or the laws of humanity, are liable to criminal prosecution." And it pointed out—with evident satisfaction—that Hitler himself had justified his invasion of Czechoslovakia on the ground that "[t]he alleged

---

[126] *Ministries*, Order and Memorandum of the Tribunal Dismissing Count Four, 26 Mar. 1948, XIII TWC 116.

[127] *Einsatzgruppen*, IV TWC 458–9.

[128] *Justice*, III TWC 982.   [129] Ibid., 983.   [130] Ibid., 980.

persecution of racial Germans by the government of that country was a matter of international concern warranting intervention by Germany."[131]

It is a difficult question whether the *Justice* tribunal was correct to claim that Law No. 10's extension of the London Charter was consistent with customary international law. Taylor believed that it was, rejecting claims that the extension violated the principle of non-retroactivity by insisting that the London Charter was not intended "to be a complete statement of the entire content of international penal law" and that, as a result, the NMTs were free to differ from the IMT concerning the reach of a particular international principle.[132] Bassiouni, by contrast, disagrees. In his opinion, Law No. 10's elimination of the London Charter's nexus requirement "overreaches" and "strains the principle of legality"[133] because—as noted above—pre-war crimes against humanity that were not connected to the war, though reprehensible, did not transgress the "moral and legal principles" underlying the Hague Regulations.

This debate, however, is merely academic. Although Law No. 10's criminalization of invasions led to actual convictions, no NMT defendant was ever convicted of a peacetime crime against humanity that was not connected to war crimes or crimes against peace.

4. Criminal Membership

Neither the IMT nor the NMTs ever considered whether membership in a criminal organization was a crime under international law prior to World War II. The IMT's silence was not problematic, because it convicted the organizations themselves, not individual members of those organizations. The NMTs, by contrast, convicted more than 70 individuals of the crime. Unless criminal membership was prohibited by either conventional or customary law, therefore, those convictions violated the principle of non-retroactivity.

Interestingly, not long after the NMT trials ended, one of the judges in the *Hostage* case, Edward Carter, revealed that it was no accident that the tribunals had not addressed the retroactivity issue. According to Carter, although the judges were skeptical that criminal membership was an international crime, they felt bound to honor its inclusion in Law No. 10.[134] Judge Carter himself was certainly dubious of the crime: in his view, "the IMT applied a retroactive pronouncement to this phase of the case," because "the holding that the Nazi party or the SS is a criminal organization and that membership in either was criminal [was] not based on any source of international law known to the writer, existing prior to the London Charter."[135]

---

[131] Ibid., 982.   [132] Taylor, *Final Report*, 9.
[133] Bassiouni, 34.
[134] Edward F. Carter, "The Nurnberg Trials: A Turning Point in the Enforcement of International Law," 28 *Neb. L. Rev.* 370, 374 (1949).
[135] Ibid., 373–4.

The question was more complicated than Judge Carter acknowledged, however, because it was at least arguable that the crime of criminal membership was "a fundamental principle of criminal law accepted by nations generally," which qualified as international law according to his own tribunal.[136] Justice Jackson had mentioned a number of states that had criminalized criminal membership during the organizational phase of the IMT, a list that included all of the Allies[137] and could have been expanded to include Belgium and Switzerland.[138] He had also pointed out that the German Penal Code of 1891 had criminalized "participation in an organisation, the existence, constitution or purposes of which are to be kept secret from the Government," that in 1922 the German Parliament had criminalized membership in Nazi-like associations, and that German courts had declared the entire German Communist Party a criminal organization in 1927 and 1928.[139]

The customary status of criminal membership also drew some support from national laws criminalizing conspiracy. The IMT held that "[a] criminal organisation is analogous to a criminal conspiracy in that the essence of both is cooperation for criminal purposes."[140] That description was only partially accurate; as we will see in Chapter 12, criminal membership was actually a hybrid of conspiracy and common-plan liability. Nevertheless, the fact that conspiracy was an integral part of the common law and was far more widespread in civil-law systems than commonly acknowledged[141]—including in Germany[142]—indicates that the crime of criminal membership "cannot be regarded as entirely new law."[143]

V. Personal Jurisdiction

The NMTs, in short, are best understood as inter-allied special tribunals that applied international law. One question thus remains: did the tribunals have "the legal right to take jurisdiction over the German defendants and to hold them individually responsible for their crimes under international law?"[144]

Any attempt at an answer must begin with the fact that, unlike Japan, Germany never consented to Allied prosecution of German war criminals in its instrument of surrender.[145] As noted earlier, a tribunal based on an agreement between states is international only in the most literal sense, because it is entitled "to the combined

---

[136] *Hostage*, XI TWC 1235.

[137] XIII LRTWC 46.

[138] Glaser, in Mettraux, 67.

[139] XIII LRTWC 46.

[140] IMT Judgment, 67.

[141] See, e.g., Wienczyslaw J. Wagner, "Conspiracy in Civil Law Countries," 42 *J. Crim. L., Criminology & Police Sci.* 171, 175–7 (1951).

[142] See, e.g., ibid., 171–82.

[143] Woetzel, 209. The existence of conspiracy in Germany and in civilian systems generally is discussed in more detail in Chapter 12.

[144] Ibid., 241.

[145] A.R. Carnegie, "Jurisdiction Over Violations of the Laws and Customs of War," 39 *Brit. Y.B. Int'l L.* 402, 416 (1963).

powers of jurisdiction of the contracting parties, but no more."[146] If that is correct, we cannot assume that the IMT and the NMTs had jurisdiction over the German war criminals simply by virtue of the Allies' decision to sign the Charter or enact Law No. 10. In each case, we would need to show that the individual Allies would have had jurisdiction over Germans had they created their own military tribunals.

That said, Woetzel argued that there are two situations in which a tribunal can exercise jurisdiction over nationals of a non-contracting state regardless of the contracting state's individual jurisdiction: where the tribunal qualifies as genuinely international, because it has the consent and approval of the international community; and where "exceptional circumstances" justify setting aside the general rule of consent.[147] The first exception would validate the IMT's jurisdiction over Germans, because the IMT qualified as a genuinely international tribunal. But it would not validate the NMTs' jurisdiction, because the international community never consented to or approved Law No. 10.

The second exception, by contrast, might justify the tribunals' jurisdiction. As discussed earlier, the dissolution of the German government and the High Command's unconditional surrender meant that the Allied Control Council was entitled to act as the supreme legislative authority in Germany. It is thus possible to argue that Law No. 10's assertion of jurisdiction over German war criminals was justified in one of two different ways: (1) Germany's consent to Law No. 10 was irrelevant, because Germany had ceased to exist as a state; or (2) as the *de facto* German government, the Control Council was entitled to consent to Law No. 10 on Germany's behalf. Kelsen endorsed the first argument[148]; Woetzel, the second.[149]

Only one tribunal specifically addressed its personal jurisdiction over German war criminals. In the *Justice* case, Tribunal III acknowledged that, as a general rule, no international authority could "establish judicial machinery for the punishment of those who have violated the rules of the common international law" if the criminals were nationals of "a state having a national government presently in the exercise of its sovereign powers." It pointed out, however, that the general rule did not prohibit the Control Council from enacting Law No. 10, because the German government had ceased to exist.[150]

Although plausible, both arguments seem designed less to announce a general rule of international law than to find a coherent *ex post* justification for the Allied war-crimes program. The second argument appears particularly unseemly: the idea of the Allies using their defeat of Germany to consent on Germany's behalf to the prosecution of German war criminals is more than a little redolent of victor's justice. It is thus reasonable to consider Woetzel's primary basis for the NMTs' jurisdiction—the "combined powers of jurisdiction of the contracting parties" to Law No. 10. If each of the Allies could have individually prosecuted Germans for the crimes contained in Law No. 10, there is—as explained earlier—no reason they could not have prosecuted them together.

---

[146] Woetzel, 42–3.   [147] Ibid., 86–7.   [148] Kelsen, *Legal Status*, 525.
[149] Woetzel, 77–8.   [150] *Justice*, III TWC 971.

That inquiry begins with the *Lotus Case*, in which the Permanent Court of International Justice held that international law provides states "a wide measure of discretion" to extend their jurisdiction to acts committed outside of their territory.[151] By World War II, international law already recognized, to varying degrees, four bases of criminal jurisdiction other than territorial: active nationality, passive personality, protective, and universal.[152] Territorial and active nationality jurisdiction were not at issue in the NMT trials—although Carnegie noted in the early 1960s that it is possible to justify the Allies' jurisdiction on the ground that, regardless of the consent issue, the Control Council was entitled as the *de facto* government of Germany to exercise territorial jurisdiction over crimes committed in Germany and active nationality jurisdiction over crimes committed outside of it.[153] The three remaining bases, by contrast, all help explain the tribunals' right to prosecute German war criminals.

A. War Crimes

Two tribunals specifically relied on passive-personality jurisdiction to justify their jurisdiction over Germans accused of war crimes. In the *Justice* case, Tribunal III held that, with regard to "war crimes in the narrow sense," it had "always been recognized that tribunals may be established and punishment imposed by the state into whose hands the perpetrators fall. These rules of international law were recognized as paramount, and jurisdiction to enforce them by the injured belligerent government, whether within the territorial boundaries of the state or in occupied territory, has been unquestioned."[154] Similarly, in *Einsatzgruppen*, Tribunal II affirmed that individuals who violated the laws of war "were subject to trial and prosecution by both the country whose subjects they were and by the country whose subjects they maltreated."[155] That position had been endorsed prior to the war by the UNWCC and by Hersh Lauterpacht.[156]

There is, of course, one problem with this argument: many of the crimes the NMTs prosecuted were not committed against American nationals. Insofar as the victims were nationals of another member of the Control Council, it can be persuasively argued that, by enacting Law No. 10, each member constructively consented to the others exercising passive-nationality jurisdiction on its behalf. Both the British[157] and the *Einsatzgruppen* tribunal made that argument explicitly.[158] A similar argument can also be made concerning the tribunals' jurisdiction over crimes whose victims were not nationals of a member of the Control Council.

---

[151] *Lotus Case*, PCIJ Series A No. 10 (1927), at 19.

[152] Harvard Research, "Jurisdiction with Respect to Crime," 29 *Am. J. Int'l L. Supp.* 439, 445 (1935).

[153] Carnegie, 418.

[154] *Justice*, III TWC 970.

[155] *Einsatzgruppen*, IV TWC 496.

[156] XV LRTWC 26; Hersh Lauterpacht, "The Law of Nations and the Punishment of War Crimes," 21 *Brit. Y.B. Int'l L.* 58, 63 (1944).

[157] Carnegie, 420.   [158] *Einsatzgruppen*, IV TWC 460.

As the UNWCC pointed out, numerous Allies held trials for "offences committed against the nationals of another Ally or of persons treated as Allied nationals," including Britain, the United States, Australia, Norway, and China.[159] Those prosecutions can only be explained as relying on transferred passive-personality jurisdiction or—even more dramatically—universal jurisdiction.

In the *Hostage* case, in fact, Tribunal V specifically relied on universal jurisdiction to justify its prosecution of war crimes:

An international crime is such an act universally recognized as criminal, which is considered a grave matter of international concern and for some valid reason cannot be left within the exclusive jurisdiction of the state that would have control over it under ordinary circumstances. The inherent nature of a war crime is ordinarily itself sufficient justification for jurisdiction to attach in the courts of the belligerent into whose hands the alleged criminal has fallen ... Such crimes are punishable by the country where the crime was committed or by the belligerent into whose hands the criminals have fallen, the jurisdiction being concurrent.[160]

Although not uncontroversial,[161] there was significant support for the *Hostage* tribunal's position. The UNWCC endorsed universal jurisdiction over war crimes, as did Lord Wright in his foreword to the Commission's Report.[162] Numerous other scholars agreed, both German and non-German, including Hans-Heinrich Jescheck, Sheldon Glueck, and William Cowles, whose 1945 essay "Universality of Jurisdiction over War Crimes" was cited by the UNWCC.[163]

B. Crimes Against Peace

None of the tribunals specifically defended their ability to prosecute crimes against peace. That jurisdiction, however, can be justified on the basis of the protective principle, according to which "[a] State has jurisdiction with respect to any crime committed outside its territory by an alien against the security, territorial integrity, or political independence of that State."[164] The protective principle was recognized by international law long before World War II,[165] and numerous scholars writing during and after the war claimed that the principle permitted states to prosecute crimes against peace, including Quincy Wright, Alexander Sack, Lauterpacht, Carnegie, and Woetzel.[166]

It is clear that the states who were directly victimized by Nazi aggression would have had protective jurisdiction over the crimes against peace committed against

---

[159] XV LRTWC 43.   [160] *Hostage*, XI TWC 1241.

[161] See, e.g., Carnegie, 421; von Knieriem, 68.

[162] XV LRTWC 26; Lord Wright, "Foreword," XV LRTWC x.

[163] Hans-Heinrich Jescheck, *Die Verantwortlichkeit der Staatsorgane nach Völkerstrafrecht* 163 (1952); Glueck, 1087; Willard B. Cowles, "Universality of Jurisdiction Over War Crimes," 33 *Cal. L. Rev.* 177, 218 (1945).

[164] Harvard Research, 543.   [165] Ibid.

[166] Wright, *Law of the Nuremberg Trial*, in Mettraux, 330; Alexander N. Sack, "War Criminals and the Defense of Act of State In International Law," 5 *Law. Guild Rev.* 288, 299 (1945); Lauterpacht, 63; Carnegie, 410; Woetzel, 62.

them. The issue is whether the NMTs, as agents of the Control Council, could prosecute those crimes on their behalf. The argument is easiest to make—analogizing to the British and *Einsatzgruppen* position mentioned above—regarding the Soviet Union, which was a signatory to Law No. 10. But there is no reason to assume that the "constructive consent" argument does not work for the other victimized states as well, given that most of them adhered to the London Charter, which provided for international prosecutions of those responsible for waging aggressive war against them, and that few if any of those states could have prosecuted crimes against peace in their domestic courts.[167] Alternatively, it is reasonable to contend that the Nazis' desire to conquer all of Europe directly threatened each Ally, permitting them to assert protective jurisdiction over any of those acts of aggression. Indeed, even a critic like von Knieriem acknowledged that because "an act directed against an ally may be considered a violation of a nation's own interests and may thus be subjected to the state's own criminal law under the principle of protection... every state which actively participated in the war against Germany could judge by its own law acts committed against itself as well as against its allies."[168]

C. Crimes Against Humanity

The NMTs' jurisdiction over crimes against humanity is more problematic. The first category—mass war crimes in occupied territory—can be justified in the same way as "war crimes in the narrow sense," via passive-personality jurisdiction. That basis of jurisdiction, however, only justifies the second category—acts committed outside of occupied territory but in connection with the war—if we make the assumption that the Control Council, acting as the *de facto* government of Germany, consented to the tribunals' exercising passive-nationality jurisdiction over crimes against the Jews on Germany's behalf. But if we make that assumption, why not simply assume either that the Control Council consented to the tribunals' jurisdiction *in toto* on Germany's behalf or that, as Carnegie suggested, the Control Council was entitled to exercise territorial jurisdiction over the crimes against the Jews?

The protective principle, by contrast, provides a more satisfying justification for the NMTs' jurisdiction over the second category of crimes against humanity—a suggestion made by Quincy Wright before the war and by Carnegie after it.[169] Such crimes might not have directly threatened the security of the members of the Control Council, but there is no question that many of them *indirectly* threatened their security by materially increasing the Nazis' ability to wage aggressive wars. Tribunal IV made that point in *Ministries*, noting that although the Aryanization of Jewish agricultural property took place before the war, it was "of undoubted

---

[167] See, generally, XV LRTWC 28–48.   [168] Von Knieriem, 83.
[169] Wright, *Law of the Nuremberg Trial*, in Mettraux, 331; Carnegie, 410.

assistance in financing aggressive plans."[170] The same is true of the use of Jewish slave labor in Germany before the war.

That rationale, however, would not justify the tribunals' jurisdiction over the third category—atrocities and persecutions committed prior to the war that did not satisfy the nexus requirement. There are only two possible bases for that jurisdiction: the debellatio rationale discussed above or universal jurisdiction. Kelsen explicitly embraced the former solution, arguing that the disappearance of the German government meant that the Control Council had the authority to prosecute Germans for any international crime, "even if the crime is not exactly a war crime in the usual sense of the term, such as certain atrocities, committed in no direct connection with the war, by the Nazis against their own fellow citizens."[171] Sack, by contrast, defended the latter solution, arguing in 1945 that universal jurisdiction existed for any crime that was "universally recognized to be wrong," that "seriously affect[ed] or concern[ed] the community of nations," and that could not "be left within the exclusive jurisdiction of the government which would ordinarily have jurisdiction."[172] That is precisely the definition of a crime against humanity adopted in *Einsatzgruppen*, which strongly suggests that Tribunal II believed that universal jurisdiction justified the prosecution of such crimes even in the absence of a connection to war.[173]

Conclusion

The NMTs viewed themselves as international tribunals. That characterization, however, is inaccurate: unlike the IMT, which qualified as international because the London Charter was approved by the international community, the NMTs were based on a multinational agreement, Law No. 10, that never received such approval. The tribunals are thus better understood as inter-allied special tribunals created by the Control Council in its capacity as the *de facto* government of Germany. That distinction is anything but academic, because—as discussed in Chapter 16—uncertainty about the legal character of the NMTs has directly affected the willingness of modern courts and tribunals to rely on the their judgments.

Although the tribunals were not international, they applied international law. They could not apply the law of occupation, because the High Command's unconditional surrender meant that the Allies were no longer belligerently occupying Germany. They could not apply American law, because the source of their authority was Law No. 10, enacted by the Control Council to create "a uniform legal basis in Germany for the prosecution of war criminals." And they could not apply German law, because Law No. 10 was based on the London Charter, which

---

[170] *Ministries*, XIV TWC 557.   [171] Kelsen, *Legal Status*, 525.
[172] Sack, 297.
[173] *Einsatzgruppen*, IV TWC 498. The *Hostage* tribunal also adopted that definition in its discussion of universal jurisdiction over war crimes. *Hostage*, XI TWC 1241.

had been transformed into international law by the international community and at least arguably reflected pre-war customary international law.

That said, Law No. 10 went beyond the London Charter in a number of respects, the most important of which were the criminalization of invasions and the elimination of the nexus requirement for crimes against humanity. Those extensions likely violated the principle of non-retroactivity, particularly given that—with the exception of the *Justice* tribunal—the NMTs viewed non-retroactivity as a limit on sovereignty, not as a principle of justice. That was a moot point regarding the nexus requirement, because no defendant was ever convicted of a crime against humanity that was not connected to war crimes or crimes against peace. But it calls into question the *Ministries* tribunal's decision to convict two defendants of crimes against peace for their roles in the invasions of Austria and Czechoslovakia.

6

Evidence

Introduction

The NMTs derived their rules of evidence from three sources. The most important was Article VII of Ordinance No. 7, which read in relevant part:

The tribunals shall not be bound by technical rules of evidence. They shall adopt and apply to the greatest possible extent expeditious and nontechnical procedure, and shall admit any evidence which they deem to have probative value . . . The tribunal shall afford the opposing party such opportunity to question the authenticity or probative value of such evidence as in the opinion of the tribunal the ends of justice require.

The tribunals also applied the evidentiary provisions of the Uniform Rules of Procedure (URP),[1] which Tribunal I drafted and adopted in the *Medical* case pursuant to Article V(f) of Ordinance No. 7. Article V(f) authorized the tribunals to adopt whatever procedural rules they felt were necessary for the orderly and expeditious conduct of the trials, subject to the proviso that they be "not inconsistent with this Ordinance." The URP were amended a number of times during the life of the NMTs.

Finally, the tribunals derived rules of evidence from the "fundamental principles of justice which have been accepted and adopted by civilized nations generally."[2] As Tribunal V noted in the *Hostage* case, if "most nations in their municipal law" included a particular principle, "its declaration as a rule of international law would seem to be fully justified."[3] Such general principles, according to the tribunals, included the presumption of innocence and proof beyond a reasonable doubt.[4]

This chapter discusses the most important evidentiary issues that the tribunals addressed. Section I examines two threshold issues, admissibility and the standard of proof. Section II deals with testimonial evidence, including the tribunals' controversial practice of taking evidence via commissioners. Section III focuses on documentary evidence, particularly the widespread use of affidavits in lieu of live testimony. Section IV examines how the tribunals applied the doctrines of *res judicata* and judicial notice and dealt with the decisions of their predecessors.

---

[1] See Appendix E. [2] *Hostage*, XI TWC 1235.
[3] Ibid. [4] See, e.g., *Flick*, VI TWC 1188; *Krupp*, IX TWC 1331.

I. Admissibility and the Standard of Proof

The tribunals took a very liberal approach to admissibility. To some extent, that was the natural consequence of Article VII, which reflected the "free proof" approach to admissibility normally associated with the civil-law tradition.[5] But it also reflected the tribunals' desire to give the defendants every opportunity to prove their innocence, because the judges even admitted evidence offered by the defense that had no probative value whatsoever. In *Einsatzgruppen*, for example, the defendants wanted to introduce statements made during the war by the Kremlin, articles from a Russian encyclopedia, and various speeches given by Stalin. Tribunal II acknowledged that all of the exhibits were "strictly irrelevant and might well be regarded as a red herring drawn across the trial," but it nevertheless admitted them on the ground that "the Tribunal's policy throughout the trial has been to admit everything which might conceivably elucidate the reasoning of the defense."[6] Indeed, Judge Musmanno, the presiding judge in *Einsatzgruppen*, once remarked in open court that he would admit evidence of the social life of an Antarctic penguin if it helped establish the defendants' innocence. The defense attorneys were so pleased by what came to be known as the "Penguin Rule" that they presented Musmanno with a three-foot bronze statue of a penguin when the trial was over.[7]

The tribunals also attempted to give the benefit of the doubt to the defendants in terms of the standard of proof. Relying on Wharton, the *Krupp* tribunal stated the rule thus: "[t]he defense is not required to take up any burden until the prosecution has established every essential element of crime charged beyond a reasonable doubt. When the prosecution has finished its case, the defendant is entitled to an acquittal if the case of the prosecution is not made out beyond a reasonable doubt."[8] The tribunals agreed that proof beyond a reasonable doubt did not require "mathematical demonstration or proof beyond fanciful or factious doubt"[9]; such doubt existed, they said, when an "unbiased, unprejudiced, reflective person... could not say that he felt an abiding conviction amounting to a moral certainty of the truth of the charge."[10]

These were not mere words. Time and again, the tribunals relied on the exacting nature of proof beyond a reasonable doubt to acquit defendants whom they believed might well be guilty of the crime charged. In the *Medical* case, for example, Tribunal I held that Ruff, Romberg, and Weltz were not criminally responsible for the horrific experiments conducted at Dachau even though "[i]t cannot be denied that there is much in the record to create at least a grave suspicion that the

---

[5] See generally Mirjan Damaška, "Free Proof and Its Detractors," 43 *Am. J. Comp. L.* 343–57 (1995).

[6] *Einsatzgruppen*, IV TWC 465.   [7] Earl, 88.

[8] *Krupp*, IX TWC 1329; see also *High Command*, XI TWC 484.

[9] *Ministries*, Motion for Correction, XIV TWC 949.

[10] *Medical*, II TWC 184.

defendants" were involved in them. The problem, according to the tribunal, was that the evidence of their involvement was purely circumstantial, and circumstantial evidence only satisfied the standard of proof if it manifested "such a well-connected and unbroken chain of circumstances as to exclude all other reasonable hypotheses but that of…guilt."[11] Similarly, the *Ministries* tribunal acquitted Dietrich, the Nazi propaganda chief, of crimes against peace on the ground that the prosecution had not proved his knowledge of the Nazis' aggressive plans beyond a reasonable doubt. The tribunal admitted that it was "entirely likely that he had at least a strong inkling of what was about to take place," but it insisted that "suspicion, no matter how well founded, does not take the place of proof."[12] The tribunal went even further when it acquitted Steengracht von Moyland of similar charges, insisting that the prosecution had not satisfied its burden to prove that he "had the requisite knowledge," even though it was "of the opinion that in all likelihood he did."[13]

II. Testimonial Evidence

The tribunals dealt with three sets of issues involving testimonial evidence: (1) witness testimony; (2) taking evidence via commissioners; and (3) testimony by defendants.

A. Witness Testimony

1. Rules Governing Witness Testimony

Ordinance No. 7 and the URP were largely silent concerning the testimony of witnesses. Article XI of Ordinance No. 7 provided that both the prosecution and the defense "shall produce its evidence subject to the cross examination of its witnesses," making it clear that the trials were based on the common-law system of adversarial trials. And Rule 9 of the URP provided that witnesses were required to testify under oath or affirmation, could not be present in the courtroom when not testifying, and could not consult with other witnesses.

2. Calling Witnesses

Neither the prosecution nor the defense was ever required to call a witness— although, as we will see, the failure to call a witness could affect the admissibility of his affidavit. In the *Medical* case, for example, the defense questioned why the prosecution did not call two available witnesses instead of relying on their written correspondence. The prosecution explained that the witnesses were themselves

---

[11] Quoted in Taylor, *Final Report*, 166.
[12] *Ministries*, XIV TWC 417.
[13] Ibid., 961, Motion for Correction.

potential defendants in a later case and would be hostile to the prosecution. Tribunal I then held that "[n]either the prosecution nor the defense are obligated to call witnesses save those that they desire to put on the stand."[14]

In contrast to typical common-law practice, the tribunals reserved the right to call their own witnesses. Indeed, four tribunals called a total of nine tribunal witnesses during the trials: one in the *Medical* case, one in *Milch*, two in *Pohl*, and five in *Einsatzgruppen*. The most unusual situation concerned the testimony of Walter Neff, Rascher's assistant at Dachau, who was being held on suspicion of involvement in Rascher's medical experiments. The prosecution suggested to Tribunal I that it call Neff as a tribunal witness, so that the prosecution could avoid the unseemly spectacle of eliciting self-incriminating testimony from one of its own witnesses. It also recommended that the tribunal advise Neff that his testimony could be used against him at a later trial. The tribunal agreed, and Neff testified as a tribunal witness after being warned against self-incrimination.[15]

3. Self-Incrimination

The potential for a witness to incriminate himself was a problem throughout the trials. When that potential became evident prior to trial, the tribunals required the witness to be informed of his privilege against self-incrimination. Such warnings were given to Field Marshals von Manstein and von Rundstedt, for example, when the defense sought to call them as witnesses in *High Command*, because Tribunal V had been made aware that the British were actively preparing cases against them.[16] Both Field Marshals asserted the privilege and did not testify.[17] Similarly, when the tribunals recognized that a testifying witness had been asked a question that might incriminate him, they immediately informed the witness of his right not to answer the question. In the *Hostage* case, for example, Tribunal V warned General Hans Felber that he answered a question concerning reprisal measures at his peril. General Felber nevertheless answered the question.[18]

4. Questioning by Defendants

Examinations were normally conducted by prosecutors, defense attorneys, and judges. During the *Farben* and *Medical* trials, however, the tribunals held that the complexity of expert testimony justified permitting one or more of the defendants to personally conduct cross-examination. Those decisions represented a rejection of the IMT's position, which had ruled that a defendant represented by counsel was not entitled to question witnesses.[19]

---

[14] XV TWC 688.
[15] Ibid., 691, extract from *Medical* transcript, 17 Dec. 1946.
[16] Ibid., 381, extract from *High Command* transcript, 26 July 1948.
[17] Ibid., 366.
[18] Ibid., 709, extract from *Hostage* transcript, 11 Aug. 1947.
[19] Ibid., 342.

Over prosecution objection, two defendants in the *Medical* case, Ruff and Rose, were permitted to cross-examine Dr. Andrew Ivy, the prosecution's most important expert witness. According to Freyhofer, the cross-examinations were extremely effective. Most dramatically, Rose—an expert in tropical medicine—was able to completely discredit Ivy's claims that "American researchers, unlike the defendants, had not maltreated, tortured, or killed human subjects" and that all of the subjects had volunteered for the American experiments knowing what awaited them.[20] Indeed, as Freyhofer notes, "apparently suspecting problems, the tribunal limited examination time to thirty minutes when Rose started his questioning of Ivy," and "[m]ore than once a prosecutor, and sometimes a judge, interfered and redirected the examination in Ivy's favor."[21]

Defendants also cross-examined expert witnesses on two separate occasions in *Farben*, in each case with the prosecution's blessing. First, because of his experience as the chief of Farben's Technical Committee, Fritz ter Meer cross-examined Brigadier General J.H. Morgan concerning Allied efforts after World War I to prevent Germany from rearming in the chemical field. Later, three defendants—ter Meer again, Buetefisch, and Ambros—each cross-examined Dr. Nathaniel Ellis, a prosecution chemical expert.[22]

5. Scope of Examination

Because Ordinance No. 7 simply guaranteed the right to call witnesses, the tribunals had complete discretion to determine the scope of examination on direct, cross, and re-direct. In general, those issues were uncontroversial and followed normal American trial practice. The most significant controversy concerned limits that some of the tribunals imposed on defense and prosecution examination. One troubling example was mentioned above: limiting Rose's cross-examination of Ivy to 30 minutes, a decision that can only be explained as a deliberate attempt by the *Medical* tribunal to blunt Rose's effectiveness. More often, however, tribunals limited prosecution questioning. In *RuSHA*, the prosecution reluctantly agreed prior to trial that it would cross-examine defendants for no more than 30 minutes and defense witnesses for no more than 10 minutes[23]—neither of which seems adequate. Even more problematically, the *Farben* tribunal announced in the middle of trial that the prosecution's cross-examination of defendants and defense witnesses would be limited to 20 percent of the time the defense spent on direct examination. That limit had a significant effect on the prosecution: the judges twice cut off questioning before prosecutors had completed their questioning, once when a defendant was on the stand, and once when a critical defense witness—the most important non-defendant Farben official involved in the use of slave labor from Auschwitz—was testifying.[24]

---

[20] Freyhofer, 98. [21] Ibid., 97.
[22] XV TWC 342. [23] Ibid., 686.
[24] Ibid., 702–7, extract from *Farben* transcript, 14 Apr. 1948.

B. Taking Evidence Via Commissioners

Perhaps sensitive to the optics of cutting off the prosecution during cross-examination, the *Farben* tribunal later suggested that, if the prosecution needed more time, it could continue its cross-examination before commissioners.[25] Such out-of-court questioning was permitted by Article V(e) of Ordinance No. 7, which authorized the tribunals "to appoint officers for the carrying out of any task designated by the tribunals including the taking of evidence on commission." Article V(e) was itself based on—and identical with—Article 17(e) of the London Charter.

During the IMT trial, commissioners had heard more than 100 witnesses and received more than 1,800 affidavits concerning the "Accused Organisations."[26] The NMTs used commissions in five cases: *Justice, Flick, Farben, Krupp,* and *Ministries.* In each case, the tribunal appointed commissioners (as few as one, as many as three); representatives appeared for the prosecution and the defense; and examination proceeded as it would at trial. The transcript of the proceedings was then "considered by the Tribunal in all respects as if the proceedings had been had, the interrogations made, and the testimony given before the full Tribunal."[27]

Commissions were used sparingly in *Justice* and *Flick.* In the *Justice* case, three members of Tribunal III—two regular members and the alternate—served as commissioners, so the commission sat only when the court itself was not in session. The commissioners heard the testimony of 13 prosecution witnesses.[28] In *Flick,* a commission heard the testimony of only one witness—Albert Speer. Tribunal IV appointed John H.E. Fried to serve as the commissioner, because Speer was serving his sentence in Spandau Prison in Berlin and the OCC was unable to arrange for him to be temporarily transferred to Nuremberg.[29] Commissioners were used much more extensively in *Farben,* in most cases to hear the cross-examination of prosecution and defense witnesses who had submitted affidavits in lieu of direct testimony. Two commissioners heard the testimony of nearly 50 witnesses.

The use of commissioners led to significant controversy in *Krupp.* Toward the end of the prosecution's case-in-chief, Tribunal III appointed a commissioner, Carl I. Dietz, to hear cross-examination of a number of prosecution witnesses who had submitted affidavits in lieu of direct examination. To save time, the tribunal instructed Dietz to hold the hearings while court was in session. The defense objected vociferously to the simultaneous proceedings, arguing that they deprived the defendants of their right under Ordinance No. 7 to be present at trial. The tribunal overruled the objection, holding that the right to be present did not apply to commissions and that there were more than enough defense attorneys to cover both the trial and the commission hearings.[30] The defense continued to object until the tribunal insisted that it would hear no further argument. At that point, the

---

[25] XV TWC 706.   [26] IMT Judgment, 2.
[27] *Justice,* Order, 12 June 1947, XV TWC 595.   [28] Ibid., 587.
[29] Ibid., 588.   [30] Ibid., 614, extract from *Krupp* transcript, 16 Jan. 1948.

defense attorneys stormed out of the courtroom *en masse*,[31] the remarkable event discussed in Chapter 4.

Tribunal IV increasingly relied on commissioners as the *Ministries* trial progressed. During the prosecution's case-in-chief, commissioners heard the testimony of a number of its witnesses. The tribunal then ordered that all documentary evidence would be taken by commission and appointed two members of the tribunal, Judges Powers and Maguire, to hear evidence on behalf of defendants Otto Meissner and Friedrich Gaus. Finally, after 10 of the 21 defendants had completed their cases-in-chief, the tribunal ruled that commissioners would hear the testimony of all defense witnesses until the defendants had finished testifying and would hear all rebuttal and surrebuttal testimony until the trial was completed.[32] The defense immediately objected, arguing—not without reason—that the ruling introduced "a fundamental deviation from and challenge to the principle of direct presentation of evidence before the ruling Tribunal itself," and that the 11 defendants who had not completed their cases-in-chief were "going to be prejudiced compared with the cases in chief already presented and also compared with the case in chief of the prosecution, which has already taken place."[33] The tribunal rejected both arguments, noting with regard to the latter that it would not be able to remember the massive amount of live testimony it had heard and would thus have to rely on the same kind of transcripts that were generated by the commissions.[34]

C. Testimony by Defendants

Following IMT precedent, each NMT defendant was allowed to testify under oath during his case-in-chief and to give an unsworn statement to the tribunal after his counsel's closing argument. In almost every case, defendants availed themselves of both opportunities. The primary exception was *Krupp*, in which none of the defendants testified and only two—Alfried Krupp and Ewald Loeser—gave unsworn final statements. Seven of the 12 defendants did take the stand, however, to challenge the voluntariness of their pre-trial statements,[35] an issue discussed in the next chapter. No adverse inference could be drawn from a defendant's failure to testify under oath.[36]

Upon the conclusion of a defendant's direct testimony, counsel for his co-defendants were required to cross-examine him—the same practice the IMT followed.[37] The judges would occasionally question the defendant, as well, and in at least one case—*Pohl*—the judges even recalled a defendant during rebuttal to

[31] Ibid., 589.
[32] Ibid., 620, *Ministries*, Order, 23 July 1948.
[33] Ibid., 621–2, extract from *Ministries* transcript, 29 July 1948.
[34] Ibid., 623.
[35] *Krupp*, IX TWC 2.
[36] Letter from Brand to Young, 18 Oct. 1948, 6.
[37] Ibid., 716.

question him a second time.[38] Judge Musmanno was particularly notorious for his active questioning; as Earl notes, "when he felt that a defendant was being less than frank in his responses to the court ... he would relentlessly question a defendant until he either recanted his testimony or admitted to his actions."[39]

III. Documentary Evidence

Many scholars have noted that the IMT trial was primarily document-driven.[40] Witness testimony played a much more significant role in the NMT trials, yet nearly every trial still involved hundreds if not thousands of documents—captured German records, pre-trial statements by the defendants, witness affidavits, and so on. The fewest documents, 171, were introduced in *Milch*. The most, 3,712, were introduced in *Ministries*.[41] In all but three cases—*Milch*, *Pohl*, and *Flick*—the defense relied more heavily on documents than the prosecution, sometimes introducing more than twice as many into evidence.

The admissibility of documentary evidence was, therefore, a critical issue at the NMTs. The general rule, cited earlier, was straightforward: the tribunals were required to admit any document that had probative value, including "affidavits, depositions, interrogations and other statements, diaries, letters, the records, findings, statements and judgments of the military tribunals and the reviewing and confirming authorities of any of the United Nations." Tribunal practice, however, was far messier. As this section demonstrates, the tribunals excluded a wide variety of documentary evidence that satisfied the literal requirements of Article VII.

A. Affidavits, Depositions, Interrogations, and Other Statements

1. Statements in Lieu of Oath

The tribunals rarely distinguished between affidavits, depositions, interrogations, and other statements, normally referring to all four simply as "affidavits." There were, however, three important differences between "affidavits, depositions, and interrogations" and "other statements." First, unlike affidavits, depositions, and interrogations, "other statements" were not sworn. Second, because "other statements" were not sworn, they were admissible only if they satisfied Rule 21 of the URP, which required statements made "in lieu of oath" to be signed by the witness and certified by a defense attorney, a notary, a *Burgermeister* (Mayor), or a competent prison-camp authority. The certification requirement was designed to ensure that the person making the statement was aware that there could be consequences for testifying falsely.[42] Third, at least one tribunal—Tribunal III in the *Justice*

---

[38] Ibid., 682.   [39] Earl, 242.
[40] See, e.g., Joseph E. Persico, *Nuremberg: Infamy on Trial* 92 (2000).
[41] NMT Trial Statistics, TTP-5-1-2-25, at 1.
[42] OCCWC, Memo on Review of Rulings on Points of Procedure and Law, TTP-5-1-1-9, at 16 (Case 1, 2/12/47, 2922–3).

case—suggested that, as a general matter, sworn statements had greater probative value than unsworn statements.[43]

The tribunals almost always excluded "other statements" that did not satisfy Rule 21, even though Rule 22 permitted them to admit such statements if it was impossible or unduly burdensome for the defense to comply with Rule 21's requirements.[44] They also tended to apply Rule 21 literally, as demonstrated by the *Medical* tribunal's refusal to admit an unsworn witness statement that was made in front of a German prosecutor.[45]

2. Affidavits by Available Witnesses

The prosecution and the defense each made liberal use of affidavits in lieu of live testimony, although—as with documents generally—the defense tended to rely on them far more heavily. In *Pohl*, for example, the prosecution called 21 witnesses and introduced 95 affidavits, while the defense called 27 witnesses and introduced 416 affidavits.[46] Similarly, in *Farben*, the prosecution called 87 witnesses and introduced 419 affidavits, while the defense called 102 witnesses and introduced 2,394 affidavits.[47]

When an affiant was available and the opposing party sought to cross-examine him on the contents of the affidavit, the tribunals were uniformly willing to order the witness be produced for cross-examination by the tribunal or a commissioner.[48] The prosecution routinely waived cross-examination for all but the most important defense affiants,[49] as did the defense in some trials, such as the *Medical* case.[50] In other trials, however, the defense insisted on cross-examining a significant percentage of the prosecution's affiants. In the *Justice* case, for example, the prosecution was required to produce nearly 50 affiants, an administrative burden that Zeck estimates delayed the trial by nearly six weeks.[51] The tribunals often went to great lengths to secure cross-examination, as illustrated by the *Milch* tribunal's willingness to send a commissioner to Spandau Prison in Berlin to examine Albert Speer.

Although the tribunals were normally able to arrange for the cross-examination of available affiants, there were a number of situations in which such affiants nevertheless refused to appear. Such situations posed a difficult legal dilemma for the tribunals, because Ordinance No. 7 was unclear concerning whether the defense had a right to cross-examine witnesses who submitted affidavits in lieu of testifying. The defense insisted that it did, citing Article IV(e) of the Ordinance, which provided that a defendant "shall have the right through his counsel . . . to

[43] Ibid., 23 (Case 3, 3/24/47, 958–65).
[44] XV TWC 777.
[45] Memo on Review of Rulings, 15–6 (Case 1, 1/16/47, 1809–11).
[46] *Pohl*, V TWC 195.
[47] *Farben*, VII TWC 3.
[48] Extract from *RuSHA* transcript, 10 Nov. 1947, XV TWC 827.
[49] Taylor, *Final Report*, 99.
[50] *Medical*, II TWC 780.
[51] William Allen Zeck, "Nuremberg: Proceedings Subsequent to Goering et al.," 26 *N.C. L. Rev.* 350, 370 (1948).

cross-examine any witness called by the prosecution."[52] The prosecution disagreed, pointing out that Article VII did not condition the admissibility of affidavits on the ability of the opposing party to cross-examine the affiant.[53]

Perhaps not surprisingly, the tribunals reached different conclusions concerning the admissibility of affidavits by available witnesses who refused to testify. Of the nine tribunals that specifically considered the issue, five—two early, three late—held that such affidavits were admissible even in the absence of cross-examination: *Medical, Milch, Einsatzgruppen, Ministries,* and *High Command.* Tribunal V's statement in *High Command* was typical: although it informed the defense that it could submit written interrogatories to the available witness in question—an American officer who had certified the authenticity of the film "The Nazi Plan"—it reminded them that "these affidavits, under the basic authority, are admissible, and that would be true . . . whether or not the affiants are available for cross-examination."[54]

Four other tribunals, by contrast, refused to admit affidavits given by available witnesses who refused to appear. In *Krupp,* Tribunal III announced at the beginning of trial that, "exercising its right to construe" Ordinance No. 7, "it would not consider any affidavit unless the affiant was made available for cross-examination or unless the presentation of the affiant for cross-examination had been waived."[55] Tribunal II held likewise in *Pohl,* justifying its categorical rule on the ground that the issue "involves a rather fundamental principle of American jurisprudence; that is, a right to be confronted by your witness and to cross-examine him if he is available."[56] The *Hostage* and *Farben* tribunals reached similar conclusions,[57] the latter over the impassioned dissents of Judge Hebert[58] and the alternate, Judge Merrell.[59]

3. Affidavits by Unavailable Witnesses

The tribunals also faced a number of situations in which the prosecution or the defense offered an affidavit of a witness who was not available to testify, either because of logistical problems or because the affiant had died in the interim. As with affidavits by available witnesses, the tribunals took different positions regarding the admissibility of such affidavits.

a. Living Affiants

Not surprisingly, all of the tribunals that admitted affidavits of available witnesses also admitted the affidavits of witnesses who were alive but unavailable. In the

---

[52] See, e.g., extract from *High Command* transcript, 10 Nov. 1947, XV TWC 838.
[53] See, e.g., ibid., 886, extract from *Farben* transcript, 4 Nov. 1947.
[54] Ibid.
[55] *Krupp,* IX TWC 1328.
[56] Extract from *Pohl* transcript, 9 Apr. 1947, XV TWC 818.
[57] *Hostage,* XI TWC 1259; *Farben,* VIII TWC 1084.
[58] Extract from *Farben* transcript, 11 May 1948, XV TWC 865.
[59] Ibid., 1045, statement of Judge Merrell.

Medical case, for example, Tribunal I admitted the defense affidavit of Dr. Hans Jaedicke even though he was being held in an English internment camp and the tribunal could not make arrangements for him to be brought to Nuremberg.[60] Before admitting such affidavits, however, the tribunals normally used their "utmost endeavors" to procure cross-examination via written interrogatories prepared by the opposing party.[61]

The *Pohl* tribunal, it is worth noting, was more flexible concerning affidavits of unavailable witnesses than affidavits of available ones. The tribunal was unwilling to admit the affidavits of two prosecution witnesses being held in Dachau, because it believed that the prosecution could obtain their live testimony. But it was willing to admit the prosecution affidavit of Rudolf Hoess, the notorious commandant of Auschwitz, who was on trial in Poland. As for cross-examination, Judge Toms told the defense that it would have to be satisfied with introducing the transcript of Hoess's testimony at the IMT, because "[t]hat is the best that can be done. We cannot produce this man."[62]

Three tribunals, by contrast, categorically refused to admit affidavits of living but unavailable witnesses. The *Farben* tribunal stated in its judgment that "[i]n instances where the witnesses could not be cross-examined, counter affidavits procured, or answers to interrogatories obtained, the tribunal, on motion, struck the affidavits from the evidence."[63] The *Hostage* and *Krupp* tribunals did likewise.[64] Interestingly, Judge Wilkins, one of the judges in *Krupp*, later acknowledged that Tribunal III specifically relied on U.S. law to reject prosecution affidavits of six Polish witnesses who could not testify concerning Krupp's use of slave labor because they were trapped in East Berlin by the Russians. "Although these affidavits were admissible under international law," he wrote, "under the rules by which we were operating, we sustained the defense's objections to the admission as we felt to admit them would be contrary to our training and our American system of justice."[65]

b. Deceased Affiants

In almost every trial, either the prosecution or the defense attempted to introduce the affidavits of witnesses who had either committed suicide or been executed prior to trial. The first five tribunals—*Medical, Milch, Justice, Pohl,* and *Flick*—all admitted such affidavits, including the transcript of Hermann Goering's interrogation prior to the IMT trial, which was introduced by the prosecution in *Milch* and by the defense in *Flick*.[66] The final three tribunals—*Einsatzgruppen, Ministries,* and *High Command*—took the same approach.[67]

---

[60] Ibid., 792, extract from *Medical* transcript, 25 Feb. 1947.
[61] See, e.g., ibid., 840, extract from *High Command* transcript, 9 Mar. 1948.
[62] Ibid., 818, extract from *Pohl* transcript, 9 Apr. 1947.
[63] *Farben*, VIII TWC 1084.
[64] *Hostage*, XI TWC 1259; *Krupp*, IX TWC 830.
[65] Wilkins, 217.
[66] *Farben*, Prosecution Motion for Reconsideration, 29 Nov. 1947, XV TWC 893.
[67] Ibid., 880.

The *Farben* tribunal, by contrast, refused to distinguish between affidavits of deceased witnesses and affidavits by living but unavailable witnesses. For example, it excluded the pre-IMT interrogation of Fritz Sauckel, executed at Nuremberg, even though—as Drexel Sprecher pointed out in oral argument—both the *Milch* and *Flick* tribunals had admitted it.[68] Both Judge Herbert and the alternate, Judge Merrell, dissented from the majority's decision.[69] The *Krupp* tribunal followed the *Farben* approach.[70]

4. Probative Value of Non-Examined Witness Statements

Although the majority of tribunals admitted affidavits given by witnesses who could not be cross-examined, they agreed that the absence of cross-examination significantly diminished their probative value.[71] In *Einsatzgruppen*, for example, Tribunal II admitted an affidavit by an unlocated German soldier that identified the defendant Ruehl as the leader of a Kommando unit, but held that "the Tribunal cannot ascribe to this lone piece of evidence the strength needed to sustain so momentous a weight as the leadership of a Kommando with its concomitant responsibility for executions."[72] Indeed, the tribunals generally took the position that an affidavit that was not tested by cross-examination could not, by itself, prove a disputed issue beyond reasonable doubt. Two rulings in *Ministries* illustrate the point. The first concerned a series of affidavits given by Karl J. Burckhardt, the International Commissioner for Danzig, that incriminated the defendant von Weizsaecker regarding the invasion of Poland. Tribunal IV admitted the affidavits, but refused to rely upon them "except insofar as they are corroborated from other sources," because the judges found it "difficult to reconcile a willingness, personal or governmental, to permit an ex parte statement to be given and an unwillingness to permit inquiry as to the accuracy of the statement."[73] By contrast, the tribunal gave far more weight to an affidavit submitted by an executed witness—Gabor Vanja, the Szalasi government's Minister of the Interior—that connected the defendant Gottlob Berger to the deportation of Hungarian Jews. The tribunal noted that although it would not have convicted Berger if the case against him "rested upon the affidavit alone," in this case Vanja's affidavit was "corroborated by evidence given by Berger himself, and which already establishes that he was an active party in the program of the persecution, enslavement, and murder of the Jews."[74]

---

[68] Ibid., 887, extract from *Farben* transcript, 4 Nov. 1947.
[69] Ibid., 866, extract from *Farben* transcript, 11 May 1948; ibid., 1045, statement of Judge Merrell.
[70] Ibid., 880.
[71] Available witnesses: see, e.g., *Ministries*, XIV TWC 445. Unavailable witnesses: see, e.g., *Einsatzgruppen*, IV TWC 579. Deceased witnesses: see XV TWC 880.
[72] *Einsatzgruppen*, IV TWC 579.
[73] *Ministries*, XIV TWC 357.
[74] Ibid., 541.

5. Pre-Trial Statements by Defendants

In each of the 12 cases, the prosecution introduced into evidence statements made by the defendants prior to trial. Some of those statements were transcripts of pre-trial interrogations; others were affidavits prepared by interrogators describing an interrogation that the defendants had reviewed and signed. The tribunals did not distinguish between the two kinds of statements, referring to both simply as "affidavits."

Defendants first challenged the admissibility of such affidavits in the *Medical* case, when one objected that he had not been warned about the possibility of self-incrimination prior to interrogation. Tribunal I overruled the objection on the ground that the defendant was free to explain the circumstances of his statement when he took the stand.[75] The *Justice* tribunal rejected a similar claim, holding that the prosecution was not required to warn a suspect that incriminating statements could be used against him until he had been formally indicted.[76]

The defendants mounted their most concerted attack on the admissibility of pre-trial affidavits in *Farben*. Initially, following in the footsteps of their brethren in the *Medical* and *Justice* trials, they objected that "Anglo-Saxon trial procedure" did not permit the prosecution to use incriminating affidavits against them.[77] The *Farben* tribunal overruled the objection, pointing out that such affidavits were admissible as statements against interest. The tribunal noted, however, that it would exclude any pre-trial statement made by a defendant that was obtained under duress[78]—a ruling that would ultimately lead the tribunal to exclude incriminating statements made by the defendant Schmitz, an issue discussed in the next chapter.

Having lost the self-incrimination argument, the *Farben* defendants then focused on the fact that many of the pre-trial affidavits incriminated not only the affiant, but also one or more of the affiant's co-defendants. Citing both Article IV(e) of Ordinance No. 7 and the U.S. Constitution, they argued that unless the defendant who made the statement chose to testify—thereby opening himself to cross-examination—his affidavit was only admissible against the defendant himself. The tribunal agreed.[79]

That ruling had a significant effect on the prosecution's case. For example, the prosecution's claim that Farben's Vorstand was aware that Hitler intended to invade Poland depended heavily on a series of pre-trial admissions to that effect made by the defendant von Schnitzler. Because von Schnitzler elected not to testify at trial, the tribunal held that "his statements are evidence only as to the maker and are excluded from consideration in determining the guilt or innocence of other

---

[75] Memo on Review of Rulings, 14 (Case 1: 1/3/47, 1078–9, 2094).
[76] Ibid., 19 (Case 3, 3/27/47, 1171–2).
[77] Extract from *Farben* transcript, 28 Aug. 1947, XV TWC 855.
[78] *Farben*, VIII TWC 1084.
[79] Ibid.

defendants."[80] The tribunal then later dismissed the crimes against peace charges on the ground that the prosecution had offered "mere conjecture" concerning the defendant's knowledge of the Nazis' intent to wage aggressive war.[81]

Judge Hebert and Judge Merrell dissented from the majority's approach to pre-trial affidavits given by defendants—as they had from the majority's approach to affidavits generally. Both pointed out that the majority had provided the defendants with a perverse incentive not to testify. Regarding von Schnitzler, for example, Judge Hebert noted that "[t]he ruling of the Tribunal in this regard was tantamount to an open invitation to him to exercise his privilege of not testifying in the interest of his co-defendants. Its result was to deprive the Tribunal of the opportunity through the examination of von Schnitzler in open court to determine his credibility and to judge more intelligently what weight should be attached to these pretrial statements."[82]

Unfortunately, Judge Hebert and Judge Merrell's criticisms went unheeded. Tribunal III took the same approach to pre-trial affidavits in *Krupp*[83]—a fact that, according to Appleman, at least partially explains why none of the Krupp defendants chose to testify in the case.[84]

B. Captured Documents

Although affidavits were important, captured German documents—diaries, reports, orders, records, etc.—were the prosecution's primary source of evidence during the trials. Very few of those documents would have been admissible under common-law rules of evidence; as Tribunal V pointed out in the *Hostage* case, "the record is replete with testimony and exhibits which have been offered and received in evidence without foundation as to their authenticity and, in many cases where it is secondary in character, without proof of the usual conditions precedent to the admission of such evidence."[85] Article VII, however, provided that captured documents were automatically admissible, subject only to the proviso that a tribunal "afford the opposing party such opportunity to question the authenticity or probative value of such evidence as in the opinion of the tribunal the ends of justice require."

Although Article VII placed the burden of challenging the authenticity of a captured document on the party opposing its admission, the prosecution began all of the trials by using two affidavits to establish the general authenticity of the captured documents it intended to introduce in evidence. The first affidavit had been prepared by Major William Coogan, the Chief of the Documentation Division in Justice Jackson's office. It explained how Coogan's Field Branch had

---

[80]   *Farben*, VIII TWC 1120.

[81]   Ibid., 1115.

[82]   *Farben*, Hebert Concurrence, VIII TWC 1232. For Judge Merrell's position, see Statement of Judge Merrell, XV TWC 1048.

[83]   *Krupp*, IX TWC 1328.

[84]   Appleman, 209–10.

[85]   *Hostage*, XI TWC 1257.

collected, stored, recorded, and processed all of the documents captured in the European Theater that the prosecution had used during the IMT trial.[86] The second affidavit was prepared by Fred Niebergall, the Chief of the OCC's Document Control Branch. It described how his organization had processed all of the captured German documents that the OCC intended to use during the NMT trials that had not been introduced at the IMT.[87]

The prosecution also submitted a certificate of authenticity with each captured document it introduced at trial.[88] The certificates themselves, which were prepared by employees in the OCC's Evidence Division, described the document in question and attested that it was either the original or a true copy of "a document found in German archives, records and files captured by military forces under the command of the Supreme Commander, Allied Expeditionary Forces."[89] The defendants rarely provided certificates of authenticity for the captured documents on which they relied, and the prosecution rarely challenged a document's authenticity. When it did, however, the tribunal would admit the document subject to the defense later providing the necessary certification.[90]

The tribunals relied on Article VII to admit—usually over defense objection—a wide variety of potentially unreliable captured documents. In the *Justice* case, for example, Tribunal III admitted a document whose author and addressee were unknown[91] and a letter allegedly written by a defendant that was a copy, unsigned, and did not indicate that the defendant had ever sent the letter.[92] Similarly, in *Pohl*, Tribunal II admitted a document that was unsigned, undated, and did not identify the office from which it originated, although the tribunal indicated that it did not believe the document had much probative value.[93] The tribunals even occasionally admitted documents that did not technically qualify as captured, ruling that those documents nevertheless bore similar indicia of reliability. Tribunal III used that argument in the *Justice* case, for example, to admit unsworn statements taken by German authorities that had been reduced to writing and included in a case-file.[94]

Many of the captured documents relied on by the prosecution were extremely long. In some of the trials, the prosecution introduced such documents into evidence in their entirety. That practice was uncontroversial, although the defense in *Einsatzgruppen* challenged one of the prosecution's documents on the ground that it was not complete. The prosecution acknowledged its error and procured the missing pages from the archives in D.C.[95] In other trials, the prosecution only

---

[86] Coogan Affidavit, XV TWC 124–5.

[87] Ibid., 128, Niebergall Affidavit.

[88] See, e.g., Memo on Review of Rulings, 28 (Case 1, 3/12/47, 4807–9).

[89] See XV TWC 646. Mendelsohn questions the reliability of the prosecution's certification process, pointing out that the same employee often certified hundreds of captured documents per day. Mendelsohn, 159 & 168 n. 5.

[90] See, e.g., excerpt from the *Medical* case, 28 Feb. 1947, XV TWC 650.

[91] Memo on Review of Rulings, 30 (Case 3, 3/11/47, 432).

[92] Ibid. (Case 3, 3/27/47, 1183).

[93] Ibid., 36 (Case 4, 4/9/47, 104–8).

[94] Ibid., 24 (Case 3, 3/24/47, 993–1005).

[95] XV TWC 637.

introduced certified extracts of a long document into evidence. In such situations, the tribunals uniformly granted defense requests to introduce into evidence other parts of the document that the defense believed were relevant.[96] That process was normally unproblematic, although there were cases in which the prosecution did not always have the entire document in its possession. In the *Hostage* case, for example, the defense objected to the prosecution's attempt to introduce extracts of reports made to the Wehrmacht Commander Southeast. The prosecution admitted that it did not have the remaining pages, but insisted that the D.C. archives had forwarded all of the pages that had "a substantial bearing on the case." Tribunal V did not consider that representation to be adequate and ordered the prosecution to either have the documents transferred to Nuremberg or permit the defense to examine the documents in D.C. If it did not, the tribunal warned, "it will be presumed that the evidence withheld which could have been produced or made available to the defendants, would be unfavorable to the prosecution."[97] The prosecution arranged to have all of the documents shipped by air to Nuremberg.

IV. Judicial Notice, *Res Judicata*, and Precedent

A. Judicial Notice

Article IX of Ordinance No. 7 required the tribunals to take judicial notice of three kinds of evidence: (1) "facts of common knowledge"; (2) "official governmental documents and reports of any of the United Nations, including the acts and documents of the committees set up in the various Allied countries for the investigation of war crimes"; and (3) "the records and findings of military or of other tribunals of any of the United Nations." Judicial notice of "facts of common knowledge" never provoked controversy during the trials, and the defense challenged judicial notice of "official government documents" only in the *Medical* case, with regard to a report prepared by the Dutch War Crimes Investigation Bureau. Tribunal I overruled the objection on the ground that the Netherlands qualified as an Ally.[98]

By contrast, the defense often challenged judicial notice of the "records and findings" of other tribunals. When those challenges concerned documents that were part of the IMT record, the tribunals nearly always held that notice was proper. In the *Medical* case, for example, the defense argued that affidavits contained in a report prepared by a commission investigating atrocities committed at Dachau were not admissible under Article IX, even if the report itself was. Tribunal I admitted the affidavits on the ground that they had been received by the IMT and thus qualified as IMT "records."[99] Indeed, the only time a tribunal accepted a defense challenge was in the *Justice* case, when the prosecution made the startling argument that

[96] Memo on Review of Rulings, 10 (Case 1, 3/10/47, 3990).
[97] *Hostage*, Tribunal Order on the Defense Motion, 14 Aug. 1947, XV TWC 411.
[98] Memo on Review of Rulings, 53 (Case 1, 1/10/47, 1496).
[99] Ibid. (Case 1, 12/13/46, 413).

Tribunal III was entitled to take judicial notice of *any* item of evidence in the IMT record—any affidavit, document, or pre-trial statement—regardless of whether the IMT had relied on that evidence in its judgment. The tribunal rejected the prosecution's argument, noting that, taken to its logical conclusion, it would require the judges to take notice of documents that the IMT had received into evidence but ultimately found "to be incorrect or untrue." It thus held that the term "record" in Article IX was limited to evidence that had been specifically approved in the IMT judgment.[100]

The defendants were more successful when they challenged the admissibility of "records and findings" of other NMTs. In *Farben*, for example, the defense objected when the prosecution attempted to introduce an extract of testimony that had been given by Karl Lindemann, a member of Himmler's Circle of Friends, in *Flick*. Although that testimony was clearly admissible under Article IX, Tribunal VI nevertheless held that—as with affidavits generally—it would admit the extract only if the prosecution produced Lindemann for cross-examination.[101]

B. *Res Judicata*

Article X of Ordinance No. 7 made certain aspects of the IMT judgment binding on the NMTs. It read:

The determinations of the International Military Tribunal in the judgments in Case No. 1 that invasions, aggressive acts, aggressive wars, crimes, atrocities or inhumane acts were planned or occurred, shall be binding on the tribunals established hereunder and shall not be questioned except insofar as the participation therein or knowledge thereof by any particular person may be concerned. Statements of the International Military Tribunal in the judgment in Case No. 1 constitute proof of the facts stated, in the absence of substantial new evidence to the contrary.

Four tribunals relied on Article X to find a determination in the IMT judgment *res judicata*. The *Einsatzgruppen* tribunal recognized the IMT's finding that the invasion of Poland was an act of aggression[102]; the *Milch*, *Pohl*, and *Farben* tribunals recognized the IMT's findings concerning the deportation and use of slave labor[103]; and the *Pohl* tribunal recognized the IMT's finding that the Nazis had systematically pillaged occupied countries.[104]

It is unclear why the tribunals did not rely more heavily on Article X. The best explanation seems to be that they believed it was unfair to the defendants to recognize an IMT determination that a particular crime had been committed, even though such recognition did not relieve the prosecution of proving the defendant's individual responsibility for the crime. That explanation is consistent with the tribunals' general willingness to allow defendants to challenge IMT

[100] Extract from *Justice* transcript, 29 Apr. 1947, XV TWC 580–5.
[101] Ibid., 906, extract from *Farben* transcript, 21 Nov. 1947.
[102] *Einsatzgruppen*, IV TWC 457.
[103] *Milch*, II TWC 785; *Pohl*, V TWC 970; *Farben*, VIII TWC 1172.
[104] *Pohl*, V TWC 976.

determinations on the ground that "substantial new evidence" contradicted them—challenges that, read literally, Article X permitted only with regard to IMT "statements." The *Ministries* tribunal, for example, made no apology for allowing the defendants to challenge the IMT's determinations concerning crimes against peace:

Notwithstanding the provisions in Article X of Ordinance No. 7 . . . we have permitted the defense to offer evidence upon all these matters. In so doing we have not considered this article to be a limitation on the right of the Tribunal to consider any evidence which may lead to a just determination of the facts. If in this we have erred, it is an error which we do not regret, as we are firmly convinced that courts of justice must always remain open to the ascertainment of the truth and that every defendant must be accorded an opportunity to present the facts.[105]

Even tribunals that did rely on Article X permitted such challenges. In *Milch*, Tribunal II noted with regard to the deportation and slave-labor program that "[a]ny new evidence which was presented was in no way contradictory of the findings of the [IMT] but, on the contrary, ratified and affirmed them."[106] And in *Farben*, Tribunal VI pointed out that the defense had not even bothered to question those findings.[107]

C. Precedent

Although Article IX required a tribunal to take judicial notice of previous tribunals' "records and findings," it did not specifically require a tribunal to treat such records and findings as *res judicata*. The tribunals thus uniformly held they were free to reject the legal and factual findings of their predecessors. As Tribunal IV said in *Flick* regarding Article X's IMT provisions, "[t]here is no similar mandate either as to findings of fact or conclusions of law contained in judgments of coordinate Tribunals. The tribunal will take judicial notice of the judgments but will treat them as advisory only."[108] The prosecution agreed with that position, although it urged the tribunals to give previous legal and factual findings "great weight."[109] Ironically, that position came back to haunt the prosecution in *Farben*, when Judge Hebert relied on the acquittals in *Krupp* to justify his decision to concur in the majority's decision to acquit the defendants of crimes against peace. "I am concurring," he wrote, "though realizing that on the vast volume of credible evidence presented to the Tribunal, if the issues here involved were truly questions of first impression, a contrary result might as easily be reached by other triers of the facts more inclined to draw inferences of the character usually warranted in ordinary criminal cases."[110]

---

[105] *Ministries*, XIV TWC 317.   [106] *Milch*, II TWC 785.
[107] *Farben*, VIII TWC 1172.   [108] *Flick*, VI TWC 1190.
[109] See, e.g., *Ministries*, Oral Argument of the Prosecution on the Defense Motion to Dismiss Count Four, 2 Mar. 1948, XIII TWC 83.
[110] *Farben*, Hebert Concurrence, VIII TWC 1212.

Conclusion

Modern international tribunals have often been criticized for admitting evidence—particularly hearsay—that the common law views as unreliable.[111] On the surface, the NMTs appear to be no different: Ordinance No. 7 required the tribunals to "admit any evidence which they deem to have probative value," including documents that lacked even the most basic indicia of authenticity. In practice, however, the tribunals did everything they could to ensure that their "free proof" approach to admissibility did not undermine the fairness of the trials. They took the burden of proof seriously, acquitting defendants even when there was significant evidence of their guilt. They were willing to innovate procedurally, such as allowing defendants to conduct cross-examinations, when they believed that doing so would improve the quality of a trial. They went to great lengths to ensure that defendants were able to cross-examine the witnesses against them, even though nothing in the Ordinance No. 7 required them to do so. They refused to convict solely on the basis of hearsay. And they allowed defendants to challenge the findings and conclusions of the IMT, despite the fact that they were technically *res judicata*.

---

[111] See, e.g., Peter Murphy, "No Free Lunch, No Free Proof," 8 *J. Int'l Crim. Just.* 539, 563–4 (2010).

7

Procedure

Introduction

The procedural rules applied by the NMTs were based on the same three sources of law as the rules of evidence: Ordinance No. 7, the Uniform Rules of Procedure, and the "fundamental principles of justice which have been accepted and adopted by civilized nations generally." There was, however, an important difference between the two regimes: whereas the rules of evidence deviated substantially from the common-law tradition, "[a]ll of the tribunals . . . conducted their courts as nearly as possible in conformance with American trial practices."[1] Tribunal II specifically highlighted that distinction in *Pohl*, noting that "[t]he trial was conducted generally along the lines usually followed by the trial courts of the various states of the United States, except as to the rules of evidence, and this practice has prevailed throughout."[2]

This chapter focuses on three sets of procedural issues that were particularly controversial during the trials. Section I examines how the tribunals interpreted and applied the fair-trial rights guaranteed by Ordinance No. 7. Section II asks whether the defense had adequate resources during the trials. And Section III discusses the absence of appellate review and its substitute, joint sessions of the tribunals.

I. Fair Trial Rights

Article IV of Ordinance No. 7 guaranteed NMT defendants a range of fair trial rights, such as the right to counsel and the right to produce witnesses and documents. Paul Hebert, one of the judges in *Farben*, believed that the tribunals went to great lengths to ensure that the defendants received fair trials; indeed, he claimed after the trials were over that "in some of the cases, out of a desire to be so fair that the proceedings could not be subjected to any possible censure or criticism, there was a tendency to err in the direction of according a degree of latitude to the defense which would go far beyond anything we would consider permissible in criminal law proceedings under Anglo-American law."[3] Judge Hebert's assessment was generally

---

[1] Zeck, 368.   [2] *Pohl*, V TWC 959.
[3] Hebert, *Nurnberg Subsequent Trials*, 231.

accurate, as the following survey of how the tribunals interpreted Article IV demonstrates.

A. Indictment

As noted earlier, Article III of Ordinance No. 7 made the OCC solely responsible for deciding what charges to include in an indictment. A number of scholars have criticized the OCC's unreviewable authority. Douglass, for example, argued in the early 1970s that "[i]f there can be any criticism of a violation of due process in the trials under the Anglo-American concept of justice, it can be directed to the method of indictment of specific defendants for there were not even the rudimentary safeguards of the grand jury or other limitations on the prosecutorial authority."[4] Such criticism, however, is overstated: although the tribunals could not prevent the OCC from bringing specific charges against the defendants, they could—and often did—dismiss counts in an indictment on legal or evidentiary grounds. Tribunal IV's rejection of the pre-war crimes against humanity count in *Ministries* is an example of the former[5]; Tribunal III's decision to dismiss the crimes against peace counts in *Krupp*[6] is an example of the latter. Both decisions are discussed in later chapters.

Moreover, although no substitute for formal oversight, it is important to acknowledge that the OCC voluntarily dismissed allegations in an indictment whenever it concluded that it could not prove a defendant's guilt beyond a reasonable doubt. In *Flick*, the prosecution asked Tribunal IV to amend the indictment five separate times. Three of the changes significantly narrowed the slave-labor charges against Burkart, Terberger, and Weiss,[7] while the other two made clear that Flick was not responsible for the slave labor and spoliation charges involving the Siemag Company.[8] In *Farben*, the prosecution informed Tribunal VI at the end of its case-in-chief that, in order to assist Hoerlein prepare his defense, it was willing to stipulate with regard to Count 1 (crimes against peace) that "the evidence which it has presented has not established its burden of proof" concerning his involvement in Farben efforts to prevent the United States from developing atabrine and sulphur drugs.[9] And in *Ministries*, the prosecution not only formally withdrew the crimes against peace charges against Meissner because it concluded it could not prove them,[10] it also voluntarily dismissed the plunder and spoliation charges against him when the defense pointed out that it had not introduced "a single document to show [his] participation . . . in the offenses referred to in count six."[11]

---

[4] Douglass, 689.   [5] See Chapter 12.
[6] See Chapter 8.   [7] *Flick*, Indictment, VI TWC 14–5.
[8] Ibid., 16, 19.
[9] *Farben*, Prosecution Statement, 29 Jan. 1948, XV TWC 230.
[10] Ibid., 232, *Ministries*, Prosecution Closing Statement, 9 Nov. 1948.
[11] Ibid., *Ministries*, Order, 23 June 1948.

Ministries also involved the most unusual situation in which the prosecution voluntarily dismissed charges. Immediately after the prosecution rested, the defendant Bohle shocked the journalists present in the courtroom by asking Tribunal IV to allow him to plead guilty to two counts in the indictment, persecuting and forcibly transferring civilians (Count 5) and membership in the SS (Count 8).[12] Bohle's explanation was even more surprising: he told the media that "it would be irresponsible on my part to plead not guilty and thereby shift to others the burden of responsibility and its consequences," because "the Nurnberg courts and the courts in the American and British zones have already handed down verdicts of guilty for ... subordinates of mine."[13]

Bohle's request to change his plea might well have been sincere; he later called upon his fellow Nazis to "frankly admit the atrocities that have been committed ... and remove from the name of Germany the blot which the deeds of criminal brains have cast upon it."[14] But he also had a more practical reason: representatives of the OCC, headed by Robert Kempner, had promised to dismiss the crimes against peace charges (Counts 1 and 2) and the plunder charge (Count 6) in exchange for his guilty plea.

Unfortunately, Kempner had not bothered to discuss the deal with Taylor—and Taylor was livid when he found out about it. Kempner defended the plea bargain by arguing that the prosecution's case against Bohle was not particularly strong, that Bohle's plea would strengthen the case against the Foreign Office defendants, and—perhaps most interesting of all—that a guilty plea by a "well-known defendant" would "acknowledge the jurisdiction of the Nurnberg Courts before the U.S. and the German people."[15] Taylor, however, was "not impressed" with Kempner's defense. He rejected Kempner's jurisdiction argument, replying that "Bohle is not an expert on legal jurisdiction, and his opinion will be given weight by no one." He also did not understand how dismissing the crimes against peace charges against Bohle would strengthen the prosecution's case against the other "professional warmakers." Most importantly, though, he rejected the very idea of entering into a plea bargain with Bohle, insisting that "everyone will regard it as a 'deal', which in fact it obviously is," and that "[t]he whole business of making 'deals' has no place in the type of proceedings we are conducting here."[16]

Despite his opposition to the plea bargain, Taylor knew that the OCC's credibility depended on honoring it. With the tribunal's agreement, the prosecution attempted "to draw up a stipulation in the nature of a bill of particulars setting out the specific acts to which the defendant would plead guilty and the charges which the prosecution would withdraw."[17] When those negotiations broke down, Taylor decided to oppose Bohle's change of plea but nevertheless withdraw the

---

12 Ibid., 264–5, *Ministries*, Motion by Defendant Bohle, 27 Mar. 1948.
13 Press Release from Deane, 29 Mar. 1948, TTP-5-1-4-63.
14 Press Release from Deane, 24 July 1948, TTP-5-1-4-63, at 10.
15 Memo from Kempner to Taylor, 25 May 1948, TTP-5-1-4-63, at 1.
16 Memo from Taylor to Kempner, 25 May 1948, TTP-5-1-4-63, at 1.
17 Ibid.

charges the prosecution had agreed to drop. The prosecution's answer to Bohle's motion, however, did not hide his dissatisfaction with what had transpired:

It has never been the policy of the prosecution before any of the Nuernberg Tribunals to agree to dismiss charges appearing to the prosecution to be well founded in return for a plea of guilty in response to other charges. However, it appears that during the conferences referred to above certain representations were made by members of the prosecution staff on the basis of which counsel for the defendant Bohle may have been led to assume that the prosecution would agree to dismiss counts one, two and six of the indictment, and may have filed his plea of guilty on the basis of that assumption. Solely for that reason...the prosecution herewith respectfully moves that the name of the defendant Bohle be withdrawn from counts one, two, and six of the indictment.[18]

Bohle replied by asking the tribunal to accept his change of plea regarding his membership in the SS (Count 8) but allow him to withdraw his plea of guilty on the persecution and forcible transfer charges (Count 5).[19] The tribunal then dismissed Counts 1, 2, and 6; set aside Bohle's request to plead guilty to Count 5; and entered a plea of guilty to Count 8[20]—the first and only time during the NMT trials that a defendant pleaded guilty to one of the charges against him.

B. Right to Counsel

Article IV(c) of Ordinance No. 7 provided that "[a] defendant shall have the right to be represented by counsel of his own selection, provided such counsel shall be a person qualified under existing regulations to conduct cases before the courts of defendant's country, or any other person who may be specially authorized by the tribunal." Even if Article IV(c) had not guaranteed the right to counsel, however, the tribunal would have recognized it; as the *Krupp* tribunal pointed out, that right was a fundamental principle of justice and implicit in the very idea of a fair trial.[21]

Article IV(c) differed in one critical respect from the right-to-counsel provision in the London Charter, Article 16(d): whereas Article IV(c) required a defendant to be represented by counsel, Article 16(d) also gave a defendant "the right to conduct his own defense before the Tribunal." Nothing in the history of Ordinance No. 7 sheds light on whether the drafters intended to remove the right of self-representation, and the difference became moot when the judges adopted the Uniform Rules of Procedure. Unlike Article IV(c), Rule 7(a) of the URP returned to the Charter approach by providing that "[a] defendant shall have the right to conduct his own defense, or to be represented by counsel of his own selection."

No defendant ever chose to represent himself during the NMT trials. All of the defendants hired at least one main counsel, and many also employed one or more assistant counsel. More than 200 attorneys represented defendants during the

---

[18] *Ministries*, Answer of the Prosecution, 27 May 1948, XV TWC 266.
[19] Ibid., 267, *Ministries*, Reply of Defendant Bohle, 1 June 1948.
[20] Ibid., 268, *Ministries*, Order, 4 June 1948.
[21] *Krupp*, IX TWC 1331.

trials.[22] A few represented multiple defendants in the same trial. Alfred Seidl, for example, was main counsel to Fischer, Gebhardt, and Oberhauser in the *Medical* case. Others represented defendants in different trials, such as Carl Haensel, who was main counsel to Joel in *Justice*, Loerner in *Pohl*, Greifelt in *RuSHA*, and Steengracht von Moyland in *Ministries*.

1. German Attorneys

With the exception of two Americans and one Swiss, all of the attorneys who represented NMT defendants were German. The vast majority of the German attorneys had been associated with the Nazis either before or during the war: most had belonged to the Nazi Bar Association, and 136 had been members of either the National Socialist Party or one of its branches, including 10 members of the SS and 22 members of the SA.[23] Nevertheless, the Central Secretariat—which was responsible for securing counsel through its Defense Center—had decided prior to the first trial that Nazi affiliation, no matter how serious, would not disqualify an attorney from being appointed counsel to one of the defendants. The Secretary-General had thus negotiated an "informal understanding" with Bavarian authorities that the denazification tribunals would not initiate proceedings against any of the lawyers as long as an NMT defendant continued to retain them.[24]

Despite this general rule, an attorney's Nazi affiliation created problems for the tribunals on two occasions. The first concerned Ernst von Weizsaecker's request to have Hellmut Becker appointed as one of his counsel. When the Defense Center processed the questionnaire (*Fragenbogen*) that Becker filled out concerning his qualifications and political affiliations—a requirement for all NMT attorneys—it discovered that he had lied about not being a member of the Nazi Party, a serious violation of OMGUS policy. Von Weizsaecker was reluctant to hire a different attorney, because Becker had already spent considerable time preparing for the case. The Committee of Presiding Judges thus decided that Becker would be allowed to represent von Weizsaecker, but with the proviso that OMGUS would be free to bring charges against him after the *Ministries* trial was over.[25]

A more serious situation arose during the defense case in *Farben*. While Gajewski's main counsel, Ernst Achenbach, was away from Nuremberg on a tribunal-authorized trip, Bavarian authorities attempted to serve an arrest warrant on him that had been issued by the Nuremberg *Spruchkammer*, the local denazification board. According to the warrant, Achenbach had failed to submit the questionnaire required by the Liberation Law to the *Spruchkammer* and was believed—based on considerable evidence—to have played an important role in the extermination of French Jews

---

[22] 207 individuals appeared as counsel. In *High Command*, Schniewind's Main Counsel was a German Naval officer who was not an attorney. A few other assistant counsel did not have legal training. Taylor, *Final Report*, 47 n. 148.

[23] Ibid., 48.

[24] XV TWC 304–5.

[25] Ibid., 313, Extract from Minutes of the Committee of Presiding Judges, 2 Dec. 1947.

while he was an official in the German Embassy in Paris.[26] Achenbach refused to return to Nuremberg when he learned of the warrant and asked Tribunal VI to intervene on his behalf. Recognizing that it had no legal authority to interfere with the *Spruchkammer* but was obligated to protect Gajewski's right to counsel, the *Farben* tribunal instructed the Secretary General to ask the Bavarian authorities to delay the arrest warrant until the end of the trial. Unfortunately, the President of the Bavarian *Landesgericht* refused the request.[27] The tribunal thus had no choice but to permit Achenbach to resign as Gajewski's main counsel and replace him with Gajewski's assistant.[28]

2. Non-German Attorneys

The presence of three non-German attorneys at the NMTs distinguished them from the IMT, at which all of the defense attorneys were German.[29] The first non-German attorney appointed was Walter Vinassa, a Swiss attorney hired by Haefliger—a Swiss citizen who had acquired German citizenship during the war but renounced it afterward—in the *Farben* case. The second was Warren Magee, an American attorney hired by von Weizsaecker to serve as co-counsel for the *Ministries* trial. Hellmut Becker's motion seeking Magee's appointment argued that a "proper defense" for von Weisaecker required American as well as German counsel, because the tribunal was American, the judges and prosecutors were American, and the rules of procedure invoked both American and international law. Tribunal IV granted the motion on 29 December 1947, noting that it believed that, "as far as practicable, a defendant should be represented by counsel of his own choice." The judges emphasized, however, that the tribunal was international, not American, and that they considered the nationality of the judges and prosecutors "immaterial."[30]

The final non-German attorney was Joseph Robinson, an American attorney who represented von Buelow during the *Krupp* trial. Robinson had served during the war in the Judge Advocate General's office in D.C. and on General MacArthur's Board of Review in the Pacific Theater, an appellate military court that reviewed court-martial convictions. Tribunal III appointed Robinson as co-counsel to von Buelow's main counsel, Wolfgang Pohle, on 26 February 1948, and Robinson participated actively in the trial until April 5, when the tribunal found all the defendants not guilty on the crimes against peace charges.[31]

The tribunals also rejected the applications of two non-German attorneys. In *Farben*, the defendant von Schnitzler requested that an American attorney, Thomas

---

[26] Ibid., 318–9, Letter from the President of the Landesgericht, 10 Feb. 1948.

[27] Ibid., 317, Certificate of Secretary General Withholding Service of Warrant, 16 Feb. 1948.

[28] Ibid., 305.

[29] That was not an accident. In October 1945, senior British QCs, led by then-Attorney General Hartley Shawcross, had passed a controversial resolution condemning such representation as "contrary to the public interest." Kirsten Sellars, *The Rise and Rise of Human Rights* 25–6 (2002).

[30] *Farben*, Order, 29 Dec. 1947, XV TWC 326.

[31] Taylor, *Krupp Trial*, 198.

Allegretti, be appointed co-counsel. Allegretti was in Germany at the time as an official with the Army's European Exchange Service, but had been ordered to leave Germany by American authorities. The *Farben* tribunal informed Allegretti that his application did not adequately establish that he was still a member of the bar in good standing, and it then rejected the application when he "wholly failed" to amend it.[32]

The more dramatic rejection came in *Krupp*, when Alfried Krupp sought to hire an American attorney, Earl Carroll, to replace his original counsel, the legendary Otto Kranzbuehler. On 8 December 1947, the first day of trial, Krupp applied to the court to have the law firm "Foley and Carroll" of Hollywood, California, entered as his counsel of record. That application was accompanied by a letter signed by Earl Carroll stating only that "[a] competent associate to undertake the trial representation can be expected in Nuernberg within thirty days of the receipt." Tribunal III denied the motion the next day on the ground that, by not identifying the specific counsel who would represent Krupp, the application failed to comply with Rule 7 of the URP.[33]

On December 15, Krupp filed a second application for new counsel. This application stated that a member of Foley and Carroll was now present in Germany and ready to replace Kranzbuehler, but it still did not identify the attorney. Finally, when questioned in open court, Kranzbuehler informed the tribunal that the attorney was Earl Carroll himself. The application was then amended to reflect that fact.[34]

Four days later, the tribunal denied the second application. In the interim, the judges had learned that Carroll—whom Judge Anderson called an "ambulance chaser"[35]—had willfully violated the conditions of his entry permit into Germany. Carroll had been allowed to enter the U.S. zone to defend five American soldiers who were being court-martialed, and General Clay had informed him by letter in May 1947—nearly seven months before Krupp's first application—that he had to leave Germany after the courts-martial were concluded and could not engage in any additional legal activity while in the country.[36] In "flagrant defiance" of Clay's order, Carroll had nevertheless "appeared in other Courts Martial cases, represented a foreign liquor concern in a commercial matter, and appeared in a Military Government Court."[37] He had also attempted to file a notice of appearance with the Secretary General of the NMTs on December 17, even though Krupp had filed the second application two days earlier and the tribunal had yet to rule on it—itself a blatant violation of the URP.[38]

When the *Farben* tribunal announced its decision, Kranzbuehler attempted to resign from the case, informing the judges that Krupp "has told me that he is

---

[32] *Farben*, Order, 28 Jan. 1948, XV TWC 326–7.
[33] Ruling of Military Tribunal III, 5 Jan. 1948, NA-153-1018-9, at 2–3.
[34] Ibid., 4.
[35] Wilkins, 222.
[36] Ruling of Military Tribunal III, 5 Jan. 1948, at 4.
[37] Letter from Clay to Carroll, 30 Apr. 1947, TTP-5-1-1-4.
[38] Ruling of Military Tribunal III, 5 Jan. 1948, 2–3.

interested only in being represented by Mr. Earl J. Carroll, and that if this representation were denied to him he was not interested in being represented by anyone, not by me either." When the tribunal denied his request to withdraw, Kranzbuehler argued that Rule 7 permitted the tribunal to appoint counsel for Krupp only if he had not selected his own counsel—and Krupp had selected Earl Carroll. Unmoved, the tribunal cut him off and told him that he was free to ask the Committee of Presiding Judges for a joint session of the tribunals on that issue.[39] Kranzbuehler did so, but the Committee held that representation issues were outside of its jurisdiction.[40]

Carroll, it should be noted, revealed his true colors not long thereafter. At the end of March 1948, he wrote to President Truman to complain about the NMT trials. Carroll assured Truman "from personal experiences and investigation" that the trials were "a disgrace to the people of the United States," were "destroying German capitalism and discrediting American justice," and represented "one of the most effective communist infiltrations into American administration of Occupied Germany." He also insisted that some of the native German prosecutors in the OCC "were active communists in Germany at the outset of the Nazi regime"[41]—a claim he had first made two months earlier in an equally-incendiary letter to General Clay.[42]

C. Self-Incrimination

1. Unwarned Statements

In late November 1946, less than three weeks before the *Medical* trial began, Tribunal I ordered the OCC to warn any indicted war-crimes suspect that he had a right to remain silent during interrogation and that any statements he made could be used against him in a criminal prosecution.[43] That was a significant procedural innovation: neither the London Charter, Law No. 10, nor Ordinance No. 7 required such warnings, and prior to the *Medical* tribunal's ruling no IMT or NMT interrogator had ever given them. The OCC's Interrogations Branch immediately complied with the order, instructing its interrogators to give the warnings at "such time as the defendant or his counsel have [*sic*] received the indictment papers through the Secretary of the Tribunal."[44]

As noted in the previous chapter, no tribunal ever excluded an incriminating pretrial statement made prior to November 1946 on the ground that it violated the defendant's right to silence. NMT critics regularly denounced that practice,[45] but

---

[39] Extract from *Krupp* transcript, 19 Dec. 1947, XV TWC 335–6.

[40] Ibid., 1131–2, Order of the Committee, 12 Jan. 1948. Joint sessions are discussed in more detail in Section IV below.

[41] Letter from Carroll to President Truman, 25 Mar. 1948, NA-153-1018-9-86-2-2, at 1–2.

[42] Letter from Carroll to Clay, 12 Jan. 1948, TTP-5-1-1-4, at 4–5.

[43] Memo from Rapp to All Interrogators, 21 Nov. 1946, TTP-5-1-3-42, at 1.

[44] Ibid.

[45] See, e.g., Wurm Memorandum, 85; Von Knieriem, 144.

their vitriol was misplaced. There is no question that U.S. war-crimes officials specifically designed the interrogation process to maximize the likelihood that a defendant would make incriminating statements. The War Department, for example, initially prohibited POW camps from segregating suspects from regular detainees precisely to avoid alerting them that they were under suspicion,[46] and IMT interrogators routinely misled suspects into believing that they were viewed only as witnesses.[47] The tribunals' approach to unwarned statements was no different, however, than the approach taken by American courts. After all, the Supreme Court did not decide *Miranda v. Arizona*, requiring all suspects to be warned of their right to silence upon arrest, until 1966.[48]

NMT critics also denounced Taylor's deliberate refusal to provide suspects with defense counsel until they were formally indicted—the same position that Jackson had taken at the IMT, because he "loathed the obstructionism practiced by criminal attorneys in the U.S."[49] Taylor justified his policy on two grounds, neither of which is persuasive. The first was logistical: until late August 1946, the OCC was investigating nearly 2,500 suspects and conducting literally hundreds of interrogations per month, making it impossible to provide every suspect with counsel during every interrogation.[50] That may have been true in the early stages of the OCC's planning, but the OCC could have provided suspects with attorneys once it had reduced Peiser's list of 2,500 suspects to a more manageable 400.

Taylor's second rationale was even more problematic:

I quite agree that in normal circumstances, anyone confined should be promptly given the right of counsel. The difficulty is, of course, that information provided by people in custody is a very important source to us of determining what people should be charged with war crimes and what people can be safely released... This process would be much impaired if all persons in confinement were to be given immediate right to counsel.[51]

There is no question that suspects provide better information when they are not represented, but that does not justify denying them counsel—particularly when any incriminating statements they make can be used against them at trial. That said, Taylor's policy was consistent with American practice. Just as the Supreme Court did not require Miranda warnings until 1966, it did not hold that suspects had a right to counsel during interrogations until 1964, when it decided *Escobedo v. Illinois*.[52]

---

[46] Clio Edwin Straight, *Report of Deputy Judge Advocate Straight for War Crimes: June 1944–July 1948*, 26–7 (1949).

[47] See, e.g., Earl, 83.

[48] 384 U.S. 436 (1966). Taylor himself participated in *Miranda* as *amicus curiae* on behalf of New York. He argued against the existence of the constitutional right. Earl, 84 n.163.

[49] Earl, 86.

[50] Ibid., 85.

[51] Letter from Taylor to Rockwell, 12 Mar. 1947, cited in ibid., 86.

[52] 378 U.S. 478 (1964).

2. Duress

In early July 1946, less than a month after the Interrogation Branch was created, Walter Rapp, the chief of the Branch, distributed an "Interrogator's Guide." Paragraph 9 of the Guide made clear that interrogators were not permitted to use coercive methods to obtain incriminating statements:

These are not wartime operational interrogations where any means that served to get the information were all right. You are now connected with a legal trial where you must let yourself be guided by professional, ethical standards. If you don't, you degrade yourself to shyster status. Any form of duress is out. Equally out are any loose promises to any prisoner for supplying you with evidence . . . You cannot force a man to sign anything. He must sign voluntarily. Anything else would be indefensible in court.[53]

NMT critics alleged that OCC interrogators regularly violated these guidelines. Bishop Wurm, for example, claimed in June 1948 that "[r]eports have been increasing that statements have been made during the preliminary investigations under the influence of the after-effects of inadmissible methods of treatment, under the influence of inadmissible pressure and under the threat of long imprisonment, hanging or extradition to foreign powers."[54]

There is no evidence that interrogators regularly made use of coercive techniques. The tribunals consistently rejected such claims,[55] and even Fritz Sauter, who represented defendants in three different trials, stated that "I am bound to say that during the time I have been active in Nurnberg I did not see anything of such methods; nor did I hear anything like that either from defendants or witnesses. I do not know of a single case in which a defendant or witness was maltreated or 'tormented' during the conduct of a trial in Nurnberg."[56] Defendants also often labeled even the most innocuous interrogation techniques as "duress." When a German journalist asked one defendant claiming duress what had happened to him, the defendant responded, "[h]e offered me a cigarette, therefore leading me to believe that he was my friend."[57]

That said, Taylor's claim in his Final Report that "[t]hroughout the existence of the Subsequent Proceedings Division and OCCWC, it never came to my attention that any member of the Interrogation Branch departed from these instructions"[58] is clearly an overstatement. Taylor himself sent a memo to Kempner in August 1947 that acknowledged "various attorneys and research analysts" permitted to conduct interrogations "had violated the Interrogation Guide" by "making promises to inmates of the jail to the effect that they were to be released at such and such a time and date or were 'definitely not defendants'."[59] Moreover, there is no question

---

[53] Rapp, Interrogator's Guide, 8 July 1946, TTP-5-1-3-42, at 2.
[54] Letter from Wurm to Kempner, 5 June 1948, in Wurm Memorandum, 31.
[55] See, e.g., *Farben*, VIII TWC 1119; Earl, 87.
[56] Interview by Dr. Sauter, 1 July 1948, NA-260-199a1-162-4, at 3.
[57] Forum Discussion, "Are the Nurnberg Trials Just and Fair?," NA-260-199a1-162-4, at 25.
[58] Taylor, *Final Report*, 62.
[59] Memo from Taylor to Kempner, 20 Aug. 1947, TTP-5-1-3-42.

that—as alleged by Bishop Wurm[60]—Kempner himself coerced a witness, Friedrich Gaus, into testifying for the prosecution by threatening to turn him over to the Soviets, whom Gaus knew would almost certainly execute him. Frei points out that "Kempner's colleagues were horrified by this fiasco," particularly his superior, Charles LaFollette, who later told Clay that Kempner's "foolish, unlawyer-like methods of interrogation . . . [were] protested by those of us who anticipated the arising of a day, just such as we now have, when the Germans would attempt to make martyrs out of the common criminals on trial in Nuernberg."[61]

The tribunals were also occasionally sympathetic to claims of coercion. In *RuSHA*, for example, Tribunal I excluded a number of affidavits, including ones provided by the defendants, because the affiants testified at trial "that they were threatened, and that duress of a very improper nature was practiced by an interrogator."[62] It is not clear, however, whether the tribunal believed the affiant's claims or simply erred on the side of caution.

No such ambiguity exists concerning the *Farben* tribunal's decision to exclude pre-trial statements made by the defendant Schmitz, although the statements in question were made to an IMT interrogator in 1945, not one employed by the Interrogation Branch. When the War Department lifted its policy prohibiting the segregation of war-crimes suspects, OMGUS enacted Military Government Ordinance No. 1, which provided, *inter alia*, that "refusing to give information required by Military Government" was an offense punishable by up to life imprisonment.[63] Schmitz claimed—and the prosecution stipulated—that the IMT interrogator had told him he would be sentenced to 20 years' imprisonment under Ordinance No. 1 if he refused to cooperate. The *Farben* tribunal excluded the statements, pointing out that "[i]t would be difficult, if not impossible, to conceive of a more effective means of coercing one into giving evidence against himself than to advise him that he would be subject to life imprisonment for failure to do so, especially when the implied threat is accompanied by the showing of an official directive providing for such liability."[64]

D. Production of Witnesses and Documents

Article IV(f) of Ordinance No. 7 gave defendants the right to obtain witnesses and documents:

A defendant may apply in writing to the tribunal for the production of witnesses or of documents. The application shall state where the witness or document is thought to be located and shall also state the facts to be proved by the witness or the document and the relevancy of such facts to the defense. If the tribunal grants the application, the defendant shall be given such aid in obtaining production of evidence as the tribunal may order.

---

[60] Wurm Memorandum, 31.
[61] Norbert Frei, *Adenauer's Germany and the Nazi Past* 108 (2002).
[62] *RuSHA*, V TWC 871.
[63] Military Government Ordinance No. 1, Art. 2, sec. 33.
[64] *Farben*, Order, 25 May 1948, XV TWC 868.

How defense requests were processed depended on the location of the particular witness or document. For those located in the American zone, the Secretary General "promptly" issued a summons for the attendance of the witness or the production of the document.[65] For those located outside of the American zone—in another zone, or outside of Germany—the tribunal itself would "request through proper channels that the Allied Control Council arrange for the production of any such witness or document as the Tribunal may deem necessary to the proper presentation of the defense."[66]

1. Witnesses

The defense made liberal use of Article 4(f) with regard to witnesses. In *Milch*, the smallest of the 12 trials, the defense submitted 47 requests. In *High Command*, one of the larger trials, it submitted 165. The tribunals went to great lengths to honor those requests. In *Milch*, for example, Tribunal II granted 34 of the 47 requests without condition; granted four of the requests pending approval of the Control Council, because the witnesses were outside the American zone; granted three of the requests for deposition only; and denied six of the requests. All of the witnesses outside of the American zone—Constantin von Neurath, Erich Raeder, Albert Speer, and Karl Wolff—ultimately testified during the trial.[67] In most of the trials the Defense Administrator made arrangements for the witness to be brought to Nuremberg. That was the case in *Ministries* when Bishop Berggrav of Norway testified for von Weizsaecker, and in *High Command* when a British naval officer, Captain Russell Grenfell, testified on behalf of Schniewind.[68]

When a tribunal authorized a deposition or a witness was unable or unwilling to come to Nuremberg, the Defense Administrator tried to arrange for a representative of the defense to travel to the witness's location. "Extensive assistance" was given to the defense regarding travel within Germany, including arranging for counsel to travel by airlift to Berlin during the blockade. It was much more difficult for German counsel to travel outside of Germany, because most states still classified Germans as enemy aliens, but the Defense Administrator managed in the later trials to arrange trips to Austria, Czechoslovakia, England, Norway, and Switzerland.[69] When defense counsel could not travel to a witness's location, the Defense Center did its best to arrange for the witness to be served with interrogatories prepared by the defense.[70]

Despite these efforts, there is no question that the prosecution found it much easier to obtain witnesses than the defense. As von Knieriem rightly pointed out, "[t]he prosecution . . . had for years sought out and interrogated witnesses with a

---

[65] URP 12(c).   [66] URP 12(d).

[67] *Milch*, Table Concerning Defense Requests, XV TWC 370. Because the Control Council later changed its mind about von Neurath, Raeder, and Speer testifying in public, they testified via commissioner.

[68] Ibid., 365.   [69] Ibid., 366–7.

[70] Defense Memorandum No. 1, undated, NA-260-199a1-161-21, at 2.

staff of officials in all countries formerly occupied by Germany. It could search for witnesses or evidence in foreign countries and have the witnesses interrogated and brought to Nuremberg as soon as a person or an event was mentioned in the proceedings."[71] Two interrelated advantages were particularly glaring: the prosecution could locate witnesses, most of whom were detained in Allied POW camps, more easily than the defense; and unlike German counsel, the prosecution could—and did—travel freely outside of Germany to escort witnesses to Nuremberg or take depositions.[72]

Defense frustrations boiled over in *Farben*, when Drexel Sprecher admitted to Tribunal VI that no German lawyer had ever been allowed to travel outside of Germany. (Travel restrictions had not yet been eased.) The defense immediately moved the tribunal to strike "all affidavits and testimony of such prosecution witnesses as the prosecution secured during the trips abroad of its members," arguing that the "utterly unequal" position of the prosecution and the defense "seriously endanger[ed] the finding of the full truth about the events which constitute the basis for this trial."[73] The prosecution replied that, if relative advantages determined whether certain types of evidence were admissible, it would move to strike the more than 2,000 affidavits introduced by the defense that the prosecution had a limited ability to cross-examine.[74] The tribunal denied the motion.

The "utterly unequal" position of the defense and prosecution is indeed troubling, and there is at least some evidence that the tribunals did not do everything they could to obtain witnesses for the defense. In June 1947, for example, the Defense Administrator complained to the head of the OCC's Administrative Division that he believed the defense was being discriminated against by the "[r]efusal to send Military personnel after Defense witnesses who are in prison in other Zones or Countries" and the "[r]efusal of travel orders by OCC to personnel of the Office of the Secretary General to secure and return witnesses in custody."[75]

That said, the limits on the defense resulted far more often from the tribunals' own dependence on the willingness of the Control Council and Allied governments to cooperate with requests for witnesses. As the *Farben* tribunal noted, it was simply "not in a position to issue directives that are binding or forceful with reference to military authorities or foreign governments."[76] That was an accurate statement: France refused a defense request for a French expert in the *Medical* case[77]; Poland refused to allow important witnesses to testify in *RuSHA* because they were on trial at the time[78]; and the Soviets never honored defense requests.[79]

---

[71] Von Knieriem, 179.   [72] Ibid., 177–8.

[73] *Farben*, Defense Motion, 11 May 1948, XV TWC 384–5.

[74] Ibid., 386, Answer of the Prosecution, 13 May 1948.

[75] Memo from Wartena to Director of the Administrative Division, 10 June 1947, NA-260-194a1-134-14, at 2.

[76] Excerpt from *Farben* transcript, 17 Dec. 1947, 4686, 4688/89.

[77] Freyhofer, 97.

[78] Wurm Memorandum, 114.   [79] Ibid.

2. Documents

In general, defense requests for documents created fewer problems than requests for witnesses. OMGUS limited German access to captured documents for security reasons,[80] but both the OCC and the tribunals invested considerable time and energy ensuring that the defendants received the documents they needed to prepare their defense. In all of the cases, for example, the OCC provided the defense with significant numbers of documents in advance of trial, sometimes—as in *Farben*—even before judges had been assigned to the case.[81] The OCC also voluntarily complied with numerous defense requests for documents. In *Flick*, for example, the prosecution not only provided the defense with all of its files concerning the Reich Association Coal, it told the defense where it could find additional Association documents.[82]

For their part, the tribunals routinely granted defense requests under Article IV(f) for access to particular documents and document collections. In *Farben*, Tribunal VI permitted both ter Meer and his counsel to examine company documents stored in Frankfurt.[83] It also ordered the OCC to give the defense access to all of the Farben documents in its files that it did not intend to use for the first time on cross-examination, despite the prosecution's vehement objection that the request was nothing more than a "fishing expedition."[84] In *Ministries*, Tribunal IV not only gave the defense access to copies of German Foreign Office documents that were in the prosecution's files, it also permitted a representative of the defense to travel to the Berlin Documentation Center to examine the originals.[85] In *High Command*, Tribunal V arranged for the Secretary General to have 1,503 document folders—enough to fill 37 footlockers—shipped by air to Nuremberg for defense inspection.[86] And as noted earlier, the *Hostage* tribunal ordered the prosecution to either permit defense representatives to examine War Department archives in D.C. or arrange to have the documents requested by the defense shipped to Nuremberg.

II. Defense Resources

In his book on the NMT trials, Von Knieriem claimed that "the weapons of prosecution and defense" could only have been equalized by providing the defense with more time to prepare and vastly greater resources.[87] Ben Ferencz, by contrast, has argued that "the assistance given the Nurnberg defendants for the preparation

---

[80] XV TWC 393.
[81] Ibid., 395.
[82] Ibid., 404, *Flick*, Answer of the Prosecution, 18 June 1947.
[83] Ibid., 400, Defense Center Memorandum, 20 June 1947.
[84] Ibid., 430, *Farben*, Order, 22 Apr. 1948.
[85] Ibid., 419, *Ministries*, Order, 29 Mar. 1948.
[86] *High Command*, XI TWC 466.
[87] Von Knieriem, 185.

and presentation of their defense" was more than sufficient to guarantee the defendants a fair trial and was, in fact, "greater than that available to the average impecunious defendant in America."[88] Ferencz appears to have the better of the argument.

A. Time

NMT critics often claimed that defendants did not have sufficient time to prepare for trial. First, they pointed out that the defendants were not able to begin preparations until they were formally indicted, because only at that point were they entitled to counsel.[89] Second, they emphasized that the prosecution was under no such limitation and had begun to prepare some of its cases more than two years before trial.[90]

The second objection has a superficial attraction, but is in no way unique to the NMT trials: domestic and international prosecutors always devote considerable time and resources to building a case against a suspect before they formally indict him. And although the first objection is literally true, the question is not whether the defendants could have had more time, but whether the time they did have was sufficient to prepare an effective defense. It seems clear that it was. Rule 4 of the URP required a minimum of 30 days between service of the indictment and the beginning of trial, which Ferencz claims was "greater than that required by German or American criminal or military law."[91] Indeed, the contrast with Nazi law was particularly stark, as illustrated by a colloquy between Tribunal III and Franz Schlegelberger in the *Justice* case. After being read the indictment at the arraignment, Schlegelberger asked the tribunal, "[b]efore you sentence us, could I please say just a word in behalf of myself and my associates?" Schlegelberger thought the trial would begin immediately—standard practice under the Nazis—and was "amazed" to find out that he had 30 days to consult with his attorney.[92]

In practice, moreover, most of the defendants had far more than 30 days to prepare. Although the *Medical* and *Flick* trials started one month after the indictment was served, the average period between indictment and trial was nine weeks, including 14 weeks in *RuSHA* and 15 weeks in *Farben* and *Krupp*. It was also standard practice for the tribunal to recess the trial for three to four weeks at the close of the prosecution's case-in-chief to give the defense additional time to prepare,[93] although Musmanno deviated from that practice in *Einsatzgruppen*, calling it a "delaying tactic."[94] Finally, the tribunals liberally

---

[88] Benjamin B. Ferencz, "Nurnberg Trial Procedure and the Rights of the Accused," 39 *J. Crim. L. & Criminology* 144, 147 (1948).

[89] See, e.g., von Knieriem, 176.   [90] Ibid., 177.

[91] Ferencz, 148.   [92] Wilkins, 201.

[93] See, e.g., Hébert, *Hitler's Generals*, 181.

[94] Earl, 240.

granted shorter recesses when a particular defendant needed a few extra days to prepare his case.[95]

B. Resources

NMT critics also argued that the defendants did not have sufficient human and material resources to prepare an effective defense. Although there is no question that additional resources would have been helpful, the defendants were relatively privileged even by modern standards.

1. Counsel and Staff

Every defendant was entitled to hire two attorneys, one main counsel and one assistant counsel, as well as a secretary.[96] Nearly all hired both, although some defendants, such as Friedrich Flick, relied solely on main counsel. The tribunals also occasionally permitted defendants to hire three attorneys. In *Ministries*, for example, Paul Koerner had two assistant counsel and Otto Stuckart had an additional co-counsel. Overall, defense attorneys significantly outnumbered prosecutors: more than 200 defense attorneys represented clients during the trials, while the number of prosecutors never exceeded 100. And with the exception of *Milch*, in which there were two defense attorneys and six prosecutors, defense attorneys outnumbered than prosecutors in every trial. In *Einsatzgruppen*, for example, there were more than 40 defense attorneys and only six prosecutors.[97]

In three cases, the tribunals also appointed additional counsel and staff to assist the defendants. In *Krupp*, Tribunal III appointed the head of Krupp's legal division as "special counsel" for all of the defendants. In *Ministries*, Tribunal IV appointed a senior counselor in the German Foreign Office and three assistants (a scientific assistant, a historian, and an interpreter) to help the seven Foreign Office defendants prepare for trial. And in *Farben*, Tribunal VI not only appointed 12 "general staff" to assist the defendants—four main counsel, four assistant counsel, and four secretaries—it appointed three "special counsel," as well: a professor of international law at Heidelberg, the professor's assistant, and a member of Farben's legal division.[98]

Finally, the Defense Center made an American legal consultant available to the defendants at all times. Three men held that position, including John H.E. Fried, who also served as a legal consultant to the tribunals themselves.[99]

---

[95] See, e.g., Appleman, 153.
[96] Memo from Wartena to Secretary General for Military Tribunals, 13 June 1947, NA-260-199a1-162-7, at 1.
[97] See Taylor, *Final Report*, Appendix Q.
[98] Ibid.
[99] Final Report of the Defense Center, XV TWC 190.

2. *Material Resources*

The defendants also had significant material resources at their disposal. Financially, each main defense counsel was paid 3,500 marks per month by OMGUS, 7,000 marks per month if he represented multiple defendants.[100] Bishop Wurm complained that the monthly payment did not permit a defendant's main counsel to pay "the necessary assistant personnel,"[101] but Ferencz notes that the 3,500 marks per month was a veritable fortune compared to the 200 marks per month that the average skilled worker in Germany received at the time.[102] OMGUS also offset many of the living expenses that would normally have been incurred by defense counsel and their staff. It provided free housing for all of the defense counsel and secretaries who lived outside of Nuremberg[103]; paid for the gasoline they used to drive private vehicles to the Palace of Justice or on official defense business[104]; established a separate mess hall where, for 50 pfennigs per meal, they could get coffee and three meals a day—3900 calories daily, more than the number of calories provided to American soldiers and three times as many as average Germans managed[105]; and gave one carton of free cigarettes per week to defense counsel (which not even OMGUS employees received) and one free bar of soap to counsel and their secretaries.[106]

Providing defense teams with sufficient space proved more difficult. Space was at a premium until mid-April 1947, when renovations to the Palace of Justice allowed the Defense Center to allocate 29 rooms to the teams—"ample space for present and future needs," according to the Defense Administrator.[107] The Defense Center also provided each defense team with desks, chairs, bookshelves, filing cabinets, lamps, typewriters, and stationery, although one of the Krupp attorneys complained that his team did not have what they needed—particularly light-bulbs, which were scarce because they were necessary for working after dark—until the trial began in December 1947.[108]

Finally, the Defense Center provided the defense teams with a number of important litigation services. Attorneys were allowed to make unlimited local and long distance calls within Germany at no charge—although they complained about the number of phones throughout the trials[109]—and to send as many official cables as they wanted outside of Germany.[110] The defense teams also had the same access as prosecutors to the OCC's facilities for translation, photocopying, and mimeographing.[111]

---

[100] Ferencz, 147.
[101] Letter from Bishop Wurm to Clay, 20 May 1948, in Wurm Memorandum, 25.
[102] Ibid. [103] Final Report of the Defense Center, XV TWC 190.
[104] Ferencz, 147. [105] Ibid.
[106] Final Report of the Defense Center, XV TWC 189.
[107] Memo from Wartena to Secretary General for Military Tribunals, 13 June 1947, 1.
[108] Quoted in von Knieriem, 181.
[109] See, e.g., Letter from Bishop Wurm to Clay, 20 May 1948, in Wurm Memorandum, 25.
[110] Final Report of the Defense Center, XV TWC 190.
[111] Ferencz, 147.

III. Appeal

Article XV of Ordinance No. 7 provided that "[t]he judgments of the tribunals as to the guilt or the innocence of any defendant shall give the reasons on which they are based and shall be final and not subject to review." The inability of defendants to appeal their convictions was perhaps the most controversial aspect of the trials; Bishop Wurm spoke for nearly all of the NMT critics when he wrote to Robert Kempner in June 1948 that "[i]n view of all these circumstances it seems very discouraging that no opportunity to appeal against the Nuremberg Judgments exists. When taking into consideration the importance of the findings for international law and their serious consequences for the inflicted persons, such an appeal becomes an imperative demand."[112]

The critics' position has considerable merit, even if Ordinance No. 7 was simply following in the London Charter's footsteps.[113] Justice Jackson defended the absence of appellate review at the IMT on the ground that it would simply take too long.[114] That may well have been the case, but such pragmatic concerns do not outweigh the importance of such review, which was almost certainly a "fundamental principle of criminal law accepted by nations generally" by 1946.[115] Moreover, nothing in Law No. 10 *prohibited* the U.S. from providing appellate review; as noted earlier, each Ally had the discretion under Law No. 10 to adopt its own procedural rules. In fact, France not only permitted defendants convicted in a zonal trial to appeal their convictions, one such appeal led a higher military court to reverse Hermann Roechling's conviction for waging aggressive war.[116]

In addition to not permitting defendants to appeal their conviction, Ordinance No. 7 also initially prohibited defendants from seeking interlocutory review of tribunal decisions on points of law. That changed on 17 February 1947, when—at Telford Taylor's urging—OMGUS promulgated Ordinance No. 11, which amended Ordinance No. 7 to provide that the prosecution or defense could request a "joint session" of the tribunals then operating "to hear argument upon and to review conflicting or inconsistent final rulings contained in the decision or judgments of any of the Military Tribunals on a fundamental or important legal question, either substantive or procedural." Defendants filed numerous requests for joint sessions during the trials, but the tribunals rejected all of them.[117] Many of those requests did not involve challenges to inconsistent rulings, such as a *Farben* defendant's claim that Law No. 10 was invalid.[118] Other requests did challenge

---

[112] Letter from Bishop Wurm to Kempner, 5 June 1948, in Wurm Memorandum, 25.

[113] Ibid., 33, Letter from Clay to Bishop Wurm, 19 June 1948.

[114] See, e.g., Letter from Jackson to Petersen, 12 Sept. 1946, NA-153-1018-2-84-1, at 2.

[115] Unlike most common-law countries, however, there was no right to appeal a conviction in the United States until 1956. See *Griffin v. Illinois*, 315 U.S. 12, 18 (1956).

[116] Jonas Nilsson, "Rochling and Others," in *The Oxford Companion to Criminal Justice* 887 (Antonio Cassese ed, 2009).

[117] XV TWC 1061.

[118] Ibid., 1133, Order of the Committee of Presiding Judges, 17 Mar. 1948.

inconsistent rulings but were clearly without merit, such as a *Hostage* defendant's claim that Tribunal V's unwillingness to recognize his necessity defense was inconsistent with Tribunal IV's acquittal of a defendant in *Flick* on necessity grounds. The Committee of Presiding Judges simply—and rightly—pointed out that "[t]he basic and controlling facts of each are materially different."[119]

Although the tribunals rejected all of the defense requests, in July 1947 the Committee of Presiding Judges called a joint session of Tribunals I–V to consider whether Law No. 10 recognized conspiracy to commit a war crime or crime against humanity as a separate substantive offense. The tribunals had not yet issued conflicting rulings on that issue, making Ordinance No. 11 technically inapplicable, but defendants had challenged such charges in the *Medical, Justice,* and *Pohl* cases. The Committee thus justified convening a joint session *sua sponte* on the ground that it was "desirable that there be a uniform determination on the issue presented by such motions."[120] The Committee did not issue a ruling after hearing argument from representatives of the prosecution and defense—discussed in more detail in Chapter 12—but a few days later each tribunal dismissed the conspiracy charges.[121]

Unique problems concerning joint sessions arose after Tribunal V pronounced sentence in *High Command* on 27 October 1948 and adjourned *sine die.* Two weeks later, the defendants filed a request for joint session alleging that the tribunal's judgment conflicted with previous judgments on a number of issues, including the *tu quoque* defense and the status of hostages. The *Ministries* tribunal denied the request on November 16 on the ground that a joint session was not possible, because there was now only one tribunal still functioning in Nuremberg. The tribunal nevertheless considered the merits of the request and concluded that it did not allege an inconsistency that would have justified a joint session.[122]

A similar problem arose at the close of the *Ministries* trial. Aware that it could not call a joint session because it was the final tribunal, Tribunal IV decided to permit the defendants to file memorandums with the Secretary General "calling to the attention of the Tribunal any matters of fact or law which it is believed are in error."[123] As discussed in Chapter 4, the 19 convicted defendants each filed such a memorandum, three of which—those filed by von Weizsaecker, Woermann, and Steengracht von Moyland—were granted, at least in part. That solution was no doubt fair to the *Ministries* defendants, but it is difficult to reconcile with the absence of appellate review in the 11 other trials, even if the tribunal was reviewing its own judgment. No other defendant ever received *de novo* review of the evidence supporting their convictions.

[119] Ibid., 1105, Order of the Committee of Presiding Judges, 3 Mar.1948.
[120] Ibid., 1065, Order of the Committee of Presiding Judges, 7 July 1947.
[121] Ibid., 1061.
[122] Ibid., 1126.
[123] Ibid., 1213, *Ministries*, Order, 7 Apr. 1949.

Conclusion

The NMTs did everything they could to provide defendants with fair trials. The tribunals ensured that defendants could choose their own attorneys, even ones who were themselves war-crimes suspects. They required the OCC to inform suspects of their right not to incriminate themselves. They excluded inculpatory statements made under even a hint of duress. They went to great lengths to bring witnesses and documents to Nuremberg—and helped the defense travel outside of the American zone when they failed. And they ensured that the defendants enjoyed sufficient resources to prepare their defense, readily granting continuances and appointing extra counsel in particularly complicated cases.

That said, there were important procedural problems in the trials. The order to inform suspects about self-incrimination came far too late; by that time, most of the defendants had already given incriminating statements. The defendants were intentionally denied counsel by the OCC until after they were indicted, even though it would have been possible to make counsel available earlier. There is no question that the prosecution found it much easier than the defendants to obtain witnesses and documents. And, of course, the defendants had no right to appeal their convictions.

Some of those problems, such as the problems defense counsel faced obtaining witnesses and conducting investigations outside of the American zone, were inevitable. Others, such as the failure to provide counsel prior to indictment, could have been avoided. Overall, though, the trials were impressively fair—an assessment shared by the defendants themselves, as indicated by a statement made by Fritz Sauter, who represented five different defendants in three different cases, in a July 1948 interview:

I have often put my view to a test and asked several defendants in Nurnberg whether they would prefer being tried by a German or perhaps a French court, not to mention the courts in the Eastern countries. But everyone told me: if at all, then rather before a US Tribunal . . . judgments have been passed which we could not regard just, but which, in our opinion, were misjudgments. This, however, has nothing to do with the question of the fairness of the trials, nor with the question of the judges' endeavors to find a just verdict.[124]

That is a remarkable statement—and a testament to the dedication of the judges who served on the NMTs.

---

[124] Interview by Sauter on the Fairness of the Nurnberg Trials, 1 July 1948, 3–4.

8

Crimes Against Peace

Introduction

Article II(1)(a) of Law No. 10 recognized "each of the following acts" as a crime against peace:

Initiation of invasions of other countries and wars of aggression in violation of international laws and treaties, including but not limited to planning, preparation, initiation or waging a war of aggression, or a war of violation of international treaties, agreements or assurances, or participation in a common plan or conspiracy for the accomplishment of any of the foregoing.

The OCC charged defendants with crimes against peace in four cases: *Farben*, *Krupp*, *High Command*, and *Ministries*. In each case, the prosecution alleged both that the defendants had participated in a "common plan or conspiracy" and that they had planned, prepared, initiated, or waged aggressive wars and invasions.

Taylor himself was ambivalent about the crimes against peace charges. He had first expressed skepticism about their legal merit while working for Justice Jackson, noting in June 1945 that "[t]he thing we want to accomplish is not a legal thing but a political thing" and that it was "an interesting question" whether the crime was "presently a juridically valid doctrine."[1] He also recognized, as noted in Chapter 3, that it was much more difficult and time-consuming to prove crimes against peace than war crimes or crimes against humanity. He nevertheless brought the charges in the NMT trials "[o]ut of strong personal conviction no less than because it was my official duty to enforce the provisions of Law No. 10—including its proscription of war-making."[2] In retrospect, Taylor's skepticism was warranted: the crimes against peace charges failed completely in *Farben*, *Krupp*, and *High Command*, and although five defendants were convicted of planning, preparing, and waging invasions in *Ministries*, Tribunal IV set aside von Weizsaecker and Woermann's convictions after they filed motions to correct the judgment.

The tribunals generally followed the IMT's approach to analyzing whether a defendant had committed crimes against peace. They began by determining whether the particular aggressive wars or invasions specified in the indictment did, in fact, qualify as such crimes. They then asked whether the defendants themselves were individually criminally responsible for those aggressive acts either directly or by

---

[1] Sellars, 28.   [2] Taylor, *Final Report*, 66.

participating in a common plan or conspiracy.[3] That analytic framework structures this chapter. Section I focuses on the acts of aggression at issue in the trials, explaining why the tribunals extended crimes against peace to include invasions as well as wars. Section II discusses the elements of planning, preparing, initiating, and waging aggressive wars and invasions: the leadership requirement, the *actus reus*, and the *mens rea*. Finally, Section III explains why the tribunals uniformly rejected allegations that defendants had conspired to commit crimes against peace.

I. Aggressive Wars and Invasions

Unlike the London Charter, which criminalized only wars of aggression, Law No. 10 criminalized both wars of aggression and "invasions." That difference led the NMTs to take a much broader approach to crimes against peace than the IMT.

A. Aggressive Wars

The IMT held that ten of the Nazis' armed attacks qualified as wars of aggression: Poland, Yugoslavia, Greece, Denmark, Norway, Belgium, the Netherlands, Luxemburg, the Soviet Union, and the United States. None of the tribunals questioned those determinations. The *Ministries* tribunal did, however, clarify a curious ambiguity in the IMT judgment concerning the Nazis' attacks on the United Kingdom and France. Count Two of the IMT indictment described those attacks as "wars of aggression," and the IMT judgment noted in passing that it had decided "certain of the defendants planned and waged aggressive wars against *twelve* nations."[4] But the IMT judgment only discussed the criminality of the ten wars of aggression mentioned above—it said nothing about the attacks on the United Kingdom and France, although they had to be the other two, given that the indictment described Austria and Czechoslovakia not as aggressive wars but as "aggressive actions." The *Ministries* tribunal rectified that oversight by specifically holding that the attacks on the United Kingdom and France were, in fact, aggressive wars.[5]

B. Invasions

The IMT also addressed what it called the "invasion" of Austria and the "seizure" of Czechoslovakia. It considered those attacks, which had not resulted in armed conflict, "acts of aggression" instead of aggressive wars.[6] That distinction had significant legal consequences for the defendants. The IMT held that planning, preparing, initiating, or waging a *war* of aggression constituted a crime against

---

[3] See, e.g., *Ministries*, XIV TWC 336–7. For sake of readability, I will refer to a "common plan or conspiracy" simply as a "common plan."
[4] IMT Judgment, 36.
[5] *Ministries*, XIV TWC 336–7.
[6] IMT Judgment, 17, 106.

peace under Count Two of the indictment. By contrast, it held that planning, preparing, initiating, or waging an *act* of aggression did not constitute a crime against peace under Count Two, but could be criminal under Count One of the indictment, which prohibited conspiring to commit crimes against peace.[7] No defendant, therefore, was ever convicted under Count Two for participating in the attacks on Austria or Czechoslovakia.

Because Law No. 10 criminalized invasions as well as wars of aggression, the tribunals took a very different approach to the attacks on Austria and Czechoslovakia. In particular, the *Ministries* tribunal not only held that those attacks qualified as invasions, it convicted two defendants for participating in them: Lammers for his role in the invasion of Czechoslovakia; Keppler for his role in the invasions of both Czechoslovakia and Austria.

Those convictions were only possible, of course, because the *Ministries* tribunal concluded that Germany's attacks on Austria and Czechoslovakia qualified as invasions. Law No. 10 did not specify what distinguished aggressive wars from invasions; it simply made clear that they were different kinds of attacks. And the IMT had neither defined the term nor used it consistently, referring to the attacks on Denmark, Norway, Belgium, the Netherlands, and Luxemburg as "invasions" although it considered them aggressive wars and describing the attack on Czechoslovakia as a "seizure."

The *Ministries* tribunal was not, however, writing on a completely blank slate. Tribunal V had provided a definition of "invasion" in *High Command*, albeit in dicta because it had dismissed the crimes against peace charges—as discussed below—on the ground that the defendants did not satisfy the leadership requirement. According to the *High Command* tribunal, the difference between an aggressive war and an invasion was that the latter did not involve armed resistance:

[A]n invasion of one state by another is the implementation of the national policy of the invading state by force even though the invaded state, due to fear or a sense of the futility of resistance in the face of superior force, adopts a policy of nonresistance and thus prevents the occurrence of any actual combat.[8]

The majority in *Ministries* adopted *High Command*'s definition of invasion, noting—rightly—that there was no legal or political rationale for assuming "that an act of war, in the nature of an invasion, whereby conquest and plunder are achieved without resistance, is to be given more favorable consideration than a similar invasion which may have met with some military resistance."[9] The two judges thus had little problem determining that the attacks on Austria and Czechoslovakia qualified as invasions and were crimes against peace under Law No. 10.

---

[7] The distinction emerges most clearly in the IMT's acquittal of Schacht. After noting that the invasions of Austria and Czechoslovakia were not charged as "aggressive wars," making him ineligible for conviction under Count Two, it acquitted him under Count One because his participation in those invasions "was on such a limited basis that it does not amount to participation in the common plan." Ibid., 106.

[8] *High Command*, XI TWC 485.

[9] *Ministries*, XIV TWC 330.

With regard to Austria, they emphasized that "armed bands of National Socialist SA and SS units" had taken control of the Austrian government even before German troops crossed the border.[10] With regard to Czechoslovakia, they emphasized that Hitler had coerced Hacha into consenting to German occupation by threatening to destroy Prague by air and had "started his armed forces on the march into Bohemia and Moravia" even before Hacha had given that consent.[11] With regard to both, they noted that "[t]he fact that the aggressor was here able to so overawe the invaded countries, does not detract in the slightest from the enormity of the aggression in reality perpetrated."[12]

Judge Powers dissented from the majority's criminalization of the attacks on Austria and Czechoslovakia. He offered three basic arguments in defense of his position, none of which are compelling. To begin with, he argued that because the London Charter was made an "integral part" of Law No. 10,[13] the tribunal had to assume that the drafters of Law No. 10 did not intend to "substantially alter or change" the London Charter's definition of crimes against peace.[14] This was the same argument that both the *Flick* and *Ministries* tribunals had previously relied on to ignore Law No. 10's elimination of the nexus requirement from crimes against humanity, an issue discussed in more detail in Chapter 10. Suffice it to say here that the argument renders Article II(1)(a)'s use of the term "invasion" moot, thereby violating the basic canon of statutory construction that "every word and clause must be given effect,"[15] even though there is no evidence that the drafters of Law No. 10 did not intentionally distinguish between aggressive wars and invasions.

Perhaps aware of that problem, Judge Powers also argued that even if the two meant different things, "[a]n analysis of the language of Law 10 and its grammatical construction does not support the contention that a mere invasion is a violation of its terms." Law No. 10 referred to "initiation of invasions of other countries *and* wars of aggression"; according to Judge Powers, the use of the conjunctive meant that only an invasion that led to an aggressive war qualified as a crime against peace.[16] That was a very strained reading of Law No. 10, one that finds no support in the drafting history and reads the use of the word "and" in a very idiosyncratic way. There is nothing unusual about criminalizing different actions conjunctively; indeed, Article II(1)(c)'s defined crimes against humanity as "atrocities and offenses, including but not limited to..." Judge Powers' canon of construction would mean that all crimes against humanity had to involve both atrocities and one of the enumerated offenses, a reading that would have decriminalized a wide variety of persecutions, such as the program of Aryanization that Judge Powers' own

---

[10] *Ministries*, XIV TWC 330.   [11] Ibid., 332.

[12] Ibid., 331.   [13] See Law No. 10, Art. I.

[14] *Ministries*, Powers Dissent, XIV TWC 880.

[15] See, e.g., Karl N. Llewellyn, "Remarks on the Theory of Appellate Decision and the Rules or Canons About How Statutes are to be Construed," 3 *Vand. L. Rev.* 395, 404 (1950).

[16] *Ministries*, Powers Dissent, XIV TWC 881.

tribunal held criminal in *Ministries*.[17] Judge Powers did not dissent from that conclusion.

Finally, Judge Powers simply argued that the majority's definition of invasion—and thus, by implication, *High Command*'s definition, as well—was incorrect. In his view, there was a reason that the drafters of Law No. 10 referred to "crimes against peace" instead of to "crimes of aggression": they wanted to emphasize that aggressive acts were only criminal if they actually breached the peace.[18] That argument suffered from the same flaw as the first: it rendered the term "invasion" superfluous. The IMT almost certainly considered the attacks on Austria and Czechoslovakia to be aggressive acts instead of aggressive wars because they did not involve actual armed conflict. Requiring invasions to result in armed conflict thus collapses the distinction between invasions and aggressive wars. That is not only an implausible reading of Article II(1)(a), it contradicts the plain meaning of "invasion"—as the majority pointed out, dictionaries at the time defined an invasion as simply "a warlike or hostile entrance into the possessions or domains of another," a definition that does not require the invaded state to resist.[19]

C. Self-Defense

The *Ministries* tribunal also expanded upon the IMT's rejection of the idea that the Nazis' attacks were justified acts of self-defense. The defendants at the IMT had argued, for example, that "Germany was compelled to attack Norway to forestall an Allied invasion, and her action was therefore preventive." The tribunal disagreed, holding that preventive attacks were justified only where there was "an instant and overwhelming necessity for self-defense leaving no choice of means, and no moment of deliberation," which was not the case in Norway.[20]

The defendants made the same argument regarding Norway in *Ministries*, alleging that "newly discovered evidence proves that Germany was not the aggressor."[21] The *Ministries* tribunal rejected that claim, but not on the ground that the attack failed self-defense's necessity requirement. Instead, it held that Germany forfeited the right to claim self-defense once it committed an act of aggression, because "[i]t thereby became an international outlaw and every peaceable nation had the right to oppose it without itself becoming an aggressor."[22] It repeated that argument with regard to Germany's declaration of war against the United States, which the defendants claimed was justifiable self-defense in light of American support for the countries Germany had occupied. "A nation which engages in aggressive war," the tribunal held, "invites the other nations of the world to take measures, including force, to halt the invasion and to punish the aggressor, and if by

[17] See, for example, the conviction of Darre. Ibid., 557.

[18] Ibid., 882, Powers Dissent.

[19] Ibid., 331.

[20] IMT Judgment, 28.

[21] *Ministries*, XIV TWC 323. Von Weizsaecker did not do them any favors, because he freely admitted that all 12 of the attacks were criminal.

[22] Ibid., 336.

reason thereof the aggressor declares war on a third nation, the original aggression carries over and gives the character of aggression to the second and succeeding wars."[23]

II. Individual Criminal Responsibility

Once the tribunals determined which Nazi attacks qualified as crimes against peace, they then had to determine which defendants were criminally responsible for planning, preparing, initiating, or waging those attacks. As summarized by Judge Powers in *Ministries*, such responsibility required an affirmative answer to three questions:

1. Did he knowingly engage in some activity in support of a plan or purpose to induce his government to initiate a war?

2. Did he know that the war to be initiated was to be a war of aggression?

3. Was his position and influence, or the consequences of his activity, such that his action could properly be said to have had some influence or effect in bringing about the initiation of the war on the part of his government?[24]

Because the tribunals treated it as a threshold consideration, it is appropriate to begin with the third element—the so-called "leadership requirement."

A. The Leadership Requirement

The idea that crimes against peace could only be committed by defendants who had the authority to influence Nazi policy originated with the NMTs. Neither the London Charter nor Law No. 10 imposed a leadership requirement on such crimes; they simply prohibited participating in them.

1. The Development of the Requirement

The leadership requirement was first adopted by the *Farben* tribunal with regard to waging aggressive war. The requirement was necessary, according to the tribunal, because Article II(2) of Law No. 10 criminalized "any person" who was a principal or an accessory to one of the crimes in Article II(1), which included crimes against peace. Applied literally, Article II(2) meant that "the entire manpower of Germany could, at the uncontrolled discretion of the indicting authorities, be held to answer for waging wars of aggression," including "the private soldier in the battlefield, the farmer who increased his production of foodstuffs to sustain the armed forces, or the housewife who conserved fats for the making of munitions." The tribunal believed that such "collective guilt" was "unthinkable"; it thus held—extrapolating

---

[23] *Ministries*, XIV TWC 323.
[24] Ibid., 889, Powers Dissent. Powers disagreed with the majority's application of the test; he did not disagree with the test itself.

from the IMT judgment—that only "leaders" could be convicted of waging aggressive war:

Strive as we may, we are unable to find, once we have passed below those who have led a country into a war of aggression, a rational mark dividing the guilty from the innocent . . . Here let it be said that the mark has already been set by that Honorable Tribunal in the trial of the international criminals. It was set below the planners and leaders . . . and above those whose participation was less and whose activity took the form of neither planning nor guiding the nation in its aggressive ambitions . . . [I]ndividuals who plan and lead a nation into and in an aggressive war should be held guilty of crimes against peace, but not those who merely follow the leaders.[25]

Tribunal V then significantly expanded the leadership requirement in *High Command*. Nothing in *Farben* indicated that the leadership requirement applied to the other forms of participation in crimes against peace; on the contrary, as discussed below, the *Farben* tribunal held that it was criminal for anyone to contribute to preparing, planning, or initiating an armed attack that he knew was aggressive. The *High Command* tribunal, however, held that no individual below the "policy level" could be convicted of *any* form of participation in a crime against peace:

When men make a policy that is criminal under international law, they are criminally responsible for so doing. This is the logical and inescapable conclusion. The acts of commanders and staff officers below the policy level, in planning campaigns, preparing means for carrying them out, moving against a country on orders and fighting a war after it has been instituted, do not constitute the planning, preparation, initiation, and waging of war or the initiation of invasion that international law denounces as criminal.[26]

Although the *High Command* tribunal did not specifically address its rejection of *Farben*, it did explain why it believed that the leadership requirement applied to all forms of participation in crimes against peace. First, the tribunal claimed that because the "lawfulness or unlawfulness" of an attack was determined by the policy behind it—an unlawful attack being one motivated by a policy "criminal in its intent and purpose"—it made sense to limit individual criminal responsibility to those who helped determine that policy.[27] Second, the tribunal said that although it was convinced that crimes against peace were consistent with the principle of non-retroactivity, it believed that customary international law "had not [yet] developed to the point of making the participation of military officers below the policy making or policy influencing level into a criminal offense in and of itself."[28]

2. The Requirement Defined

Having embraced a leadership requirement, the tribunals then had to define it. The *Farben* tribunal was rather vague, simply suggesting that anyone "in the political,

---

[25] *Farben*, VIII TWC 1126.
[26] *High Command*, XI TWC 491.
[27] Ibid., 486.   [28] Ibid., 489.

military, and industrial fields" who was "responsible for the formulation and execution of policies" qualified as a leader.[29] The *High Command* tribunal was more specific, holding that "[i]t is not a person's rank or status, but his power to *shape or influence* the policy of his State, which is the relevant issue for determining his criminality under the charge of crimes against peace."[30] The *Ministries* tribunal then adopted *High Command*'s "shape or influence" standard, holding that Koerner could be convicted of crimes against peace because the evidence indicated that "the wide scope of his authority and discretion in the positions he held ... enabled him to shape policy and influence plans and preparations of aggression."[31]

Four aspects of the "shape or influence" standard are important to note. First, a defendant's ability to shape or influence policy could not simply be inferred solely from his position in the Nazi hierarchy. That was an important qualification, because Article II(2)(f) of Law No. 10 "deemed" a defendant guilty of a crime against peace "if he held a high political, civil or military (including General Staff) position in Germany or in one of its Allies, co-belligerents or satellites or held high position in the financial, industrial or economic life of any such country." Judge Hebert noted in his *Farben* concurrence that, "literally construed," Article II(2)(f) imposed strict liability for crimes against peace.[32] The tribunals rejected that idea, as the quote from *High Command* indicates. The OCC also disclaimed it,[33] although the prosecution did argue in *Farben*—unsuccessfully—that a defendant who held one of the specified "high positions" had "the burden of countering" the "legitimate and reasonable inferences" that could be drawn from his status.[34]

Second, a defendant's ability to "shape or influence" policy was not all-or-nothing. Some defendants were sufficiently powerful that they could be convicted of any crime against peace in which they knowingly participated. Paul Koerner, who was Goering's plenipotentiary in the Four Year Plan, is an example.[35] Other defendants, however, satisfied the leadership requirement for some crimes against peace but not others. The *Ministries* tribunal held, for example, that von Weizsaecker had the ability to shape or influence the invasion of Czechoslovakia,[36] but not the invasions of Denmark and Norway.[37]

Third, the tribunals were divided over whether a defendant had to *actually* influence Nazi policy in order to satisfy the leadership requirement. The *Farben* tribunal defined a leader as someone who was "responsible for the formulation and execution of policies," implying that the mere *ability* to influence policy was not enough. The *High Command* and *Ministries* tribunals, by contrast, assumed that any substantial participation in a crime against peace was criminal as long as the

---

[29] *Farben*, VIII TWC 1124.
[30] *High Command*, XI TWC 489 (emphasis added).
[31] *Ministries*, XIV TWC 425.
[32] *Farben*, Hebert Concurrence, VIII TWC 1299.
[33] Taylor, *Final Report*, 72.
[34] *Farben*, Prosecution Opening Statement, VII TWC 118.
[35] *Ministries*, XIV TWC 425–6.
[36] Ibid., 354.   [37] Ibid., 370.

defendant had the ability to influence policy. In *High Command*, for example, Tribunal V wrote that "[t]hose who commit the crime are those who participate at the policy making level in planning, preparing, or in initiating war. After war is initiated, and is being waged... [t]he crime at this stage likewise must be committed at the policy making level."[38] More concretely, in *Ministries*, Tribunal IV convicted Koerner of the attack on Russia because he "participated in the plans, preparations, and execution of the Reich's aggression against Russia" while being at the policy level, not because he shaped or influenced the policy itself.[39]

Fourth, although no industrialist was ever convicted of crimes against peace, the tribunals consistently emphasized that industrialists could satisfy the leadership requirement. As noted earlier, the *Farben* tribunal held that anyone "in the political, military, and industrial fields" could qualify as a leader. The *Krupp* tribunal echoed that position, insisting when it dismissed the crimes against peace charges that "[w]e do not hold that industrialists, as such, could not under any circumstances be found guilty upon such charges."[40] Their position was sound—after all, Article II(2)(f) specifically extended crimes against peace to include individuals who "held high position in the financial, industrial or economic life" of a country involved in aggression.

3. The Effect of the Requirement

The leadership requirement had a profound impact on the trials. In *Farben*, Tribunal VI's decision to adopt the requirement for waging an aggressive war doomed the crimes against peace charges, because it believed that "[t]he defendants now before us were neither high public officials in the civil government nor high military officers. Their participation was that of followers and not leaders."[41] That conclusion was questionable, to say the least. Von Schnitzler himself, the chairman of Farben's Commercial Committee, provided the prosecution with numerous affidavits detailing the extent to which Farben influenced Hitler's aggressive plans; indeed, he freely admitted that "[f]or twelve years the Nazi foreign policy and the I.G. foreign policy were largely inseparable" and expressed his belief that "I. G. was largely responsible for Hitler's foreign policy."[42] The tribunal simply ignored von Schnitzler's damning admissions, attributing them to "mental confusion" caused by the war and perversely citing his willingness to cooperate with the prosecution as evidence that the admissions had "questionable evidentiary value."[43] Judge Hebert, however, drew essentially the same conclusions as von Schnitzler in his concurrence, rejecting Farben's claims of duress on the ground that they were "at variance with numerous instances of Farben's ability to influence the course of

---

[38] *High Command*, XI TWC 490.
[39] *Ministries*, XIV TWC 434.
[40] *Krupp*, Order Acquitting the Defendants of the Charges of Crimes Against Peace, 5 Apr. 1948, IX TWC 393.
[41] *Farben*, VIII TWC 1126.
[42] DuBois, *Generals*, 54.
[43] *Farben*, VIII TWC 1120.

events where such action was deemed to be in the interest either of Farben or of the government program."[44]

The crimes against peace charges in *Krupp* also failed because of the leadership requirement. Tribunal III dismissed the charges at the close of the prosecution's case because—in the words of Judge Anderson—none of the defendants "had any voice in the policies that led their nation into aggressive war; nor were any of them privies to that policy. None had any control over the conduct of the war or over any of the armed forces; nor were any of them parties to the plans pursuant to which the wars were waged."[45] Notably, Judge Wilkins stated in his concurrence that he would have been willing to conclude that Gustav Krupp—whom the OCC had not charged because he had still not recovered his mental faculties—qualified as a leader for purposes of crimes against peace.[46]

The leadership requirement proved no less insuperable in *High Command*. Having held that the requirement applied to all of the forms of participation in crimes against peace, Tribunal V summarily dismissed those charges on the ground that the defendants "were not on the policy level."[47] That conclusion, however, is difficult to reconcile with the IMT judgment. As Taylor later asked rhetorically, "[w]ere Keitel (convicted by the IMT), Hitler's military administrative assistant, with little or no influence on strategy, and Doenitz (also convicted by the IMT), a rear admiral in command of submarines, 'policy makers' any more than Admiral Schniewind...the Chief of the Naval War Staff within which the plan for the invasions of Norway and Denmark originated?"[48]

B. *Actus Reus*

In addition to qualifying as a leader, a defendant also had to satisfy the *actus reus* of crimes against peace: planning, preparing, initiating, or waging an aggressive war or invasion. Such participation had to be substantial; Tribunal IV held in *Ministries* that "[t]o say that any action, no matter how slight, which in any way might further the execution of a plan for aggression, is sufficient to warrant a finding of guilt would be to apply a test too strict for practical purposes."[49] The tribunal took that requirement seriously, acquitting Woermann of helping prepare the invasion of Czechoslovakia because his actions—which had involved little more than ordering the seizure of equipment and files in the Czech Foreign Office—though knowing, were simply too *de minimis* to justify conviction.[50]

Before examining the four forms of direct participation in a crime against peace, it is important to emphasize that, because they took the position that a defendant did not have to actually influence policy to satisfy the leadership requirement,

---

[44] *Farben*, VIII TWC, 1298, Hebert Concurrence.
[45] *Krupp*, Anderson Concurrence, IX TWC 449.
[46] Ibid., 465–6, Wilkins Concurrence.
[47] *High Command*, XI TWC 491.
[48] Taylor, *Final Report*, 222.
[49] *Ministries*, Motion for Correction, XIV TWC 966.
[50] Ibid., 392–3.

the *High Command* and *Ministries* tribunals each held that an omission could satisfy the "substantial participation" requirement. In *High Command*, for example, Tribunal V held that "[i]f after the policy to initiate and wage aggressive wars was formulated, a defendant came into possession of knowledge that the invasions and wars to be waged were aggressive and unlawful, then he will be criminally responsible if he, being on the policy level, could have influenced policy and failed to do so."[51] Similarly, Tribunal IV insisted in *Ministries*—in the context of acquitting von Weizsaecker with regard to the war against the Soviet Union—that "[w]e are not to be understood as holding that one who knows that a war of aggression has been initiated is to be relieved from criminal responsibility if he thereafter wages it, or if, with knowledge of its pendency, he does not exercise such powers and functions as he possesses to prevent its taking place."[52]

The *Ministries* tribunal emphasized, however, that the duty to protest was not unlimited. Most importantly, a protest did not have to have an actual effect. For example, although the *Ministries* tribunal recognized that von Weizsaecker's protests failed to "prevent the catastrophe" brought about by the invasion of Poland, it nevertheless insisted that "his lack of success is not the criteria."[53] The duty to protest was also a purely internal one; the tribunal specifically held with regard to von Weizsaecker and the invasion of the Soviet Union that "the failure to advise a prospective enemy of the coming aggression in order that he may make military preparations which would be fatal to those who in good faith respond to the call of military duty does not constitute a crime."[54]

Even those limits were not enough for Judge Powers. He dissented from the majority's omission argument in *Ministries*, insisting that the failure of a defendant "to do anything to prevent the proceedings, even if he had had an opportunity, cannot be regarded as a crime. He does not commit a crime against peace in any event, by inaction. Something affirmative is required."[55]

1. Planning, Preparing, Initiating

The tribunals normally discussed planning, preparing, and initiating an aggressive attack separately from waging an aggressive war or invasion, an analytic framework that Judge Anderson believed was consistent with the IMT's approach to crimes against peace.[56] In many cases, the tribunals did not even distinguish between the three preliminary stages of the crime; the *Ministries* tribunal, for example, simply convicted Koerner for participating "in the plans, preparations, and executions of the Reich's aggression against Russia."[57] The tribunals did, however, highlight some important differences between the three stages.

---

[51] *High Command*, XI TWC 488–9.
[52] *Ministries*, XIV TWC 383.
[53] Ibid., 369.   [54] Ibid., 383.
[55] Ibid., 893, Powers Dissent.
[56] *Krupp*, Anderson Concurrence, IX TWC 426.
[57] *Ministries*, XIV TWC 434.

a. Planning

The key issue with planning—the earliest stage of a crime against peace—is whether the tribunals believed that there was a difference between planning as a part of a "common plan" to commit a crime against peace and planning as form of direct participation in a particular aggressive war or an invasion. The London Charter and Law No. 10 each referred to both "planning" and the "common plan," implying that the two were different. The IMT, however, effectively treated them as synonymous. The traditional interpretation of the judgment is that the Tribunal distinguished between Count One and Count Two in terms of specificity of planning: whereas "common plan" under Count One involved "making long-term plans and arrangements for waging wars of aggression in the future"[58] and required either a close relationship with Hitler (Hess)[59] or presence at one of the four key meetings held by Hitler between 1937 and 1939 at which he disclosed his aggressive intentions (Goering),[60] "planning" under Count 2 involved the "specific planning... of an aggressive war against a specific country."[61] In fact, all of the IMT defendants who were convicted of *planning* specific wars of aggression under Count Two were also convicted of participating in the common plan under Count One; the four defendants who were convicted under Count Two because they had *prepared* or *waged* aggressive war—Funk, Frick, Doenitz, and Seyss-Inquart—were each acquitted under Count One. Funk had participated in "the economic preparation" for the attack on the Soviet Union[62]; Frick and Seyss-Inquart had waged aggressive war by administering the occupied territories[63]; and Doenitz had waged aggressive war with his submarine fleet.[64]

The *Farben* tribunal also treated "planning" and "common plan" as synonymous. It began by noting that, to be guilty of a crime against peace, "it must be shown that the [defendants] were parties to the plan, or, knowing of the plan, furthered its purpose and objective by participating in the *preparation* for aggressive war"[65]—a formulation that leaves no room for planning independent of the common plan. It then acquitted Krauch (the only Farben defendant it discussed concerning planning) on the ground that "[n]o opportunity was afforded to him to participate in the planning, either in a general way or with regard to any of the specific wars charged in count one," because "[t]he plans were made by and within a closely guarded circle. The meetings were secret. The information exchanged was confidential. Krauch was far beneath membership in that circle."[66] The *Farben* tribunal clearly believed, therefore, that all of the planning for aggressive war was

---

[58] United Nations War Crimes Commission, *History of the United Nations War Crimes Commission and the Development of the Laws of War* 248 (1948).

[59] IMT Judgment, 87.

[60] Ibid., 14–7.

[61] UNWCC History, 249.

[62] IMT Judgment, 103.

[63] Ibid., 99 (Frick), 120 (Seyss-Inquart).

[64] Ibid., 107.

[65] *Farben*, VIII TWC 1108 (emphasis added).

[66] Ibid., 1110.

carried out by the members of the Nazi "common plan"; anyone who was not a member of that common plan had simply "prepared" aggressive war.

The *Ministries* tribunal, by contrast, held that a defendant could plan an aggressive attack even if he was not part of the common plan. That distinction is most evident concerning Lammers, who was convicted of being "a criminal participant in the *formulation*, implementation and execution of the Reich's plans and preparations of aggression" against seven different countries.[67] Lammers had, for example, played an active role in determining how the occupying authorities would deal with the "Jewish question" in Poland within weeks of the 23 May 1939 meeting at which Hitler announced his intention to invade the country.[68]

The tribunal's conviction of Koerner is also instructive. It emphasized that Koerner was Goering's deputy in the Four Year Plan, which was "an instrumentality for the planning and carrying on of aggressions,"[69] and was Deputy Chairman of the General Council, which "became a very important and active agency for certain phases of planning in connection with subsequent invasions and other aggressions."[70] Specifically, the tribunal convicted Koerner of "planning... the aggression against Russia" because, once the decision to invade the Soviet Union had been made, he and Goering had created an "economic staff" to manage the economic affairs of Operation Barbarossa.[71]

The *Ministries* tribunal, in short, adopted a broader definition of planning than either the IMT or the *Farben* tribunal. The latter considered an individual to have planned a crime against peace only if he was involved in Hitler's decision to launch an aggressive war or invasion against that country. The former, by contrast, expanded planning to include individuals who were not involved in the decision to launch an aggressive attack, but formulated the policies necessary to ensure that the attack succeeded—what the IMT and the *Farben* tribunal would have considered "preparing."

b. Preparing

The second stage of a crime against peace, "preparing," began where planning (however defined) ended: once the decision to launch an aggressive war or invasion had been made. Preparing, in other words, involved "implementing" aggressive plans, not formulating them. That distinction is evident in the *Ministries* tribunal's acquittal of Woermann for the invasion of Yugoslavia, which it justified on the ground that the evidence did not show "that Woermann either initiated or implemented the plans for such aggression."[72] The tribunal particularly emphasized what it called "diplomatic preparations" for aggression—efforts by the defendants to deceive other countries into believing that Hitler's aims were not aggressive.[73] Such efforts were at the heart of von Weizsaecker's conviction, later

[67] *Ministries*, XIV TWC 416 (emphasis added).
[68] Ibid., 408.   [69] Ibid., 421.
[70] Ibid., 402.   [71] Ibid., 432.
[72] Ibid., 398.   [73] Ibid., 396.

reversed on factual grounds,[74] for the invasion of Czechoslovakia. The tribunal acknowledged that von Weizsaecker "did not originate this invasion, and that his part was not a controlling one," but it insisted that he had helped prepare for the invasion through diplomatic negotiations designed to knowingly deceive Czechoslovakia, France, and Britain into believing that Germany did not intend to invade.[75]

The *Farben* tribunal dealt with preparation in the context of the company's participation in the rearmament of Germany prior to the invasion of Austria. The tribunal ultimately acquitted Krauch and the other defendants because they lacked *mens rea*, but it made clear that "by contributing to her economic strength and the production of certain basic materials of great importance in the waging of war," Farben had prepared Germany for aggressive wars and invasions.[76]

c. Initiating

The tribunals rarely referred to the third stage of a crime against peace, "initiating" an aggressive war or invasion. The *Farben* tribunal refused to convict Krauch of initiating any of the wars of aggression or invasions because "he was informed of neither the time nor the method of initiation."[77] That statement suggests that a defendant was guilty of initiating aggressive wars or invasions if he helped determine either "the strategic moment for their execution"[78] or the precise manner in which they would begin. Keppler's conviction for the invasion of Austria is likely an example of the latter form of initiation: the *Ministries* tribunal convicted him because he had delivered Hitler's ultimatum to President Miklas that the German army would invade unless Seyss-Inquart was appointed Chancellor.[79] It was that ultimatum that had led Schuschnigg to resign and the Austrian National Socialists to assume power.[80]

2. Waging

"Waging" referred to the final stage of a crime against peace—actions taken after a war or invasion had been initiated that furthered the aggressive purposes of the attack. The *Ministries* tribunal cited a number of different ways in which defendants like Lammers and Koerner "waged" war: signing decrees that altered the legal status of occupied territory, such as the decree that that incorporated Poland into the Reich[81]; establishing Nazi authority over an invaded country, such as installing Frank as the Governor-General of Poland[82]; and taking steps to ensure that occupied territory would be economically exploited, such as transforming the economic staff that planned Operation Barbarossa into an organization responsible for "extracting the maximum quantities of goods required for the war effort."[83] The

---

[74] Ibid., 955, von Weizsaecker Order.   [75] Ibid., 354.
[76] *Farben*, VIII TWC 1112.   [77] Ibid.
[78] *Ministries*, XIV TWC 378.   [79] Ibid., 387.
[80] IMT Judgment, 18.   [81] *Ministries*, XIV TWC 408.
[82] Ibid.   [83] Ibid., 434.

Krupp and *Farben* tribunals discussed waging in the context of rearmament, which obviously continued even after Germany invaded Poland, making clear Hitler's aggressive aims.[84]

The key issue with waging an aggressive war or invasion was not what actions qualified as waging, but under what conditions a defendant could be held responsible for that particular form of participation in a crime against peace. The *High Command* and *Ministries* tribunals simply held that—as with all forms of participation—a defendant could be convicted of waging an aggressive war or invasion only if he satisfied the leadership requirement. In *High Command*, recall, Tribunal V held that "after war is initiated, and is being waged . . . [t]he crime at this stage likewise must be committed at the policy making level." The *Ministries* tribunal did not make that requirement explicit, but it is evident in its decisions concerning individual defendants. Lammers, for example, was convicted of waging aggressive war because he signed the decree that installed Frank as Governor-General of Poland. Stuckart, by contrast, was acquitted of waging aggressive war even though he not only actually held "many responsible positions in the administration of the occupied territories," but also "drafted or assisted in the preparation of decrees related to them."[85] The difference between the two was that Lammers, unlike Stuckart, had the ability to shape and influence Nazi policy.[86]

The *Farben* tribunal also emphasized the leadership requirement when it discussed whether rearmament qualified as waging an aggressive war or invasion. As noted earlier, however, the *Farben* tribunal—unlike the *High Command* and *Ministries* tribunals—held that the *ability* to shape or influence policy was not enough; the defendant had to actually be "responsible for the formulation and execution of policies." That difference had an important practical effect: it meant that an industrialist could not be convicted of waging an aggressive war or invasion unless he had previously played a role in planning, preparing, or initiating that war or invasion. In the absence of that nexus, rearmament was simply "in aid of the war effort in the same way that other productive enterprises aid in the waging of war."[87]

The *Krupp* tribunal, by contrast, adopted a broader conception of waging. In its order dismissing the crimes against peace charges, Tribunal III simply—and unhelpfully—stated that "[i]f Speer's activities were found not to constitute 'waging aggressive war' we most certainly cannot find these defendants guilty of it."[88] Judge Anderson's concurring opinion, however, makes clear that the tribunal was not holding that rearmament could never qualify as "waging aggressive war." Instead, it indicates that the tribunal believed that rearmament qualified as waging as long as that rearmament began *before* the aggressive war was initiated and the defendant *knew at the time* that it was aggressive. As Judge Anderson said, although he could understand "how a private citizen can be held indictable if he was privy to the plans

---

[84] See *Farben*, VIII TWC 1125; *Krupp*, Order Acquitting the Defendants, IX TWC 398.
[85] *Ministries*, XIV TWC 416.
[86] Cf. ibid., 406, with ibid., 416.
[87] *Farben*, VIII TWC 1126–7.
[88] *Krupp*, Order Acquitting the Defendants, IX TWC 398.

which led his country into a war that he knew would be a war of aggression and aided in the execution of those plans," he did not believe that "a citizen not privy to the prewar plans, but who after the war has begun is called upon to aid in the war effort, must determine in advance and at his peril whether the war is a justifiable one and refuse his aid if he concludes that it was not."[89]

Both the *Farben* and *Krupp* tribunals believed, in short, that the responsibility of an industrialist for post-war rearmament depended on his actions prior to the war. The two differed only in terms of what actions were required: the *Farben* tribunal held that the industrialist had to actually influence the formulation and execution of the policies that led to the aggressive war or invasion, while the *Krupp* tribunal assumed that it was enough for the industrialist to be involved in pre-war rearmament knowing that his arms would be used for aggressive purposes—a much less restrictive standard.

C. *Mens Rea*

The IMT paid little attention to the *mens rea* of crimes against peace. The judgment clearly indicates, though, that a defendant could be convicted of planning, preparing, initiating, or waging an aggressive war only if he was aware of the war's aggressive nature—a *mens rea* of knowledge. The IMT convicted von Neurath because he participated in various acts of aggression "with knowledge of Hitler's aggressive plans"[90] and Hess because his relationship with Hitler was such that he "must have been informed of Hitler's aggressive plans when they came into existence."[91] Conversely, the IMT acquitted Schacht because the prosecution had failed to prove "that Schacht did in fact know of the Nazi aggressive plans"[92] and acquitted Bormann because the evidence did not show "that Bormann knew of Hitler's plans to prepare, initiate or wage aggressive wars."[93]

The NMTs also adopted knowledge as the *mens rea* of crimes against peace, with one minor exception discussed below. The *Ministries* tribunal stated that "[o]ur task is to determine which, if any, of the defendants, knowing there was an intent to so initiate and wage aggressive war, consciously participated in either plans, preparations, initiations of those wars, or so knowing, participated or aided in carrying them on."[94] The *High Command* tribunal held that, to convict a defendant of a crime against peace, "[t]here first must be actual knowledge that an aggressive war is intended and that if launched it will be an aggressive war."[95] And the *Farben* tribunal described the "question of knowledge" as the issue that was "decisive of the guilt or innocence of the defendants" for the charged crimes against peace.[96]

[89] Ibid., 449, Anderson Concurrence.   [90] IMT Judgment, 125.
[91] Ibid., 87.   [92] Ibid., 106–7.   [93] Ibid., 128.
[94] *Ministries*, XIV TWC 337.
[95] *High Command*, XI TWC 488.
[96] *Farben*, VIII TWC 1113.

1. *The Definition of Knowledge*

The IMT treated the definition of "knowledge" as self-evident. The *Ministries* tribunal, by contrast, explored the definition in some detail. To begin with, it emphasized that knowledge required a defendant to be virtually certain that a war or invasion was aggressive—"it is not sufficient that he have suspicions."[97] The tribunal took that requirement seriously, acquitting Dietrich, the Reich press chief, of crimes against peace even though it considered it "entirely likely that he had at least a strong inkling of what was about to take place." The tribunal emphasized that such suspicion, "no matter how well founded, does not take the place of proof."[98]

Judge Hebert, it is worth noting, agreed with the *Ministries* tribunal that "knowledge" required virtual certainty that a war or invasion was aggressive. He stated in his *Farben* concurrence that the prosecution had been able to prove that the defendants had participated in the rearmament of Germany "on a gigantic scale with reckless disregard of the consequences, under circumstances strongly suspicious of individual knowledge of Hitler's ultimate aim to wage aggressive war." He nevertheless concluded that the defendants had to be acquitted, because recklessness "does not meet the extraordinary standard" required by the IMT judgment.[99]

The *Ministries* tribunal also insisted, almost certainly speaking for all of the tribunals, that "knowledge" required a defendant to make a *legal* evaluation of the war or invasion in question. It was not enough for the defendant to know that the Nazis intended to use armed force against another country; he also had to subjectively recognize that the intended attack would violate international law. The tribunal thus held that, in contrast to war crimes or crimes against humanity, a defendant could argue mistake of law as a defense to a crime against peace:

While we hold that knowledge that Hitler's wars and invasions were aggressive is an essential element of guilt under count one of the indictment, a very different situation arises with respect to...war crimes and crimes against humanity. He who knowingly joined or implemented, aided, or abetted in their commission as principal or accessory cannot be heard to say that he did not know the acts in question were criminal.[100]

The *Ministries* tribunal applied that knowledge requirement strictly. Although it acknowledged that many of Schwerin von Krosigk's activities as Reich Minister of Finance "dealt with waging war," for example, the tribunal nevertheless held that "in the absence of proof that he knew these wars were aggressive and therefore without justification, no basis for a judgment of guilty exists."[101]

[97] *Ministries*, XIV TWC 337.   [98] Ibid., 417.
[99] *Farben*, Hebert Concurrence, VIII TWC 1213.
[100] *Ministries*, XIV TWC 339.
[101] Ibid., 418.

2. *The* Mens Rea *of Rearmament*

The only disagreement between the tribunals concerning the *mens rea* of crimes against peace involved rearmament. The *Farben* and *Krupp* tribunals did not distinguish between rearmament and other preparations for crimes against peace; they simply applied the regular knowledge requirement. The *Farben* tribunal held that "the rearmament of Germany was not a crime on the part of any of the defendants in this case, unless that rearmament was carried out, or participated in, with knowledge that it was a part of a plan or was intended to be used in waging aggressive war."[102] And the *Krupp* tribunal asked simply—if rather awkwardly— whether it could be said "that the defendants in doing whatever they did do prior to 1 September 1939 did so, knowing they were participating in, taking a consenting part in, aiding and abetting the invasions and wars?"[103]

The *Ministries* tribunal, by contrast, specifically held that rearmament was criminal only if a defendant both *knew* that his arms production would be used for aggressive purposes and *intended* them to be used in that way. That higher *mens rea* emerges clearly in the tribunal's acquittal of Pleiger, the head of the Hermann Goering Works. According to the tribunal, "rearmament, in and of itself is no offense against international law. It can only be so when it is undertaken with the intent and purpose to use the rearmament for aggressive war."[104]

Although the *Ministries* tribunal's position was in the minority, it was supported by judges in both *Krupp* and *Farben*. In his concurrence in *Krupp*, Judge Anderson insisted—contra the majority—that "activities relied upon as constituting waging war must have been pursued with knowledge of the criminal objective and with the intention of aiding in its accomplishment."[105] Similarly, in his concurrence in *Farben*, Judge Anderson said that the critical issue regarding crimes against peace was whether the prosecution had proved "that the acts of the defendants in preparing Germany for war were done with knowledge of Hitler's aggressive aims and with the criminal purpose of furthering such aims."[106] Neither judge ever explained, however, why industrialists should be held to a different *mens rea* than other types of defendants.

3. *The Effect of the* Mens Rea *Requirement*

Like the leadership requirement, the *mens rea* requirement had a profound impact on the trials. The *Ministries* tribunal acquitted a number of defendants of crimes against peace on the ground that they had been unaware of the Nazis' aggressive plans. Dietrich's acquittal has already been mentioned; other acquitted defendants included Ritter, the liaison between the High Command and the Foreign Office, and Schwerin von Krosigk, the Reich Minister of Finance. Lack of knowledge played a

[102] *Farben*, VIII TWC 1112–3.
[103] *Krupp*, Order Acquitting Defendants, IX TWC 396.
[104] *Ministries*, XIV TWC 435.
[105] *Krupp*, Anderson Concurrence, IX TWC 448.
[106] *Farben*, Hebert Concurrence, VIII TWC 1217.

particularly important role in Schwerin von Krosigk's acquittal, because the tribunal acknowledged "that many of his activities and those of his department dealt with waging war."[107]

The *mens rea* requirement also doomed the crimes against peace charges in *Farben*. Tribunal VI categorically rejected the prosecution's contention that the defendants knew the Nazis intended to use Farben's industrial production for aggressive purposes. The tribunal not only held that "common knowledge of Hitler's plans did not prevail in Germany, either with respect to a general plan to wage aggressive war, or with respect to specific plans to attack individual countries,"[108] it also held that none of the defendants had individual knowledge of those plans, describing the prosecution's proof as "mere conjecture." The tribunal was particularly derisive of the idea that it should infer the requisite knowledge from the "magnitude of the rearmament effort." The defendants were not "military men," the tribunal pointed out, and thus could not be expected to know at what point rearmament for defensive purposes turned into rearmament for aggressive war.[109]

Judge Hebert ultimately concurred with the acquittal of the Farben defendants, but he planned on dissenting until nearly the day before the judgment was announced.[110] His private notes are replete with references to his belief that the defendants were aware that Hitler intended to use their weapons to commit aggression. On one occasion, he stated that he could not "reach any conclusion but that this was known to persons in the position of these defendants."[111] On another, he reminded himself that it was not even necessary "to rely upon the inference of knowledge established from the nature and scope of their activities and from the positions which they held," because "[t]he record establishes that knowledge of plans for aggressive war in which they were participating was brought home in a more direct fashion on a number of occasions."[112] Indeed, Judge Hebert went so far as to draft a dissenting opinion when he believed that his colleagues intended to grant the motion to dismiss the crimes against peace charges that the defendants filed when the prosecution rested.[113]

In the end, a number of factors convinced Judge Hebert to concur instead of dissent: the IMT's acquittal of Schacht and Speer; the decision of France's General Tribunal to acquit high-ranking Roechling officials of planning and preparing aggressive war; Tribunal III's acquittal of the Krupp defendants; and "a most liberal application of the rule of reasonable doubt."[114] His concurrence, however, made clear that he believed his colleagues were far too credulous toward the Farben

[107] *Ministries*, XIV TWC 418.
[108] *Farben*, VIII TWC 1107.
[109] Ibid., 1112.
[110] Zuppi, 514.
[111] Hebert Archives, Exhibit 196.
[112] Ibid., Exhibit 241.
[113] Ibid., Exhibit 54. The tribunal ultimately decided to delay ruling on the motion until the judgment.
[114] *Farben*, Hebert Concurrence, VIII TWC 1212.

defendants' claim to have been innocent dupes of Hitler. He described the evidence, for example, as "truly so close as to cause genuine concern as to whether or not justice has actually been done."[115] And he suggested that "[i]f a single individual had combined the knowledge attributable to the corporate entity and had engaged in the course of action under the same circumstances as that attributable to the corporate entity, it is extremely doubtful that a judgment of acquittal could properly be entered."[116]

Unlike the *Farben* tribunal, the *Krupp* tribunal did not specifically rely on the *mens rea* requirement to dismiss the crimes against peace charges. The two concurrences, however, both discussed the defendants' knowledge. Judge Anderson emphasized that there was no evidence in the record to suggest that the defendants knew their arms would be used for aggressive purposes. In particular, echoing the *Farben* tribunal, he emphasized that the requisite knowledge could not be inferred "from the inherent nature and extent of the Krupp firm's activities in the rearmament field," such as the fact that Krupp had primarily produced offensive weapons for the Nazis. In Judge Anderson's view, that was "not of determinative significance," because "[o]ffensive warfare and aggressive war are not the same thing. Offensive weapons may be, and frequently are, employed by a nation in conducting a justifiable war."[117]

Judge Wilkins was more sympathetic to the prosecution. He believed that it was "inescapable" that "the Krupp firm under the leadership of Gustav Krupp played a vital and very substantial role in preparing Germany for its wars of aggression, as well as in the waging of these wars, and that, prior to the attack on Poland in September 1939, the huge armament production of the firm was contemplated to be used for purposes of aggression."[118] He nevertheless concluded that there were two fatal flaws with the crimes against peace charges. First, and most obviously, Gustav Krupp was not on trial. Second, although the evidence that some of the defendants shared Gustav's knowledge of the Nazis' aggressive aims was "well nigh compelling," he agreed with the tribunal that—as discussed earlier—none of the charged defendants satisfied the leadership requirement.[119]

III. Common Plan or Conspiracy

As noted earlier, the prosecution alleged a common plan or conspiracy in all four of the cases that involved crimes against peace. The tribunals did not have to determine whether such a common plan existed; the IMT had already held that it did, a determination that the tribunals accepted as *res judicata* under Article X of Law No 10.[120] The only issue, therefore, was whether the individual defendants had

[115] Ibid.   [116] Ibid., 1214.
[117] *Krupp*, Anderson Concurrence, IX TWC 439.
[118] Ibid., 465–6, Wilkins Concurrence.
[119] Ibid., 466, Wilkins Concurrence.
[120] See, e.g., *Farben*, VIII TWC 1127; *Krupp*, Anderson Concurrence, IX TWC 435.

participated in the common plan. Such responsibility, according to the tribunals, required the prosecution to prove that a defendant had knowledge of the plan and took steps to carry it out.[121] The requisite knowledge could be established by proof that a defendant was either "in such close relationship with Hitler that he must have been informed of Hitler's aggressive plans ... or attended at least one of the four secret meetings at which Hitler disclosed his plans for aggressive war"—a standard that the tribunals derived from the IMT judgment.[122]

The "common plan or conspiracy" charges were summarily dismissed in both *High Command* and *Farben*. Once the *High Command* tribunal concluded that none of the defendants satisfied the leadership requirement for planning, preparing, initiating, and waging aggressive wars or invasions, it was a foregone conclusion that they could not be convicted of participating in the common plan. In fact, Tribunal V did not even address those charges.[123] Similarly, given that the *Farben* tribunal equated "planning" and "common plan," it had to dismiss the common-plan charges once it concluded that none of the defendants had participated—much less knowingly participated—in planning any of the Nazis' aggressive wars or invasions.[124]

The *Ministries* tribunal also dismissed the "common plan or conspiracy" charges, holding that "[n]o evidence has been offered to substantiate a conviction of the defendants in a common plan and conspiracy."[125] That conclusion is open to question, however, given that Tribunal IV convicted both Koerner and Lammers of planning crimes against peace. Koerner's acquittal is the more defensible of the two. First, he did not participate in any of the four conferences at which Hitler revealed his aggressive aims. And second, although he held extremely significant positions in the Nazi government, he did not seem to have the "close relationship" with Hitler that led to Hess's conviction. Indeed, Koerner's situation seems almost precisely analogous to Funk's, given that both worked under Goering in the Four Year Plan and both were members of the Central Planning Board. If Funk could not be convicted of participating in the common plan, it is difficult to see how Koerner could have been.

Lammers, however, is a different story. Although he did not attend any of the four conferences, the *Ministries* tribunal recognized that, as Reich Minister and Chief of the Reich Chancellery, Lammers "occupied a position of influence and authority through which he collaborated with and greatly helped Hitler and the Nazi hierarchy in their various plans of aggression and expansion." Indeed, it noted that Hitler and Goering had personally asked him to help draft the Four Year Plan, a fact that it said "indicates graphically how dependent they were upon him for the proper formulation and efficient implementation of that and following schemes."[126] He also participated in numerous conferences at which plans for

---

[121] See, e.g., *Farben*, VIII TWC 1102.
[122] Ibid.
[123] See *High Command*, XI TWC 491.
[124] *Farben*, VIII TWC 1128.
[125] *Ministries*, XIV TWC 436.
[126] Ibid., 401.

specific aggressive wars and invasions were discussed, including conferences concerning Austria, Czechoslovakia, Poland, Denmark, the Low Countries, and the Soviet Union.[127] The "common plan or conspiracy" case against Lammers thus seems at least as strong, if not actually stronger, than the case against von Ribbentrop, who was convicted on Count One of the IMT indictment because his "diplomatic efforts were so closely connected with war that he could not have remained unaware of the aggressive nature of Hitler's actions."[128]

The "common plan or conspiracy" charges fared no better in *Krupp*. Tribunal III dismissed the charges—and the crimes against peace charges as a whole—prior to the defense case, stating simply that it could not find the defendants guilty even if it assumed that all of the prosecution's evidence was credible.[129] There was, however, a unique angle to the prosecution's allegations against the Krupp defendants: it not only claimed that the defendants had participated in the *Nazis'* conspiracy to commit aggressive wars and invasions, it also argued that the defendants had *conspired among themselves* to do so. As the prosecution wrote in its response to the defendants' motion to dismiss, "[t]he conspiracy charged here is not the 'Nazi conspiracy' charged in count one of the indictment filed before [the IMT], with which its judgment deals, but is a conspiracy to do the acts of the character charged under count two of that indictment," namely, preparing and waging aggressive war.[130]

The prosecution's argument concerning the defendants' responsibility for a separate "Krupp conspiracy" had two basic elements. To begin with, it claimed that the members of the Krupp firm had independently conspired to prepare Germany for aggressive war from the end of World War I until the Nazis came to power, at which point in time the Krupp conspiracy and the Nazi conspiracy merged.[131] It then argued that, under basic principles of conspiracy, "Alfried Krupp, Loeser, and other defendants who dominated the Krupp firm and controlled it in the latter years of the conspiracy, are as liable for those activities as those of the defendants who were in the conspiracy from the beginning."[132] That was a critical claim, because only three of the defendants in Krupp had been with the firm in 1919, and the prosecution conceded that "none of them occupied a sufficiently important position to justify charging them with the responsibility for decisions taken at the end of 1920."[133]

The prosecution's argument was creative but unsuccessful: Tribunal III refused to conclude "that there were two or more separate conspiracies to accomplish the same end, one the 'Nazi conspiracy' and the other the 'Krupp conspiracy'."[134] The tribunal did not explain why the prosecution's argument failed in its order

127 Ibid., 406–15.
128 IMT Judgment, 190.
129 *Krupp*, Order Acquitting Defendants, IX TWC 393.
130 Ibid., 371, Prosecution Response.
131 Ibid., 369, Prosecution Response.
132 Ibid., 371, Prosecution Response.
133 *Krupp*, Anderson Concurrence, IX TWC 411.
134 Ibid., 400, Order Acquitting Defendants.

dismissing the crimes against peace charges. Instead, both Judge Anderson and Judge Wilkins addressed that issue in their concurring opinions.

Judge Anderson focused on the first element of the prosecution's argument, the existence of a Krupp conspiracy dating back to 1919. He argued that the alleged conspiracy was best understood not as a conspiracy to wage aggressive war, but as a conspiracy to preserve Krupp's armament potential in case "some future government embarked upon a rearmament program in support of a national policy of aggrandizement."[135] Such a conspiracy could not be considered criminal, however, because the IMT had specifically held that a conspiracy had to be "clearly outlined in its criminal purpose" and could not be "too far removed from the time of decision and of action."[136] Judge Anderson then pointed out that even if the Krupp conspiracy could be considered criminal, the crime itself was complete in 1919, when the members of Krupp agreed to rearm Germany. But if that was the case, the conspiracy presented "a serious question of jurisdiction"—not even the most liberal interpretation of Law No. 10 criminalized actions taken more than two decades before the Nazis came to power.[137]

Judge Wilkins, in turn, focused on the second element of the prosecution's argument, the idea that the defendants could be held liable for the actions of their predecessors. He was much more sympathetic to the prosecution's argument than Judge Anderson. He believed, for example, that the prosecution had established that Krupp had knowingly and intentionally supported the Nazis' aggressive aims during the early years of Hitler's regime.[138] He also acknowledged that had the tribunal adopted the "widely accepted, less conservative theory of conspiracy" the prosecution had proposed, the defendants would likely have been convicted, because he believed that the defendants were fully aware of Krupp's support for the Nazis when they assumed positions of importance in the company. He nevertheless supported the tribunal's decision to dismiss the conspiracy charges, agreeing with his brethren that a more conservative approach to the doctrine of conspiracy was warranted because the tribunal was acting "in a comparatively new field of international law."[139]

Conclusion

The crimes against peace charges in the trials were a spectacular failure: of the 66 defendants who faced such charges, only three were ever finally convicted of them. The tribunals nevertheless made a number of important contributions to the development of what the IMT called "the supreme international crime." First, unlike the IMT, the tribunals systematically identified the crime's four essential

---

[135] Ibid., 412, Anderson Concurrence.
[136] IMT Judgment, 43.
[137] *Krupp*, Anderson Concurrence, IX TWC 420–1.
[138] Ibid., 457, Wilkins Concurrence.
[139] Ibid.

elements: a state act of aggression; sufficient authority to satisfy the leadership requirement; participation in the planning, preparing, initiating or waging of the aggressive act; and *mens rea*. Second, although Lammers' and Keppler's convictions likely violated the principle of non-retroactivity, the tribunals established that a bloodless invasion qualified as an act of aggression. Third, the tribunals provided a clear and workable definition of the leadership requirement—and made clear that, the acquittals notwithstanding, private economic actors could be complicit in aggression. Finally, the tribunals disentangled the various forms of participation in an act of aggression, particularly with regard to "waging."

9

War Crimes

Introduction

Article II(1)(a) of Law No. 10 recognized the following acts as war crimes:

Atrocities or offenses against persons or property constituting violations of the laws or customs of war, including but not limited to, murder, ill treatment or deportation to slave labour or for any other purpose, of civilian population from occupied territory, murder or ill treatment of prisoners of war or persons on the seas, killing of hostages, plunder of public or private property, wanton destruction of cities, towns or villages, or devastation not justified by military necessity.

This chapter examines the tribunals' war-crimes jurisprudence. Section I explores when the Hague and Geneva Conventions applied, how the tribunals defined "occupation," and whether the applicability of the Conventions was affected by the illegality of a particular war or invasion. Section II discusses two issues involved in the summary execution of partisans: when partisans could qualify as lawful combatants, and whether unlawful combatants could be summarily executed. Section III focuses on crimes against prisoners of war. Section IV examines crimes against civilians. Finally, Section V addresses the crime against property of plunder/spoliation.

I. The Application of the Laws and Customs of War

A. The General Applicability of the Conventions

The tribunals derived "the laws and customs of war" from two primary sources: the Regulations annexed to the Hague Convention IV of 1907, and the Geneva Convention of 1929. Like their predecessors at the IMT, the NMT defendants challenged the general applicability of the Conventions. The Hague Regulations did not apply, they contended, because some of the belligerents were not parties to it, thereby running afoul of the "general participation" requirement in Article 2 of the Convention.[1] And they argued that the Geneva Convention did not apply, at least with regard to the war between Germany and the Soviet Union, because the latter had denounced

---

[1] See, e.g., *High Command*, XI TWC 532.

adherence to the Convention.[2] Those arguments were no more successful than they had been at the IMT: without exception, the tribunals held that the Hague and Geneva Conventions were binding because—in the words of the *High Command* tribunal—"they were in substance an expression of international law as accepted by the civilized nations of the world."[3]

That said, multiple tribunals questioned whether all of the provisions in the Conventions qualified as customary international law. The *High Command* tribunal focused on POWs, pointing out that "[i]n stating that the Hague and Geneva Conventions express accepted usages and customs of war, it must be noted that certain detailed provisions pertaining to the care and treatment of prisoners of war can hardly be so designated."[4] The *Farben* tribunal focused on the means and methods of warfare, suggesting that "[t]echnical advancement in the weapons and tactics used in the actual waging of war may have made obsolete, in some respects, or may have rendered inapplicable, some of the provisions of the Hague Regulations having to do with the actual conduct of hostilities and what is considered legitimate warfare."[5] The *Flick* tribunal agreed regarding means and methods, claiming that the obsolescence of the Hague Regulations made plain "the necessity of appraising the conduct of defendants with relation to the circumstances and conditions of their environment." Guilt, the tribunal insisted, "may not be determined theoretically or abstractly. Reasonable and practical standards must be considered."[6]

B. The Specific Applicability of the Conventions

Once the tribunals determined that the Hague and Geneva Conventions applied during the war, they then had to determine whether they applied to specific wars and invasions. Four questions were particularly important. First, did the Conventions apply to "peaceful" invasions, or was actual armed conflict required? Second, at what point did a war or invasion develop into a belligerent occupation? Third, did the Conventions protect Germans who fought in wars or invasions that qualified as crimes against peace? And fourth, did violations of the laws of war release opposing forces from the obligation to comply with those laws?

1. Actual Conflict

The tribunals uniformly held that the Hague and Geneva Conventions did not apply unless an invasion resulted in actual armed conflict. That issue was first addressed in *Farben*, when the defendants moved to dismiss plunder allegations in

---

[2] See, e.g., *Milch*, Musmanno Concurrence, II TWC 821.
[3] *High Command*, XI TWC 534; see also *Farben*, VIII TWC 1138; *Einsatzgruppen*, IV TWC 459.
[4] *High Command*, XI TWC 535.
[5] *Farben*, VIII TWC 1138.
[6] *Flick*, VI TWC 1208.

Austria and the Sudetenland on the ground that the prosecution had failed to prove that a "state of actual warfare" existed in those locations. Tribunal VI acknowledged "the force of the argument that property situated in a weak nation which falls a victim to the aggressor because of incapacity to resist should receive a degree of protection equal to that in cases of belligerent occupation when actual warfare has existed." It nevertheless granted the motion, arguing that it was required "to apply international law as we find it."[7]

Two other tribunals reached similar conclusions. In *Krupp*, Tribunal III dismissed plunder charges in Austria for want of jurisdiction.[8] And in *Ministries*, Tribunal IV dismissed plunder charges in the Sudetenland on the ground that, because Germany occupied the Sudetenland as a result of the Munich Pact, "the occupation of the territory ... did not create a situation of belligerent occupancy subject to the restrictions of the Hague Convention."[9]

Judge Wilkins dissented from Tribunal III's holding in *Krupp*—and from the general idea that peaceful invasions did not trigger the Hague Regulations. He made two points, both of which are persuasive. First, he noted that the "actual warfare" requirement was inconsistent with the IMT, which had specifically held that the laws of war applied in the Sudetenland[10] and had not reached the same conclusion regarding Austria only because the prosecution had not alleged that war crimes were committed there.[11] Second, he noted that, as a matter of policy, it made no sense to exempt an aggressor from the restrictions of the Hague Regulations simply because the state that it invaded was too militarily weak to resist.[12] The latter objection is particularly important, because the "actual warfare" requirement imposed by the *Farben*, *Krupp*, and *Ministries* tribunals meant that the invasions of Austria and Czechoslovakia were crimes against peace but could not involve the commission of war crimes—an asymmetry that is difficult to reconcile with the IMT's insistence that aggression is the "supreme international crime" because "it contains within itself the accumulated evil of the whole."[13]

2. Belligerent Occupation

The tribunals also had to determine when actual warfare, which was sufficient to make the Hague and Geneva Conventions generally applicable, developed into a belligerent occupation, thus triggering the rules contained in Articles 42–56 of the Hague Regulations. That issue was first discussed at length in the *Hostage* case concerning the invasions of Greece, Yugoslavia, and Norway. Tribunal V distinguished between "invasion" and "occupation" as follows:

---

[7] *Farben*, VIII TWC 1130. [8] *Krupp*, IX TWC 1373.
[9] *Ministries*, XIV TWC 684. [10] IMT Judgment, 125.
[11] *Krupp*, Wilkins Dissent, IX TWC 1459.
[12] Ibid., 1460, Wilkins Dissent.
[13] IMT Judgment, 13.

Whether an invasion has developed into an occupation is a question of fact. The term invasion implies a military operation while an occupation indicates the exercise of governmental authority to the exclusion of the established government. This presupposes the destruction of organized resistance and the establishment of an administration to preserve law and order. To the extent that the occupant's control is maintained and that of the civil government eliminated, the area will be said to be occupied.[14]

The tribunal emphasized—echoing Article 42 of the Hague Regulations—that the rules of occupation applied only to territory that the occupying power actually controlled and continued to apply only while the occupant maintained its control.[15] It nevertheless rejected the defendants' claim that any sustained partisan activity in a country that temporarily disrupted an occupant's control meant the territory was no longer belligerently occupied. Regarding such activity in Yugoslavia and Greece, for example, the tribunal held that belligerent occupation survived temporary control of territory, because "the Germans could at any time they desired assume physical control of any part of the country."[16]

The tribunals also rejected the defense argument that Germany's "annexation" of various occupied countries meant that those countries were no longer belligerently occupied. The IMT had pointed out that the doctrine of annexation "was never considered to be applicable so long as there was an army in the field attempting to restore the occupied countries to their true owners," as had been the case throughout World War II.[17] The tribunals agreed. In *RuSHA*, for example, Tribunal I held that "the Incorporated Eastern Territories" remained belligerently occupied, because "[a]ny purported annexation of territories of a foreign nation, occurring during the time of war and while opposing armies were still in the field," was "invalid and ineffective."[18] The *Farben*, *Ministries*, and *Justice* tribunals took the same position—although the latter pointed out, on a realist note, that attempts to annex territory are always "dependent upon the final successful outcome of the war," because once a war succeeds, "no one questions the validity of the annexation."[19]

3. Jus ad Bellum *vs.* Jus in Bello

The prosecution argued in two cases that Germany's decision to initiate aggressive wars and invasions meant that it forfeited the protections of the Hague and Geneva Conventions. In the *Justice* case, it argued that German laws that prohibited "undermining military efficiency," which would have been legal in a defensive war, were criminal because they were connected to wars of aggression.[20] And in the *Hostage* case, it argued that the German army was not entitled to exercise the rights of an occupant in Yugoslavia and Greece because the occupations had resulted from illegal invasions.[21]

---

[14] *Hostage*, XI TWC 1243.   [15] Ibid.   [16] Ibid.
[17] IMT Judgment, 65.   [18] *RuSHA*, V TWC 154.
[19] *Farben*, VIII TWC 1137; *Ministries*, XIV TWC 685; *Justice*, III TWC 1027.
[20] *Justice*, III TWC 1025–6.   [21] *Hostage*, XI TWC 1246.

The tribunals disagreed. The *Hostage* tribunal specifically reaffirmed the traditional independence of the *jus ad bellum* and the *jus in bello*, noting that "international law makes no distinction between a lawful and an unlawful occupant in dealing with the respective duties of occupant and population in occupied territory. There is no reciprocal connection between the manner of the military occupation of territory and the rights and duties of the occupant and population to each other after the relationship has in fact been established."[22] The *Justice* tribunal took the same position, adding that eliminating the distinction between the *jus ad bellum* and *jus in bello* would mean "that every soldier who marched under orders into occupied territory or who fought in the homeland was a criminal and a murderer," making the defendants' trial—and all similar trials—"a mere formality."[23]

4. Reciprocity

Finally, the *Ministries* tribunal affirmed the idea that a belligerent is obligated to respect the laws of war even if its adversary does not. Von Weizsaecker was charged with participating in the distribution of an order from Hitler directing Norwegian, Finnish, and Danish soldiers who entered Norway across Sweden's neutral borders to be deemed guerrillas and executed. His defense was that the Geneva Convention's POW provisions did not apply to the executions, because the affected soldiers had violated Article 2 of the Hague Convention V of 1907—concerning the rights and duties of neutral powers during land wars—which provided that "[b]elligerents are forbidden to move troops or convoys of either munitions of war or supplies across the territory of a neutral power." The *Ministries* tribunal rejected that argument, holding that such violations could not justify either murdering the soldiers or "depriving them of the status of prisoners of war and the protection afforded by the Geneva Convention."[24]

II. Summary Execution of Unlawful Combatants

Hitler's order to summarily execute non-Norwegian soldiers captured in Norway was never carried out. Unfortunately, that was the exception, not the rule: as Taylor noted in his Final Report, "the outright slaughter" of individuals who resisted German aggression was a regular occurrence during World War II.[25] When those individuals qualified as POWs, their murder was obviously criminal. Article 4 of the Hague Regulations required POWs to be "humanely treated," and Article 2 of the Geneva Convention provided that POWs had to be "at all times humanely treated and protected, particularly against acts of violence."

NMT defendants charged with executing POWs, however, consistently argued that their victims were unlawful combatants—partisans, guerrillas, bandits,

---

[22] Ibid., 1247. [23] *Justice*, III TWC 1027.
[24] *Ministries*, XIV TWC 464. [25] Taylor, *Final Report*, 66.

francs-tireurs—who were not protected by the Hague and Geneva Conventions.[26] That defense was anything but frivolous; as Adam Roberts has pointed out, it is difficult to contend that, during World War II, "there was a clear, precise, and effective body of law relating to the problem of resistance in occupied territories."[27] Addressing the defendants' argument, therefore, required the tribunals to answer two basic questions. First, under what circumstances did partisans qualify as lawful combatants entitled to be treated as POWs? Second, if partisans did not qualify as lawful combatants, were the Nazis entitled to summarily execute them upon capture?

A. Lawful Combatants

The right of the inhabitants of an invaded country to resist their invader was the source of significant debate during the conferences that led to the adoption of the 1907 Hague Convention IV. States with large armies insisted that lawful-combatant status should extend only to organized military forces and to members of a *levée en masse* who met the same requirements as regular combatants. Less powerful states, by contrast, wanted to ensure that the definition of lawful combatant did nothing—in the words of a British proposal offered at the 1899 Hague Conference—"to modify or suppress the right which a population of an invaded country possesses of fulfilling its duty of offering the most energetic national resistance to the invaders by every means in its power."[28] The impasse was ultimately solved by adopting a two-pronged approach to lawful combatancy. First, the Convention would not specifically exclude groups from the definition of lawful combatant; instead, it would detail the requirements for two specific kind of armed groups—irregular forces and individuals involved in a *levée en masse*—to qualify as lawful combatants. Second, the Convention would make clear that the requirements for lawful combatancy were not exclusive.[29]

The first aspect of the compromise led to the adoption of Articles 1 and 2 of the Hague Regulations. Article 1 addressed irregular forces such as militia and volunteer corps. It provided that such forces were entitled to lawful-combatant status if they satisfied four conditions: (1) they were commanded by a person responsible for his subordinates; (2) they had a fixed and distinctive emblem that was recognizable at a distance; (3) they carried arms openly; and (4) they conducted their operations in a manner consistent with the laws and customs of war. Article 2 dealt with a *levée en masse*, providing that the inhabitants of invaded territory who spontaneously took up arms to resist their invader qualified as lawful combatants as long as they carried arms openly and respected the laws and customs of war. The Preamble to the Hague Convention then addressed the second aspect of the

---

[26] See, e.g., *Einsatzgruppen*, IV TWC 492; *Ministries*, XIV TWC 530.

[27] Adam Roberts, "Land Warfare: From Hague to Nuremberg," in *The Laws of War*, 116, 133 (Michael Howard et al. eds, 1994).

[28] Lester Nurick & Roger W. Barrett, "Legality of Guerrilla Forces Under the Laws of War," 40 *Am. J. Int'l L.* 563, 565 (1946).

[29] Ibid., 566.

compromise, providing that "in cases not included in the Regulations adopted by them, the inhabitants and the belligerents remain under the protection and the rule of the principles of the law of nations"—the Martens Clause.

In addressing whether partisans qualified as lawful combatants, the NMTs embraced a very conservative reading of the Hague Regulations. None of the tribunals ever acknowledged the Martens Clause; on the contrary, they uniformly held that a partisan could qualify as a lawful combatant only if he satisfied the requirements of either Article 1 or 2 of the Regulations. In *High Command*, for example, Tribunal V simply quoted the two Articles and then held that "[a] failure to meet these requirements deprives one so failing on capture of a prisoner of war status."[30] The *Hostage* tribunal reached a similar conclusion, even though it acknowledged the debates at the 1899 Hague Conference and the earlier 1874 Brussels Conference. Indeed, the tribunal insisted that "[a] review of the positions assumed by the various nations" was pointless, because it believed—erroneously, in light of the Martens Clause—that Articles 1 and 2 of the Regulations represented the compromise between the two sides of the debate and "remained the controlling authority in the fixing of a legal belligerency. If the requirements of the Hague Regulation, 1907, are met, a lawful belligerency exists; if they are not met, it is an unlawful one."[31]

Having identified the applicable legal standards, the tribunals then had to address specific claims that the defendants' victims did not qualify as lawful combatants. Only one such claim ever succeeded, regarding the status of partisan units active in Yugoslavia and Greece. The *Hostage* tribunal held that the "greater portion" of those units—whose members were executed in the thousands—had failed to comply with the requirements of Article 1, because they had no common uniform, generally wore civilian clothes, used a distinctive emblem (the Soviet star) that could not be seen at a distance, and only carried their arms openly when it was in their advantage to do so. The partisans were thus *francs-tireurs* who were not entitled to be treated as POWs upon capture.[32]

Three tribunals, by contrast, categorically rejected unlawful-combatant claims. In *Einsatzgruppen*, Tribunal II held that there was no justification for the defendants labeling thousands of their victims in the Soviet Union as partisans, because the killing-squads' own reports indicated that "combatants were indiscriminately punished only for having fought against the enemy."[33] In *Ministries*, Tribunal IV rejected Woermann's argument that the non-Norwegian soldiers found in Norway were unlawful combatants, despite complying with Article 1, because they were not organized on Norwegian soil. The tribunal noted that Article 1 did not contain such a requirement—and pointed out that "[i]f a belligerent may grant or refuse prisoner-of-war status to members of enemy forces because in its judgment the prisoner had not been lawfully inducted into the enemy army, the very purpose of the provisions of the Hague Convention would be defeated."[34] Finally, in *High Command*, Tribunal V refused to even consider defense claims that the Barbarossa

[30] *High Command*, XI TWC 529–30.   [31] *Hostage*, XI TWC 1247.
[32] Ibid., 1244.   [33] *Einsatzgruppen*, IV TWC 493.
[34] *Ministries*, XIV TWC 465–6.

Jurisdiction Order had led only to the execution of unlawful combatants, because it held that the order categorized "partisans" in such an overbroad manner relative to Article 1 that it could not possibly be legal. For example, the order authorized the summary execution of "[e]very civilian who impedes or incites others to impede the German Wehrmacht," a criterion that "clearly opens the way for arbitrary and bloody implementation."[35]

B. Summary Execution

The second issue that the tribunals had to address was whether partisans who were unlawful combatants, and thus not protected by the Hague or Geneva Conventions, could be summarily executed upon capture. They had little trouble concluding that unlawful combatants could be *executed*. The *Hostage* tribunal pointed out, for example, that guerillas who did not satisfy either Article 1 or Article 2 of the Hague Regulations were placed "much in the same position as a spy. By the law of war it is lawful to use spies. Nevertheless, a spy when captured may be shot because the belligerent has the right, by means of an effective deterrent punishment, to defend against the grave dangers of enemy spying. The principle therein involved applies to guerrillas who are not lawful belligerents."[36] The *Einsatzgruppen* tribunal was even more blunt, noting that "under these provisions, an armed civilian found in a treetop sniping at uniformed soldiers is not such a lawful combatant and can be punished even with the death penalty if he is proved guilty of the offense."[37]

The "proved guilty" qualification, however, was critical. The tribunals uniformly agreed that captured partisans could not be *summarily* executed; their captors first had to determine through some sort of fair judicial process that they were, in fact, unlawful combatants.[38] In the *Hostage* case, for example, Tribunal V held Rendulic responsible for the execution of hostages, reprisal prisoners, and partisans because "[c]ourt martial proceedings were not held as required." Instead, the victims were simply killed "without even the semblance of a judicial hearing."[39] Similarly, in *Einsatzgruppen*, Tribunal II rejected Haensch's claim that Sonderkommando 4b's execution of hundreds of partisans in Russia was legal on the ground that there was no evidence in the record that status hearings had been held prior to the executions, much less that such hearings had "conformed to the accepted trial requirements, recognized by the rules of war and international law."[40]

Unfortunately, the tribunals were maddeningly vague concerning what the "accepted trial requirements" actually were. The *High Command* tribunal expressed skepticism that a court procedure was required, suggesting that a quasi-judicial hearing before a military officer would suffice.[41] That officer, however, had to be of

---

[35] *High Command*, XI TWC 530.
[36] *Hostage*, XI TWC 1245.
[37] *Einsatzgruppen*, IV TWC 392.
[38] See, e.g., ibid., 549; *High Command*, XI TWC 531.
[39] *Hostage*, XI TWC 1290.
[40] *Einsatzgruppen*, IV TWC 549.
[41] *High Command*, XI TWC 523.

significant rank; the tribunal held that permitting a junior officer to conduct the proceedings would be criminal.[42] Regardless of who conducted the hearing, the decision-maker could neither presume that the suspect was an unlawful combatant nor require the suspect to prove that he was not.[43] The decision-maker also had to apply a substantial standard of proof; mere suspicion that the suspect was an unlawful combatant was not enough.[44]

If a hearing satisfied the minimum requirements of international law, the officer conducting the hearing would not be guilty of a war crime simply because he mistakenly deprived a suspect of POW status. On the contrary, the *Hostage* tribunal specifically held that "[i]n determining the guilt or innocence of an army commander when charged with a failure or refusal to accord a belligerent status to captured members of the resistance forces, the situation as it appeared to him must be given the first consideration . . . Where room exists for an honest error in judgment the commander is entitled to the benefit thereof by virtue of the presumption of his innocence."[45] That said, the tribunal made clear that blind deference was also not required: a commander would not be permitted "to ignore obvious facts in arriving at a conclusion." Indeed, the tribunal pointed out that "[o]ne trained in military science will ordinarily have no difficulty in arriving at a correct decision."[46]

III. Crimes Against Prisoners of War

Taylor noted in his Final Report that crimes against POWs played a less significant role in the NMT trials than crimes against civilians.[47] The tribunals did pay significant attention, however, to three crimes involving POWs: murder, use in the war effort, and mistreatment. The murder of POWs was obviously criminal, as discussed above. This section will thus focus on issues of use in the war effort and mistreatment.

A. Use of POWs in the War Effort

Tribunal V noted in *High Command* that the Hague Regulations and the Geneva Convention did not take a consistent approach to the use of POWs in the war effort. Article 6 of the Hague Regulations provided that the labor of POWs "shall have no *connection* with the operations of war." Article 31 of the Geneva Convention, by contrast, provided that POW labor "shall have no *direct connection* with the operations of the war." That inconsistency, however, did not prevent the tribunals from concluding that two categories of POW labor clearly violated both Article 6 and Article 31: using POWs in the production of armaments and other weapons of war, such as airplanes, regardless of whether the "employer" was a government

---

[42] Ibid.   [43] Ibid., 531.   [44] Ibid.
[45] *Hostage*, XI TWC 1245–6.   [46] Ibid., 1246.
[47] Taylor, *Final Report*, 65.

institution[48] or a private corporation[49]; and using POWs in any kind of war-related work that was inherently dangerous, such as loading ammunition, mine-clearing, and manning anti-aircraft guns.[50]

Defendants accused of violating Articles 6 and 31 offered two defenses for their actions. The first was that the state of which the POWs were nationals had authorized their use in the war effort. The *Krupp* defendants made that argument with regard to the Vichy government and French POWs used in Krupp plants to manufacture armaments. Tribunal III rejected the defense, noting that such an agreement—which the judges did not believe existed—"was void under the law of nations," because it would have been made at a time when France and Germany were still technically at war, having signed an armistice but not a treaty of peace.[51]

Defendants also claimed that the POWs involved in the war effort had consented to being used in that way. In *Ministries*, for example, Schellenberg made that argument regarding "Operation Zeppelin," in which Soviet POWs had been used to conduct espionage in areas that the Germans had not yet occupied. The prosecution did not contest that the Soviet POWs had voluntarily spied on their countrymen; instead, it insisted that their consent was irrelevant. The *Ministries* tribunal rejected the prosecution's position, holding that "the cited prohibitions of the Hague Convention prohibit[ing] the use of prisoners of war in connection with war operations . . . apply only when such use is brought about by force, threats, or duress, and not when the person renders the services voluntarily."[52]

B. Mistreatment of POWs

The tribunals also devoted considerable attention to the mistreatment of POWs. Such mistreatment fell into two basic categories: forcing POWs to work in inhumane and dangerous conditions; and denying POWs accused of criminal activity a fair trial.

1. Inhumane and Dangerous Conditions

Both the Hague Regulations and the Geneva Conventions required POWs to be "humanely treated."[53] The Geneva Convention also contained a number of more specific provisions that prohibited the use of POWs in inhumane and dangerous labor conditions, such as Article 32's insistence that POWs not be given "unhealthy or dangerous" work. In *High Command*, Tribunal V specifically held that all of

---

[48] See, e.g., *Milch*, II TWC 785.
[49] See, e.g., *Krupp*, IX TWC 1376.
[50] See, e.g., *High Command*, XI TWC 601 (ammunition and mines); *Milch*, II TWC 785 (anti-aircraft guns).
[51] *Krupp*, IX TWC 1395.
[52] *Ministries*, XIV TWC 667–8.
[53] Hague Regulations, Art. 4; Geneva Conventions, Art. 2.

these provisions were declaratory of customary international law and that their violation was a war crime.[54]

a. Inhumane Conditions

A number of tribunals focused on the war crime of forcing POWs to work in inhumane conditions. In *Krupp*, Tribunal III condemned the company's practice of using Soviet POWs in "heavy work" for which, "due to undernourishment, they were totally unfit physically."[55] Indeed, the tribunal emphasized that Krupp had treated the Soviet POWs so poorly that both plant managers and officers in the German army who were responsible for POW labor had protested.[56] Similarly, the *High Command* tribunal concluded that German treatment of Russian POWs was based on the "economic principle that it was better to work them to death than to merely let them die" and was thus criminal.[57]

The *Farben* tribunal, by contrast, was unimpressed by the prosecution's claim that POWs forced to work at Auschwitz III were criminally mistreated. The tribunal concluded that they were "treated better than other types of workers in every respect," because "[t]he housing, the food, and the type of work they were required to perform would indicate that they were the favored laborers of the plant site." Any "isolated instances of ill-treatment," it thus held, did not result from Farben policy or from acts for which Farben was responsible.[58]

b. Dangerous Conditions

In *Krupp*, Tribunal III convicted defendants for violating Article 9 of the Geneva Convention, which prohibited POWs from being sent to areas where they "would be exposed to the fire of the fighting zone." According to the tribunal, Krupp had established POW camps in Essen despite anticipating (correctly) that the city would be the target of Allied bombing attacks and had failed to provide the POWs with "adequate air raid protection"—a failure that the tribunal held aggravated the crime.[59]

2. Unfair Trials

Although none of the tribunals questioned Germany's right to try captured POWs for violations of the laws of war, they agreed that—in the words of the *Ministries* tribunal—"[w]here a captured enemy is suspected or charged with violation of the rules of war, he has the right to be tried in accordance with those rules."[60] The failure to provide POWs with a fair trial led to a number of convictions. In *Ministries*, Tribunal IV held that Schellenberg was criminally responsible for permitting his subordinates to execute Soviet POWs who had voluntarily served in Operation Zeppelin "without trial or notice of any offense of which they were alleged to be guilty," a policy that the tribunal described as "a flagrant violation of

---

[54] *High Command*, XI TWC 538.   [55] *Krupp*, IX TWC 1388.   [56] Ibid., 1366.
[57] *High Command*, XI TWC 538.   [58] *Farben*, VIII TWC 1183.
[59] *Krupp*, IX TWC 1393.   [60] *Ministries*, XIV TWC, 441.

international law."[61] In the *Justice* case, Tribunal III convicted Lautz for bringing high-treason charges against Polish POWs for attempting to escape from the Reich, because such charges "represented an unwarrantable extension of the concept" and meant that POWs would be executed "for a minor offense."[62] And in *High Command*, Tribunal V held that the mere act of turning over POWs to the SD was a war crime, because the defendants "must have...suspected or known" that the "murderous organization" would execute the POWs without trial.[63]

IV. Crimes Against Civilians

War crimes against civilians played a central role in the trials. This section focuses on five of the most important crimes: hostage-taking and reprisals; use in the war effort; deportation; slave labor; and mistreatment.

A. Hostage-Taking and Reprisals

As Taylor noted in his Final Report, Germany's "wholesale execution of hostages under the guise of pacification" in occupied territory "perhaps aroused the bitterest and widespread condemnation during the war."[64] Tribunal V shared in that condemnation in the *Hostage* case—but nevertheless upheld the right of an occupier to execute civilian hostages in certain circumstances. It began by distinguishing between "hostages" and "reprisal prisoners":

> For the purposes of this opinion the term "hostages" will be considered as those persons of the civilian population who are taken into custody for the purpose of guaranteeing with their lives the future good conduct of the population of the community from which they were taken. The term "reprisal prisoners" will be considered as those individuals who are taken from the civilian population to be killed in retaliation for offenses committed by unknown persons within the occupied area.[65]

The tribunal then held that the execution of hostages was governed by different rules than the execution of reprisal prisoners.

1. Hostages

The *Hostage* tribunal based its approach on a "theory of collective responsibility" that applied to both the occupying power and the inhabitants of occupied territory. Occupation conferred on the occupying power the "right of control for the period of the occupation within the limitations and prohibitions of international law." Conversely, occupation obligated the inhabitants of occupied

---

[61] Ibid., 668.   [62] *Justice*, III TWC 1028.
[63] *High Command*, XI TWC 538.
[64] Taylor, *Final Report*, 68.
[65] *Hostage*, XI TWC 1249.

territory "to refrain from all injurious acts toward the troops or in respect to their military operations." The occupying power was thus entitled to respond to "injurious acts" by the inhabitants of occupied territory by taking hostages "to guarantee . . . peaceful conduct" and then, if peaceful conduct did not follow, to shoot them "as a last resort."[66]

The "last resort" language, however, was critical. The tribunal rejected the defendants' claim that hostages could be taken "as a matter of military expediency." On the contrary, it insisted that the occupying power was "required to use every available method to secure order and tranquility before resort may be had to the taking and execution of hostages." Prior to taking hostages, the occupying power was required to issue regulations designed to convince the inhabitants of occupied territory to not interfere with the occupation, such as imposing restrictions on their movement, evacuating "troublesome" areas, imposing monetary fines, etc. Hostage-taking was justified only if all of those less-Draconian steps failed to pacify the population.[67]

The tribunal also restricted who could be taken hostage when such taking was justified, holding that, because deterrence was the goal of executing hostages, "there must be some connection between the population from whom the hostages are taken and the crime committed."[68] Ideally, the hostages taken would come from the specific population resisting occupation. The tribunal accepted, however, that "[n]ationality or geographic proximity" was acceptable when such a narrow geographic nexus was impracticable.[69]

Finally, the tribunal imposed three procedural restrictions on the execution of hostages. First, the occupying power had to publish a proclamation that identified the hostages taken and informed the affected population that future acts of resistance would lead to their execution. Second, the actual execution order had to be based "upon the finding of a competent court martial that necessary conditions exist and all preliminary steps have been taken which are essential to the issuance of a valid order." Third, and finally, the number of hostages executed had to be proportionate to "the severity of the offenses the shooting is designed to deter."[70]

2. Reprisal Prisoners

The *Hostage* tribunal also held that it was legal for an occupying power to execute inhabitants of occupied territory in reprisal for violations of the laws of war.[71] As with hostages, however, it imposed a number of requirements on such executions. First, the same connection between the affected population and the perpetrators of the offense had to exist. Second, the occupying power had to publish a statement identifying the offense that ostensibly justified the reprisal. Third, the occupying power had to provide the affected population with a reasonable opportunity to identify the perpetrators of the offense. Fourth, executions had to be preceded by a

---

[66] Ibid.   [67] Ibid., 1249–50.   [68] Ibid., 1250.
[69] Ibid.   [70] Ibid.   [71] Ibid., 1253.

judicial finding that the executions were warranted, unless "the necessity for the reprisal require[d] immediate reprisal action to accomplish the desired purpose and which would be otherwise defeated by the invocation of judicial inquiry." Finally, the reprisal could not be excessive in comparison to the underlying crime.[72]

3. Fixed Ratios

Although the *Hostage* tribunal accepted the general idea that hostages and reprisal prisoners could be executed in the right circumstances, it had no trouble concluding that "[t]he extent to which the practice has been employed by the Germans exceeds the most elementary notions of humanity and justice."[73] An example was the execution of thousands of Serbian civilians in "reprisal" for a partisan attack that had killed 22 German soldiers near Topola. The tribunal held that List was responsible for "plain murder," because there was "no evidence of any connection whatever, geographical, racial, or otherwise between the persons shot and the attack at Topola," no judicial finding was ever made, and the executions were not even remotely proportionate to the underlying crime.[74]

The tribunal was particularly appalled by the German military's regular use of "fixed ratios"—orders that required or permitted the execution of a certain number of civilians for every German soldier killed by partisan activity. At Topola, for example, the ratio was 100:1. Such fixed ratios, the tribunal held, were per se criminal.[75]

No doubt anticipating this holding, Hans Laternser, List's main counsel, attempted to prove that the Allies had also relied on fixed ratios for reprisals. In particular, he alleged that on 25 November 1944, following the liberation of Paris, General Jacques Philippe LeClerc, the commander of the 2nd French Armored Division, had ordered the execution of five German hostages for each French soldier killed. The tribunal responded by ordering General Eisenhower to submit an affidavit confirming or denying the allegation. Eisenhower ultimately confirmed that the order had been given, but pointed out that LeClerc's successor had rescinded the illegal order less than a week later and had informed the Germans "that future orders would conform strictly to the principles of international law."[76]

4. Status Under Customary International Law

The *Hostage* tribunal's approach to hostage-taking provides a striking example of the NMTs' general willingness to disregard substantive provisions of Law No. 10 that they believed were inconsistent with international law. The "killing of hostages" was specifically criminalized by Article II(1)(b) of Law No. 10, as it had been by Article 6(b) of the London Charter. The tribunal, however, did not even *mention* Article II(1)(b) when it upheld the right of occupying powers to execute hostages and reprisal prisoners. On the contrary, it looked exclusively to conven-

---

[72] Ibid., 1252–3.   [73] Ibid., 1252.   [74] Ibid., 1270.
[75] Ibid.   [76] Eisenhower Affidavit, 1 Dec. 1947, NA-153–1018-7-86-1-1, at 1–2.

tional and customary international law, noting that "[i]nternational law is prohibitive law and no conventional prohibitions have been invoked to outlaw this
barbarous practice."[77]

Although regrettable, the tribunal's holding was likely correct. Killing hostages
was the second war crime included on the list prepared by the Commission on
Responsibilities at the end of World War I, but scholars generally accept that the
absence of *opinio juris* and state practice meant that such executions were permitted
by customary international law.[78] The American Rules of Land Warfare, for
example, specifically provided that "[h]ostages taken and held for the declared
purpose of insuring against unlawful acts by the enemy forces or people may be
punished or put to death if the unlawful acts are nevertheless committed."[79]

B. Use in the War Effort

The tribunals held that two different methods of using civilians in the war effort
constituted war crimes: forced conscription into the armed forces; and forced labor
related to military operations.

1. Conscription

Three tribunals condemned the Nazi practice of forcibly conscripting the inhabitants of occupied territory into the German military. The *Hostage* tribunal convicted General von Leyser for his role in the forcible conscription of Croatian
civilians into the Waffen Ustasha and the Croatian Wehrmacht. As the tribunal
noted, "occupation forces have no authority to conscript military forces from the
inhabitants of occupied territory. They cannot do it directly, nor can they do it
indirectly."[80] The *RuSHA* tribunal convicted Lorenz, the head of VoMi, for
permitting "tens of thousands of foreign nationals" to be removed from VoMi
camps and conscripted into the Waffen SS and the German army.[81] And the
Ministries tribunal convicted Berger for participating in forced conscription in ten
different countries, emphasizing that although it was not illegal to permit civilians
to voluntarily enlist, "pressure or coercion to compel such persons to enter into the
armed services obviously violates international law."[82]

2. Military Operations

Article 52 of the Hague Regulations provides that "[r]equisitions in kind and
services shall not be demanded from municipalities or inhabitants except for the

---

[77] *Hostage*, XI TWC 1252.
[78] See, e.g., A.R. Albrecht, "War Reprisals in the War Crimes Trials and in the Geneva Conventions of 1949," 47 *Am. J. Int'l L.* 590, 601–2 (1953).
[79] U.S. Army Rules of Land Warfare, Field Manual 27-10, at 89–90 (1940).
[80] *Hostage*, XI TWC 1305.
[81] *RuSHA*, V TWC 144.
[82] *Ministries*, XIV TWC 549.

needs of the army of occupation. They shall ... be of such a nature as not to involve the inhabitants in the obligation of taking part in military operations against their own country." Belligerents traditionally distinguished between "military operations" and "military preparations," excluding from the ambit of Article 52 "compulsion upon inhabitants to render assistance in the construction of military roads, fortifications, and the like behind the front, or in any other works in preparation for military operations."[83] The IMT rejected that distinction, expanding Article 52 to include not only "military preparations" but also any work that directly assisted an enemy's "war effort" or "war economy."[84]

The NMTs continued the IMT's expansion of Article 52. In *Krupp*, for example, Tribunal III held that the company had violated the Article by using civilians to produce arms, noting that "in the latter years of the war the production of armament on a substantial scale reached could not have been carried on without their labor."[85] Even more dramatically, the *High Command* tribunal convicted General Reinhardt for forcing civilians to engage in various kinds of labor within the area under his command.[86] According to the tribunal, Article 52 meant that "the compulsory labor of the civilian population *for the purpose* of carrying out military operations against their own country was illegal"[87]—a construction that indicates just how far the "military operation" language in Article 52 had evolved.

The *Milch* tribunal also held that forcing French civilians to engage in "war work," such as building airplanes for the military, was a war crime.[88] More notable, though, is the tribunal's rejection of two alleged justifications for such labor. First, anticipating the *Krupp* tribunal's similar position with regard to POWs, the tribunal held that it was irrelevant that the civilian laborers had been supplied by the French government pursuant to an agreement with Germany, because "the Vichy Government was a mere puppet set up under German domination, which, in full collaboration with Germany, took its orders from Berlin."[89] Second, it dismissed the defendants' insistence that the French civilians had voluntarily engaged in war work as "purely fictitious," asking "[d]oes anyone believe that the vast hordes of Slavic Jews who labored in Germany's war industries were accorded the rights of contracting parties?" The tribunal answered its own question: "[t]hey were slaves, nothing less."[90]

C. Deportation

Article II(1)(b) of Law No. 10 criminalized "deportation to slave labour or for any other purpose, of civilian population from occupied territory." The tribunals did not have to devote much effort to determining whether civilians had, in fact, been deported to Germany; as noted in Chapter 6, the *Milch, Pohl,* and *Farben* tribunals considered the IMT's conclusion that occupation authorities had deported "at least

---

[83] UNWCC History, 227.   [84] Ibid., 228–9.
[85] *Krupp*, IX TWC 1431.   [86] *High Command*, XI TWC 609.
[87] Ibid., 540.   [88] *Milch*, II TWC 788.
[89] Ibid.   [90] Ibid., 789.

5,000,000 persons to Germany to serve German industry and agriculture"[91] to be *res judicata*. The tribunals were thus left to address whether those deportations were criminal—an issue the IMT had essentially taken for granted.

The illegality of deportations arose for the first time in *Milch*, because many of the employees in the factories under the defendant's control had been deported from France and the Incorporated Eastern Territories. Tribunal II convicted Milch, but it said very little about the circumstances in which deportations were illegal. That silence led Judge Phillips to write separately to clarify the issue. In his view, deportation was a war crime in three different situations. First, it was criminal when conducted without "legal title," such as the deportation of civilians from occupied territory. Article 52 of the Hague Regulations limited requisitions in "services" to the "needs of the army of occupation"; by definition, civilians deported to labor outside of occupied territory were not working to satisfy such needs. Second, it was criminal when the purpose of the deportation was illegal, such as deportations designed to force civilians to participate in military operations against their own country. Third, it was criminal "whenever generally recognized standards of decency and humanity [we]re disregarded. This flows from the established principle of law that an otherwise permissible act becomes a crime when carried out in a criminal manner."[92]

Judge Phillips' concurring opinion had a significant influence on later trials. Tribunal III explicitly adopted his tripartite categorization of illegal deportation in *Krupp*,[93] and three other tribunals—in *Justice*, *RuSHA*, and *High Command*—held that the deportation of civilians from occupied territory was criminal on similar grounds.[94] The tribunals also had little trouble condemning specific deportations as criminal, such as Krupp's use of Jewish labor deported from Poland in its Bertha Works,[95] the Night and Fog program,[96] and the systematic deportation of ethnic Germans from occupied territories for Germanization.[97]

Unfortunately, the tribunals failed to conclusively resolve three important legal issues. To begin with, it is unclear whether deportation was limited to relocating civilians from one state to another or included relocations within a state. The *High Command* tribunal was the only tribunal that explicitly addressed the issue. It held that "there is no international law that permits the deportation . . . either within the area of the army . . . or to rear areas or to the homeland of the occupying power,"[98] implying that both deportation and transfer were war crimes. The *RuSHA* tribunal also implied that cross-border relocation was not required, referring to relocations from incorporated Poland to the Government General as deportation.[99]

---

[91] IMT Judgment, 57.
[92] *Milch*, Phillips Concurrence, II TWC 865–6.
[93] *Krupp*, IX TWC 1432.
[94] *Justice*, III TWC 1057; *RuSHA*, V TWC 126; *High Command*, XI TWC 603.
[95] *Krupp*, IX TWC 1417.
[96] *Justice*, III TWC 1057.
[97] *RuSHA*, V TWC 126.
[98] *High Command*, XI TWC 603.
[99] *RuSHA*, V TWC 126.

It is also unclear whether the tribunals uniformly believed that deportations had to be *forcible*. They most likely did: the *High Command* tribunal specifically held that the deportations had to be "against the will" of the affected civilians,[100] and the tribunals generally refused to condemn genuinely consensual acts that would have been criminal in the absence of consent. That said, the Article 52 rationale for criminalizing deportations articulated by Judge Phillips and adopted by the *Krupp* tribunal—that the labor of deported civilians would not be directed toward the needs of the occupying army—would apply to both voluntary and forcible deportations.

Finally, the tribunals left open the possibility that otherwise-criminal deportations could be justified on two different grounds. First, in the context of rejecting a "state security" defense of the Night and Fog program, the *Justice* tribunal suggested that an occupying power could remove civilians from occupied territory if doing so "was necessary to protect the security of the occupant forces"[101]—a potentially broad exception. Second, the *RuSHA* tribunal refused to condemn deportations that were carried out "by virtue of treaties entered into by Germany and the country concerned by the resettlement action,"[102] thus suggesting an exception to the tribunals' general refusal to recognize the right of governments to authorize the criminal treatment of their nationals.

D. Slave Labor

Slave-labor charges played a central role in seven of the 12 NMT trials: *Milch*, *Pohl*, *Flick*, *Farben*, *Krupp*, *High Command*, and *Ministries*. In part, their centrality simply reflected the fact that the Nazis had enslaved at least 5,000,000 civilians from occupied territories, a number that the *Pohl* tribunal stated "had been repeatedly and conclusively proved before this and other Tribunals,"[103] most notably the IMT. Taylor acknowledged in his Final Report, however, that the OCC's emphasis on slave labor was also motivated by political concerns:

[T]he problem of forced-labor was of current importance and particular significance in view of rumors and reports that it was prevalent in one or more countries of eastern Europe. It seemed to me that vigorous prosecution of those who were guilty of deporting and enslaving foreign workers under the Third Reich would make it clear beyond doubt that the United States did not condone such practices at any time or under any circumstances.[104]

In each of the seven cases, the OCC charged the defendants' use of slave labor as both a war crime and a crime against humanity. That practice could have become an issue during the trials: although Law No. 10 specifically designated "enslavement" as a crime against humanity, it only prohibited "deportation to slave labor"

---

[100] *High Command*, XI TWC 603.
[101] *Justice*, III TWC 1059.
[102] *RuSHA*, V TWC 126.
[103] *Pohl*, V TWC 970.
[104] Taylor, *Final Report*, 67.

as a war crime. Indeed, Judge Phillips acknowledged that distinction in his concurring opinion in *Milch*.[105] The tribunals nevertheless treated both enslavement and "deportation to slave labor" as independent war crimes.[106]

The tribunals also insisted, quite progressively, that the war crime of enslavement was different than the war crime of "ill treatment" of a civilian population. As Tribunal II noted in *Pohl*, "[s]lavery may exist even without torture. Slaves may be well fed, well clothed, and comfortably housed, but they are still slaves if without lawful process they are deprived of their freedom by forceful restraint... There is no such thing as benevolent slavery."[107] That view was echoed by the *High Command* tribunal, which held that giving "extra rations or extra privileges" to enslaved civilians "could be considered, if at all, only in mitigation of punishment and not as a defense to the crime."[108]

Although all of the tribunals condemned the use of slave labor, the slave-labor charges themselves met with mixed success. Three cases resulted in all or nearly all of the defendants being convicted. In *Milch*, the defendant was convicted for using slaves in the airplane factories that he controlled.[109] In *Pohl*, all of the defendants were convicted for their roles in the WVHA, which "managed and controlled a vast number of economic enterprises" that "were operated almost entirely by the use of concentration camp labor."[110] And in *Krupp*, all of the defendants except Pfirsch were convicted for participating in the company's willing use of slave labor at Auschwitz, the Bertha Works, and other factories.[111]

The charges were much less successful in *Flick*, *High Command*, *Ministries*, and *Farben*. The *Flick* tribunal acknowledged that the company had made widespread use of slaves,[112] but nevertheless acquitted four of the six defendants on the ground that they had a valid necessity defense—a questionable decision discussed in Chapter 13—and convicted the other two, Flick himself and Weiss, only for their roles in securing Russian POWs to produce freight cars for the company's Linke-Hoffman Works.[113] The *High Command* tribunal acquitted eight of 13 defendants, only convicting those who, like Field Marshal von Kuechler and General Reinhardt, commanded occupied areas from which large numbers of slaves were "recruited" and used.[114] And the *Ministries* tribunal convicted five of 14 defendants, limiting responsibility to those who either helped shape the slave-labor policy, like Lammers,[115] or actually used slaves, like Pleiger, the head of the Hermann Goering Works.[116]

---

[105] *Milch*, Phillips Concurrence, II TWC 866.
[106] See, e.g., *Farben*, VIII TWC 1174.
[107] *Pohl*, V TWC 970.
[108] *High Command*, XI TWC 603.
[109] *Milch*, II TWC 828.   [110] *Pohl*, V TWC 966.
[111] *Krupp*, IX TWC 1449.
[112] *Flick*, VI TWC 1196.   [113] Ibid., 1198.
[114] See, e.g., *High Command*, XI TWC 607.
[115] *Ministries*, XIV TWC 809.
[116] Ibid., 843.

The *Farben* trial led to similar results. Only five of the 23 defendants were convicted, even though the tribunal concluded that the company had employed thousands of slaves at Auschwitz and other Farben plants.[117] Three of the defendants—Ambros, Butefisch, and Duerrfeld—were convicted because they were the Farben officials "most directly responsible" for the construction at Auschwitz III.[118] Krauch was convicted because, as a member of the Central Planning Board, he was involved in allocating slave laborers to Auschwitz and to other non-Farben chemical factories,[119] while ter Meer was Ambros' superior and had steered Farben toward Auschwitz because of the ready supply of slave labor there.[120]

The other 18 defendants were acquitted for various reasons. Those defendants divided into three categories: members of the Vorstand who managed individual Farben plants as members of the Technical Committee (TEA); members of the Vorstand who were not part of TEA; and lower-level officials who were not members of either the Vorstand or TEA. The tribunal held that the eight defendants in the first category were entitled to a defense of necessity for using slaves in the plants that they managed and had not known that slave laborers would be used at Auschwitz III when they approved its construction.[121] It held that the seven defendants in the second category, despite being aware of Farben's widespread use of slave labor in other plants, were not directly involved in the "allocation or recruitment" of slaves and knew even less about the use of slaves at Auschwitz III than the members of TEA.[122] And the tribunal summarily acquitted the three defendants in the third category for lack of evidence.[123]

The acquittals provoked an angry dissent from Judge Hebert. Although he concurred with the acquittals of the three non-Vorstand defendants, he insisted that the members of the Vorstand were not entitled to a necessity defense[124] and that they knew full well slave labor was being used at Auschwitz III—a fact Krauch himself had freely admitted in a pre-trial affidavit (one that the majority had conveniently decided to ignore).[125] More importantly, though, Judge Hebert categorically rejected the idea that members of the Vorstand could only be convicted if they had been directly involved in recruiting or allocating slave labor. In his view, the role they had played in formulating and approving Farben's general "corporate policy" of using slaves made them criminally responsible for the results of that policy.[126]

E. Mistreatment of Civilians

Law No. 10 specifically designated the "ill treatment" of civilians as a war crime. As interpreted by the tribunals, that war crime encompassed three different kinds of

---

[117] *Farben*, VIII TWC 1186–7.   [118] Ibid., 1187.   [119] Ibid., 1189.
[120] Ibid., 1192.   [121] Ibid., 1193–4.   [122] Ibid., 1195.   [123] Ibid., 1196.
[124] Ibid., 1312, Hebert Dissent.   [125] Ibid., 1318, Hebert Dissent.
[126] Ibid., 1312–13, Hebert Dissent. Judge Hebert's views on the responsibility of corporate officials are explored in more detail in Chapter 11.

mistreatment: inhumane labor conditions; medical experimentation; and the deprivation of fundamental rights.

1. Inhumane Labor Conditions

Mistreatment charges played a central role in the three industrialist cases: *Flick*, *Krupp*, and *Farben*. The IMT had specifically condemned the conditions in the Krupp Works in Essen,[127] so it is not surprising that the charges were most successful in *Krupp*. Tribunal III convicted all of the defendants but Pfirsch for abusing civilians—nearly all of whom were slaves—employed by Krupp factories and housed in Krupp-controlled penal camps. It noted, for example, that the workers imprisoned in the company's Dechenschule camp had their heads shaved, were forced to wear "convict clothing" and painful wooden shoes, subsisted on liquid food, lived in rat-infested quarters, were regularly beaten with truncheons, received almost no medical care, and were assigned an air-raid trench that was unsafe and too small to protect all of the workers.[128]

By contrast, the mistreatment charges failed completely in *Flick*. Tribunal IV not only rejected the prosecution's description of the "inhuman" conditions in Flick's plants as "not sustained by the evidence," it went out of its way to praise the company for doing everything it could "to provide healthful housing for such laborers, to provide them with not only better but more food than permitted by governmental regulations, to give them adequate medical care and necessary recreation and amusement."[129]

The *Farben* majority was equally sympathetic to the defendants, acquitting them of mistreatment with regard to all of Farben's plants other than Auschwitz III on the ground that, "as a general policy, Farben attempted to carry out humane practices in the treatment of its workers and that these individual defendants did what was possible under then existing conditions to alleviate the miseries inherent in the system of slave labor."[130] Not even the *Farben* majority, however, could completely overlook the miserable conditions in which the company's Auschwitz slaves labored under the watchful eye of the SS—the inadequate food and clothing, the endless heavy and dangerous labor, the regular beatings, the constant threat of being transferred to Birkenau for extermination if they were unable to work.[131] It thus convicted Ambros, Butefisch, and Duerrfeld on the mistreatment charges, holding that they were so deeply involved in the operations of Auschwitz III that they shared responsibility for the conditions in the camp with the SS.[132]

Judge Hebert dissented on the mistreatment charges. In his view, just as the Vorstand was collectively responsible for the use of slaves in the Auschwitz III, it was also collectively responsible for their mistreatment.[133] He additionally rejected the majority's claim that only three of the 20 members of the Vorstand were aware of the conditions in Auschwitz III, noting that they "were so horrible that it is

---

[127] IMT Judgment, 59. [128] *Krupp*, IX TWC 1400–03.
[129] *Flick*, VI TWC 1199. [130] *Farben*, VIII TWC 1194.
[131] Ibid., 1184. [132] Ibid., 1185. [133] Ibid., 1315, Hebert Dissent.

utterly incredible to conclude that they were unknown to the defendants, the principal corporate directors, who were responsible for Farben's connection with the project."[134]

2. Medical Experimentation

The *Medical* tribunal had little trouble concluding that the notorious medical experiments conducted by the Nazis on civilians imprisoned in concentration-camps—involving everything from infecting the prisoners with deadly diseases to forcibly sterilizing them—violated the laws and customs of war. The tribunal did not hold that those experiments were criminal per se; instead, it articulated ten principles that determined whether a particular experiment was lawful, such as that the subject consented and the experiment was designed to avoid unnecessary suffering—what is now known as the "Nuremberg Code."[135] Without exception, however, the Nazis' experiments had violated those principles:

In every single instance appearing in the record, subjects were used who did not consent to the experiments . . . All of the experiments were conducted with unnecessary suffering and injury and but very little, if any, precautions were taken to protect or safeguard the human subjects from the possibilities of injury, disability, or death.[136]

Because the prosecution alleged that the experiments violated both the laws of war and the "general principles of criminal law as derived from the criminal laws of all civilized nations," Tribunal I permitted the prosecution to call Dr. Andrew Ivy to testify concerning the conduct of medical experimentation in "civilized nations." As noted in Chapter 6, that decision backfired—although Ivy testified on direct examination that he knew of no experiments conducted in the United States during the war that did not comply with the Nuremberg Code, the defendants forced him to admit on cross-examination that he had personally conducted dangerous experiments on prisoners and conscientious objectors.

3. Denial of Rights

Although not specifically prohibited by Article II(1)(b) of Law No. 10, the tribunals held that depriving civilians in occupied territory of certain fundamental rights—particularly the right to a fair trial, the right to private property, the right to nationality, or the right to freedom of religion—was a war crime. Some of those rights were expressly protected by Article 46 of the Hague Regulations, which provided that "[f]amily honor and rights, the lives of persons and private property, as well as religious convictions and practice, must be respected. Private property cannot be confiscated." The others, according to the tribunals, were implicitly protected by Article 23(h), which provided that it was forbidden "[t]o declare abolished, suspended, or inadmissible in a court of law the rights and actions of the

---

[134] *Farben*, VIII TWC 1322, Hebert Dissent.
[135] *Medical*, II TWC 181–2.   [136] Ibid., 183.

nationals of the hostile party," and by Article 43, which provided that an occupying power was required to take "all the measures in his power to restore, and ensure, as far as possible, public order and safety, while respecting, unless absolutely prevented, the laws in force in the country."

i. Right to a Fair Trial

The *Justice* tribunal held that a variety of German decrees concerning the prosecution of civilians in occupied territory violated the Hague Regulations, making participation in their formulation or execution a war crime. Three decrees were particularly important: the Law Against Poles and Jews, the Law to Change the Penal Code, and the Night and Fog Decree.

The Law Against Poles and Jews, which was enacted on 4 December 1941, extended German criminal law to Poles and Jews in the Incorporated Eastern Territories and mandated the death penalty for a wide range of offenses.[137] The *Justice* tribunal condemned a number of aspects of the law. First, it held that the very act of suspending the domestic law in occupied territory in favor of German criminal law violated not only Articles 23(h), 43, and 46 of the Hague Regulations, but also the Martens Clause.[138] Second, it held that the law breached the *nullem poena sine lege* principle, because it permitted courts to impose the death penalty on Jews and Poles "even where such punishment was not prescribed by law," as long as the evidence indicated that they had "particularly objectionable motives."[139] Third, the law violated the principle of non-retroactivity, because the law was made applicable—through a decree issued by Schlegelberger on 31 January 1942—"to offenses committed before the [law] came into force."[140]

The Law to Change the Penal Code, issued by Hitler on 28 June 1935, provided that an act that was not specifically criminal under German criminal law "shall be punished according to the law whose underlying principle can be most readily applied to the act." The *Justice* tribunal held that the law was a flagrant violation of the *nullem crimen sine lege* principle, because its adoption of criminalization by analogy "constituted a complete repudiation of the rule that criminal statutes should be definite and certain"[141] and meant that civilians in occupied territory "could have no possible conception of the acts which would constitute criminal offenses."[142]

Finally, the Night and Fog decree, which was enacted on 7 December 1941, required civilians in occupied territory who were suspected of committing offenses against either the Reich or German occupation forces to be secretly transferred to Germany for trial and punishment. The criminality of the deportations the Night and Fog decree authorized was discussed above. Here it is important to note that the *Justice* tribunal held that the trials conducted pursuant to the decree—which led to thousands of executions—deprived the civilian defendants of their right under the Hague Regulations to a fair trial:

---

[137] *Justice*, III TWC 995–6.　　[138] Ibid., 1076–7.
[139] Ibid., 1063–4.　　[140] Ibid., 1085.
[141] Ibid., 990.　　[142] Ibid., 1083.

The accused NN persons were arrested and secretly transported to Germany and other countries for trial. They were held incommunicado. In many instances they were denied the right to introduce evidence, to be confronted by witnesses against them, or to present witnesses in their own behalf. They were tried secretly and denied the right of counsel of their own choice, and occasionally denied the aid of any counsel. No indictment was served in many instances and the accused learned only a few moments before the trial of the nature of the alleged crime for which he was to be tried. The entire proceedings from beginning to end were secret and no public record was allowed to be made of them.[143]

ii. Right to Property
The *Pohl* tribunal held that, in light of Article 46 of the Hague Regulations, it was a war crime to confiscate the personal property of civilians in occupied territory. The tribunal focused on Action Reinhardt, the Nazi program of systematically looting the property of Jews imprisoned and murdered in concentration camps and transferring that property to Germany. As the tribunal pointed out, "everything that could be lifted was moved," most notoriously human hair and dental gold.[144]

iii. Right to Nationality
The *RuSHA* tribunal held that "Germanization" was a criminal violation of the rights protected by the Hague Regulations.[145] That process—defined as subjecting civilians to measures designed "to strengthen the German nation and the so-called 'Aryan' race at the expense of... other nations and groups by imposing Nazi and German characteristics upon individuals selected therefrom"[146]—involved a variety of criminal acts: "[d]eportation of Poles and Jews; the separation of family groups and the kidnapping of children for the purpose of training them in Nazi ideology; confiscation of all property of Poles and Jews for resettlement purposes; the destruction of the economic and cultural life of the Polish population; and the hampering of the reproduction of the Polish population."[147] Those crimes, which the prosecution alleged were part of "a systematic program of genocide," are discussed in more detail in the next chapter.

iv. Right to Religion
Finally, the *Ministries* tribunal condemned the Nazi regime's "campaign of perse-cution of the Catholic Church, its dignitaries, priests, nuns, and communicants," a campaign that included removing priests from occupied territory to deprive its inhabitants of religious teaching and comfort.[148] The tribunal held that such acts violated not only the right to "religious convictions and practice" protected by Article 46 of the Hague Regulations, but also violated Article 56's mandate that "institutions dedicated to religion" must be treated by an occupying power as private property.[149]

---

[143] Ibid., 1047.   [144] *Pohl*, V TWC 977–8.
[145] *RuSHA*, V TWC 153.   [146] *RuSHA*, Indictment, para. 2, IV TWC 609–10.
[147] *RuSHA*, V TWC 96.   [148] *Ministries*, XIV TWC 520.   [149] Ibid., 522.

V. Crimes Against Property

Law No. 10 designated the "plunder of public or private property" a war crime. That crime—which the prosecution variously referred to as both plunder and spoliation, terms that the *Farben* tribunal said were synonymous[150]—was at issue in five of the 12 trials: *Pohl, Flick, Farben, Krupp,* and *Ministries.*

A. Private Property

The tribunals uniformly held that plundering private property violated the Hague Regulations.[151] Three Regulations were particularly important: Article 46, which provided, as noted, that "private property ... cannot be confiscated"; Article 47, which provided that "[p]illage is formally forbidden"; and Article 52, which provided in relevant part that "[r]equisitions in kind and services shall not be demanded from municipalities or inhabitants except for the needs of the army of occupation. They shall be in proportion to the resources of the country." The Regulations thus protected two different kinds of rights in occupied territory: the *individual* right of civilians to enjoy private property (Articles 46 and 47); and the *collective* right of the occupied state to maintain an economy that would be viable after the occupation ended (Article 52).

All of the tribunals agreed that it was a war crime to violate the individual right. They disagreed, however, over the status of the collective right. The *Krupp* tribunal specifically held that violating the collective right was a war crime,[152] convicting the defendants involved in appropriating Dutch factories on the ground that the plunder had been conducted—quoting the IMT—"in the most ruthless way, without consideration of the local economy."[153] The *Ministries* tribunal agreed, convicting Darre because he had applied the Reich Food Estate Law to the Incorporated Eastern Territories with "utter disregard for the provisions of Article 52."[154]

In criminalizing violations of Article 52, the *Krupp* and *Ministries* tribunals were simply following the lead of the IMT, which (as the quote above indicates) had reached the same conclusion. The *Farben* tribunal nevertheless specifically limited the war crime of plunder to violations of the individual right to private property, holding that the collective impact of acquisitions on the local economy was irrelevant as long as the property was acquired with the owner's consent. "We look in vain," the tribunal wrote, "for any provision in the Hague Regulations which would justify the broad assertion that private citizens of the nation of the military occupant may not enter into agreements respecting property in occupied

---

[150] *Farben,* VIII TWC 1133.
[151] See, e.g., ibid., 1131; *Krupp,* IX TWC 1341.
[152] *Krupp,* IX TWC 1342.
[153] Ibid., 1370. Interestingly, the tribunal also held that the defendants could not have relied on Art. 52 even if the plunder had been consistent with it, because a private corporation did not belong "to the army of occupation." Ibid., 1345.
[154] *Ministries,* XIV TWC 710.

territories when consent of the owner is, in fact, freely given."[155] The *Farben* tribunal thus not only rejected the IMT's position, it quite literally read Article 52 out of existence.

The *Farben* tribunal did, however, take a progressive approach to the question of what made a civilian's decision to sell property "voluntary." It acknowledged that the mere fact that property was transferred during an occupation did not negate voluntariness as a matter of law. But it also emphasized that numerous transactions that did not involve overt violence should be considered involuntary, holding that when an owner's "consent" was obtained "by threats, intimidation, pressure, or by exploiting the position and power of the military occupant under circumstances indicating that the owner is being induced to part with his property against his will," the Hague Regulations were violated.[156]

The *Farben* tribunal also took a progressive approach to other aspects of plunder. First, it insisted—and the *Krupp* tribunal agreed[157]—that the Hague Regulations applied not only to the non-consensual acquisition of tangible property, such as a factory or machines, but also to the non-consensual acquisition of intangible property, such as stocks or legal title.[158] Second, and conversely, it rejected the defendants' contention that the Hague Regulations did not prohibit seizing tangible property "as long as no definite transfer of title was accomplished." In its view, an occupant did not "respect" private property if its actions in any way deprived the owner of "lawfully exercising his prerogative as owner."[159] Third, it held that as long as an acquisition was non-consensual, the fact that the occupant paid for the property or provided "other adequate consideration" for it did not render the transaction legal.[160]

The plunder charges involving private property were relatively successful. Tribunal VI convicted nine Farben defendants of illegally acquiring factories and machinery in Poland, Norway, Alsace-Lorraine, and France through "the everpresent threat of forceful seizure of the property by the Reich or other similar measures, such, for example, as withholding licenses, raw materials, the threat of uncertain drastic treatment in peace treaty negotiations."[161] Tribunal III convicted six Krupp defendants for seizing plants and machinery in France and the Netherlands,[162] with Judge Wilkins insisting in dissent that the majority wrongly held that it had no jurisdiction over the seizure of a metalwork plant in Austria and that the defendants should have been convicted for confiscating mining properties in France and Yugoslavia.[163] And Tribunal IV convicted nine defendants in *Ministries* for being involved in plunder throughout the Incorporated Eastern Territories, such as

---

[155] *Farben*, VIII TWC 1135.   [156] Ibid., 1135–6.

[157] *Krupp*, IX TWC 1347.

[158] *Farben*, VIII TWC 1134; see also *Krupp*, IX TWC 1346.

[159] *Farben*, VIII TWC 1345.

[160] Ibid., 1132.   [161] Ibid., 1140.

[162] See, e.g., *Krupp*, IX TWC 1357–8.

[163] Ibid., 1455, Wilkins Dissent.

the German Resettlement Trust's systematic theft of property—farms, estates, houses, businesses—from civilians who were deported to the Reich, a program that involved more than 250,000 separate transactions.[164]

B. Public Property

The tribunals also agreed that the plunder of public property violated the Hague Regulations. Two Regulations were particularly important: Article 53, which limited an army of occupation to seizing state property—such as arms and vehicles—that were of use in military operations; and Article 55, which provided that "[t]he occupying State shall be regarded only as administrator and usufructuary of public buildings, real estate, forests, and agricultural estates belonging to the hostile State."[165] Article 53 was important as a counterweight to the defense argument in *Ministries* that state-owned property, unlike private property, could be seized regardless of military use.[166] Article 55 was important to cabin the general principle, accepted by the tribunals, that state-owned property could be seized for the benefit of the occupying power for the duration of the occupation. As the *Ministries* tribunal pointed out, that right did not permit the occupying power to "strip off the property involved" or to "so use the property as to ruin or destroy the economy of the occupied territories."[167]

Plunder of public property resulted in convictions in two cases. In *Farben*, von Schnitzler and ter Meer were convicted of illegally acquiring a dyestuffs plant in Poland owned by the Polish government.[168] In *Ministries*, a number of defendants were convicted of plundering state-owned property in occupied territory. Lammers, for example, was convicted for participating in the formulation and execution of the Nazis' plan "to assure the highest utilization and development of existing stores and capacities" of the Soviet Union for the benefit of Germany.[169] Similarly, Stuckart was convicted for creating the Main Trustee Office East, which was responsible for seizing property not only from Poles and Jews, but also from the Polish state.[170]

Conclusion

Most of the NMTs' jurisprudence concerning war crimes was very progressive. The tribunals held that the rules of belligerent occupation applied even if territory was annexed and insisted on the strict separation of the *jus ad bellum* and *jus in bello*. They required judicial process to determine whether a captured partisan was entitled to POW status or whether a POW had violated the laws of war. And they held that enslavement did not require slaves to be mistreated, articulated far-

---

[164] *Ministries*, XIV TWC 584.
[165] See, e.g., *Krupp*, IX TWC 1338–9; *Ministries*, XIV TWC 746.
[166] *Ministries*, XIV TWC 746.   [167] Ibid., 747.
[168] *Farben*, VIII TWC 1141–3.
[169] *Ministries*, XIV TWC 712.   [170] Ibid., 720.

reaching principles for the use of humans in medical experimentation, and criminalized the deprivation of rights even though such deprivation was not specifically prohibited by Article II(1)(b).

Other aspects of the tribunals' jurisprudence, however, were problematic. In some cases, the tribunals articulated the law better than they applied it. The *Flick* and *Farben* tribunals, for example, accepted that enslavement and mistreatment of civilians was criminal, yet acquitted a number of defendants despite overwhelming evidence of their guilt. In other cases, the law itself was the problem. Two examples stand out: the tribunals' insistence—over Judge Wilkins' dissent—that a bloodless invasion was a crime against peace but did not trigger the Hague and Geneva Conventions; and the willingness of the tribunals to tolerate the execution of civilians as hostages and in reprisal. Fortunately, as discussed in Chapter 16, the 1949 Geneva Conventions rejected both of those positions.

10

Crimes Against Humanity

Introduction

The OCC charged defendants with crimes against humanity in all 12 trials.[1] Those crimes were enumerated in Article II(1)(c) of Law No. 10:

Atrocities and offenses, including but not limited to murder, extermination, enslavement, deportation, imprisonment, torture, rape, or other inhumane acts committed against any civilian population, or persecutions on political, racial or religious grounds whether or not in violation of the domestic laws of the country where perpetrated.

Although Article II(1)(c) overlapped considerably with Article II(1)(b), the war-crimes provision, there were two important differences. First, Article II(1)(c) criminalized "persecutions" as well as atrocities and offenses. Second, whereas Article II(1)(b) applied to war crimes committed against "civilian population from occupied territory," Article II(1)(c) applied to "any civilian population," indicating that crimes against humanity could be committed outside of occupied territory.

As noted in Chapter 5, there was also a critical difference between Article II(1)(c) and its equivalent in the London Charter, Article 6(c). Article 6(c) required crimes against humanity to be committed "in execution of or in connection with any crime within the jurisdiction of the Tribunal"—the "nexus" requirement. That requirement was conspicuously absent from Article II(1)(c), leaving open the possibility that the NMTs would reject the IMT's position that none of the acts committed against German Jews prior to 1 September 1939—the date Germany invaded Poland—qualified as crimes against humanity.

This chapter discusses the tribunals' interpretation of Article II(1)(c). Sections I–III examine the three categories of crimes against humanity that were addressed by the tribunals: (1) atrocities and persecutions committed in occupied territory that also qualified as war crimes; (2) wartime atrocities and persecutions committed outside of occupied territory; and (3) atrocities and persecutions committed before the war. Section IV then discusses the contextual elements that the tribunals applied to all three categories of crimes against humanity—their widespread and systematic commission pursuant to a government policy. Finally, Section V focuses

---

[1] Taylor, *Final Report*, 69.

on the specific crimes against humanity enumerated in Article II(1)(c), with an emphasis on genocide.

I. Acts in Occupied Territory

The IMT held that war crimes "committed on a vast scale" in occupied territory also constituted crimes against humanity.[2] The NMTs took a similar approach to the relationship between the two crimes, although they insisted that large-scale war crimes qualified as crimes against humanity only if they were also systematic and committed pursuant to a government policy—an issue discussed below.

The tribunals condemned a wide variety of atrocities and persecutions committed in occupied territory as both war crimes and crimes against humanity: the crimes committed pursuant to the Night and Fog program in the *Justice* case[3]; the Germanization program and the systematic plunder of the "incorporated and occupied territories" in *RuSHA*[4]; slave labor and the plunder of Jewish property in *Pohl*[5]; Sonderkommando executions in *Einsatzgruppen*[6]; the persecution of the Catholic Church[7] and forced conscription of civilians in *Ministries*.[8] In fact, the *Pohl* tribunal held that slave labor and plunder in the "Eastern occupied territories" were crimes against humanity even though the indictment limited such crimes to acts committed *outside* of occupied territory.[9]

Read literally, Article II(1)(c) limited "murder-type" crimes against humanity to acts committed against civilians. That limitation reflected the position of the UNWCC's Legal Committee, which had concluded that "[o]ffences committed against members of the armed forces were outside the scope of this type"—and were likely outside the scope of persecution-type crimes against humanity as well.[10] The *High Command* tribunal nevertheless convicted Warlimont of a murder-type crime against humanity for participating in the "illegal plan of the leaders of the Third Reich fostering the lynching of Allied flyers."[11]

II. Wartime Acts Outside of Occupied Territory

The NMTs held that wartime atrocities and persecutions committed against two different kinds of civilian populations outside of occupied territory qualified as crimes against humanity: (1) civilians in countries that were not belligerently occupied by Germany; and (2) German civilians.

---

[2] IMT Judgment, 65.   [3] *Justice*, III TWC 1134.   [4] *RuSHA*, V TWC 152.
[5] *Pohl*, V TWC 997.   [6] *Einsatzgruppen*, IV TWC 548, 554–5.
[7] *Ministries*, XIV TWC 522.
[8] Ibid., 549.   [9] See *Pohl*, Indictment, para. 24, V TWC 207.
[10] UNWCC History, 179.   [11] *High Command*, XI TWC 679.

A. Non-German Civilians

The tribunals agreed that atrocities and offenses committed against civilians in countries that were not belligerently occupied qualified as crimes against humanity. In *Milch*, for example, the defendant was charged not only with the war crime of enslaving civilians in occupied territory, but also with the crime against humanity of enslaving "German nationals and nationals of other countries." Tribunal II rejected the prosecution's proof regarding German nationals, but concluded that "[a]s to such crimes against nationals of other countries, the evidence shows that a large number of Hungarian Jews and other nationals of Hungary and Romania, which countries were occupied by Germany but were not belligerents, were subjected to the same tortures and deportations as were the nationals of Poland and Russia." It thus concluded that "the same unlawful acts of violence which constituted war crimes under count one of the indictment also constitute crimes against humanity as alleged in count three of the indictment."[12]

The *Ministries* tribunal reached a similar conclusion regarding the deportation of Jews from Hungary. Veesenmayer contended that "he could not commit war crimes against Hungarians inasmuch as Hungary was a military ally of Germany."[13] The tribunal agreed that war crimes could only be committed in occupied territory, but pointed out that Count 5 was not concerned with war crimes, but dealt with crimes against humanity "irrespective of the nationality of the victims."[14]

B. German Civilians

Although Article II(1)(c) provided that murder-type crimes against humanity could be committed "against any civilian population" and that persecution-type crimes against humanity were criminal "whether or not in violation of the domestic laws of the country where perpetrated," the tribunals split concerning the criminality of wartime atrocities and persecutions committed against German civilians. Most of the tribunals held that, in fact, they did qualify as crimes against humanity. The *Justice* tribunal specifically relied on the text of Article II(1)(c) to conclude that "acts by Germans against German nationals may constitute crimes against humanity within the jurisdiction of this Tribunal to punish."[15] It thus held that crimes committed pursuant to the "nationwide government-organized system of cruelty and injustice" were crimes against humanity "when enforced in the Alt Reich against German nationals."[16] The *Einsatzgruppen* tribunal did likewise, condemning Einsatzgruppe A's executions of more than 20,000 German Jews as crimes against humanity on the ground that Article II(1)(c) was "not restricted as to nationality of the accused or of the victim, or to the place where committed."[17] The *Ministries* tribunal took a similar position.[18]

---

[12] *Milch*, II TWC 791.   [13] *Ministries*, XIV TWC 653.
[14] Ibid., 654.   [15] *Justice*, III TWC 973.   [16] Ibid., 1081.
[17] *Einsatzgruppen*, IV TWC 499.   [18] *Ministries*, XIV TWC 654.

The *Medical* tribunal, by contrast, rejected the idea that medical experiments conducted during the war on German nationals qualified as crimes against humanity, even though it had no trouble accepting that such crimes could be committed against non-German civilians in countries that were not belligerently occupied.[19] The crimes against humanity count in the indictment alleged that the Nazis' euthanasia program involved the murder of "hundreds of thousands of human beings, including German civilians, as well as civilians of other nations."[20] The tribunal did not question the idea that the program had involved German civilians, but it nevertheless held that only "the deaths of non-German nationals" outside of occupied territory were criminal.[21]

Michael Marrus has attributed the *Medical* tribunal's erroneous approach to crimes against humanity to the OCC's decision to focus the trial on medical experiments involving non-Germans—a decision, in his opinion, that meant "the trial suffered grievously as a chronicle of the medical crimes."[22] If so, the OCC did not learn its lesson, because the *RuSHA* tribunal reached the same conclusion regarding the euthanasia program the following year. The crimes against humanity count in the indictment charged Hildebrandt for participating in "the extermination of thousands of German nationals pursuant to the so-called 'Euthanasia Program' of the Third Reich, from September 1939 to February 1940"[23]—namely, *after* the invasion of Poland. The tribunal nevertheless acquitted him on the ground that the prosecution had not contended "that this program, insofar as Hildebrandt might have been connected with it, was extended to foreign nationals." In its view, "euthanasia, when carried out under state legislation against citizens of the state only, does not constitute a crime against humanity."[24]

III. Acts Committed Before the War

A. Background

Article 6(c) of the London Charter limited crimes against humanity that took place before the war to atrocities and persecutions committed "in execution of or in connection with any crime within the jurisdiction of the Tribunal."[25] Early American proposals for the London Charter did not contain a nexus requirement; the final American proposal before the London Conference, dated 14 June 1945, simply criminalized "[a]trocities and offenses, including atrocities and persecutions on racial or religious grounds, committed since 1 January 1933 in violation of any applicable provision of the domestic law of the country in which committed."[26] Those proposals, however, treated crimes against humanity as domestic crimes; as

---

[19] See, e.g., *Medical*, II TWC 227.   [20] *Medical*, Indictment, para. 14, I TWC 16–17.
[21] *Medical*, II TWC 289.   [22] Marrus, *Nuremberg Doctors' Trial*, 114–5.
[23] *RuSHA*, Indictment, para. 26, IV TWC 617.   [24] *RuSHA*, V TWC 161–2.
[25] IMT Judgment, 65.
[26] Roger S. Clark, "Crimes Against Humanity," in *The Nuremberg Trial and International Law* 177, 182 (G. Ginsburgs & V.N. Kudriavtsev eds, 1990).

soon as the Allies decided at the London Conference to limit the IMT's jurisdiction to violations of international law, nearly every draft of what would become Article 6(c) required the nexus.[27] That restriction was more than acceptable to Justice Jackson, who took the position that "the way Germany treats its inhabitants...is not our affair any more than it is the affair of some other government to interpose itself in our programs. The reason that this program of extermination of Jews and destruction of the rights of minorities becomes an international concern is this: it was a part of a plan for making an illegal war."[28]

The nexus requirement doomed the pre-war crimes against humanity charges in the IMT indictment. The tribunal had "no doubt whatever" that "[t]he policy of persecution, repression and murder of civilians in Germany before the war of 1939...was most ruthlessly carried out" against Jews, communists, and other undesirables. It nevertheless refused to criminalize those actions, concluding that "revolting and horrible as many of these crimes were, it has not been satisfactorily proved that they were done in execution of, or in connection with, any such crime."[29]

Unlike Article 6(c), of course, Article II(1)(c) did not contain a nexus requirement. That absence complicated Taylor's planning for the NMT trials. He was convinced that the drafters of Law No. 10 had intentionally eliminated the requirement. Yet, like Jackson, he was skeptical that acts committed by Germans against German nationals—particularly non-violent persecutions—violated international law in the absence of the nexus. As he wrote to Howard Petersen, the Assistant Secretary of War, in February 1947, "[m]y own view is that departures from democratic systems as may exist in some countries and discrimination, even quite aggravated such as may exist against negroes in certain countries, should not even, in these enlightened times, constitute crimes at international law."[30] Taylor was not alone in that belief: the following month, the State Department told Taylor that although it believed Law No. 10 criminalized pre-war acts that did not satisfy the nexus requirement, "as a matter of policy the United States should not prosecute a crime against humanity alone but only in conjunction with a crime against peace or war crimes."[31]

Despite his concerns, Taylor ultimately alleged peacetime crimes against humanity in two cases. The *Flick* indictment charged Flick, Steinbrinck, and Kaletsch with responsibility for acts of Aryanization committed "[b]etween January 1936 and April 1945"[32] and charged Flick and Steinbrinck with responsibility for a variety of SS crimes committed "[b]etween 30 January 1933 and April 1945."[33] Similarly, the *Ministries* indictment accused 13 defendants of having participated in atrocities and persecutions committed "during the period from January 1933 to September 1939."[34]

---

[27] Ibid., 183.   [28] Quoted in ibid., 186.   [29] IMT Judgment, 65.
[30] Memo from Taylor to Petersen, 19 Feb. 1947, NA-153–1018-1-84-1.
[31] Memo from Petersen to Taylor, 4 Mar. 1947, NA-153–1018-1-84-1.
[32] *Flick*, Indictment, para. 13, VI TWC 21.   [33] Ibid., 23, para. 17.
[34] *Ministries*, Indictment, para. 30, XII TWC 38.

B. The Tribunal's Response

Although pre-war crimes against humanity were charged only in *Flick* and *Ministries*, five tribunals addressed the nexus requirement. The *Justice* and *Einsatzgruppen* tribunals rejected the requirement, albeit in dicta, while the *Pohl*, *Flick*, and *Ministries* tribunals accepted it.

1. No Nexus Required

The first tribunal that addressed the nexus requirement—Tribunal III in the *Justice* case—rejected it. The tribunal began with the text of Law No. 10, pointing out that because Article 6(c)'s nexus requirement had been "deliberately omitted" from Article II(1)(c), there was no question that Law No. 10 did not require pre-war atrocities and persecutions to be committed "in execution of, or in connection with" war crimes or crimes against peace.[35] It then rejected the defendants' argument that peacetime crimes against humanity violated the principle of non-retroactivity, insisting that as long as the acts in question satisfied the crime's contextual elements—discussed below—they violated international law as it existed prior to the war:

[T]he statute is limited by construction to the type of criminal activity which prior to 1939 was and still is a matter of international concern. Whether or not such atrocities constitute technical violations of laws and customs of war, they were acts of such scope and malevolence, and they so clearly imperiled the peace of the world that they must be deemed to have become violations of international law.[36]

The tribunal concluded by noting, in a nice rhetorical move, that Hitler himself accepted the criminality of peacetime crimes against humanity, having "expressly justified his early acts of aggression against Czechoslovakia on the ground that the alleged persecution of racial Germans by the government of that country was a matter of international concern warranting intervention by Germany."[37]

The *Einsatzgruppen* tribunal rejected the nexus requirement on similar grounds. It also emphasized that the absence of the requirement in Article II(1)(c) meant that "the present Tribunal has jurisdiction to try all crimes against humanity as long known and understood under the general principles of criminal law," regardless of when, where, or against whom they were committed.[38] And it also justified the criminalization of peacetime crimes against humanity on the ground that "the law of humanity" was "not restricted to events of war," but envisaged "the protection of humanity at all times" against "acts committed in the course of wholesale and systematic violation of life and liberty."[39]

---

[35] *Justice*, III TWC 974.   [36] Ibid., 982.   [37] Ibid.
[38] *Einsatzgruppen*, IV TWC 499.   [39] Ibid., 497–8.

2. Nexus Required

Three tribunals, by contrast, limited pre-war crimes against humanity to those that satisfied the nexus requirement. The *Pohl* tribunal emphasized the sovereignty of the German state, insisting—with regard to the infamous 1933 decree suspending key provisions of the Weimar Constitution—that international law had nothing to say about how a government treated its own people:

> It is to be assumed that if this is the kind of national government the people of Germany preferred, they were entitled to it. If they consented to surrender their human liberties to a police force, that was their privilege, and any outsider who intruded could well be told to mind his own affairs. But when the attempt is made to make the provisions of such a decree extra-territorial in their effect and to apply their totalitarian and autocratic police measures to non-Germans and in non-German territory, they thereby invaded the domain of international law.[40]

The *Flick* tribunal reached the same conclusion, but by different means. It relied solely on the language of Law No. 10, finding "no support" for the prosecution's argument that the absence of the nexus was intentional. First, the tribunal held that any ambiguity in Article II(1)(c) had to be resolved in favor of the defendants, because "[j]urisdiction is not to be presumed. A court should not reach out for power beyond the clearly defined bounds of its chartering legislation."[41] Second, the tribunal insisted that, in fact, the meaning of Article II(1)(c) was not ambiguous at all, because Article I of Law No. 10 made the Moscow Declaration and the London Charter an "integral part" of the document, and "[i]mplicit in all of this chartering legislation is the purpose to provide for punishment of crimes committed during the war or in connection with the war."[42]

Two months after the *Flick* tribunal issued its decision, the defendants in *Ministries* filed a motion with Tribunal IV—a panel that included *Flick*'s Judge Christianson, now the Presiding Judge—to dismiss Count 4 of the indictment, which alleged the commission of crimes against humanity between January 1933 and September 1939. Oral argument was held on the motion on 2 March 1949, in the middle of the prosecution's case-in-chief. The defense was represented by Egon Kuboschok, Rasche's main counsel. The prosecution was represented by Taylor.

a. The Defense Argument

The defense motion essentially repeated Tribunal IV's reasoning in *Flick*. It began by arguing that Article II(1)(c) did not have to mention the nexus requirement, because the Preamble to Law No. 10 stated that the document's purpose was to "give effect" to the London Charter, which specifically limited pre-war crimes

---

[40] *Pohl*, V TWC 991–2.   [41] *Flick*, VI TWC 1212–3.   [42] Ibid., 1213.

against humanity to those committed in connection with war crimes or crimes against peace. It then claimed that, in light of the "close connection" between the Charter and Law No. 10, the drafters of the latter could have extended Article II(1) (c) to include peacetime crimes against humanity only by expressly stating their desire to do so. Deleting the "in connection with" language was not enough, according to the motion, because Article II(1)(c) had also eliminated Article 6(c)'s "before or during the war" language, yet the OCC had repeatedly claimed that Article II(1)(c) applied to crimes against humanity committed prior to 1 September 1939. "If one thing was omitted intentionally, surely the other thing was omitted, too."[43]

In his oral presentation, Kuboschok focused on an additional argument for reading the nexus requirement into Article II(1)(c): the principle of non-retroactivity. In his view, it was precisely the nexus requirement that prevented Article 6(c) from violating that principle: "crimes against humanity perpetrated between 1933 and 1939" that did not satisfy the requirement would not have violated any law that existed prior to the war, "be it either codified law or customary law, the Kellogg-Briand Pact and the provisions of international law, codified as well as customary law." Kuboschok also pointed out—very cleverly—that the prosecution had defended Article 6(c) at the IMT on precisely that ground.[44]

b. The Prosecution Argument

Taylor entered his oral argument with three objectives. First, in response to the argument made in the defense motion, he had to demonstrate that Article II(1)(c) applied to pre-war crimes against humanity even though it did not contain Article 6(c)'s "before or during the war" language. Second, he had to establish that the drafters of Law No. 10 had, in fact, intentionally removed the nexus requirement. Third, he had to show that nexus-less crimes against humanity would not violate the principle of non-retroactivity.

The first objective was the easiest. Article II(5) of Law No. 10 provided that "[i]n any trial or prosecution for a crime herein referred to, the accused shall not be entitled to the benefits of any statute of limitation in respect of the period from 30 January 1933 to 1 July 1945." As Taylor pointed out, that provision made no sense if the drafters of Law No. 10 wanted to limit the prosecution of crimes against humanity to those committed after the invasion of Poland on 1 September 1939.[45]

Taylor devoted most of his argument to the second objective, which was obviously much more complicated. He began by claiming that the IMT had wrongly interpreted Article 6(c) of the London Charter. In his view, the "in connection with" language was not intended to limit the prosecution of pre-war crimes against humanity to those that were actually connected to war crimes or

---

[43] *Ministries*, Defense Motion to Dismiss Count Four of the Indictment, 26 Feb. 1948, XIII TWC 77–8.

[44] Ibid., 80–1, Defense Argument.   [45] Ibid., 93–4, Prosecution Argument.

crimes against peace, but was designed "to make it clear that the definition was not meant to embrace private or occasional crimes or local petty persecutions but only such wholesale campaigns of eradication."[46] That was a bold argument—and one that directly contradicted the drafting history of Article 6(c), which indicates that the drafters included the nexus because they believed that the connection to crimes against peace was necessary to distinguish a domestic crime from an international crime against humanity.[47]

Perhaps recognizing the weakness of his interpretation, Taylor also argued that the IMT's interpretation of the nexus requirement was irrelevant to the defendant's motion, because "[j]ust as the IMT was bound by the definitions in the London Charter, so . . . this Tribunal is bound by the definition of Law No. 10." Law No. 10 had been enacted by the Control Council and was "the fountain of jurisdiction" of the NMTs. No individual tribunal, therefore, had the power to "set aside and disregard any provisions of Law No. 10"—including the nexus requirement.[48]

That argument depended, of course, on the idea that the drafters of Law No. 10 had deliberately rejected Article 6(c)'s nexus requirement. Taylor thus argued exactly that:

[T]he very fact that this clause appeared in the definition of the London Charter, but not in the definition of Law No. 10, we think serves only to emphasize the clear and unambiguous meaning of Law No. 10 . . . [T]he London Charter was in the hand of those who promulgated Law No. 10, as the preamble and Article I of Law No. 10 make abundantly clear, and it is a well recognized principle of construction that changes in language are presumed to be meaningful rather than meaningless.[49]

Taylor supported his argument by citing the *Justice* tribunal's conclusion that the nexus requirement had been "deliberately omitted" from Article II(1)(c). He then addressed Tribunal IV's decision in *Flick*, which had reached the opposite conclusion. With regard to the *Flick* tribunal's nexus argument, he insisted that "it is one thing to resolve ambiguities in favor of the accused, and quite another to create ambiguities where none in fact exist, and with all respect we believe that is what had been done in that case."[50] With regard to the tribunal's Article I argument, he claimed that the drafters made the Moscow Declaration and London Charter an "integral part" of Law No. 10 not to prevent Law No. 10 from deviating from the Charter, but to give effect to provisions in the Charter that were "essential to the implementation of Law No. 10," most notably the three Articles—Articles 9, 10, and 11—governing the prosecution of members of organizations that the IMT had deemed criminal. Indeed, he pointed out that "to give the London Charter such over-riding effect would be in direct contravention of the London Agreement itself," which provided in Article 6 that "[n]othing in this agreement shall prejudice the jurisdiction or the powers of any national or occupation court

---

[46] Ibid., 92.   [47] Clark, in Ginsburgs & Kudriavtsev, 187–8.
[48] *Ministries*, Prosecution Argument, XIII TWC 85.   [49] Ibid., 93.   [50] Ibid., 92.

established or to be established in any Allied territory or in Germany for the trial of war criminals."[51]

Taylor's statutory interpretation argument was by far his strongest. As he pointed out, the drafters of Law No. 10—primarily Charles Fahy's legal team in the American Legal Division of the Control Council—modeled Article II(1)(c) on Article 6(c). It thus seems highly unlikely either that the deletion of the nexus requirement was accidental or, if deliberate, was not intended to expand the category of crimes against humanity to include those that were not connected to war crimes or crimes against peace. Indeed, the NMT defendants and the *Flick* tribunal were alone in their insistence that Article II(1)(c) still required the nexus— that interpretation was rejected not only by Taylor and the State Department, but also by the UNWCC, which stated that the only possible interpretation of the "striking difference" between Article 6(c) and Article II(1)(c) was that the latter did not require the nexus.[52]

Although Taylor did not cite it in his argument, an exchange between Alvin Rockwell, the director of OMGUS's Legal Division, and Col. C.B. Mickelwait, the Theater Judge Advocate, indicates that the deletion of the nexus requirement was intentional. On 12 November 1946, Rockwell sent a memo to Mickelwait proposing that the U.S. offer certain amendments to Law No. 10. One of those amendments proposed amending Article II(1)(c) to read, in relevant part, as follows:

(c) Crimes against Humanity. Atrocities and offenses committed on or after 30 January 1933, *whether or not connected with the crimes set out in (a) or (b) above* or in violation of the domestic laws of the country where perpetrated.[53]

Mickelwait responded on November 20 that the Theater Judge Advocate's office concurred with OMGUS's proposal.[54] The amendment was never adopted by the Control Council, but that does not undermine its importance. As Rockwell made clear in his memo, the amendment was not designed to expand the substantive reach of Article II(1)(c). On the contrary, OMGUS wanted to offer it "merely for clarification of subsection (c)"—"to remove any doubt that crimes against humanity may be charged which occurred after the Nazi seizure of power and which were not directly related to crimes against peace or war crimes."[55]

Having argued that the drafters intentionally eliminated the nexus requirement, Taylor turned to his third and final objective: demonstrating that a nexus-less Article II(1)(c) would not violate the principle of non-retroactivity. He accepted that the principle applied—and referenced a working draft of the Universal Declaration of Human Rights, then being debated by UN Commission on Human Rights, to that effect.[56] But he insisted that atrocities and persecutions

[51] *Ministries*, Prosecution Argument, XIII TWC, 95–6.
[52] History of the UNWCC, 213.
[53] Memo from Rockwell to Mickelwait, 12 Nov. 1946, NA-549–2236-1, at 2 (emphasis added).
[54] Memo from Mickelwait to Rockwell, 20 Nov. 1946, NA-549–2236-1, at 1.
[55] Ibid.   [56] *Ministries*, Prosecution Argument, XIII TWC 88.

that were not connected to war crimes or crimes against peace had been criminal even prior to World War II. He began by discussing the trial of Peter von Hagenbach in 1474, claiming that "[t]he acts of which he was accused were not committed during actual hostilities or in time of war and, therefore, under our modern terminology would be akin more to crimes against humanity than to war crimes."[57] He then cited the *Justice* tribunal's belief that peacetime crimes against humanity "constituted violations not alone of statute but also of common international law"[58] and recalled the examples of peacetime humanitarian interventions that the tribunal had provided in its decision, such as the American intervention in Cuba in 1898.[59]

c. The Tribunal's Decision

Although Taylor had argued his position well, the *Ministries* tribunal held that Article II(1)(c) only criminalized pre-war atrocities and persecutions that were connected to war crimes or crimes against peace. Its disappointing order, which ran less than five pages and contained very little analysis, simply parroted Kuboschok's main arguments. The tribunal agreed that Law No. 10's "give effect" and "integral part" language indicated that the drafters of Law No. 10 did not intend to expand the NMTs' jurisdiction beyond the limits of the London Charter. It defended that conclusion by pointing out that, if the tribunal did not read the nexus requirement into Article II(1)(c), it "would be according to this and similar tribunals jurisdiction over crimes of the character described, whenever and wherever committed"[60]—an absurd argument, given that Law No. 10's Preamble specifically limited the tribunals' personal jurisdiction to German war criminals and that Article II(5) made clear their temporal jurisdiction began on 30 January 1933, when Hitler was appointed Chancellor of Germany.

The tribunal also agreed with Kuboschok that peacetime crimes against humanity "were not, when committed, crimes against international law."[61] That may well have been the correct decision; a number of scholars, both past and present, have reached the same conclusion.[62] But it is still unfortunate that the *Ministries* tribunal did not bother to address, much less distinguish, the numerous examples of unilateral humanitarian interventions cited by the *Justice* tribunal and by Taylor during his presentation. Instead, the tribunal simply noted that "[s]uch arguments and observations rather serve to emphasize the urgent need of comprehensive legislation by the family of nations, with respect to individual human rights."[63]

Although the order dismissing Count 4 was issued by Tribunal IV as a whole, it is clear that Judge Maguire disagreed with his colleagues' interpretation of Article II(1)(c). Indeed, he expressed his disagreement to his friend Judge Brand, the presiding judge in the *Justice* case, who encouraged him "not to go along" with a

---

[57] Ibid., 97.   [58] See *Justice*, III TWC 979.
[59] *Ministries*, Prosecution Argument, XIII TWC 97–8.
[60] Ibid., 115, Order Dismissing Count Four, 26 Mar. 1948.
[61] Ibid., 116.
[62] See, e.g., Bassiouni, 80.
[63] *Ministries*, Order Dismissing Count Four, XIII TWC 117.

"narrow construction of crimes against humanity committed by a government against its own nationals"[64]—the same construction, of course, that the *Justice* tribunal had already rejected, if only in dicta. In the end, though, Judge Maguire chose not to dissent from the majority's holding, for reasons that he never publicly or privately explained.

Finally, it is important to note that the *Ministries* tribunal was willing to criminalize peacetime atrocities and persecutions that *did* satisfy the nexus requirement. It convicted Darre for his role in the theft of Jewish agricultural property, for example, even though the thefts were completed a few months prior to the invasion of Poland. That conviction was justified, according to the tribunal, because it was "unquestionable" that "the proceeds of the Aryanization of farms and other Jewish property were in aid of and utilized in the program of rearmament and subsequent aggression."[65]

IV. The Contextual Elements

The IMT was generally silent concerning the contexual elements of crimes againt humanity, emphasizing only that the difference between a war crime and a crime against humanity was that the latter involved acts "committed on a vast scale." The NMTs, by contrast, not only systematically developed the contextual elements, they adopted a very strict approach to them. Specifically, they limited all three categories of crimes against humanity to atrocities and persecutions that were committed pursuant to government policy and were both large-scale and systematic.

A. Government Policy

The policy requirement was articulated most forcefully by the *Justice* tribunal with reference to peacetime crimes against humanity:

As we construe it, [Article II(1)(c)] provides for punishment of crimes committed against German nationals only where there is proof of conscious participation in systematic government organized or approved procedures amounting to atrocities and offenses of the kind specified in the act and committed against populations or amounting to persecutions on political, racial, or religious grounds.[66]

That requirement followed naturally from the tribunal's insistence that the Nazis' pre-war atrocities and persecutions violated international law even though they were not connected to war crimes or crimes against peace. Such acts violated international law *precisely because* they were the product of government policy. In the words of the tribunal, "governmental participation is a material element of the crime against humanity" because "[o]nly when official organs of sovereignty

---

[64] Quoted in Maguire, 176.   [65] *Ministries*, XIV TWC 557.   [66] *Justice*, III TWC 982.

participated in atrocities and persecutions did those crimes assume international proportions."[67]

The *Einsatzgruppen* tribunal also viewed the policy requirement as a substitute for the nexus requirement. Although it concluded that Article II(1)(c) was not "limited to offenses committed during war," it insisted that such peacetime offenses violated international law only if the Nazi regime had been in some sense responsible for their commission:

Crimes against humanity are acts committed in the course of wholesale and systematic violation of life and liberty. It is to be observed that insofar as international jurisdiction is concerned, the concept of crimes against humanity does not apply to offenses for which the criminal code of any well-ordered state makes adequate provision. They can only come within the purview of this basic code of humanity because the state involved, owing to indifference, impotency or complicity, has been unable or has refused to halt the crimes and punish the criminals.[68]

As the quotes indicate, the *Einsatzgruppen* tribunal took a slightly broader approach to the policy requirement than the *Justice* tribunal. The latter held that the requirement was satisfied as long as the crimes in question were "government organized or approved." The former, by contrast, held that the requirement was satisfied by government "indifference, impotence, or complicity." The *Einsatzgruppen* tribunal thus suggested that the perpetrators of crimes against humanity did not have to be formally or informally connected to the government as long as their ability to commit the crimes depended on the government being too weak to stop them.

The *Einsatzgruppen* and *Justice* tribunals each discussed the policy requirement primarily in the context of peacetime crimes against humanity. The *Justice* tribunal made clear, however, that the requirement applied to the other categories of crimes against humanity, as well. First, it specifically held that "the adoption and application of systematic government-organized and approved procedures amounting to atrocities and offenses of the kind made punishable by C. C. Law 10 qualified as crimes against humanity "when carried out in occupied territory."[69] Second, when the defendants claimed that they could not be convicted of committing crimes against humanity against German civilians during the war because they were simply applying then-existing German law, the tribunal rejected that argument on the ground that "[i]t can scarcely be said that governmental participation, the proof of which is necessary for conviction, can also be a defense to the charge."[70] In practice, therefore, the *Justice* tribunal applied the policy requirement to all three categories of crimes against humanity.

The *Ministries* tribunal also strongly implied that the policy requirement applied to acts committed during the war. The tribunal condemned the Nazis' "campaign of persecution of the Catholic Church" as a crime against humanity on the ground

---

[67] Ibid., 984.
[68] *Einsatzgruppen*, IV TWC 498.
[69] *Justice*, III TWC 1081.   [70] Ibid., 984.

that it "did not consist of isolated acts of individual citizens," but had been "adopted as a matter of policy by the Third Reich."[71] That campaign had involved acts that substantively qualified as all three categories of crimes against humanity: persecutions of priests who resided in occupied territory; persecutions of priests from countries allied with Germany, such as Hungary; and persecutions of German priests prior to the war.[72] The tribunal nevertheless limited the criminality of the campaign to wartime acts in the first and second categories; it dismissed the pre-war acts in the third category when it dismissed Count 4. It could not, therefore, have believed that the policy requirement applied only to pre-war acts.

B. Large-Scale and Systematic Acts

The NMTs also insisted that atrocities and persecutions qualified as crimes against humanity only if they were both large-scale and systematic. As Tribunal III said in the *Justice* case:

It is not the isolated crime by a private German individual which is condemned, nor is it the isolated crime perpetrated by the German Reich through its officers against a private individual. It is significant that the enactment employs the words "against any civilian population" instead of "against any civilian individual." The provision is directed against offenses and inhumane acts and persecutions on political, racial, or religious grounds systematically organized and conducted by or with the approval of government.[73]

The other tribunals took similar positions. The *Einsatzgruppen* tribunal simply defined crimes against humanity as governmental acts involving the "wholesale and systematic violation of life and liberty."[74] The *Ministries* tribunal condemned the persecution of the Catholic Church as a crime against humanity because persecutory acts "were committed on a large scale . . . were planned and were a part of the program adopted as a matter of policy by the Third Reich."[75] And the *Medical* tribunal considered the Nazis' medical experiments to be crimes against humanity because they were "not the isolated and casual acts of individual doctors and scientists working solely on their own responsibility," but were "carried out on a large scale" as "the product of coordinated policy-making and planning at high governmental, military, and Nazi Party levels."[76]

Unfortunately, except for insisting that isolated acts could not qualify as crimes against humanity, the tribunals provided little interpretive guidance concerning the scale and systematicity requirements. The absence of discussion is not surprising, though, given the nature of the crimes committed by the Nazis. Those crimes were almost invariably large-scale and systematic; the OCC thus had no incentive to allege crimes against humanity that had any chance of running afoul of the contextual elements.

---

[71] *Ministries*, XIV TWC 522.   [72] Ibid., 520–1.
[73] *Justice*, III TWC 973.   [74] *Einsatzgruppen*, IV TWC 498.
[75] *Ministries*, XIV TWC 522.   [76] *Medical*, II TWC 181.

C. Connection Between the Act and the Attack

Finally, it is worth noting that the tribunals required the prosecution to prove that a defendant's specific acts were, in fact, committed as part of a larger attack on a civilian population. In *Ministries*, for example, the OCC alleged that during the war Meissner had illegally acquired a property interest in the Berlin Hippodrome by causing the owner, a German industrialist, "to be arrested by the Gestapo and threatened with imprisonment in a concentration camp unless he should consent to the transaction." The tribunal did not question the idea that the Nazis had engaged in large-scale, systematic plunder of private property during the war. It nevertheless acquitted Meissner of a crime against humanity because it concluded that "[t]he transaction, whatever it may have been, was purely personal" and had no connection to the larger Nazi policy of plunder.[77]

V. Substantive Law

Although the tribunals devoted most of their attention to the jurisdictional and contextual elements of crimes against humanity, they also discussed the substantive aspects of those crimes, particularly persecution-type crimes against humanity and genocide.

A. Murder-Type

The tribunals rarely addressed the substantive aspects of the murder-type crimes against humanity listed in Article II(1)(c), because nearly all of them qualified as war crimes under Article II(1)(b) when committed in occupied territory[78] and were thus discussed in that context. The primary exception was rape, which was unique to the crimes against humanity provision, but—as many feminist scholars have noted—never charged in the NMT trials.[79]

B. Persecution-Type

The tribunals focused on three basic issues concerning persecution-type crimes against humanity: (1) whether political, racial, and religious persecution was also a war crime when committed in occupied territory; (2) whether even "minor" acts of persecution qualified as crimes against humanity; and (3) whether the deprivation of private property was not only a war crime, but a crime against humanity as well.

---

[77] *Ministries*, XIV TWC 606.

[78] See UNWCC History, 194; Schwelb, in Mettraux, 131.

[79] See, e.g., Kelly D. Askin, "Prosecuting Wartime Rape and Other Gender-Related Crimes Under International Law: Extraordinary Advances, Enduring Obstacles," 21 *Berkeley J. Int'l L.* 288, 301–2 (2003).

1. Persecution as a War Crime

The most striking difference between Article II(1)(c) and Article II(1)(b) was, of course, that only the crimes against humanity provision criminalized "persecutions on political, racial, or religious grounds." The tribunals nevertheless held that racial and religious persecutions qualified as war crimes when committed in occupied territory. The *Ministries* tribunal relied on Article 46 of the Hague Regulations— which protected "religious convictions and practice"—to hold that the persecution of Catholic priests from occupied countries was a war crime.[80] And the *Justice* tribunal held in no uncertain terms that atrocities and offenses "amounting to persecution on racial grounds"—a category in which the tribunal included all acts of persecution against Jews[81]—qualified as war crimes "when carried out in occupied territory."[82] No tribunal ever addressed the status of political persecutions in occupied territory, largely because Taylor made a conscious decision to avoid charging defendants with political persecution whenever possible[83]; the only defendant ever convicted of such persecution—Oeschey in the *Justice* case, discussed below—committed the crime in Germany during the war.[84] There is no reason to assume, though, that the *Justice* tribunal would have treated political persecution any differently than racial persecution; after all, unlike religious freedom, the Hague Regulations did not guarantee either racial integrity or political opinion.[85]

2. Minor Forms of Persecution

The *Justice* tribunal made clear that laws did not qualify as crimes against humanity simply because they "could be and were applied in a discriminatory manner."[86] In particular, the tribunal refused to criminalize German laws that imposed the death penalty on habitual criminals, on looters, on hoarders, and on individuals whose statements undermined "military efficiency." Such laws, the judges insisted, may be "revolting to our sense of justice." But that did not mean that they were crimes against humanity, particularly given that they were adopted in response to the exigencies of war. The tribunal upheld the anti-looting laws, for example, by claiming that "[a]nyone who has seen the utter devastation of the great cities of Germany must realize that the safety of the civilian population demanded that the werewolves who roamed the streets of the burning cities, robbing the dead, and plundering the ruined homes should be severely punished."[87] Similarly, with regard to the military efficiency laws, the tribunal noted that "even under the protection of the Constitution of the United States a citizen is not wholly free to attack the Government or to interfere with its military aims in time of war."[88]

---

[80] *Ministries*, XIV TWC 522.   [81] *Justice*, III TWC 1063.   [82] Ibid., 1081.

[83] Memo from WDSCA for Taylor, 28 Mar. 1947, NA-153–1018-1-84-1, at 1.

[84] *Justice*, III TWC 1164.

[85] Many scholars at the time believed that all three forms of persecution were war crimes. See, e.g., Schwelb, in Mettraux, 132.

[86] *Justice*, III TWC 1027.   [87] Ibid., 1026.   [88] Ibid.

Although the peacetime/wartime distinction was obviously critical to the *Justice* tribunal, the fact that none of those "Draconic laws" directly involved political, racial, or religious persecution also seems to have been important. The tribunal was more than willing to condemn acts that involved such persecution even when the acts themselves were relatively minor. Two examples are particularly illustrative. First, the tribunal held that Oeschey had committed a crime against humanity when, in the final weeks of the war, he sentenced a German count to death for insulting Hitler and expressing approval of the attempt on his life. It acknowledged that "the mere fact alone that Montgelas was prosecuted for remarks hostile to the Nazi regime may not constitute a violation of C. C. Law 10," but insisted that "Montgelas was not convicted for undermining the already collapsed defensive strength of the defeated nation, but...as a last vengeful act of political persecution."[89] Second, the tribunal held that even "lesser forms of racial persecution" such as denying Jews the right to engage in civil litigation without advancement of costs qualified as crimes against humanity. The tribunal recognized that such laws might appear "as a small matter compared to the extermination of Jews by the millions," but pointed out that they were nevertheless "part of the government-organized plan for the persecution of the Jews."[90]

3. Deprivation of Property

The most contentious issue was whether depriving civilians of property on political, racial, or religious grounds qualified as the crime against humanity of persecution. The tribunals agreed that the theft of personal property could qualify, but disagreed concerning the theft of industrial property.

a. Industrial Property

The *Flick* and *Farben* tribunals both held that depriving civilians of industrial property on the basis of race qualified as a war crime but not as a crime against humanity.[91] The *Flick* tribunal offered two rationales for that limitation. To begin with, it argued that "it nowhere appears in the judgment that IMT considered, much less decided, that a person becomes guilty of a crime against humanity merely by exerting anti-Semitic pressure to procure by purchase or through state expropriation industrial property owned by Jews."[92] That was an unpersuasive interpretation: the IMT had declined to criminalize the seizure of Jewish businesses— discussed in the section of the judgment entitled "Persecution of the Jews"—not because of the nature of the plundered property, but because it could not conclude that the seizures were connected to the Nazis' aggressive wars.[93] Indeed, the IMT made clear that it would have considered the pre-war persecution of the Jews to be a crime against humanity had the nexus been satisfied.[94]

The *Flick* tribunal also argued that Article II(1)(c) excluded offenses committed against industrial property. It pointed out that all of the "atrocities and offenses"

---

[89] Ibid., 1164.   [90] Ibid., 1114.   [91] *Flick*, VI TWC 1216; *Farben*, VIII TWC 1129.
[92] *Flick*, VI TWC 1215.   [93] IMT Judgment, 65.   [94] Ibid.

that qualified as murder-type crimes against humanity involved "offenses against the person." It then insisted that, "[u]nder the doctrine of *ejusdem generis* the catch-all words 'other persecutions' must be deemed to include only such as affect the life and liberty of the oppressed peoples."[95] That was an equally unpersuasive argument, one that depended on a significant misstatement of Article II(1)(c). The crimes against humanity provision did not mention "other persecutions" after listing the murder-type atrocities and offenses; it simply mentioned "persecutions." The difference was critical: although the expression "other persecutions" might have implied that Article II(1)(c) intended to criminalize persecutions "of the same kind" as the atrocities and offenses, the more generic term "persecutions" gives rise to no such implication. Indeed, given that the provision mentioned atrocities or offenses "or" persecutions, the far more natural reading of the provision is that *any* persecution on one of the prohibited grounds constituted a crime against humanity.

For reasons that are unclear—and may have been strategic—Taylor took the same position as the *Flick* and *Farben* tribunals in his oral argument in *Ministries*.[96] Fortunately, the *Ministries* tribunal itself did not. As noted above, it not only condemned the Nazis' systematic theft of Jewish agricultural property—farms, livestock, etc.—as a crime against humanity, it convicted Darre, the Minister of Food and Agriculture, for participating in those thefts.[97] Similarly, the *Pohl* tribunal convicted Frank of a crime against humanity for participating in Action Reinhardt, "an ambitious and profitable undertaking for Germany" in which Jews "were herded into concentration camps as slaves and their entire worldly possessions confiscated." The tribunal noted that an integral part of Action Reinhardt was the WVHA's systematic theft of Jewish real property.[98]

b. Personal Property

Undermining its own argument, the *Flick* tribunal suggested that, in terms of Article II(1)(c), "[a] distinction could be made between industrial property and the dwellings, household furnishings, and food supplies of a persecuted people."[99] A number of other tribunals specifically held that the theft of personal property on political, racial, or religious grounds was a crime against humanity. The *Pohl* tribunal's condemnation of Action Reinhardt is one example: the program involved the looting of Jewish personal property as well as Jewish real property—everything from blankets to baby carriages to jewelry.[100] Other examples include the *RuSHA* tribunal's criminalization of the Germanization program, which involved the "confiscation of all property of Poles and Jews for resettlement purposes,"[101] and the *Ministries* tribunal's conviction of Schwerin von Krosigk for permitting his

---

[95] *Flick*, VI TWC 1215.

[96] *Ministries*, Prosecution Argument, XIII TWC 100.

[97] *Ministries*, XIV TWC 556–7. Judge Powers dissented from the majority's legal conclusion, agreeing with the *Flick* and *Farben* tribunals that "[a] persecution . . . must involve some act of violence against the person of the persecuted." Ibid., 917, Powers Dissent.

[98] *Pohl*, V TWC 977–8.   [99] *Flick*, VI TWC 1214.

[100] *Pohl*, V TWC 977.   [101] *RuSHA*, V TWC 96.

subordinates in the Ministry of Finance to confiscate "money, securities, jewelry, furniture, clothing, [and] works of art" owned by German Jews and by Jews who lived in Belgium, the Netherlands, and occupied France.[102]

C. Genocide

The concept of genocide was first mentioned in Telford Taylor's opening argument in the *Medical* case. At this point in the trials, genocide had no legal function; Taylor simply used the term to describe the Nazis' systematic persecution of various groups:

Mankind has not heretofore felt the need of a word to denominate the science of how to kill prisoners most rapidly and subjugated people in large numbers. This case and these defendants have created this gruesome question for the lexicographer. For the moment we will christen this macabre science "thanatology," the science of producing death. The thanatological knowledge, derived in part from these experiments, supplied the techniques for genocide, a policy of the Third Reich, exemplified in the "euthanasia" program and in the widespread slaughter of Jews, gypsies, Poles, and Russians.[103]

The OCC did not rely on genocide as a legal concept until Case No. 8—*RuSHA*. Count 1 of the *RuSHA* indictment, concerning crimes against humanity, alleged that "[t]he acts, conduct, plans and enterprises charged in paragraph 1 of this count were carried out as part of a systematic program of genocide, aimed at the destruction of foreign nations and ethnic groups, in part by murderous extermination, and in part by elimination and suppression of national characteristics."[104] Very similar language then appeared in the *Einsatzgruppen* and *Ministries* indictments.[105]

American war-crimes officials made a conscious decision during the *Medical* case to try to establish genocide as a crime against humanity in the later trials. As the prosecution was nearing the end of its case-in-chief, Raphael Lemkin, the Polish Jew who coined the term "genocide," wrote to David Marcus, the head of the War Department's War Crimes Branch, to stress "the necessity of developing the genocide concept" in the case.[106] Lemkin's memo came too late, but it led John H.E. Fried, then a legal consultant to the Secretary of War, to submit his own memo to the OCC promoting the idea of developing genocide in subsequent cases.[107] That memo, in turn, was reinforced by the Departments of State and War, which informed Taylor during the defense's case-in-chief that insofar as he intended "to formulate accusations in [later] indictments charging crimes against

---

[102] *Ministries*, XIV TWC 677–8.
[103] *Medical*, Prosecution Opening Argument, I TWC 38.
[104] *RuSHA*, Indictment, para. 2, IV TWC 609–10.
[105] *Einsatzgruppen*, Indictment, para. 2, IV TWC 15; *Ministries*, Indictment, para. 39, XII TWC 44.
[106] Memo from Lemkin to Marcus, 19 Jan. 1947, 1, NA-153–1018-10–86-3-1, at 1.
[107] John H.E. Fried, Memorandum on the Necessity to Develop the Concept of Genocide in the Proceedings, Undated, TTP-5-1-1-2, at 1.

humanity in terms of persecutions on religious and racial grounds," they wanted him to describe those persecutions as acts of genocide.[108]

Despite the OCC's best efforts, the tribunals barely addressed genocide in their judgments. The *RuSHA* and *Ministries* tribunals mentioned genocide only when they quoted the indictments, although Judge Powers was obviously skeptical of the idea, arguing in his *Ministries* dissent the remarkable proposition that it was incorrect "to assume that every reference to the 'Final Solution' of the Jewish Question means extermination."[109] The *Einsatzgruppen* tribunal mentioned genocide twice—to note that the Einsatzgruppen had set up a school to teach "the fine art of genocide"[110] and that "the genocide program was in no way connected with the protection of the *Vaterland*"[111]—but did not consider genocide as a legal concept.

By contrast, Tribunal III specifically held that genocide was a crime against humanity in the *Justice* case—an ironic result, given that the OCC did not mention genocide either in the indictment or in its opening argument. Three aspects of the tribunal's decision are particularly notable. First, it singled out genocide as the "prime illustration" of a crime that, "by reason of its magnitude and international repercussions," qualified as a crime against humanity even in the absence of a nexus to war crimes or crimes against peace.[112] Second, it cited the recently adopted General Assembly Resolution 96(I) in defense of that conclusion, stating that the Assembly, though not "an international legislature," was "the most authoritative organ in existence for the interpretation of world opinion."[113] Third, it specifically convicted two defendants—Lautz and Rothaug—of genocide for participating in "the established governmental plan" for the extermination of Poles and Jews.[114]

Conclusion

The NMTs made an invaluable contribution to the development of crimes against humanity. First, unlike the IMT, the tribunals systematically distinguished between the three different geographic and temporal categories of crimes against humanity: acts that took place in occupied territory; acts that took place outside of occupied territory during the war; and acts that took place prior to the war. Second, they laid the groundwork for the eventual elimination of the nexus requirement, even though the *Pohl, Flick,* and *Ministries* tribunals wrongly held that Law No. 10 required the nexus. Third, they developed the contextual elements that are at the heart of modern doctrine and that definitively distinguish crimes against humanity from war crimes. Finally, they provided the first comprehensive analysis of persecution as a crime against humanity and were the first tribunals—international or domestic—to convict defendants of genocide. All of those contributions are discussed in more detail in Chapter 16.

---

[108] Memo from WDSCA for Taylor, 28 Mar. 1947, at 1.
[109] *Ministries*, Powers Dissent, XIV TWC 909.
[110] *Einsatzgruppen*, IV TWC 450.   [111] Ibid., 469–70.   [112] *Justice*, III TWC 983.
[113] Ibid.   [114] Ibid., 1128 (Lautz), 1156 (Rothaug).

11

Modes of Participation

Introduction

The previous chapters focused on how the tribunals interpreted the war crimes and crimes against humanity enumerated in Article II(1)—the "special part" of Law No. 10. That was, of course, only half of the story; the tribunals had to determine not only "whether certain acts infringe[d] international law, but also whether criminal responsibility attache[d] to an individual for such infringement."[1] The latter determination was governed by Article II(2), Law No. 10's "general part":

Any person without regard to nationality or the capacity in which he acted, is deemed to have committed a crime as defined in paragraph 1 of this Article, if he was (a) a principal or (b) was an accessory to the commission of any such crime or ordered or abetted the same or (c) took a consenting part therein or (d) was connected with plans or enterprises involving its commission or (e) was a member of any organization or group connected with the commission of any such crime or (f) with reference to paragraph 1 (a) if he held a high political, civil or military (including General Staff) position in Germany or in one of its Allies, co-belligerents or satellites or held high position in the financial, industrial or economic life of any such country.[2]

Chapter 8 noted that the tribunals discarded Article II(2)(f), because it implied strict liability for crimes against peace. They also devoted little attention to Article II(2)(a), because—to quote Taylor's final trial program—"[m]ost of the defendants in these cases occupied very high positions in the government or economic structure of Germany. Very few of them ever committed a murder or crime with their own hands."[3] The critical modes of participation in the trials were thus those that involved secondary liability, Article II(2)(b)–(e): ordering, abetting, taking a consenting part, being connected to a criminal enterprise, and membership in a criminal organization.

This chapter and the next discuss the tribunals' jurisprudence concerning the modes of participation in a war crime or a crime against humanity.[4] This chapter focuses on the modes of participation in Article II(2)(b) and (c). Section I examines a number of threshold issues concerning criminal responsibility, such as liability for omissions and the liability of corporations. Sections II–IV discuss ordering, taking a consenting part, and command responsibility, respectively.

---

[1] *High Command*, XI TWC 510.   [2] Law No. 10, Art. II(2).   [3] Third Trial Program, 4.
[4] Chapter 8 discussed the modes of participation in a crime against peace, which were *sui generis*.

Finally, Section V addresses two modes of participation referenced only in passing by the tribunals—perpetration by means and incitement—as well as the tribunals' rejection of attempt.

I. General Principles

A. Basic Structure of Criminal Responsibility

Von Knieriem pointed out in his book on the NMT trials that reading the judgments with regard to individual responsibility is often an exercise in frustration:

[M]ost of the Nuremberg Tribunals did not even take the trouble to state clearly on which of the alternatives enumerated in [Article II(2)] their sentences were based in a particular case. Frequently it is impossible to ascertain whether a sentence is based on the fact that somebody was a principal or an accessory, or whether he was regarded as having participated in the crime only by consenting. In most of the cases where more than one person acted, the opinions say no more than that a certain defendant "took part in the act." It is then left to the reader to ponder which of the various alternatives of CCL No. 10 may have been applicable.[5]

The *Medical* case is an excellent example. In convicting Karl Brandt for his role in the Nazis' barbaric medical experiments, Tribunal I simply held that he "was responsible for, aided and abetted, took a consenting part in, and was connected with plans and enterprises involving medical experiments conducted on non-German nationals against their consent, and in other atrocities."[6]

Despite the imprecision of many of the judgments, however, it is clear that individual criminal responsibility consisted of three basic elements: (1) the commission of a crime specified in the indictment; (2) the defendant's knowledge of the crime; and (3) the defendant's participation in the crime in a manner proscribed by Article II(2).[7] In *Farben*, for example, Tribunal VI began by establishing the corporation's involvement in plundering private property in occupied territory and then held that, "[a]s the action of Farben in proceeding to acquire permanently property interests in the manner generally outlined is in violation of the Hague Regulations, any individual who knowingly participated in any such act of plunder or spoliation with the degree of connection outlined in Article II, paragraph 2 of Control Council Law No. 10, is criminally responsible therefore."[8]

What it meant to "knowingly participate" in a crime differed, of course, depending on the particular mode of participation. Two considerations nevertheless applied to all of the modes. First, the tribunals insisted that the requisite knowledge could not be inferred from the defendant's official position. The *Pohl* tribunal, for example, noted "the necessity of guarding against assuming criminality, or even culpable responsibility, solely from the official titles which the several

---

[5] Von Knieriem, 211. [6] *Medical*, II TWC 198.
[7] *Justice*, III TWC 1093. [8] *Farben*, VIII TWC 1141.

defendants held."[9] Similarly, the *Krupp* tribunal specifically held that "guilt must be personal. The mere fact without more that a defendant was a member of the Krupp Directorate or an official of the firm is not sufficient."[10]

Second, the tribunals agreed that the participation requirement could be satisfied either by an act or by an omission. Tribunal V's statement in the *Hostage* case was typical: "[i]n determining the guilt or innocence of these defendants, we shall require proof of a causative, overt act or omission from which a guilty intent can be inferred before a verdict of guilty will be pronounced."[11] The tribunals emphasized, however, that an omission was "not sufficient to warrant a conviction except in those instances where an affirmative duty exists to prevent or object to a course of action."[12] Liability for omission was thus limited in practice—as discussed below—to taking a consenting part in a crime and command responsibility.

B. Corporate Criminal Responsibility

A number of scholars believe that the NMT trials provide precedent for corporate criminal responsibility. Anita Ramasastry, for example, has argued that "[a] parsing of the judgments rendered . . . involving industrialists and other commercial actors reveals an underlying implication that the corporations for which they worked had also committed international war crimes."[13] Such interpretations are misguided. First, and most obviously, none of the trials involved allegations that juristic persons had committed war crimes, crimes against humanity, or crimes against peace, even though neither Law No. 10 nor Ordinance No. 7 expressly limited the tribunals' jurisdiction to natural persons.[14] The *Farben* tribunal, for example, specifically pointed out that "the corporate defendant, Farben, is not before the bar of this Tribunal and cannot be subjected to criminal penalties in these proceedings."[15] Judge Wilkins made a similar statement regarding Krupp in his concurring opinion.[16]

Second, the tribunals unequivocally rejected the idea that individual criminal responsibility was in any way derivative of a corporation's collective responsibility for a crime. Ramasastry argues that "[b]ecause of Farben's liability, individual directors could be convicted by virtue of their affiliation with Farben."[17] In fact, the *Farben* tribunal specifically noted that although it had "used the term 'Farben' as descriptive of the instrumentality of cohesion in the name of which the enumerated acts of spoliation were committed," the prosecution was still required to prove "that an individual defendant was either a participant in the illegal act or that,

---

[9] *Pohl*, V TWC 980.   [10] *Krupp*, IX TWC 1448.
[11] *Hostage*, XI TWC 1261.   [12] *Ministries*, XIV TWC 625.
[13] Anita Ramasastry, "Corporate Complicity: From Nuremberg to Rangoon," 20 *Berkeley J. Int'l L.* 91, 105 (2002); see also Andrew Clapham, "The Question of Jurisdiction Under International Criminal Law Over Legal Persons," in *Liability of Multinational Corporations Under International Law* 139, 140 (Menno T. Kamminga & Saman Zia-Zarifi eds, 2000).
[14] See Bush, *Conspiracy*, 1223.
[15] *Farben*, VIII TWC 1153. Strangely, the corporation itself was represented by an attorney during the trial. That attorney even gave a closing argument on behalf of Farben. See Bush, *Conspiracy*, 1224.
[16] *Krupp*, Wilkins Concurrence, IX TWC 455.   [17] Ramasastry, 107.

being aware thereof, he authorized or approved it. Responsibility does not automatically attach to an act proved to be criminal merely by virtue of a defendant's membership in the Vorstand."[18] The *Krupp* tribunal took the same position, as the quote above indicates.

Third, and finally, nothing in the judgments supports the idea that a corporation's "collective intent"—to use Ramasastry's phrase—was in any way attributable to an individual official when determining the extent of his knowledge of the corporation's criminal activity. In fact, according to Judge Hebert, nearly all of the *Farben* defendants had to be acquitted precisely because the tribunal rejected any such attribution: "[i]f a single individual had combined the knowledge attributable to the corporate entity and had engaged in the course of action under the same circumstances as that attributable to the corporate entity, it is extremely doubtful that a judgment of acquittal could properly be entered."[19]

C. Principals and Accessories

As von Knieriem noted, the tribunals never systematically distinguished between principals and accessories to a crime. That is perhaps not surprising: although Article II(2) implied that principal liability was limited to those who personally committed the *actus reus* of a crime, it specifically provided that any defendant whose actions fell within the parameters of Article II(2) was "deemed to have committed" a war crime, crime against humanity, or crime against peace. The principal/accessory distinction was thus generally irrelevant, although one tribunal held that the modes of participation enumerated in Article II(2) were listed in descending order of culpability, an issue discussed in Chapter 14.

II. Ordering

Because crimes committed pursuant to notorious Nazi orders were at the heart of a number of NMT trials—the Commando Order, the Commissar Order, the Night and Fog Decree—the tribunals devoted considerable attention to ordering as a mode of participation. According to the tribunals, a defendant was responsible for ordering a crime if three requirements were satisfied: (1) an illegal order had been issued by a superior to a subordinate; (2) the defendant was responsible in some way for that order; and (3) the defendant knew or should have known that the order was illegal.

A. Illegal Order

Responsibility for ordering a crime depended on the existence of an illegal order. The tribunals generally considered the idea of an "order" to be self-evident, perhaps

---

[18] *Farben*, VIII TWC 1153.   [19] Ibid., 1214, Hebert Concurrence.

because most of the orders considered in the trials were issued by individuals whose authority to require obedience from their subordinates was unquestioned, such as Hitler, high-ranking SS officials, and military officers. Two tribunals, however, addressed the nature of the ordering relationship. In *Pohl*, Tribunal II emphasized that a superior/subordinate relationship was a necessary element of ordering—the orderer had to have the right to demand the orderee comply with his instructions.[20] And in *High Command*, Tribunal V held that the requisite superior/subordinate relationship could exist either *de jure* or *de facto*: as long as the defendant's orders were "binding upon subordinate units to whom they were directed," it was irrelevant whether the subordinates were under the defendant's "direct command authority."[21] Reinecke argued, for example, that he could not give orders to civilian concentration-camp personnel because they were not formally subordinate to him. The tribunal rejected that claim, pointing out that the concentration-camp personnel felt "compelled to comply" with his directives.[22]

Ordering also required the order in question to be either "criminal on its face"[23] or capable of being applied in a criminal manner.[24] The Commando Order was an example of the former, because it was nothing more than "an order to commit murder."[25] The Barbarossa Jurisdiction Order, by contrast, was an example of the latter. The order had two parts: the first permitted the execution of civilians without adequate process; the second relieved field commanders of the obligation to prosecute crimes committed by their subordinates against civilians. The first part of the order was facially criminal, but the criminality of the second part depended on its implementation, because a field commander could satisfy his obligation to protect the civilian population by disciplining his subordinates instead of by prosecuting them. The criminality of the Barbarossa Jurisdiction Order, therefore, depended upon how a field commander implemented it.[26]

B. *Actus Reus*

To be responsible for "ordering" a crime, a defendant also had to be involved in issuing, drafting, or transmitting an illegal order—the mode of participation's *actus reus*. The nature of those activities differed, however, depending on whether the order was military or civilian.

1. *Military Orders*

a. Issuing

Defendants who used their authority to issue illegal orders were obviously responsible for the crimes committed pursuant to them. In *High Command*, for example, von Roques was convicted for ordering his soldiers to collectively punish—through mass executions and the destruction of villages—civilians in occupied territory who

---

[20] *Pohl*, V TWC 983.   [21] *High Command*, XI TWC 651.   [22] Ibid.
[23] Ibid., 512.   [24] Ibid., 560–1.   [25] Ibid., 481.   [26] Ibid., 525.

were suspected of supporting partisans.[27] Similarly, in the *Hostage* case, Kuntze was convicted for issuing an order that established a fixed ratio for reprisal killings of 100 Serbian civilians for every German soldier killed.[28]

b. Drafting

Military commanders, however, rarely drafted written orders themselves. Instead, they relied on staff officers to translate their "ideas and general directives" into "properly prepared orders."[29] According to the *High Command* tribunal, that function was criminal if the order was illegal: "[i]f the basic idea is criminal under international law, the staff officer who puts that idea into the form of a military order, either himself or through subordinates under him ... commits a criminal act under international law."[30] The tribunal did, however, impose a substantive limit on the responsibility of staff officers for drafting an illegal order: if the staff officer functioned solely as a stenographer, "merely transcribing" his superior's order, he was not responsible for it.[31] In other words, preparing an unlawful order qualified as ordering only if the staff officer exercised "personal initiative" during the drafting process, using his intelligence and skills to translate an amorphous (but illegal) directive from his superior into a written order specific enough that subordinate officers would be able to carry it out.[32]

A number of *High Command* defendants were held responsible for drafting illegal orders issued by their superiors. Warlimont, for example, was convicted for participating in the Commissar Order because "he contributed his part to moulding it into its final form."[33] Similarly, Lehmann—a civilian who was the chief legal advisor to the OKW—was convicted for participating in the Barbarossa Jurisdiction Order because he "became the main factor in determining the final form into which the criminal ideas of Hitler were put" and "modified those ideas within his own sphere up to a certain point and placed the whole into an effective military order."[34] By contrast, the *Hostage* tribunal acquitted von Geitner for preparing an order to commit illegal reprisals because he was simply carrying out his superior's instructions.[35]

The *High Command* tribunal's emphasis on personal initiative, it is worth noting, created a Catch-22 for defendants accused of drafting an illegal order. From a sentencing perspective, it was important for defendants to emphasize that they had done everything in their power to ameliorate the order's unlawfulness. Arguing that they had done so, however, required them to admit that they had not functioned simply as stenographers. As the tribunal noted, "if defendants were able to modify the specific desires of their superiors in the interests of legality and humanity ... the same power could be exercised for other ends and purposes and they were not mere transcribers of orders."[36] Warlimont learned that lesson when

---

[27] *High Command*, XI TWC 645.　　[28] *Hostage*, XI TWC 1277–8.
[29] *High Command*, XI TWC 513.　　[30] Ibid.　　[31] See, e.g., ibid., 515, 651.
[32] Ibid., 683.　　[33] Ibid., 665.　　[34] Ibid., 693.
[35] *Hostage*, XI TWC 1288.　　[36] *High Command*, XI TWC 515.

the tribunal rejected his claim to have softened the Commissar Order and then used his admission of initiative to convict him for drafting it.[37]

c. Transmitting

Finally, the *High Command* tribunal held that a commander was responsible for ordering a crime if he transmitted an unlawful order issued by one of his superiors to officers subordinate to himself. "The transmittal through the chain of command constitutes an implementation of an order. Such orders carry the authoritative weight of the superior who issues them and of the subordinate commanders who pass them on for compliance."[38]

Transmission was criminal for two different kinds of orders. When an order was criminal on its face, the mere act of transmission qualified as ordering. Von Salmuth, for example, was convicted for passing an obviously illegal order down the chain of command that required the execution of any civilian found in the vicinity of partisan activity.[39]

The issue was more complicated when an order (or part of an order) was not criminal on its face, but was capable of being applied in a criminal manner. The *High Command* tribunal held that, in such situations, it was criminal for a commander to transmit the order "without proper safeguards as to its application."[40] Von Leeb was thus convicted for participating in the Barbarossa Jurisdiction Order because there was no evidence that "it was in any way clarified or that instructions were given in any way to prevent its illegal application."[41]

Although the *High Command* tribunal took a broad approach to transmission, it insisted that a commander could not be held responsible for transmitting an illegal order if he was outside the chain of command. The rationale for criminalizing transmission was, as noted, that the subordinate commander lent his authority to an unlawful order by passing it along. That rationale did not apply when a superior authority simply used a subordinate commander's headquarters to distribute an illegal order to military units in the field. In such a situation, transmission was a "mere intermediate administrative function" for which the subordinate commander could not be held responsible.[42]

2. Civilian Orders

The tribunals held that civilians could also be criminally responsible for ordering war crimes and crimes against humanity. As in the military context, issuing was the least problematic form of ordering. In *RuSHA*, for example, Rudolf Creutz, Greifelt's deputy in the RKFDV, was convicted for issuing binding instructions to his subordinates to Germanize children in Polish orphanages who were considered to be Aryan.[43] And in the *Justice* case, Schlegelberger was convicted

[37] Ibid., 665. [38] Ibid., 510. [39] Ibid., 617.
[40] Ibid., 525. [41] Ibid., 560–1. [42] Ibid., 510.
[43] *RuSHA*, V TWC 106.

for ordering the execution of a Jew who had been sentenced to prison for stealing eggs.[44]

Civilian defendants were convicted for transmitting illegal orders, as well. In *Ministries*, for example, Lammers, Reich Minister and Chief of the Reich Chancellery, was convicted for transmitting a secret circular issued by Thierack that prohibited the prosecution of Germans civilians who participated in lynching downed Allied flyers.[45] As with military transmission, however, "personal initiative" was required. The *Ministries* tribunal emphasized that "Lammers was not a mere postman, but acted freely and without objection as a responsible Reich Minister carrying out the functions of his office."[46]

C. Mens Rea

Finally, a defendant had to have participated in issuing, drafting, or transmitting an illegal order with the necessary *mens rea*. According to *High Command* tribunal, that requirement was satisfied if the defendant knew that the order was illegal or, because the order was "criminal on its face," should have known that it was:

Military commanders in the field with far reaching military responsibilities cannot be charged under international law with criminal participation in issuing orders which are not obviously criminal or which they are not shown to have known to be criminal under international law . . . He cannot be held criminally responsible for a mere error in judgment as to disputable legal questions. It is therefore considered that to find a field commander criminally responsible for the transmittal of such an order, he must have passed the order to the chain of command and the order must be one that is criminal upon its face, or one which he is shown to have known was criminal.[47]

That statement of ordering's *mens rea* applied specifically to transmitting an order that was illegal on its face or was capable of being illegally applied. The tribunal made clear, however, that the same *mens rea* applied to issuing and drafting such orders, as well.[48]

D. A Substantive Crime?

Article II(2)(b) considered ordering a mode of participation in a crime, not a substantive crime in itself. The tribunals uniformly followed that approach when an illegal order was executed, holding a defendant responsible for the crimes committed pursuant to the order.[49] They split, however, over whether a defendant could be held criminally responsible for participating in an illegal order that was never executed.

Two tribunals took a conservative approach to that issue. In *Einsatzgruppen*, Tribunal II held that an order was criminal only if it was executed, contrasting Law

---

[44] *Justice*, III TWC 1085.   [45] *Ministries*, XIV TWC 462.
[46] Ibid., 463.   [47] *High Command*, XI TWC 511.
[48] Ibid., 512.   [49] See, e.g., ibid., 531.

No. 10 with Article 47 of the German Military Penal Code, according to which it was "sufficient if the order aims at the commission of a crime or offense."[50] Similarly, in *RuSHA*, Tribunal I acquitted Brueckner of submitting a draft of an illegal order involving the forced conscription of civilians because there was no evidence that the order was adopted or carried out.[51]

The *Hostage* tribunal, by contrast, specifically held that a defendant could be held responsible for participating in an illegal order even if it was not executed. Rendulic, for example, was convicted of transmitting the Commissar Order even though, as he contended, there was no evidence that "captured commissars were shot by troops under his command." That fact, according to the tribunal, was "a mitigating circumstance but [did] not free him of the crime of knowingly and intentionally passing on a criminal order."[52]

The *High Command* tribunal took the most unusual position. It held that a defendant could not be convicted for participating in an order that was not executed, as illustrated by Reinhardt's acquittal for distributing the Commissar Order.[53] But it also held that a defendant who issued an executed order was not only responsible for the crimes committed pursuant to it, but was also guilty of issuing the illegal order itself, thus treating ordering as a substantive crime. With regard to Reinhardt's involvement in deportations, plunder, and forced labor, for example, the tribunal held that "[t]he orders to do those things were criminal orders, and they were fully implemented by him. He is criminally responsible for issuing the orders *and* for the acts done in implementation of them."[54]

III. Consenting Part

Article II(2)(c) established criminal responsibility for taking a "consenting part" (TCP) in a war crime or crime against humanity. TCP was first mentioned in the Moscow Declaration, which promised punishment for Nazis who "have been responsible for or have taken a consenting part in…atrocities, massacres and executions." It also appeared in Article 3(b) of JCS 1023/10 and in the Preamble to the London Agreement, although it was not included in the London Charter itself.

The Joint Chiefs of Staff apparently considered TCP to be functionally equivalent to command responsibility. A 21 October 1944 draft of JCS 1023/10 provided that the term "war criminals" specifically included "persons who have taken a consenting part in war crimes" and then gave the example of "a superior officer who has failed to take action to prevent a war crime when he had knowledge of its contemplated commission and was in a position to prevent it."[55] By contrast, the tribunals considered TCP either as another name for participating in a criminal

---

[50] *Einsatzgruppen*, IV TWC 487.   [51] *RuSHA*, V TWC 147.
[52] *Hostage*, XI TWC 1294.   [53] *High Command*, XI TWC 615–6.
[54] Ibid., 614 (emphasis added).
[55] Draft Directive on Apprehension of War Criminals, in Taylor, *Final Report*, 247 (Appendix C).

enterprise or—more interestingly—as a *sui generis* mode of participation in a crime similar to, but not equivalent with, command responsibility.

The critical difference was whether TCP required a positive act or could be satisfied by an omission. The *Pohl* tribunal took the first position, holding that "[t]here is an element of positive conduct implicit in the word 'consent'. Certainly, as used in the ordinance, it means something more than 'not dissenting'."[56] The requirement of a positive act then determined which defendants were convicted for taking a consenting part in a crime. Volk was convicted of mistreating concentration-camp inmates, for example, even though he had not personally committed the mistreatment and "did not have the power" to prevent it. The tribunal held that "[i]f Volk was part of an organization actively engaged in crimes against humanity, was aware of those crimes and yet voluntarily remained a part of that organization, lending his own professional efforts to the continuance and furtherance of those crimes, he is responsible under the law."[57] By contrast, the tribunal acquitted Vogt of taking a consenting part in similar charges because "[t]he only consent claimed arises from imputed knowledge—nothing more. But the phrase, 'being connected with' a crime means something more than having knowledge of it... There is an element of positive conduct implicit in the word 'consent'."[58] That formulation drew an explicit parallel between TCP and enterprise liability.

Unlike the *Pohl* tribunal, the *Einsatzgruppen*, *Farben*, and *Ministries* tribunals specifically viewed TCP as an omission-based mode of participation. In their view, a defendant had taken a consenting part in a crime if three conditions were satisfied: (1) he knew that a crime had been or was going to be committed; (2) because of his authority, he was in a position to object to the criminal activity; and (3) he nevertheless failed to object to it. TCP was thus broader than command responsibility.

A. Knowledge

The tribunals emphasized that a defendant accused of TCP must have known that a crime had been or was going to be committed. The *Einsatzgruppen* tribunal, for example, noted that von Radetzky "knew that Jews were executed by Sonderkommando 4a because they were Jews" when it convicted him of taking a consenting part in those executions.[59] Similarly, the *Farben* tribunal relied on the fact that Schmitz "knew of Farben's program to take part in the spoliation of the French dyestuffs industry" to convict him of taking a consenting part in that spoliation.[60] There is no indication in any of the judgments that the tribunals would have applied a negligence standard to TCP, which—as we will see—partially distinguishes TCP from command responsibility. That distinction makes sense: because effective control over the perpetrators of the crime was not an essential element of TCP, it would have been manifestly unfair to convict a defendant for failing to

---

[56] *Pohl*, V TWC 1002.   [57] Ibid., 1048.   [58] Ibid., 1002.
[59] *Einsatzgruppen*, IV TWC 577.   [60] *Farben*, VIII TWC 1155.

object to a crime of which he was unaware. The defendant's duty was to object to the crime, not to prevent it.

B. Authority

According to the tribunals, failing to object to a crime qualified as TCP only if the defendant had been in a position to influence the organization or individuals responsible for its commission. In *Einsatzgruppen*, for example, Fendler was convicted for failing to object to executions because, "as the second highest ranking officer in the Kommando, his views could have been heard in complaint or protest against what he now says was a too summary procedure."[61] Similarly, in *Farben*, Schmitz's conviction depended on the fact that he failed to object to the company's spoliation activities even though "[h]e was in a position to influence policy and effectively to alter the course of events."[62] By contrast, the *Einsatzgruppen* tribunal refused to convict Ruehl for taking a consenting part in Sonderkommando 10b's executions because, although he knew about them, the prosecution had failed to prove "that he was in a position to control, prevent, or modify the severity of [the] program."[63]

The "authority" requirement of TCP, it is important to note, differed from the superior/subordinate requirement of command responsibility. None of the defendants convicted of taking a consenting part in a crime had either *de jure* or *de facto* effective control over the individuals who committed it, which is what makes TCP a unique mode of participation. Schmitz might have been *primus inter pares* as the Chairman of Farben's Vorstand, but he did not have the power to approve or disapprove the activities of his colleagues. Fendler was an SD officer in Division III of Sonderkommando 4b, while the executions themselves were committed by units subordinate to the Gestapo officers in Division IV.[64] Von Radetzky was in the same position in Sonderkommando 4a—and the *Einsatzgruppen* tribunal specifically declined to find that he had taken *de facto* control of Sonderkommando 4a when Blobel was absent because of illness.[65] Most revealing of all, however, is the *Einsatzgruppen* tribunal's explanation of why it convicted Ott for executions committed by Sonderkommando 7b:

In view of the fact that Ott arrived in Bryansk on 19 February for the specific purpose of taking over control of Sonderkommando 7b, it is not clear why he should have waited until 15 March to assume leadership of the unit. But even if this unexplained delay in the technical assumption of command were a fact, this would not of itself exculpate Ott from responsibility for the operation involved. Under Control Council Law No. 10 one may be convicted for taking a "consenting part in the perpetration of crimes" and it would be difficult to maintain that Ott, while actually with the Kommando, did not (*even though technically not its commanding officer*) consent to these executions.[66]

---

[61] *Einsatzgruppen*, IV TWC 572.   [62] *Farben*, VIII TWC 1155.
[63] *Einsatzgruppen*, IV TWC 581.   [64] Ibid., 571–2.
[65] Ibid., 577.   [66] Ibid., 560 (emphasis added).

This interpretation of the difference between TCP and command responsibility is confirmed by Judge Powers' dissent in *Ministries*. Judge Powers derisively described TCP as convicting a defendant for the "failure to either openly protest or go on a sit-down strike in time of war, after receiving knowledge that somebody somewhere in the government committed a crime."[67] That was a mischaracterization of TCP even as endorsed by *Ministries* itself; the majority had acquitted von Weizsaecker of taking a knowing and consenting part in Einsatzgruppen atrocities precisely because it concluded that "the Foreign Office had no jurisdiction or power to intervene" in the program.[68] Judge Powers' statement nevertheless indicates that he did not view TCP as equivalent to command responsibility. Indeed, he insisted in the next paragraph that he believed the majority should have considered the two equivalent: "[a]ny person who can order a crime committed can consent to its commission with equal effect and with equal responsibility. To take a consenting part means no more than that."[69]

C. Failure to Object

If a defendant had knowledge of a crime and the authority to influence it, the tribunals agreed that he had a duty to use his authority to try to "control, prevent, or modify the severity" of the crime.[70] It was the existence of that duty that justified holding the defendant responsible for an omission.[71] Fendler was thus convicted because, as noted earlier, he did nothing even though "his views could have been heard in complaint or protest."[72]

IV. Command Responsibility

A number of tribunals relied on the doctrine of command responsibility to convict military and civilian defendants of crimes committed by their subordinates. Article II(2) of Law No. 10 did not expressly include command responsibility as a mode of participation; the tribunals derived the availability of that mode from international law. In the *Medical* case, for example, Tribunal I held that "[t]he law of war imposes on a military officer in a position of command an affirmative duty to take such steps as are within his power and appropriate to the circumstances to control those under his command for the prevention of acts which are violations of the law of war."[73] None of the tribunals, however, identified the precise "law of war"—conventional or customary—that justified imposing criminal responsibility on a military commander who failed to properly supervise his subordinates, much less on a civilian

---

[67] *Ministries*, Powers Dissent, XIV TWC 874–5. [68] Ibid., 472–3.
[69] Ibid., 875, Powers Dissent. [70] *Einsatzgruppen*, IV TWC 580.
[71] See, e.g., *Ministries*, XIV TWC 625.
[72] *Einsatzgruppen*, IV TWC 572; see also *Pohl*, V TWC 1011; *High Command*, XI TWC 543–4.
[73] *Medical*, II TWC 207.

superior. Instead, they simply cited *Yamashita*, decided by the U.S. Supreme Court in 1946, for the existence of the mode of participation.[74]

The tribunals' failure to discuss the conventional or customary basis for command responsibility is surprising, given how often they stressed the need to take a conservative approach to international law. It is also troubling, because a number of scholars have convincingly argued that—in the words of Bing Bing Jia—"there had existed nothing like a custom of command responsibility prior to the *Yamashita* case."[75] A vague notion of command responsibility existed in Articles 1 and 43 of the Hague Regulations, in Article 10 of the 1907 Hague Convention (X) for the Adaptation to Maritime Warfare of the Principles of the Geneva Convention, and in Article 26 of the 1929 Convention for the Amelioration of the Condition of the Wounded and Sick in Armed Forces in the Field. None of those Conventions, however, imposed criminal liability for breaches of their provisions. Moreover, although the Commission on the Responsibility of the Authors of the War endorsed such criminal liability after World War I, that endorsement—even when combined with scattered references to command responsibility in the Leipzig Trials—hardly amounted to a customary rule.[76]

Nor did *Yamashita* help the tribunals' cause. The tribunals relied on the Supreme Court's analysis of the state of international law on the eve of World War II; they did not view the decision as establishing a new rule of international law or as binding precedent.[77] But as Bing Bing Jia has pointed out, "[l]ooking at the *Yamashita* case, it is plain that there was no reference to a clear basis in international law that required that a commander be held personally responsible in such a case."[78] His conclusion is sound: the Supreme Court simply cited the three Conventions mentioned above and the practice of American military tribunals for the idea that a military commander was criminally liable for failing to properly supervise his troops.[79]

Because there is little support for the idea that command responsibility existed as a mode of participation under international law during World War II, the convictions obtained via command responsibility during the NMT trials at least arguably violated the principle of non-retroactivity. The tribunals' jurisprudence nevertheless remains an important contribution to the development of the doctrine. According to the tribunals, command responsibility for a war crime or crime against humanity had three elements: (1) the defendant and the perpetrators of the crime were in a superior/subordinate relationship; (2) the defendant either knew or should have known that crimes had been or were going to be committed; and (3) the defendant failed to take the necessary steps to prevent or punish the crime.

---

[74] See, e.g., *Pohl*, V TWC 1011.

[75] Bing Bing Jia, "The Doctrine of Command Responsibility Revisited," 3 *Chinese J. Int'l L.* 1, 12 (2004).

[76] Ibid., 11–12.

[77] See, e.g., *High Command*, XI TWC 544.

[78] Bing Bing Jia, 8.

[79] *In re Yamashita*, 327 U.S. 1, 15–16 (1946).

A. Superior/Subordinate Relationship

1. *Military Superiors*

In discussing the nature of the superior/subordinate relationship in the military context, the tribunals distinguished between commanding generals, tactical commanders, and Chiefs of Staff.

a. Commanding Generals

According to the tribunals, the superior responsibility of a commanding general in occupied territory had two aspects. Like all commanders, he was responsible for the actions of the military units directly subordinate to him. But he also exercised "executive authority" over the territory under his command, charging him—in the words of the *Hostage* tribunal—"with the duty of maintaining peace and order, punishing crime, and protecting lives and property within the area of his command. His responsibility [was] coextensive with his area of command."[80] The latter duty was particularly important, because it meant that a commanding general was responsible for the actions of *any* military unit that operated within his area of command, even those that were not directly subordinate to him.[81]

Nor was the commanding general's superior responsibility limited to military units. Because of his executive authority, he also had an obligation to control the actions of civilian organizations operating in his area of command.[82] In the *Hostage* case, for example, List argued that he could not be held responsible for the execution of thousands of civilians in reprisal because "many of these executions were carried out by units of the SS, the SD, and local police units which were not tactically subordinated to him." Tribunal V convicted List despite accepting his factual claim, pointing out that "it must be borne in mind that in his capacity as commanding general of occupied territory, he was charged with the duty and responsibility of maintaining order and safety."[83]

b. Tactical Commanders

The tribunals agreed that, unlike commanding generals, tactical commanders were responsible only for the actions of military units directly subordinate to them. As the *Hostage* tribunal put it, "[t]he matter of subordination of units as a basis of fixing criminal responsibility becomes important in the case of a military commander having solely a tactical command."[84] The tribunals nevertheless interpreted the idea of "subordination" very expansively. First, a tactical commander was responsible not only for the actions of combat units under his command, but also for the actions of his subordinate commanders.[85] A tactical commander could thus be criminally responsible for failing to prevent his subordinate commanders from unlawfully applying an order that was not criminal on its face.[86]

---

[80] *Hostage*, XI TWC 1271.   [81] Ibid., 1257.   [82] *High Command*, XI TWC 546.
[83] *Hostage*, XI TWC 1272.   [84] Ibid., 1260.   [85] Ibid., 1303.   [86] Ibid.

Second, subordination could exist either *de jure* or *de facto*: as long as a tactical commander exercised effective control over a military unit or civilian organization, he was superior to it for purposes of command responsibility. In *High Command*, for example, Reinicke argued that he was not responsible for the mistreatment of POWs because he did not have "direct command authority" over the soldiers who had committed the mistreatment. Tribunal V rejected that argument:

This Tribunal is not concerned with fine formalities or divisions of authority. The evidence establishes overwhelmingly the over-all control and supervision of the defendant Reinecke as to prisoners of war under the supreme authority of the OKW and his power over prisoner of war camps and prisoner of war affairs. The evidence shows that he exercised that authority by issuing orders; that he had the right of inspection both in himself and his subordinate; that such inspection was a duty entrusted to him and carried out by him; that he had the sources of knowledge and the duty was placed upon him to know and supervise what took place in these camps, and that he did know and supervise what took place therein and directed certain operations in such camps.[87]

As noted earlier, the *High Command* tribunal used the same reasoning to reject Reinecke's related claim that he could not be held responsible for ordering mistreatment. Reinecke's conviction thus suggests that the tribunal believed the same test of "effective control" applied to both ordering and command responsibility. The *Hostage* tribunal appears to have taken the same position. In acquitting von Leyser of responsibility for reprisal executions, it noted that "[a] corps commander must be held responsible for the acts of his subordinate commanders in carrying out his orders and for acts which the corps commander knew or ought to have known about," indicating that the ability to order implied the obligation to properly supervise.[88]

c. Chiefs of Staff

As discussed above, a Chief of Staff could be convicted for participating in the drafting or issuing of an illegal order. By contrast, the *High Command* tribunal specifically held that a Chief of Staff could not be held responsible for the acts of military units subordinate to his commanding general, because he "has no command authority over subordinate units nor is he a bearer of executive power."[89]

2. Civilian Superiors

The tribunals had little difficulty extending command responsibility to civilians who exercised effective control over subordinates. The easiest cases were those involving paramilitary organizations like the SS, which had clearly demarcated chains of command. Pohl, for example, attempted to disclaim responsibility for the mistreatment of slave labor in concentration camps by arguing that his office, the WVHA, had exercised "formal," not "actual," control over Amtsgruppe D

---

[87] *High Command*, XI TWC 653–4.   [88] *Hostage*, XI TWC 1303.
[89] *High Command*, XI TWC 684.

(which had engaged in the mistreatment) because the office had continued to take orders from Himmler. Tribunal II rejected Pohl's argument, noting simply that "[t]he fact remains...that Pohl as head of the WVHA was the superior of Gluecks and Maurer and was in a position to exercise and did exercise substantial supervision and control over Amtsgruppe D."[90] Similarly, the *Pohl* tribunal convicted Mummenthey for the mistreatment of slave labor because it concluded—despite his self-description as a "private business man"—that he "was a definite integral and important figure in the whole concentration camp set-up, and, as an SS officer, wielded military power of command. If excesses occurred in the industries under his control he was in a position not only to know about them, but to do something."[91]

Government officials could also qualify as superiors for purposes of command responsibility. In the *Medical* case, Karl Brandt was held responsible for the sulfanilamide experiments conducted at Ravensbrueck because "[i]n the medical field [he] held a position of the highest rank directly under Hitler. He was in a position to intervene with authority on all medical matters; indeed, it appears that such was his positive duty."[92] And in the *Justice* case, Joel was held responsible for the illegal sentences imposed in the Night and Fog trials because "[i]t was his task to supervise the work of all prosecutors assigned to his office."[93]

The ability of government officials to qualify as superiors was, however, subject to an important qualification: the official in question had to have exercised actual control over the subordinates who committed a crime; *de jure* authority was not enough. That restriction emerges clearly in the *Ministries* tribunal's analysis of Berger's responsibility for racial examinations conducted by RuSHA. The tribunal acknowledged that Berger was formally superior to the examiners, but it nevertheless acquitted him because, "[i]n making the so-called racial examination, these men were not subject to Berger's control, but to that of the bureau from which they were detailed."[94] Similarly, the *Ministries* tribunal acquitted Steengracht von Moyland for failing to prevent his subordinate in the Foreign Office, Best, from forcibly deporting Jews from Denmark—a flagrant violation of international law—because it could not rule out the possibility that "Best was acting on orders from Hitler and Himmler which Steengracht von Moyland could not overcome."[95]

B. *Mens Rea*

The tribunals did not take a consistent approach to the *mens rea* of command responsibility. Some held that a superior had to have actually known that his subordinates had committed or were going to commit crimes. Others held that negligence sufficed. And one—the *High Command* tribunal—held that different standards applied depending on the nature of the underlying crimes.

---

[90] *Pohl*, V TWC 981–2.　　[91] Ibid., 1052.　　[92] *Medical*, II TWC 193.
[93] *Justice*, III TWC 1137.　　[94] *Ministries*, XIV TWC 546–7.　　[95] Ibid., 518.

1. Knowledge

Two tribunals required knowledge. In *Milch*, Tribunal II stated that the "controlling legal question" concerning the defendant's responsibility for failing to prevent or stop illegal medical experiments conducted by his subordinates was whether the experiments were "conducted with prior knowledge on his part that they might be excessive or inhuman."[96] The tribunal then acquitted Milch on the ground that, although he knew that experiments were planned, the evidence failed to show "any knowledge on his part that unwilling subjects would be forced to submit to them or that the experiments would be painful and dangerous to human life."[97] Similarly, the *Pohl* tribunal acquitted Tschentscher of responsibility for murders of Polish and Ukrainian Jews committed by members of his supply column because "[t]here is some evidence that he had constructive knowledge of the participation of members of his command, but absolutely no evidence that he had actual knowledge of such facts."[98]

Tribunals that adopted a *mens rea* of knowledge were, however, willing to infer the requisite knowledge from the nature of subordinates' criminal activity. The *High Command* tribunal, for example, convicted Reinhardt for tolerating the forcible deportation of civilian workers from occupied territory under his control because the deportations were "of such long continued and general practice, that even were there no orders signed by the defendant authorizing it, he must be held to have had knowledge of the practice and of its extent."[99] Conversely, the *Pohl* tribunal justified its unwillingness to infer that Tschentscher knew about the execution of Jews by pointing out that the participation of his subordinates in those executions "was not of sufficient magnitude or duration to constitute notice to the defendant, and thus give him an opportunity to control their actions."[100]

2. Negligence

Two tribunals specifically held that negligence sufficed for command responsibility. The *Hostage* tribunal held simply that "[a] corps commander must be held responsible...for acts which the corps commander knew or ought to have known about."[101] And the *Medical* tribunal convicted Genzken for illegal typhus experiments conducted by his subordinates because he should have known that the experiments were illegal: "[h]ad he made the slightest inquiry, he would have discovered that many of the human subjects used were non-German nationals who had not given their consent to the experiments."[102]

The *Ministries* tribunal also implicitly adopted a negligence standard, as indicated by Schellenberg's conviction for permitting the execution of more than 200 Soviet POWs who had participated in Operation Zeppelin, which he commanded.

---

[96] *Milch*, II TWC 774.   [97] Ibid., 776.   [98] *Pohl*, V TWC 1011.
[99] *High Command*, XI TWC 609.   [100] *Pohl*, V TWC 1011.
[101] *Hostage*, XI TWC 1303.   [102] *Medical*, II TWC 222.

The tribunal was deeply suspicious of Schellenberg's claim that he had not ordered the executions and had been unaware of them. But it held that he was responsible for the executions even if he was telling the truth, because they would still have been attributable to his negligent supervision of his subordinates: "[i]f Weissgerber and Grafe ordered these executions, their action can only be accounted for if the defendant had permitted an utterly callous attitude toward human life to grow up and become established in his division."[103]

It is not completely clear why some tribunals adopted a knowledge standard for command responsibility while others adopted negligence. The best explanation seems to be that tribunals in the latter category believed that a superior not only had a general duty to properly supervise his subordinates, but also had a positive duty to obtain information about their activities. If such a duty existed, a superior's negligent failure to discover that his subordinates were committing or were about to commit crimes was obviously criminal.

The *Medical* tribunal explicitly relied on the duty to discover. It convicted Karl Brandt for failing to prevent his subordinates from conducting the illegal sulfanil-amide experiments because "the duty rested upon him to make some adequate investigation concerning the medical experiments which he knew had been, were being, and doubtless would continue to be, conducted in the concentration camps."[104] Even more dramatically, the *Hostage* tribunal held that a commanding general was not only obliged to "require adequate reports of all occurrences that come within the scope of his power," he also had a duty, "if such reports are incomplete or otherwise inadequate . . . to require supplementary reports to apprise him of all the pertinent facts."[105]

3. High Command

In an article after the war, Judge Brand—a member of Tribunal III in the *Justice* case—noted that the *High Command* judgment oscillated between knowledge and negligence when addressing issues of command responsibility.[106] Judge Brand could not explain the inconsistency, but a close reading of the judgment reveals that the *High Command* tribunal actually took a principled approach to command responsibility's *mens rea*, determining whether negligence or knowledge applied by reference to the nature of the underlying crimes.

In the first category were crimes committed pursuant to illegal orders that a defendant knew had been issued by his superiors. The defendant was obviously responsible for ordering those crimes if he had personally transmitted the illegal order. But even if he had not transmitted the order, he was still obligated to prevent his subordinates from carrying it out and to discover if they were. Negligence with

---

[103] *Ministries*, XIV TWC 669.   [104] *Medical*, II TWC 194.

[105] *Hostage*, XI TWC 1271.

[106] G. Brand, "The War Crimes Trials and the Laws of War," 26 *Brit. Y.B. Int'l L.* 414, 425 (1949).

regard to those obligations was thus criminal, as the tribunal made clear in its discussion of command responsibility for the Commissar Order:

Can these defendants escape liability because this criminal order originated from a higher level? They knew it was directed to units subordinate to them. Reports coming in from time to time from these subordinate units showed the execution of these political functionaries. It is true in many cases they said they had no knowledge of these reports. They should have had such knowledge.[107]

Knowledge then applied to crimes committed by a defendant's subordinates either spontaneously or pursuant to superior orders that the defendant did not know existed. The latter was the case, for example, with regard to executions committed by the Einsatzgruppen in the areas under the defendants' control. The *High Command* tribunal acknowledged that, with regard to the Einsatzgruppen (as opposed to the Wehrmacht), "no superior orders transmitted to the defendant field commanders show the mass murder program of the Third Reich."[108] It thus held that the "sole question" for those defendants was "whether or not they knew of the criminal activities of the Einsatzgruppen... and neglected to suppress them."[109]

C. Efforts to Prevent or Punish

The tribunals agreed that superiors had a non-derogable duty to properly supervise their subordinates. A superior was thus criminally liable for his subordinates' crimes if he failed to prevent them, failed to prevent their recurrence, or failed to punish those responsible for them.

1. Failure to Prevent

The *Hostage* tribunal held that a superior was obligated to take "effective steps" to prevent his subordinates from committing crimes.[110] In practice, the failure to prevent was an issue in the first *High Command* scenario mentioned above: when a superior became aware that his superiors had issued illegal orders that his subordinates were likely to execute. According to the *Hostage* tribunal, a superior in such a situation was "required to rescind [the] illegal orders" as long as time permitted it.[111]

2. Failure to Prevent Recurrence

A superior was also required to take effective steps to prevent his subordinates from continuing to commit crimes once he became aware that they had been committed.[112] If a superior knew those crimes had been committed pursuant to illegal

---

[107] *High Command*, XI TWC 520.   [108] Ibid., 548.   [109] Ibid., 547.
[110] *Hostage*, XI TWC 1257.   [111] Ibid., 1271.
[112] See, e.g., *High Command*, XI TWC 632; *Einsatzgruppen*, IV TWC 513; *Medical*, II TWC 206.

orders, the superior was obligated to rescind those orders as soon as possible. In *Einsatzgruppen*, for example, Jost was held responsible for failing to revoke the Fuhrer Order after he learned upon taking command of Einsatzgruppe A that it was leading to illegal executions.[113] The superior was also required to issue new orders to ensure that, in the future, his subordinates would act lawfully. In the *Hostage* case, for example, Lanz was convicted for failing to prevent his subordinates from continuing to engage in illegal executions because, "with full knowledge of what was going on," he "did absolutely nothing about it. Nowhere does an order appear which has for its purpose the bringing of the hostage and reprisal practice within the rules of war."[114]

A superior had a similar obligation if his subordinates were committing crimes either spontaneously or pursuant to illegal orders of which he was unaware. In such a situation, the superior was required to take affirmative steps to ensure that his subordinates acted lawfully in the future. Genzken was held responsible for the typhus experiments, for example, because "he did nothing to insure that such research would be conducted with permissible legal limits."[115]

3. Failure to Punish

Finally, as part of his obligation to prevent the recurrence of crimes, a superior was required to punish the subordinates who had committed them. In the *Hostage* case, for example, Tribunal V held List responsible for illegal reprisal executions because "[n]ot once did he condemn such acts as unlawful. Not once did he call to account those responsible for these inhumane and barbarous acts."[116] The *High Command* tribunal emphasized, however, that the form of punishment was irrelevant as long as the punishment itself protected civilians from the commission of further crimes. As it said, "[w]hether this protection be assured by the prosecution of soldiers charged with offenses against the civilian population, or whether it be assured by disciplinary measures or otherwise, is immaterial from an international standpoint."[117]

D. Causation

In two places in its judgment, the *Medical* tribunal emphasized that a defendant's failure to properly supervise his subordinates had played a causal role in their commission of crimes. First, it concluded that Karl Brandt's "dereliction" with regard to the Nazis' euthanasia program had "contributed" to the extermination of non-German nationals.[118] Second, it pointed out that if Handloser had exercised his authority over the typhus experiments at Buchenwald, "later deaths would have been prevented."[119] Neither the *Medical* tribunal nor any other tribunal, however,

---

[113] *Einsatzgruppen*, IV TWC 513. [114] *Hostage*, XI TWC 1311.
[115] *Medical*, II TWC 222. [116] *Hostage*, XI TWC 1272.
[117] *High Command*, XI TWC 524. [118] *Medical*, II TWC 198. [119] Ibid., 206.

ever suggested that a causal relationship was a necessary condition of a defendant's responsibility for the failure to prevent the occurrence or recurrence of crimes.

E. Independent Crime or Mode of Participation?

The tribunals occasionally referred to a superior's failure to properly supervise his subordinates as a "dereliction of duty."[120] There is no question, however, that they viewed command responsibility as a mode of participation, not as an independent crime. Once the *Medical* tribunal concluded that Karl Brandt had failed to prevent the euthanasia program, for example, it held that he was "criminally responsible in the program."[121] Similarly, the *Ministries* tribunal held Schellenberg responsible for the Operation Zeppelin executions after finding that he had permitted them to occur.[122]

V. Other Modes

Although devoting comparatively little attention to them, the tribunals also discussed two other modes of participation, incitement and indirect perpetration, as well as the inchoate crime of attempt.

A. Incitement

Article II(2) did not specify that incitement was a mode of participation in a crime. The *Ministries* tribunal nevertheless convicted Dietrich, the Reich press chief, for orchestrating "a well thought-out, oft-repeated, persistent campaign to arouse the hatred of the German people against Jews." Through that campaign, the tribunal held, "Dietrich consciously implemented, and by furnishing the excuses and justifications, participated in, the crimes against humanity regarding Jews."[123]

B. Perpetration by Means

Article 25(3)(a) of the Rome Statute adopts the German concept of "perpetration by means," whereby an individual commits an international crime through another by means of his "control over an organized apparatus of power."[124] That mode of participation has four elements: a superior/subordinate relationship; sufficient "authority and control" by the defendant—normally because of his capacity to "hire, train, impose discipline, [or] provide resources"—to ensure that his orders

---

[120] See, e.g., *Hostage*, XI TWC 1271.   [121] *Medical*, II TWC 198.
[122] *Ministries*, XIV TWC 671.   [123] Ibid., 576.
[124] See *Prosecutor v. Katanga*, Case No. ICC-01/04-01/07, Decision on the Confirmation of Charges, para. 510 (30 Sept. 2008).

will be carried out; the defendant's use of the apparatus to actually commit a crime; and the defendant's awareness of his control over the apparatus.[125]

Scholars have argued that the Rome Statute's reliance on perpetration by means is a novelty in international criminal law.[126] It is thus interesting to note that the *Ministries* tribunal relied on an analogous concept to hold Berger responsible for the crimes against humanity committed by the notorious Dirlewanger Brigade:

> While in the field the unit was not under his tactical direction, it was organized by him, trained by the man whom he selected, the idea was his, he kept it and its commander under his protection, he was repeatedly informed of its savage and uncivilized behavior, which he not only permitted to continue, but attempted to justify... That one of the purposes for which the brigade was organized was to commit crimes against humanity, and that it did so to an extent which horrified and shocked even Nazi commissioners and Rosenberg's Ministry for the Eastern Territories.[127]

The similarity between the tribunal's explanation of Berger's conviction and perpetration by means is striking.

C. Attempt

Outside of the context of issuing an illegal order, the tribunals rarely discussed whether attempting to commit a crime was itself criminal. That is not surprising; after all, given the Nazis' systematic criminality, the OCC had no reason to pursue inchoate crimes other than conspiracy. The primary exception involved plunder: the prosecution charged the *Flick* and *Farben* defendants with attempting to illegally obtain title to factories in occupied territory. Those efforts failed, however, because both tribunals held that an attempt to plunder public or private property was not criminal, even if the defendants had intended to complete the criminal act.[128] As the *Flick* tribunal colorfully put it, "[t]o covet is a sin under the Decalogue but not a violation of the Hague Regulations nor a war crime."[129]

Conclusion

The NMTs were the first tribunals to systematically identify the essential elements of ordering and command responsibility, two modes of participation that are at the heart of modern international criminal law. Their definition of command responsibility has had a profound effect on modern tribunals, an issue discussed in Chapter 16. Their definition of ordering, by contrast, has been largely ignored. That is unfortunate, because the NMTs took a very innovative approach to the

---

[125] Ibid., paras 512–4.
[126] See, e.g., Florian Jessberger & Julian Geneuss, "On the Application of a Theory of Indirect Perpetration in *Al Bashir*: German Doctrine at the Hague?," 6 *J. Int'l Crim. Just.* 853, 867 (2008).
[127] *Ministries*, XIV TWC 545–6.
[128] *Flick*, VI TWC 1210; *Farben*, VIII TWC 1147.
[129] *Flick*, VI TWC 1210.

concept. First, the tribunals held that *de facto* authority to command established the necessary superior/subordinate relationship, making it clear that civilians could be held responsible for ordering international crimes. Second, the tribunals extended ordering to include not only orders that were illegal on their face, but also orders that were capable of being criminally applied. Third, the tribunals defined the *actus reus* of ordering very broadly, prohibiting drafting and transmitting illegal orders as well as issuing them. Fourth, and perhaps most interesting of all, the *Hostage* tribunal held that issuing an illegal order was an inchoate crime, not simply a mode of participation—an idea that a number of scholars have endorsed.[130]

---

[130] See, e.g., Robert Cryer, "General Principles of Liability in International Criminal Law," in *The Permanent International Criminal Court: Legal and Policy Issues* 242–7 (McGoldrick et al. eds, 2004).

12

Conspiracy, Enterprise Liability, and Criminal Membership

Introduction

The previous chapter bracketed two modes of participation included in Article II(2) of Law No. 10: being "connected with plans or enterprises" involving the commission of a crime—enterprise liability—and abetting a crime. This chapter rectifies those omissions by discussing those modes of participation in the context of conspiracy and criminal membership, two substantive crimes that are closely related to enterprise liability. Section I discusses the OCC's failed efforts to prosecute conspiracy to commit war crimes and crimes against humanity. Section II then explores enterprise liability, noting that the tribunals treated abetting as a form of participation in a criminal enterprise instead of as a mode of participation in its own right. Finally, Section III focuses on the crime of criminal membership, which is best understood as a hybrid of conspiracy and enterprise liability.

I. Conspiracy to Commit War Crimes and Crimes Against Humanity

The London Charter contained two provisions concerning conspiracy: Article 6(a) criminalized "participation in a common plan or conspiracy" to commit a crime against peace, and the final sentence of Article 6 criminalized "participating in a common plan or conspiracy to commit any of the foregoing crimes." Those "foregoing crimes" included both war crimes and crimes against humanity; read literally, therefore, the London Charter criminalized conspiring to commit all three of the crimes listed in Article 6 of the Charter.

Despite the catch-all provision in Article 6, the IMT held that "the Charter does not define as a separate crime any conspiracy except the one to commit acts of aggressive war." In its view, the catch-all provision did not "add a new and separate crime to those already listed," but simply established "the responsibility of persons participating in a common plan."[1] In other words, although conspiring to commit

---

[1] IMT Judgment, 44.

crimes against peace was criminal in itself, conspiring to commit war crimes or crimes against humanity was simply a mode of participation in those crimes.

Unlike the London Charter, Law No. 10 gave no indication that conspiring to commit war crimes or crimes against humanity was an independent crime—there was no equivalent to Article 6 in either Article II(1) or Article II(2). That absence, however, did not prevent the OCC from alleging such conspiracies in its first three multi-defendant cases: *Medical*, *Justice*, and *Pohl*. In the *Medical* case, for example, Count 1 of the indictment was entitled "The Common Design or Conspiracy" and alleged in paragraph 1 that "all of the defendants herein, acting pursuant to a common design, unlawfully, willfully, and knowingly did conspire and agree together and with each other and with divers other persons, to commit war crimes and crimes against humanity, as defined in Control Council Law No. 10, Article II."[2] The other two indictments contained nearly identical language.

The defendants filed motions to dismiss the conspiracy charges in all three cases. Believing that it was "desirable that there be a uniform determination on the issue presented by such motions," the Committee of Presiding Judges responded by holding a joint session on the conspiracy issue on 9 July 1947[3]—the first and only joint session that involved oral argument. Telford Taylor argued on behalf the OCC. Carl Haensel, who represented Joel in the *Justice* case and Loerner in the *Pohl* case, argued on behalf of the defendants.

A. The Defense Argument

Haensel offered six arguments in support of his position that conspiring to commit war crimes or crimes against humanity was not an independent crime under Law No. 10. He began by noting that such conspiracies were not mentioned in *either* the London Charter or Law No. 10.[4] That was clearly true for Law No. 10, which mentioned conspiracy only with regard to crimes against peace, but Haensel simply ignored the catch-all provision in Article 6, which criminalized conspiring to commit any of the crimes listed in the Charter. The oversight was minor, however, because he immediately pointed out—his second argument—that the IMT had limited conspiracy as an independent crime to crimes against peace.[5]

Haensel's third argument distinguished Article II(2)(d)'s "connected with plans or enterprises" provision. He noted that the subparagraph did not mention conspiracy and that, in any case, enterprise liability was a mode of participation, not an independent crime.[6] His fourth argument then addressed the curious fact that although Law No. 10 did not have an equivalent to the catch-all provision in Article 6, the first article of Ordinance No. 7 specified that the NMTs would have "the power to try and punish persons charged with offenses recognized as crimes in Article II of Control Council Law No. 10, *including conspiracies to commit any such crimes.*"[7] Haensel claimed that Article I had to be read down to exclude conspiracies

---

[2] *Medical*, Indictment, para. 1, I TWC 10.   [3] XV TWC 1060.
[4] Transcript of Conspiracy Oral Argument, 9 July 1947, NA-238-196-2-17, at 6.
[5] Ibid., 6–7.   [6] Ibid., 7–8.   [7] Ordinance No. 7, Art. I (emphasis added).

to commit war crimes and crimes against humanity, because permitting the tribunals to prosecute conspiracies that were not included in Article II would undermine the "uniform legal basis in Germany" that Law No. 10 was designed to establish.[8] That was a good argument, given that the other Allies had adopted Article II verbatim.[9] Haensel could also have pointed out that Law No. 10 gave Zone Commanders the right to adopt rules of procedure that were unique to their zone, but said nothing about adopting idiosyncratic interpretations of Article II's substantive crimes.

Haensel's fifth argument was that the tribunals were not permitted to deviate from the substantive provisions of Law No. 10 by applying the American common law of conspiracy. Haensel claimed—explicitly invoking debellatio and the resulting Allied condominium—that "Germany is subject to the united occupation powers as represented in the Control Council, but not to the Russian, the English, the French, or the American law as such. The individual occupying power did not transfer the law of its own country attached to its banners into this country."[10] That argument made sense—and as discussed in Chapter 5, a number of the tribunals, including Tribunal III in the *Justice* case, later adopted it.

Haensel's sixth and final argument was that recognizing conspiracy to commit war crimes and crimes against humanity would violate the principle of non-retroactivity, which the IMT had recognized as a principle of justice.[11] That argument proceeded in two steps. Haensel first claimed that, because German law applied prior to the Allied occupation of Germany, conspiracy to commit war crimes or crimes against humanity was consistent with the principle of non-retroactivity only if "German law had known this crime previous to the occupation." He then argued that "[t]here will hardly be one among the high judges of the Court who had met so far a German jurist who would call conspiracy to commit war crimes and crimes against humanity a recognized crime in German penal law."[12]

This was the weakest of Haensel's arguments. To begin with, the IMT had *rejected* the idea that the principle of non-retroactivity required the crimes in the London Charter to have been criminal before the war, under German law or otherwise.[13] But even if it had agreed with Haensel's interpretation of the principle, his conspiracy claim would still have failed: although pre-war German criminal law did not specifically consider conspiring to commit a war crime or crime against humanity to be an independent crime, it had long accepted the idea that the mere agreement to commit certain kinds of violent acts was criminal. The Criminal Code of 1871 prohibited conspiring to commit treason and high treason "irrespective of whether the intention of the conspirators was attempted to be carried out."[14] The Protection of the Republic Act, in force between 1922 and 1929, prohibited conspiring to kill government officials.[15] Article 49b of the Criminal Code, enacted

---

[8] Transcript, 12.   [9] See, e.g., *Rochling Appeal Judgment*, XIV TWC 1099–1100.
[10] Transcript, 10–1.   [11] Ibid., 14.   [12] Ibid., 20.
[13] See Chapter 5.   [14] Wagner, 175.
[15] John H.E. Fried, Forms of Committing War Crimes and Crimes Against Humanity, TTP-5-1-1-2, at 15.

in 1932, prohibited entering into "a combination or agreement" whose object was "the commission of major crimes against life."[16] That article was then amended in 1943 to prohibit not only entering into "an agreement to commit a major crime," but even entering "into serious negotiation to do so."[17]

B. The Prosecution Argument

Taylor's presentation was not his finest moment—his arguments were disjointed, repetitive, confusing, and above all unpersuasive. He opened by attempting to explain why, if the London Charter and Law No. 10 recognized conspiracies to commit war crimes and crimes against humanity, the relevant provisions did not specifically mention such conspiracies. According to Taylor, the explanation was simple: because the common law had always accepted the idea that it was criminal to conspire to commit acts of violence, the drafters did not need to refer to conspiring to commit war crimes and crimes against humanity "any more than they felt it necessary to make express reference to the liability of accessories and accomplices or to the law of attempts. All these things adhere to such crimes automatically."[18] That was a curious argument, given that the drafters of both the London Charter and Law No. 10 *had*, in fact, made express reference to accomplice liability.

They had also, of course, made express reference to conspiring to commit crimes against peace. Taylor's second argument thus attempted to explain why, if conspiracy "automatically" adhered to crimes of violence, the drafters had included that reference. In his view, the drafters had singled out such conspiracies to emphasize the collective nature of crimes against peace: "while war crimes and crimes against humanity can certainly be committed by a single individual, it is hard to think of any one man as committing the crime of waging an aggressive war as a solo venture. It is peculiarly a crime brought about by the confederation or conspiracy of a number of men acting pursuant to well-laid plans."[19] That argument, however, actually cut the other way: if conspiracy "automatically" adhered to crimes of violence, why would it be necessary to specifically mention conspiracy with regard to crimes that, by their very nature, were collective endeavors? Would it not have made more sense for the drafters to emphasize that war crimes and crimes against humanity, more often the product of individual will, could also be the object of conspiracy?

Taylor's third argument addressed perhaps his greatest obstacle: the IMT's decision to limit conspiracy to crimes against peace. With admirable forthrightness, he claimed that the IMT "was clearly wrong, and overlooked the express language of the Charter."[20] He was referring, of course, to the catch-all provision in Article 6. According to Taylor, the tribunal had taken "the easy way out" by ignoring that provision—a result he attributed to "mistaken and misapplied suspicion of the whole concept" of conspiracy on the part of the judges.[21] Taylor then pointed out

---

[16] Wagner, 177.   [17] Ibid.   [18] Transcript, 7.
[19] Ibid., 8.   [20] Ibid., 11.   [21] Ibid.

that Ordinance No. 7 did not make the IMT's decisions on points of law binding on the NMTs, permitting the Committee of Presiding Judges to reach a "contrary result" for Law No. 10.[22]

There was, of course, a significant problem with that claim: there was no equivalent to Article 6's catch-all provision in Law No. 10. That might well have been an oversight; as soon as the IMT released its judgment, OMGUS and the Theater Judge Advocate's Office had both suggested amending Law No. 10 to make clear that it criminalized conspiring to commit war crimes or crimes against humanity no less than conspiring to commit crimes against peace.[23] The proposed amendment was never adopted, however, so Taylor was forced to explain the absence of the catch-all provision. His response was another version of his earlier "no need" argument: conspiracy to commit war crimes and crimes against humanity was "implicit" in Law No. 10, because its purpose was "to recognize the criminal liability of those who are substantially connected with the commission of a crime, even though the final criminal act is performed by someone else."[24] In his view, Article II(2) was "more than broad enough to comprehend the criminal liabilities which are held to attach to those who enter into a criminal conspiracy."[25]

That argument, however, elided the critical distinction between conspiracy as an independent crime and conspiracy as a mode of participation. Taylor was supposed to be defending counts in the *Medical, Justice,* and *Pohl* indictments that criminalized the mere act of agreeing to commit war crimes or crimes against humanity; separate counts sought to hold the defendants responsible for being connected with plans or enterprises that actually committed those crimes. Yet Taylor was now implying—as he had at the beginning of his argument and would again at its end—that conspiracy was just another mode of participation under Article II(2), undermining his basic point.

Taylor's fifth argument was perhaps his most radical: that even if conspiring to commit war crimes and crimes against humanity was not implicitly prohibited by Law No. 10, the tribunals were still free to criminalize such conspiracies. In Taylor's view, neither the London Charter nor Law No. 10 represented "a complete, or even a nearly complete codification of international penal law." And that was particularly true, he insisted, with regard to "the necessary degree of connection with a crime," where the provisions in the Charter and Law No. 10 were "illustrative rather than exhaustive attempts at statutory definition."[26] There was nothing inherently wrong with that argument, but it was unlikely to succeed—as we have seen, although the tribunals were willing to use conventional and customary international law to *limit* Law No. 10, they were far less willing to use such sources of law to *supplement* it. Attempt is an excellent example: although Taylor specifically invoked attempt as an inchoate crime that was not mentioned in Law No. 10 but was clearly part of international law,[27] the tribunals uniformly declined to criminalize attempts to commit war crimes or crimes against humanity.[28]

---

[22] Ibid., 11–2.   [23] Memo from Rockwell to Mickelwait, 12 Nov. 1946, 2.
[24] Transcript, 13.   [25] Ibid.   [26] Ibid., 15.
[27] Ibid.   [28] See Chapter 11.

Taylor concluded his presentation by explicitly arguing that conspiracy was a mode of participation, not an independent crime. According to Taylor, "[c]onspiracy, to achieve an unlawful objective or to use unlawful means to attain an objective, is not, properly speaking, a separate crime at all; it is a test of the degree of connection with crime necessary to establish guilt."[29] That claim, it is safe to say, cost Taylor the oral argument. First, as noted above, it completely undermined the conspiracy counts in the *Medical, Justice*, and *Pohl* indictments. And second, it did not explain why the tribunals should read conspiracy as mode of participation into Law No. 10 when Article II(2) already prohibited being "connected with plans or enterprises" involving the commission of war crimes or crimes against humanity. In the absence of such an explanation—which Taylor never provided—the Committee of Presiding Judges had no incentive to rule in Taylor's favor.

C. The Outcome

In fact, the Committee never ruled at all. Instead, the *Medical, Justice*, and *Pohl* tribunals simply dismissed the conspiracy counts, each holding that they had "no jurisdiction to try any defendant upon a charge of conspiracy considered as a separate substantive offense."[30]

D. The OCC's Response

Despite the dismissal of the conspiracy counts, the OCC was not quite ready to abandon the idea that it was criminal to conspire to commit war crimes or crimes against humanity. It thus tried a new tack in four later cases, folding such accusations into counts that alleged conspiracies to commit crimes against peace. Count 5 of the *Farben* indictment, for example, alleged that the defendants had participated in "a common plan or conspiracy to commit, or which involved the commission of, crimes against peace (including the acts constituting war crimes and crimes against humanity which were committed as an integral part of such crimes against peace) as defined by Control Council Law No. 10."[31] Similar language appeared in the *Krupp, Ministries*, and *High Command* indictments.

Though clever, the OCC's new approach was no more successful than its initial one. As the *High Command* tribunal pointed out when it dismissed the charges, conspiracy to commit war crimes and crimes against humanity functioned in the new omnibus count as a mode of participation, not as an independent crime, because the count alleged the actual commission of such crimes. The conspiracy allegations thus added nothing to the counts that alleged the defendants were responsible for war crimes and crimes against humanity, because they were "connected with plans or enterprises" involving their commission.[32]

---

[29] Transcript, 15.   [30] See, e.g., *Justice*, Order, 11 July 1947, XV TWC 235.
[31] *Farben*, Indictment, para. 146, VII TWC 59.   [32] *High Command*, XI TWC 483.

II. Enterprise Liability

The tribunals, in short, disregarded conspiracy as an independent crime in favor of being "connected with plans or enterprises" as a mode of participation. Enterprise liability, according to the tribunals, had four elements: (1) the existence of a criminal enterprise; (2) the commission of a war crime or crime against humanity pursuant to the criminal enterprise; (3) the defendant's knowledge of the criminal enterprise; and (4) the defendant's participation in the criminal enterprise. As we will see, the tribunals took an exceptionally broad approach to enterprise liability's *mens rea* and *actus reus*, making it unlikely that the failure of the conspiracy charges actually handicapped Taylor and the OCC.

A. The Criminal Enterprise

1. Nature

The tribunals identified a wide variety of criminal enterprises. Some had a relatively narrow scope, such as the "campaign of persecution of the Catholic Church," which "was a definite governmental plan . . . to separate the worshippers from the Church and its priests [and] destroy its leadership."[33] But most were much larger. Some extended throughout Germany, such as the enterprise famously condemned in the *Justice* case: "a nationwide government-organized system of cruelty and injustice, in violation of the laws of war and of humanity, and perpetrated in the name of law by the authority of the Ministry of Justice, and through the instrumentality of the courts."[34] Others extended throughout the Nazi empire. The Germanization program discussed in *RuSHA*, for example, reflected a government policy that "was put into practice in all of the countries, twelve in number, as they were ruthlessly overrun by Hitler's armed forces."[35] Similarly, the *Pohl* tribunal treated the entire concentration-camp system as a criminal enterprise designed to carry out "a broad categorical Nazi political policy" of slavery and "wholesale extermination."[36]

No matter how large or small, those criminal enterprises had a common denominator: they relied on a sophisticated division of labor to accomplish their objectives. As the *Pohl* tribunal pointed out with regard to the Final Solution:

An elaborate and complex operation, such as the deportation and extermination of the Jews and the appropriation of all their property, is obviously a task for more than one man. Launching or promulgating such a program may originate in the mind of one man or a group of men. Working out the details of the plan may fall to another. Procurement of personnel and the issuing of actual operational orders may fall to others. The actual execution of the plan in the field involves the operation of another. Or it may be several other persons or groups. Marshaling and distributing the loot, or allocating the victims, is

---

[33] *Ministries*, XIV TWC 520.   [34] *Justice*, III TWC 985.
[35] *RuSHA*, V TWC 96.   [36] *Pohl*, V TWC 969.

another phase of the operation which may be entrusted to an individual or a group far removed from the original planners.[37]

2. Horizontal and Vertical Enterprises

OCC indictments often alleged multiple criminal enterprises. In some cases, the enterprises were pleaded horizontally, with no relationship to each other. The *Milch* indictment is an example: Count 1 alleged that the defendant was connected to "plans and enterprises involving slave labor and deportation to slave labor," while Count 2 alleged that the defendant was connected to unrelated "plans and enterprises involving medical experiments without the subjects' consent."[38] In other cases, the criminal enterprises were pleaded vertically, nesting a series of smaller, interrelated enterprises inside of a larger, overarching one. The *RuSHA* indictment alleged, for example, that the defendants had participated in the Nazis' "systematic program of genocide" through their connection to "plans and enterprises" involving, *inter alia,* kidnapping the children of Eastern workers, Germanization of enemy nationals, and persecuting Jews.[39] Similarly, the indictment in the *Justice* case operationalized the "nationwide government-organized system of cruelty and injustice" by alleging that the defendants were connected to various aspects of that system, such as the Night and Fog program or the enforcement of the Law Against Poles and Jews.[40]

The OCC's rationale for pleading such vertically nested criminal enterprises was clear: it wanted to use proof that a defendant had been involved in a small enterprise to hold him responsible for participating in the overarching one. That strategy, however, was only partially successful. Some tribunals accepted it. The *Justice* tribunal, for example, specifically held that "[t]he record is replete with evidence of specific criminal acts, but they are not the crimes charged in the indictment. They constitute evidence of the intentional participation of the defendants and serve as illustrations of the nature and effect of the greater crimes charged in the indictment."[41] The tribunal thus convicted Rothenberger for taking part in the "system of cruelty and injustice" because he had taken a consenting part in the Night and Fog program.[42] Similarly, the *Ministries* tribunal held Puhl responsible for the Nazis' "program of extermination" because he had participated in Action Reinhardt. As the tribunal noted, "[i]t would be a strange doctrine indeed, if, where part of the plan and one of the objectives of murder was to obtain the property of the victim, even to the extent of using the hair from his head and the gold of his mouth, he who knowingly took part in disposing of the loot must be exonerated and held not guilty as a participant in the murder plan."[43] By contrast, the *RuSHA* tribunal limited defendants' responsibility to the specific enterprises in

[37] *Pohl*, V TWC 1173, Supplemental Judgment.
[38] *Milch*, Indictment, paras 1, 8, II TWC 360, 362.
[39] *RuSHA*, Indictment, para. 2, IV TWC 609.
[40] *Justice*, Indictment, paras 11–15, III TWC 20–2.
[41] Ibid., 985. [42] Ibid., 1118.
[43] *Ministries*, XIV TWC 611.

which they had participated. Creutz, for example, was convicted of participating in kidnapping alien children, forced resettlement, forced Germanization, and slave labor, but was not held responsible for the overarching "systematic program of genocide."[44]

B. Commission of a Crime

Because enterprise liability was a mode of participation, not an independent inchoate crime, the tribunals required the prosecution to prove that the criminal enterprise had actually resulted in the commission of at least one war crime or crime against humanity. Although rarely contentious, the tribunals took that requirement seriously. In *Ministries*, for example, Tribunal IV concluded that both von Weizsaecker and Woermann had participated in a Foreign Office plan to strip Italian Jews of their citizenship. It nevertheless acquitted them because there was no evidence "that their efforts ever reached fruition, or that the crime was consummated."[45]

C. *Mens Rea*

The tribunals consistently emphasized that knowledge was sufficient to satisfy the *mens rea* of enterprise liability. In *Ministries*, Tribunal IV began its analysis of von Weizsaecker and Woermann's responsibility for the mass deportation of Jews following the Wannsee Conference by stating that "[t]he question is whether they knew of the program and whether in any substantial manner they aided, abetted, or implemented it."[46] In the *Justice* case, Tribunal III said that the defendants' responsibility for the Night and Fog program depended solely on whether they had participated in it, because "[a]ll of the defendants who entered into the plan or scheme, or who took part in enforcing or carrying it out knew that its enforcement violated international law of war."[47] And in *Pohl*, Tribunal II held Frank responsible for participating in the concentration-camp system because he "knew that the slave labor was being supplied by the concentration camps on a tremendous scale."[48]

What is particularly striking about these examples—and there are numerous others—is the complete absence of any reference to the defendant's intent to commit the crimes contemplated by the criminal enterprise. Indeed, the *Ministries* tribunal made clear that a defendant could be convicted of participating in a criminal enterprise even if he did not subjectively desire the commission of its crimes. With regard to von Weizsaecker and Woermann's responsibility for the deportation program, for example, the tribunal specifically acknowledged that they "neither originated it, gave it enthusiastic support, nor in their hearts approved of it."[49] Even more dramatically, the tribunal held Puhl responsible for the

---

[44] *RuSHA*, V TWC 155.   [45] *Ministries*, XIV TWC 560.
[46] Ibid., 478.   [47] *Justice*, III TWC 1038.
[48] *Pohl*, V TWC 995, 1015.   [49] *Ministries*, XIV TWC 478.

extermination program even though it believed that Action Reinhardt "was probably repugnant to him" and that he would not have participated in the extermination program itself "even under orders." The fact that he "knew that what was to be received and disposed of was stolen property and loot taken from the inmates of concentration camps" was enough.[50]

Although not requiring intent, the tribunals rejected the idea that the requisite knowledge could be inferred from the defendant's position in the Nazi hierarchy. In *Pohl*, the prosecution argued that the defendants had to have known that crimes were being committed in the concentration camps, because they each held important positions in the WVHA. That argument was only partially successful. The tribunal categorically rejected the idea that knowledge of a criminal enterprise could be inferred "solely from the official title" that a defendant held.[51] It thus acquitted Scheide because it concluded that "the only evidence on the part of the prosecution to sustain . . . conviction would be the organizational charts of the WVHA, which show (and the defendant admits it) that he was the chief of Amt B V."[52] The tribunal did acknowledge, however, that a defendant's authority had some probative value regarding his knowledge of a criminal enterprise.[53] It thus held Fanslau responsible for participating in the concentration-camp system because "[h]is claim that he was unaware of what was going on in the organization and in the concentration camps which it administered is utterly inconsistent with the importance and indispensability of his position" as chief of Amtsgruppe A.[54]

D. *Actus Reus*

Once a tribunal determined that a defendant had knowledge of a criminal enterprise that had led to the commission of a crime, "the remaining question" was whether he had participated in the enterprise.[55] The tribunals took an extremely broad approach to a defendant's participation in a criminal enterprise, holding that it was immaterial to a defendant's responsibility for the enterprise's crimes whether he "originated or executed them, or merely implemented them, justified them to the world, or gave aid and comfort to their perpetrators."[56]

The tribunals did not, however, treat all participants in a criminal enterprise equally. On the contrary, they distinguished between defendants who were involved in *creating* the enterprise and defendants who simply *executed* an enterprise created by others: whereas creating an enterprise automatically satisfied the participation requirement, executing an enterprise satisfied it only if the defendant possessed a certain amount of authority and discretion in his professional activities. As the *Ministries* tribunal wrote, the question was whether the defendants "participated in the initiation or formulation of such spoliation program, or whether they . . . were vested with responsibility for execution thereof, and in such positions

---

[50] Ibid., 620–1.   [51] *Pohl*, Supplemental Judgment, V TWC 1171.
[52] Ibid., 1017–18.   [53] Ibid., 1171, Supplemental Judgment.
[54] Ibid., 998.   [55] *Justice*, III TWC 981.   [56] *Ministries*, XIV TWC 472.

of responsibility, influenced or played a directing role in the carrying out of such criminal program."[57]

1. Creators

The tribunals convicted numerous defendants for participating in the "initiation or formulation" of criminal enterprises. The *RuSHA* tribunal held Creutz responsible for the kidnapping of alien children because he had "issued instructions for the carrying out of a 'children's operation', which meant the bringing of children into Germany for Germanization."[58] The *Pohl* tribunal held Pohl responsible for the Eastern Industries Limited Liability Company's systematic theft of Jewish property because he was "an original incorporator" of the program and had served as its "directing head and chief executive."[59] And the *Einsatzgruppen* tribunal held Haensch responsible for a series of executions committed by his Sonderkommando even though he was on leave at the time, noting that "[a] high ranking officer who plans an operation or participates in the planning and has control over officers taking part in the movement certainly cannot escape responsibility for the action by absenting himself the day of execution of the plan."[60]

The tribunals also included defendants who either drafted or issued decrees that gave rise to criminal enterprises in the category of "creators." In *Ministries*, for example, Stuckart was held responsible for the extermination program because he had "drafted and approved" legislation and regulations that gave shape to the program. The tribunal specifically noted that "if those who implemented or carried out the orders for the deportation of Jews to the East are properly tried, convicted, and punished ... then those who in the comparative quiet and peace of ministerial departments, aided the campaign by drafting the necessary decrees, regulations, and directives for its execution are likewise guilty."[61]

2. Executors

Unlike creating a criminal enterprise, executing a criminal enterprise had two requirements: (1) action in connection with the enterprise; and (2) sufficient authority or discretion concerning that action.

a. Action

Nearly any activity that was connected to an enterprise satisfied the "action" requirement. Four categories of actions were particularly common. The first included defendants who had administered criminal programs formulated and initiated by others, such as Mettgenberg in the *Justice* case, who had overseen the execution of the Night and Fog program,[62] and Loerner in *Pohl*, who had "helped administer" the slave-labor program "in an active and responsible fashion."[63]

---

[57] Ibid., 684.   [58] *RuSHA*, V TWC 106.   [59] *Pohl*, V TWC 991.
[60] *Einsatzgruppen*, IV TWC 549.   [61] *Ministries*, XIV TWC 645–6.
[62] *Justice*, III TWC 1128.   [63] *Pohl*, V TWC 1107–8.

The second category, related to the first, included defendants who had applied decrees enacted by others. The *Justice* tribunal, for example, held that the action requirement was satisfied by Lautz "zealously" enforcing the Night and Fog Decree,[64] by Klemm supervising the enforcement of the Law Against Poles and Jews in terms of clemency decisions,[65] and by Rothaug serving as "an instrument" of his superiors by subjecting Night and Fog prisoners to unfair trials.[66]

The third category included defendants who had provided resources necessary for the effective implementation of a criminal enterprise. The *Pohl* tribunal convicted Pohl for participating in the medical-experimentation program because he had supplied the subjects from his concentration camps, even though that was his only connection to the program.[67] The *Ministries* tribunal convicted Berger for participating in the concentration-camp program because he had "furnished the exterior guards" for the camps.[68] And the *Einsatzgruppen* tribunal convicted Klingelhofer for participating in the "Einsatzgruppe operation" because he had been involved "in locating, evaluating and turning over lists of Communist party functionaries to the executive department of his organization."[69]

The fourth and final category included defendants who had participated in distributing the proceeds of criminal enterprises involving the plunder of property. Pohl was thus responsible for Action Reinhardt because it "was a broad criminal program, requiring the cooperation of many persons, and Pohl's part was to conserve and account for the loot."[70] In *Ministries*, Puhl was held responsible for Action Reinhardt for similar reasons.[71]

b. Authority and Discretion

The NMTs also specifically limited responsibility for executing a criminal enterprise to defendants who possessed a certain degree of authority and discretion with regard to the actions that connected them to the enterprise. That limitation is both implicit and explicit in the judgments. It is implicit in the tribunals' consistent emphasis on the authority and discretion of the defendants they convicted for executing a criminal enterprise. In the *Justice* case, Tribunal III noted that Mettgenberg "exercised wide discretion and had extensive authority"[72] and von Ammon "held an executive position of responsibility involving the exercise of personal discretion" concerning the Night and Fog program.[73] In *Pohl*, Tribunal II pointed out that Tschentscher "was not a mere employee of the WVHA, but held a responsible and authoritative position in this organization,"[74] and that Loerner "was more than a mere bookkeeper," because "he exercised discretion and judgment and made many important decisions."[75] And in *Ministries*, Tribunal IV convicted Ritter for participating in the plan to murder downed Allied flyers because he was "selected to occupy a position of considerable delicacy," not

---

[64] *Justice*, III TWC 1120.   [65] Ibid., 1095.   [66] Ibid., 1155.
[67] *Pohl*, V TWC 998.   [68] *Ministries*, XIV TWC 548.
[69] *Einsatzgruppen*, IV TWC 569.   [70] *Pohl*, V TWC 989.
[71] *Ministries*, XIV TWC 611.   [72] *Justice*, III TWC 1128.   [73] Ibid., 1134.
[74] *Pohl*, V TWC 1000.   [75] Ibid., 1014.

"a mere messenger boy,"[76] and convicted Lammers for participating in the perversion of the Ministry of Justice because he was not "a notary public certifying the acts of others," but "possessed sufficient rank to interpose and exercise judgment and power."[77]

The tribunals also explicitly relied on the "authority and discretion" requirement to acquit defendants accused of executing a criminal enterprise. Two examples are particularly notable. The first is the *Ministries* tribunal's explanation of why Schwerin von Krosigk could not be held responsible for helping to implement the concentration-camp program:

> As Minister of Finance the defendant furnished the means by which the concentration camps were purchased, constructed, and maintained, but it is clear that he neither originated nor planned these matters, and the funds were provided by him on Hitler's express orders. They were Reich funds and not Schwerin von Krosigk's, and he had no discretion with respect to their disposition. His act in disbursing them for these purposes was actually clerical, and we cannot charge him with criminal responsibility in this matter.[78]

The tribunal's explanation is revealing in two respects. First, it explicitly grounded the "authority and discretion" requirement in the fact that Schwerin von Krosigk did not plan or originate the concentration-camp program. Second, it indicates that the tribunals viewed the requirement as conjunctive, not disjunctive: although Schwerin von Krosigk did not have discretion concerning the funds, as Minister of Finance he clearly had the authority to disburse them.

The other notable example is the *Pohl* tribunal's explanation of why, despite the fact that they were both auditors in the WVHA, Vogt was acquitted of participating in the concentration-camp program while Hohberg was convicted. The difference, according to the tribunal, concerned the extent of their authority and discretion: "Vogt at no time was anything but an auditor, whereas Hohberg, in addition to being an auditor, was an active participant in the economic enterprises of the SS in the several capacities of chief of staff W, financial director, and economic advisor."[79]

E. "Abetting" a Criminal Enterprise

Article II(2)(b) of Law No. 10 enumerated abetting as an independent mode of participation in a crime. The tribunals, however, addressed abetting solely in the context of enterprise liability, considering defendants who had executed a criminal enterprise to have abetted it: Rothenberger "aided and abetted" the perversion of the Nazi justice system[80]; the question was whether von Weizsaecker and Woermann "aided, abetted, or implemented" the deportation program, because they had not "originated" it[81]; Pohl did not "have a decisive part in formulating" the extermination program, but was guilty if he "was an accessory to or abetted" it[82]; etc.

---

[76] *Ministries*, XIV TWC 441.   [77] Ibid., 604.   [78] Ibid., 676.
[79] *Pohl*, V TWC 1042.   [80] *Justice*, III TWC 1118.   [81] *Ministries*, XIV TWC 478.
[82] *Pohl*, Supplemental Judgment, V TWC 1174.

F. The Responsibility of Private Economic Actors

As we have seen in previous chapters, the tribunals were generally more lenient toward private economic actors—bankers and industrialists—than toward military and government defendants. That lenience extended to enterprise liability. To begin with, most of the economic defendants who were accused of being "connected with plans or enterprises" involving war crimes or crimes against humanity were acquitted. Despite convicting Flick of plunder and the use of slave labor, for example, the *Flick* tribunal refused to consider him a member of either the "program of systematic plunder" or the slave-labor program. In its (questionable) view, Flick had not been aware of the former[83] and had not taken part in the "formation, administration, or furtherance" of the latter.[84] Similarly, although the *Ministries* tribunal acknowledged that Puhl—the Vice President of the Reichsbank—had financed SS enterprises that he knew made use of slave-labor, it nevertheless acquitted him of participating in the slave-labor program because it did not believe that he had played "a decisive role in the granting of such loans."[85]

The tribunals were also willing to ignore their own jurisprudence when doing so favored an economic defendant. As we have seen, the *Ministries* tribunal convicted a variety of military and government defendants who had knowingly used their authority and discretion to execute a criminal enterprise. The tribunal nevertheless refused to hold Rasche—the head of the Dresdner Bank—responsible for helping implement the slave-labor program by making loans to SS enterprises, even though it believed that he knew the enterprises were using slaves *and* that he had authority and discretion concerning the loans:

> The real question is, is it a crime to make a loan, knowing or having good reason to believe that the borrower will us[e] the funds in financing enterprises which are employed in using labor in violation of either national or international law? . . . A bank sells money or credit in the same manner as the merchandiser of any other commodity. It does not become a partner in enterprise, and the interest charged is merely the gross profit which the bank realizes from the transaction, out of which it must deduct its business costs, and from which it hopes to realize a net profit.[86]

The *Ministries* tribunal's unprincipled lenience toward Rasche is particularly striking in light of its willingness to convict Keppler and Kehrl on the ground that their corporation, Deutsche Umsiedlungs-Treuhandgesellschaft (DUT), had been "an important component in the scheme of German resettlement and in the crimes charged in count five relating to it."[87] The difference between the situations was

---

[83] *Flick*, VI TWC 1208.
[84] Ibid., 1198.
[85] *Ministries*, XIV TWC 852. The *Krupp* tribunal, it is worth noting, did not consider enterprise liability even though the indictment alleged that the defendants had participated in the slave-labor and plunder programs. See *Krupp*, Indictment, paras. 36, 48, IX TWC 25, 30.
[86] *Ministries*, XIV TWC 622.
[87] Ibid., 588.

that, unlike the Dresdner Bank, DUT was "in form a private, limited liability corporation," but "was in fact a governmental agency."[88]

G. The Responsibility of Legal Advisors

A number of defendants in the NMT trials were legal advisors: the *Justice* case's Klemm, Mettgenberg, Joel, and von Ammon advised the Reich Minister of Justice; *Farben*'s von Knieriem was the corporation's chief lawyer; *Ministries*' von Weizsaecker and Woermann advised the Nazi government on behalf of the Foreign Office; and *High Command*'s Lehmann was a legal advisor to the OKW. As we saw in the previous chapter, such advisors could be convicted of ordering a crime if they helped draft an illegal order; that was Lehmann's fate, for example, with regard to the Night and Fog Decree.[89] The tribunals also had little difficulty holding legal advisors responsible for crimes committed pursuant to a criminal enterprise when they had been directly involved in creating the enterprise or had used their authority and discretion to carry it out. Klemm was convicted of helping execute the "nationwide system of cruelty and injustice," for example, because he had issued the letter that denied the protection of German's juvenile law to Jews, Poles, and gypsies.[90] Similarly, von Ammon was convicted of implementing that system because he had used his "executive position of responsibility involving the exercise of personal discretion" to ensure that Night and Fog defendants were executed as quickly and efficiently as possible.[91]

The more difficult question is whether the tribunals believed that a legal advisor satisfied enterprise liability's participation requirement simply by providing inaccurate legal advice in response to an official query. The three tribunals that addressed the issue took different positions. The *Justice* tribunal implied that providing such advice would not satisfy the participation requirement. In holding Klemm responsible for participating in the perversion of the justice system, for example, it specifically pointed out that the letter limiting the ambit of Germany's juvenile law was "an expression of Party policy," not "a legal opinion," with regard to Poles and Jews, and that it could "hardly be construed as a legal opinion as to gypsies in view of the statement therein made that a special regulation will come into effect" as a result of the letter.[92] Those statements suggest that, had Klemm simply offered an opinion about the legality of the proposed policy, the tribunal would not have convicted him.

By contrast, the *Farben* tribunal suggested that providing inaccurate legal advice *could* satisfy the participation requirement. When it acquitted von Knieriem of participating in the Nazis' spoliation program, the tribunal noted that there was no evidence "that he was consulted for legal advice" in connection with Farben's plunder in Poland and emphasized that "[h]is action in a legal capacity in the establishment of the eastern corporations for possible operations in Russia [was] not

---

[88] Ibid., 583.   [89] *High Command*, XI TWC 693.   [90] *Justice*, III TWC 1095.
[91] Ibid., 1041–2.   [92] Ibid., 1095.

connected with any completed act of spoliation."[93] Both statements imply that, in the right circumstances, providing legal advice would be criminal.

Finally, the *Ministries* tribunal held in no uncertain terms that legal advisors could participate in a criminal enterprise simply by providing inaccurate legal advice. On 9 and 11 March 1942, Eichmann wrote the Foreign Office to ask whether the SS could deport thousands of French and stateless Jews to Auschwitz. Nine days later, von Weizsaecker and Woermann replied in a signed order that the Foreign Office had "no objection"—language von Weizsaecker had changed from Woermann's "no misgivings."[94] The tribunal held that, as the Reich's principal legal advisors, both men had an absolute duty to object to the deportations when Eichmann asked them to assess their legality. Their failure to do so was thus criminal:

The Foreign Office was the only official agency of the Reich which had either jurisdiction or right to advise the government as to whether or not proposed German action was in accordance with or contrary to the principles of international law. While admittedly it could not compel the government or Hitler to follow its advice, the defendants von Weizsaecker and Woermann had both the duty and responsibility of advising truthfully and accurately . . .

Unfortunately for Woermann and his chief von Weizsaecker, they did not fulfill that duty. When Woermann approved the language "the Foreign Office has no misgivings" and von Weizsaecker changed it to the phrase "has no objections," which phrases so far as this case is concerned are almost synonymous, they gave the "go ahead" signal to the criminals who desired to commit the crime.[95]

The *Ministries* tribunal also emphasized that providing inaccurate legal advice satisfied enterprise liability's participation requirement even if accurate advice would not have prevented the commission of war crimes or crimes against humanity. The tribunal had "no doubt" that the SS would have deported the French Jews even if von Weizsaecker and Woermann had objected to the deportation. It nevertheless reiterated that "[i]f the program was in violation of international law, the duty was absolute to so inform the inquiring branch of the government."[96]

III. Criminal Membership

Article II(1)(d) of Law No. 10 recognized as a crime "[m]embership in categories of a criminal group or organization declared criminal by the International Military Tribunal." Eighty-seven defendants in the NMT trials were charged with membership in one of the four organizations that the IMT had declared criminal: the SS, the SD, the Gestapo, and the Leadership Corps of the Nazi Party.[97] None were charged solely with criminal membership; Taylor decided early on to leave pure

---

[93] *Farben*, VIII TWC 1159.   [94] *Ministries*, XIV TWC 496.
[95] Ibid., 958–9, Motion for Correction.   [96] Ibid., 959.
[97] Jesse Joseph Silverglate, *The Role of the Conspiracy Doctrine in the Nuremberg War Crimes Trials* 215 (1969).

membership cases to the denazification tribunals.[98] Seventy-four of the 87 were convicted of criminal membership,[99] ten of whom were acquitted of all other charges.[100]

A. Nature of the Crime

Most scholars have described the crime of criminal membership as a form of conspiracy.[101] That description accords with the IMT judgment, which described a criminal organization as "analogous to a criminal conspiracy in that the essence of both is cooperation for criminal purposes. There must be a group bound together and organised for a common purpose. The group must be formed or used in connection with the commission of crimes denounced by the Charter."[102] As the "formed *or* used" language indicates, such organizations could have been held criminal even if they had never committed a crime.

It is also possible, however, to view criminal membership as a form of enterprise liability. Article 9 of the London Charter provided that "[a]t the trial of any individual member of any group or organization the Tribunal may declare (in connection with any act of which the individual may be convicted) that the group or organization of which the individual was a member was a criminal organization." The parenthetical language implies that a conviction for membership required proof that a defendant was responsible for at least one criminal act committed by the organization of which he was a member. Indeed, that was Justice Jackson's view: he specifically argued at the IMT that a criminal organization "must have committed crimes against the peace or war crimes or crimes against humanity."[103] As the UNWCC pointed out, "[v]iewed in this light, membership resembles more the crime of acting in pursuance of a common design that it does that of conspiracy."[104]

B. Elements of the Crime

The IMT touched only briefly on the elements of criminal membership, recommending that "[m]embership alone" not be considered criminal and that the crime "should exclude persons who had no knowledge of the criminal purposes or acts of the organization and those who were drafted by the State for membership, unless they were personally implicated in the commission of acts declared criminal by Article 6 of the Charter as members of the organisation."[105] The tribunals distilled those statements into a test for criminal membership that had three elements: (1)

---

[98] Taylor, *Final Report*, 17.   [99] Silverglate, 216.   [100] Ibid., 221.

[101] See, e.g., Carl Haensel, *Das Organisationsverbrechen: Nürnberger Betrachtungen zum Kontrollratsgesetz Nr. 10*, 54–5 (1947).

[102] IMT Judgment, 67.

[103] XXII Nuremberg Trial Proceedings 240 (29 Aug. 1946).

[104] XIII LRTWC 99.

[105] IMT Judgment, 67.

membership in a criminal organization; (2) voluntary membership; and (3) know-ledge of the organization's criminal purposes.

1. Membership

The membership requirement, which the *Farben* tribunal described as a threshold test,[106] was rarely problematic. The easiest cases were defendants who had not been members of organizations deemed criminal by the IMT or had been members of non-criminal subgroups within criminal organizations. Rothaug was an example of the former: the *Justice* tribunal acquitted him because he had been a member of the Lawyer's League, which was connected to the Nazi Party but was not part of the Leadership Corps.[107] Von der Heyde was an example of the latter: he was acquitted in *Farben* because he had been a member of an SS Riding Unit, which the IMT had exempted from criminal liability.[108]

The more difficult cases involved honorary members of the SS—civilian defend-ants who had received an honorary rank in the organization after the Nazis seized power.[109] The tribunals held that whether an honorary member of the SS satisfied the membership requirement was a functional test, "determined by a consideration of his actual relationship to [the SS] and its relationship to him."[110] The *Farben* tribunal thus acquitted Buetefisch of criminal membership because he had not taken the SS oath, had never attended SS functions, and had refused to wear an SS uniform,[111] while the *Ministries* tribunal convicted Lammers because he had re-mained an honorary member of the SS long after learning of its criminal nature.[112]

2. Voluntariness

The OCC advanced a remarkably expansive concept of "voluntariness"—one that, as Silverglate notes, effectively rendered "the defense of involuntary membership meaningless."[113] First, it argued that the tribunals should rely on Article X of Ordinance No. 7 to irrebuttably presume that a defendant was a voluntary member of any organization that the IMT had considered "entirely voluntary"[114]—a description that, conveniently enough, applied to all four of the organizations the IMT had declared criminal. Second, it contended that, in the alternative, the tribunals should limit the category of "involuntary" membership to being drafted into a criminal organization; "threats of political and economic retaliation" for failing to join should not qualify.[115] Third, and finally, it argued that the tribunals should not consider involuntary the membership of a defendant who had unsuc-cessfully attempted to resign from an organization once he learned of its criminal nature, as long as he had originally joined voluntarily.[116]

---

[106] *Farben*, VIII TWC 1200.   [107] *Justice*, III TWC 1144.
[108] *Farben*, VIII TWC 1201–2.   [109] *Ministries*, XIV TWC 855.
[110] See, e.g., *Farben*, VIII TWC 1201.   [111] Ibid., 1199.
[112] *Ministries*, XIV TWC 859–60.   [113] Silverglate, 218.
[114] Ibid.   [115] Ibid.   [116] Ibid., 220.

Voluntariness issues rarely arose during the trials—and when they did, the OCC's arguments generally fell on deaf ears. The *Ministries* tribunal, for example, was "not impressed" by the OCC's resignation argument, thus acquitting Darre of membership in the SS because Himmler and Hitler had refused to let him resign from the organization.[117] That said, the *Einsatzgruppen* tribunal relied on the first two arguments to reject Graf's claim that he had not been a voluntary member of the SD. In its view, although there was evidence that his membership involved "compulsion and constraint," the IMT's declaration that the SD "was a voluntary organization and that membership therein was voluntary" foreclosed acquitting him. The tribunal thus relegated compulsion and constraint to mitigation of sentence.[118]

A more common involuntariness issue concerned defendants who had been drafted into a criminal organization. As noted above, the IMT had excluded such defendants from the crime of criminal membership unless "they were personally implicated in the commission of acts declared criminal by Article 6 of the Charter as members of the organisation." Two tribunals applied that qualification literally: the *Einsatzgruppen* tribunal convicted von Radetzky of criminal membership in the SD because he had taken a consenting part in executions as a member of the organization,[119] while the *Ministries* tribunal acquitted von Weizsaecker of criminal membership in the SS because, although he was responsible for war crimes and crimes against humanity, he had committed those crimes in his capacity as an official in the Foreign Office, not as a member of the SS.[120] By contrast, a third tribunal—*Pohl*—acquitted Volk of criminal membership in the SS simply because he was drafted into the organization,[121] ignoring the fact that (as the tribunal itself found) he had participated in the concentration-camp program as a member of the organization.[122] That acquittal was clearly incorrect.

3. Knowledge

In adopting knowledge as the *mens rea* of criminal membership, the IMT had specifically rejected Justice Jackson's argument at trial that the lack of knowledge of an organization's criminal purpose should "weigh in mitigation rather than in complete defense."[123] The OCC nevertheless attempted to convince the tribunals to disregard the IMT's knowledge requirement in favor of a simple negligence standard—knew or "reasonably should have known."[124] That effort failed: all of the tribunals required actual knowledge instead of negligence.[125]

The tribunals emphasized, however, that the requisite knowledge could be inferred from the scope of an organization's crimes and the defendant's rank. The *Justice* tribunal convicted Alstoetter of membership in the SS, for example, because the SS's crimes were "of so wide a scope that no person of the defendant's

---

[117] *Ministries*, XIV TWC 862.   [118] *Einsatzgruppen*, IV TWC 587.   [119] Ibid.
[120] *Ministries*, XIV TWC 857.   [121] *Pohl*, V TWC 1051.   [122] Ibid., 1058.
[123] VIII Nuremberg Trial Proceedings 443 (1 Mar. 1946).   [124] Silverglate, 219.
[125] See, e.g., *Pohl*, V TWC 1018.

intelligence, and one who had achieved the rank of Oberfuehrer in the SS, could have been unaware of its illegal activities."[126] Similarly, the *Flick* tribunal justified convicting Steinbrinck of membership in the SS by pointing out that it was impossible for "a man of Steinbrinck's intelligence and means of acquiring information could have remained wholly ignorant of the character of the SS under the administration of Himmler."[127]

The OCC also tried to convince the tribunals that voluntary membership in a criminal organization created a rebuttable presumption that the defendant was aware of the organization's criminal purpose.[128] That was the official American position, as demonstrated by an OMGUS proposal in late 1946 to amend Law No. 10 "to make clear that the burden of proving lack of knowledge ... is upon the accused."[129] No such amendment was ever adopted, most likely because the British rejected the idea that the burden of proving knowledge could be shifted to the defendant.[130] The OCC's argument was no more successful: all of the tribunals assumed that the prosecution had to prove the defendant's knowledge beyond a reasonable doubt.[131] Indeed, the *Farben* tribunal explicitly endorsed that position.[132]

Conclusion

The NMTs devoted comparatively little attention to conspiracy and criminal membership. They spent more time discussing what it meant for a defendant to be "connected with plans or enterprises" involving the commission of a crime. As we will see in Chapter 16, that jurisprudence not only anticipated the modern concept of joint criminal enterprise, it is in at least one important respect—its fine-grained approach to culpability—superior to the modern concept.

---

[126] *Justice*, III TWC 1175.   [127] *Flick*, VI TWC 1217.   [128] *Farben*, VIII TWC 1198.
[129] Memo from Rockwell to Mickelwait, 12 Nov. 1946, 2.
[130] Memo from Ferencz to British Liaison Officer, 3 June 1947, NA-260-183a1-13–15, at 1.
[131] See, e.g., *Pohl*, V TWC 1018.   [132] *Farben*, VIII TWC 1198.

13

Defenses

Introduction

A leading treatise on international criminal law describes defenses to criminal conduct as "an oft-forgotten aspect" of international criminal law.[1] As this chapter explains, that description does not apply to the NMTs, which generated an extensive jurisprudence concerning a number of important defenses. Section I discusses "jurisdictional" defenses, such as *tu quoque*. Section II focuses on substantive defenses that emphasized the defendant's lack of responsibility for a particular crime, such as superior orders and mistake of law. Finally, Section III discusses the defense of military necessity, which functioned either as a failure of proof defense or as a justification, depending on the circumstances.

I. Jurisdictional Defenses

Defendants invoked three defenses that would have required the tribunals to dismiss the charges against them for lack of jurisdiction: immunity, selective prosecution, and *tu quoque*. None were successful.

A. Immunity

Two tribunals considered arguments that defendants were immune from prosecution by virtue of their official positions. In the *Justice* case, the judicial defendants claimed that they were entitled to immunity for actions that they had taken in their capacity as judges. The tribunal had little trouble rejecting that defense. First, it noted that the common-law doctrine of judicial immunity presumed the existence of "an independent judiciary administering impartial justice," which had clearly not existed in Nazi Germany. Second, it pointed out that immunity did not prevent the prosecution of a judge for "malfeasance in office," particularly of the kind in which the defendants had engaged. And third, it claimed that "the sinister influences which were in constant interplay between Hitler, his ministers, the Ministry of Justice, the Party, the Gestapo, and the courts" meant that the courts over which

---

[1] Robert Cryer et al., *An Introduction to International Criminal Law and Procedure* 402 (2nd edn, 2010).

the defendants presided were "judicial only in a limited sense."[2] In the tribunal's view, those courts were better viewed as "administrative tribunals" whose powers were "quasi-judicial" at best.[3]

The *Ministries* case involved a claim of diplomatic immunity. The defendant Veesenmayer argued that he was immune from prosecution for his role in the deportation of Jews from Hungary because, at the time of the deportations, he had been accredited as Minister and Plenipotentiary General for the Greater German Reich in the country. The tribunal acknowledged the existence of diplomatic immunity, but nevertheless rejected Veesenmayer's claim. It began by noting that his diplomatic immunity, as immunity *ratione personae*, ended when he left office. It then adopted the customary position—endorsed not long before by the IMTFE[4]—that diplomatic immunity protected the diplomat only from prosecution in the courts of the state to which he was accredited, making such immunity inapplicable in an international prosecution for an international crime.[5]

B. Selective Prosecution

In *Pohl*, one of the defense attorneys argued that his client (never named) "should not be tried or sentenced unless and until his superior officer has been indicted and tried and judgment entered against him." Tribunal II rejected that claim in its supplemental judgment, pointing out that "[t]he sole province of the Tribunal is to judge those who are brought before it by the duly constituted prosecuting authorities who are entirely independent of the Tribunals. The judicial power does not extend to the institution or launching of criminal proceedings."[6]

That conclusion was no doubt correct; Telford Taylor had exclusive authority under Ordinance No. 7 to "determine the persons to be tried by the tribunals." But there is no question that whether certain individuals were prosecuted depended heavily on which war-crimes tribunal had jurisdiction over them. Consider, for example, the very different fates that awaited the German and Japanese doctors who had engaged in barbaric medical experiments during the war. Freyhofer notes that the Japanese experiments were similar to the German experiments, "not only with respect to the kinds of medical subjects explored, but also with respect to the scope and brutality of execution."[7] Nevertheless, whereas many of the defendants in the *Medical* case were executed or sentenced to life imprisonment, many of the Japanese doctors received immunity from prosecution in exchange for information about their crimes.[8]

---

[2] *Justice*, III TWC 1024–5.   [3] Ibid., 1025.

[4] Neil Boister & Robert Cryer, *The Tokyo International Military Tribunal: A Reappraisal* 47 (2008).

[5] *Ministries*, XIV TWC 660–2.

[6] *Pohl*, Supplemental Judgment, V TWC 1171–2.

[7] Freyhofer, 93.

[8] Ibid.

C. *Tu Quoque*

The selective-prosecution defense challenged the fact that the tribunals prosecuted only a small fraction of the tens of thousands of Nazi officials and soldiers who had committed serious international crimes. The *tu quoque* defense, by contrast, challenged the right of the tribunals to prosecute specific crimes against peace, war crimes, and crimes against humanity that the Allies had themselves committed. That defense was thus quintessentially political, designed to paint the NMTs as "victor's justice" by revealing the (alleged) hypocrisy underlying the entire proceedings.

The *Ministries* tribunal specifically addressed the "victor's justice" aspect of the *tu quoque* defense. It openly acknowledged that fairness required applying the same standards of conduct to both the Germans and the Allies:

These Tribunals were not organized and do not sit for the purpose of wreaking vengeance upon the conquered. Was such the purpose, the power existed to use the firing squad, the scaffold, or the prison camp without taking the time and putting forth labor which have been so freely expended on them, and the Allied Powers would have copied the methods which were too often used during the Third Reich. We may not, in justice, apply to these defendants because they are Germans standards of duty and responsibility which are not equally applicable to the officials of the Allied Powers and to those of all nations. Nor should Germans be convicted for acts or conducts which, if committed by Americans, British, French, or Russians would not subject them to legal trial and conviction.[9]

The tribunal emphasized, however, that the defendants were not contending that their actions would have been legal if they had been committed by the Allies. Instead, they were claiming that it was unfair to prosecute them for crimes that the Allies had also committed. That was a very different proposition, the tribunal pointed out, and one that had to be rejected: "[i]t has never been suggested that a law duly passed becomes ineffective when it transpires that one of the legislators whose vote enacted it was himself guilty of the same practice or that he himself intended, in the future, to violate the law."[10]

The *Ministries* tribunal addressed *tu quoque* in the context of crimes against peace, rejecting a defense claim that the secret protocol of the 1939 Molotov-Ribbentrop Pact, which permitted Germany's invasion of Poland and made clear the Soviet Union's intention to invade the country as well, disqualified the Soviets from enacting the London Charter and Law No. 10 and rendered both instruments invalid.[11] Tribunal V rejected a similar argument in *High Command*, reiterating that it was irrelevant whether the Soviets had waged aggressive war against Poland, because "[u]nder general principles of law, an accused does not exculpate himself from a crime by showing that another committed a similar crime, either before or after the alleged commission of the crime by the accused."[12] The *Einsatzgruppen* tribunal reached the same conclusion.[13]

---

[9] *Ministries*, XIV TWC 317.   [10] Ibid., 323.   [11] Ibid., 322.
[12] *High Command*, XI TWC 482.   [13] *Einsatzgruppen*, IV TWC 456.

Defendants also invoked *tu quoque* in two other contexts. In *Ministries*, the defendants claimed that they could not be prosecuted for violations of the Hague Regulations concerning belligerent occupation, particularly those requiring occupants to respect national laws, because the Allies had committed similar violations during their occupation of Germany. The tribunal did not even feel it necessary to reiterate the general rule against *tu quoque*; instead, it reminded the defendants that—as discussed in Chapter 5—Germany's unconditional surrender and the subsequent debellatio meant that the Allies were not bound by the Hague Regulations.[14]

Finally, in both *Einsatzgruppen* and the *Hostage* case, defendants claimed that they could not be convicted of war crimes and crimes against humanity for killing innocent civilians because—to quote *Einsatzgruppen*—"every Allied nation brought about the death of noncombatants through the instrumentality of bombing."[15] That was a clever argument; the Allies were so sensitive about the attacks on Dresden, Berlin, Hiroshima, and Nagasaki that they had deliberately avoided charging IMT defendants with crimes related to the bombing of London.[16] Both tribunals nevertheless rejected the defense, the *Hostage* tribunal noting that even if the Allied bombings were illegal, "they can give no comfort to these defendants as recriminatory evidence."[17]

There is no question that the tribunals correctly rejected *tu quoque*; no national criminal-law system accepts the defense,[18] and not even von Knieriem, otherwise so critical of the NMTs, argued that it should have been recognized.[19] It is nevertheless easy to understand Sienho Yee's claim that the *tu quoque* defense "troubles the human soul when it is presented in a fitting situation."[20] The *Medical* case again provides a compelling example. There was nothing unjust about convicting the defendants for conducting the medical experiments revealed during the trial. But it is impossible to ignore that, as discussed in previous chapters, both the prosecution and the judges themselves did everything they could to obscure the fact that American doctors and scientists had engaged in medical experiments during the war that differed in degree, but certainly not in kind. Indeed, the hypocrisy was even greater, because some of the *Medical* defendants were prosecuted for experiments that they had continued to conduct after the war on behalf of the U.S. military. Ruff, for example, had engaged in high-altitude research for the Air Force using the same kind of low-pressure chamber that he had previously used in Dachau—research that involved multiple fatalities.[21]

[14] *Ministries*, XIV TWC 690.
[15] *Einsatzgruppen*, IV TWC 467.
[16] Chris Jochnick & Roger Normand, "The Legitimation of Violence: A Critical History of the Laws of War," 35 *Harv. Int'l L.J.* 49, 91–2 (1994).
[17] *Hostage*, XI TWC 1317.
[18] See Sienho Yee, "The Tu Quoque Argument as a Defence to International Crimes, Prosecution or Punishment," 3 *Chinese J. Int'l L.* 87, 94 (2004).
[19] Von Knieriem, 23.   [20] Yee, 87.   [21] Freyhofer, 92.

II. Substantive Defenses

The NMTs took an unsystematic approach to defenses that negatived the defendant's responsibility for a crime. The tribunals not only failed to distinguish between justifications, excuses, and failure-of-proof defenses, they also generally ignored the issue of whether the prosecution or the defense bore the burden of proof with regard to a defense. They did, however, discuss a number of substantive defenses in great detail.

A. Burden of Proof

Only one tribunal discussed burden of proof issues. In *Krupp*, Tribunal III cited with approval Wharton's approach to "confession and avoidance" defenses— defenses that admitted the elements of the crime, but argued that the defendant's commission of that crime was either justified or excused. That approach placed the burden of proof on the defendant, requiring him to introduce evidence sufficient to raise a reasonable doubt of his guilt.[22]

B. Superior Orders

As noted above, Article II(4)(b) of Law No. 10 provided that "[t]he fact that any person acted pursuant to the order of his Government or of a superior does not free him from responsibility for a crime, but may be considered in mitigation." In *Einsatzgruppen*, Tribunal II provided the classic explanation of why superior orders should not be considered a complete defense:

The obedience of a soldier is not the obedience of an automaton. A soldier is a reasoning agent. He does not respond, and is not expected to respond, like a piece of machinery. It is a fallacy of wide-spread consumption that a soldier is required to do everything his superior officer orders him to do . . . If every military person were required, regardless of the nature of the command, to obey unconditionally, a sergeant could order the corporal to shoot the lieutenant, the lieutenant could order the sergeant to shoot the captain, the captain could order the lieutenant to shoot the colonel, and in each instance the executioner would be absolved of blame.[23]

Although the tribunals took a remarkably consistent approach to superior orders, they disagreed about two aspects of the defense.

1. Source

To begin with, they disagreed concerning the source of law that justified rejecting superior orders as a complete defense. The *High Command* tribunal simply relied

---

[22] *Krupp*, IX TWC 1437, citing *Wharton's Criminal Evidence* 236–7 (11th edn, 1935).
[23] *Einsatzgruppen*, IV TWC 470.

on the existence of Article II(4)(b), noting that "we are bound by it as one of the basic authorities under which we function as a judicial tribunal"[24]—a rare example of a tribunal applying a specific provision of Law No. 10 without considering its conventional or customary foundation. The *Hostage* tribunal, by contrast, specifically held that "[t]he rule that superior order is not a defense to a criminal act is a rule of fundamental criminal justice that has been adopted by civilized nations extensively" and thus "properly may be declared as an applicable rule of international law."[25] In reaching that conclusion, the tribunal acknowledged—as argued by the defendants—that Oppenheim, the British Manual of Military Law, and the American Rules of Land Warfare each endorsed superior orders as a complete defense. It nevertheless dismissed Oppenheim as a "decidedly minority view" and held that military regulations were "not competent for any purpose in determining whether a fundamental principle of justice has been accepted by civilized nations generally," because they were "neither legislative nor juridical pronouncements."[26] The tribunal also noted that the military regulations of other Allied countries rejected the defense of superior orders, which would have precluded recognizing the defense as a general principle of justice even if military regulations were a competent source of law.[27]

2. Scope and Effect

The tribunals also disagreed about the scope and effect of the defense. The seemingly clear language of Article II(4)(b) actually masked a fundamental ambiguity. Did the *mere existence* of a superior order entitle the defendant to a sentence reduction? Or were only *some kinds* of superior orders mitigating?

The tribunals divided into three camps. The *Pohl* tribunal took the position that a defendant who committed a criminal act pursuant to any superior order, even a clearly illegal one, was entitled to at least some degree of sentence mitigation. Bobermin, for example, attempted to justify the use of concentration-camp labor at his plant near Auschwitz on the ground that he was simply following Pohl's orders. The tribunal held that "[w]here outright criminality is involved, superior orders are in themselves no excuse, although they may be argued in mitigation of punishment."[28]

Two tribunals, by contrast, held that the mere existence of a superior order did not entitle a defendant to a reduced sentence. In their view, a defendant was entitled to rely on Article II(4)(b) only if the order was not clearly illegal—the conditional liability approach discussed in detail below. The *Einsatzgruppen* tribunal held that "[t]he subordinate is bound only to obey the lawful orders of his

[24] *High Command*, XI TWC 508.   [25] *Hostage*, XI TWC 1236.   [26] Ibid., 1236–7.
[27] Ibid., 1238. The *Hostage* tribunal clearly distinguished here between rules of customary international law and general principles of justice. It acknowledged that, had the military regulations been put into practice—acquitting soldiers who committed crimes pursuant to superior orders—they might have helped establish a customary rule permitting superior orders to serve as a complete defense. Ibid., 1237.
[28] *Pohl*, V TWC 1058.

superior and if he accepts a criminal order and executes it with a malice of his own, he may not plead superior orders in mitigation of his offense."[29] The *Medical* tribunal reached a similar conclusion with regard to Gebhardt's claim that Himmler had ordered him to participate in medical experimentation, holding that Gebhardt was not entitled to mitigation because he had not satisfied the requirements of the defense.[30]

Finally, although the *Hostage* tribunal rejected the *respondeat superior* approach to the defense of superior orders, it also rejected the idea that legitimate reliance on a superior order was nothing more than a mitigating factor. On the contrary, it held that a defendant who relied on a superior order that was not clearly illegal was entitled to *acquittal*, not simply a sentence reduction: "if the illegality of the order was not known to the inferior, and he could not reasonably have been expected to know of its illegality, *no wrongful intent necessary to the commission of a crime exists* and the inferior will be protected."[31] That position was clearly inconsistent with Article II(4)(b).

3. Conditional Liability

With the exception of the *Pohl* tribunal, then, all of the tribunals adopted a conditional liability approach to the defense of superior orders. That approach required a defendant to satisfy five requirements. First, a superior/subordinate relationship had to exist between the individual who gave the order and the defendant who relied on it.[32] Formal superiority, however, was not required: "[s]uperior means superior in capacity and power to force a certain act. It does not mean superiority only in rank. It could easily happen in an illegal enterprise that the captain guides the major, in which case the captain could not be heard to plead superior orders in defense of his crime."[33]

Second, the order had to be binding on the defendant. As the *Medical* tribunal pointed out, the defense of superior orders "has never been held applicable to a case where the one to whom the order is given has free latitude of decision whether to accept the order or reject it."[34] That requirement doomed a number of superior-orders claims. In the *Medical* case, for example, Sievers argued that he was not criminally responsible for participating in the infamous murder of 112 Jews at Auschwitz whose skeletons were requested by the Reich University of Strasbourg, because he had been ordered to participate by Brandt and Himmler. The tribunal rejected his defense, pointing out that although "the basic policies or projects which he carried through were decided upon by his superiors ... in the execution of the details Sievers had an unlimited power of discretion."[35]

---

[29] *Einsatzgruppen*, IV TWC 471.
[30] *Medical*, II TWC 227.
[31] *Hostage*, XI TWC 1236 (emphasis added).
[32] *Einsatzgruppen*, IV TWC 480.
[33] Ibid.
[34] *Medical*, II TWC 227; see also *Einsatzgruppen*, IV TWC 471.
[35] *Medical*, II TWC 262–3.

Third, the order had to relate to "military duty." An order to steal, for example, would not qualify for the defense of superior orders.[36]

Fourth, the defendant must have honestly believed that the order was legal.[37] The *Medical* tribunal rejected Fischer's superior-orders claim regarding his participation in sulfanilamide experiments, for example, because he "acted with most complete knowledge that what he was doing was fundamentally criminal, even though directed by a superior."[38]

Finally, the order must not have been "manifestly"[39] or "patently"[40] illegal. That was, as the *Hostage* tribunal made clear, a simple negligence test: the defense of superior orders did not apply if the defendant "knew or should have known" of the order's illegality.[41] The *Hostage* tribunal also suggested that the experience and rank of the defendant should be taken into account when determining whether a defendant "could reasonably have been expected to know" that an order was illegal.[42] List, for example, argued that he had reasonably believed that the Commissar Order—which required the immediate execution of captured Soviet commissars—was legal. The tribunal rejected that claim, noting simply that "a field marshal of the German Army with more than 40 years of experience as a professional soldier knew or ought to have known of its criminal nature."[43]

C. Necessity

The defense of "necessity"—a term the tribunals used interchangeably with "duress"—played an important role in at least half of the NMT trials. The necessity defense had two important advantages over the defense of superior orders. First, it did not require the defendant to prove that he neither knew nor should have known that a particular order was illegal; the defense applied to even the most patently illegal order. Second, all of the tribunals agreed that a legitimate necessity defense required acquittal, not simply mitigation of sentence. Defendants thus had a powerful incentive to admit that they knew a particular order was illegal, but claim that the "dire consequences" of non-compliance forced them to carry it out.

The tribunals imposed five conditions on the defense of necessity. First, the defendant's criminal act had to have been a response to a "serious evil."[44] The tribunals did not specifically define that term, but it is clear that the evil had to involve the possibility of physical violence. A number of tribunals emphasized the possibility that non-compliance with superior orders could have led to death or

---

[36] *Einsatzgruppen*, IV TWC 470.
[37] *Hostage*, XI TWC 1236.
[38] *Medical*, II TWC 296.
[39] *Einsatzgruppen*, IV TWC 471.
[40] *Pohl*, Supplemental Judgment, V TWC 1250.
[41] *Hostage*, XI TWC 1271.
[42] Ibid., 1236.   [43] Ibid., 1271.
[44] *Krupp*, IX TWC 1436.

serious bodily harm,[45] while the *Krupp* tribunal insisted—again citing Wharton—that "fear of the loss of property will not make the defense of duress available."[46]

Second, the serious evil had to be "imminent, real, and inevitable."[47] The *Einsatzgruppen* tribunal emphasized, however, that the imminence requirement had to be applied reasonably; the defense of necessity did not require the criminal act to be committed with the proverbial gun to the head.[48]

Third, the defendant must not have had any alternative to committing the criminal act—"no other adequate means of escape," in the words of the *Krupp* tribunal.[49] That requirement, according to Tribunal II in *Pohl*, required the defendant to prove that he had actively resisted the order: "[a]nyone ordered to perform a patently illegal and inhuman act is charged by law to protest the order to the extent of his ability, short of endangering his own security. If he fails to do so he will be required to answer for the execution of the illegal act."[50]

Fourth, the harm caused by the criminal act had to be proportionate to the harm threatened by the serious evil.[51] The *Krupp* tribunal took a narrow approach to that requirement, stating that it would not have recognized a necessity defense for the use of slave labor even if it believed the defendants' claim (which it did not) that the failure to comply with Nazi production quotas would have resulted in internment in a concentration camp, because "[t]he defendants in a concentration camp would not have been in a worse plight than the thousands of helpless victims whom they daily exposed to danger of death."[52] The *Einsatzgruppen* tribunal, by contrast, took a more generous approach, specifically holding that necessity was available even as a defense to murder. "No court," it said, "will punish a man who, with a loaded pistol at his head, is compelled to pull a lethal lever."[53]

Fifth, the threat of the serious evil must have actually deprived the defendant of the ability not to commit the criminal act—the *mens rea* requirement. In the words of the *Krupp* tribunal, "[u]nder the rule of necessity, the contemplated compulsion must actually operate upon the will of the accused to the extent he is thereby compelled to do what otherwise he would not have done."[54] This is the well-known "moral choice"[55] requirement: if the defendant would have committed the criminal act even in the absence of the threat, he was not entitled to a defense of necessity.[56] Here, too, the defendant's efforts to resist carrying out an illegal order were relevant: "[t]he failure to attempt disengagement from so catastrophic an assignment

---

[45] See, e.g., *Flick*, VI TWC 1197; *Einsatzgruppen*, IV TWC 480.
[46] *Krupp*, IX TWC 1445.
[47] *Einsatzgruppen*, IV TWC 480.   [48] Ibid.
[49] *Krupp*, IX TWC 1436.
[50] *Pohl*, Supplemental Judgment, V TWC 1250.
[51] See, e.g., *Einsatzgruppen*, IV TWC 471.
[52] *Krupp*, IX TWC 1446.
[53] *Einsatzgruppen*, IV TWC 480.
[54] *Krupp*, IX TWC 1439.
[55] See IMT Judgment, 42; *Farben*, VIII TWC 1179.
[56] *Krupp*, IX TWC 1439.

might well spell the conclusion that the defendant involved had no deep-seated desire to be released."[57]

Finally, it is important to note that the tribunals divided over whether the *mens rea* of necessity was subjective or objective. The *High Command* tribunal held that the defense required the defendant to show not only that the serious evil had actually deprived him of his moral choice, but also "that a reasonable man would apprehend that he is in such imminent physical peril as to deprive him of freedom to choose the right and refrain from the wrong."[58] The *Krupp* tribunal, by contrast, insisted that "[t]he effect of the alleged compulsion is to be determined not by objective but by subjective standards."[59]

Although all of the tribunals recognized the defense of necessity, actual invocations of the defense met with mixed results. The *Krupp* tribunal rejected the idea that the defendants had no choice but to use slave labor in its factories, concluding that "the guilty individuals were not acting under compulsion or coercion exerted by the Reich authorities within the meaning of the law of necessity."[60] The *Einsatzgruppen* tribunal was similarly hostile to the defendants' claims that refusing to participate in the execution of Jews would have led to their own execution. The tribunal noted that the proffered "serious evil" did not actually exist, because the defendants themselves had admitted on the stand that the punishment for refusing to kill Jews was *transfer*, not death.[61] That had been the result, for example, of Graf's refusal to take command of a Subkommando group in 1942.[62]

The necessity defense was relatively more successful in *Flick* and *Farben*. The *Flick* tribunal rejected Flick and Weiss' claim that the Reich authorities compelled them to use Soviet POWs to construct freight cars for the Linke-Hofmann Works, concluding that their actions "were not taken as a result of compulsion or fear, but admittedly for the purpose of keeping the plant as near capacity production as possible,"[63] but it acquitted the other four defendants on the slave-labor charges. In its view, those defendants did not want to use slave labor in Flick plants and did so only because they were aware that "[t]he Reich, through its hordes of enforcement officials and secret police, was always 'present', ready to go into instant action and to mete out savage and immediate punishment against anyone doing anything that could be construed as obstructing or hindering the carrying out of governmental regulations or decrees."[64] That was a questionable assessment of the situation, to say the least. Bower has pointed out, for example, that when Friedrich Flick testified for the defense at the *Farben* trial, he was unable to name even one German industrialist who had been punished for refusing to use slave labor.[65]

The scorecard was also mixed in *Farben*. As discussed in Chapter 9, the tribunal rejected the necessity defense with regard to the use of slave labor at Auschwitz and Fuerstengrube, holding that "these were wholly private projects operated by Farben, with considerable freedom and opportunity for initiative on the part of Farben

---

[57] *Einsatzgruppen*, IV TWC 482.   [58] *High Command*, XI TWC 509.
[59] *Krupp*, IX TWC 1438.   [60] Ibid.
[61] *Einsatzgruppen*, IV TWC 481–2.   [62] Ibid., 585.
[63] *Flick*, VI TWC 1202.   [64] Ibid., 1201.   [65] Bower, 356.

officials connected therewith."[66] It nevertheless acquitted the eight members of the Technical Committee (TEA) for using slave labor in the plants they controlled, concluding that the defendants had not taken the initiative in obtaining the slaves and had used them only because they knew that "the defiant refusal of a Farben executive to carry out the Reich production schedule or to use slave labor to achieve that end would have been treated as treasonous sabotage and would have resulted in prompt and drastic retaliation."[67]

Judge Hebert dissented from the acquittals. To begin with, he simply disagreed with the majority's insistence that the TEA defendants had no "moral choice" but to accept slave labor. In his view, the Farben Vorstand as a whole had willingly cooperated in the slave-labor program because "there was no other solution" to Farben's "manpower problems."[68] More importantly, though, he rejected the very idea that defendants in the NMT trials could rely on the defense of necessity. First, he argued that the defense was inconsistent with Law No. 10, which indicated "quite clearly that governmental compulsion is merely a matter to be considered in mitigation and does not establish a defense to the fact of guilt." Second, he said that it made no sense to allow industrialist defendants to rely on the defense, given that the IMT had not recognized necessity "as applied to defendants who were subject to strict military discipline and subject to the most severe penalties for failure to carry out the criminal plans decreed and evolved by Hitler." Third, and finally, he believed that *Flick*'s recognition of the defense represented "unbridled license for the commission of war crimes and crimes against humanity on the broadest possible scale through the simple expediency of the issuance of compulsory governmental regulations combined with the terrorism of the totalitarian or police state."[69]

Judge Hebert's first argument is unconvincing. Not even the *Einsatzgruppen* tribunal, which was rarely sympathetic to defense claims, believed that there was no difference between the defense of superior orders and the defense of necessity. His second and third arguments, however, have considerable merit. The Nazis were far more dependent on German industrialists than they were on individual members of the German armed forces, even high-ranking ones; as Judge Hebert noted, for example, Farben "carried out activities indispensable to creating and equipping the Nazi war machine."[70] It is thus difficult to believe that refusing to use slave labor would have met with more serious repercussions than refusing to execute Jews, even assuming the threat of punishment had actually existed.

D. Self-Defense

In *Einsatzgruppen*, the defendants attempted to rely on two different versions of self-defense to justify their systematic slaughter of the Jews. They began by invoking *Staatshilfe*, defense of state, arguing that their crimes were necessary to

---

[66] *Farben*, VIII TWC 1186–7.   [67] Ibid., 1175.
[68] Ibid., 1204, Statement of Judge Hebert.
[69] Ibid., 1309–10, Hebert Dissent.
[70] Ibid., 1297, Hebert Concurrence.

defend Germany against the "Jews in the East," who were—in the words of the defendant Braune—"the decisive bearers of Communism and its illegal manner of fighting."[71] Tribunal II had little trouble rejecting that defense. First, it noted that threats to the security of a state did not justify violating the laws of war, which prohibited killing of civilians simply because they were viewed as "dangerous"— another example of a tribunal insisting on the strict separation of the *jus ad bellum* and the *jus in bello*. Second, it pointed out that none of the defendants had even attempted to show how, "assuming the Jews to be disposed towards bolshevism, this *per se* translated itself into an attack on Germany." Third, it noted that the Einsatzgruppen had killed Jews indiscriminately, not simply those suspected of communism, which indicated that the *Staatshilfe* argument was nothing more than an *ex post* rationalization for cold-blooded murder.[72]

Perhaps recognizing the absurdity of the *Staatshilfe* argument, the defendants also attempted to rely on *Putativnothilfe*, "presumed" self-defense, according to which they were entitled to acquittal as long as they honestly believed that they were acting in the defense of Germany.[73] The *Einsatzgruppen* tribunal dismissed that argument as well, noting derisively that it did not correspond "with any accepted tenets of international law" and would render the laws of war irrelevant.[74]

Individual self-defense—as opposed to "self-defense" of state—played a minor role in *Krupp*. Although the defendants relied exclusively on the defense of necessity, Tribunal III strongly implied that it believed self-defense was available, at least in theory, with regard to a war crime or crime against humanity.[75] It also made clear that the two defenses were closely related, the "principal distinction" between them being that "[s]elf-defense excuses the repulse of a wrong, whereas the rule of necessity justifies the invasion of a right"—the only example of a tribunal distinguishing between a justification and an excuse. More importantly, the tribunal specifically held that, as with necessity, the *mens rea* of self-defense was purely subjective: whether the defendant's act was necessary had to be determined "from the standpoint of the honest belief of the particular accused in question."[76]

E. Mistake of Law

The tribunals consistently emphasized that the defendants were fully aware that their actions were illegal. In the *Justice* case, for example, Tribunal III noted with regard to the crimes committed pursuant to the Night and Fog Decree that "[a]ll of the defendants who entered into the plan or scheme, or who took part in enforcing or carrying it out, knew that its enforcement violated international law of war."[77] Similarly, in *Einsatzgruppen*, Tribunal II said that it was "apparent" that all of the

---

[71] Earl, 202.

[72] *Einsatzgruppen*, IV TWC 464. The last rationale emerged out of an exchange at trial between Judge Musmanno and Braune. Musmanno forced Braune to admit that he did not believe all of the Jews were Bolsheviks, just the "vast majority." According to Earl, when Musmanno asked Braune why, then, even the non-communist Jews were murdered, he had no response. Earl, 202.

[73] *Einsatzgruppen*, IV TWC 463.   [74] Ibid., 463–4.

[75] *Krupp*, IX TWC 1438.   [76] Ibid.   [77] *Justice*, III TWC 1038.

defendants involved in executing Heydrich's Operational Order No. 8, which ordered the mass murder of POWs and civilians held in POW camps, "were aware of its illegality."[78]

The tribunals made clear, however, that the maxim *ignorantia legis nihil excusat* applied to both war crimes and crimes against humanity. Analogizing to domestic law, for example, the *Krupp* tribunal specifically held that the "criminal intent" required by such crimes did not include knowledge that a particular act was illegal:

> We know of no system under which ignorance of the law excuses crime... The rule that every man is presumed to know the law necessarily carries with it as a corollary the proposition that some persons may be found guilty of a crime who do not know the law and consequently that they may have imputed to them criminal intent in cases of which they have no realization of the wrongfulness of the act, much less an actual intent to commit the crime. A general criminal intent is sufficient in all cases in which a specific or other particular intent or mental element is not required by the law defining the crime.[79]

The *Ministries*, *Pohl*, and *Justice* tribunals took similar positions. In *Ministries*, Tribunal IV held that "[h]e who knowingly joined or implemented, aided, or abetted" the commission of a war crime or crime against humanity "cannot be heard to say that he did not know the acts in question were criminal."[80] In *Pohl*, Tribunal II noted that it had to be "conclusively presumed" that a defendant who was aware of the Nazis' slave-labor program also knew that "slavery constituted a crime against humanity."[81] And in the *Justice* case, Tribunal III stated that Joel was "chargeable with knowledge that the Night and Fog program from its inception to its final conclusion constituted a violation of the laws and customs of war."[82]

By contrast, as noted in Chapter 8, the *Ministries* tribunal held that crimes against peace required the prosecution to prove that a defendant knew a particular war or invasion qualified as aggressive. "One can be guilty only where knowledge of aggression in fact exists," the tribunal wrote, which meant that "it is not sufficient that he have suspicions that the war is aggressive."[83]

It is also possible that the tribunals would have allowed legal advisors to argue mistake of law. As discussed in the previous chapter, the *Ministries* tribunal convicted von Weizsaecker and Woermann of war crimes and crimes against humanity for approving the deportation of thousands of French Jews to Auschwitz. In reaching that conclusion, the tribunal emphasized that "when an official inquiry was made as to whether or not the Foreign Office had any objection to these deportations they answered in the negative, in face of the fact that *they both knew and realized that the proposal was a clear violation of international law*."[84] That emphasis is not itself dispositive, of course, given the tribunals' continual insistence that defendants knew that their actions were illegal. But there are two reasons to believe—or at least suspect—that the *Ministries* tribunal would not have convicted von Weizsaecker and Woermann had they honestly believed that they were

---

[78] *Einsatzgruppen*, IV TWC 441.   [79] *Krupp*, IX TWC 1378.
[80] *Ministries*, XIV TWC 339.   [81] *Pohl*, V TWC 945.
[82] *Justice*, III TWC 1138.   [83] *Ministries*, XIV TWC 337.
[84] Ibid., 956–7, Motion for Correction (emphasis added).

providing the Foreign Office with accurate legal advice. To begin with, Judge Powers' dissent implies that the majority convicted them because they knew their advice violated international law. His basic objection to their conviction was that, in his view, they had not given the Foreign Office inaccurate legal advice. But he emphasized that, "whether it was or not, there is nothing to indicate that it was not given in good faith, and honestly. A mistake in the interpretation or application of the law, fortunately, is not a crime."[85] Judge Powers might have been speaking only for himself, but the categorical phrasing of the statement implies that the absence of good faith was critical to the majority's decision to convict von Weizsaecker and Woermann.

That interpretation of *Ministries* is also consistent with the *Justice* tribunal's condemnation of the notorious "Judges' Letters"—letters written by Otto Thierack, the Reich Minister of Justice, that provided judges with guidance concerning the "administration of justice" under the Nazis. The tribunal held that "the evidence satisfies us beyond reasonable doubt that the purpose of the judicial guidance was sinister and was known to be such by the Ministry of Justice and by the judges who received the directions."[86] That conclusion depended, however, on the tribunal's belief that Thierack had written the letters knowing that he was encouraging the judiciary to engage in illegal acts: it specifically noted that "[i]f the letters…had been written in good faith, with the honest purpose of aiding independent judges in the performance of their duties, there would have been no occasion for the carefully guarded secrecy with which the letters were distributed."[87] The tribunal's statement strongly suggests that it believed providing legal advice in "good faith" was not criminal, even if the advice itself was incorrect.

III. Military Necessity

Defendants claimed in more than half of the trials that their actions were justified by the principle *Kriegsraison geht vor Kriegsrecht*—"military necessity in war overrides the law of war."[88] That argument took two basic forms. Most radically, they claimed in *Krupp* that World War II was a "total war" to which the Hague Convention IV simply did not apply. The *Krupp* tribunal "emphatically rejected" that idea, holding—as had the IMT—that the Convention was binding on Germany as both conventional and customary law.[89]

Defendants also claimed that *Kriegsraison* justified violating specific provisions of the Hague Regulations. In *High Command*, they argued that military necessity justified forcibly recruiting labor from occupied territory either for use in military operations or for deportation to Germany, despite Article 45 of the Regulations.[90] In *Krupp*, they argued that their plunder of the occupied territories was "justified by the great emergency in which the German war economy found itself," despite

---

[85] Ibid., 913, Powers Dissent.   [86] *Justice*, III TWC 1018.   [87] Ibid., 1019.
[88] See Gary D. Solis, *The Law of Armed Conflict* 265 (2010).
[89] *Krupp*, IX TWC 1340.   [90] *High Command*, XI TWC 541.

Articles 46, 47, and 50.[91] And in *Einsatzgruppen* and the *Hostage* case they argued that military necessity justified the extermination of the Jews, despite Articles 46, 47, and 50.[92]

The tribunals' response to such claims depended on the nature of the Hague Regulation in question. When the text of a Regulation did not specifically take military necessity into account, the tribunals uniformly held that defendants could not invoke *Kriegsraison* as a defense. The *Hostage* tribunal's rejection of military necessity as a defense to murder was typical:

We do not concur in the view that the rules of warfare are anything less than they purport to be. Military necessity or expediency do not justify a violation of positive rules. International law is prohibitive law. Articles 46, 47, and 50 of the Hague Regulations of 1907 make no such exceptions to its enforcement. The rights of the innocent population therein set forth must be respected even if military necessity or expediency decree otherwise.[93]

The *Krupp* and *High Command* tribunals took the same position,[94] the former pointing out that the drafters of the Hague Regulations were fully aware that they were limiting the effectiveness of belligerents by adopting Regulations that did not acknowledge military necessity. "It is an essence of war that one or the other side must lose," the *Krupp* tribunal wrote, "and the experienced generals and statesmen knew this when they drafted the rules and customs of land warfare. In short these rules and customs of warfare are designed specifically for all phases of war. They comprise the law for such emergency."[95]

The tribunals were more sympathetic to defense claims when the Hague Regulation in question *did* specifically make exception for military necessity. Regulation 23(g), for example, provided that it was forbidden "[t]o destroy or seize the enemy's property, unless such destruction or seizure be imperatively demanded by the necessities of war." In *High Command*, the defendant Hollidt was charged with the equivalent war crime in Article II(1)(b), "devastation not justified by military necessity," for ordering his Sixth Army to remove or destroy "everything which could be usable to the enemy in the area" during its retreat from the Soviet Union. That order led to vast amounts of cattle, poultry, and agricultural machinery being seized and more than 4,000 tons of corn being dumped into the Dnieper River, significantly harming the civilian population. Tribunal V nevertheless acquitted Hollidt because it could not conclude "that the measures applied were not warranted by military necessity under the conditions of war in the area under the command of the defendant."[96]

The tribunals also permitted defendants to argue military necessity when defendants were charged with war crimes or crimes against humanity involving methods of warfare that were not specifically regulated by the Hague Regulations. In such situations, the tribunals held, "[m]ilitary necessity permits a belligerent . . . to apply any amount and kind of force to compel the complete submission of the enemy

---

[91] Ibid., 1345–7. [92] *Hostage*, XI TWC 1255–6. [93] Ibid.
[94] *Krupp*, IX TWC 1347; *High Command*, XI TWC 541.
[95] *Krupp*, IX TWC 1347. [96] *High Command*, XI TWC 628.

with the least possible expenditure of time, life, and money."[97] The siege of Leningrad by von Leeb's Army Group North, considered in *High Command*, is a striking example of that rule. The goal of the siege was to starve the civilian population of the city into surrendering, which von Leeb accomplished by, *inter alia*, ordering his artillery units to drive civilians who attempted to flee through German lines back into the city. The siege lasted more than two years and led to hundreds of thousands of civilian deaths. The *High Command* tribunal nevertheless acquitted von Leeb of the siege-related charges on the ground of military necessity, citing Hyde for the proposition that nothing in the Hague Regulations prohibited using starvation as a weapon of war. "We might wish the law were otherwise," the tribunal said, "but we must administer it as we find it."[98]

Equally striking is the *Einsatzgruppen* tribunal's rather defensive discussion of the U.S. decision to drop atomic bombs on Hiroshima and Nagasaki. As noted earlier, both the *Einsatzgruppen* and *Hostage* tribunals held that the defendants could not argue *tu quoque* with regard to the Nazis' extermination program *even if* those bombings were illegal. The *Einsatzgruppen* tribunal nevertheless went to great lengths to show that, because so-called "morale bombing" was not prohibited by the laws of war—a position that was generally accepted at the time by both belligerents and scholars[99]—the bombings of Hiroshima and Nagasaki were fully justified by military necessity:

It was argued in behalf of the defendants that there was no normal distinction between shooting civilians with rifles and killing them by means of atomic bombs. There is no doubt that the invention of the atomic bomb, when used, was not aimed at noncombatants. Like any other aerial bomb employed during the war, it was dropped to overcome military resistance. Thus, as grave a military action as is an air bombardment, whether with the usual bombs or by atomic bomb, the one and only purpose of the bombing is to effect the surrender of the bombed nation. The people of that nation, through their representatives, may surrender and, with the surrender, the bombing ceases, the killing is ended.[100]

Depending on the circumstances, in short, military necessity functioned as either a failure of proof defense (when a Hague Regulation incorporated necessity) or as a justification (when the Hague Regulations were silent concerning necessity). In both cases, however, the tribunals imposed some objective limits on what military necessity would justify. First, they were very sensitive to pretextual invocations of the defense. In *RuSHA*, for example, Tribunal I convicted Greifelt for his role in the systematic plunder of personal and real property in Poland because it concluded

---

[97] *Hostage*, XI TWC 1253.

[98] *High Command*, XI TWC 563. Hyde's view was widely accepted at the time. See, e.g., Lester Nurick, "The Distinction Between Combatant and Noncombatant in the Law of War," 39 *Am. J. Int'l L.* 680, 686 (1945)..

[99] See, e.g. Nurick, 695; C.P. Philips, "Air Warfare and Law: An Analysis of the Legal Doctrines, Practices and Policies," 21 *Geo. Wash. L. Rev.* 311, 327–8 (1953). Taylor took the same position in his Final Report. Taylor, *Final Report*, 65. Years later, however, Taylor conceded that the bombings of Nagasaki and Dresden were war crimes, "tolerable in retrospect only because their malignancy pales in comparison to Dachau, Auschwitz, and Treblinka." Taylor, *Anatomy*, 143.

[100] *Einsatzgruppen*, IV TWC 467.

that "[t]hese confiscations were not carried out by reason of military necessity, but mainly were a part of a preconceived plan to strip the Polish population of the Eastern territories of all their property and in turn to make the property available to resettlers."[101] Second, with regard to non-pretextual uses of the defense, they insisted that there had to be some objective relationship between a defendant's acts and military necessity—a "reasonable connection," in the words of the *Hostage* tribunal.[102]

That said, the tribunals also made clear that the existence of the requisite "reasonable connection" had to be determined from the perspective of the defendant—a rule that effectively transformed military necessity into a purely subjective test. In the *Hostage* case, for example, General Rendulic was charged with "the wanton destruction of private and public property in the province of Finmark, Norway, during the retreat of the 20th Mountain Army commanded by him." Tribunal V acknowledged that the evidence indicated that, objectively, there had been no military necessity for Rendulic's "scorched earth" policy. It nevertheless acquitted him, concluding that "the conditions as they appeared to the defendant at the time were sufficient upon which he could honestly conclude that urgent military necessity warranted the decision made."[103]

Conclusion

The NMTs provided comprehensive analyses of a number of defenses that are now routinely applied by modern tribunals. Two of those analyses have proven particularly important. First, the tribunals systematically distinguished between the defense of superior orders and the defense of necessity. Second, the tribunals limited the defense of military necessity to violations of the laws of war that specifically took such necessity into account. The tribunals' jurisprudence was far from perfect; a number of tribunals suggested, for example, that the *mens reas* of necessity and military necessity were purely subjective. But there is no question that the judgments significantly furthered the development of a particularly important area of international criminal law.

---

[101] *RuSHA*, V TWC 147–8.   [102] *Hostage*, XI TWC 1254.   [103] Ibid., 1296–7.

14

Sentencing

Introduction

Law No. 10 provided little guidance to the tribunals concerning sentencing. Article II(3) simply specified that any defendant found guilty of a crime should be "punished as shall be determined by [a] tribunal to be just" and provided that such punishment could consist of "one or more" of six penalties:

(a) Death.
(b) Imprisonment for life or a term of years, with or without hard labor.
(c) Fine, and imprisonment with or without hard labour, in lieu thereof.
(d) Forfeiture of property.
(e) Restitution of property wrongfully acquired.
(f) Deprivation of some or all civil rights.

The NMT trials resulted in 142 convictions. Twenty-four defendants were sentenced to death, all in *Medical*, *Pohl*, and *Einsatzgruppen*. Twenty defendants were sentenced to life imprisonment. Ninety-seven defendants were sentenced to imprisonment for a term of years. One defendant sentenced to a term of years—Alfried Krupp—was also required to forfeit his property. No defendant was ever fined, imprisoned in lieu of a fine, or deprived of his or her civil rights.[1]

This chapter explores the sentencing practices of the 12 tribunals. Section I discusses the failure of the tribunals to develop general sentencing principles. Section II compares sentences *within* cases, assessing the consistency of the sentences that the defendants received. Sections III and IV discuss aggravating and mitigating sentencing factors. Finally, Section V draws on the previous sections to compare sentences *between* cases, questioning the accepted wisdom that the sentences became increasingly lenient over time.

I. General Principles

Mark Drumbl has criticized the IMT for imposing sentences without "providing a framework or heuristic to account for the exercise of discretion."[2] The NMTs were no different. The tribunals never explained how they determined the sentences they

---

[1] Review of Sentences by Military Governor and U.S. High Commissioner for Germany, XV TWC 1141–2.
[2] Mark A. Drumbl, *Atrocity, Punishment, and International Law* 50 (2007).

imposed—even when the sentence was death. In *Einsatzgruppen*, for example, Tribunal II simply informed Otto Ohlendorf that, "on the counts of the indictment on which you have been convicted, the Tribunal sentences you to death by hanging."[3] The judges then repeated the same statement 14 more times over the next few minutes for the other condemned defendants.

Two tribunals did comment on the general sentencing principles they applied. Unfortunately, those principles directly contradicted each other. In its supplemental judgment, the *Pohl* tribunal held that the seven modes of participation in Article II(2) were enumerated "in a descending order of culpability"—principals being more culpable than orderers, orderers being more culpable than individuals who had taken a consenting part in a crime, and so on.[4] The *RuSHA* tribunal, by contrast, reversed the relationship between principals and orderers, specifically holding with regard to defendants who ordered illegal deportations that "[w]hile in such a case the defendant might not have actually carried out the physical evacuation in the sense that he did not personally evacuate the population, he nevertheless is responsible for the action, and his participation by instigating the action is more pronounced than that of those who actually performed the deed."[5] The existence of such dramatically different approaches to culpability raises serious questions about the ability of the tribunals to sentence defendants consistently across cases, an issue discussed in more detail below.

II. Within-Case Comparisons

Although the process was anything but transparent, there is no reason to believe that the judges did not do their best to impose sentences that were both fair and consistent. On the contrary, Judge Wilkins' description of the *Krupp* tribunal's efforts—which involved a bitter dissent on sentencing issues by Judge Anderson— likely applied to all of the tribunals:

We three judges spent days carefully reviewing the evidence against all defendants and the extent of their personal guilt. We gave much thought to what would be appropriate sentences to impose upon the 11 defendants who were found guilty. Coming from widely separated areas in America (Judge Daly from Connecticut, Judge Anderson from Tennessee and I from Washington State), we sought not only to impose a sentence that would fit the guilt of the individual defendant but also bring about uniformity in the sentences which we judges strive to obtain throughout this country.[6]

This section attempts to explain the tribunals' sentencing decisions in the 11 trials that involved multiple defendants. (*Milch*, of course, involved only one.) As we will see, although many of the sentences were consistent, some were either too lenient

[3] *Einsatzgruppen*, IV TWC 587.
[4] *Pohl*, Supplemental Judgment, V TWC 1229.
[5] *RuSHA*, V TWC 153.
[6] Wilkins, 215.

or too punitive relative to the sentences imposed on similarly-situated co-defendants.

A. *Medical*

Sixteen of the 23 defendants in the *Medical* case were convicted. Seven were sentenced to death, five were sentenced to life, and four were sentenced to terms of imprisonment longer than 10 years. All 16 were convicted of both war crimes and crimes against humanity; nine of those 16 were additionally convicted of membership in the SS.

Two factors seem to have determined whether a defendant was sentenced to death: membership in the SS, and responsibility for at least one type of medical experiment (typhus, high-altitude, etc.) that involved fatalities. Six out the seven condemned defendants satisfied those criteria, and the one defendant who did not—Brack, who had been involved only in sterilization experiments—had played a central role in the Nazi's murderous "euthanasia" program, which did not even pretend to have a medical purpose.[7]

The tribunal did not, however, mechanistically determine sentences. Two of the five defendants sentenced to life imprisonment, Fischer and Genzken, satisfied the two death criteria: both were members of the SS, and both had been involved in lethal experiments. Fischer seems to have received life instead of death because the tribunal accepted his claim that Gebhardt, his superior (sentenced to death), had ordered him to conduct the sulfanilamide experiments[8]—a striking example of superior orders as a mitigating factor. By contrast, Genzken appears to have avoided the gallows because he had not been directly involved in the typhus experiments; his conviction was based on command responsibility.[9]

The idea that the tribunal viewed direct involvement in experiments as more culpable than responsibility as a superior is reinforced by a comparison between Genzken and Rose's life sentences. Both were held responsible for only one type of experiment, itself the same (typhus), but only Genzken was a member of the SS. Why, then, did Rose not receive a lesser sentence? The answer seems to be that Rose, unlike Genzken, had personally ordered the typhus experiments at Buchenwald.[10]

B. *Justice*

Of the 14 defendants in the *Justice* case, 10 were convicted. Four were sentenced to life (Schlegelberger, Klemm, Oeschey, and Rothaug), four to ten years' imprisonment (von Ammon, Mettgenberg, Lautz, and Joel), and two to between five and seven years. Seven of the eight defendants who received either life or a ten-year sentence were convicted of both war crimes and crimes against humanity; Rothaug was convicted solely of crimes against humanity. Two of the eight were

---

[7] *Medical*, II TWC 281.   [8] Ibid., 296.
[9] Ibid., 222.   [10] Ibid., 269.

also convicted of criminal membership: Joel for membership in the SS; Oeschey for membership in the Leadership Corps of the Nazi Party.

The differences between the sentences appear to reflect two primary factors: the defendant's position in the Nazi hierarchy, and whether he was convicted of criminal membership. Two of the life sentences were given to the most important defendants in the case: Schlegelberger, who had been the acting Reich Minister of Justice; and Klemm, the Ministry's State Secretary. A third was given to Oeschey, who was not as high-ranking—he was the presiding judge of the Special Court in Nuremberg during the war—but unlike Schlegelberger and Klemm was also convicted of criminal membership. The final life sentence is more difficult to understand: Rothaug held the least important position of the four (he was a public prosecutor at the People's Court in Berlin) and had been acquitted of membership in the Leadership Corps. He seems to have received a life sentence because he was "a sadistic and evil man" who "gave himself utterly" to carrying out the Final Solution.[11] Indeed, he was one of only two defendants in the trials specifically convicted of genocide.

Given the *Justice* tribunal's emphasis on position and criminal membership, it is understandable why Von Ammon and Mettgenberg were sentenced to 10 years instead of to life imprisonment: although they were deeply involved in administering the Night and Fog program, both were primarily legal advisors in the Ministry of Justice, and neither was convicted of membership in a criminal organization. The other ten-year sentences, however, are more difficult to explain. A strong case can be made that Lautz deserved the same sentence as Rothaug, given that he was Rothaug's superior in the Berlin People's Court and was the other defendant convicted of genocide. His lesser sentence, therefore, must reflect the fact that, as discussed below, the tribunal found "much to be said in mitigation of punishment" for him.[12] An even stronger case can be made that Joel's ten-year sentence was too lenient: he had served as the Ministry of Justice's liaison to the SS, SD, and Gestapo until 1943 and as a chief prosecutor in two Special Courts after that; he was convicted of membership in the SS; and the tribunal found no mitigating factors that justified reducing his sentence.

C. *Pohl*

Fifteen of the 18 defendants in *Pohl* were convicted. Three were sentenced to death (Pohl, Eirenschmalz, and Sommer); three were sentenced to life (Loerner, Frank, and Mummenthey); and nine were sentenced to 10 or 15 years' imprisonment. Thirteen of the convicted defendants were also convicted of membership in the SS (Volk was acquitted and Hohberg was not charged).

As officials in the WVHA, all of the defendants had been intimately involved in the administration of the concentration camps. Whether a defendant was sentenced to death appears to have been determined by the degree of his connection to the

---

[11] *Justice*, III TWC 1156.   [12] Ibid., 1127.

extermination program. Pohl oversaw the camps even though he knew that many of them were executing prisoners in gas chambers and crematoria[13]; Eirenschmalz was responsible for building the crematoria at Dachau, Buchenwald, and other camps and knew that they were being used to carry out the Final Solution[14]; Sommer's Amtsgruppe D "played an important part in the commission of these atrocities and murders."[15] By contrast, although both Frank and Mummenthey were aware of the extermination program, neither was involved in its creation. Indeed, the *Pohl* tribunal noted in its supplemental judgment that it sentenced Mummenthey to life instead of death because he was "too lacking in imagination to conjure up the planning of murder and equivalent enormities."[16]

Loerner's life sentence is more difficult to understand. He was initially sentenced to death, but the tribunal reduced his sentence to life on the ground that there were no relevant differences between him and Frank.[17] Even that sentence, however, seems unduly harsh. Unlike Frank and Mummenthey, Loerner was not aware of the extermination program[18]; unlike Frank, he was not convicted of participating in Action Reinhardt[19]; and unlike Mummenthey, he participated in the slave labor program but was not responsible for (and might not have even known about) the mistreatment of slaves.[20] Loerner thus seems little different from Fanslau, who received a 15-year sentence for his role in the slave-labor program and who was, in fact, a higher-ranking SS officer.

D. *Flick*

Three of the six defendants were convicted in *Flick*. Flick himself was sentenced to seven years' imprisonment; Steinbrinck was sentenced to five years; and Weiss was sentenced to 2½ years. Those sentences were actually relatively harsh, given the acts for which the defendants were held responsible. (The real problem with the case, as discussed in previous chapters, was the *Flick* tribunal's unwillingness to convict the defendants of various crimes in the first place.) Friedrich Flick, for example, was convicted of slave labor and plunder, but the tribunal found that he had voluntarily used slave labor only in the company's Linke-Hofmann Works,[21] had not mistreated the company's slaves,[22] and had engaged in only one act of plunder that was not connected to the Nazi's larger program.[23] Flick was also entitled to some mitigation based on his fear of reprisal by the Nazis and his misunderstanding of French property law, as discussed below.

E. *Hostage*

Of the 10 defendants in the *Hostage* case, eight were convicted. Two were sentenced to life imprisonment (List and Kuntze); the other sentences ranged from twenty years

---

[13] *Pohl*, V TWC 984.   [14] Ibid., 1030.
[15] Ibid., 1034.   [16] Ibid., 1239, Supplemental Judgment.
[17] Ibid., 1183, Supplemental Judgment.   [18] Ibid., 1007.
[19] Ibid., 1010.   [20] Ibid., 1007.   [21] *Flick*, VI TWC 1202.
[22] Ibid., 1199.   [23] Ibid., 1207.

(Rendulic and Speidel) to seven years (Dehner). List's sentence reflected both his importance—he was the fifth-ranking Field Marshal in the German Army—and his acts, particularly his distribution of illegal orders calling for the execution of civilian hostages pursuant to fixed ratios[24] and his failure to prevent or even condemn the thousands of such executions committed by his subordinates.[25] Kuntze was only a Lt. General, but he replaced List for nearly a year while List was ill and equally failed to prevent his subordinates from illegally executing civilian hostages.[26] Kuntze was also convicted of deporting Jews to slave labor,[27] unlike List—which perhaps offset the fact that he was acquitted of distributing illegal orders.[28]

It is difficult to explain why Rendulic was sentenced to 20 years instead of to life. He was higher-ranking than Kuntze and was, like List, convicted of both distributing illegal orders and failing to prevent illegal executions.[29] The *Hostage* tribunal also did not find any mitigating factors for Rendulic, in contrast to List and Kuntze. The only reasonable inference is that the tribunal did not feel a life sentence for Rendulic was warranted given that he was responsible for a much smaller area of occupied territory and fewer soldiers than either List or Kuntze.

These factors also explain why Dehner received the shortest sentence, despite being convicted of permitting the same illegal executions as Rendulic.[30] Dehner was Rendulic's subordinate, he was acquitted of distributing illegal orders and participating in deportation to slave labor, and—likely most important—the tribunal found in mitigation that he had consistently attempted "to correctly apply the rules of warfare as they apply to guerrilla warfare in occupied territory," even in the face of orders to the contrary.[31]

F. *Farben*

Eleven of the 21 defendants in *Farben* were convicted. The longest sentences, for slave labor, were eight years (Ambros and Duerrfeld); the shortest sentences, all for plunder, were two years or less (Oster, Buergin, Haefliger, Jaehne). The most interesting question is why ter Meer was given a shorter sentence (seven years) than Ambros and Duerrfeld, given that he was convicted of both slave labor and plunder and had played a leading role in the latter.[32] The answer seems to be that ter Meer was much less involved in the construction of Auschwitz III than Ambros and Duerrfeld,[33] was convicted for slave labor solely on the basis of command responsibility,[34] and had not known that Farben had mistreated the workers it used to build the plant.[35]

G. *Einsatzgruppen*

All of the defendants in *Einsatzgruppen* were convicted of war crimes, crimes against humanity, and membership in the SS. Fifteen were sentenced to death; two were

---

[24] *Hostage*, XI TWC 1265.   [25] Ibid., 1272.   [26] Ibid., 1275.
[27] Ibid., 1280.   [28] Ibid., 1276–7.   [29] Ibid., 1290.
[30] Ibid., 1297.   [31] Ibid., 1300.   [32] *Farben*, VIII TWC 1160.
[33] Ibid., 1180.   [34] Ibid., 1190.   [35] Ibid., 1192.

sentenced to life (Nosske and Jost); and six were sentenced to between time served and 20 years. Those were by far the most severe sentences in the trials.

Two factors appear to have determined whether a defendant was sentenced to life instead of to death: rank in the SS and direct involvement in executions. Most satisfied both criteria: all but two of the condemned defendants were high-ranking members of the SS—Lt. Colonel and higher—and all of those defendants either ordered[36] or supervised[37] executions. The two lower-ranking members of the SS, Schubert (a 1st Lieutenant) and Klingelhofer (a Major), were each directly involved in executions: Schubert supervised the murder of 700–800 Jews and Russians at Simferopol[38]; and Klingelhofer, the opera singer, personally executed 30 Jews for leaving a ghetto without permission.[39] By contrast, although Nosske was a high-ranking member of the SS—a Lt. Colonel—he had not been directly involved in executions; his conviction was based on command responsibility.[40] Two other factors also pointed toward life instead of death: his Kommando unit was responsible for a comparatively small number of executions, and he had refused to carry out at least one order that he considered illegal.[41]

Jost's life sentence is more difficult to understand, given that he was a Brigadier General in the SS and was the only commander of an Einsatzgruppen who was not sentenced to death. The explanation appears to be that he was convicted on the basis of command responsibility and that most of Einsatzgruppen A's executions had been committed before he took control of the group.[42] Earl additionally notes that, unlike all of the other condemned defendants, Jost never admitted to the crime of murder[43]—an important consideration for Judge Musmanno, whose personal opposition to the death penalty was based on concerns that the defendant might be innocent.[44]

Rank and direct involvement also explain why Fendler received the lightest sentence—10 years—despite the fact that he was convicted on all three counts and that the Subkommando he commanded was responsible for a significant number of executions. Fendler was a Major in the SS, the second-lowest rank in the trial, and had not been involved in planning, ordering, or committing executions.[45] In fact, he was not even convicted on the basis of command responsibility; the tribunal found that he had taken a consenting part in the executions instead, indicating that it considered TCP a less serious mode of participation in a crime.[46]

H. *RuSHA*

All but one of the 14 defendants were convicted in *RuSHA*. The five defendants convicted solely of membership in the SS were all sentenced to time served; the eight defendants convicted of war crimes and crimes against humanity as well were

---

[36] See, e.g., *Einsatzgruppen*, IV TWC 560 (Ott).   [37] See, e.g., ibid., 585 (Biberstein).
[38] Ibid., 582.   [39] Ibid., 569.   [40] Ibid., 556 (Nosske).
[41] Ibid., 558.   [42] Ibid., 513.   [43] Earl, 263.
[44] Ibid.   [45] *Einsatzgruppen*, IV TWC 570.   [46] Ibid., 572.

sentenced to life (Greifelt), 25 years (Hofmann and Hildebrandt), or between 10 and 20 years.

The defendant's sentences generally correlated with the position they held in the various SS organizations and the number of criminal enterprises in which they had participated (kidnapping alien children, forced Germanization, slave labor, etc.). Greifelt, for example, was the head of the RKFDV and convicted of six of the nine enterprises.[47] By contrast, the second lowest sentence—15 years—was given to Heubner, who was chief of an RKFDV branch office and convicted of only two enterprises.[48]

That said, it is not easy to explain why Hoffman and Hildebrandt were sentenced to 25 years instead of life. Both had served as the head of RuSHA, and both were convicted of all of the criminal enterprises except plunder.[49] The difference between them and Greifelt seems to be that the RKFDV was (in the words of the indictment) the "driving force" of the Germanization program as a whole, while RuSHA was responsible for only a "portion" of the program.[50] Indeed, the *RuSHA* tribunal emphasized that, as head of the RKFDV, Greifelt was second only to Himmler regarding Germanization.[51]

I. *Krupp*

Eleven of the 12 *Krupp* defendants were convicted. Alfried Krupp, Mueller, and von Buelow received the longest sentences, 12 years; Lehmann and Korschan received the shortest sentences, six years. Alfried Krupp was also forced to forfeit his industrial empire—the only case in which a tribunal punished a defendant with forfeiture.

Two aspects of the case are particularly interesting. To begin with, despite days of conference, the judges disagreed bitterly about the appropriate sentences. Judge Anderson not only rejected the order of forfeiture, he also insisted that the tribunal ignored mitigating factors that justified substantial reductions in most of the sentences.[52] He was particularly incensed by Loeser's seven-year sentence, because Loeser had resigned from Krupp in 1943 and had been part of the "underground movement to overthrow Hitler and the Nazi Party" since 1937.[53] Judge Wilkins later expressed regret that he did not agree to sentence Loeser to time served, noting that because Krupp's lawyers did not file a clemency petition on Loeser's behalf with McCloy's Advisory Board[54]—the result of friction caused by his resignation from the company—Loeser remained in Landsberg prison longer than any of his co-defendants, despite his relatively short sentence.[55]

The other interesting issue concerns the range of sentences imposed on defendants convicted solely of slave labor—12 years for von Buelow, nine for Ihn, and six

[47] *RuSHA*, V TWC 154–5.
[48] Ibid., 155.   [49] Ibid., 160 (Hofmann), 161 (Hildebrandt).
[50] *RuSHA*, Indictment, para. 8, IV TWC 612.   [51] *RuSHA*, V TWC 154.
[52] He agreed with Krupp's prison sentence and Kupke's release for time served.
[53] *Krupp*, Anderson Dissent, IX TWC 1453.
[54] The Advisory Board is discussed at length in Chapter 15.   [55] Wilkins, 221.

for Korschan and Lehmann. The three shorter sentences correlate with the defendants' relatively low rank in Krupp: Ihn was a deputy member of both the Direktorium and Vorstand; Korschan was a deputy member of the Vorstand; and Lehmann was Ihn's assistant. Von Buelow, however, was not a member of either the Direktorium or Vorstand. His longer sentence seems to reflect the fact that, as head of Krupp's plant police, he was primarily responsible for the mistreatment of Eastern workers, which was second in severity only to the mistreatment of concentration-camp inmates.[56] Von Buelow was also Krupp's liaison to the Gestapo and the SS.[57]

J. *Ministries*

It is almost impossible to compare the sentences in *Ministries*, because the trial included defendants whom the OCC had originally intended to try in six different cases. Nineteen of the 21 defendants were convicted; the longest sentence was 25 years (Berger), while the shortest was time served (Stuckart).

Given the magnitude of their crimes, it is surprising that Berger and Lammers did not receive life sentences. Berger, for example, was a Lt. General in the SS; was directly involved in the cold-blooded murder of a French general, Mesny[58]; knew about the Final Solution[59]; personally organized the Dirlewanger Brigade, which was responsible for hundreds of thousands of illegal executions[60]; and conscripted children into slave labor.[61] The only explanation for his 25-year sentence is that the *Ministries* tribunal gave him substantial credit for risking his life at the end of the war to save Allied officers and soldiers.[62]

Lammers' 20-year sentence is even more difficult to understand. Lammers was "one of the most important figures in the Reich government"[63]; was convicted of aggression for his involvement in the invasions of Czechoslovakia, Poland, the Low Countries, Belgium, the Netherlands, Luxembourg, and Russia[64]; was involved in issuing the lynch law[65] and drafting many of the most anti-Semitic laws, such as the Law Against Poles and Jews[66]; was responsible for mass deportations[67]; knew about the Final Solution[68]; and helped plan the slave-labor program.[69] The tribunal also failed to identify any factors warranting mitigation of his sentence.

K. *High Command*

Twelve of the 14 defendants in *High Command* were convicted. Two were sentenced to life imprisonment (Warlimont and Reinecke); the others received sentences ranging from 22 years (von Roques) to time served (von Leeb). Rank had

---

[56] *Krupp*, IX TWC 1405.   [57] Ibid., 1411.
[58] *Ministries*, XIV TWC 454.   [59] Ibid., 535.
[60] Ibid., 542.   [61] Ibid., 817.
[62] Ibid., 552.   [63] Ibid., 589.
[64] Ibid., 401–6.   [65] Ibid., 462.
[66] Ibid., 600.   [67] Ibid., 599.
[68] Ibid., 602.   [69] Ibid., 806.

little impact on the sentences: all of the defendants were at least Lt. Generals, and the highest-ranking convicted defendant, von Leeb, received the lightest sentence. Instead, the sentences reflected the number and gravity of the crimes the defendants committed. Warlimont, for example, helped draft the Commissar Order and the lynch law, contributed ideas to the Commando Order, was connected to the Barbarossa Jurisdiction Order and the Hostage Order, was involved in the deportation and enslavement of civilians, and knew about the extermination program.[70]

That said, some of the sentences seem inconsistent. It is difficult to understand, for example, why Reinecke was sentenced to life imprisonment while von Kuechler was sentenced to only 20 years. Reinecke's crimes were clearly very serious: he was directly involved in the murder and mistreatment of POWs, forced POWs to engage in labor connected to the war effort, and was responsible for plunder.[71] But he does not seem more culpable than von Kuechler, who distributed the Commando and Barbarossa Jurisdiction Orders, approved the use of POWs and civilians in improper and dangerous work, failed to prevent the execution and mistreatment of POWs, and was responsible for the deportation of massive numbers of civilians to slave labor.[72] Von Kuechler was also a higher rank—a Field Marshal instead of a Lt. General. The difference seems to be that, as noted below, the tribunal believed that Reinecke had precisely the kind of vicious character that justified a longer sentence.

III. Aggravating Factors

The tribunals rarely mentioned factors that warranted an increase in a defendant's sentence, most likely because, as Bill Schabas has pointed out, "[g]iven the horror of the crimes over which such tribunals had jurisdiction, discussion of aggravating factors must have seemed superfluous."[73] They do, however, appear to have implicitly recognized four aggravating factors. The first, and perhaps the most important, was membership in the SS. No defendant who was not a member of the SS was ever sentenced to death, not even those who—like Berger in *Ministries*—were responsible for hundreds, if not thousands, of murders.

The tribunals also appear to have penalized defendants who had a particularly vicious character, even by Nazi standards. Rothaug, for example, seems to have been sentenced to life instead of a term of years primarily because he had been a particularly enthusiastic proponent of the Final Solution. Similarly, in sentencing Reinecke to life imprisonment—one of only two such sentences in *High Command*—Tribunal V emphasized that he had been responsible for "the Nazification of the various services, particularly of the army" and had served as a lay judge during

---

[70] *High Command*, XI TWC 665–81.
[71] Ibid., 659–61.
[72] Ibid., 567–77.
[73] William A. Schabas, "Sentencing by International Tribunals: A Human Rights Approach," 7 *Duke J. of Comp. & Int'l L.* 461, 483 (1997).

the trial of the German officers who tried to assassinate Hitler in 1944, "perhaps the most infamous travesty on human justice ever so completely recorded in the annals of man."[74]

Conversely, the tribunals seem to have sentenced defendants more harshly who were particularly educated and cultured—the idea being that they should have known better than to collaborate with the Nazis. In *Einsatzgruppen*, for example, Tribunal II justified the severity of its sentences with the following statement:

> The defendants are not untutored aborigines incapable of appreciation of the finer values of life and living. Each man at the bar has had the benefit of considerable schooling. Eight are lawyers, one a university professor, another a dental physician, still another an expert on art. One, as an opera singer, gave concerts throughout Germany before he began his tour of Russia with the Einsatzkommandos. This group of educated and well-bred men does not even lack a former minister, self-unfrocked though he was.[75]

Finally, the tribunals appear to have treated a defendant's consistent evasiveness during trial as an aggravating factor. The *Pohl* tribunal, for example, specifically noted with regard to Eirenschmalz, one of the three defendants sentenced to death, that "[t]hroughout the entire trial he has endeavored to hide in every way possible his responsibility and participation in concentration camp construction-maintenance affairs."[76] Similarly, Judge Young complained in a letter home that Warlimont, one of two defendants sentenced to life in *High Command*, "is cagy, never could answer a question in precision, always go all the way around Robin-Hood's barn, alibi—alibi—alibi."[77]

IV. Mitigating Factors

Unlike aggravating factors, all of the tribunals specifically identified factors that warranted reducing a defendant's sentence. Analogizing to the defenses, those factors can be divided into justifications and excuses. The first category focused on actions that indicated that, despite his crimes, the defendant never completely lost his humanity during the war. The second category focused on aspects of a defendant's crimes that were not morally praiseworthy, but at least partially mitigated the defendant's culpability.

A. Justifications

Justifications for a reduced sentence clustered around two basic themes: (1) independence from the Nazis; and (2) active resistance to the Nazi regime.

---

[74] *High Command*, XI TWC 660–1.
[75] *Einsatzgruppen*, IV TWC 500.
[76] *Pohl*, V TWC 1030.
[77] Quoted in Hébert, *Hitler's Generals*, 135.

1. Independence

A number of tribunals rewarded defendants for maintaining professional and ideological independence from the Nazis. The *Justice* tribunal cited as mitigating the fact that Lautz "was not active in Party matters" and "resisted all efforts of Party officials to influence his conduct."[78] The *High Command* tribunal pointed out that von Leeb "was not a friend or follower of the Nazi party or its ideology,"[79] while the *Hostage* tribunal stated that the record supported Kuntze's claim that he "was not in high favor with Hitler and the Nazi Party."[80] And the *Flick* tribunal emphasized that although Flick and Steinbrinck both joined the Nazi Party, they "participated in no Party activities and did not believe in its ideologies," were not "pronouncedly anti-Jewish," and "did not approve nor . . . condone the atrocities of the SS." Indeed, the tribunal said that it was "unthinkable that Steinbrinck, a U-boat commander who risked his life and those of his crew to save survivors of a ship which he had sunk, would willingly be a party to the slaughter of thousands of defenseless persons."[81]

2. Resistance

The tribunals also rewarded defendants who had actively resisted the Nazis. First, three tribunals highlighted a defendant's opposition to Hitler himself: the *Pohl* tribunal credited Hohberg with playing "an active part" in the "underground movement working against the regime"[82]; the *Flick* tribunal pointed out that Flick himself "knew in advance of the plot on Hitler's life in July 1944, and sheltered one of the conspirators"[83]; and the *Ministries* tribunal accepted von Weizsaecker's claim that he remained in the Foreign Office so that "he might thereby continue to be at least a cohesive factor in the underground opposition to Hitler."[84]

Second, a number of tribunals focused on a defendant's efforts to prevent the issuance of illegal orders. The *Hostage* tribunal, for example, said that Kuntze was entitled to mitigation because he had regularly protested the harshness of orders he received concerning the execution of hostages.[85] Similarly, the *High Command* tribunal gave von Leeb significant credit for his repeated attempts to prevent Hitler from issuing the Commissar Order, which he believed to be both "stupid" and "in violation of international law."[86]

Third, multiple tribunals acknowledged that defendants had either attempted to prevent the commission of crimes or had softened illegal orders and decrees. The *Flick* tribunal noted that Steinbrinck had prevented "several instances" of pillaging.[87] The *Hostage* tribunal found that Dehner's attempts to ensure that his soldiers

---

[78] *Justice*, III TWC 1128. [79] *High Command*, XI TWC 563.
[80] *Hostage*, XI TWC 1280. [81] *Flick*, VI TWC 1222.
[82] *Pohl*, V TWC 1042. [83] *Flick*, VI TWC 1222.
[84] *Ministries*, XIV TWC 497. [85] *Hostage*, XI TWC 1280.
[86] *High Command*, XI TWC 555. [87] *Flick*, VI TWC 1203.

complied with the laws of war "warrant[ed] mitigation of punishment."[88] The *Ministries* tribunal said that it would "not ignore" Kehrl's efforts "to alleviate the harshness of the slave-labor program by a policy which would thus restrict deportations from the occupied territories into Germany."[89] And the *High Command* tribunal credited Reinhardt for partially countermanding the Commando Order in the area he controlled by issuing an order "that parachutists are lawful combatants and are to be treated as prisoners of war."[90]

Finally, three tribunals credited defendants with saving individuals from the Nazis. The *Flick* tribunal noted that Steinbrinck and Flick had each helped Jewish friends emigrate from Germany and that Steinbrinck had twice interceded to prevent the internment of Pastor Niemoeller, of whose congregation he was a member.[91] The *Einsatzgruppen* tribunal concluded that von Radetzky had occasionally attempted "to assist potential victims of the Fuehrer Order and in one particular instance issued passes which allowed some persons to escape from the camp in which they were being held."[92] And the *Ministries* tribunal acknowledged that Berger had exposed himself to considerable danger in the final months of the war in order to save the lives "of American, British, and Allied officers and men whose safety was gravely imperiled by orders of Hitler that they be liquidated or held as hostages,"[93] while Schellenberg had rendered "actual and notable aid" to individuals suffering from "imprisonment, oppression, and persecution in the Third Reich."[94] Interestingly, the *Ministries* tribunal took a strictly utilitarian approach to Schellenberg's mitigation, insisting that it was irrelevant whether his actions "arose from true benevolence or from a desire to curry favor with the then imminent victors," because "[h]is motives made no difference to the beneficiaries of his acts."[95]

B. Excuses

The tribunals identified four different clusters of factors that helped excuse a defendant's crimes, thereby warranting a reduced sentence: (1) superior orders; (2) military considerations; (3) legal clarity; and (4) personal characteristics. The *Hostage* tribunal emphasized, however, that excuse-based mitigation did not "in any sense of the word reduce the degree of the crime," but was "more a matter of grace than of defense."[96]

1. Superior Orders

The first cluster of excuses centered on crimes that were committed by subordinates in hierarchical organizations. As noted in Chapter 12, Article II(4)(b) of Law No. 10 entitled the tribunals to reduce a defendant's sentence on the ground that he had

---

[88] *Hostage*, XI TWC 1300.   [89] *Ministries*, XIV TWC 580.
[90] *High Command*, XI TWC 600.   [91] *Flick*, VI TWC 1222.
[92] *Einsatzgruppen*, IV TWC 578.   [93] *Ministries*, XIV TWC 522.
[94] Ibid., 861.   [95] Ibid.   [96] *Hostage*, XI TWC 1317.

committed his crimes pursuant to superior orders. A number did so, including the *High Command*, *Hostage*, and *Pohl* tribunals.[97] Superior orders was a mitigating factor even for defendants as high-ranking as von Leeb,[98] and the existence of such orders meant the difference between life and death for Mummenthey in *Pohl*.[99] Similarly, in the civilian context, the *Justice* tribunal reduced Lautz's sentence for participating in the Nazis' nationwide system of cruelty and injustice because he honestly believed that, as a prosecutor, he was ethically bound to apply all properly enacted German laws, even those he considered unjust.[100]

2. Military Considerations

The second cluster of excuses focused on the military context in which a defendant committed a particular crime. The *High Command* tribunal identified three such factors. First, it held that although *tu quoque* was not a defense to a crime, it could be considered in mitigation. It thus reduced Woehler's sentence for forcing POWs to engage in work connected to the war because it was convinced that the Allies had used German POWs in a similar manner.[101] Second, it suggested that Hollidt was entitled to some degree of mitigation for forcing POWs to work in dangerous conditions because the "difficult and deplorable condition" in which his army found itself during its retreat from Russia had made such danger nearly impossible to avoid.[102] Third, it reduced von Leeb's sentence for the crimes committed by his subordinates pursuant to the Barbarossa Jurisdiction Order on the ground that no field commander "engaged in a stupendous campaign with responsibility for hundreds of thousands of soldiers, and a large indigenous population spread over a vast area," could ever completely prevent the commission of war crimes.[103]

3. Legal Clarity

The third cluster of excuses concerned the clarity of the law that governed a defendant's actions. Although the *Hostage* tribunal condemned the Nazis execution of civilian hostages and reprisal prisoners, it also criticized "[t]he failure of the nations of the world to deal specifically with the problem of hostages and reprisals by convention, treaty, or otherwise, after the close of World War I." The resulting legal uncertainty, according to the tribunal, "mitigate[d] to some extent the seriousness of the offense."[104] The *Flick* tribunal, by contrast, focused on domestic law instead of international law. It held that although the maxim *ignorantia legis*

---

[97] *High Command*, XI TWC 567 (von Kuechler); *Hostage*, XI TWC 1280, 1299 (Kuntze, Dehner); *Pohl*, Supplemental Judgment, V TWC 129 (Mummenthey).
[98] *High Command*, XI TWC 563.
[99] *Pohl*, Supplemental Judgment, V TWC 1239.
[100] *Justice*, III TWC 1128.
[101] *High Command*, XI TWC 685.
[102] Ibid., 627.
[103] Ibid., 563.
[104] *Hostage*, XI TWC 1274.

applied to both international and domestic law, a defendant's failure to understand the domestic law of a state other than his own—in this case, Friedrich Flick's knowledge of French property law—could be considered in mitigation.[105]

4. Personal Characteristics

The final cluster of excuses focused on a defendant's personal characteristics. The *Flick* tribunal held that Friedrich Flick's fear that the Nazis would retaliate against him if he did not participate in the slave-labor program, though not rising to the level of necessity, nevertheless justified reducing his sentence.[106] And the *Ministries* tribunal relied on Stuckart's serious medical condition to sentence him to time served, noting that even a short period of imprisonment "would be equivalent to the death sentence," a penalty that his crimes—though serious—did not warrant.[107] Surprisingly, only one tribunal ever mentioned remorse as a mitigating factor: the *Pohl* tribunal gave Hohberg "generous credit" for repenting "the dynamic part he played in the operation of a machine which crushed human beings spiritually and physically."[108] By contrast, remorse is often considered mitigating by modern international tribunals.[109]

V. Between-Case Comparisons

A. Are Comparisons Possible?

It is extremely difficult to compare sentences between cases. As the *Pohl* tribunal noted in its supplemental judgment:

[T]he facts in no two cases are identical. Similarities may exist to a greater or lesser degree, but not absolute identity. Nor is it possible to assure entire unanimity in the findings of separate Tribunals. Disparity in conclusions, or findings of fact, may result from the disparity in emphasis which separate Tribunals may accord to the evidence. A single document may in the opinion of one Tribunal assume controlling force, and in the opinion of another Tribunal be given lesser weight. One Tribunal may find the testimony of one witness true, and another Tribunal may discredit it. In appraising the preponderance of the proof for and against the defendant, one Tribunal may find the scales to be tipped in one direction and another Tribunal in the other.[110]

The structure of the judgments further complicates productive comparison. First, most defendants were convicted of multiple crimes, making it difficult to generalize about specific crimes. It seems to be the case, for example, that the

---

[105] *Flick*, VI TWC 1208–9.
[106] Ibid., 1221.
[107] *Ministries*, XIV TWC 869–70.
[108] *Pohl*, Supplemental Judgment, V TWC 1225.
[109] See, e.g., Schabas, *Sentencing*, 496.
[110] *Pohl*, Supplemental Judgment, V TWC 1187–8.

tribunals generally viewed plunder as the least serious war crime: no defendant convicted solely of plunder received a sentence longer than six years (Krauch in *Farben*), and many defendants convicted of both plunder and slave labor— clearly the more serious crime—received relatively short sentences, such as Friedrich Flick (seven years) and Loeser (seven years) in *Krupp*. But *Farben* was the only case in which a defendant was convicted solely of plunder, and for every Flick and Loeser there is a defendant sentenced to a much longer sentence for plunder and slave labor: Frank received life in *Pohl*; Pleiger received 15 years in *Ministries*; Alfried Krupp and Mueller each received 12 years in *Krupp*. The longer sentences likely reflect the defendants' greater participation in slave labor, not different conceptions of plunder's gravity, but that is nothing more than an educated guess.

Second, as noted in Chapter 11, the tribunals rarely identified the modes of participation they used to convict defendants of specific crimes. It is thus very difficult to determine whether the tribunals generally agreed with the *Pohl* tribunal's belief that personally committing a crime was more serious than ordering its commission or the *RuSHA* tribunal's insistence that the opposite was true—and even more difficult to generalize about the modes of participation as a whole. The one exception is command responsibility: it seems clear that the tribunals generally viewed failing to prevent crimes as less serious than personally committing them, ordering them, or being connected to a criminal enterprise involving them, given the lighter sentences imposed on Genzken in the *Medical* case, ter Meer in *Farben*, and Jost in *Einsatzgruppen*.

Finally, although the tribunals identified a wide variety of mitigating factors, their failure to explain the connection between those factors and individual sentences complicates inter-tribunal comparison. The most that can be said is that, in general, the tribunals seem to have agreed that a justificatory mitigating factor warranted a significant reduction in a defendant's sentence. In at least six cases, defendants credited with such factors received very light sentences: Lautz's ten-year sentence was the lowest in the *Justice* case; Hohberg's ten-year sentence was the lowest in *Pohl*; Dehner's seven-year sentence was the lowest in the *Hostage* case; von Radetzky's 20-year sentence was the second lowest in *Einsatzgruppen*; Schellenberg's six-year sentence was the third lowest in *Ministries*; and von Leeb's sentence of time served was the lowest in *High Command*.

B. Did the Sentences Become More Lenient?

Telford Taylor argued in his Final Report that, "[o]n the whole, it was apparent to anyone connected with the entire series of trials under Law No. 10 that the sentences became progressively lighter as time went on." Taylor attributed that trend to a number of factors, including "waning interest on the part of the general public and the shift in the focus of public attention resulting from international events and circumstance."[111] The historian Peter Maguire agrees, writing that after

---

[111] Taylor, *Final Report*, 92.

February 1948—when the *Hostage* tribunal delivered its judgment—"the sentences handed down at Nuremberg grew increasingly lenient... due to a combination of Cold War pressure and legitimate discomfort with the radical implications" of Law No. 10.[112]

Some of the sentences imposed in the later trials support these claims. It seems likely, for example, that earlier tribunals would have sentenced Lammers and von Kuechler to life imprisonment, not to the 20 years they received from the *Ministries* and *High Command* tribunals, respectively. Nevertheless, it seems more accurate to say that individual tribunals were particularly lenient than that the sentences became increasingly lenient over time. Consider the cases decided after Maguire's February 1948 date: *RuSHA, Einsatzgruppen, Krupp, Ministries,* and *High Command.* The latter two tribunals were indeed lenient—but *Einsatzgruppen* and *Krupp* were not. More defendants were sentenced to death in *Einsatzgruppen* than in all of the other cases combined, and the defendants in *Krupp* received far longer sentences than their industrialist counterparts in *Flick* and *Farben.*

An analysis of specific crimes also calls into question the idea that the sentences became increasingly lenient. Consider, for example, the sentences that the tribunals imposed on defendants convicted solely of membership in a criminal organization—a crime that Taylor cited in defense of the leniency hypothesis[113]:

Case	Trial End	Defendant	Sentence
Medical	August 1947	Poppendick	10 years
Justice	December 1947	Alstoetter	5 years
Flick	December 1947	Steinbrinck	5 years
RuSHA	March 1948	Meyer-Hetling	2½ years
RuSHA	March 1948	Ebner	2½ years
RuSHA	March 1948	Schwarzenberger	2½ years
RuSHA	March 1948	Sollman	2½ years
RuSHA	March 1948	Tesch	2½ years
Einsatzgruppen	April 1948	Ruehl	10 years
Einsatzgruppen	April 1948	Graf	2½ years
Ministries	April 1949	Bohle	5 years

These sentences do not indicate that sentences for criminal membership became increasingly lenient. Instead, they suggest that the *RuSHA* tribunal viewed the crime—for reasons it never explained—as less serious than the other tribunals. After all, Ruehl received the same sentence in Case No. 8 that Poppendick received in Case 1, while Bohle received the same sentence in Case No. 11 that Alstoetter and Steinbrinck received in Case 3 and Case 4, respectively. Moreover, the "lenient" later sentences given to Graf and Bohle would likely have been longer

---

[112] Maguire, 190.
[113] See Taylor, *Final Report*, 179 n. 145.

but for mitigating circumstances: the *Einsatzgruppen* tribunal found that Graf's membership in the SD "was not without compulsion and constraint,"[114] and Bohle pleaded guilty to membership in the SS.[115]

Conclusion

Reading the judgments with regard to sentencing is an exercise in frustration. The tribunals never adopted a consistent set of sentencing principles, and they rarely explained their sentencing decisions in any detail. A close reading of the judgments indicates, however, that individual sentences were significantly affected by the presence of aggravating or mitigating factors; that the sentences within cases were generally consistent; and that—contrary to the received wisdom—sentences did not become increasingly lenient over time.

[114] *Einsatzgruppen*, IV TWC 587.
[115] *Ministries*, XIV TWC 856.

15

Aftermath

Introduction

Peter Maguire has written that 1949 inaugurated a "second phase" of U.S. war-crimes policy, one in which "American and West German leaders fashioned two American policies—one public and one private. The public policy was designed to defend the legal validity of the American trials from widespread German attack, while the private policy sought to release war criminals as quickly and quietly as the political and legal circumstances would allow."[1] As this chapter explains, that "private policy" led to what can only be described as the complete collapse of the U.S. commitment to the NMT trials. When the trials drew to a close in April 1949, many of the 142 convicted defendants were facing execution or significant prison sentences: 24 had been sentenced to death; 20 had been sentenced to life; and 18 had been sentenced to more than 20 years. A mere six years later, however, only 12 of the 25 death sentences had been carried out and only seven of the prisoners serving sentences of 20 years or more remained in prison. Indeed, the last NMT defendant walked out of Landsberg Prison a free man in 1958.

The chapter is divided into three sections. Section I recounts the events that preceded John J. McCloy's appointment as High Commissioner of Germany in June 1949, focusing on General Clay's review of the NMT convictions and the deactivation of the OCC. Section II then discusses McCloy's creation of the Advisory Board on Clemency for War Criminals, which likely violated Law No. 10, and his decision in mid-1951 to grant clemency to the nearly all of the convicted NMT defendants. Finally, Section III explores the events that followed McCloy's clemency decisions, focusing on the work of the U.S.-German Interim Mixed Parole and Clemency Board and its permanent successor.

I. Events Preceding McCloy's Appointment as High Commissioner

A. General Clay's Review

As discussed in Chapter 7, Article XV of Ordinance No. 7 provided that "[t]he judgments of the tribunals as to the guilt or the innocence of any defendant shall

---

[1] Maguire, 210.

give the reasons on which they are based and shall be final and not subject to review." Ordinance No. 7 did, however, vest considerable discretion in the Military Governor—General Clay—to modify a convicted defendant's sentence. Article XVII(a) gave the Military Governor "the power to mitigate, reduce or otherwise alter the sentence imposed by the tribunal," as long as he did not "increase the severity thereof." And Article XVIII provided that "[n]o sentence of death shall be carried into execution unless and until confirmed in writing by the Military Governor."

Between November 1947 and March 1949, General Clay reviewed the sentences in all of the NMT cases except *Ministries*, whose judgment was still not final when OMGUS was terminated and McCloy was appointed High Commissioner of Germany (HICOG). Clay confirmed all of the sentences in eight of the 11 cases he reviewed: *Medical, Milch, Justice, Flick, Hostage, RuSHA, Einsatzgruppen*, and *High Command*. In each of the other three cases, he confirmed all of the sentences except one. In *Pohl*, he reduced Karl Sommer's death sentence to life imprisonment. In *Farben*, he reduced Paul Haefliger's two-year sentence to time served because his time in confinement had been incorrectly calculated. And in *Krupp* he made a very slight modification to the forfeiture order imposed on Alfried Krupp, clarifying that the order applied only to Krupp's real and personal property on the date of the tribunal's judgment and sentence.[2]

Although Clay confirmed 23 of the 24 death sentences he reviewed, in each case he stayed the executions "[p]ending actions on petitions filed by the defendant with authorities other than the Office of Military Government for Germany"[3]—a reference to the fact that the condemned defendants in the three trials involving death sentences (*Medical, Pohl*, and *Einsatzgruppen*) had immediately filed petitions for habeas with the U.S. Supreme Court. On 16 February 1948, with Justice Jackson not participating and with Justices Black, Murphy, and Rutledge "of the opinion that the petitions should be set for hearing on the question of the jurisdiction of this court," the Supreme Court denied the petitions filed by the defendants in the *Medical* case. Clay lifted the stays of execution on May 14 and the sentences were carried out on June 2.[4] The following year, on 2 May 1949, the Supreme Court denied the *Pohl* and *Einsatzgruppen* defendants leave to file their habeas petitions; the vote was 4-4, with Chief Justice Vinson and Justices Reed, Frankfurter, and Burton concluding that "there is want of jurisdiction," and Justices Black, Douglas, Murphy, and Rutledge arguing that "argument should be heard... in order to settle what remedy, if any, the petitioners have."[5] As discussed below, because he was set to resign as Military Governor less than two weeks later, Clay never lifted the stays of execution in *Pohl* and *Einsatzgruppen*, turning that responsibility over to McCloy.

---

[2] XV TWC 1144–5.   [3] Ibid., 1145.   [4] II TWC 330.
[5] V TWC 1256. Justice Jackson once again did not participate in the decision.

B. Attacks on the War Crimes Program

In late 1948, Clay confessed regret that his lot as Military Governor was "to have ... to sign many death warrants and to approve many life imprisonments."[6] His willingness to confirm nearly all of the NMT sentences was thus particularly remarkable, given that opposition to the U.S. war-crimes program—from Germans and Americans—had become particularly acute by early 1948, when he began to review them.

Attacks on the war-crimes program were, of course, nothing new. In America, Chief Justice Harlan Fiske Stone had famously denounced the IMT in January 1946 as a "high-grade lynching party in Nuremberg" that presented a "false façade of legality,"[7] and in July 1947 Congressman Dondero had attacked Patterson, the Secretary of War at the time, for failing to prevent "Communist sympathizers" from infiltrating the Army.[8] Meanwhile, in Germany, church leaders like Hans Meiser, the Evangelical *Landesbishop* of Bavaria, had spent much of 1947 agitating about supposed flaws in the Dachau trials.[9]

Nevertheless, 1948 proved to be a particularly banner year for war-crimes critics. On February 11, Senator William Langer, a Republican from North Dakota, informed Clay that he intended to introduce a resolution authorizing the Senate Judiciary Committee to investigate whether the Army's "conduct of trials and treatment of prisoners ... have been in accordance with American concepts of justice."[10] Senate Resolution 39—which Langer did not formally submit to the Senate until the following January—was specifically directed at the Malmedy trial, a Dachau trial in which 73 members of the SS had been convicted of murdering nearly 90 American POWs during the Battle of the Bulge in 1944. A number of the defendants had alleged during the two-month trial, which ran from May to July 1946, that their American captors had tortured them into confessing. Those allegations had been amplified by Willis M. Everett, Jr., the defendants' court-appointed American attorney, who claimed in 1947 that more than 80 percent of the confessions had been obtained illegally.[11]

By the time he received Langer's cable, General Clay was already mired in the Malmedy controversy. Indeed, the cable arrived just as two Army review boards were completing very different reports on the trial. Three days earlier, on February 8, a board created by the Theater Judge Advocate, James L. Harbaugh, had submitted a very critical report, finding "much evidence" of improper investigative techniques, including the use of mock trials, and condemning procedural rulings by

---

[6] Quoted in Buscher, 39.

[7] Quoted in Gary Jonathan Bass, "War Crimes and the Limits of Legalism," 97 *Mich. L. Rev.* 2103, 2105 (1999).

[8] See Chapter 2.

[9] Frei, 99.

[10] Quoted in James J. Weingartner, *Crossroads of Death: The Story of the Malmedy Massacre and Trial* 198 (1979).

[11] Buscher, 38.

the tribunal that had limited the defense's ability to examine witnesses.[12] By contrast, three days after Langer's cable, on February 14, Clay's own Administration of Justice Review Board, which he had created in August 1947 to review the work of U.S. military courts,[13] submitted a report that largely exonerated the Malmedy trial. The Review Board acknowledged that mock trials, violence, and "stool pigeons" had occasionally been used to convince defendants to confess, but it "blamed this more on the tough caliber of the defendants than the intentions of the American investigators." It also found no evidence to support any of the other allegations of prosecutorial misconduct.[14]

Langer's cable, which included a request that Clay stay executions pending Senate consideration of Resolution 39, forced Clay to make a decision on the fate of the Malmedy prisoners. On March 20, he commuted 31 of the 43 death sentences to life imprisonment, released 13 prisoners, and reduced the sentences of most of the others.[15]

February 1948 also witnessed an attack more specifically directed at the NMT trials: Judge Charles Wennerstrum's interview with the *Chicago Tribune*, discussed in Chapter 4, in which he denounced the trials as "victor's justice." Although Wennerstrum's criticisms were ably rebutted by Taylor, they nevertheless "inevitably kindled further German anti-Nuremberg sentiment. For those Germans opposed to the trial program, the fact that the Americans were publicly debating these trials seemed to indicate decreasing U.S. commitment to the proceedings."[16] Indeed, German critics immediately stepped up their attacks on the NMT and Dachau trials. On March 25, Johannes Neuhausler, the Auxiliary Bishop of Munich who had spent time in a concentration camp during the war, wrote to various members of Congress complaining about the alleged mistreatment of the Malmedy prisoners and asking them to launch additional investigations of the trial.[17] A month later, Bishop Wurm, the chairman of Germany's Protestant Church Council, launched a "massive and sweeping attack" on the war-crimes program, claiming in an open letter to the OCC's Kempner—who had taken Wurm on a tour of the Nuremberg prison on Easter 1948—that "in trial preparations in those cases thus far ending with death sentences, criminal methods and repellent tortures have been applied in order to extort statements and confessions."[18] Wurm's political motivations were particularly evident, because he had admitted to Kempner after the tour that his "fears that the care and treatment of the prisoners was cause for great concern were groundless."[19]

The next major attack came on 20 May 1948, when a group of Evangelical church leaders in the American zone, led by Bishop Wurm, submitted a "chilly" anti-NMT petition to Charles LaFollette, the former OCC prosecutor who was now the head of Wurttemberg-Baden's military government. The petition contained a potpourri of complaints about the NMT trials: that the working

---

[12] Weingartner, 180–1.
[13] Andrew Szanajda, *The Restoration of Justice in Postwar Hesse, 1945–1949*, 98 (2007).
[14] Buscher, 39–40.   [15] Weingartner, 185.   [16] Buscher, 36.
[17] Cited in ibid., 93.   [18] Quoted in Frei, 108.   [19] Cited in ibid.

conditions of the German defense attorneys were inadequate; that witness detention was foreign to German law; that the law being applied was *ex post facto*; that military instead of civilian judges should have been used, particularly in the *High Command* trial; and so forth. But most important—because it initiated a critical theme that would persist for the next five years—the petition claimed that there was an "undeniable need" to create either an American or an international appellate court empowered to review war-crimes convictions.[20] In fact, Wurm repeated that criticism twice in the next two weeks. On June 1, Wurm cabled Clay to demand that the Dachau death sentences be stayed "until the definite clearance through an appointed court of appeals."[21] And on June 5, Wurm wrote to Kempner claiming that, "[w]hen taking into consideration the importance of the findings for international law and their serious consequences for the inflicted persons, such an appeal becomes an imperative demand."[22]

LaFollette forwarded Bishop Wurm's petition to Clay on June 8, along with a five-page letter rebutting the Evangelicals' criticisms of the war-crimes program. He was particularly adamant in his rejection of the need for an appellate court, contending that the existing procedures for granting clemency were sufficient and pointing out that the creation of an appellate court would undoubtedly be seen by the Germans as a tacit admission that the NMT and Dachau trials were procedurally flawed.[23]

LaFollette's letter greatly influenced Clay's reaction to the petition. Clay zealously defended the NMT trials and the absence of appellate review in a June 19 letter to Bishop Wurm, insisting that "[n]ever in history has evidence so convicted those in high places for their actions. It is difficult to understand how any review of the evidence of those yet to be sentenced could provide a basis for sentimental sympathy for those who brought suffering and anguish to untold millions." Clay was particularly incensed by the attacks on the *High Command* trial, which he described—correctly—as designed "to discredit a court which with high intent is endeavoring to establish precedents in international law which may serve to prevent again a world being plunged into chaos."[24]

Perhaps anticipating a negative response, Bishop Wurm did not wait to hear from Clay before launching a new round of attacks on the Malmedy trial. Further embellishing earlier claims, Wurm now began to refer to the Army's treatment of the SS defendants as a "crime against humanity" and to insist that many of the convicted defendants were actually innocent.[25] Wurm's strategy was obvious: "to link reproaches aimed at Nuremberg with those aimed at Dachau in order to demand a review of all sentences by a review body."[26] But it was also very a intelligent line of attack, because it was all too easy for American officials to lose sight of the fact that the NMT trials were far more procedurally sound than the Dachau trials.[27] Indeed, "[t]he accusations surrounding the Dachau trials made some Nuremberg personnel nervous that they also would be marked with the same taint."[28] Sprecher, for example, would

---

[20] Cited in ibid., 105.   [21] Cited in Buscher, 98.
[22] Letter from Bishop Wurm to Kempner, 5 June 1948, in Wurm Memorandum, 25.
[23] Cited in Frei, 106.   [24] Cited in ibid., 107.   [25] Ibid., 109.
[26] Ibid.   [27] Hébert, *Hitler's Generals*, 53.   [28] Ibid.

later describe German attempts to blur the lines between the two sets of trials as "a good strategy."[29]

C. The Simpson Commission

Wurm's efforts quickly paid off. In mid-July 1948, General Clay ordered his Administration of Justice Review Board to once again investigate the Malmedy trial.[30] Even more dramatically, on July 30, Royall not only stayed the execution of all the Dachau prisoners sentenced to death—including the 12 Malmedy prisoners whose sentences Clay had affirmed in March—he announced that he was appointing Gordon Simpson, a member of the Texas Supreme Court, to review all of the Dachau trials.[31]

If Clay and Royall believed that their actions would defuse criticism of the war-crimes program, they were mistaken. Bishop Neuhausler responded by expanding his attacks beyond Malmedy, alleging that American prosecutors had relied on "professional witnesses" in a number of the Dachau trials and demanding that Clay create a review board with the power to overturn the verdicts issued by both the Dachau and the NMT tribunals.[32] Neuhausler's demand for an appellate court was seconded on August 26 by the Fulda Bishops Conference, which meant that—as Buscher points out—"the fight against American war crimes trials was now the official policy of the German Catholic Church."[33]

On September 14, the Simpson Commission released its report on the Dachau trials. The Report was a mixed bag for the critics. The Commission found "no general or systematic use of improper methods to secure prosecution evidence for use at the trials" and concluded that the 12 remaining Malmedy death sentences were justified. But it also condemned the use of mock trials to obtain confessions and recommended that, in light of the procedural irregularities in the Malmedy trial, the death sentences be commuted to life imprisonment.[34]

Royall responded to the Simpson Commission's report by lifting—no doubt reluctantly, because he had long since lost faith in the war-crimes program[35]—the stays of execution that he had ordered in July.[36] His decision was met with immediate outrage by the Bishops, who launched a "large-scale political-journalistic offensive" against the executions, one that featured a new rhetorical innovation: referring to the convicted defendants as "war criminals," in quotation marks, instead of simply as war criminals.[37] The Bishops also received support from an unlikely source: Edward Van Roden, a Pennsylvania judge who had served on the Simpson Commission. A few days before executions resumed on October 15, Van Roden told reporters in the United States that Gordon Simpson had suppressed evidence indicating that the Malmedy defendants had, in fact, been physically abused by Army interrogators. The German press immediately republished his statements throughout Germany.[38]

[29] Ibid., 53.   [30] Buscher, 38.   [31] Earl, 274.
[32] Buscher, 94.   [33] Ibid.   [34] Cited in Frei, 111–2.
[35] Ibid., 112.   [36] Ibid.   [37] Ibid., 113.   [38] Ibid., 112.

D. Landsberg Prison and the Baldwin Subcommittee

Faced with renewed controversy, Clay stayed the 12 remaining Malmedy death sentences on October 25.[39] As before, however, his concession simply emboldened his critics. In early December, Bishop Neuhausler orchestrated a letter-writing campaign to Clay about the living conditions and treatment of the inmates at Landsberg prison,[40] where all of the defendants convicted in the NMT and Dachau trials were now being held.[41] Clay responded to the campaign by asking Taylor to investigate the situation at the prison. After visiting Landsberg on February 14, Taylor reported back to Clay that the prison was "fairly and efficiently administered and that (given the general circumstances which prevail throughout Germany at the present time) conditions . . . are generally satisfactory."[42]

Clay was evidently convinced by Taylor's report, because on two separate occasions in March 1949 he asked Royall to permit him to lift the stays of execution he had imposed the previous October. That was a remarkably selfless request, because—as noted earlier—Clay had long since tired of signing death warrants. He nevertheless felt obligated not to bequeath the responsibility for approving executions to his successor. "I would not like to have a mass execution," he wrote, "and yet I do want to free my successor from this thankless task to give him a clearer and more constructive task."[43] Clay also recognized that the "punitive" phase of the occupation was rapidly giving way to the "constructive" phase, which would mean that the pressure on his successor to commute the remaining death sentences would only increase.[44]

Royall, however, refused to let Clay execute the remaining Malmedy prisoners. Between Clay's two requests, the Senate Armed Services Committee had authorized yet another review of the Malmedy trial, this time in the form of a three-person Subcommittee headed by Raymond Baldwin, a Republican senator from Connecticut. Both Baldwin and another member of the Subcommittee, Estes Kefauver, a Democrat from Tennessee, had ties to individuals involved in the Malmedy trial through their law firms, so a fourth Senator was soon added—Joseph McCarthy, the infamous red-baiting Republican from Wisconsin, who viewed the Baldwin Subcommittee as an opportunity to thrust himself further into the national spotlight.[45] The Subcommittee's creation provided Royall with a ready-made excuse to prevent Clay from carrying out the remaining executions before he stepped down as Military Governor.

---

[39] Buscher, 94.   [40] Earl, 273 n. 42.
[41] Taylor, *Final Report*, 97–8.   [42] Ibid., 98.
[43] Quoted in Thomas Alan Schwartz, *America's Germany: John J. McCloy and the Federal Republic of Germany* 158 (1991).
[44] Ibid., 158–9.   [45] Frei, 116.

E. The *Ministries* Dissent

While the Baldwin Subcommittee prepared for its public hearings, a new development refocused German and U.S. attention on the NMT trials: Judge Powers angrily dissented from the majority's judgment in the *Ministries* case. In his view, most of the convictions—particularly those for crimes against peace—were "incomprehensible," devoid of legal reasoning, and "not justified by the law or the facts."[46] Even worse, according to Judge Powers, the prosecution's entire theory of the case had been predicated on a retrograde notion of collective responsibility:

These attitudes reflect impatience with the idea that these defendants, as individuals, must be shown to have personally committed crimes according to the usual and customary standards or tests. They may also indicate a realization that the evidence in many instances is insufficient to establish guilt by such standards. They represent a concept of mass or collective guilt, under which men should be found guilty of a crime even though they knew nothing about it when it occurred, and it was committed by people over whom they had no responsibility or control.[47]

Judge Powers was not the first judge to dissent during the trials: Judge O'Connell had dissented from a number of sentences in *RuSHA*, and Judge Hebert had dissented from the overly-lenient judgment in *Farben*. But no judge had ever questioned the propriety of one of the NMT's convictions, so it was not surprising that Judge Powers' words were "more than enough evidence to convince the German clergy that along with the Army's proceedings, all war crimes trials carried out by the United States, including the Subsequent Nuremberg Proceedings, were tainted."[48] Within weeks, Bishop Wurm and Bishop Meiser flooded Clay's office with petitions attacking the NMT trials and demanding that the convicted defendants—particularly von Weizsaecker and Schwerin von Krosigk—be released.[49]

Powers' dissent also emboldened Joseph McCarthy to use the Baldwin Subcommittee, whose mandate was limited to the Malmedy trial, to attack the NMTs. Indeed, McCarthy opened the Subcommittee's first public session on 4 May 1949 by savagely attacking Judge Maguire and Judge Christianson's majority opinion in *Ministries*, particularly with regard to von Weizsaecker's conviction. McCarthy insisted that von Weizsaecker's good-motives defense was legitimate, claiming that it was "uncontradicted" that he "was the most valuable undercover man which the Allies had in Germany, starting in 1936." McCarthy also demanded that the panel force Maguire and Christianson to testify, arguing that "I think this committee should see what type of morons—and I use that term advisedly—are running the military court over there."[50]

Eleven days later, on May 15, General Clay's tenure as Military Governor came to an end. The death sentences against six Malmedy defendants were still pending, as were the 16 death sentences in *Pohl* and *Einsatzgruppen*, the Supreme Court

---

[46] XIV TWC 877–8.   [47] Ibid., 874.   [48] Earl, 275.
[49] Hébert, *Hitler's Generals*, 54.   [50] Maguire, 205.

having denied the condemned NMT defendants' habeas petitions on May 2. Clay would later apologize to McCloy for saddling him with the unpleasant responsibility, as High Commissioner, of deciding the fates of those men.[51]

F. The Deactivation of the OCC

It was in this toxic environment that the OCC was formally deactivated on 20 June 1949. The Central Secretariat remained in existence to deal with the paperwork associated with McCloy's impending review of the convictions in *Ministries*; it would be dissolved on November 15.[52]

On August 15, Taylor submitted his Final Report to Royall, the Secretary of the Army. In the "Unfinished Business" section, he emphasized the need to ensure that three categories of major war criminals whom the OCC had not been able to prosecute did not escape punishment entirely. First, there were the high-ranking Reich officials closely connected with the extermination program whom he had declined to include in the *Ministries* case.[53] Second, there were the individuals whom the OCC would have indicted but for the fact that it had been unable to extradite them from one of the occupied countries. As an example, Taylor mentioned General Hans Felber, the chief military commander in Serbia in 1943 and 1944, whom the OCC had wanted to include in the *Hostage* case.[54] Third, there were the five individuals who had been indicted in Nuremberg but never stood trial. Two of the five could not be tried: Gustav Krupp remained mentally unfit, and Otto Rasch, who had been indicted in *Einsatzgruppen*, had since died. Taylor considered a third, Max Brueggeman, a *Farben* indictee with a heart problem, to be relatively unimportant. But Taylor insisted that two others— Karl Engert and Field Marshal von Weichs—"should certainly stand trial if in the future their physical conditions permits." Engert, who had been indicted in the *Justice* case, had been Chief of the Penal Administration Division in the Reich Ministry of Justice and a Vice President of the People's Court. Von Weichs, who had been indicted in *High Command*, had been the head of all the German armed forces in the Balkans from 1943 to 1945 and thus "the commanding officer of Generals Rendulic, Felmy, Lanz, Dehner, von Leyser, and Speidel, all of whom were convicted and sentenced to long prison terms for transgressions of the laws of war."[55]

Taylor was understandably skeptical that these individuals would ever be brought to justice. He knew that it was too late to form additional tribunals, and he believed that Engert and von Weichs' crimes were too serious to be dealt with by denazification tribunals. That left German tribunals as the only option—and Taylor was fully aware that German opposition to the war-crimes program made prosecutions unlikely. He nevertheless urged Royall to push the German

---

[51] Thomas Alan Schwartz, "John J. McCloy and the Landsberg Cases," in *American Policy and the Reconstruction of West Germany* 433, 436 (Hartmut Lehmann ed., 1993).
[52] Taylor, *Final Report*, 94.   [53] Ibid.   [54] Ibid.   [55] Ibid., 95.

government anyway, cannily recognizing that the failure to prosecute would have its own didactic value:

> It is true that the prevailing trend and climate of political opinion in Germany makes it quite unlikely that the German authorities will eagerly pursue this course of action. But if the situation in Germany is indeed such that the Germans will not bring to trial men such as those who were deeply implicated in the extermination of European Jewry, the sooner that fact is apparent and generally understood the better it will be for all concerned.[56]

There is no evidence that Royall ever heeded Taylor's advice.

II. John J. McCloy and the Advisory Board on War Criminals

A. McCloy's Appointment

On 2 September 1949, McCloy became the High Commissioner for Germany. McCloy, a graduate of Harvard Law School, had spent the war as an Assistant Secretary in the War Department, a position in which he had dealt with some of the most difficult—and most controversial—military issues of the day. On some of those issues, he had been quite progressive. His Advisory Committee on Negro Troop Policies (the "McCloy Committee"), for example, had ultimately concluded that the use of segregated units undermined "military efficiency" and recommended, in March 1944, that black soldiers be used in combat.[57] On other issues, however, his views had been retrograde—with painful consequences. He had supported President Roosevelt's decision to intern the Japanese and had helped administer the program, notoriously telling Attorney General Biddle in early 1942 that "if it is a question of the safety of our country [and] the constitution why the constitution is just a scrap of paper to me."[58] He had also rejected the plaintive requests of Jewish groups to bomb Auschwitz, insisting—inaccurately, as more recent research has shown—that such an attack was "impracticable" and would divert resources from "decisive operations elsewhere."[59]

McCloy had also been deeply involved in the war-crimes program and the postwar reconstruction of Germany. He had turned down the position of High Commissioner in 1945, because he believed that a soldier was better suited to the role that would eventually become Military Governor; he had recommended that FDR appoint General Clay instead.[60] McCloy had also played an important role in the promulgation of JCS 1067/6, ensuring that it was neither too punitive nor too lenient and insisting that "denazification and demilitarization" were essential components of U.S. policy.[61] He had then later traveled to London to lobby the British to drop their desire to summarily execute the major war criminals.[62]

By the time McCloy assumed office, commuting the Dachau and NMT death sentences and freeing all of the remaining war criminals had become the official

---

[56] Taylor, *Final Report*, 94.   [57] Schwartz, *America's Germany*, 14.   [58] Ibid., 15–6.
[59] Ibid., 17.   [60] Ibid., 21.   [61] Ibid.   [62] Ibid., 21–2.

policy of the German government: the Federal Republic of Germany had been formed out of the French, British, and American occupation zones in May 1949, and one of the new Adenauer government's first acts was to publicly announce its intention to propose a general amnesty for defendants whose crimes were "committed in the confusion and economic distress."[63] The Adenauer government did not have the authority, however, to enact such an amnesty itself: the Occupation Statute of Germany, signed on 12 May 1949, had specifically reserved to the occupying powers "control of the care and treatment in German prisons of persons charged before or sentenced by the courts or tribunals of the occupying Powers or occupation authorities; over the carrying out of sentences imposed on them; and over questions of amnesty, pardon or release in relation to them."[64] The fate of the NMT and Dachau defendants thus remained in American hands.

The German government and the German church leaders almost immediately began to lobby McCloy to commute the NMT death sentences—unlike Clay, McCloy had jurisdiction only over the defendants convicted by the NMTs; General Thomas Handy, the Commander-in-Chief of the United States European Command (EUCOM) and Clay's successor, had jurisdiction over the defendants convicted in the Dachau trials.[65] Adenauer personally appealed to McCloy, citing the length of time the *Pohl* and *Einsatzgruppen* defendants had been awaiting execution—which was, of course, due largely to German lobbying—and the fact that Germany's new Basic Law, adopted on May 8, prohibited the death penalty.[66] Adenauer's appeals were echoed by his coalition partners, the Free Democrats and the German Party, and by Cardinal Joseph Frings, the head of the Fulda Bishops Conference, who insisted that the actions of the condemned prisoners did "not stem from a criminal disposition."[67]

Publicly, McCloy took a hard line on the Germans' requests, insisting that a general amnesty for the NMT defendants would "be taken as an abandonment of the principles established in the trials" and would imply that "those crimes have ... been sufficiently atoned for [and] that the German people should be allowed to forget them."[68] Privately, though, McCloy believed that a "solution" to the war-criminals problem was necessary, because the growing Soviet threat to Europe had put a premium on improved German-American relations.[69]

McCloy was far from alone in that belief among U.S. authorities. Between early 1948 and late 1949, fear of the Soviet Union had grown exponentially: Czechoslovakia had fallen in a shockingly brutal Soviet-backed coup in March 1948; the Soviets had withdrawn from the Control Council shortly thereafter; and—most dramatically—the Soviets had blockaded Berlin for nearly a year. At the same time, American sympathy

---

[63] Letter from the German Federal Government to the High Commissioner, undated, cited in Earl, 278.

[64] Occupation Statute, Art. 2(i).

[65] See Executive Order No. 10144, 21 July 1950.

[66] Schwartz, *America's Germany*, 159.

[67] Schwartz, *McCloy and Landsberg*, 438.

[68] Cited in Schwartz, *America's Germany*, 160.

[69] Earl, 278.

toward the Germans was growing as the public became aware that there had been significant, if ultimately futile, resistance to the Nazis within Germany.[70] Even Clay, who was far more uncompromising than McCloy, acknowledged that OMGUS's "growing awareness" of the resistance movement "tended to create a greater respect toward the German people and therefore a greater disposition to accelerate a revival of German governmental controls."[71]

In this climate, the temptation to use parole and clemency programs as a means of improving American-German relations was nearly overwhelming. But the new willingness to consider such programs was not merely strategic: occupation authorities also sincerely believed that "efforts to ensure fairness in trying and sentencing war criminals" would also re-educate and democratize ordinary Germans by demonstrating "the superior moral standards of a democratic society."[72] That was a tragic miscalculation.

B. Creation of the War Crimes Modification Board

Formal efforts to consider clemency began in July 1949 on the EUCOM side, with a committee of the War Crimes Branch recommending the creation of a five-member War Crimes Modification Board that would have the authority to "equalize" the sentences imposed in the Dachau trials—precisely what the Simpson Commission had recommended months earlier—and to grant medical parole, where appropriate, to seriously ill prisoners. The committee emphasized that the board would need to avoid undue leniency: "sentences should be reduced to minimum levels consistent with maintaining respect for the occupying powers who represent the victorious United Nations; penalties as reduced must still be severe enough to act as punishment for the offenders and to deter future would-be violators of the rules of warfare."[73] And it insisted that the board must not function, overtly or covertly, as an appellate court: although "defense counsel and counsel representing the Government" could be heard, "[t]he case will not be retried" and "[n]o new witnesses will be heard or other evidence submitted. The re-argument will be made on the record of the case as it now exists."[74]

Even that limited mandate troubled some officials in the Theater Judge Advocate's Office. Lt. Col. John Awtry, the Assistant Chief of the War Crimes Branch, believed that it was "illogical and unsound" to create different clemency boards for the Dachau and NMT prisoners and unwise for the United States to review sentences unilaterally, without consulting the French and the British, given that the war-crimes program had always been an inter-allied undertaking.[75] Similarly, Awtry's superior in the War Crimes Branch, Colonel Wade M. Fleischer, believed that releasing Dachau prisoners would not promote democratization and re-education,

[70] Schwartz, *America's Germany*, 158.
[71] Cited in ibid., 158 n. 3.
[72] Buscher, 50.
[73] Memo from Awtry to Chief, War Crimes Division, 1 June 1949, NA-549–2236-3, at 1–2.
[74] Memo from Awtry to Fleischer, 10 May 1949, NA-549–2236-3, at 1.
[75] Memo from Awtry to Record, 28 July 1949, NA-549–2236-3, at 2.

because those individuals would "undoubtedly commence to work against the occupation authorities in Western Germany."[76]

Fleischer's concern was echoed by the Baldwin Subcommittee's final report, which was released on October 13. The Subcommittee acknowledged—as had been found by previous investigations—that mock trials and physical force had occasionally been used to convince defendants to confess, but it concluded that there was absolutely no evidence that any of the defendants had been tortured.[77] More dramatically, the Subcommittee insisted that "attacks on the war-crimes trials in general and the Malmedy trial in particular" were motivated, in large part, by the desire to revive German nationalism and to discredit the American occupation of Germany.[78] Indeed, ironically turning the tables on its former member, Joseph McCarthy, the Subcommittee claimed that "[t]here is evidence that at least a part of this effort is attempting to establish a close liaison with Communist Russia"—a "sensational thesis" that Frei insists was "by no means as absurd as public opinion would have had it."[79]

None of these concerns, however, were enough to derail American plans to offer clemency to the Dachau prisoners. On November 28, EUCOM formally created the War Crimes Modification Board.[80] EUCOM avoided using the word "clemency" in the name of the board, "to prevent erroneous impression that all prisoners may anticipate substantial reduction or remission of all or part of their sentences."[81]

C. McCloy's Advisory Board on Clemency for War Criminals

The creation of the War Crimes Modification Board for the Dachau prisoners made it nearly inevitable that a similar review mechanism would be created for the NMT prisoners—as reflected by Awtry's comment, both EUCOM and HICOG were sensitive to the criticism that differential treatment of the two would evoke.[82] That development, however, was still a few months away. In the interim, on 20 December 1949, McCloy and Handy created a good-conduct program for the Dachau and NMT prisoners that reduced sentences five days per month.[83] McCloy insisted that the program was "in no sense an indication of any attitude of unwarranted leniency on my part towards war criminals," but it meant that 60 prisoners would be released before Christmas, including at least five NMT defendants: Josef Alstoetter from *Justice*, Georg von Schnitzler from *Farben*, Ernst-Wilhelm Bohle and Emil Puhl from *Ministries*, and Karl Hollidt from *High Command*.[84] McCloy would later increase the reduction to ten days per month, leading to the release of nearly all of the remaining *Flick* and *Farben* defendants by

---

[76] Cited in Buscher, 59.   [77] Frei, 117.   [78] Ibid., 118.
[79] Ibid.   [80] Buscher, 59.
[81] Memo from Johnson to Secretary of Army, Washington, 14 Dec. 1949, NA-549-2236-3, at 1.
[82] Buscher, 59.
[83] Ibid., 60.
[84] OCCWC, List of Defendants of the United States Tribunals, Nuernberg, With Disposition Made in Each Case, undated, NA-238-213-1.

September 1950[85]—an act that caused such controversy that even the State Department, which had enthusiastically supported EUCOM and HICOG's clemency programs, told McCloy to warn it before releasing any additional NMT prisoners.[86]

Once the good-conduct program was in place, McCloy began to push for a full-fledged NMT clemency program. His efforts were no doubt furthered by Tribunal IV's decision in early December, discussed in Chapter 4, to set aside von Weiszaecker and Woermann's convictions for crimes against peace and Steengracht von Moyland's conviction for the war crimes of murder and mistreatment of prisoners of war.[87] Judge Christianson dissented from all three decisions, insisting that the evidence was more than sufficient to sustain their convictions. Indeed, he stated that "[a] re-examination of the evidence with respect to the actions of defendant von Weizsaecker in connection with the aggression against Czechoslovakia deepens my conviction that said defendant is guilty under said count one."[88]

Judge Powers had originally dissented from the convictions, so the decision to set them aside indicated that Judge Maguire had changed his mind at some point between April 11, when the judgment was released, and December 12, when the convictions were set aside. William Caming, one of the prosecutors in *Ministries*, wrote decades later that "Judge Maguire's Memorandum Opinion is embarrassingly vague and devoid of any rationale for his change of heart. I can only surmise what the impelling personal factors were."[89] Peter Maguire, the Judge's grandson, suspects that the "personal factors" included a desire "to appease the right wing of the Republican Party"—Judge Maguire had decided to run for the Oregon Supreme Court as a Republican in the fall of 1949.[90] (He lost.)

A week after the reconsideration of *Ministries* and the predictable German rejection of von Weizsaecker's continued imprisonment—Theo Kordt, a leader of the German resistance, immediately described von Weizsaecker's situation as "a new Dreyfus case"[91]—McCloy urged General Handy to expand the jurisdiction of the War Crimes Modification Board to include the NMT prisoners. That effort failed, however, because Dean Acheson, the Secretary of State, opposed it. Acheson insisted that the nature of the Dachau and NMT trials were too different to justify a joint clemency board and that a joint board would facilitate German efforts to use the problems with the Malmedy trial to taint the NMT trials.[92]

McCloy was undeterred. Although he continued to publicly criticize German attempts to discredit the war-crimes program and their demands for a general amnesty,[93] he privately promised Cardinal Frings that he would create a board to review all of the NMT sentences and "prepare a practical solution."[94] He made good on that promise in February 1950, when he convinced a reluctant Acheson to give him permission to create his own "War Crimes Clemency Board." Acheson was particularly worried that "individual groups" would misunderstand the

---

[85] Schwartz, *McCloy and Landsberg*, 439.   [86] Ibid., 439 n. 28.   [87] XIV TWC 946.
[88] Ibid., 960, Christianson Separate Memorandum.
[89] Cited in Maguire, 208.   [90] Ibid.   [91] Ibid.
[92] Memo from Acheson to McCloy, 9 Feb. 1950, NA-549–2237-2, at 1.
[93] Buscher, 60.   [94] Cited in ibid.

decision to create the Board—"a veiled reference to their concern that Jewish organizations would criticize any further review" of the NMT sentences.[95] McCloy thus promised to take "special precautions" to avoid negative publicity.[96]

McCloy established his review board—officially named the Advisory Board on Clemency for War Criminals, ignoring EUCOM's conclusion that referring to clemency would inflate German expectations—on 18 July 1950. Unfortunately, his public announcement betrayed a fundamental uncertainty about the Advisory Board's mandate. On the one hand, McCloy pointed out that "[t]he availability to the individual defendant of an appeal to executive clemency is a salutary part of the administration of justice"—a justification that reflected the traditional conception of clemency as an act of grace. But he also insisted that "[i]t is particularly appropriate that the cases of defendants convicted of war crimes be given an executive review because no appellate court review has been provided."[97] It was thus unclear from the Advisory Board's inception whether it was intended to function as a clemency board, as an appellate court, or as both—a lack of clarity that would have disastrous consequences.

The Board's mandate was further muddied by McCloy's staffing decisions. After Chief Justice Vinson refused to allow him to recruit federal judges, McCloy appointed David W. Peck as the Board's chairman. At the time, Peck was serving as the Presiding Justice of the New York Supreme Court's Appellate Division—a strange choice for a Board that was not supposed to function as an appellate body. McCloy then rounded out the "Peck Panel" by appointing Conrad Snow, an Assistant Legal Advisor to the State Department who had served on an earlier War Department clemency board for U.S. soldiers, and Frederick A. Moran, who was the chairman of the New York State Board of Parole.[98] Moran had a background in social work and was a fervent believer in parole as "an instrument of rehabilitation."[99]

McCloy's decision to create the Peck Panel outraged the OCC. Reacting to the possibility that McCloy would commute the death sentences of the 16 "red jackets" in Landsberg Prison—the name given to the condemned NMT defendants on account of the distinctive jackets they wore[100]—Taylor angrily (and presciently) complained to a reporter for the *New York Post* that "[t]he retreat from Nuremberg is on. I fear such a review would work to the benefit of those who have wealthy and powerful influences behind them."[101] Nor was outrage limited to the prosecution. Michael Musmanno, the presiding judge in *Einsatzgruppen*, told the same reporter that the death sentences imposed in the case were "eminently just and proper" and insisted that the tribunal had "leaned over backwards to give the defendants every possible opportunity" to prove their innocence.[102]

[95] Schwartz, *America's Germany*, 160–1.   [96] Schwartz, *McCloy and Landsberg*, 441.
[97] Cited in Maguire, 212.   [98] Schwartz, *America's Germany*, 162.
[99] Maguire, 216.   [100] Earl, 278.
[101] John Hohenberg, "Stalling Baffles U.S. Prosecutor," *New York Post*, 3 Feb. 1950, A2.
[102] John Hohenberg, "Nuremberg Judge Upholds Doom on 16 Nazis Who Killed Million Jews," *New York Post*, 3 Feb. 1950, A2.

D. The Work of the Advisory Board

McCloy set out the parameters of the Advisory Board's authority in a July 18 memo—the same day that he announced the Board's creation. The memo made clear that the Board could not review the defendants' convictions: the Panel was prohibited from considering either "questions relating to the jurisdiction or composition of the Tribunals before which the defendants were tried" or the tribunals' decisions on "questions of law and fact."[103] What the Board *could* do, however, was far more uncertain. On the one hand, it was authorized "to consider disparities among sentences for comparable offenses and such other facts as tend to show that the sentence imposed on the defendant was excessive"—a vague mandate that was somewhat akin to traditional clemency review. But it was also authorized to take into account "the physical condition and family situation of the particular defendant"—a power that "came dangerously close to a parole board function."[104]

The Board officially began work in Munich on 11 July 1950. Over the next six weeks, Peck, Snow, and Moran "heard 50 counsel representing 90 of the defendants" and "read the judgments (over 3,000 pages) in the cases of 104 defendants now in confinement as a result of the [NMT] trials, the appeals filed by counsel, the petitions for clemency and all supporting documents."[105] The Board also received recommendations from a panel of eight German consultants appointed by the West German Federal Ministry of Justice, who were given access to the same documents.[106] The hearings themselves, which began on August 4, unfolded "at a dizzying pace": counsel for the defendants were given 30 minutes to speak, and then the Board deliberated for 15 minutes before reaching a decision. Neither the oral arguments nor the deliberations were transcribed.[107]

There were a number of problems with the Board's operating procedure. Most obviously, although the Board considered the views of both the lawyers for the defendants and the German consultants, it never heard—either orally or in writing—from the judges or the prosecution.[108] In fact, the Board simply ignored Ben Ferencz's offer to consult with it, even though Ferencz was still in Germany.[109] Had the Board reviewed the trial transcripts and the evidence considered by the judges, that failure might not have been so problematic. By the Board's own admission, though, in nearly every case it limited itself to reading the judgments, which contained only a fraction of the evidence that supported the convictions.[110]

---

[103] McCloy, Establishment of Advisory Board on Clemency, 18 July 1950, NA-238-213-1.
[104] Buscher, 62.
[105] Review of Sentences by Military Governor and U.S. High Commissioner for Germany, XV TWC 1157.
[106] Hébert, *Hitler's Generals*, 161.
[107] Cited in ibid.
[108] Goetz, 672.
[109] Kai Bird, *The Chairman: John J. McCloy and the Making of the American Establishment* 365 (1992).
[110] Schwartz, *America's Germany*, 164. The Board referred to the trial record "in only two or three instances." Schwartz, *McCloy and Landsberg*, 446.

Nothing prevented the Board from conducting a more thorough review; as Ferencz later pointed out, the records of the *Einsatzgruppen* trial were stored in the basement of the same house in Munich in which the Board met throughout the hearings.[111] The Board's failure to go beyond the judgments was thus indefensible, particularly given that—as we will see below—the Board's "clemency" decisions were often based on its disagreement with the tribunals' assessment of the strength of the prosecution's evidence.

E. The Advisory Board's Recommendations

The Advisory Board submitted its report to McCloy on 28 August 1950. Not surprisingly, the Board disagreed with the vast majority of the sentences imposed by the tribunals and affirmed by General Clay, recommending that McCloy commute the sentences of seven of the 15 defendants sentenced to death and reduce the sentences of 77 of the 90 defendants sentenced to terms of imprisonment.[112] Many of the suggested reductions were significant, such as the Board's recommendation that McCloy reduce Milch's sentence from life to 15 years[113] and reduce Gerhard Nosske's sentence—imposed because the Einsatzkommando he commanded had executed hundreds of Jews—from life to ten years. Even more dramatically, the Board recommended that McCloy commute Heinz Schubert and Willy Seibert's death sentences to time served.[114] Both Seibert and Schubert (a descendant of the legendary composer) were high-ranking officers in Ohlendorf's Einsatzgruppe D, which Ohlendorf admitted had killed more than 90,000 Jews.

The Advisory Board's recommendations met significant resistance from U.S. officials involved in the war-crimes program. John Raymond, a State Department official who had been one of Clay's legal advisors for the sentence reviews, believed that the proposed reductions were so lenient—particularly for Siebert and Schubert—that they would undermine the legitimacy of the NMTs.[115] Robert Bowie, HICOG's general counsel and McCloy's trusted advisor, was even more critical. He agreed with Raymond about the potential impact of the report: "certain statements by the Board suggest that they have striven to be as lenient as possible, and I am concerned lest the report as a whole create the impression of a repudiation of the Nuremberg trials." He was particularly incensed by the Board's recommendation of clemency for Hermann Reinecke, Walter Warlimont, and Georg von Kuechler, defendants in *High Command*, because of their "alleged subordinate positions"—as he pointed out, von Kuechler was a Field Marshal and Warlimont and Reinecke were Lieutenant Generals.[116] And he was so disturbed by the Board's soft-pedaling of the crimes committed by the defendants in the *Medical* case and *Einsatzgruppen* that he directed his staff to prepare their own reports for McCloy explaining why the defendants did not deserve significant sentence reductions.[117]

---

[111] Bower, 370–1.   [112] Cited in Hébert, *Hitler's Generals*, 163.
[113] Advisory Board on Clemency Report, 28 Aug. 1950, TTP-5-3-2-11, at 3.
[114] Earl, 283.   [115] Quoted in Maguire, 218.
[116] Schwartz, *McCloy and Landsberg*, 446.   [117] Ibid.

Raymond and Bowie's concerns were valid, because the Board's approach to sentence equalization was no less flawed than its operating procedures. The Board justified equalization reductions for a number of high-ranking defendants by arguing that "although their titles may have sounded impressive... in reality they were little more than common members of a criminal organization."[118] To reach that conclusion, the Board had grouped all of the petitioners together and then placed them "in proper relation to each other and the programs in which they participated," ostensibly revealing the "differences in authority and action" between them.[119] That procedure inevitably understated the culpability of the defendants at the bottom of the pyramid, no matter how grave their crimes: as Schwartz points out, "[w]hen compared with men like Otto Ohlendorf or Paul Blobel, who supervised and directed thousands of murders, the bureaucrats and industrialists seemed far less criminal and deserving of punishment."[120]

To be sure, it was appropriate for the Board to compare the defendants horizontally, ensuring that defendants who had committed the same crimes received roughly similar sentences. That is what Tribunal II had done in *Pohl* when it concluded that Georg Loerner and August Frank deserved equal sentences in light of their "similarity in length of service with WVHA, and as deputy to Pohl, a consideration of their respective ranks, and of the counts on which they were found guilty."[121] The Board, however, could not have made accurate horizontal comparisons simply by reading the judgments; as the *Einsatzgruppen* tribunal made clear, because the evidence against many of the defendants went far beyond what was needed to convict, the judgments did not need to recount all of a defendant's criminal acts:

[W]hile emphasis throughout the trial has been on the subject of murder, the defendants are charged also in counts one and two with crimes against humanity and violations of laws or customs of war which include but are not limited to atrocities, enslavement, deportation, imprisonment, torture, and other inhumane acts committed against civilian populations. Thus, if and where a conclusion of guilt is reached, such conclusion is not based alone on the charge of murder but on all committed acts coming within the purview of crimes against humanity and war crimes. In each adjudication, without its being stated, the verdict is based upon the entire record.[122]

The Board's equalization procedure also led to excessively lenient sentences even when defendants were similarly situated. The Board recommended reducing the sentences in *Krupp*, for example, because they were considerably longer than the sentences in *Farben* and *Flick*. But the *Krupp* sentences were not the problem—the problem was that the *Farben* and *Flick* sentences were far too lenient, because the tribunals had acquitted the defendants of crimes they had clearly committed. Nevertheless, because the Board was not empowered to increase sentences,

118   Advisory Board on Clemency Report, 12.
119   Cited in Schwartz, *America's Germany*, 163–4.
120   Ibid., 164.
121   *Pohl*, Supplemental Judgment, V TWC 1183.
122   *Einsatzgruppen*, IV TWC 509–10.

"equalization" required it to reduce the *Krupp* sentences to match the ones in *Farben* and *Flick*.

In addition to adopting flawed equalization procedures, the Board also ignored its mandate not to reconsider the tribunals' decisions on "questions of law and fact." Time and again, the Board concluded "that the facts as stated in the judgments themselves are not sufficient to establish beyond a reasonable doubt the defendant's responsibility for specific crimes."[123] Its treatment of Franz Six, convicted of war crimes and crimes against humanity in *Einsatzgruppen* for his role as Chief of Vorkommando Moscow, is a striking example: the Board justified its recommendation that his sentence be reduced from 20 years to time served by arguing the war crimes and crimes against humanity charges were "not proved beyond a reasonable doubt."[124] How the Board convinced itself of that fact is a mystery, given that—as Earl notes—"they neither reviewed the trial transcript nor any of the evidence submitted by the prosecution in reaching their decision."[125] Instead, the Board simply relied on Tribunal II's discussion of Six's guilt, which ran all of five pages in the *Einsatzgruppen* judgment.

The Advisory Board's willingness to reweigh the evidence was based on its curious interpretation of its mandate. Although it acknowledged that it was required to accept the tribunal's "judgments on the law or the facts," the Board nevertheless claimed "that the authority to review sentences required a differentiation between specific facts found and established in the evidence and conclusions that may have been drawn therefrom. We have considered ourselves bound by the former but not by the latter."[126] In other words, the Board believed that it was required to accept a tribunal's factual findings (such as that a defendant personally executed Jews) and its legal conclusions (that executing Jews was a war crime or crime against humanity), but was nevertheless free to reject the tribunal's conclusion that the facts and applicable law meant that the defendant was guilty. But that was nonsensical: the only way to acquit a defendant in such a situation was to either reject the facts (insisting that the evidence did not prove that the defendant personally executed Jews) or reject the law (that executing Jews was not necessarily a war crime or crime against humanity)—precisely what the Board's mandate prohibited.

F. McCloy's Clemency Decisions

Although McCloy created the Advisory Board in February 1950 and received its report that August, he did not make final decisions on clemency until the end of January 1951. Much had changed in the interim. Most obviously, on 25 June 1950, North Korean troops had launched an "all-out offensive" against the Republic of

---

[123] Cited in Schwartz, *McCloy and Landsberg*, 444.
[124] Earl, 284.
[125] Ibid.
[126] Advisory Board on Clemency Report, 3.

South Korea, an aggressive act that, by September, had led to a "full-scale war" involving American troops.[127]

The outbreak of the Korean War had a profound effect on McCloy, convincing him to drop his long-standing opposition to German rearmament.[128] It had a similar effect on the U.S and its allies in the West,[129] who responded to North Korea's aggression—supported, of course, by Russia and China—by developing plans for consolidating the military forces of Western European states, including Germany, into a European Defense Community (EDC). Such a community, they hoped, would be able to rearm Germany while preventing it from acting on any imperial ambitions it might still possess.[130]

Western Europe's plans for an EDC doomed the war-crimes program. The United States and its allies needed Germany now more than ever—and the German government knew it, rarely missing an opportunity to remind McCloy that its willingness to contribute "to the defense of the West" might depend upon the United States' willingness to free the NMT and Dachau prisoners, particularly those facing execution. Adenauer's chief advisors on rearmament, Generals Adolf Heusinger and Hans Speidel (the brother of Wilhelm Speidel, convicted in the *Hostage* case), told McCloy's liaison in Bonn that "if the prisoners at Landsberg were hanged, Germany as an armed ally against the East was an illusion."[131] That claim was echoed by a group from the Bundestag that represented all of Germany's important non-communist political parties, who insisted to McCloy in early January that the West's desire for a military alliance with Germany justified commuting the death sentences.[132]

McCloy responded to the German pressure—which included death threats that forced him to have bodyguards assigned to his children[133]—with admirable openness, traveling around Germany to speak to ordinary people about the cases, considering evidence and petitions no matter their source, even meeting personally with some of the NMT prisoners in Landsberg.[134] At the same time, however, he expressed frustration at the Germans' repeated attempts to delegitimize the war-crimes program. During the meeting with the Bundestag deputies mentioned above, for example, McCloy reminded the group that the NMT and Dachau trials were reactions to the Nazis' "spasm of criminality" and decried the desire "to put things under the carpet and refuse to acknowledge what really happened."[135]

---

[127] Maguire, 216.   [128] Schwartz, *McCloy and Landsberg*, 444.

[129] Taylor was one of the leading dissenters from this view. As he wrote in a 1950 issue of *Harper's Magazine*, "[s]urely the withdrawal of American troops from Germany would open up to the Russians opportunities beyond their wildest present imaginings, and this would be so whether or not we were to leave behind us a West German 'army'. For the Russians are not to be frightened by five or ten or even twenty German divisions. They are presently held in check by fear of war with the United States and our allies." Telford Taylor, "Arms and the Germans," *Harper's*, Mar. 1950, at 25–6.

[130] Hébert, *Hitler's Generals*, 164–5.

[131] Cited in Schwartz, *McCloy and Landsberg*, 445.

[132] Cited in ibid.

[133] Schwartz, *America's Germany*, 166.

[134] Ibid., 167.

[135] Quoted in Hébert, *Hitler's Generals*, 166.

At the end of January 1951, McCloy retreated to his home to "wrestl[e] with his soul and his heart" about the clemency decisions.[136] Finally, on January 31— one day after Heusinger and Speidel visited him to make a last-ditch plea for clemency—McCloy went public with his decisions. Claiming that he had "striven to temper justice with mercy," he released the following statement:

Sentences have been reduced in a very large number of cases. They have been reduced wherever there appeared a legitimate basis for clemency. Such reductions have been granted where the sentence was out of line with sentences for crimes of similar gravity in other cases; where the reduction appeared justified on the ground of the relatively subordinate authority and responsibility of the defendants; where new evidence, not available to the court, supported such clemency... In certain cases my decision to grant clemency has been influenced by the acute illness of the prisoner or other special circumstances of a similar nature.[137]

All in all, McCloy reduced the sentences of 77 of the 89 defendants who had submitted clemency petitions. (Fifteen defendants considered by the Advisory Board had since been released through the good-conduct program.[138]) Of the 69 petitioners sentenced to terms of imprisonment, only five were denied clemency: Wilhelm List and Walter Kuntze in the *Hostage* case, both of whom McCloy suggested might be eligible for medical parole[139]; and Hermann Reinecke, Hermann Hoth, and Hans Reinhardt in *High Command*. Of the 15 petitioners sentenced to death, only five were denied commutation: Otto Ohlendorf, Paul Blobel, Werner Braune, and Erich Naumann in *Einsatzgruppen*, and Oswald Pohl.

The most striking aspect of McCloy's "Landsberg Report" is that, with very few exceptions, he avoided explaining individual clemency decisions in favor of general comments about each of the 10 NMT cases he considered.[140] Indeed, perhaps revealing his biases, McCloy spent far more time discussing why he had decided *not* to grant clemency to the five defendants sentenced to death. A complete list of McCloy's decisions can be found in Appendix A. What follows is an overview of his most important—and often quite problematic—decisions in each case:

Medical

There was nothing McCloy could do for the seven condemned defendants, because they had already been executed. But he reduced the sentences of all nine petitioners, noting that although it was "difficult to find room for clemency," he agreed with the Advisory Board's finding that "lack of primary responsibility, age, and limited participation" justified the reductions.[141] Some of the reductions were quite

---

[136] Ibid., 167.

[137] Statement of McCloy, 31 Jan. 1951, TTP-5-3-2-11, at 2.

[138] Telford Taylor, "The Nazis Go Free," *The Nation*, 24 Feb. 1951, at 171.

[139] McCloy Clemency Decisions, 31 Jan. 1951, TTP-5-3-2-11, at 7. McCloy directed that medical examinations be conducted on the two men. Why he had not previously done so is unclear, because he was willing to immediately release Schlegelberger on medical parole. Ibid., 4.

[140] All of the defendants in *Flick* and *Farben* had either been released or were already eligible for parole. Ibid., 6.

[141] Ibid., 2.

significant: Oskar Schroeder's life sentence was reduced to 15 years, despite Tribunal I finding that he had used his position as Chief of the Luftwaffe's Medical Service to initiate the sea-water experiments and promote the typhoid experiments at Dachau[142]; Gerhard Rose's life sentence was reduced to 15 years even though the tribunal found that he had instigated and directly participated in the typhus experiments conducted at Buchenwald and Natzweiler.[143]

Milch

The Advisory Board had recommended reducing Milch's life sentence to 15 years because of his "instability of temperament due to nervous strain, aggravated by a head injury." McCloy acknowledged Milch's "almost violent advocacy of and pressure for slave labor and disregard for the life and health of workers," but nevertheless agreed with the Board's "sharp reduction."[144]

Justice

McCloy "had difficulty in finding a justification for clemency in any of these cases." He nevertheless significantly reduced the sentences of all seven petitioners "for reasons such as limited responsibility": three from life to 20 years; one from life to immediate release for medical reasons; and three from ten years to time served. Two of the life-sentence decisions are particularly notable. McCloy reduced Oswald Rothaug's sentence to 20 years—the same Oswald Rothaug who, according to Tribunal III, had "identified himself" with and "gave himself utterly to" the Nazi program of racial persecution and had "participated in the crime of genocide."[145] And he released Franz Schlegelberger, who bore "primary responsibility" for the Night and Fog Decree,[146] on medical parole.

Pohl

As noted, McCloy found "no basis" for commuting Oswald Pohl's death sentence. But he did reduce the 14 other sentences, including one from death to nine years, four from life to either 15 or 20 years, and seven from 10, 15, or 20 years to time served. McCloy acknowledged that reducing Franz Eirenschmalz's sentence from death to nine years was a "radical commutation," but he insisted that the reduction was warranted "due to the introduction of new evidence dissociating him from the offenses on which the original death sentence was chiefly based," which had rendered "his individual connection with exterminations . . . remote."[147] McCloy never disclosed the new evidence—nor did he explain how it undercut Tribunal II's conclusion that Eirenschmalz ordered and supervised the construction of concentration-camp crematoria despite knowing that they would be used to carry out the Final Solution.[148]

---

[142] *Medical*, II TWC 210–6.   [143] Ibid., 267–71.
[144] McCloy Clemency Decisions, 3.   [145] *Justice*, III TWC 1156.
[146] Ibid., 1083.   [147] McCloy Clemency Decisions, 5.   [148] *Pohl*, V TWC 1030–1.

Hostage

Although McCloy refused to reduce the sentences given to List and Kuntze, he reduced all of the other sentences on the ground that the "other officers charged with excessive reprisals...had lesser responsibility or, in some cases, showed evidence of humane considerations."[149] Both rationales were questionable. Wilhelm Speidel received the most significant reduction, from 20 years to time served, despite Tribunal V's conclusion that he was responsible, as Military Governor of Greece, for more than 1,000 illegal executions[150]—a stunning act of clemency that at least one commenter attributed not to "lesser responsibility" or "humane considerations," but to the fact that Speidel was the brother of Hans Speidel, the Adenauer advisor who was then involved in negotiating German rearmament with the Allies.[151] Ernst Dehner also had his sentence reduced from seven years to time served, even though his soldiers had executed hundreds of civilians.[152] Dehner's sentence was already lenient, given the gravity of his crimes; a further reduction on the ground of "lesser responsibility" was hardly warranted. Moreover, although there were, in fact, "human considerations" justifying a lesser sentence—Dehner had attempted to mitigate the harshness of some of the orders he received from his superiors—Tribunal V had already taken them into account.[153] In fact, the tribunal made clear that it had taken mitigating factors such as "humane considerations" into account for all of the defendants.[154]

RuSHA

McCloy significantly reduced the sentences of all six petitioners, in three instances from 10 or 15 years to time served, based on "the relatively restricted nature of the relationship of these defendants to the crimes, their relatively subordinate roles, and certain other extenuating circumstances."[155] It is unfortunate that McCloy did not discuss his specific decisions, because it is difficult to see why—to take only one example—Heinz Brueckner deserved to have his 15-year sentence reduced to time served. Tribunal I found that Brueckner, who was the Chief of the VoMI department dedicated to "Safeguarding German Folkdom in the Reich," had "in the course of the immense VoMI operations bec[o]me deeply involved in measures carried out under the Germanization program," including forced evacuation and resettlement, Germanization, and the use of slave labor.[156]

Einsatzgruppen

As noted above, McCloy commuted 10 of the 15 death sentences—four to life imprisonment, one to 25 years, one to 20 years, two to 15 years, and two to 10 years. In doing so—and allegedly "with difficulty"—McCloy went beyond the recommendations of the Advisory Board and commuted three death sentences that

---

[149] McCloy Clemency Decisions, 8.   [150] *Hostage*, XI TWC 1315–7.
[151] Anatole Goldstein, "The Burial of Nuremberg," Institute of Jewish Affairs, Records of the World Jewish Congress, Subseries 1, Box 121, Document 17, at 6.
[152] *Hostage*, XI TWC 1297–8.   [153] Ibid., 1299.   [154] Ibid., 1317.
[155] McCloy Clemency Decisions, 8.   [156] *RuSHA*, V TWC 140, 159–60.

the Board had recommended confirming: Waldemar Klingelhoefer, Adolf Ott, and Martin Sandberger.[157] McCloy did, however, reject the Board's recommendation that Siebert and Schubert's death sentences be commuted to time served; they received 15 and 10 years, respectively.

Once again, McCloy relied on undisclosed "new evidence" to justify his clemency decisions. McCloy claimed, for example, that "injustice would be done" by executing Haensch and Steimle, because "new and persuasive evidence which has recently been made available" substantially lessened "the directness of their connection with the crimes." He thus commuted Haensch's death sentence to 15 years and Steimle's death sentence to 20 years.[158]

Krupp

McCloy's most dramatic clemency decisions benefited the seven *Krupp* petitioners. He not only reduced all of the sentences to time served, he also—echoing Judge Anderson's dissenting opinion[159]—countermanded the confiscation of Alfried Krupp's property. In defense of those reductions, McCloy insisted that Tribunal III's judgment made it "extremely difficult to allocate individual guilt among the respective defendants" and argued that "whatever guilt these defendants may have shared for having taken a consenting part in either offense, it was no greater in these cases than that involved in the *Farben* and *Flick* cases."[160]

The problem with the latter rationale was discussed earlier: the *Krupp* sentences were not too tough; the *Farben* and *Flick* judgments were too lenient, because the defendants had been wrongly acquitted of a number of crimes. The former rationale, however, was even less persuasive. The most significant problem with McCloy's "allocation of guilt" rationale was that Tribunal III's sentences were based on the evidence presented at trial, whereas McCloy—like the Advisory Board before him—reviewed only the tribunal's judgment. Moreover, the judgment itself was anything but ambiguous: although the indictment discussed the crimes of the Krupp firm as a whole, the 122-page judgment provided a comprehensive and detailed accounting of each defendant's responsibility for the firm's crimes. Indeed, the tribunal specifically held that "[t]he mere fact without more that a defendant was a member of the Krupp Directorate or an official of the firm is not sufficient" for criminal responsibility,[161] and insisted—in the final paragraph of the judgment—that "[t]he nature and extent" of the defendants' participation "was not the same in all cases and therefore these differences will be taken into consideration in the imposition of the sentences upon them."[162]

McCloy defended returning Alfried Krupp's property on two grounds. First, he argued that, because "even those guilty of participation in the most heinous crimes have not suffered confiscation of their property," he believed that "confiscation in this single case constitutes discrimination against this defendant unjustified by any

---

[157] Earl, 287.   [158] McCloy Clemency Decisions, 10.
[159] *Krupp*, Anderson Dissent, IX TWC 1453.
[160] McCloy Clemency Decisions, 13.
[161] *Krupp*, IX TWC 1448.   [162] Ibid., 1449.

considerations attaching peculiarly to him." Second, he noted that confiscation of property "is repugnant to American concepts of justice."[163]

The first ground was literally correct, although it conveniently overlooked the difference between confiscating the property of an industrialist and confiscating the property of a soldier or government official. But the second ground was irrelevant. As discussed in Chapter 5, U.S. law did not apply to the NMT trials and Law No. 10 specifically empowered the tribunals to order the "forfeiture of property."[164] Invoking U.S. law to trump a specific provision of Law No. 10 was thus *ultra vires*.

The Krupp petitioners, it is worth noting, expected to be granted clemency. As Bower points out, they knew full well what German rearmament meant for them:

A room had been set aside at Landsberg for the Krupp directors to discuss corporate business, and directors and officials would come from Essen with the necessary documents to plan the company's programme for rapid expansion to meet Western demands in Korea. Eating and drinking the best food and wines available, Alfried and his fellow convicts took pleasure in insulting the very people who put them there.[165]

The return of Krupp's fortune also benefited Earl Carroll, the lawyer Tribunal IIII had refused to permit Alfried to hire prior to trial. Carroll worked with Krupp's German attorney, Otto Kranzbuehler, on Alfried's petition for clemency. According-ing to William Manchester, "[t]he terms of Caroll's employment were simple. He was to get Krupp out of prison and get his property restored. The fee was to be 5 percent of everything he could recover. Carroll got Krupp out and his fortune returned, receiving for his five-year job a fee of, roughly, $25 million."[166]

Ministries

McCloy followed the recommendations of the Advisory Board and reduced the sentences of all the petitioners, including three 10- and 15-year sentences to time served. Gottlob Berger's reduction from 25 to 10 years is particularly illuminating, because McCloy openly admitted that he believed he had the authority to provide appellate review of the tribunals' judgments, disapproving convictions with which he disagreed. Berger's sentence was based in part on the murder of a French General, Gustave-Marie-Maurice Mesny, while in transit between two POW camps. Tribunal IV discussed Berger's responsibility for the murder at length, concluding that Berger, as the Chief of POW affairs, had jurisdiction over Mesny at the time of the murder, knew that the murder was being planned by his subordin-ates, and yet did nothing to prevent it[167]—a classic case of command responsibility. McCloy nevertheless decided to "eliminate entirely from the consideration of the weight of his sentence any participation in the Mesny murder," because he had concluded that "Berger appears to have been unjustly convicted of participation in the murder."[168] McCloy did not bother to explain how he could reach that conclusion without examining the evidence on which the tribunal relied, nor did

---

[163] McCloy Clemency Decisions, 14.   [164] Law No. 10, Art. II(3)(c).
[165] Bower, 372.   [166] Wilkins, 222.
[167] *Ministries*, XIV TWC 447–54.   [168] McCloy Clemency Decisions, 15.

he explain how disregarding that one incident and crediting Berger with attempting to save Allied officers at the end of the war—acts for which the tribunal had already given him credit[169]—justified dramatically reducing the sentence of the man who had created the Dirlewanger Brigade, whose viciousness "shocked even Nazi commissioners" for the specific purpose of committing crimes against humanity.[170]

High Command

As noted above, McCloy refused to modify Hermann Reinecke's life sentence or Hans Reinhardt and Hermann Hoth's 15-year sentences. He did, however, grant clemency to the other three petitioners as a result of "more detached responsibility and other extenuating circumstances brought out mainly since the trials."[171] The result represented a split decision for Robert Bowie, who had angrily protested the Board's decision to recommend clemency for Reinecke, Walter Warlimont, and Georg von Kuechler because of their "alleged subordinate positions": although McCloy deviated from the Board concerning Reinecke, he ignored Bowie and reduced Warlimont's life sentence to 18 years and von Kuechler's 20-year sentence to 12 years. McCloy specifically noted that he reduced the 70-year-old von Kuechler's sentence "so as to give [him], with time served and time off for good behavior, a chance of release of prison during his lifetime."[172]

G. Were the Good-Conduct and Clemency Programs *Ultra Vires?*

McCloy created the good-conduct program and the Advisory Board on Clemency for War Criminals on the basis of a legal opinion by the HICOG General Counsel that he had the authority to reduce the sentences imposed by the NMTs.[173] It is far from clear whether that opinion was correct. First, Law No. 10 may not have authorized General Clay's review of the NMT sentences, much less McCloy's good-conduct and clemency programs. Second, it is unlikely that McCloy had the right to create those programs without the assent of the High Commission as a whole.

1. Ordinance No. 7

Article XVII(a) of Ordinance No. 7 specifically authorized the Military Governor "to mitigate, reduce or otherwise alter the sentence imposed by the tribunal, but may not increase the severity thereof." That provision was adopted pursuant to Article III(2) of Law No. 10, which provided that "[t]he tribunal by which persons charged with offenses hereunder shall be tried and the rules and procedure thereof shall be determined or designated by each Zone Conmmander for his respective Zone." But did the latter justify the former?

---

[169] *Ministries*, XIV TWC 552.　　　[170] Ibid., 546.
[171] McCloy Clemency Decisions, 17.　　　[172] Ibid., 18.
[173] Schwartz, *America's Germany*, 160.

There are two problems here, one narrow and one broad. The narrow problem is that it is unclear whether the Control Council intended Article III(2) to authorize zone commanders to review the sentences imposed by the tribunals they created. It seems unlikely, given that Article III(5) of Law No. 10 specifically prohibited zone commanders from deferring "the execution of death sentences" by more than one month "after the sentence ha[d] become final." Article III(5) seems to suggest that the Control Council did not view rules permitting sentence modifications as the kind of rule or procedure that Article III(2) permitted zone commanders to adopt.

The broader problem involves the relationship between Law No. 10 and the IMT Charter. As noted in Chapter 10, the *Ministries* tribunal held that Law No. 10 could not extend the jurisdiction of the NMTs beyond the Charter's provisions—to include crimes against humanity that did not satisfy the nexus requirement, for example—because Law No. 10 stated in its preamble that it was enacted "to give effect to the terms of the London Agreement of 8 August 1945."[174] The London Charter made the "Control Council for Germany" as a whole responsible for modifying sentences of defendants convicted by the IMT; individual Allies had no such authority. The logic of *Ministries* thus suggests that insofar as the Control Council wanted to authorize individual Allies to modify the sentences imposed in their zonal trials, it had to condition such modifications on the agreement of all four Allies. Such a limitation would have been procedurally cumbersome, but it would not have been irrational—after all, Law No. 10 was specifically enacted "to establish a uniform legal basis in Germany for the prosecution of war criminals and other similar offenders, other than those dealt with by the International Military Tribunal."[175] Giving each Ally the unlimited and unreviewable right to release defendants convicted in Control Council trials was obviously inconsistent with that goal.

2. The High Commission

Even if General Clay did have the authority to modify the NMT sentences as Military Governor, that does not mean McCloy had the authority to create the good-conduct and clemency programs. Indeed, Joseph L. Haefle, a Major in EUCOM's Office of the Judge Advocate, expressly rejected that idea in a 1949 memo to the Judge Advocate himself. Haefle pointed out that McCloy was not the Military Governor when he created the programs in December 1949 and July 1950, respectively; that position had been abolished with the creation of HICOG the previous September. The question, therefore, was whether McCloy's decision to create the good-conduct and clemency programs were justified "by the succession of a High Commissioner to certain of the powers and authority previously exercised by General Clay as Military Governor and representative of the United States Government on the Allied Control Council."[176]

---

[174] *Ministries*, Order and Memorandum of the Tribunal Dismissing Count Four, XIV TWC 114.
[175] Law No. 10, Preamble.
[176] Memo from Haefle to Judge Advocate, European Command, 22 Aug. 1949, NA-549-2237-2, at 1-2.

Haefle concluded that they were not. The problem, in his view, was that the authority to modify the sentences imposed by tribunals established pursuant to Law No. 10 belonged not to the individual High Commissioners, but to the Allied High Commission—as the successor to the Allied Control Council—as a whole. The High Commission, which had been created by the United States, Britain, and France on 8 April 1949,[177] was responsible for exercising the powers that the Allies had reserved in the Occupation Statute.[178] One of those powers, as discussed earlier, was "control over ... questions of amnesty, pardon or release in relation to" sentences imposed by "courts or tribunals of the occupying powers." The Agreement, however, did not authorize individual High Commissioners to exercise the reserved powers; on the contrary, Article 9 provided that "[a]ll powers of the Allied High Commission shall be uniformly exercised in accordance with tripartite policies and directives," and Article 6 provided that, on all matters other than amending Germany's Federal Constitution (which required unanimity), "action shall be a majority vote."[179]

Because all decisions concerning "amnesty, pardon, or release" required the majority vote of the High Commission, Haefle insisted that McCloy could not create the good-conduct and clemency programs unilaterally:

In essence then, there must be further agreement by the body most nearly comparable to the Allied Control Commission and having authority to legislate in this field, which body is the High Commission, as successor to the Allied Control Council in the Western Zones of Germany, to which is specifically reserved the authority with reference to disposition of war criminals. It is considered the directives to the High Commission by their governments preclude unilateral action on this subject by any one of the High Commissioners, at least until the procedures for joint agreement have been exhausted.[180]

Haefle submitted his memo on 22 August 1949, before McCloy created the good-conduct and clemency programs. He thus recommended that "assent to the proposed program[s] be obtained from the High Commission to whom the matter should be presented under the provisions of the 'Tripartite Agreement'."[181] McCloy ignored his recommendation.

H. The Response to the Decisions

The Allied response to McCloy's decisions was overwhelmingly negative. Some attacked McCloy's overall approach to clemency, such as Hartley Shawcross, the IMT prosecutor who had become the British Attorney General, who claimed that

---

[177] Agreement as to Tripartite Controls, 8 Apr. 1949, para. 1.

[178] Ibid., para. 2.

[179] Article II(1) of the Charter of the Allied High Commission, enacted on 22 June 1949, specifically required the High Commission to "reach its decisions" concerning reserved powers "in accordance with the provisions of the Agreement as to Tripartite Controls."

[180] Memo from Haefle to Judge Advocate, 22 Aug. 1949, at 9.

[181] Ibid., 10.

the decisions reflected McCloy's "mistaken ideas of political expediency or . . . the wholly false view that these sentences were no more than vengeance wreaked by the victors upon the vanquished."[182] Others focused on specific decisions—in particular McCloy's decision to release Alfried Krupp and restore his property. Atlee and Churchill each condemned Alfried's release on the floor of Parliament.[183] Ben Ferencz attributed McCloy's excessive sympathy for Krupp to his background as a Wall Street lawyer.[184] And William Wilkins, one of the judges in the *Krupp* case, wrote an angry letter to McCloy protesting Alfried's release.[185] In Wilkins' view, McCloy's decisions were dictated solely by "political expediency" and had the effect of "recogniz[ing] Hitler's Lex Krupp decree as valid." Wilkins also insisted that McCloy did not have the authority to restore Krupp's fortune, because the return of property did not fall within "the category of clemency."[186]

The most incisive attack on McCloy's clemency decisions, however, came from Telford Taylor himself. On 24 March 1951, Taylor published an article in *The Nation* entitled "The Nazis Go Free." Echoing Shawcross, Taylor condemned McCloy's report as nothing more than

the embodiment of political expediency, distorted by a thoroughly unsound approach to the law and the facts, to say nothing of the realities of contemporary world politics. Mr. McCloy paints his action as an effort to iron out discrepancies in severity and to consider individual circumstances justifying clemency. Analysis shows, however, that what he has done approximates blanket commutation of sentences.[187]

Taylor was incensed by much of McCloy's report, particularly its patently false claim that although Krupp plants had used and mistreated vast number of slave laborers, "the industrial concern and its management were not primarily responsible for this treatment"[188]—an idea that Taylor described as "bad logic and worse law."[189] More importantly, though, Taylor insisted that the clemency decisions would deal a severe blow both to the legitimacy of the U.S. war-crimes program and to the development of international criminal law:

It appears to me that Mr. McCloy has been deluded into the belief that the Germans will regard his "clemency" as a demonstration of American fairness and good-will. We shall soon see how wide of the mark he has shot. True democrats in Germany will not applaud the release of Krupp directors and S.S. concentration-camp administrators. Nor will German nationalist sentiment be appeased. For the ultra-nationalists, Nurnberg has become an invaluable whipping boy. These commutations will be seized upon as tantamount to a confession that the trials were the product of Allied vengeance and hate rather than the embodiment of law.[190]

---

[182] Maguire, 232–3.

[183] Bower, 373. According to Bower, McCloy thought that Atlee and Churchill were being hypocritical, given Britain's reluctance to avoid trying Krupp itself. Ibid.

[184] Maguire, 231.   [185] Wilkins, 217.   [186] Ibid., 218.

[187] Taylor, *The Nazis Go Free*, 171.   [188] McCloy Clemency Decisions, 12–3.

[189] Taylor, *The Nazis Go Free*, 171–2.   [190] Ibid., 172.

McCloy was evidently stung by such criticism, but his attempts to defend himself only deepened skepticism toward his decisions. McCloy published an open letter to Eleanor Roosevelt, for example, in which he claimed that the clemency program was justified because "unlike criminal cases in the U.S. and England, there was no provision for further court review of these cases for possible errors of law or fact after the court of first instance passed on them"[191]—an open admission that he believed he was entitled to provide the NMT prisoners with appellate review. McCloy's letter prompted a personal response from Taylor, who pointed out its "numerous inaccuracies"—such as McCloy's contention that General Clay "for one reason or another had been unable to dispose of [the cases] finally"[192]—and reminded Roosevelt that, contrary to U.S. clemency practice, McCloy and the Advisory Board had made its decisions without ever soliciting input from the prosecution.[193] McCloy also doubled down on his defense of Alfried Krupp, describing him as a "playboy" who "hadn't had much responsibility" for the decisions of the firm,[194] despite all the evidence to the contrary. Finally, McCloy attempted to rebut the idea that his decisions were driven by the need to convince the Germans to rearm by claiming that he "received the [Advisory] Board's conclusion...many months before there was any question of German rearmament." As Schwartz points out, that was simply untrue: the Board submitted its final report two weeks before the New York Conference at which U.S, British, and French representatives agreed to support rearming Germany.[195]

The German reaction to McCloy's decisions was equally disappointing, although for a very different reason. As Taylor predicted, the decisions failed to legitimize the NMT trials or the war-crimes program in the eyes of ordinary Germans. A State Department survey conducted in Bavaria in early February 1951 concluded that "[a] fairly general public view seems to be that all the decisions were a political maneuver rather than an expression of American justice."[196] The following month, a HICOG survey of public opinion in all four occupation zones found that "the legal considerations motivating the American decisions in the Landsberg cases, apparently completely failed to impress the German public." Instead, most of the Germans surveyed believed that the U.S. authorities had been so lenient because "[t]hey realize the injustice of the trials."[197] Similar attitudes were also exhibited by German officials: a March survey of *Burgermeisters* throughout Germany found that "[t]he prevailing interpretations are either that the basic injustice of Nuremberg is now being conceded, or that the revisions were prompted by a desire to win German allegiance." More than 90 percent of those mayors also believed that Alfried Krupp had done "no more than war industrialists in other countries"[198]—an opinion that no doubt helps explain why Krupp "was greeted as a returning national hero" upon his release.[199]

---

[191] Ibid., 172.

[192] General Clay had, of course, reviewed all of the NMT sentences except those in *Ministries*.

[193] Letter from Taylor to Eleanor Roosevelt, 19 June 1951, TTP-14-4-3-53, at 1.

[194] Quoted in Bower, 373.   [195] Schwartz, *America's Germany*, 165.

[196] Cited in Maguire, 229.   [197] Ibid.

[198] Quoted in ibid.   [199] Bower, 373.

The Germans also continued to advocate on behalf of the NMT prisoners McCloy did not release, particularly the five men whose death sentences he confirmed. McCloy received more than 1,000 letters in the five weeks after he announced his decision, nearly all of which asked him to stay the executions, which were scheduled for 16 February 1951.[200] More proactively, the Federal Republic's Main Office for the Legal Protection of War Criminals, which was headed by the attorney who had defended Erich Naumann in the *Einsatzgruppen* trial, hired Warren Magee, von Weizsaecker's attorney in *Ministries*, to challenge the executions in the United States.

On February 14, two days before the executions, Magee filed habeas petitions on behalf of the five men in the U.S. District Court for the District of Columbia. McCloy refused to stay the executions pending the disposition of the petitions, even after Adenauer personally requested that he do so. Nevertheless, the executions did not take place on time: a few hours before they were set to begin, Secretary of State Acheson informed McCloy that he "should not proceed with executions until further advised."[201] The stays elicited a new round of lobbying by the Germans. Letters continued to stream into McCloy's office asking for clemency for the condemned men, and he received a petition for clemency signed by more than 600,000 Germans.[202] McCloy was unmoved, however, because he believed that commuting the death sentences would "further undermine the moral and legal principles established at the Nuremberg Trials" and would "strike another blow at the prospects for a democratic Germany, provide the communists with a powerful propaganda weapon to use against us and make a mockery of American standards of justice and law."[203]

Magee was no more successful on the legal front. The District Court rejected the habeas petitions not long after he filed them, and when he appealed, "the U.S. Solicitor General, the Assistant Solicitor General, the Judge Advocate General of the Army and legal counsel for the State Department all showed up at the Court of Appeals to oppose his motion"[204]—an impressive, and all too rare, show of support for the NMT trials. Magee lost again, and the Supreme Court denied his petition for certiorari on May 22. McCloy then—with Acheson's permission—lifted the stays of execution and ordered the executions take place on May 25.[205]

Magee still refused to give up. He filed another petition in federal district court, this one seeking a permanent injunction against the executions on the ground that the Federal Republic's Basic Law prohibited capital punishment—an argument that the Germans had been making since the Law was enacted in May 1949. That petition convinced the judge to stay the executions until June 5, but he ultimately denied Magee's petition on jurisdictional grounds. Magee appealed, but the U.S. Court of Appeals for the D.C. Circuit affirmed the district court. The Supreme Court then refused to grant certiorari or extend the stay of execution on June 4.[206]

---

[200] Earl, 288.   [201] Ibid., 289.   [202] Ibid., 290.   [203] Quoted in ibid.
[204] Earl, 289.   [205] Ibid., 291.   [206] Ibid.

The condemned men were now out of options—and on June 7, after saying goodbye to their wives the night before, Pohl, Ohlendorf, Naumann, Blobel, and Braune were hanged at Landsberg Prison. According to Maguire, "[w]hen Ohlendorf was lowered into the grave, the mourners gave the Nazi salute."[207]

III. The Clemency Boards

McCloy's clemency decisions ushered in a new phase of the U.S. war-crimes program, one in which the "problem" of the remaining NMT and Dachau prisoners "was now seen purely as a political one, in which the U.S. government sought to appease German demands while not unduly aggravating its own public opinion."[208] The new goal was straightforward: release the remaining prisoners as quickly and as quietly as possible.

German critics, of course, were anything but quiet. After Pohl and the *Einsatzgruppen* defendants were executed, the critics shifted their attention to a new cause—the ten German generals still in Landsberg, six of whom had been convicted in the NMT trials: Walter Kuntze (*Hostage*), Hermann Hoth, Hans Reinhardt, Hans van Salmuth, Hermann Reinecke, and Walter Warlimont (*High Command*). Time and again, the defense of the generals sounded a common theme: that the civilian judges who presided over the NMT and Dachau trials had no understanding of what was necessary during war—especially one involving a ruthless "Bolshevistic enemy" who routinely violated the laws and customs of war. Lieutenant Colonel Gerhard Matzky, for example, wrote on behalf of an association of German soldiers employed by the U.S Army that the "non-war experienced" judges had been unable to appreciate the "conscientiousness and seriousness" the German generals had shown during the war, because they "were lacking experience with an enemy whose complete recklessness they only very recently had an opportunity to feel for themselves."[209] As Hebert points out, Matkzy was making "veiled reference" to alleged American war crimes committed against communist partisans fighting in the Korean War, which continued to rage. Other critics were less subtle: in a February 2 letter to McCloy, Bishop Wurm justified further sentence reductions for the generals on the ground that "[r]eports on the warfare in Korea raise the question in many instances whether the first sentences passed upon the generals were not perhaps based on insufficient knowledge of present-day partisan warfare."[210]

To his credit, McCloy rejected the Korean analogy, reminding Bishop Wurm that "[t]here was no military reason behind the slaughter of Jews as such," and that he could be certain "no 'Fuehrer' order was issued in Korea."[211] The constant comparisons nevertheless further delegitimized the war-crimes program in the eyes of ordinary Germans. A 1952 poll found that only 37 percent believed that

---

[207] Maguire, 234.   [208] Schwartz, *McCloy and Landsberg*, 453.
[209] Quoted in Hébert, *Hitler's Generals*, 171.
[210] Quoted in ibid., 172.   [211] Quoted in ibid.

the incarcerated generals were guilty and that only 10 percent supported the war-crimes program.[212]

The continued erosion of German support created a significant problem for the Allies, who were in the process of negotiating the "Convention on the Settlement of Matters Arising out of the War and the Occupation" with the Adenauer government. With the support of nearly all of Germany's political parties, Adenauer conditioned Germany's contribution to the EDC upon the release of all of the remaining war-prisoners in Allied custody. The Allies responded by giving Adenauer a choice: the German government could take custody of the prisoners, provided that they recognized the legitimacy of their convictions and guaranteed that they would serve the remainder of their sentences; or the prisoners could remain in Allied custody while a mixed German-Allied clemency board addressed the possibility of further sentence reductions. Adenauer desperately wanted control over the prisoners, but he was unwilling to guarantee that the German government would not review their sentences.[213] As a result, when the Convention was signed on 26 May 1952, Article 6 specifically established a "Mixed Board" whose mandate would be, "without calling in question the validity of the convictions, to make recommendations for the termination or reduction of sentences, or for parole, in respect of persons convicted by a tribunal of an allied power ... and confined the Three Powers in prisons in the Federal Republic."[214]

The Mixed Board failed to satisfy the German critics, who condemned the Convention and continued to agitate for a general amnesty. A coalition of 11 POW and veterans organizations submitted a petition to HICOG that insisted "no German can be expected to don a military uniform again until the question of 'war criminals' has been satisfactorily settled"; the petition was signed by more than 2,000,000 Germans.[215] German newspapers published editorial after editorial insisting (seemingly without recognizing the contradiction) that no war crimes had been committed during the war and that the prisoners had just followed orders.[216] Most dramatically—and most indicative of how little the Germans had learned from their recent past—the Foreign Ministry condemned the Mixed Board on the ground that it was not an *Endlosung*, a Final Solution, to the war-criminals problem.[217]

A. The Interim Mixed Parole and Clemency Board

Although HICOG officials were no more impressed by these arguments than before, by the end of 1952 they believed that German demands for a general amnesty threatened both the Bundestag's ratification of the Convention and the re-election of the Adenauer government, which was set to face the electorate in September 1953 and was under relentless attack for accepting the Mixed Board.[218]

---

[212] Sellars, 25.   [213] Maguire, 236–7.
[214] Convention on the Settlement of Matters Arising out of the War and Occupation, 26 May 1952, Art. VI.
[215] Maguire, 240.   [216] Hébert, *Hitler's Generals*, 176.
[217] Frei, 190.   [218] Buscher, 106–8.

The officials also realized that the Mixed Board would not solve the war-criminals problem even if the Convention was signed by Germany, because Allied ratification would require at least another couple of years—and France was already intimating that it might not sign the Convention at all.[219]

The State Department's solution was to acknowledge the obvious: that there was no way to address the political problem created by Landsberg Prison without abandoning the principles upon which the war-crimes program was based. Department officials thus recommended creating an Interim Mixed Board, one that would release all of the remaining war criminals within nine months by administering "a more lenient system of sentence reduction and parole" than previous boards. The officials did not pretend that the interim board would be anything other than a political solution to a political problem; indeed, they openly stated that the board should begin by releasing prisoners—the generals convicted in *High Command* foremost among them—"whose retention will continue to occasion major outcry."[220]

The State Department's recommendation encountered significant opposition. John Raymond argued that it "unwittingly accept[ed] the very German psychology which it criticizes"—namely, the idea that the prisoners were convicted because they were soldiers, not because they were murderers. Similarly, John Auchincloss, an international relations officer in the State Department, suggested that the solution "would remove all legal basis for the trials by showing what little respect we have for them."[221] Both men additionally believed—not without reason—that the creation of yet another clemency board, even a "more lenient" one, would not satisfy German demands that the United States acknowledge that the NMT and Dachau prisoners had been unjustly convicted.[222]

Raymond and Auchincloss's concerns, however, went unheeded: on 31 August 1953, James B. Conant, the new High Commissioner—McCloy had stepped down a year earlier[223]—formally created the Interim Mixed Parole and Clemency Board. The five-person Interim Board consisted of three Americans and two Germans and was chaired by Henry Shattuck, who had served in the House of Representatives from 1942 to 1948. The Interim Board's mandate was based on the proposed mandate for the Mixed Board: "without questioning the validity of the convictions and sentences, to make recommendations to the competent U.S. authorities for the termination or reduction of sentences or for the parole of persons convicted by the War Crimes Tribunals."[224] In terms of clemency, the Board would consider the number of the prisoner's crimes; his position when he

---

[219] Maguire, 242.

[220] Quoted in Hébert, *Hitler's Generals*, 186.

[221] Quoted in Maguire, 244–5.

[222] Ibid., 248.

[223] One of McCloy's final acts regarding the NMT prisoners was to release Hans Reinhardt. Reinhardt's daughter had tried to commit suicide in November 1950, perhaps as a reaction to her father's imprisonment, and Reinhardt had then applied for compassionate parole. McCloy granted the application in June 1952, although he warned his subordinates at HICOG that "there should be no publicity" about Reinhardt's release. Hébert, *Hitler's Generals*, 190.

[224] Quoted in Maguire, 251.

committed them; the existence of superior orders; and disparities between sentences imposed on similarly-situated offenders. In terms of parole, the Board would take into account the prisoner's age, health, and "overall character." New evidence would be considered, but only insofar as it provided "insight into the character of the applicant and the likelihood of his successful integration into society."[225]

When the Interim Board began work on October 27, there were 431 war criminals in U.S. custody: 312 in Landsberg, including 31 who had been convicted in the NMT trials, and 119 elsewhere. Between October 27 and 11 August 1955, when the Mixed Board replaced it, the Interim Board recommended parole or clemency for 347 of those prisoners—239 of the 259 who applied for parole, and 108 of the 172 who applied for clemency. EUCOM approved all but six of the parole recommendations and all but eight of the clemency recommendations. As summarized by an undated HICOG memo, "practically all of the war criminal convicts . . . who could show any mitigating factor in connection with the commission of the crimes for which they were convicted, had their sentences reduced and were released on parole."[226]

B. The Mixed Parole and Clemency Board

As specified by Article 6 the Convention on the Settlement of Matters Arising out of the War and the Occupation, the Mixed Parole and Clemency Board consisted of six people, three Germans and one representative from each of the Three Powers. The American representative was Edwin Plitt, a career officer in the State Department who had also served on the Interim Board. Unlike the Interim Board, the Mixed Board was a quasi-judicial body whose parole and clemency decisions were binding when unanimous.[227]

When the Mixed Board began work, 34 Dachau defendants and 10 NMT defendants remained in Landsberg Prison—the "hard-core" war criminals, as they were known. Almost immediately, the Board was plunged into controversy: in late 1955, a unanimous vote of the Board led to the parole of Sepp Dietrich, the commander of the SS units involved in the Malmedy Massacre. Dietrich's release infuriated veterans groups and important politicians in the United States, particularly Senator Kefauver, who had been a member of the Baldwin Subcommittee. Kefauver denounced Dietrich's release as a "serious mistake" and demanded a Senate investigation. The State Department attempted to defuse the controversy by emphasizing the Board's independence and the conditional nature of parole, but such legalistic considerations were no more persuasive to the Americans than they had been in other contexts to the Germans.[228]

[225] Hébert, *Hitler's Generals*, 189.
[226] Summary of U.S. War Crimes Program in Germany, undated, NA-549–2236-3, at 4.
[227] Settlement of Matters Convention, Art. 6(3)(b).
[228] Maguire, 265.

The fallout from the Dietrich controversy ultimately cost Plitt his position on the board; the State Department blamed him for casting the vote that made the parole decision unanimous and thus binding. Unfortunately, Plitt's replacement, Senator Robert Upton of New Hampshire, proved no more successful: after casting the lone vote against the parole plan the Board had approved the previous October for Joachim Peiper, whose *Kampfgruppe* had personally carried out the Malmedy massacre, Upton resigned from the Mixed Board in June 1956, less than three months after he had joined it. Explaining his decision to quit so suddenly, Upton claimed that the Mixed Board was functioning not as a genuine parole board, but as a "device" for releasing war criminals as quickly and as efficiently as possible. He was particularly aggrieved by his fellow Board members' insistence that the gravity of a prisoner's crimes had no bearing on whether he should be granted parole.[229]

Once Upton resigned, it was only a matter of time before the Mixed Board emptied Landsberg Prison completely. His replacement, Spencer Phenix—a State Department lifer who had helped draft the Kellogg-Briand Pact of 1928—fully understood "that the objective of the final phase of American war crimes policy was to release the remaining war criminals," and he was happy to be the scapegoat for the anger of U.S. veterans and politicians like Kefauver by pretending that he was making decisions without the approval of the State Department.[230] Not long after he was appointed, Phenix submitted two memos to the Department concerning the remaining Landsberg prisoners. Memo A pointed out that maintaining the Mixed Board's current approach to parole would mean that it "would continue in operation until the deaths of the six individuals serving life terms, or, barring prior death, until 1985." Not surprisingly, Phenix opposed that option, seeing no "political, practical, or sociological advantage" for the United States in keeping the worst of the worst in prison that long.[231] Memo B thus detailed his "preferred method" for the "rapid liquidation of the war crimes problem": reducing the number of years a prisoner had to serve before he was eligible for parole; eliminating the cumbersome oversight of parolees that went far beyond what the French or British required; and quietly commuting the parolees' sentences to time served after they were released.

The State Department—including John Raymond, who had evidently tired of fighting a losing battle on behalf of the NMT and Dachau trials—enthusiastically supported Phenix's solution. The German Foreign Office then "coincidentally" recommended a very similar proposal to the State Department. Phenix took the plan to the Mixed Board on 10 April 1957, and the Board unanimously approved the plan the following day.

By the end of 1957, all but four of the Landsberg prisoners had been released under the relaxed parole requirements, including Joachim Peiper. The remaining prisoners were the "ultimate hard core" and included, not surprisingly, three of the *Einsatzgruppen* defendants who had been originally sentenced to death: Adolf Ott, Ernst Biberstein, and Martin Sandberger. The Mixed Board refused to grant parole

---

[229] Maguire, 272.   [230] Ibid., 273.   [231] Quoted in ibid., 275.

to those men, but it was willing "to approve the individual clemency requests with the result that it was recommended unanimously that the sentences of the four be reduced to time served"—thereby achieving the same result. On 9 May 1958, Ott, Biberstein, Sandberger walked out of Lansdberg Prison as free men.[232] The U.S. war-crimes program was officially over.

[232] Ibid., 281–2.

16

Legacy

Introduction

The previous chapters examined the origins of the Nuremberg Military Tribunals, the law they applied, and the fate of the defendants they convicted. This chapter examines the legacy of the tribunals through the prism of the goals the trials were designed to achieve. Section I focuses on retribution, the judges' primary goal. It asks—extending the discussion in Chapters 14 and 15—whether the defendants convicted in the trials received their just deserts. Section II questions whether the trials achieved the two interrelated goals that Telford Taylor viewed as equally, if not more important, than retribution: creating an enduring historical record of the atrocities of the Nazi regime, and exposing the German people to those atrocities. Finally, Section III asks whether the NMT trials have had a positive impact on the development of international criminal law.

I. Retribution

The NMT judgments reflect a single-minded, if not entirely successful, devotion to the idea that the principal goal of a criminal trial is to separate the guilty from the innocent and impose sentences that reflect the moral culpability of the convicted.[1] That devotion is evident in every aspect of the tribunals' jurisprudence, from their rigorous application of the presumption of innocence to their desire— recalling Judge Wilkins' description—"not only to impose a sentence that would fit the guilt of the individual defendant but also bring about uniformity in the sentences."

Did the tribunals achieve retributive justice? A categorical answer to that question is not possible, because retributive justice is not a unitary phenomenon. On the contrary, it has at least four indices in the context of a criminal trial: (1) whether suspects selected for trial were more deserving of prosecution than suspects who were not selected[2]; (2) whether convicted defendants were, in fact guilty;

---

[1] *R. v. M.(C.A.)* [1996] 1 S.C.R. 500, quoted in *Prosecutor v. Kordić and Čerkez*, IT-95-14/2-A, Judgment, para. 1075 (17 Dec. 2004).
[2] Drumbl, 151.

(3) whether acquitted defendants were, in fact, innocent; and (4) whether the sentences imposed on guilty defendants reflected their culpability.[3]

A. Selectivity

As Mark Drumbl has noted, the retributive function of international tribunals is often "hobbled by the fact that only some extreme evil gets punished, whereas much escapes its grasp, often for political reasons anathema to Kantian deontology."[4] The NMTs were no different, for all of the reasons discussed in Chapter 3. Most obviously, of the 2,500 "major war criminals" identified by the OCC, only 177 ever stood trial—a mere 7 percent. That retributive shortfall would have been troubling even if the 177 defendants had represented the most major of the "major war criminals." But that seems unlikely, given how many important suspects were not prosecuted solely for financial, temporal, or logistical reasons—Fritz Bartels, the head of the Reich Central Office of Health Leadership, because he arrived in Nuremberg after the indictment in *RuSHA* had already been filed; Karl Wolff, Himmler's Chief of Staff, because Dulles has promised him immunity; Field Marshals von Brauchitsch, von Manstein, and von Rundstedt, because Clay ordered Taylor not to prosecute them; and so on.

B. Convicting the Innocent

In general, the convictions themselves appear to have been retributively just. There is no obvious example of a defendant in the trials who should have been acquitted but was not, and the tribunals acquitted 35 of the 177 defendants, an acquittal rate (20 percent) that exceeds both the IMT's (13 percent) and the ICTY's (15 percent). The tribunals also acquitted another 11 defendants (6 percent) on all charges other than criminal membership. Those statistics do not exclude the possibility of a wrongful conviction, but they at least indicate that the judges took their obligation to avoid convicting the innocent very seriously.

C. Acquitting the Guilty

By contrast, the tribunals' high rate of acquittal does suggest that guilty defendants might have avoided conviction. There is no question that the reliability of the OCC's selection process was undermined by the office's lack of time and personnel, the amount of evidence that the attorneys and analysts had to process, and the questionable reliability of some of that evidence. As noted in Chapter 3, for example, Marrus argues that "overly hasty prosecution" based on "insufficient evidence" explains the high number of acquittals (seven) in the *Medical* case. That said, given the vast number of major war criminals the OCC had to choose from, it seems unlikely that one out of every five indicted suspects (and one out of

---

[3] See, e.g., Charles K.B. Barton, *Getting Even: Revenge as a Form of Justice* 49–50 (1999).
[4] Drumbl, 151.

every four, if we limit consideration to the crimes against peace, war crimes, and crimes against humanity) was factually innocent of the charges against him. Indeed, although it is always difficult to identify wrongful convictions, at least some wrongful acquittals are readily apparent, such as the 12 defendants in *Flick* and *Farben* who were acquitted of slave-labor charges because the tribunals believed—despite all evidence to the contrary—that they were entitled to a defense of necessity.[5]

D. Just Punishment

Finally, it is difficult to argue that the punishment the convicted defendants received was retributively just. The sentences themselves were generally consistent, even if some defendants deserved longer sentences (Joel in the *Justice* case; Lammers in *Ministries*), while others deserved shorter ones (Loerner in *Pohl*). But were they fair? Drumbl has pointed out that although international crimes are considered more serious than their domestic counterparts, "sentences for multiple international crimes are generally not lengthier than what national jurisdictions award for a serious ordinary crime."[6] That disparity is particularly glaring concerning the sentences imposed by the NMTs. It is difficult to imagine that a court in Poland or the United States would have sentenced a defendant who worked thousands of slaves to death to 12 years in prison (Alfried Krupp's sentence) or a defendant who was responsible for the murder of thousands to 15 years (General Felmy's sentence in *High Command*).

Despite such concerns, the NMTs deserve praise for at least attempting to impose fair and consistent sentences. The same cannot be said of McCloy's clemency decisions, which left an indelible stain on the tribunals' legacy. It is impossible to argue that Willy Seibert deserved 15 years' imprisonment instead of death, given that he had been Ohlendorf's deputy in Einsatzgruppen D, which murdered at least 90,000 Soviet Jews. Similarly, there was no retributive justification for reducing the sentence of Gottlob Berger, the architect of the vicious Dirlewanger Brigade, from 25 years (itself overly lenient) to a mere 10 years.

Worse still, because of the liberal good-conduct and parole programs created by the United States after the tribunals shut down, very few of the convicted defendants ever served even a fraction of their modified sentences. To take only the most obvious example, seven defendants were facing life sentences after McCloy's clemency decisions in January 1951: List and Kuntze from the *Hostage* case; Biberstein, Klingelhofer, Ott, Sandberger from *Einsatzgruppen*; and Reinecke from *High Command*. List was released from prison in late 1952; Kuntze was released in early 1953; Klingelhofer was released in late 1956; and the others were all released in early 1958. In practice, therefore, a life sentence meant as few as three and no more than 10 years—a result that is impossible to reconcile with retributive principles.

---

[5] See Chapter 9.　　[6] Drumbl, 155.

II. The Documentary and Didactic Functions

Taylor agreed with the judges that it was critically important for "just punishment [to] be imposed on the guilty."[7] But he made clear in the opening minutes of the *Medical* trial that he had far greater ambitions:

The mere punishment of the defendants, or even of thousands of others equally guilty, can never redress the terrible injuries which the Nazis visited on these unfortunate peoples. For them it is far more important that these incredible events be established by clear and public proof, so that no one can ever doubt that they were fact and not fable . . . It is our deep obligation to all peoples of the world to show why and how these things happened.[8]

This statement articulated two different but interrelated goals. The first was documentary: creating a historical record of the Nazis' atrocities. The second was didactic: educating a still-skeptical public about those atrocities.

By any standard, the documentary goal was a spectacular success. As noted in the Introduction, more than 1,300 witnesses testified during the trials, the parties introduced more than 30,000 documents into evidence, and the judgments run more than 3,800 pages. In the aftermath of the trials, only the most committed apologist could maintain that the Holocaust—and the Nazis' other crimes beyond number—were "fable, not fact."

The didactic goal, however, was an equally spectacular failure. When Taylor spoke about the "peoples of the world," he was thinking about the German people in particular—as he said later in his opening argument, "I do not think the German people have as yet any conception of how deeply the criminal folly that was Nazism bit into every phase of German life, or of how utterly ravaging the consequences were. It will be our task to make these things clear."[9] It is difficult, of course, to determine precisely what effect the NMT trials had on the views of ordinary Germans; the trials were only one part of the U.S. war-crimes program, extending the work of the IMT and functioning alongside the much-maligned concentration-camp trials and the increasingly unpopular denazification boards.[10] But it is clear that the war-crimes program as a whole failed to reduce either support for National Socialism or the prevalence of racist attitudes toward Jews and other minorities—two critical indicia of whether the program was having its desired didactic effect. OMGUS conducted a series of public-opinion polls on both subjects in Germany between 1945 and 1949. In 1946, an average of 40 percent of Germans believed that National Socialism was a good idea badly carried out. By 1948, the average had risen to 55.5 percent.[11] At the same time, the percentage of Germans who believed

---

[7] *Medical*, Prosecution Opening Argument, I TWC 27.   [8] Ibid.   [9] Ibid., 29.

[10] Merritt and Merritt note that acceptance of denazification among ordinary Germans declined from approximately half in the winter of 1945 to little more than a sixth in January 1949. Anna J. Merritt & Richard L. Merritt, *Public Opinion in Occupied Germany: the OMGUS Surveys, 1945–49*, 37 (1980).

[11] Ibid., 295, Survey 175, June 1949.

that National Socialism was a bad idea dropped from a high of 41 percent to a low of 30 percent.[12] Racist views did not show a similar increase, but they also did not markedly decrease: 61 percent of Germans held racist views in December 1946, and 59 percent still held such views in mid-1948.[13]

Given the Germans' unyielding resistance to the war crimes program, American efforts to use the NMT trials for educational purposes might have been doomed from the beginning. The Americans did not help themselves, though, by failing to make the trials' vast documentary record available to the Germans in their own language. Taylor had always been convinced that the didactic function of the trials depended on the documentary function; he began to lobby the American government to publish the proceedings in both German and English as early as May 1948, arguing in a report to Royall, the Secretary of War, that although the "re-education of Germany" would be "far from easy," the one thing that the Army could do was "make the facts available to German historians, so that future generations of Germans will be able to grasp the full and malignant import of the Third Reich."[14] Indeed, he warned Royall that the entire NMT project would be "truncated and incomplete" if the documentary record of the trials was "left in the dust on the top shelf out of reach."[15]

Unfortunately, the Army was never committed to a German publication project. Although Royall allocated $317,000 to the OCC in July 1948 to prepare selected trial proceedings in both languages, the project called for an English set that was twice as long as the German one and did not guarantee publication of the German set.[16] The Army later agreed to equalize the length of the German and English volumes, which the OCC dutifully prepared, and briefly entertained the possibility—at the OCC's urging—of having a German publishing house underwrite the publication project.[17] Nevertheless, in October 1949, the Army pulled the plug on the project completely, claiming that the German volumes were "of insufficient value to the military to warrant their publication."[18]

That rationale was, in fact, Army-speak for the belief that publishing the trial proceedings would needlessly complicate American efforts to enlist Germany in the fight against communism.[19] Indeed, as the occupation of Germany wore on, American occupation authorities became increasingly open about why they wanted to allow the trial proceedings to—as Taylor put it—"sink into oblivion."[20] In July 1952, for example, Samuel Reber, the Assistant High Commissioner, argued against restarting the German publication project on the ground that publishing trial materials would remind Germans of the "war-criminals problem" at a time when "[i]t is our primary purpose...to prevent this issue from becoming an obstacle to ratification of the Bonn Agreements and European Defense Treaty

---

[12] Ibid., 32.   [13] Ibid., 239–40, Survey 122, 22 May 1948.
[14] Quoted in Taylor, *Final Report*, 116 (Appendix A).   [15] Ibid., 115, 117.
[16] Hébert, *Hitler's Generals*, 179.   [17] Ibid.
[18] Ibid., 180. The Army discontinued publication of the American volumes at the same time, but reversed itself when Congress allocated additional funds for the project. Ibid.
[19] See ibid., 181–2.   [20] Taylor, *Final Report*, 111.

and to forestall its developing into a serious impediment to future military cooperation."[21]

Because the publication project was never revived, the Germans had almost no access to the trial proceedings. As of August 1952, only two German institutions had a significant collection of German-language materials. The University of Goettingen possessed a complete set of trial records and made them available to the public, but they were unbound and unindexed. The University of Heidelberg had about 75 percent of the transcripts and exhibits, although some of them were in English instead of German. The University paid to have the records bound and was preparing indexes by hand, but had no plans to make them publicly available.[22] Indeed, ironically enough, the most widely available American war-crimes document was McCloy's Landsberg Report, which presented the trials in an extremely unflattering light. According to Hébert, the translation of the Landsberg Report quickly became the "authoritative" German document on the trials.[23]

The German publication project was not the only casualty of the Cold War. The Army also did everything it could to avoid publicizing Taylor's Final Report, which criticized OMGUS for its "lack of planned effort to utilize the documents and other evidence disclosed at the trials so as to advance the purposes of the occupation"[24] and claimed that any effort to "soft pedal" Nuremberg to protect German-American relations would, in fact, "play into the hands of those Germans who do not want a democratic Germany."[25] Taylor submitted the report to the Secretary of the Army in August 1949, but the Army did not inform the press that it was available until early November. The Army also made only one copy of the report available for inspection and required reporters to read it at the Pentagon—a significant deviation from standard Army practice, which was to provide copies of important reports to reporters well in advance of their official release date.[26] The Army's slow-walking of the report had its intended effect: as a *New York Post* article entitled "Taylor Report on Nazi Crimes Buried Without Honor" noted, the national press largely ignored it.[27]

III. The Origins of International Criminal Law

Although Taylor grew increasingly pessimistic about the didactic function of the trials, he never wavered in his belief that the tribunals' jurisprudence would have a profound influence on the development of international criminal law. As he said in a 12 May 1948 report to Secretary Royall:

Many perplexing problems of international legal procedure have been met and answered in the course of these trials, and many profoundly important substantive questions have

---

[21] Quoted in Hébert, *Hitler's Generals*, 182.   [22] Ibid., 182–3.
[23] Ibid., 181.   [24] Taylor, *Final Report*, 106.   [25] Ibid., 112.
[26] Charles van Devander, "Taylor Report on Nazi Crimes Buried Without Honor," *New York Post*, 21 Nov. 1949, TTP-5-3-3-24, at 4.
[27] Ibid.

received the considered judgment of experienced jurists. International penal law—like the Anglo-Saxon common law, from which our most cherished legal institutions derives—is growing by the case method. The trials of major war criminals at Nurnberg... will be looked to by diplomats and international jurists just as the decisions of our own courts are looked to by our statesmen and lawyers.[28]

As Taylor predicted, "diplomats and international jurists" have indeed consistently relied on the judgments when addressing new and difficult jurisprudential issues. Most often, that reliance has been positive. The modern conception of crimes against humanity, for example, is deeply indebted to the judgments in the *Justice* and *Einsatzgruppen* trials. In some cases, though, reliance on the judgments has had a negative effect. The Rome Statute's reliance on a subjective *mens rea* for the war crime of "excessive incidental death, injury, or damage," for example, reflects the *Hostage* tribunal's problematic acquittal of Lothar Rendulic.

A. Customary International Law

Although international and domestic courts have consistently relied on the NMT judgments to determine the state of customary international law,[29] they have exhibited considerable uncertainty about their authority. A number of courts have simply finessed the issue, stating that the judgments "contribute" to customary international law without identifying the weight of their contribution.[30] Other courts have viewed the judgments as evidence of U.S. practice, no more important than the decisions of any national court. And still others have treated the judgments as the decisions of an international tribunal, entitling them to considerably more authority than national decisions.

The disagreement between the majority and Judge Cassese in *Erdemović* provides a striking example of the debate. The primary issue in the case was whether customary international law permitted a defendant to invoke duress as a defense to murder. In rejecting the existence of such a customary rule, Judges McDonald and Vohrah—writing for the majority—acknowledged the *Einsatzgruppen* tribunal's statement that "[n]o court will punish a man who, with a loaded pistol at his head, is compelled to pull a lethal lever." They nevertheless held that the judgment was no more authoritative than the decisions of British and Canadian military tribunals that had reached the opposite conclusion, because the NMTs were of "questionable" international character and had applied American law instead of "purely international law."[31] By contrast, as part of his argument that customary international law did permit duress as a defense to murder, Judge Cassese insisted that the NMT judgments were entitled to much greater weight than decisions of

---

[28] Quoted in Taylor, *Final Report*, 116 (Appendix A).

[29] See, e.g., *Prosecutor v. Hadžihasanović*, IT-01-47-T, Judgment, para. 72 (15 Mar. 2006); *Karins v. Parliament of Latvia*, Constitutional Review, Case No. 2007-10-0102, para. 25.5 (2007).

[30] See, e.g., *Khulumani v. Barclay Nat'l Bank, Ltd.*, 504 F.3d 254, 273 (2nd Cir. 2007).

[31] *Prosecutor v. Erdemović*, IT-96-22-T*bis*, Joint Separate Opinion of Judges McDonald and Vohrah, paras 53–4 (7 Oct. 1997).

national military tribunals. In his view, because Law No. 10 was "an international agreement among the four Occupying Powers (subsequently transformed, to a large extent, into customary international law), the action of the courts established or acting under that Law acquire[d] an international relevance that cannot be attributed to national courts pronouncing solely on the strength of national law."[32]

The ICTY Appeals Chamber reaffirmed McDonald and Vohrah's position in *Kunarac*,[33] and some domestic courts have reached the same conclusion. In *Polyukhovich*, for example, the High Court of Australia refused to consider *Justice* an "authoritative statement of customary international law" because "Law No. 10 and the tribunals which administered it were not international in the sense that the Nuremberg Charter and the International Military Tribunal were international."[34] Other courts, however, have adopted Cassese's position. The ECCC, for example, held in *Case No. 2* that the NMTs "offer an authoritative interpretation of their constitutive instruments and can be relied upon to determine the state of customary international law."[35] Similarly, the Second Circuit held in *Doe v. Unocal* that, in Alien Tort Claims Act cases, it "should apply international law as developed in the decisions of international criminal tribunals such as the Nuremberg Military Tribunals for the applicable substantive law."[36]

With regard to the substantive crimes and modes of participation enumerated in Law No. 10, Cassese's position is clearly the superior one. Although McDonald and Vohrah are correct that the NMTs were not international tribunals, that does not mean, as Cassese notes, that they were domestic American courts that applied domestic American law. On the contrary, they were inter-allied special tribunals that applied Law No. 10, which itself reflected—according to the tribunals— customary international law. As a result, although the NMT judgments may not carry the same weight as the IMT judgment, they are certainly more authoritative than the decisions of "ordinary" national military tribunals concerning substantive international crimes and modes of participation.

The situation is more complicated, however, concerning defenses. The NMTs did not base their willingness to apply particular defenses on customary international law; they looked instead to "fundamental principles of justice which have been accepted by civilized and adopted by civilized nations generally." The *Krupp* and *Flick* tribunals were willing to permit the defendants to argue duress, for example, because they concluded that "the rule finds recognition in the systems of various nations"[37] and that "[t]his principle has had wide acceptance in American and English courts and is recognized elsewhere."[38] Similarly, the *Hostage* tribunal

---

[32] Ibid., para. 27, Separate and Dissenting Opinion of Judge Cassese.

[33] See *Prosecutor v. Kunarac*, IT-96-23 & IT-96-23/1-AAC, Judgment, para. 98 n. 188 (12 June 2002).

[34] *Polyukhovich v. Commonwealth*, 172 CLR 501, Opinion of Justice Brennan, para. 62 (14 Aug. 1991).

[35] *Case No. 2*, 002/19-09-2007-ECCC/OCIJ (PTC 38, Public Appeals Decision on Joint Criminal Enterprise, para. 60 (20 May 2010).

[36] See, e.g., *Doe v. Unocal*, 395 F.3d 932, 948 (9th Cir. 2002).

[37] *Krupp*, IX TWC 1436–7.

[38] *Flick*, VI TWC 1200.

accepted the defense of superior orders because "the municipal law of civilized nations generally sustained the principle at the time the alleged criminal acts were committed."[39] That is a critical difference: because the tribunals were applying municipal law instead of "purely international law" with regard to the defenses, their decisions regarding the availability and interpretation of specific defenses—including duress—are entitled to no more weight than the decisions of national military tribunals.[40]

Cassese, it is important to note, is not the only judge who has overestimated the value of NMT decisions when determining the customary status of a particular rule or principle. A number of international and domestic courts—including the ICTY in other cases—have made the same mistake. In *Rwamakuba*, for example, the ICTR Appeals Chamber relied exclusively on *Justice* and *RuSHA* to hold that customary international law permitted a defendant to be convicted of genocide via joint criminal enterprise.[41] Similarly, in *Blagojevic and Jokic*, four NMT judgments were the only pre-1993 legal sources that the ICTY's Trial Chamber I-A cited to establish that customary international law criminalized "other inhumane acts" as a "residual category of crimes against humanity."[42] Neither decision is necessarily incorrect, but the truncated nature of their analyses of customary international law is nevertheless impossible to justify.[43] Far better in this regard is *Abdullahi v. Pfizer, Inc.*, in which the Second Circuit cited the *Medical* tribunal's condemnation of nonconsensual medical experimentation as a crime against humanity and then pointed out that, "since Nuremberg, states throughout the world have shown through international accords and domestic law-making that they consider the prohibition . . . identified at Nuremberg as a norm of customary international law."[44]

B. The Principle of Non-Retroactivity

Despite the fact that the NMTs were the first tribunals to insist that the principle of non-retroactivity was a limit on sovereignty, not simply a principle of justice, courts have only occasionally mentioned the judgments when addressing retroactivity issues. In *Vasiljević*, an ICTY Trial Chamber cited the *Justice* case for the proposition that the principle requires a charged crime to be "defined with sufficient clarity under international law . . . to have been sufficiently foreseeable and accessible."[45] That citation is incorrect: the *Justice* tribunal was the only tribunal that considered

---

[39] *Hostage*, XI TWC 1236.

[40] See Claus Kress, *Erdemović*, in Oxford Companion, 661.

[41] *Prosecutor v. Rwamakuba*, ICTR-98-44-AR72.4, Decision on Interlocutory Appeal Regarding Application of Joint Criminal Enterprise to the Crime of Genocide, paras 16–22 (22 Oct. 2004).

[42] *Prosecutor v. Blagojević*, IT-02-60, Judgment, para. 624 (17 Jan. 2005). Even worse, the Trial Chamber cited to the *indictments* in those cases, not to the judgments, despite claiming that the NMTs had entered convictions for other inhumane acts. Ibid., para. 624 n. 2027.

[43] See generally Darryl Robinson, "The Identity Crisis of International Criminal Law," 21 *Leiden J. Int'l L.* 925, 933–46 (2008).

[44] 562 F.3d 163, 179 (2nd Cir. 2009).

[45] *Prosecutor v. Vasiljević*, IT-98-32-T, Judgment, para. 201 (29 Nov. 2002).

non-retroactivity to be a principle of justice—and a relaxed principle at that, one that was satisfied as long as the defendant should have known his act was wrongful.[46] The ICTY Appeals Chamber made the same mistake in *Milutinović*, with the same judgment, when it held that convicting a defendant of "serious criminal offenses" via JCE did not run afoul of the *nullum crimen* principle.[47] By contrast, in *Polyukhovich*, the High Court of Australia correctly cited the *Hostage* case for the idea that a defendant "may not be charged with crime for committing an act which was not a crime at the time of its commission."[48]

C. Evidence and Procedure

Courts have largely ignored the NMT judgments with regard to evidence and procedure—and the primary exception is problematic. In *Tadić*, the Appeals Chamber held that it had the "inherent power" to punish "conduct which interferes with its administration of justice," even though the ICTY Statute was silent concerning contempt. In defense of that conclusion—which has been criticized by scholars[49]—it noted that the NMTs had "interpreted their powers as including the power to punish contempt of court."[50] That was a misleading statement, because Article VI(c) of Ordinance No. 7 specifically empowered the tribunals to "deal summarily with any contumacy." Their contempt power, therefore, was anything but "inherent."

D. Aggression

The NMT judgments have had an important impact on the development of the crime of aggression. Most notably, there is now no question that invasions—armed attacks that are not resisted by the attacked State—are acts of aggression that can give rise to individual criminal responsibility. The International Law Commission's 1954 Draft Code of Offences Against the Peace and Security of Mankind criminalized "[a]ny act of aggression, including the employment by the authorities of a State of armed force against another State for any purpose other than national or collective self-defence."[51] The Draft Code's definition of aggression went far beyond Article 6(a) of the Nuremberg Charter, which was limited to wars of aggression,[52] but it was very much in keeping with the tribunals' criminalization of the invasions of Austria and Czechoslovakia. Article 8*bis*(2) of the Rome Statute,

---

[46] See Chapter 5.

[47] *Prosecutor v. Milutinović*, IT-99-37-AR72, Decision on Motion Challenging Jurisdiction—Joint Criminal Enterprise, para. 39 (21 May 2003).

[48] *Polyukhovich*, para. 46.

[49] See generally Michael Bohlander, "International Criminal Tribunals and Their Power to Punish Contempt and False Testimony," 12 *Crim. L. Forum* 91–118 (2001).

[50] *Prosecutor v. Tadić*, IT-94-1-A-AR77, Appeals Judgment on Allegations of Contempt, para. 14 (27 Feb. 2001).

[51] Draft Code of Offences Against the Peace and Security of Mankind with Commentaries, Art. 2 (1954).

[52] See Yoram Dinstein, *War, Aggression, and Self-Defense* 125 (2001).

adopted in 2010, also specifically includes "[t]he invasion or attack by the armed forces of a State of the territory of another State" in the category of acts of aggression that can give rise to individual criminal responsibility.[53] Article 8*bis*(2)'s criminalization of invasions reflects the influence of the NMTs—although the language is borrowed from General Assembly Resolution 3314, Article 5(2) of the Resolution limited "crimes against international peace" to "wars of aggression."

The criminalization of invasions has influenced national courts, as well. In *Karins v. Parliament of Latvia*, Latvia's Constitutional Court considered whether the Soviet Union's peaceful deployment of troops in Latvia in June 1940, to which the Latvian Parliament had consented under duress, constituted an act of aggression. The Court held that it did, specifically citing *Ministries* for the proposition that "lack of resistance to the invasion of another State does not necessarily mean that no such invasion has taken place."[54]

The tribunals' adoption of a leadership requirement for crimes against peace has also had a significant impact on modern doctrine. Article 16 of the 1996 Draft Code of Crimes specified that aggression could only be committed by a "leader or organizer," which the ILC defined as someone who had "the necessary authority or power to be in a position potentially to play a decisive role in committing aggression."[55] Similarly, Article 8*bis*(1) of the Rome Statute limits the crime to individuals who were "in a position effectively to exercise control over or to direct the political or military action" of the State responsible for an act of aggression.

The drafters of the Rome Statute's definition of aggression have claimed that Article 8*bis*(1) is consistent with the jurisprudence of the NMTs.[56] In fact, the Article's "control or direct" requirement is considerably more restrictive than the "shape or influence" requirement adopted by the tribunals. As I have noted elsewhere, the "control or direct" requirement excludes the prosecution of private economic actors such as industrialists, even though the tribunals—and the IMT— insisted that such actors could be complicit in aggression.[57]

Article 8*bis* and the jurisprudence of the NMTs also differ in terms of *mens rea*. As discussed in Chapter 8, the tribunals held that participating in an act of aggression was criminal only if the defendant knew that the act was illegal under international law, a requirement that permitted a defendant to argue mistake of law. By contrast, Element 2 of the Elements of Crimes, adopted alongside Article 8*bis*, specifically provides that "[t]here is no requirement to prove that the perpetrator has made a legal evaluation as to whether the use of armed force was inconsistent with the Charter of the United Nations."[58] In contrast to the leadership requirement,

[53] Resolution RC/Res. 6, 11 June 2010, at 2.

[54] *Karins v. Parliament of Latvia*, para. 25.5.

[55] International Law Commission, Draft Code of Crimes Against the Peace and Security of Mankind with Commentaries, Art. 16, at 43 (1996).

[56] See, e.g., Proposal submitted by Belgium, Cambodia, Sierra Leone, and Thailand, PCNICC/2002/WGCA/DP.5 (8 July 2002).

[57] Kevin Jon Heller, "Retreat from Nuremberg: The Leadership Requirement in the Crime of Aggression," 18 *Eur. J. Int'l L.* 477, 489–91 (2007).

[58] Resolution RC/Res. 6, at 5.

the drafters of Article 8*bis* do not claim that Element 2 is consistent with the NMTs' jurisprudence. But they also have not explained why they have deviated from the *mens rea* adopted by the tribunals, whose analysis of the essential elements of aggression remains unequalled in its systematicity.

E. War Crimes

The NMT judgments have made significant contributions to three areas of modern war-crimes jurisprudence: (1) the treatment of unlawful combatants; (2) hostage-taking and reprisals; and (3) the definitions of individual war crimes.

1. Lawful Combatants

In his Final Report, Taylor claimed that the *Hostage* tribunal's refusal to extend belligerent status to "ununiformed guerrillas and franc-tireurs" would "stimulate efforts to reconsider the provisions of the Hague and Geneva Conventions relating to this controversial question."[59] Once again his predictive skills were lacking: although the Third Geneva Convention of 1949 (GC III) makes clear that "militias and other volunteer corps" that are not part of the armed forces can qualify as lawful combatants, Article 4(2) requires partisans to satisfy the same four requirements as Article 1 of the Hague Regulations. That said, the tribunals likely influenced the drafters of the Article 4(2) concerning partisan activity in occupied territory. According to Pictet, it was "generally considered" that the Hague Regulations permitted partisans to be recognized as lawful combatants only during the period of invasion.[60] Article 4(2), by contrast, explicitly permits partisan groups that qualify as lawful combatants to operate "in or outside their own territory, even if this territory is occupied." That change is consistent with the NMT judgments, which never relied on the invasion/occupation distinction to deny partisans combatant status. Indeed, the *Hostage* tribunal specifically held that "certain band units in both Yugoslavia and Greece complied with the requirements of international law entitling them to the status of a lawful belligerent" even though it considered both countries to be occupied at the time.[61]

The NMTs also likely influenced the adoption of Article 5 of GC III, which provides that "[s]hould any doubt arise as to whether persons, having committed a belligerent act and having fallen into the hands of the enemy, belong to any of the categories enumerated in Article 4, such persons shall enjoy the protection of the present Convention until such time as their status has been determined by a competent tribunal." That provision had no analogue in the Hague Regulations, but it is consistent with the judgments, which uniformly held that captured

---

[59] Taylor, *Final Report*, 223.
[60] Jean S. Pictet, *Commentary on the Geneva Convention Relative to the Protection of Prisoners of War* 59 (1960).
[61] *Hostage*, XI TWC 1244.

partisans were entitled to a fair judicial process to determine whether they were, in fact, unlawful combatants.

2. Hostage-Taking and Reprisals

The tribunals were notoriously less progressive regarding the execution of civilian hostages and reprisal prisoners, although it is clear that they upheld the practice only because they believed that customary international law permitted it.[62] Indeed, the *Hostage* tribunal decried "the complete failure on the part of the nations of the world to limit or mitigate the practice by conventional rule" and stated that it was "self-evident" that "international agreement is badly needed in this field."[63]

Unlike Taylor with partisans, the tribunal got its wish: Article 33 of the Fourth Geneva Convention of 1949 (GC IV) prohibits subjecting civilians to reprisals,[64] and Article 34 prohibits taking civilians hostage.[65] It is very likely that those provisions were motivated by the NMT judgments. Taylor noted in his Final Report that the *Hostage* judgment generated widespread outrage in Europe and the United Kingdom,[66] and Pictet's commentary on Article 34 cites Lord Wright's seminal article on the killing of civilian hostages,[67] which severely criticized the *Hostage* judgment for approving the practice.[68]

3. Individual Crimes

The ICTY has often relied, not always accurately, on the NMT judgments or on Law No. 10 when analyzing specific war crimes. In some cases, the tribunal has used those sources to establish the criminality of a particular act under customary international law. In *Blaškić*, for example, the Appeals Chamber relied on *High Command* to hold that forcing POWs to perform dangerous work is a war crime.[69] Similarly, in *Furundžija*, the Appeals Chamber held that "the international community has long recognized rape as a war crime" based in part on the fact that "rape was prosecuted as a war crime under Control Council Law No. 10"[70]—an erroneous claim, given that Law No. 10 only prohibited rape as a crime against humanity and that none of the defendants in the trials were ever charged with rape.[71]

In other cases, the ICTY has relied on the judgments or on Law No. 10 to establish the definition of a particular war crime. In *Naletilić and Martinović*, Trial Chamber I cited *Krupp* for the idea that plunder applies not only to "acts of appropriation committed by individual soldiers for their private gain," but also to "large-scale seizures of property within the framework of systematic economic exploitations of

---

[62] Ibid., 1251.   [63] Ibid., 1251–2.   [64] GC IV, Art. 34.

[65] Ibid., Art. 33.   [66] Taylor, *Final Report*, 108.   [67] Lord Wright, 309.

[68] Pictet, *Commentary on GC III*, 229.

[69] *Prosecutor v. Blaškić*, IT-95-14-A, Judgment, para. 589 (29 July 2004).

[70] *Prosecutor v. Furundžija*, IT-95-17/1-A, Judgment, para. 210 (21 July 2000).

[71] The *Čelebići* trial judgment made a similar error, wrongly claiming that the London Charter prohibited rape as a crime against humanity. *Čelebići*, Trial Judgment, para. 476. Rape made its first appearance as a crime against humanity in Law No. 10.

occupied territory."[72] And in *Kordić and Čerkez*, the Appeals Chamber justified not limiting the war crime of plunder to occupied territory by pointing out that Law No. 10 did not contain such a requirement.[73] That was a questionable citation: as discussed in Chapter 9, the *Farben, Krupp,* and *Ministries* tribunals each dismissed plunder charges on the ground that the acts in question took place outside of occupied territory.[74]

The NMTs' most important contribution to war-crimes jurisprudence concerns medical experimentation. The *Medical* tribunal's articulation of the "Nuremberg Code," particularly its first principle that experiments can only be conducted with the subject's "voluntary consent,"[75] led the drafters of the Geneva Conventions of 1949 to prohibit medical experimentation as a grave breach of the Conventions in both international and non-international armed conflicts.[76] Those provisions, in turn, led to the adoption of Articles 8(2)(b)(x) and 8(2)(e)(xi) of the Rome Statute, which deem such experimentation a war crime in both international and non-international armed conflict. The Nuremberg Code has also been adopted in the United States by the Department of Defense, the American Medical Association, and the National Institutes of Health.[77]

F. Crimes Against Humanity

The modern conception of crimes against humanity owes an incalculable debt to the work of the NMTs, particularly concerning the disappearance of the nexus requirement and the development of the contextual elements of crimes against humanity—although, as noted below, the ICTY's reliance on the judgments has been both selective and problematic. The judgments have also had a significant effect on the definition of specific crimes.

1. The Nexus Requirement

International tribunals have consistently cited the NMTs as evidence that customary international law no longer requires crimes against humanity to be committed "in execution of or in connection with" war crimes or crimes against peace. At the ICTY, the *Tadić* Appeals Chamber relied on the text of Law No. 10 for the disappearance of the nexus,[78] while the *Kupreškić* Trial Chamber cited Law No. 10 and the *Einsatzgruppen* and *Justice* judgments for that proposition.[79] At the ECCC, the Trial Chamber in *Case No. 1* relied on the same three sources as

---

[72] *Prosecutor v. Naletilić and Martinović*, IT-98-34-T, Judgment, para. 619 (31 Mar. 2003).

[73] *Kordić and Čerkez*, Appeals Judgment, para. 78.

[74] See Chapter 9.

[75] *Medical*, II TWC 181.

[76] See Jean S. Pictet, *Commentary on the Geneva Convention Relative to the Protection of Civilian Persons in Time of War* 224 (1958).

[77] See *In re Cincinnati Radiation Litigation*, 874 F. Supp. 796, 821 (S.D. Ohio 1995).

[78] *Prosecutor v. Tadić*, IT-94-1-A, Decision on the Defence Motion for Interlocutory Appeal on Jurisdiction, para. 140 (2 Oct. 1995); see also *Prosecutor v. Tadić*, IT-94-1-T, Decision on the Defence Motion on Jurisdiction, para. 79 (10 Aug. 1995) (citing *Einsatzgruppen*).

[79] *Prosecutor v. Kupreškić et al.*, IT-95-16-T, Judgment, para. 577 (14 Jan. 2000).

Kupreškić.[80] And in *Arellano et al. v. Chile*, the Inter-American Court of Human Rights relied solely on the *Justice* case.[81]

These citations are problematic, however, because all three courts failed to acknowledge that the *Pohl*, *Flick*, and *Ministries* tribunals read the nexus requirement into Law No. 10. Neither *Tadić* nor *Arellano* cite those judgments at all, while *Kupreškić* and *Case No. 1* ignore *Pohl* and *Ministries* and relegate *Flick* to a footnote. Such selective citation would be impossible to justify even if *Justice* and *Einsatzgruppen* were as authoritative as *Pohl*, *Flick*, and *Ministries*. But that is clearly not the case, given that *Justice* and *Einsatzgruppen* addressed the nexus requirement only in dicta. It is thus an open question to what extent the NMTs support the elimination of the nexus from the customary definition of crimes against humanity.

2. Contextual Elements

a. Widespread or Systematic

Modern tribunals have also ignored the NMTs' insistence that an attack on a civilian population must be both widespread *and* systematic to qualify as a crime against humanity. Indeed, in *Kordić and Čerkez*, the ICTY's Trial Chamber III summarily rejected a defense claim that, in light of the *Justice* case, customary international law required a conjunctive test. According to the Chamber, it was "generally accepted that the requirement that the occurrence of crimes be widespread or systematic is a disjunctive one."[82]

That claim, however, reflects an unconvincing description of the state of customary international law at the time the ICTY was created. The Chamber justified its position by citing to the trial judgments in *Tadić* and *Blaškić*, but *Blaškić* cited no pre-1993 legal sources in defense of the disjunctive test,[83] and *Tadić* cited only one: the IMT's comment in the judgment that the persecution of the Jews before the war was "a record of consistent and systematic inhumanity on the greatest scale."[84] That statement, however, was not only dicta—as the Trial Chamber itself recognized by quoting the ILC to that effect[85]—it is actually phrased *conjunctively*.

In light of the ICTY's failure to cite a single pre-1993 source of law that actually supports its "widespread or systematic" requirement, it is impossible to defend the Tribunal's decision to ignore the NMT judgments. After all, the Chambers have consistently relied on the judgments in other contexts; the NMTs were the first tribunals to develop the contextual elements of crimes against humanity in a systematic fashion; and in contrast to the split over the nexus requirement, the tribunals uniformly agreed that the test was conjunctive. The ICTY's adoption of a disjunctive requirement thus seems to have been driven not by methodological

---

[80] *Case No. 1*, 001/18-07-2007/ECCC/TC, Judgment, para. 292 (26 July 2010).
[81] *Arellano et al. v. Chile*, IACHR Series C, No. 154, Preliminary Objections, para. 96 (26 Sept. 2006).
[82] *Prosecutor v. Kordić and Čerkez*, IT-95-14/2, Judgment, paras 175, 178 (26 Feb. 2001).
[83] *Prosecutor v. Blaškić*, IT-95-14-T, Judgment, para. 207 (3 Mar. 2000).
[84] IMT Judgment, 60.
[85] *Prosecutor v. Tadić*, IT-94-1-T, Judgment, para. 648 (7 May 1997).

concerns, but by the desire to make crimes against humanity as easy as possible to prosecute—a prototypical example of what Darryl Robinson has pejoratively described as the Tribunal's "victim-focused teleological reasoning."[86]

The ICC has also adopted the "widespread or systematic" requirement. A small number of delegations, including France and the United Kingdom, favored a conjunctive test at the Rome Conference, but did not object to a disjunctive test once the Conference agreed to adopt a definition of "attack" that included a policy requirement.[87] The inclusion of the policy requirement in Article 7(2)(a) means that, as discussed below, the ICC's conception of crimes against humanity is closer to the NMTs' than to the ICTY's.

b. The Policy Requirement

In *Kunarac*, the ICTY Appeals Chamber rejected the defense's claim that crimes against humanity had to be committed pursuant to a "plan or policy." In its view, "[t]here was nothing in the Statute or in customary international law at the time of the alleged acts"—1992–1993—"which required proof of the existence of a plan or policy to commit those crimes."[88] It cited a variety of legal sources in defense of that conclusion, ranging from Article 6(c) of the London Charter to the Secretary-General's Report on the Security Council resolution that created the ICTY.[89]

Bill Schabas has convincingly demonstrated that the Appeals Chamber misrepresented the vast majority of the sources it cited in "famous footnote" 114 and conveniently omitted a number of sources that would have undermined its claim that the pre-ICTY customary definition of crimes against humanity did not contain a policy requirement.[90] Although not mentioned by Schabas, *Kunarac* similarly misused Law No. 10 and the NMT judgments. The Appeals Chamber cited Law No. 10 as evidence that a policy was not required, but failed to mention that it was designed to "give effect to the terms" of the London Charter,[91] which specifically limited the category of potential defendants to persons "acting in the interests of the European Axis countries, whether as individuals or as members of organizations."[92] Even worse, the Chamber simply disregarded the *Justice* tribunal's adoption of the policy requirement—a position taken by the *Einsatzgruppen*, *Ministries*, and *Medical* tribunals, as well—on the ground that *Polyukhovich*, the High Court of Australia case, had ostensibly shown that the judgment did not constitute "an authoritative statement of customary international law." As discussed earlier, however, *Polyukhovich* wrongly assumed that the NMTs were national courts applying domestic law. The Appeals Chamber was also willing, a mere 25 paragraphs later, to

---

[86] Robinson, 933.

[87] William Schabas, *The International Criminal Court: A Commentary on the Rome Statute* 143 (2010).

[88] *Kunarac*, Appeals Judgment, para. 98.

[89] Ibid., para. 98 n. 114.

[90] See William A. Schabas, "State Policy as an Element of International Crimes," 98 *J. Crim. L. & Criminology* 953, 960–7 (2008).

[91] Law No. 10, Preamble.

[92] London Charter, Art. VI.

rely exclusively on *Pohl* to hold that enslavement as a crime against humanity did not require mistreatment.[93]

Unlike the ICTY, the ICC has specifically adopted a policy requirement for crimes against humanity. According to Article 7(2)(a) of the Rome Statute, an "attack against any civilian population" means the commission of multiple acts "pursuant to or in furtherance of a State or organizational policy." The Elements of Crimes add that "[s]uch a policy may, in exceptional circumstances, be implemented by a deliberate failure to take action, which is consciously aimed at encouraging such attack. The existence of such a policy cannot be inferred solely from the absence of governmental or organizational action."[94] Read together, the Rome Statute and Elements of Crimes adopt a definition of "State policy" that is essentially equivalent to the one adopted by the *Justice* tribunal, which held that the policy in question must be "government organized or approved." It is slightly narrower, however, than the *Einsatzgruppen* tribunal's policy requirement, which expanded the definition to include "indifference" and "impotence." *Justice* criminalizes widespread and systematic attacks that are tolerated by the government but not actively encouraged, while *Einsatzgruppen* expands the category of crimes against humanity to include attacks committed by non-state actors that the government would like to prevent but cannot.

The NMTs' approach to the policy requirement is particularly interesting in light of the Rome Statute's extension of crimes against humanity to include attacks committed pursuant to an "organizational policy." According to the ICC Pre-Trial Chamber, any non-state actor that is capable of committing a widespread or systematic attack can satisfy the "organizational policy" requirement.[95] That is a controversial interpretation: some scholars believe that Article 7 excludes non-state actors completely,[96] while others believe that it includes only "state-like" non-state actors such as FARC or the Palestinian Authority.[97] Although obviously not binding on the ICC, which is a treaty-based tribunal, *Justice* supports the former approach, while *Einsatzgruppen* supports the latter. Both judgments agree, however, that the international community's interest in prosecuting crimes against humanity does not extend to attacks committed by non-state actors that can be adequately addressed by the affected state.

---

[93] *Kunarac*, Appeals Judgment, para. 123.

[94] Elements of Crimes, Art. 7, Introduction, para. 3 n.6.

[95] See, e.g., *Prosecutor v. Katanga and Chui*, ICC-01/04-01/07, Decision on the Confirmation of Charges, 30 Sept. 2008, para. 398.

[96] See, e.g., M. Cherif Bassiouni, I *The Legislative History of the International Criminal Court: Introduction, Analysis, and Integrated Text* 151–2 (2005).

[97] See Schabas, *State Policy*, 972; see also Kevin Jon Heller, "Situational Gravity Under the Rome Statute," in *Future Perspectives on International Criminal Justice* 227, 237 (Carsten Stahn & Larissa van den Herik, eds, 2010). Judge Kaul took the same position in his dissenting opinion in *Situation in Republic of Kenya*. See *Situation in Republic of Kenya*, ICC-01/09, Dissenting Opinion of Judge Hans-Peter Kaul, 31 Mar. 2010, para. 51.

3. Individual Crimes

Courts have consistently cited the NMT judgments and Law No. 10 when addressing specific crimes against humanity. In some cases, they have relied on those sources to interpret an element common to all such crimes. In *Tadić*, for example, the Appeals Chamber relied, *inter alia*, on the text of Article II(1)(c) of Law No. 10 to reverse the Trial Chamber's holding that all crimes against humanity have to be committed with discriminatory intent.[98] More often, though, courts have relied on those sources to establish the customary existence or customary definition of a specific crime against humanity.

a. Extermination

In *Vasiljević*, Trial Chamber II relied on Law No. 10 as evidence that customary international law criminalizes extermination as a crime against humanity.[99] It also cited the *Medical, Justice*, and *Einsatzgruppen* judgments for the idea that a defendant is guilty of extermination only if he was personally responsible—however remotely or indirectly—for a significant number of deaths.[100]

b. Enslavement

Two courts have cited *Pohl* for the proposition that enslavement as a crime against humanity does not require the individuals enslaved to be mistreated: the ICTY Appeals Chamber in *Kunarac*,[101] and the Economic Community of West African States' Community Court of Justice in *Korau v. Niger*.[102] The Community Court of Justice went even further, rightly using *Pohl* to insist that "involuntary servitude" is slavery even "with the provision of square meals, adequate clothing, and comfortable shelter."[103]

c. Deportation

In *Stakić*, the ICTY Appeals Chamber relied primarily on Judge Phillips' concurrence in *Milch* and the *Krupp* tribunal's subsequent adoption of that concurrence to hold that deportation requires the forcible displacement of persons across a *de jure* or *de facto* state border.[104] As noted in Chapter 9, however, the *High Command* tribunal specifically held that cross-border transfer was not required.[105] Judge Schomburg also noted in his separate and partially dissenting opinion in *Naletilić and Martinović*, which agreed with *Stakić* on the cross-border requirement, that the

---

[98] *Tadić*, Appeals Judgment, para. 289. Interestingly, the Trial Chamber had imposed the requirement despite acknowledging that neither Law No. 10 nor the *Medical* tribunal imposed it. See *Tadić*, Trial Judgment, para. 651.
[99] *Vasiljević*, Trial Judgment, para. 221.
[100] Ibid., para. 222.
[101] *Kunarac*, Appeals Judgment, para. 123.
[102] *Korau v. Niger*, Merits, ECW/CCJ/JUD/06/08, para. 79 (27 Oct. 2008).
[103] Ibid.
[104] *Prosecutor v. Stakić*, IT-97-24-A, Judgment, para. 291 (22 Mar. 2006).
[105] See Chapter 9.

RuSHA tribunal convicted defendants of forcible evacuations that had taken place solely within Poland and Germany.[106]

d. Imprisonment

In *Krnojelac*, Trial Chamber II relied on Law No. 10 to establish the customary status of imprisonment as a crime against humanity.[107]

e. Torture and Rape

A number of courts have relied on Law No. 10 to establish that torture is a crime against humanity under customary international law, including the ICTY in *Furundžija*,[108] the Inter-American Court of Human Rights,[109] and a federal district court in the United States.[110] The same ICTY Trial Chamber and the same district court also relied on Law No. 10 to establish the customary status of rape as a crime against humanity.[111]

f. Persecution

The NMT judgments have had a particularly significant impact on the ICTY's understanding of the crime against humanity of persecution. In *Kupreškić*, for example, Trial Chamber II relied on *High Command* and *Ministries* to hold that any of the acts listed in Article 5 of the ICTY Statute, such as murder and deportation, can also qualify as persecution when committed with discriminatory intent[112]; relied on *Justice* and *Flick* to hold that "lesser forms" of persecution not covered by Article 5, such as "attacks on political, social, and economic rights," qualify as crimes against humanity as long as they are "of an equal gravity" to the acts in Article 5[113]; and relied on the *Justice* case to hold that the gravity of lesser acts of persecution "must not be considered in isolation but examined in their context and weighed for their cumulative effect."[114] Similarly, in *Kvočka*, the Trial Chamber cited *Ministries*' condemnation of persecutory acts such as excluding Jews from educational opportunities for the idea that "acts that are not inherently criminal may nonetheless become criminal and persecutorial if committed with discriminatory intent."[115]

Those are all accurate citations. By contrast, in *Tadić*, the Trial Chamber cited *Flick* for the proposition that "offences against industrial property" cannot qualify

---

[106] *Prosecutor v. Naletelić and Martinović*, IT-98-34-A, Judgment, Separate and Partially Dissenting Opinion of Judge Schomburg, para. 12 (3 May 2006).

[107] *Prosecutor v. Krnojelac*, IT-97-25-T, Judgment, para. 109 (15 Mar. 2002).

[108] *Prosecutor v. Furundžija*, IT-95-17/1-T, Judgment, para. 137 (10 Dec. 1998).

[109] *Mehinovic v. Vuckovic*, 198 F. Supp. 2d 1322, 1353 (N.D. Ga. 2002).

[110] *Castro Prison v. Peru*, IAHCR Series C, No. 160, Merits, para. 402 (25 Nov. 2006).

[111] *Furundžija*, Trial Judgment, para. 168; *Mehinovic*, 198 F. Supp. 2d at 1353.

[112] *Kupreškić*, Trial Judgment, paras 594–8.

[113] Ibid., paras 611–19.

[114] Ibid., para. 615. Trial Chamber II cited the prosecution's opening argument, not the judgment. The judgment nevertheless supports the Trial Chamber's conclusion. See *Justice*, III TWC 1063.

[115] *Prosecutor v. Kvočka*, IT-98-30/1-T, Judgment, para. 186 (2 Nov. 2001).

as persecution even when committed with discriminatory intent.[116] That is a correct reading of *Flick*—but it overlooks the fact that, as discussed in Chapter 10, both *Ministries* and *Pohl* reached the opposite conclusion.[117] The Appeals Chamber made an even more glaring mistake in *Blaškić* when it used *Flick* to question whether the plunder of industrial or personal property was sufficiently grave to qualify as persecution. That use not only ignored *Ministries* and *Pohl* concerning industrial property, it ignored the fact that *Ministries, Pohl,* and *RuSHA* all agreed—and *Flick* itself suggested—that the discriminatory theft of personal property is a crime against humanity.

G. Genocide

The NMTs have had little impact on the modern crime of genocide, most likely because the judgments dealt with genocide as a crime against humanity. The international community was also negotiating the terms of the Genocide Convention at the same time as the trials were being held. That said, the *Justice* case represents the first example of a trial in which defendants were specifically convicted of genocide—a symbolically important development. The ICTR Appeals Chamber also rightly cited the *Justice* case in *Rwamakuba* for the idea that genocide "was treated as a crime under customary international law" during World War II.[118]

H. Conspiracy and Criminal Membership

The NMTs' approach to conspiracy and criminal membership played a small role in *Hamdan v. Rumsfeld*, in which the U.S. Supreme Court held that the military commissions created by the Bush administration violated both the Uniform Code of Military Justice and Common Article 3 of the Geneva Conventions. Justice Stevens, writing for a plurality of the Court, cited the trials as evidence that conspiracy is not a war crime triable by a military commission.[119] By contrast, Justice Thomas argued in his dissent that the criminal-membership convictions in the *Medical* case justified charging Hamdan with criminal membership in Al-Qaeda.[120] That was a clever but irrelevant use of the *Medical* case, because Hamdan was not actually charged with criminal membership.

I. Modes of Participation

The NMT judgments have influenced the current definitions of four different modes of participation in a crime: (1) ordering; (2) joint criminal enterprise; (3) aiding and abetting; and (4) command responsibility. "Taking a consenting part" has also played a minor—and somewhat confused—role at the ICTY.

---

[116] *Tadić*, Trial Judgment, para. 707.   [117] See Chapter 10.
[118] *Rwamakuba*, Appeals Judgment, para. 22.
[119] 548 U.S. 557, 611 n. 40 (2006).
[120] Ibid., 696 (Thomas, J., dissenting).

1. Ordering

In *Blaškić*, the ICTY Trial Chamber relied on *High Command* to hold that ordering does not require a military commander to give the order directly to the soldier who commits the *actus reus* of the crime.[121] It also used *High Command* to suggest that commanders who pass along orders of their superiors that they knew were criminal or were criminal on their face are equally guilty of ordering the underlying crime.[122]

2. Joint Criminal Enterprise

The NMTs' jurisprudence concerning enterprise liability has had relatively little effect on modern JCE doctrine. International tribunals have generally relied on the NMTs to establish the customary status of particular forms of JCE. In *Tadić*, the ICTY Appeals Chamber cited *Einsatzgruppen* as an example of "basic" JCE (JCE I)—a correct interpretation of the tribunal's position, although the Chamber actually cited the prosecution's opening argument instead of the judgment.[123] In *Case No. 2*, the ECCC relied on Law No. 10, *Justice*, and *RuSHA* for the existence of JCE I and "systemic" JCE (JCE II) under customary international law.[124] Finally, in *Rwamakuba*, the ICTR Appeals Chamber cited *Justice* and *RuSHA* as evidence that customary international law permits a defendant to be convicted of genocide via JCE I.[125]

These citations are clearly justified, although it is important to note that the tribunals did not specifically distinguish between "basic" and "systemic" JCEs. That does not mean that *Case No. 2* was wrong to cite the NMT judgments for the customary status of JCE II; the *Pohl* tribunal clearly considered the concentration-camp system to be a systemic JCE, as indicated by its rejection of Fanslau's claim that convicting him for playing a "minor" role in the system constituted guilt by association:

As the officer in charge of personnel, [Fanslau] was as much an integral part of the whole organization and as essential a cog in its operation as any other of Pohl's subordinates. He was in command of one of the essential ingredients of successful functioning. This has no relation to "group condemnation," which has been so loudly decried. Personnel were just as important and essential in the whole nefarious plan as barbed wire, watch dogs, and gas chambers. The successful operation of the concentration camps required the coordination of men and materials, and Fanslau to a substantial degree supplied the men.[126]

The ICTY takes the position that JCE II is "a variant" of JCE I, because it equally relies on a complex and carefully designed division of labor.[127] The *Pohl* tribunal's

---

121 *Blaškić*, Trial Judgment, para. 282.   122 Ibid., para. 282 n. 508.
123 *Tadić*, Appeals Judgment, para. 200 and n. 245.
124 *Case No. 2*, Appeals Decision on JCE, paras 65–9.
125 *Rwamakuba*, Appeals Judgment, paras 15–22.
126 *Pohl*, V TWC 998.
127 See, e.g., *Prosecutor v. Vasiljevic*, IT-98-32-A, Judgment, para. 98 (25 Feb. 2004).

emphasis on the "coordination" that was required to execute the "nefarious plan" behind the concentration camps indicates that it likely would have agreed.

One ICTY case has also relied on the NMT judgments to define the elements of JCE. In *Brđanin*, the Appeals Chamber relied on *Justice* and *RuSHA* to hold that the principal perpetrator of a crime does not have to be a member of the JCE and that, as a result, the prosecution does not have to prove that the defendant and the principal perpetrator agreed to commit the crime.[128] It also relied on *Einsatzgruppen* and *Justice* to reject a defense claim that JCE applies only to small-scale enterprises.[129]

It is not surprising that international tribunals have not relied more extensively on the NMTs' enterprise jurisprudence, given the significant differences between that jurisprudence and modern JCE. Most obviously, they differ in terms of *mens rea*: whereas enterprise liability required the prosecution to prove only that the defendant knew about the criminal enterprise, JCE I requires the prosecution to prove that the defendant intended to commit the planned crimes[130] and JCE II requires the prosecution to prove that the defendant intended "to further the criminal purpose of th[e] system."[131] Moreover, unlike modern JCE,[132] the *Pohl* tribunal rejected the idea that the requisite knowledge of a criminal enterprise could be inferred "solely from the official title" that a defendant held.

Enterprise liability and JCE also differ in terms of their *actus reus*. Modern JCE does not impose a qualitative limitation on the *actus reus*: except in the rare situation of an "opportunistic visitor" to a prison camp,[133] any contribution to the functioning of a JCE will satisfy the participation requirement, regardless of the defendant's position in the enterprise.[134] By contrast, the NMTs specifically limited responsibility for executing a criminal enterprise to defendants who possessed a certain degree of authority and discretion with regard to the actions that connected them to the enterprise.

It is unfortunate that international tribunals have largely ignored the NMTs' approach to enterprise liability. Jens Ohlin has convincingly argued that the ICTY's refusal to distinguish between "co-perpetrating" and "aiding and abetting" a JCE[135]—insisting that "minor participants are just as guilty as architects, hangers-on just as liable as organizers"—is inconsistent with the principle of culpability.[136]

---

[128] *Prosecutor v. Brđanin*, IT-99-36-A, paras 414–5 (3 Apr. 2007).

[129] Ibid., para. 422.

[130] *Tadić*, Appeals Judgment, 228.

[131] *Prosecutor v. Kvočka*, IT-98-30/1-A, para. 198 (28 Feb. 2005).

[132] See, e.g., *Stakić*, Appeals Judgment, para. 65.

[133] See *Kvočka*, Appeals Judgment, para. 599.

[134] See ibid., para. 97.

[135] The ICTY Trial Chamber drew that distinction in *Kvočka*, holding that members of a JCE who shared the intent to commit the planned crimes qualified as co-perpetrators, while members who did not share that intent but knowingly contributed to the JCE qualified as aiders-and-abettors. *Kvočka*, Trial Judgment, paras 282, 284. The Appeals Chamber disagreed, insisting on the traditional undifferentiated approach to JCE. *Kvočka*, Appeals Judgment, para. 91.

[136] Jens D. Ohlin, "The Co-Perpetrator Model of Joint Criminal Enterprise," 14 *Annotated Leading Cases of the Int'l Crim. Tribs.* 739, 742 (2008).

By contrast, as we have seen, the NMTs insisted on precisely that distinction: the co-perpetrator/aider-and-abettor distinction mirrors the creator/executor distinction that was central to enterprise liability. From a culpability standpoint, therefore, enterprise liability is far superior to JCE.

3. Aiding and Abetting

International and domestic courts have often looked to the NMT judgments for guidance concerning aiding and abetting, but they have rarely done so accurately. To begin with, courts have often misunderstood how the tribunals distinguished between different modes of participation. In *Čelebići*, for example, the ICTY Appeals Chamber cited *High Command* for the idea that a Chief of Staff could be held "directly liable for aiding and abetting" if he was involved in drafting illegal orders issued by his commanding officer.[137] In fact, all of the tribunals considered such drafting as a form of ordering, not as aiding and abetting—a difference that could have a significant impact on sentencing. The ICTY Trial Chamber made a related error in *Furundžija*, using Fendler's conviction in *Einsatzgruppen*, among others, to argue that the tribunals adopted a "substantial effect" test for the *actus reus* of aiding and abetting.[138] In fact, Fendler was convicted because he took a consenting part in the extermination program, not because he aided and abetted it.

Furundžija's problems, however, go even deeper. The NMT judgments actually provide almost no support for aiding and abetting's substantial-effect requirement,[139] however minimal,[140] because—as discussed in Chapter 12—the tribunals considered abetting as a form of participation *in a criminal enterprise*, not as an independent mode of participation in a crime. If the principles were the same, the mistake would be unimportant. But that is not the case: the tribunals not only held that the *actus reus* of enterprise liability was satisfied by *any* contribution to a criminal enterprise, they also limited enterprise liability to defendants who possessed sufficient "authority and discretion" regarding their contribution. Even having a "substantial effect" on a crime, therefore, would not have been enough for the tribunals to hold a defendant responsible for participating in a criminal enterprise; indeed, although Schwerin von Krosigk "furnished the means by which the concentration camps were purchased, constructed, and maintained"—which clearly had a substantial effect on the crimes committed in the camps—the *Ministries* tribunal acquitted him because he had no discretion concerning the funds he disbursed.

---

[137] *Prosecutor v. Delalić (Čelebići)*, IT-96-21-A, Judgment, para. 260 (20 Feb. 2001).

[138] *Furundžija*, Trial Judgment, para. 218.

[139] The *Ministries* tribunal asked whether von Weizsaecker or Woermann "in any *substantial* manner . . . aided, abetted, or implemented" the deportation of Jews following the Wannsee Conference. *Ministries*, XIV TWC 478 (emphasis added). The tribunal did not suggest, however, that a defendant who acted with authority and discretion but did not make a substantial contribution to the criminal enterprise would have to be acquitted.

[140] Cryer et al., 375.

Domestic courts have also incorrectly found a substantial-effect requirement for aiding and abetting in the NMT judgments—often, not surprisingly, simply by citing *Furundžija*. An example is *In re South African Apartheid Litigation*,[141] which then compounded its mistake by erroneously using Rasche's acquittal in *Ministries* to claim that the provision of "fungible resources" such as money and building materials to the perpetrator of a crime cannot qualify as "substantial assistance."[142] That conclusion is impossible to reconcile with *Pohl*, in which Tribunal II held Tschentscher responsible for participating in the concentration-camp program because he had used his authority and discretion to allocate "food and clothing" to the camps.[143]

Courts have generally done a better job with the *mens rea* of aiding and abetting. *Furundžija* correctly cited *Einsatzgruppen* for the idea that the defendant possesses the requisite mental state as long as he knows his actions will assist the principal perpetrator commit a crime; the intent to assist is not required.[144] *In re South African Apartheid Litigation* used *Flick*, *Einsatzgruppen*, and *Ministries* to reach the same conclusion.[145] By contrast, as noted in the Introduction, *Talisman Energy*— which implicitly overruled *In re South African Apartheid Litigation*—incorrectly relied on *Ministries* to hold that "international law at the time of the Nuremberg trials recognized aiding and abetting liability only for purposeful conduct."[146]

4. Command Responsibility

The NMTs have had a profound effect on the development of command responsibility. To begin with, the judgments helped establish the doctrine in both conventional and customary international law. The delegates to the 1977 Diplomatic Conference in Geneva included command responsibility in Article 87 of the First Additional Protocol—the first conventional recognition of command responsibility[147]—in part because of the *Hostage* case.[148] The ILC cited *Hostage* and *High Command* as a reason to include "responsibility of the superior" in the 1996 Draft Code of Crimes.[149] And in *Čelebići*, the ICTY Trial Chamber relied on *Hostage*, *High Command*, and the *Medical* case to establish the customary existence of command responsibility,[150] and relied on *Flick* to extend command responsibility "to individuals in non-military positions of superior authority."[151]

The ICTY has also consistently relied on the judgments to define the elements of command responsibility: (1) the existence of a superior/subordinate relationship;

[141]   617 F. Supp. 2d 228, 258 (S.D.N.Y. 2009).
[142]   Ibid.
[143]   *Pohl*, V TWC 1015.
[144]   *Furundžija*, Trial Judgment, para. 237.
[145]   617 F. Supp. 2d at 260.
[146]   582 F.3d 244, 259 (2nd Cir. 2009).
[147]   Richard L. Lael, *The Yamashita Precedent: War Crimes and Command Responsibility* 134 (1982).
[148]   Yves Sandoz et al., *Commentary on the Additional Protocols* 1020 (1987).
[149]   1996 Draft Code, Commentaries, at 25.
[150]   *Prosecutor v. Delalić (Čelebići)*, IT-96-21-T, Judgment, para. 138 (16 Nov. 1998).
[151]   Ibid., paras 359–60, 363.

(2) the superior's awareness of his subordinates' crimes; and (3) the superior's failure to prevent or punish his subordinates.

a. Superior/Subordinate Relationship

In *Čelebići*, Trial Chamber II cited *Hostage*, *High Command*, and *Pohl* for the proposition that a superior's *de facto* authority over subordinates is sufficient for command responsibility; *de jure* authority is not required.[152] It also rejected the prosecution's argument, which was based on the *Hostage* case, that *de facto* authority exists as long as the superior has the ability to exercise "substantial influence" over an alleged subordinate. The Chamber rightly pointed out that the prosecution was citing to the *Hostage* tribunal's discussion of the responsibility of commanding generals, not tactical commanders. According to the Chamber, unlike commanding generals, who have responsibility over all of the units in the territory under their control, tactical commanders are responsible only for the actions of units under their "effective control."[153] The Appeals Chamber later interpreted the *Hostage* judgment the same way.[154]

The Appeals Chamber also relied on the *Hostage* judgment in *Hadžihasanović*. The prosecution argued that a superior could be held responsible for failing to punish crimes that were committed by subordinates before he assumed command over them. The Chamber correctly rejected that argument, citing the *Hostage* tribunal's conviction of Kuntze—which was based on crimes committed by his troops after he replaced Field Marshal List as the Commander-in-Chief of the 12th Army—as evidence that customary international law did not support such a dramatic extension of command responsibility.[155]

b. *Mens Rea*

The ICTY has rarely relied on the NMT judgments for the *mens rea* of command responsibility, most likely because the tribunals did not take a consistent position on that issue. The primary exception is *Čelebići*, in which the Trial Chamber used *High Command* to reject the prosecution's claim that a superior could be presumed to have knowledge of widespread criminal acts by his subordinates,[156] and the Appeals Chamber used *Hostage* and *Pohl* to hold that superiors do not have a duty under customary international law to discover crimes committed by their subordinates.[157] The Appeals Chamber's conclusion, it is important to note, is based on an incorrect reading of the *Hostage* judgment: Tribunal V specifically held that a commanding general is obligated "to require and obtain complete information" about crimes committed in the territory under his command[158] and that "[a] corps commander must be held responsible ... for acts which the

---

[152] Ibid., paras 372–4.   [153] Ibid., para. 648.
[154] *Čelebići*, Appeals Judgment, para. 258.
[155] *Prosecutor v. Hadžihasanović*, IT-01-47-AR72, Decision on Interlocutory Appeal Challenging Jurisdiction in Relation to Command Responsibility, para. 50 (16 July 2003).
[156] *Čelebići*, Trial Judgment, paras 385–8.
[157] *Čelebići*, Appeals Judgment, para. 229.
[158] *Hostage*, II TWC 1271.

corps commander knew or ought to have known about."[159] The *Medical* tribunal also imposed a duty to discover on superiors, which the Appeals Chamber failed to mention.

c. Failure to Prevent or Punish

In *Blaškić*, the Appeals Chamber relied on the *Hostage* tribunal's statement that "a commanding general of occupied territory is charged with the duty of maintaining peace and order, punishing crime, and protecting lives and property within the area of his command" to hold that failing to prevent crimes and failing to punish their perpetrators were separate theories of liability.[160] Trial Chambers have also often relied on *Hostage* and *High Command* to identify specific omissions that qualify as the failure to prevent (such as the "failure to issue orders bringing the relevant practices into accord with the rules of war"[161]) and the failure to punish (such as the failure "to conduct an effective investigation"[162]).

5. Taking a Consenting Part

The idea of "taking a consenting part" in a crime, which was included in Law No. 10 and regularly applied by the NMTs, has disappeared from international criminal law. It is not clear why, although it may well be that TCP's "ability to influence" requirement, which is obviously broader than command responsibility's "effective control" requirement, casts too wide a net for modern sensibilities. Interestingly, the prosecution blurred the lines between TCP and command responsibility in *Čelebići*, citing the *Hostage* case for the idea that an individual's ability to exert "substantial influence" over someone who was not a *de jure* or *de facto* subordinate was enough to establish command responsibility.[163] Both the Trials Chamber and the Appeals Chamber rejected that argument, insisting—correctly—that effective control was the minimum required.[164]

J. Defenses

Courts have used the NMT judgments to determine the limits of three defenses: (1) *tu quoque*, (2) necessity/duress, and (3) military necessity.

1. Tu Quoque

In *Kupreškić*, Trial Chamber II cited *High Command* as evidence that the defense of *tu quoque* was "universally rejected" by the post-World War II tribunals.[165]

---

[159] Ibid., 1303.   [160] *Blaškić*, Appeals Judgment, para. 82.

[161] See, e.g., *Prosecutor v. Halilović*, IT-01-48, Judgment, para. 89 (16 Nov. 2005) (citing *Hostage*).

[162] See, e.g., *Prosecutor v. Strugar*, IT-01-42, Judgment, para. 376 (31 Jan. 2005) (citing *High Command*).

[163] *Čelebići*, Trial Judgment, para. 648.

[164] *Čelebići*, Appeals Judgment, para. 258.

[165] *Kupreškić*, Trial Judgment, para. 516.

2. Necessity/Duress

Courts have consistently looked to the NMT judgments to determine the elements of duress. In *Finta*, the Supreme Court of Canada followed *Einsatzgruppen* by holding that a defendant could invoke duress only if he had been faced by an "imminent, real, and inevitable" threat to his life.[166] In *Doe v. Unocal*, the U.S. Court of Appeals for the Ninth Circuit adopted the *Krupp* tribunal's definition of necessity and suggested that, like Krupp, Unocal had pushed to expand its operations in Myanmar knowing that doing so "would require the employment of forced labor."[167] And in *Erdemović*, the ICTY Trial Chamber relied on *Einsatzgruppen*, *Flick*, and *High Command* to hold that a defendant could argue duress only if he had been "deprived of his moral choice" by the threat of "imminent physical danger."[168]

Erdemović, of course, involved a defendant accused of participating in a mass execution of civilians. The debate in the Appeals Chamber over whether duress was available as a defense to murder focused, to a significant extent, on the NMT judgments. Judges McDonald and Vohrah, rejecting that idea for the majority, acknowledged that the *Einsatzgruppen* tribunal accepted such a defense, but it insisted that the judgment was inconsistent with other authorities from the World War II era.[169] By contrast, Judge Cassese argued—wrongly, as discussed above—that *Einsatzgruppen* was more authoritative than the national cases cited by the majority and that the judgment indicated that customary international law did not create a "murder" exception to the general availability of the necessity defense.[170]

Although Cassese overstated the authority of the NMT judgments regarding defenses, the *Einsatzgruppen* approach to duress has had a considerable influence on the ICC. In contrast to ICTY jurisprudence, Article 31(1)(d) of the Rome Statute specifically permits a defendant to invoke duress as a defense to murder.

3. Military Necessity

In *Galić*, Trial Chamber I correctly cited the *Hostage* case for the idea that a defendant cannot invoke military necessity as a defense to a violation of a rule of IHL that does not specifically take such necessity into account—there, the categorical prohibition of intentional attacks on civilians or civilian objects.[171] In *Krstić*, by contrast, the Trial Chamber erroneously relied on *Hostage* to suggest that whether military necessity justified a defendant's actions is an objective test.[172] In fact, the

---

[166] *R v. Finta* [1994] 1 S.C.R. 701, 837.
[167] *Unocal*, 395 F.3d at 948.
[168] *Prosecutor v. Erdemović*, IT-96-22-T, Sentencing Judgment, paras 17–8 (29 Nov. 1996).
[169] *Erdemović*, Appeals Judgment, McDonald and Vohrah Separate Opinion, paras 43–5.
[170] Ibid., Separate and Dissenting Opinion of Judge Cassese, paras 27–8.
[171] *Prosecutor v. Galić*, IT-98-29-T Judgment, para. 44 (5 Dec. 2003).
[172] *Prosecutor v. Krstić*, IT-98-33-T, Judgment, para. 526 (2 Aug. 2001).

Hostage tribunal held that a defendant was entitled to acquittal as long as he "honestly conclude[d]" that his actions were militarily necessary.

Although *Krstić* misread *Hostage*, its conclusion was sound. A strong case can be made that a subjective test of military necessity underprotects civilians against disproportionate attacks.[173] Unfortunately, the *Hostage* tribunal's rejection of a "reasonable military commander" test continues to have a pernicious impact on international criminal law. The Rome Statute's "war crime of excessive incidental death, injury, or damage," for example, requires the defendant to "make the value judgment" that a planned attack would be disproportionate, thus requiring the acquittal of a commander who honestly believed that the attack's expected incidental harm was not clearly excessive relative to the expected military advantage.[174]

K. Sentencing

The NMT judgments also played a role in *Erdemović* concerning the relative gravity of war crimes and crimes against humanity. McDonald and Vohrah took the position for the majority that crimes against humanity were more serious than war crimes, citing Telford Taylor's explanation in *Einsatzgruppen* that the difference between the two categories of crimes is that the former, unlike the latter, can be committed in peacetime and require "systematic violations of fundamental human rights."[175] Judge Li disagreed in his separate and dissenting opinion, arguing that war crimes were more serious than crimes against humanity by contrasting the death sentences imposed by the IMT for the former with Rothaug's life sentence for the latter in the *Justice* case.[176] Li's argument is questionable, to say the least: none of the defendants were sentenced to death in the *Justice* case, not even those that were convicted of war crimes, and all of the defendants sentenced to death by the NMTs were convicted of *both* war crimes and crimes against humanity.

That does not mean, of course, that the NMTs considered crimes against humanity to be more serious than war crimes. Indeed, in his separate opinion in *Tadić*, Judge Robinson cited *Milch* and *Hostage* for the idea that the two categories of crimes are equally serious.[177] That is a plausible reading of the judgments; after all, Lautz was sentenced to 10 years in the *Justice* case despite being one of two

---

[173] See Jessica C. Lawrence & Kevin Jon Heller, "The First Ecocentric Environmental War Crime: The Limits of Article 8(2)(b)(iv) of the Rome Statute," 20 *Geo. Int'l Env. L. Rev.* 61, 78 (2007).

[174] Rome Statute, Element of Crimes, Art. 8(2)(b)(iv), 132 n. 37. Some delegations insisted at PrepCom that whether an attack was "clearly excessive" should be determined from the perspective of the reasonable military commander. See Knut Dörmann, "Preparatory Commission for the International Criminal Court: The Elements of War Crimes," 82 *Int'l Rev. Red Cross* 461, 473–4 (2001). Footnote 37, however, specifically creates an exception to the general rule in the Elements of Crimes that mental elements do not require a perpetrator to make value judgments. Rome Statute, Element of Crimes, General Introduction, para. 4.

[175] *Erdemović*, Appeals Judgment, McDonald and Vohrah Separate Opinion, para. 24.

[176] Ibid., Li Separate and Dissenting Opinion, para. 22.

[177] *Prosecutor v. Tadić*, IT-94-1-T*bis*-R117, Sentencing Judgment, Separate Opinion of Judge Robinson, 4 (11 Nov. 1999).

defendants in the trials convicted of genocide. McDonald and Vohrah's position in *Erdemović* is nevertheless not without merit, given the tribunals' insistence that crimes against humanity, unlike war crimes, had to be widespread, systematic, *and* committed pursuant to government policy.[178]

The ICTY has also relied on the judgments with regard to less controversial issues. In *Čelebići*, the Appeals Chamber relied on the *Justice* case for the idea that a defendant can be convicted of both war crimes and crimes against humanity for the same acts, because the two categories of crimes have different elements.[179] And in *Erdemović*, the Trial Chamber cited with approval the *Hostage* tribunal's statement that mitigation "is more a matter of grace than of defence"[180] and relied on *Einsatzgruppen* and *High Command* to support its conclusion that the existence of superior orders is a mitigating factor[181]—a questionable interpretation of the former, given that the *Einsatzgruppen* tribunal acknowledged superior orders as mitigating only if the order in question was not manifestly illegal.

---

[178] The ICTY currently considers the two categories of crimes to be equally grave. The ICTR, by contrast, considers crimes against humanity to be more serious than war crimes. See Allison Danner, "Constructing a Hierarchy of Crimes in International Criminal Law Sentencing," 87 *Va. L. Rev.* 415, 469–70 (2001).

[179] *Čelebići*, Appeals Judgment, para. 411.

[180] *Erdemović*, Sentencing Judgment, para. 46.

[181] Ibid., para. 52.

Conclusion

It is always tempting to look back at an international tribunal and ask whether it was successful. The answer to that question, however, depends on the criteria that one uses to measure success. The NMTs pursued a variety of different goals, the most important of which were achieving retributive justice, educating the German people, creating a historical record, and contributing to the development of international criminal law. Some of those goals were achieved; others were not.

In terms of retributive justice, the verdict is clearly mixed. The first phase of the NMT program, the construction of the trials, receives low marks: the OCC was able to bring charges against only a fraction of the German war criminals that deserved to be prosecuted. No tribunal, of course, can prosecute every deserving suspect. But it is undeniable that the OCC's inadequate budget, lack of staff, and oppressive calendar combined to unnecessarily limit the ambition of Taylor's plan for the trials. There is also reason to believe that many high-value suspects—the Wolffs and von Mansteins—escaped prosecution for reasons that had little to do with the quantity or quality of the evidence against them.

The second phase of the NMT program, the trials themselves, achieved much better results. The judges were committed to retributive justice—acquitting the innocent, convicting the guilty, and imposing appropriate sentences. Overall, they succeeded. There is little evidence that any of the defendants were wrongly convicted, although the law was occasionally deficient concerning specific counts.[1] Some of the defendants were wrongly acquitted, particularly the industrialists in *Flick* and *Farben*, but excessive credulousness toward defense claims was a problem that affected individual tribunals, not the trials as a whole. And the sentences that the judges imposed were generally consistent within cases and over time, even if the tribunals that were the most inclined to acquit were also the most inclined to sentence leniently.

The defendants, of course, were also concerned with retributive justice. For them, the fairness of the trials was paramount—a wrongful conviction meant the loss of their freedom, even their life. Here, too, the trials were a success. There is no question that the OCC enjoyed significant material and logistical advantages over the defense, and it is difficult not to be troubled by the fact that prosecutors

---

[1] The best example being Keppler and Lammers's convictions for participating in the invasions of Austria and Czechoslovakia, which almost certainly violated the principle of non-retroactivity.

relied heavily on incriminating statements made by the defendants without the benefit of counsel. But it is equally clear that, with very few exceptions, the tribunals did everything they could to provide the defendants with fair trials. There may not have been complete equality of arms between the two sides, but the scales of justice were balanced more evenly than at most international tribunals.[2] Dr. Sauter, the defense attorney, said it best: no German suspect would have chosen to be prosecuted by a different court, because at the NMTs he could at least be confident that the judges wanted to reach "a just verdict."

Retributive justice, however, requires more than imposing an appropriate sentence on defendants convicted after a fair trial. The convicted defendants must also actually serve their sentences. From that perspective, the third phase of the NMT program—the post-trial phase—has to be viewed as a complete failure. Once the NMTs shut down, American war-crimes officials did everything they could to release the convicted defendants as quickly and as quietly as possible. In public, those officials, particularly McCloy, insisted that their decisions were motivated solely by retributive concerns. In private, however, they openly acknowledged that the need to release the convicted defendants was driven by the politics of the Cold War, not by legal considerations. The American government believed that it needed Germany as an ally in the war on communism, and the cost of German cooperation was nothing less than a general amnesty—*de facto* if not *de jure*—for the convicted NMT defendants.

Telford Taylor agreed that the trials needed to provide retributive justice, but he also hoped that the trials would create a historical record of Nazi atrocities that would have a transformative effect on ordinary Germans. From that perspective, the scorecard is mixed. The collapse of the U.S. government's commitment to the NMTs fatally undermined the didactic goal of the trials: although convincing ordinary Germans to reject the atrocities committed in their name would have been difficult under the best of circumstances, whatever possibility for education did exist was effectively destroyed by the government's decision to bury the records of the 12 trials. By contrast, from a documentary perspective, the trials were a resounding success—"the greatest history seminar ever held," as Robert Kempner described them. The trials provided unprecedented detail about Hitler's rise to power, the inner workings of the Nazi regime, the planning and preparation of Germany's wars and invasions, and the execution of the Final Solution. That vast historical record, more than 130,000 pages long, will be of use to lawyers and historians for decades to come.

The tribunals' greatest success, however, remains their inestimable contribution to the form and substance of international criminal law. It is now second nature to speak about international criminal law's "special" and "general" parts, but that was not always the case: although the IMT established individual criminal responsibility under international law, it said relatively little about its basic principles. The NMTs, by contrast, took the raw materials provided to them—the London

---

[2] See generally Jacob Katz Cogan, "International Criminal Courts and Fair Trials: Difficulties and Prospects," 27 *Yale J. Int'l L.* 111–40 (2002).

Charter, the IMT judgment, Law No. 10—and honed them into a coherent system of criminal law, one in which crimes were divided into elements, modes of participation were precisely identified, and defenses were made available but cabined within reasonable limits. The NMTs, in other words, were committed to treating international criminal law as criminal law first and international law second.

That commitment almost certainly explains why judges who had little knowledge of international law were able, far more often than not, to reach substantive decisions concerning crimes, modes of participation, and defenses that remain good law more than 60 years later. Extending crimes against peace to bloodless invasions and deeming aggression a leadership crime; requiring legal process for captured partisans and criminalizing non-consensual medical experiments; developing contextual elements for crimes against humanity and prohibiting genocide; adopting knowledge as the *mens rea* of aiding and abetting and extending command responsibility to non-military superiors; distinguishing necessity from the defense of superior orders and rejecting the idea of Total War—each decision has left an indelible mark on modern jurisprudence. The NMTs might not have given birth to international criminal law, but they clearly nurtured it into adolescence.

APPENDIX A

Table of Defendants

Defendant	Position	Indictment	Verdict	Sentence	McCloy Revision	Released
		United States of America vs. Karl Brandt, et al. (*Medical* case)				
Hermann Becker-Freyseng	Captain, Medical Service of the Air Force; Chief of the Department for Aviation Medicine of the Chief of the Medical Service of the Luftwaffe	1. Conspiracy to Commit War Crimes & Crimes Against Humanity	Dismissed by Tribunal	20 Years	10 Years	1952
		2. War Crimes: Medical Experimentation on POWs and Civilians in Occupied Territory	Convicted			
		3. Crimes Against Humanity: Medical Experimentation on German Nationals and Nationals of Other Countries	Convicted			
Wilhelm Beigleboeck	Consulting Physician to the Luftwaffe	1. Conspiracy to Commit War Crimes & Crimes Against Humanity	Dismissed by Tribunal	15 Years	10 Years	1951
		2. War Crimes: Medical Experimentation on POWs and Civilians in Occupied Territory	Convicted			
		3. Crimes Against Humanity: Medical Experimentation on German Nationals and Nationals of Other Countries	Convicted			

continued

Defendant	Position	Indictment	Verdict	Sentence	McCloy Revision	Released
Kurt Blome	Deputy Reich Health Leader; Plenipotentiary for Cancer Research in the Reich Research Council	1. Conspiracy to Commit War Crimes & Crimes Against Humanity	Dismissed by Tribunal			
		2. War Crimes: Medical Experimentation on POWs and Civilians in Occupied Territory	Acquitted			
		3. Crimes Against Humanity: Medical Experimentation on German Nationals and Nationals of Other Countries	Acquitted			
Viktor Brack	Chief Administrative Officer in the Chancellery of the Fuehrer of the NSDAP	1. Conspiracy to Commit War Crimes & Crimes Against Humanity	Dismissed by Tribunal	Death		
		2. War Crimes: Medical Experimentation on POWs and Civilians in Occupied Territory	Convicted			
		3. Crimes Against Humanity: Medical Experimentation on German Nationals and Nationals of Other Countries	Convicted			
		4. Membership in a Criminal Organization: SS	Convicted			
Karl Brandt	Personal Physician to Adolf Hitler; Reich Commissioner for Health and Sanitation	1. Conspiracy to Commit War Crimes & Crimes Against Humanity	Dismissed by Tribunal	Death		
		2. War Crimes: Medical Experimentation on POWs and Civilians in Occupied Territory	Convicted			

Name	Position	Charge	Verdict	Sentence	
		3. Crimes Against Humanity: Medical Experimentation on German Nationals and Nationals of Other Countries	Convicted		
		4. Membership in a Criminal Organization: SS	Convicted		
Rudolf Brandt	Personal Administrative Officer to Reichsfuehrer SS Himmler; Ministerial Counsellor and Chief of the Ministerial Office in the Reich Ministry of the Interior	1. Conspiracy to Commit War Crimes & Crimes Against Humanity	Dismissed by Tribunal	Death	
		2. War Crimes: Medical Experimentation on POWs and Civilians in Occupied Territory	Convicted		
		3. Crimes Against Humanity: Medical Experimentation on German Nationals and Nationals of Other Countries	Convicted		
		4. Membership in a Criminal Organization: SS	Convicted		
Fritz Fischer	Assistant Physician to the Defendant Gebhardt at the Hospital at Hohenlychen	1. Conspiracy to Commit War Crimes & Crimes Against Humanity	Dismissed by Tribunal	Life	15 Years 1954
		2. War Crimes: Medical Experimentation on POWs and Civilians in Occupied Territory	Convicted		
		3. Crimes Against Humanity: Medical Experimentation on German Nationals and Nationals of Other Countries	Convicted		
		4. Membership in a Criminal Organization: SS	Convicted		

continued

Defendant	Position	Indictment	Verdict	Sentence	McCloy Revision	Released
Karl Gebhardt	Personal Physician to Reichsfuehrer SS Himmler; Chief Surgeon of the Staff of the Reich Physician SS and Police; President of the German Red Cross	1. Conspiracy to Commit War Crimes & Crimes Against Humanity	Dismissed by Tribunal	Death		
		2. War Crimes: Medical Experimentation on POWs and Civilians in Occupied Territory	Convicted			
		3. Crimes Against Humanity: Medical Experimentation on German Nationals and Nationals of Other Countries	Convicted			
		4. Membership in a Criminal Organization: SS	Convicted			
Karl Genzken	Chief of the Medical Department of the Waffen SS	1. Conspiracy to Commit War Crimes & Crimes Against Humanity	Dismissed by Tribunal	Life	20 Years	1954
		2. War Crimes: Medical Experimentation on POWs and Civilians in Occupied Territory	Convicted			
		3. Crimes Against Humanity: Medical Experimentation on German Nationals and Nationals of Other Countries	Convicted			
		4. Membership in a Criminal Organization: SS	Convicted			
Siegfried Handloser	Lieutenant General, Medical Service; Medical Inspector of the Army;	1. Conspiracy to Commit War Crimes & Crimes Against Humanity	Dismissed by Tribunal	Life	20 Years	1953 (Illness)

Name	Position	Charges	Verdict	Sentence
	Chief of the Medical Services of the Armed Forces	2. War Crimes: Medical Experimentation on POWs and Civilians in Occupied Territory	Convicted	
		3. Crimes Against Humanity: Medical Experimentation on German Nationals and Nationals of Other Countries	Convicted	Death
Waldemar Hoven	Chief Doctor of the Buchenwald Concentration Camp	1. Conspiracy to Commit War Crimes & Crimes Against Humanity	Dismissed by Tribunal	
		2. War Crimes: Medical Experimentation on POWs and Civilians in Occupied Territory	Convicted	
		3. Crimes Against Humanity: Medical Experimentation on German Nationals and Nationals of Other Countries	Convicted	
		4. Membership in a Criminal Organization: SS	Convicted	Death
Joachim Mrugowsky	Chief Hygienist of the Reich Physician SS and Police; Chief of the Hygienic Institute of the Waffen SS	1. Conspiracy to Commit War Crimes & Crimes Against Humanity	Dismissed by Tribunal	
		2. War Crimes: Medical Experimentation on POWs and Civilians in Occupied Territory	Convicted	
		3. Crimes Against Humanity: Medical Experimentation on German Nationals and Nationals of Other Countries	Convicted	
		4. Membership in a Criminal Organization: SS	Convicted	Death

continued

Defendant	Position	Indictment	Verdict	Sentence	McCloy Revision	Released
Herta Oberheuser	Physician at the Ravensbrueck Concentration Camp; Assistant Physician to Defendant Gebhardt at the Hospital at Hohenlychen	1. Conspiracy to Commit War Crimes & Crimes Against Humanity	Dismissed by Tribunal	20 Years	10 Years	1952
		2. War Crimes: Medical Experimentation on POWs and Civilians in Occupied Territory	Convicted			
		3. Crimes Against Humanity: Medical Experimentation on German Nationals and Nationals of Other Countries	Convicted			
Adolf Pokorny	Physician, Specialist in Skin and Venereal Diseases	1. Conspiracy to Commit War Crimes & Crimes Against Humanity	Dismissed by Tribunal			
		2. War Crimes: Medical Experimentation on POWs and Civilians in Occupied Territory	Acquitted			
		3. Crimes Against Humanity: Medical Experimentation on German Nationals and Nationals of Other Countries	Acquitted			
Helmut Poppendick	Chief of the Personal Staff of the Reich Physician SS and Police	1. Conspiracy to Commit War Crimes & Crimes Against Humanity	Dismissed by Tribunal	10 Years	Time Served	1951
		2. War Crimes: Medical Experimentation on POWs and Civilians in Occupied Territory	Acquitted			

Name	Position	Charge	Verdict	Sentence	Reduced Sentence	Release
		3. Crimes Against Humanity: Medical Experimentation on German Nationals and Nationals of Other Countries	Acquitted			
		4. Membership in a Criminal Organization: SS	Convicted			
Hans Wolfgang Romberg	Doctor on Staff of the Department for Aviation Medicine, German Experimental Institute for Aviation	1. Conspiracy to Commit War Crimes & Crimes Against Humanity	Dismissed by Tribunal			
		2. War Crimes: Medical Experimentation on POWs and Civilians in Occupied Territory	Acquitted			
		3. Crimes Against Humanity: Medical Experimentation on German Nationals and Nationals of Other Countries	Acquitted			
Gerhard Rose	Brigadier General, Medical Service of the Air Force; Vice President, Chief of the Department for Tropical Medicine; Hygienic Advisor for Tropical Medicine to the Chief of the Medical Service of the Luftwaffe	1. Conspiracy to Commit War Crimes & Crimes Against Humanity	Dismissed by Tribunal			
		2. War Crimes: Medical Experimentation on POWs and Civilians in Occupied Territory	Convicted			
		3. Crimes Against Humanity: Medical Experimentation on German Nationals and Nationals of Other Countries	Convicted	Life	15 Years	1955
Paul Rostock	Chief Surgeon of the Surgical Clinic in Berlin; Surgical Advisor to the	1. Conspiracy to Commit War Crimes & Crimes Against Humanity	Dismissed by Tribunal			

continued

Defendant	Position	Indictment	Verdict	Sentence	McCloy Revision	Released
	Army; Chief of the Office for Medical Science and Research Under Defendant Karl Brandt	2. War Crimes: Medical Experimentation on POWs and Civilians in Occupied Territory	Acquitted			
		3. Crimes Against Humanity: Medical Experimentation on German Nationals and Nationals of Other Countries	Acquitted			
Siegfried Ruff	Director of the Department for Aviation Medicine at the German Experimental Institute for Aviation	1. Conspiracy to Commit War Crimes & Crimes Against Humanity	Dismissed by Tribunal			
		2. War Crimes: Medical Experimentation on POWs and Civilians in Occupied Territory	Acquitted			
		3. Crimes Against Humanity: Medical Experimentation on German Nationals and Nationals of Other Countries	Acquitted			
Konrad Schaefer	Doctor on the Staff of the Institute for Aviation Medicine in Berlin	1. Conspiracy to Commit War Crimes & Crimes Against Humanity	Dismissed by Tribunal			
		2. War Crimes: Medical Experimentation on POWs and Civilians in Occupied Territory	Acquitted			
		3. Crimes Against Humanity: Medical Experimentation on German Nationals and Nationals of Other Countries	Acquitted			

Name	Position	Charge	Verdict	Sentence		
Oskar Schroeder	Lieutenant General Medical Service; Chief of Staff of the Inspectorate of the Medical Service of the Luftwaffe; Chief of the Medical Service of the Luftwaffe	1. Conspiracy to Commit War Crimes & Crimes Against Humanity	Dismissed by Tribunal			
		2. War Crimes: Medical Experimentation on POWs and Civilians in Occupied Territory	Convicted	Life	15 Years	1954
		3. Crimes Against Humanity: Medical Experimentation on German Nationals and Nationals of Other Countries	Convicted			
Wolfram Sievers	Reich Manager of the "Ahnenerbe" Society and Director of Its Institute for Military Scientific Research; Deputy Chairman of the Managing Board of Directors of the Reich Research Council	1. Conspiracy to Commit War Crimes & Crimes Against Humanity	Dismissed by Tribunal			
		2. War Crimes: Medical Experimentation on POWs and Civilians in Occupied Territory	Convicted	Death		
		3. Crimes Against Humanity: Medical Experimentation on German Nationals and Nationals of Other Countries	Convicted			
		4. Membership in a Criminal Organization: SS	Convicted			
Georg August Weltz	Lieutenant Colonel, Medical Service of the Air Force; Chief of the Institute for Aviation Medicine in Munich	1. Conspiracy to Commit War Crimes & Crimes Against Humanity	Dismissed by Tribunal			
		2. War Crimes: Medical Experimentation on POWs and Civilians in Occupied Territory	Acquitted			
		3. Crimes Against Humanity: Medical Experimentation on German Nationals and Nationals of Other Countries	Acquitted			

continued

Defendant	Position	Indictment	Verdict	Sentence	McCloy Revision	Released
United States of America vs. Erhard Milch						
Erhard Milch	State Secretary in the Reich Air Ministry; Inspector General of the Air Force; Deputy to the Commander in Chief of the Air Force; Field Marshal in the Luftwaffe; Member of the Central Planning Board; Chief of the Jaegerstab	1. War Crimes: Slave Labor 2. War Crimes: Medical Experimentation 3. Crimes Against Humanity: Slave Labor	Convicted Acquitted Convicted	Life	15 Years	1954
United States of America vs. Josef Altstoetter, et al. (*Justice* case)						
Josef Altstoetter	Chief of the Civil Law and Procedure Division of the Reich Ministry of Justice	1. Conspiracy to Commit War Crimes and Crimes Against Humanity 2. War Crimes 3. Crimes Against Humanity 4. Membership in a Criminal Organization: SS	Dismissed by Tribunal Acquitted Acquitted Convicted	5 Years	1950	
Wilhelm von Ammon	Ministerial Counsellor of the Criminal Legislation and Administration Division the Reich Ministry of Justice	1. Conspiracy to Commit War Crimes and Crimes Against Humanity 2. War Crimes 3. Crimes Against Humanity	Dismissed by Tribunal Convicted Convicted	10 Years	Time Served	1951
Paul Barnickel	Senior Public Prosecutor of the People's Court	1. Conspiracy to Commit War Crimes and Crimes Against Humanity 2. War Crimes 3. Crimes Against Humanity	Dismissed by Tribunal Acquitted Acquitted			

Name	Position	Charges	Verdict	Sentence	Released
Hermann Cuhorst	Chief Justice of the Special Court in Stuttgart; Chief Justice of the First Criminal Senate of the District Court in Stuttgart	1. Conspiracy to Commit War Crimes and Crimes Against Humanity 2. War Crimes 3. Crimes Against Humanity 4. Membership in a Criminal Organization: SS and Leadership Corps of the Nazi Party	Dismissed by Tribunal Acquitted Acquitted Acquitted		
Karl Engert	Chief of the Penal Administration Division and of the Secret Prison Inmate Transfer Division of the Reich Ministry of Justice; Vice President of the People's Court	1. Conspiracy to Commit War Crimes and Crimes Against Humanity 2. War Crimes 3. Crimes Against Humanity 4. Membership in a Criminal Organization: SS	Mistrial Declared Due to Illness		
Guenther Joel	Legal Advisor to the Reich Minister of Justice Concerning Criminal Prosecutions; Chief Public Prosecutor of Westphalia at Hamm	1. Conspiracy to Commit War Crimes and Crimes Against Humanity 2. War Crimes 3. Crimes Against Humanity 4. Membership in a Criminal Organization: SS and SD	Dismissed by Tribunal Convicted Convicted Convicted	10 Years	1951
Herbert Klemm	State Secretary of the Reich Ministry of Justice; Chief of the Legal Education and Training Division in the Ministry of Justice	1. Conspiracy to Commit War Crimes and Crimes Against Humanity 2. War Crimes 3. Crimes Against Humanity	Dismissed by Tribunal Convicted Convicted	Life	1957
Ernst Lautz	Chief Public Prosecutor of the People's Court	1. Conspiracy to Commit War Crimes and Crimes Against Humanity 2. War Crimes 3. Crimes Against Humanity	Dismissed by Tribunal Convicted Convicted	10 Years	1951

continued

Defendant	Position	Indictment	Verdict	Sentence	McCloy Revision	Released
Wolfgang Mettgenberg	Representative of the Chief of the Criminal Legislation and Administration Division of the Reich Ministry of Justice	1. Conspiracy to Commit War Crimes and Crimes Against Humanity 2. War Crimes 3. Crimes Against Humanity	Dismissed by Tribunal Convicted Convicted	10 Years		Died in Prison, 1950
Guenther Nebelung	Chief Justice of the Fourth Senate of the People's Court	1. Conspiracy to Commit War Crimes and Crimes Against Humanity 2. War Crimes 3. Crimes Against Humanity 4. Membership in a Criminal Organization: SS	Dismissed by Tribunal Acquitted Acquitted Acquitted			
Rudolf Oeschey	Judge of the Special Court in Nuremberg and Successor to the Defendant Rothaug as Chief Justice of the Special Court in Nuremberg	1. Conspiracy to Commit War Crimes and Crimes Against Humanity 2. War Crimes 3. Crimes Against Humanity 4. Membership in a Criminal Organization: Leadership Corps of the Nazi Party (NSDAP)	Dismissed by Tribunal Guilty Guilty Guilty	Life	20 Years	1955
Hans Petersen	Lay Judge of the First Senate of the People's Court; Lay Judge of the Special Senate of the People's Court	1. Conspiracy to Commit War Crimes and Crimes Against Humanity 2. War Crimes 3. Crimes Against Humanity	Dismissed by Tribunal Acquitted Acquitted			
Oswald Rothaug	Senior Public Prosecutor of the People's Court; Formerly Chief Justice of	1. Conspiracy to Commit War Crimes and Crimes Against Humanity	Dismissed by Tribunal	Life	20 Years	1956

	Position	Charges	Verdict	Sentence	Modification	Year
	the Special Court in Nuremberg	2. War Crimes	Acquitted			
		3. Crimes Against Humanity	Convicted			
		4. Membership in a Criminal Organization: SS, Party Leadership Corps	Acquitted			
Curt Rothenberger	State Secretary of the Reich Ministry of Justice; Deputy President of the Academy of German Law	1. Conspiracy to Commit War Crimes and Crimes Against Humanity	Dismissed by Tribunal	7 Years		1950
		2. War Crimes	Convicted			
		3. Crimes Against Humanity	Convicted			
Franz Schlegelberger	State Secretary; Acting Reich Minister of Justice	1. Conspiracy to Commit War Crimes and Crimes Against Humanity	Dismissed by Tribunal	Life	Released on Medical Parole	1951
		2. War Crimes	Convicted			
		3. Crimes Against Humanity	Convicted			
Carl Westphal	Ministerial Counsellor of the Criminal Legislation and Administration Division of the Reich Ministry of Justice	1. Conspiracy to Commit War Crimes and Crimes Against Humanity	Died Prior to Commencement of Trial			
		2. War Crimes				
		3. Crimes Against Humanity				

United States of America vs. Oswald Pohl, et al.

	Position	Charges	Verdict	Sentence	Modification	Year
Oswald Pohl	Chief of the WVHA; Chief of Division W of the WVHA	1. Conspiracy to Commit War Crimes & Crimes Against Humanity	Acquitted	Death	No Modification	
		2. War Crimes: Atrocities and Offenses Against Civilian Populations in Occupied Territory and POW's	Convicted			

continued

Defendant	Position	Indictment	Verdict	Sentence	McCloy Revision	Released
		3. Crimes Against Humanity: Atrocities and Offenses Against German Civilians and Nationals of Other Countries	Convicted			
		4. Membership in a Criminal Organization: SS	Convicted			
August Frank	Deputy Chief of the WVHA; Chief of Division A of the WVHA	1. Conspiracy to Commit War Crimes & Crimes Against Humanity	Acquitted	Life	15 Years	1954
		2. War Crimes: Atrocities and Offenses Against Civilian Populations in Occupied Territory and POWs	Convicted			
		3. Crimes Against Humanity: Atrocities and Offenses Against German Civilians and Nationals of Other Countries	Convicted			
		4. Membership in a Criminal Organization: SS	Convicted			
Georg Loerner	Deputy Chief of the WVHA; Chief of Division B of the WVHA; Deputy Chief of Division W of the WVHA	1. Conspiracy to Commit War Crimes & Crimes Against Humanity	Acquitted	Death; Reduced to Life on Post-Trial Motion	15 Years	1954
		2. War Crimes: Atrocities and Offenses Against Civilian Populations in Occupied Territory and POWs	Convicted			
		3. Crimes Against Humanity: Atrocities and Offenses Against German Civilians and Nationals of Other Countries	Convicted			
		4. Membership in a Criminal Organization: SS	Convicted			

Name	Position	Charge	Verdict	Sentence		
Heinz Karl Fanslau	Chief of Division A of the WVHA	1. Conspiracy to Commit War Crimes & Crimes Against Humanity	Acquitted	25 Years; Reduced to 20 Years on Post-Trial Motion	15 Years	1954
		2. War Crimes: Atrocities and Offenses Against Civilian Populations in Occupied Territory and POW's	Convicted			
		3. Crimes Against Humanity: Atrocities and Offenses Against German Civilians and Nationals of Other Countries	Convicted			
		4. Membership in a Criminal Organization: SS	Convicted			
Hans Loerner	Chief of Office I of Division A of the WVHA	1. Conspiracy to Commit War Crimes & Crimes Against Humanity	Acquitted	10 Years	Time Served	1951
		2. War Crimes: Atrocities and Offenses Against Civilian Populations in Occupied Territory and POW's	Convicted			
		3. Crimes Against Humanity: Atrocities and Offenses Against German Civilians and Nationals of Other Countries	Convicted			
		4. Membership in a Criminal Organization: SS	Convicted			
Josef Vogt	Chief of Office IV of Division A of the WVHA	1. Conspiracy to Commit War Crimes & Crimes Against Humanity	Acquitted			
		2. War Crimes: Atrocities and Offenses Against Civilian	Acquitted			

continued

Defendant	Position	Indictment	Verdict	Sentence	McCloy Revision	Released
		Populations in Occupied Territory and POWs				
		3. Crimes Against Humanity: Atrocities and Offenses Against German Civilians and Nationals of Other Countries	Acquitted			
		4. Membership in a Criminal Organization: SS	Acquitted			
Erwin Tschentscher	Chief of Division B of the WVHA	1. Conspiracy to Commit War Crimes & Crimes Against Humanity	Acquitted	10 Years	Time Served	1951
		2. War Crimes: Atrocities and Offenses Against Civilian Populations in Occupied Territory and POWs	Convicted			
		3. Crimes Against Humanity: Atrocities and Offenses Against German Civilians and Nationals of Other Countries	Convicted			
		4. Membership in a Criminal Organization: SS	Convicted			
Rudolf Scheide	Chief of Office V of Division B of the WVHA	1. Conspiracy to Commit War Crimes & Crimes Against Humanity	Acquitted			
		2. War Crimes: Atrocities and Offenses Against Civilian Populations in Occupied Territory and POWs	Acquitted			
		3. Crimes Against Humanity: Atrocities and Offenses Against German Civilians and Nationals of Other Countries	Acquitted			

Name	Position	Charge	Verdict	Sentence	Modified Sentence	Released
		4. Membership in a Criminal Organization: SS	Acquitted			
Max Kiefer	Chief of Office II of Division C of the WVHA	1. Conspiracy to Commit War Crimes & Crimes Against Humanity	Acquitted	Life; Reduced to 20 Years on Post-Trial Motion	Time Served	1951
		2. War Crimes: Atrocities and Offenses Against Civilian Populations in Occupied Territory and POWs	Convicted			
		3. Crimes Against Humanity: Atrocities and Offenses Against German Civilians and Nationals of Other Countries	Convicted			
		4. Membership in a Criminal Organization: SS	Convicted			
Franz Eirenschmalz	Chief of Office VI of Division C of the WVHA	1. Conspiracy to Commit War Crimes & Crimes Against Humanity	Acquitted	Death	9 Years	1951
		2. War Crimes: Atrocities and Offenses Against Civilian Populations in Occupied Territory and POWs	Convicted			
		3. Crimes Against Humanity: Atrocities and Offenses Against German Civilians and Nationals of Other Countries	Convicted			
		4. Membership in a Criminal Organization: SS	Convicted			
Karl Sommer	Deputy Chief of Office II of Division D of the WVHA	1. Conspiracy to Commit War Crimes & Crimes Against Humanity	Acquitted	Death; Commuted to Life by	20 Years	1953

continued

Defendant	Position	Indictment	Verdict	Sentence	McCloy Revision	Released
		2. War Crimes: Atrocities and Offenses Against Civilian Populations in Occupied Territory and POWs	Convicted	General Clay		
		3. Crimes Against Humanity: Atrocities and Offenses Against German Civilians and Nationals of Other Countries	Convicted			
		4. Membership in a Criminal Organization: SS	Convicted			
Hermann Pook	Chief Dentist of the WVHA, Office III, Division D	1. Conspiracy to Commit War Crimes & Crimes Against Humanity	Acquitted	10 Years	Time Served	1951
		2. War Crimes: Atrocities and Offenses Against Civilian Populations in Occupied Territory and POWs	Convicted			
		3. Crimes Against Humanity: Atrocities and Offenses Against German Civilians and Nationals of Other Countries	Convicted			
		4. Membership in a Criminal Organization: SS	Convicted			
Hans Heinrich Baier	Executive Officer of Division W of the WVHA	1. Conspiracy to Commit War Crimes & Crimes Against Humanity	Acquitted	10 Years	Time Served	1950
		2. War Crimes: Atrocities and Offenses Against Civilian Populations in Occupied Territory and POWs	Convicted			

Name	Position	Charge	Verdict	Sentence	Reduced Sentence	Year
		3. Crimes Against Humanity: Atrocities and Offenses Against German Civilians and Nationals of Other Countries	Convicted			
		4. Membership in a Criminal Organization: SS	Convicted	10 Years	Time Served	1951
Hans Hohberg	Executive Officer of Division W of the WVHA	1. Conspiracy to Commit War Crimes & Crimes Against Humanity	Acquitted			
		2. War Crimes: Atrocities and Offenses Against Civilian Populations in Occupied Territory and POWs	Convicted			
		3. Crimes Against Humanity: Atrocities and Offenses Against German Civilians and Nationals of Other Countries	Convicted			
Leo Volk	Personal Advisor on Pohl's Staff; Head of Legal Section in the Executive Office of Division W of the WVHA	1. Conspiracy to Commit War Crimes & Crimes Against Humanity	Acquitted	10 Years	8 Years	1952
		2. War Crimes: Atrocities and Offenses Against Civilian Populations in Occupied Territory and POWs	Convicted			
		3. Crimes Against Humanity: Atrocities and Offenses Against German Civilians and Nationals of Other Countries	Convicted			
		4. Membership in a Criminal Organization: Waffen SS	Acquitted			

continued

Defendant	Position	Indictment	Verdict	Sentence	McCloy Revision	Released
Karl Mummenthey	Chief of Office I of Division W of the WVHA; Director & Manager of DEST	1. Conspiracy to Commit War Crimes & Crimes Against Humanity	Acquitted	Life	20 Years	1953
		2. War Crimes: Atrocities and Offenses Against Civilian Populations in Occupied Territory and POWs	Convicted			
		3. Crimes Against Humanity: Atrocities and Offenses Against German Civilians and Nationals of Other Countries	Convicted			
		4. Membership in a Criminal Organization: SS	Convicted			
Hans Bobermin	Chief of Office II of Division W of the WVHA	1. Conspiracy to Commit War Crimes & Crimes Against Humanity	Acquitted	20 Years; Reduced to 15 Years on Post-Trial Motion	Time Served	1951
		2. War Crimes: Atrocities and Offenses Against Civilian Populations in Occupied Territory and POWs	Convicted			
		3. Crimes Against Humanity: Atrocities and Offenses Against German Civilians and Nationals of Other Countries	Convicted			
		4. Membership in a Criminal Organization: SS	Convicted			
Horst Klein	Chief of Office VIII of Division W of the WVHA	1. Conspiracy to Commit War Crimes & Crimes Against Humanity	Acquitted			

		2. War Crimes: Atrocities and Offenses Against Civilian Populations in Occupied Territory and POWs	Acquitted		
		3. Crimes Against Humanity: Atrocities and Offenses Against German Civilians and Nationals of Other Countries	Acquitted		
		4. Membership in a Criminal Organization: SS	Acquitted		

United States of America vs. Friedrich Flick, et al.

Friedrich Flick	Principal Proprietor of the Flick Concern; Military Economy Leader; Member of the Official Bodies for Regulation of the Coal, Iron and Steel Industries; Member of the "Small Circle" and the "Circle of Friends"; Member of the Administrative Board of the Berg-und-Huettenwerke Ost	1. War Crimes and Crimes Against Humanity: Slave Labor	Convicted	7 Years	1950
		2. War Crimes and Crimes Against Humanity: Plunder	Convicted		
		3. Crimes Against Humanity: Aryanization	Dismissed by Tribunal		
		4. War Crimes and Crimes Against Humanity: SS Atrocities	Convicted		
Otto Steinbrinck	Principal Assistant to Flick; Plenipotentiary for Coal in the Occupied Western Territories; Plenipotentiary General for Steel Industry in Northern France, Belgium, and Luxembourg	1. War Crimes and Crimes Against Humanity: Slave Labor	Acquitted	5 Years	Died in Prison, 1949
		2. War Crimes and Crimes Against Humanity: Plunder	Acquitted		
		3. Crimes Against Humanity: Aryanization	Dismissed by Tribunal		

continued

Defendant	Position	Indictment	Verdict	Sentence	McCloy Revision	Released
		4. War Crimes and Crimes Against Humanity: SS Atrocities	Convicted			
		5. Membership in a Criminal Organization: SS	Convicted			
Bernhard Weiss	Sole Owner of Siemag (from 1941); Plenipotentiary General of the Flick Concern Ruhr Bituminous Coal Plants	1. War Crimes and Crimes Against Humanity: Slave Labor	Convicted	2½ Years		1948
		2. War Crimes and Crimes Against Humanity: Plunder	Acquitted			
Odilo Burkart	Official of Flick Enterprises	1. War Crimes and Crimes Against Humanity: Slave Labor	Acquitted			
		2. War Crimes and Crimes Against Humanity: Plunder	Acquitted			
Konrad Kaletsch	Official of Flick Enterprises; Principal Official and Owner of Siemag (until 1941)	1. War Crimes and Crimes Against Humanity: Slave Labor	Acquitted			
		2. War Crimes and Crimes Against Humanity: Plunder	Acquitted			
		3. Crimes Against Humanity: Aryanization	Dismissed by Tribunal			
Herman Terberger	Official of Flick Enterprises	1. War Crimes and Crimes Against Humanity: Slave Labor	Acquitted			

United States of America vs. Carl Krauch, et al. (*Farben*)

| Carl Krauch | Chairman of the Aufsichtsrat; General | 1. Crimes Against Peace | Acquitted | 6 Years | | 1950 |

Name	Position	Charge	Verdict	Sentence	Year
	Plenipotentiary for Special Questions of Chemical Production in the Office of the Four Year Plan	2. War Crimes & Crimes Against Humanity: Plunder	Acquitted		
		3. Crimes Against Humanity: Slave Labor	Convicted		
		5. Conspiracy to Commit Crimes Against Peace	Acquitted		
Hermann Schmitz	Chairman of the Vorstand; Member of the Reichstag; Director of the Bank of International Settlements	1. Crimes Against Peace	Acquitted	4 Years	1950
		2. War Crimes & Crimes Against Humanity: Plunder	Convicted		
		3. Crimes Against Humanity: Slave Labor	Acquitted		
		5. Conspiracy to Commit Crimes Against Peace	Acquitted		
Georg von Schnitzler	Member of the Central Committee of the Vorstand; Chief of the Commercial Committee of the Vorstand	1. Crimes Against Peace	Acquitted	5 Years	1949
		2. War Crimes & Crimes Against Humanity: Plunder	Convicted		
		3. Crimes Against Humanity: Slave Labor	Acquitted		
		5. Conspiracy to Commit Crimes Against Peace	Acquitted		
Fritz Gajewski	Member of the Central Committee of the Vorstand; Manager of "Agfa" plants	1. Crimes Against Peace	Acquitted		
		2. War Crimes & Crimes Against Humanity: Plunder	Acquitted		
		3. Crimes Against Humanity: Slave Labor	Acquitted		
		5. Conspiracy to Commit Crimes Against Peace	Acquitted		
Heinrich Hoerlein	Member of the Central Committee of the Vorstand of Farben; Chief of Chemical Research; Manager of the Elberfeld Plant	1. Crimes Against Peace	Acquitted		
		2. War Crimes & Crimes Against Humanity: Plunder	Acquitted		
		3. Crimes Against Humanity: Slave Labor	Acquitted		
		5. Conspiracy to Commit Crimes Against Peace	Acquitted		

continued

Defendant	Position	Indictment	Verdict	Sentence	McCloy Revision	Released
August von Knieriem	Member of the Central Committee of the Vorstand of Farben; Chief Counsel of Farben; Chairman, Legal and Patent Committees	1. Crimes Against Peace 2. War Crimes & Crimes Against Humanity: Plunder 3. Crimes Against Humanity: Slave Labor 5. Conspiracy to Commit Crimes Against Peace	Acquitted Acquitted Acquitted Acquitted			
Fritz ter Meer	Member of the Central Committee of the Vorstand; Chief of the Technical Committee; Chief of Division II	1. Crimes Against Peace 2. War Crimes & Crimes Against Humanity: Plunder 3. Crimes Against Humanity: Slave Labor 5. Conspiracy to Commit Crimes Against Peace	Acquitted Acquitted Convicted Acquitted	7 Years		1950
Christian Schneider	Member of the Central Committee of the Vorstand; Chief of Division I; Chief of Central Personnel Department; Chief of Intelligence Agents; Chief of Plant Leaders	1. Crimes Against Peace 2. War Crimes & Crimes Against Humanity: Plunder 3. Crimes Against Humanity: Slave Labor 4. Membership in a Criminal Organization: SS 5. Conspiracy to Commit Crimes Against Peace	Acquitted Acquitted Acquitted Acquitted Acquitted			
Otto Ambros	Member of the Vorstand; Chief of Chemical Warfare Committee of the Ministry of Armaments and War Production; Production Chief for Buna and Poison Gas; Manager of Auschwitz Plant	1. Crimes Against Peace 2. War Crimes & Crimes Against Humanity: Plunder 3. Crimes Against Humanity: Slave Labor 5. Conspiracy to Commit Crimes Against Peace	Acquitted Acquitted Convicted Acquitted	8 Years		1952

Name	Position	Charge	Verdict	Sentence	Year
Max Brueggemann	Member and Secretary of the Vorstand; Member of the Legal Committee; Deputy Plant Leader of the Leverkusen Plant; Deputy Chief of the Sales Combine Pharmaceuticals; Director of the Legal, Patent, and Personnel Departments of the Works Combine Lower Rhine		Dismissed from Trial Due to Ill Health		
Ernst Buergin	Member of the Vorstand; Chief of Works Combine Central Germany; Plant Leader at Bitterfeld and Wolfen-Farben Plants	1. Crimes Against Peace 2. War Crimes & Crimes Against Humanity: Plunder 3. Crimes Against Humanity: Slave Labor 5. Conspiracy to Commit Crimes Against Peace	Acquitted Convicted Acquitted Acquitted	2 Years	1948
Heinrich Buetefisch	Member of the Vorstand; Manager of Leuna Plants; Production Chief at Auschwitz and Moosbierbaum; Member of the Circle of Friends of Himmler	1. Crimes Against Peace 2. War Crimes & Crimes Against Humanity: Plunder 3. Crimes Against Humanity: Slave Labor 4. Membership in a Criminal Organization: SS 5. Conspiracy to Commit Crimes Against Peace	Acquitted Acquitted Convicted Acquitted Acquitted	6 Years	1951
Paul Haefliger	Member of the Vorstand; Member of the Commercial Committee; Chief, Metals Departments, Sales Combine Chemicals	1. Crimes Against Peace 2. War Crimes & Crimes Against Humanity: Plunder 3. Crimes Against Humanity: Slave Labor 5. Conspiracy to Commit Crimes Against Peace	Acquitted Convicted Acquitted Acquitted	2 Years	1948

continued

Defendant	Position	Indictment	Verdict	Sentence	McCloy Revision	Released
Max Ilgner	Member of the Vorstand; Chief of Berlin N.W. 7 Office Directing Intelligence, Espionage, and Propaganda Activities; Member of the Commercial Committee	1. Crimes Against Peace 2. War Crimes & Crimes Against Humanity: Plunder 3. Crimes Against Humanity: Slave Labor 5. Conspiracy to Commit Crimes Against Peace	Acquitted Convicted Acquitted Acquitted	3 Years (Time Served)		1948
Friedrich Jaehne	Member of the Vorstand; Chief Engineer in Charge of Construction; Chairman of the Engineering Committee; Deputy Chief, Works Combine Main Valley	1. Crimes Against Peace 2. War Crimes & Crimes Against Humanity: Plunder 3. Crimes Against Humanity: Slave Labor 5. Conspiracy to Commit Crimes Against Peace	Acquitted Convicted Acquitted Acquitted	1½ Years (Time Served)		1948
Hans Kuehne	Member of the Vorstand; Chief of the Works Combine Lower Rhine; Plant Leader at Leverkusen, Elberfeld, Uerdingen, and Dormagen Plants; Chief of the Inorganics Committee	1. Crimes Against Peace 2. War Crimes & Crimes Against Humanity: Plunder 3. Crimes Against Humanity: Slave Labor 5. Conspiracy to Commit Crimes Against Peace	Acquitted Acquitted Acquitted Acquitted			
Karl Lautenschlager	Member of the Vorstand; Chief of Works Combine Main Valley; Plant Leader at Hoechst, Griesheim, Mainkur, Gersthofen, Offenbach, Eystrup, Marburg, Neuhausen Plants	1. Crimes Against Peace 2. War Crimes & Crimes Against Humanity: Plunder 3. Crimes Against Humanity: Slave Labor 5. Conspiracy to Commit Crimes Against Peace	Acquitted Acquitted Acquitted Acquitted			

Name	Position	Charges	Verdict	Sentence	Year
Wilhelm Mann	Member of the Vorstand; Member of the Commercial Committee; Chief of the Sales Combine Pharmaceuticals	1. Crimes Against Peace 2. War Crimes & Crimes Against Humanity: Plunder 3. Crimes Against Humanity: Slave Labor 5. Conspiracy to Commit Crimes Against Peace	Acquitted Acquitted Acquitted Acquitted		
Heinrich Oster	Member of the Vorstand; Member of the Commercial Committee; Manager of the Nitrogen Syndicate	1. Crimes Against Peace 2. War Crimes & Crimes Against Humanity: Plunder 3. Crimes Against Humanity: Slave Labor 5. Conspiracy to Commit Crimes Against Peace	Acquitted Convicted Acquitted Acquitted	2 Years	1948
Karl Wurster	Member of the Vorstand; Chief of the Works Combine Upper Rhine; Plant Leader at Ludwigshafen and Oppau Plants; Production Chief for Inorganic Chemicals	1. Crimes Against Peace 2. War Crimes & Crimes Against Humanity: Plunder 3. Crimes Against Humanity: Slave Labor 5. Conspiracy to Commit Crimes Against Peace	Acquitted Acquitted Acquitted Acquitted		
Walter Duerrfeld	Director and Construction Manager of the Auschwitz Plant; Director and Construction Manager of the Monowitz Concentration Camp; Chief Engineer at the Leuna Plant	1. Crimes Against Peace 2. War Crimes & Crimes Against Humanity: Plunder 3. Crimes Against Humanity: Slave Labor 5. Conspiracy to Commit Crimes Against Peace	Acquitted Acquitted Convicted Acquitted	8 Years	1951
Heinrich Gattineau		1. Crimes Against Peace	Acquitted		

continued

Defendant	Position	Indictment	Verdict	Sentence	McCloy Revision	Released
	Chief of the Political-Economic Policy Department, "WIPO," of Berlin N.W. 7 Office; Member of Southeast Europe Committee; Director of A.G. Dynamit Nobel, Pressburg, Czechoslovakia	2. War Crimes & Crimes Against Humanity: Plunder 3. Crimes Against Humanity: Slave Labor 5. Conspiracy to Commit Crimes Against Peace	Acquitted Acquitted Acquitted			
Erich von der Heyde	Member of the Political-Economic Policy Department of Berlin N.W. 7 Office; Deputy to the Chief of Intelligence Agents; Member of the Military Economics and Armaments Office of the High Command of the Wehrmacht	1. Crimes Against Peace 2. War Crimes & Crimes Against Humanity: Plunder 3. Crimes Against Humanity: Slave Labor 4. Membership in a Criminal Organization: SS. 5. Conspiracy to Commit Crimes Against Peace	Acquitted Acquitted Acquitted Acquitted Acquitted			
Hans Kugler	Member of the Commercial Committee; Chief of the Sales Department Dyestuffs for Hungary, Romania, Yugoslavia, Greece, Bulgaria, Turkey, Czechoslovakia, and Austria; Public Commissar for the Falkenau and Aussig Plants	1. Crimes Against Peace 2. War Crimes & Crimes Against Humanity: Plunder 3. Crimes Against Humanity: Slave Labor 5. Conspiracy to Commit Crimes Against Peace	Acquitted Convicted Acquitted Acquitted	1½ Years (Time Served)		1948

United States of America vs. Wilhem List, et al. (*Hostage* case)

Name	Position	Charges	Verdict	Sentence	Modification	Year
Wilhelm List	General of the Army; Commander in Chief 12th Army; Armed Forces Commander Southeast; Commander in Chief Army Group A	1. War Crimes and Crimes Against Humanity: Hostage-Taking	Convicted	Life	No Modification	1952 (Illness)
		2. War Crimes and Crimes Against Humanity: Plunder	Acquitted			
		3. War Crimes and Crimes Against Humanity: Murder and Mistreatment of POWs	Convicted			
		4. War Crimes and Crimes Against Humanity: Murder and Mistreatment of Civilians	Acquitted			
Walter Kuntze	Lieutenant General, Engineers; Acting Commander in Chief 12th Army	1. War Crimes and Crimes Against Humanity: Hostage-Taking	Convicted	Life	No Modification	1953
		2. War Crimes and Crimes Against Humanity: Plunder	Acquitted			
		3. War Crimes and Crimes Against Humanity: Murder and Mistreatment of POWs	Convicted			
		4. War Crimes and Crimes Against Humanity: Murder and Mistreatment of Civilians	Convicted			
Lothar Rendulic	General; Commander in Chief 2nd Panzer Army; Commander in Chief 20th Mountain Army; Armed Forces Commander North;	1. War Crimes and Crimes Against Humanity: Hostage-Taking	Convicted	20 Years	10 Years	1951
		2. War Crimes and Crimes Against Humanity: Plunder	Acquitted			

continued

Defendant	Position	Indictment	Verdict	Sentence	McCloy Revision	Released
	Commander in Chief Army Group North; Commander in Chief Army Group Courland; Commander in Chief Army Group South	3. War Crimes and Crimes Against Humanity: Murder and Mistreatment of POWs	Convicted			
		4. War Crimes and Crimes Against Humanity: Murder and Mistreatment of Civilians	Convicted			
Ernst Dehner	Lieutenant General, Infantry; Commander LXIX Army Reserve Corps	1. War Crimes and Crimes Against Humanity: Hostage-Taking	Convicted	7 Years	Time Served	1951
		2. War Crimes and Crimes Against Humanity: Plunder	Acquitted			
		3. War Crimes and Crimes Against Humanity: Murder and Mistreatment of POWs	Acquitted			
		4. War Crimes and Crimes Against Humanity: Murder and Mistreatment of Civilians	Acquitted			
Ernst von Leyser	Lieutenant General, Infantry; Commander XV Mountain Army Corps; Commander XXI Mountain Army Corps	1. War Crimes and Crimes Against Humanity: Hostage-Taking	Acquitted	10 Years	Time Served	1951
		2. War Crimes and Crimes Against Humanity: Plunder	Acquitted			
		3. War Crimes and Crimes Against Humanity: Murder and Mistreatment of POWs	Convicted			
		4. War Crimes and Crimes Against Humanity: Murder and Mistreatment of Civilians	Convicted			

Name	Position	Charges	Verdict	Sentence	Time Served	Release
Hubert Lanz	Lieutenant General, Mountain Troops; Commander 1st Mountain Division; Commander XXII Mountain Army Corps	1. War Crimes and Crimes Against Humanity: Hostage-Taking	Convicted	12 Years	Time Served	1951
		2. War Crimes and Crimes Against Humanity: Plunder	Acquitted			
		3. War Crimes and Crimes Against Humanity: Murder and Mistreatment of POWs	Convicted			
		4. War Crimes and Crimes Against Humanity: Murder and Mistreatment of Civilians	Acquitted			
Helmuth Felmy	Lieutenant General, Air Force; Commander Southern Greece; Commander LXVIII Army Corps	1. War Crimes and Crimes Against Humanity: Hostage-Taking	Convicted	15 Years	10 Years	1955
		2. War Crimes and Crimes Against Humanity: Plunder	Convicted			
		3. War Crimes and Crimes Against Humanity: Murder and Mistreatment of POWs	Acquitted			
		4. War Crimes and Crimes Against Humanity: Murder and Mistreatment of Civilians	Acquitted			
Wilhelm Speidel	Lieutenant General Air Force; Commander Southern Greece; Military Commander Greece	1. War Crimes and Crimes Against Humanity: Hostage-Taking	Convicted	20 Years	Time Served	1951
		2. War Crimes and Crimes Against Humanity: Plunder	Acquitted			
		3. War Crimes and Crimes Against Humanity: Murder and Mistreatment of POWs	Acquitted			
		4. War Crimes and Crimes Against Humanity: Murder and Mistreatment of Civilians	Acquitted			

continued

Defendant	Position	Indictment	Verdict	Sentence	McCloy Revision	Released
Hermann Foertsch	Lieutenant General, Infantry; Chief of Staff 12th Army; Chief of Staff Army Group E; Chief of Staff Army Group F	1. War Crimes and Crimes Against Humanity: Hostage-Taking	Acquitted			
		2. War Crimes and Crimes Against Humanity: Plunder	Acquitted			
		3. War Crimes and Crimes Against Humanity: Murder and Mistreatment of POWs	Acquitted			
		4. War Crimes and Crimes Against Humanity: Murder and Mistreatment of Civilians	Acquitted			
Kurt von Geitner	Brigadier General; Chief of Staff to the Commanding General in Serbia; Chief of Staff to the Military Commander of Serbia and Military Commander Southeast	1. War Crimes and Crimes Against Humanity: Hostage-Taking	Acquitted			
		2. War Crimes and Crimes Against Humanity: Plunder	Acquitted			
		3. War Crimes and Crimes Against Humanity: Murder and Mistreatment of POWs	Acquitted			
		4. War Crimes and Crimes Against Humanity: Murder and Mistreatment of Civilians	Acquitted			
Maximilian von Weichs	General of the Army; Commander in Chief 2nd Army; Commander in Chief Army Group B; Commander in Chief Army Group F and Supreme Commander Southeast	1. War Crimes and Crimes Against Humanity: Hostage-Taking	Dismissed from Trial Due to Ill Health			
		2. War Crimes and Crimes Against Humanity: Plunder				

Defendant	Position	Charges	Verdict	Sentence		Release
Franz Boehme	Lieutenant General, Mountain Troops; Commander XVIII Mountain Army Corps; Plenipotentiary Commanding General in Serbia; Commander in Chief 2nd Panzer Army; Commander in Chief 20th Mountain Army and Armed Forces Commander North	3. War Crimes and Crimes Against Humanity: Murder and Mistreatment of POWs 4. War Crimes and Crimes Against Humanity: Murder and Mistreatment of Civilians 1. War Crimes and Crimes Against Humanity: Hostage-Taking 2. War Crimes and Crimes Against Humanity: Plunder 3. War Crimes and Crimes Against Humanity: Murder and Mistreatment of POWs 4. War Crimes and Crimes Against Humanity: Murder and Mistreatment of Civilians	Committed Suicide Prior to Arraignment			

United States of America vs. Ulrich Greifelt, et al. *(RuSHA)*

Defendant	Position	Charges	Verdict	Sentence		Release
Ulrich Greifelt	Chief of the Staff Main Office of the Reich Commissioner for the Strengthening of Germanism; Deputy to Himmler	1. Crimes Against Humanity: Atrocities and Offenses Against Civilians and POWs 2. War Crimes: Atrocities and Offenses Against POWs and Civilians in Occupied Territory 3. Membership in a Criminal Organization: SS	Convicted Convicted Convicted	Life		Died in Prison, 1949
Rudolf Creutz	Deputy to Greifelt, Chief of Amtsgruppe "A" of the Staff Main Office of the Reich Commissioner for the	1. Crimes Against Humanity: Atrocities and Offenses Against Civilians and POWs	Convicted	15 Years	10 Years	1955

continued

Defendant	Position	Indictment	Verdict	Sentence	McCloy Revision	Released
	Strengthening of Germanism	2. War Crimes: Atrocities and Offenses Against POWs and Civilians in Occupied Territory	Convicted			
		3. Membership in a Criminal Organization: SS	Convicted			
Konrad Meyer-Hetling	Chief of the Planning Office in the Staff Main Office of the Reich Commissioner for the Strengthening of Germanism	1. Crimes Against Humanity: Atrocities and Offenses Against Civilians and POWs	Acquitted	2 Years, 10 Months (Time Served)		1948
		2. War Crimes: Atrocities and Offenses Against POWs and Civilians in Occupied Territory	Acquitted			
		3. Membership in a Criminal Organization: SS	Convicted			
Otto Schwarzenberger	Chief of Finance in the Staff Main Office of the Reich Commissioner for the Strengthening of Germanism	1. Crimes Against Humanity: Atrocities and Offenses Against Civilians and POWs	Acquitted	2 Years, 10 Months (Time Served)		1948
		2. War Crimes: Atrocities and Offenses Against POWs and Civilians in Occupied Territory	Acquitted			
		3. Membership in a Criminal Organization: SS	Convicted			
Herbert Huebner	Chief of Poznan Office of the Reich Commissioner for the Strengthening of Germanism and	1. Crimes Against Humanity: Atrocities and Offenses Against Civilians and POWs	Convicted	15 Years	Time Served	1951

Name	Position	Charge	Verdict	Sentence		Year
	Representative of the Race and Settlement Main Office in Western Poland	2. War Crimes: Atrocities and Offenses Against POWs and Civilians in Occupied Territory	Convicted			
		3. Membership in a Criminal Organization: SS	Convicted			
Werner Lorenz	Chief of the Repatriation Office for Ethnic Germans	1. Crimes Against Humanity: Atrocities and Offenses Against Civilians and POWs	Convicted	20 Years	15 Years	1954
		2. War Crimes: Atrocities and Offenses Against POWs and Civilians in Occupied Territory	Convicted			
		3. Membership in a Criminal Organization: SS	Convicted			
Heinz Brueckner	Chief of Office of Safeguarding of German Folkdom in the Reich	1. Crimes Against Humanity: Atrocities and Offenses Against Civilians and POWs	Convicted	15 Years	Time Served	1951
		2. War Crimes: Atrocities and Offenses Against POWs and Civilians in Occupied Territory	Convicted			
		3. Membership in a Criminal Organization: SS	Convicted			
Otto Hofmann	Chief of the Race and Settlement Main Office	1. Crimes Against Humanity: Atrocities and Offenses Against Civilians and POWs	Convicted	25 Years	15 Years	1954
		2. War Crimes: Atrocities and Offenses Against POWs and Civilians in Occupied Territory	Convicted			
		3. Membership in a Criminal Organization: SS	Convicted			

continued

Defendant	Position	Indictment	Verdict	Sentence	McCloy Revision	Released
Richard Hildebrandt	Chief of the Race and Settlement Main Office	1. Crimes Against Humanity: Atrocities and Offenses Against Civilians and POWs	Convicted	25 Years		Extradited to Poland; Executed 1951
		2. War Crimes: Atrocities and Offenses Against POWs and Civilians in Occupied Territory	Convicted			
		3. Membership in a Criminal Organization: SS	Convicted			
Fritz Schwalm	Chief of Staff of the Race and Settlement Main Office and Head of the Immigration Centre in Lodz	1. Crimes Against Humanity: Atrocities and Offenses Against Civilians and POWs	Convicted	10 Years	Time Served	1951
		2. War Crimes: Atrocities and Offenses Against POWs and Civilians in Occupied Territory	Convicted			
		3. Membership in a Criminal Organization: SS	Convicted			
Max Sollman	Chief of Main Department A of the Lebensborn Society	1. Crimes Against Humanity: Atrocities and Offenses Against Civilians and POWs	Acquitted	2 Years, 8 Months (Time Served)		1948
		2. War Crimes: Atrocities and Offenses Against POWs and Civilians in Occupied Territory	Acquitted			
		3. Membership in a Criminal Organization: SS	Convicted			
Gregor Ebner	Chief of the Main Health Department of the Lebensborn Society	1. Crimes Against Humanity: Atrocities and Offenses Against Civilians and POWs	Acquitted	2 Years, 8 Months		1948

Name	Position	Charge	Verdict	Sentence	
		2. War Crimes: Atrocities and Offenses Against POWs and Civilians in Occupied Territory	Acquitted	(Time Served)	
		3. Membership in a Criminal Organization: SS	Convicted		
Guenther Tesch	Chief of the Main Legal Department of the Lebensborn Society	1. Crimes Against Humanity: Atrocities and Offenses Against Civilians and POWs	Acquitted	2 Years, 10 Months (Time Served)	1948
		2. War Crimes: Atrocities and Offenses Against POWs and Civilians in Occupied Territory	Acquitted		
		3. Membership in a Criminal Organization: SS	Convicted		
Inge Vermietz	Deputy Chief of Main Department A of the Lebensborn Society	1. Crimes Against Humanity: Atrocities and Offenses Against Civilians and POWs	Acquitted		
		2. War Crimes: Atrocities and Offenses Against POWs and Civilians in Occupied Territory	Acquitted		

United States of America vs. Otto Ohlendorf, et al. (*Einsatzgruppen*)

Name	Position	Charge	Verdict	Sentence	
Otto Ohlendorf	Commanding Officer of Einsatzgruppe D	1. Crimes Against Humanity: Atrocities and Offenses Against German Nationals and Nationals of Other Countries	Convicted	Death	No Modification
		2. War Crimes: Murder and Mistreatment of POWs & Civilian Populations in Occupied Territory	Convicted		

continued

Defendant	Position	Indictment	Verdict	Sentence	McCloy Revision	Released
		3. Membership in a Criminal Organization: SS & SD	Convicted			
Heinz Jost	Commanding Officer of Einsatzgruppe A	1. Crimes Against Humanity: Atrocities and Offenses Against German Nationals and Nationals of Other Countries	Convicted	Life	10 Years	1951
		2. War Crimes: Murder and Mistreatment of POWs & Civilian Populations in Occupied Territory	Convicted			
		3. Membership in a Criminal Organization: SS & SD	Convicted			
Erich Naumann	Commanding Officer of Einsatzgruppe B	1. Crimes Against Humanity: Atrocities and Offenses Against German Nationals and Nationals of Other Countries	Convicted	Death	No Modification	
		2. War Crimes: Murder and Mistreatment of POWs & Civilian Populations in Occupied Territory	Convicted			
		3. Membership in a Criminal Organization: SS & SD	Convicted			
Otto Rasch	Commanding Officer of Einsatzgruppe C	1. Crimes Against Humanity: Atrocities and Offenses Against German Nationals and Nationals of Other Countries	Dismissed from Trial Due to Ill Health			

Name	Charges	Verdict	Sentence	Modified Sentence	Year
Erwin Schulz	Commanding Officer of Einsatzkommando 5 of Einsatzgruppe C				
	2. War Crimes: Murder and Mistreatment of POWs & Civilian Populations in Occupied Territory				
	3. Membership in a Criminal Organization: SS, SD & Gestapo				
	1. Crimes Against Humanity: Atrocities and Offenses Against German Nationals and Nationals of Other Countries	Convicted	20 Years	15 Years	1954
	2. War Crimes: Murder and Mistreatment of POWs & Civilian Populations in Occupied Territory	Convicted			
	3. Membership in a Criminal Organization: SS	Convicted			
Franz Six	Commanding Officer of Vorkommando Moscow of Einsatzgruppe B				
	1. Crimes Against Humanity: Atrocities and Offenses Against German Nationals and Nationals of Other Countries	Convicted	20 Years	10 Years	1952
	2. War Crimes: Murder and Mistreatment of POWs & Civilian Populations in Occupied Territory	Convicted			
	3. Membership in a Criminal Organization: SS & SD	Convicted			
Paul Blobel	Commanding Officer of Sonderkommando 4a of Einsatzgruppe C				
	1. Crimes Against Humanity: Atrocities and Offenses Against German Nationals	Convicted	Death	No Modification	

continued

Defendant	Position	Indictment	Verdict	Sentence	McCloy Revision	Released
		and Nationals of Other Countries				
		2. War Crimes: Murder and Mistreatment of POWs & Civilian Populations in Occupied Territory	Convicted			
		3. Membership in a Criminal Organization: SS & SD	Convicted			
Walter Blume	Commanding Officer of Sonderkommando 7a of Einsatzgruppe B	1. Crimes Against Humanity: Atrocities and Offenses Against German Nationals and Nationals of Other Countries	Convicted	Death	25 Years	1951
		2. War Crimes: Murder and Mistreatment of POWs & Civilian Populations in Occupied Territory	Convicted			
		3. Membership in a Criminal Organization: SS, SD & Gestapo	Convicted			
Martin Sandberger	Commanding Officer of Einsatzkommando 1a of Einsatzgruppe A	1. Crimes Against Humanity: Atrocities and Offenses Against German Nationals and Nationals of Other Countries	Convicted	Death	Life	1958
		2. War Crimes: Murder and Mistreatment of POWs & Civilian Populations in Occupied Territory	Convicted			
		3. Membership in a Criminal Organization: SS & SD	Convicted			

Name	Position	Charge	Verdict	Sentence	Modification	Date
	Einsatzgruppe D	Atrocities and Offenses Against German Nationals and Nationals of Other Countries	Convicted			
		2. War Crimes: Murder and Mistreatment of POWs & Civilian Populations in Occupied Territory	Convicted			
		3. Membership in a Criminal Organization: SS & SD	Convicted			
Eugen Steimle	Commanding Officer of Sonderkommando 7a of Einsatzgruppe B; Commanding Officer of Sonderkommando 4a of Einsatzgruppe C	1. Crimes Against Humanity: Atrocities and Offenses Against German Nationals and Nationals of Other Countries	Convicted	Death	20 Years	1954
		2. War Crimes: Murder and Mistreatment of POWs & Civilian Populations in Occupied Territory	Convicted			
		3. Membership in a Criminal Organization: SS & SD	Convicted			
Ernst Biberstein	Commanding Officer of Einsatzkommando 6 of Einsatzgruppe C	1. Crimes Against Humanity: Atrocities and Offenses Against German Nationals and Nationals of Other Countries	Convicted	Death	Life	1958
		2. War Crimes: Murder and Mistreatment of POWs & Civilian Populations in Occupied Territory	Convicted			
		3. Membership in a Criminal Organization: SS, SD & Gestapo	Convicted			
Werner Braune	Commanding Officer of Sonderkommando 11b of Einsatzgruppe D	1. Crimes Against Humanity: Atrocities and Offenses Against German Nationals	Convicted	Death	No Modification	

continued

Defendant	Position	Indictment	Verdict	Sentence	McCloy Revision	Released
		and Nationals of Other Countries				
		2. War Crimes: Murder and Mistreatment of POWs & Civilian Populations in Occupied Territory	Convicted			
		3. Membership in a Criminal Organization: SS, SD & Gestapo	Convicted			
Walter Haensch	Commanding Officer of Sonderkommando 4b of Einsatzgruppe C	1. Crimes Against Humanity: Atrocities and Offenses Against German Nationals and Nationals of Other Countries	Convicted	Death	15 Years	1955
		2. War Crimes: Murder and Mistreatment of POWs & Civilian Populations in Occupied Territory	Convicted			
		3. Membership in a Criminal Organization: SS & SD	Convicted			
Gustav Nosske	Commanding Officer of Einsatzkommando 12 of Einsatzgruppe D	1. Crimes Against Humanity: Atrocities and Offenses Against German Nationals and Nationals of Other Countries	Convicted	Life	10 Years	1951
		2. War Crimes: Murder and Mistreatment of POWs & Civilian Populations in Occupied Territory	Convicted			
		3. Membership in a Criminal Organization: SS & Gestapo	Convicted			

Name	Position	Charges	Verdict	Sentence	Commuted	Notes/Year
Adolf Ott	Commanding Officer of Sonderkommando 7b of Einsatzgruppe B	1. Crimes Against Humanity: Atrocities and Offenses Against German Nationals and Nationals of Other Countries 2. War Crimes: Murder and Mistreatment of POWs & Civilian Populations in Occupied Territory 3. Membership in a Criminal Organization: SS & SD	Convicted Convicted Convicted	Death	Life	1958
Eduard Strauch	Commanding Officer of Einsatzkommando 2 of Einsatzgruppe A	1. Crimes Against Humanity: Atrocities and Offenses Against German Nationals and Nationals of Other Countries 2. War Crimes: Murder and Mistreatment of POWs & Civilian Populations in Occupied Territory 3. Membership in a Criminal Organization: SS & SD	Convicted Convicted Convicted	Death		Extradited to Belgium & Sentenced to Death; Sentence Not Carried Out Because of Mental Illness
Emil Haussmann	Officer of Einsatzkommando 12 of Einsatzgruppe D	1. Crimes Against Humanity: Atrocities and Offenses Against German Nationals and Nationals of Other Countries 2. War Crimes: Murder and Mistreatment of POWs & Civilian Populations in Occupied Territory 3. Membership in a Criminal Organization: SS & SD	Committed Suicide Prior to Arraignment			
Waldemar Klingelhoefer	Member of Sonderkommando 7b of Einsatzgruppe B; Commanding Officer of Vorkommando Moscow	1. Crimes Against Humanity: Atrocities and Offenses Against German Nationals and Nationals of Other Countries	Convicted	Death	Life	1956

continued

Defendant	Position	Indictment	Verdict	Sentence	McCloy Revision	Released
		2. War Crimes: Murder and Mistreatment of POWs & Civilian Populations in Occupied Territory	Convicted			
		3. Membership in a Criminal Organization: SS & SD	Convicted			
Lothar Fendler	Deputy Chief of Sonderkommando 4b of Einsatzgruppe C	1. Crimes Against Humanity: Atrocities and Offenses Against German Nationals and Nationals of Other Countries	Convicted	10 Years	8 Years	1951
		2. War Crimes: Murder and Mistreatment of POWs & Civilian Populations in Occupied Territory	Convicted			
		3. Membership in a Criminal Organization: SS & SD	Convicted			
Waldemar von Radetzky	Deputy Chief of Sonderkommando 4a of Einsatzgruppe C	1. Crimes Against Humanity: Atrocities and Offenses Against German Nationals and Nationals of Other Countries	Convicted	20 Years	Time Served	1951
		2. War Crimes: Murder and Mistreatment of POWs & Civilian Populations in Occupied Territory	Convicted			
		3. Membership in a Criminal Organization: SS & SD	Convicted			
Felix Ruehl	Officer of Sonderkommando 10b of Einsatzgruppe D	1. Crimes Against Humanity: Atrocities and Offenses Against German Nationals	Acquitted	10 Years	Time Served	1951

Name	Position	Charge	Verdict	Sentence	Year
		and Nationals of Other Countries			
		2. War Crimes: Murder and Mistreatment of POWs & Civilian Populations in Occupied Territory	Acquitted		
		3. Membership in a Criminal Organization: SS & Gestapo	Convicted		
Heinz Schubert	Officer of Einsatzgruppe D	1. Crimes Against Humanity: Atrocities and Offenses Against German Nationals and Nationals of Other Countries	Convicted	Death	1951
		2. War Crimes: Murder and Mistreatment of POWs & Civilian Populations in Occupied Territory	Convicted		
		3. Membership in a Criminal Organization: SS & SD	Convicted	10 Years	
Mathias Graf	Officer of Einsatzkommando 6 of Einsatzgruppe C	1. Crimes Against Humanity: Atrocities and Offenses Against German Nationals and Nationals of Other Countries	Acquitted	Time Served	1948
		2. War Crimes: Murder and Mistreatment of POWs & Civilian Populations in Occupied Territory	Acquitted		
		3. Membership in a Criminal Organization: SS & SD	Acquitted of Membership in the SS; Convicted of Membership in the SD		

continued

Defendant	Position	Indictment	Verdict	Sentence	McCloy Revision	Released
		United States of America vs. Alfried Krupp von Bohlen und Halbach, et al. *(Krupp)*				
Alfried Krupp von Bohlen und Halbach	Sole Owner, Proprietor, and Directing Head of Fried, Krupp, Essen from December 1943	1. Crimes Against Peace	Dismissed by Tribunal	12 Years and Forfeiture of Real and Personal Property	Time Served; No Forfeiture of Property	1951
		2. War Crimes and Crimes Against Humanity: Plunder	Convicted			
		3. War Crimes and Crimes Against Humanity: Slave Labor	Convicted			
		4. Conspiracy to Commit Crimes Against Peace	Dismissed by Tribunal			
Ewald Oskar Ludwig Loeser	Member of the Vorstand and Head of the Administrative and Finance Departments of Fried, Krupp A.G. until March 1943	1. Crimes Against Peace	Dismissed by Tribunal	7 Years		1951
		2. War Crimes and Crimes Against Humanity: Plunder	Convicted			
		3. War Crimes and Crimes Against Humanity: Slave Labor	Convicted			
		4. Conspiracy to Commit Crimes Against Peace	Dismissed by Tribunal			
Eduard Houdremont	Member of Direktorium and Deputy Member of the Vorstand; Head of the Metallurgical, Steel, and Machine Departments; Plant Leader Gusstahlfabrik, Essen	1. Crimes Against Peace	Dismissed by Tribunal	10 Years	Time Served	1951
		2. War Crimes and Crimes Against Humanity: Plunder	Convicted			
		3. War Crimes and Crimes Against Humanity: Slave Labor	Convicted			
		4. Conspiracy to Commit Crimes Against Peace	Dismissed by Tribunal			
Erich Mueller	Member of Vorstand and Direktorium; Head of	1. Crimes Against Peace	Dismissed by Tribunal	12 Years	Time Served	1951

Name	Position	Charge	Verdict	Sentence	Release
	Artillery Designing and Machine Construction Departments	2. War Crimes and Crimes Against Humanity: Plunder	Convicted		
		3. War Crimes and Crimes Against Humanity: Slave Labor	Convicted		
		4. Conspiracy to Commit Crimes Against Peace	Dismissed by Tribunal		
Friedrich Wilhelm Janssen	Member of Direktorium and Deputy Member of the Vorstand	1. Crimes Against Peace	Acquitted	10 Years	Time Served 1951
		2. War Crimes and Crimes Against Humanity: Plunder	Convicted		
		3. War Crimes and Crimes Against Humanity: Slave Labor	Convicted		
		4. Conspiracy to Commit Crimes Against Peace	Dismissed by Tribunal		
Karl Heinrich Pfirsch	Deputy Member of Direktorium and Vorstand	1. Crimes Against Peace	Dismissed by Tribunal		
		2. War Crimes and Crimes Against Humanity: Plunder	Dismissed by Tribunal		
		3. War Crimes and Crimes Against Humanity: Slave Labor	Acquitted		
		4. Conspiracy to Commit Crimes Against Peace	Dismissed by Tribunal		
Max Otto Ihn	Deputy Member of Direktorium and Vorstand; Deputy to Ewald Loeser and Friedrich Janssen; Deputy Plant Leader, Gusstahlfabrik, Essen	1. Crimes Against Peace	Dismissed by Tribunal	9 Years	Time Served 1951
		2. War Crimes and Crimes Against Humanity: Plunder	Acquitted		
		3. War Crimes and Crimes Against Humanity: Slave Labor	Convicted		

continued

Defendant	Position	Indictment	Verdict	Sentence	McCloy Revision	Released
		4. Conspiracy to Commit Crimes Against Peace	Dismissed by Tribunal			
Karl Adolf Ferdinand Eberhardt	Deputy Member of Direktorium and Vorstand; Successor to Karl Pfirsch as Head of War Material and Machine Sales Departments	1. Crimes Against Peace	Dismissed by Tribunal	9 Years	Time Served	1951
		2. War Crimes and Crimes Against Humanity: Plunder	Convicted			
		3. War Crimes and Crimes Against Humanity: Slave Labor	Convicted			
		4. Conspiracy to Commit Crimes Against Peace	Dismissed by Tribunal			
Heinrich Leo Korschan	Deputy Member of Vorstand; Head of the Department of Steel Plants and Deputy Head of the Metallurgical Department	1. Crimes Against Peace	Dismissed by Tribunal	6 Years	Time Served	1951
		2. War Crimes and Crimes Against Humanity: Plunder	Acquitted			
		3. War Crimes and Crimes Against Humanity: Slave Labor	Convicted			
		4. Conspiracy to Commit Crimes Against Peace	Dismissed by Tribunal			
Friedrich von Buelow	Direct Representative of Krupp with Nazi Officials, the Gestapo, and SS; Chief of the Plant Police, Gusstahlfabrik, Essen	1. Crimes Against Peace	Dismissed by Tribunal	12 Years	Time Served	1951
		2. War Crimes and Crimes Against Humanity: Plunder	Acquitted			
		3. War Crimes and Crimes Against Humanity: Slave Labor	Convicted			
		4. Conspiracy to Commit Crimes Against Peace	Dismissed by Tribunal			
Werner Wilhelm Heinrich Lehmann	Deputy to Max Ihn; Head of Labor Procurement	1. Crimes Against Peace	Dismissed by Tribunal	6 Years	Time Served	1951
		3. War Crimes and Crimes Against Humanity: Slave Labor	Convicted			

Name	Position	Charge	Verdict	Sentence	Year
		4. Conspiracy to Commit Crimes Against Peace	Dismissed by Tribunal		
Hans Albert Gustav Kupke	Head of Foreign Workers Camps	1. Crimes Against Peace	Dismissed by Tribunal		1948
		3. War Crimes and Crimes Against Humanity: Slave Labor	Convicted	2 Years, 10 Months (Time Served)	
		4. Conspiracy to Commit Crimes Against Peace	Dismissed by Tribunal		

United States of America vs. Ernst von Weizsaecker, et al. *(Ministries)*

Name	Position	Charge	Verdict	Sentence	Year
Ernst von Weizsaecker	State Secretary of German Foreign Office; Ministerial Director and Chief of the Political Division of the Foreign Office; German Ambassador to the Vatican	1. Crimes Against Peace	Convicted; Acquitted on Post-Trial Motion	7 Years; Reduced to 5 Years on Post-Trial Motion	1950
		2. Conspiracy to Commit Crimes Against Peace	Acquitted		
		3. War Crimes: Murder & Ill-treatment of Belligerents and POWs	Acquitted		
		4. Crimes Against Humanity: Persecution of German Nationals	Dismissed by Tribunal		
		5. War Crimes & Crimes Against Humanity: Atrocities & Offenses Committed Against Civilian Populations	Convicted		
		6. War Crimes & Crimes Against Humanity: Plunder	Acquitted		
		7. War Crimes & Crimes Against Humanity: Slave Labor	Acquitted		
		8. Membership in a Criminal Organization: SS	Acquitted		1950

continued

Defendant	Position	Indictment	Verdict	Sentence	McCloy Revision	Released
Gustav Steengracht von Moyland	State Secretary of the German Foreign Office, Member of German Foreign Minister's Personal Staff	3. War Crimes: Murder & Ill-treatment of Belligerents and POWs	Convicted; Acquitted on Post-Trial Motion	7 Years; Reduced to 5 Years on Post-Trial Motion		
		5. War Crimes & Crimes Against Humanity: Atrocities & Offenses Committed Against Civilian Populations	Convicted			
		6. War Crimes & Crimes Against Humanity: Plunder	Dismissed by Tribunal			
		7. War Crimes & Crimes Against Humanity: Slave Labor	Acquitted			
Wilhelm Keppler	State Secretary for Special Assignments in the German Foreign Office; Economic Advisor to Adolf Hitler	1. Crimes Against Peace	Convicted	10 Years	Time Served	1951
		2. Conspiracy to Commit Crimes Against Peace	Acquitted			
		4. Crimes Against Humanity: Persecution of German Nationals	Dismissed by Tribunal			
		5. War Crimes & Crimes Against Humanity: Atrocities & Offenses Committed Against Civilian Populations	Convicted			
		6. War Crimes & Crimes Against Humanity: Plunder	Convicted			
		8. Membership in a Criminal Organization: SS & Leadership Corps of the Nazi Party	Convicted			
Ernst Bohle	Chief of the Foreign Organization of the NSDAP; State Secretary and Chief of the Foreign Organization in the	1. Crimes Against Peace	Withdrawn by Prosecution	5 Years		1949
		2. Conspiracy to Commit Crimes Against Peace	Withdrawn by Prosecution			

	German Foreign Office; Member of the Reichstag	4. Crimes Against Humanity: Persecution of German Nationals	Dismissed by Tribunal		
		5. War Crimes & Crimes Against Humanity: Atrocities & Offenses Committed Against Civilian Populations	Acquitted		
		6. War Crimes & Crimes Against Humanity: Plunder	Withdrawn by Prosecution		
		8. Membership in a Criminal Organization: SS & Leadership Corps of the Nazi Party	Pleaded Guilty		
Ernst Woermann	Ministerial Director and Chief of the Political Division of the German Foreign Office; German Ambassador in Nanking; Chief of the International Law Section in the Legal Division of the German Foreign Office	1. Crimes Against Peace	Convicted; Acquitted on Post-Trial Motion	7 Years; Reduced to 5 Years on Post-Trial Motion	1950
		2. Conspiracy to Commit Crimes Against Peace	Acquitted		
		3. War Crimes: Murder & Ill-treatment of Belligerents and POWs	Acquitted		
		4. Crimes Against Humanity: Persecution of German Nationals	Dismissed by Tribunal		
		5. War Crimes & Crimes Against Humanity: Atrocities & Offenses Committed Against Civilian Populations	Convicted		
		6. War Crimes & Crimes Against Humanity: Plunder	Withdrawn by Prosecution		
		7. War Crimes & Crimes Against Humanity: Slave Labor	Dismissed		
		8. Membership in a Criminal Organization: SS	Acquitted		

continued

Defendant	Position	Indictment	Verdict	Sentence	McCloy Revision	Released
Karl Ritter	Ambassador for Special Assignments in the German Foreign Office; Liaison Officer Between the German Foreign Minister and the Chief of the High Command of the German Armed Forces; German Ambassador to Brazil	1. Crimes Against Peace 2. Conspiracy to Commit Crimes Against Peace 3. War Crimes: Murder & Ill-treatment of Belligerents and POWs 5. War Crimes & Crimes Against Humanity: Atrocities & Offenses Committed Against Civilian Populations 6. War Crimes & Crimes Against Humanity: Plunder 7. War Crimes & Crimes Against Humanity: Slave Labor	Acquitted Acquitted Convicted Acquitted Dismissed by Tribunal Acquitted	4 Years		1949
Friedrich von Erdmannsdorff	Embassy Councillor in China; Chief of East Asia Group at the Foreign Office; German Minister in Hungary; Deputy Chief of the Political Division of the Foreign Office	1. Crimes Against Peace 2. Conspiracy to Commit Crimes Against Peace 3. War Crimes: Murder & Ill-treatment of Belligerents and POWs 5. War Crimes & Crimes Against Humanity: Atrocities & Offenses Committed Against Civilian Populations	Withdrawn by Prosecution Withdrawn by Prosecution Withdrawn by Prosecution Acquitted			
Edmund Veesenmayer	German Minister and Plenipotentiary of the Reich in Hungary	1. Crimes Against Peace 2. Conspiracy to Commit Crimes Against Peace 4. Crimes Against Humanity: Persecution of German Nationals	Acquitted Acquitted Dismissed by Tribunal	20 Years	10 Years	1951

Name	Position	Charge	Verdict	Sentence	Year
		5. War Crimes & Crimes Against Humanity: Atrocities & Offenses Committed Against Civilian Populations	Convicted		
		7. War Crimes & Crimes Against Humanity: Slave Labor	Convicted		
		8. Membership in a Criminal Organization: SS	Convicted		
Hans Lammers	Reich Minister and Chief of the Reich Chancellery; Member of the Reich Cabinet; State Secretary in the Reich Chancellery	1. Crimes Against Peace	Convicted	20 Years	1951
		2. Conspiracy to Commit Crimes Against Peace	Acquitted	10 Years	
		3. War Crimes: Murder & Ill-treatment of Belligerents and POWs	Convicted		
		4. Crimes Against Humanity: Persecution of German Nationals	Dismissed by Tribunal		
		5. War Crimes & Crimes Against Humanity: Atrocities & Offenses Committed Against Civilian Populations	Convicted		
		6. War Crimes & Crimes Against Humanity: Plunder	Acquitted		
		7. War Crimes & Crimes Against Humanity: Slave Labor	Convicted		
		8. Membership in a Criminal Organization: SS	Convicted		
Wilhelm Stuckart	State Secretary in the Reich Ministry of the Interior; Chief of the Central Bureau in the Reich Ministry of the Interior	1. Crimes Against Peace	Acquitted	3 Years, 10 Months (Time Served)	1949
		2. Conspiracy to Commit Crimes Against Peace	Acquitted		
		4. Crimes Against Humanity: Persecution of German Nationals	Dismissed by Tribunal		

continued

Defendant	Position	Indictment	Verdict	Sentence	McCloy Revision	Released
		5. War Crimes & Crimes Against Humanity: Atrocities & Offenses Committed Against Civilian Populations	Convicted			
		6. War Crimes & Crimes Against Humanity: Plunder	Convicted			
		7. War Crimes & Crimes Against Humanity: Slave Labor	Acquitted			
		8. Membership in a Criminal Organization: SS	Convicted			
Walther Darre	Reich Minister for Food and Agriculture; Reich Peasant Leader	1. Crimes Against Peace	Acquitted	7 Years		1950
		2. Conspiracy to Commit Crimes Against Peace	Acquitted			
		4. Crimes Against Humanity: Persecution of German Nationals	Dismissed by Tribunal			
		5. War Crimes & Crimes Against Humanity: Atrocities & Offenses Committed Against Civilian Populations	Convicted			
		6. War Crimes & Crimes Against Humanity: Plunder	Convicted			
		7. War Crimes & Crimes Against Humanity: Slave Labor	Acquitted			
		8. Membership in a Criminal Organization: SS & Leadership Corps of the Nazi Party	Convicted (Leadership Corps)			

Name	Position	Charges	Verdict	Sentence	Year
Otto Meissner	Chief of the Presidential Chancellery; State Minister with the Rank of Reich Minister	1. Crimes Against Peace	Withdrawn by Prosecution		
		2. Conspiracy to Commit Crimes Against Peace	Withdrawn by Prosecution		
		4. Crimes Against Humanity: Persecution of German Nationals	Dismissed by Tribunal		
		5. War Crimes & Crimes Against Humanity: Atrocities & Offenses Committed Against Civilian Populations	Acquitted		
		6. War Crimes & Crimes Against Humanity: Plunder	Dismissed by Tribunal		
Otto Dietrich	State Secretary in the Reich Ministry of Public Enlightenment and Propaganda	1. Crimes Against Peace	Acquitted	7 Years	1950
		2. Conspiracy to Commit Crimes Against Peace	Acquitted		
		3. War Crimes: Murder & Ill-treatment of Belligerents and POWs	Acquitted		
		4. Crimes Against Humanity: Persecution of German Nationals	Dismissed by Tribunal		
		5. War Crimes & Crimes Against Humanity: Atrocities & Offenses Committed Against Civilian Populations	Convicted		
		8. Membership in a Criminal Organization: SS & Leadership Corps of the Nazi Party	Convicted		
Gottlob Berger	Chief of the SS Main Office; Liaison Officer Between the Reichsfuehrer	1. Crimes Against Peace	Acquitted	25 Years	1951
		2. Conspiracy to Commit Crimes Against Peace	Acquitted	10 Years	

continued

Defendant	Position	Indictment	Verdict	Sentence	McCloy Revision	Released
	SS and the Reich Minister for the Occupied Eastern Territories	3. War Crimes: Murder & Ill-treatment of Belligerents and POWs	Convicted			
		5. War Crimes & Crimes Against Humanity: Atrocities & Offenses Committed Against Civilian Populations	Convicted			
		6. War Crimes & Crimes Against Humanity: Plunder	Acquitted			
		7. War Crimes & Crimes Against Humanity: Slave Labor	Convicted			
		8. Membership in a Criminal Organization: SS	Convicted			
Walter Schellenberg	Chief of the Combined Civil and Military Intelligence Service of RSHA; Chief of the SD	1. Crimes Against Peace	Acquitted	6 Years		1950
		2. Conspiracy to Commit Crimes Against Peace	Acquitted			
		5. War Crimes & Crimes Against Humanity: Atrocities & Offenses Committed Against Civilian Populations	Convicted			
		8. Membership in a Criminal Organization: SS & SD	Convicted			
Schwerin von Krosigk	Reich Minister of Finance; Reich Minister of Foreign Affairs	1. Crimes Against Peace	Acquitted	10 Years	Time Served	1951
		2. Conspiracy to Commit Crimes Against Peace	Acquitted			
		4. Crimes Against Humanity: Persecution of German Nationals	Dismissed by Tribunal			
		5. War Crimes & Crimes Against Humanity: Atrocities & Offenses Committed Against Civilian Populations	Convicted			

Name	Position	Charges	Verdict	Sentence	Year
Emil Puhl	Member of the Board of Directors of the Reich Bank; Vice President of the Reich Bank	6. War Crimes & Crimes Against Humanity: Plunder	Convicted		1949
		5. War Crimes & Crimes Against Humanity: Atrocities & Offenses Committed Against Civilian Populations	Convicted	5 Years	
		7. War Crimes & Crimes Against Humanity: Slave Labor	Acquitted		
Karl Rasche	Member of the Vorstand of the Dresdner Bank	4. Crimes Against Humanity: Persecution of German Nationals	Dismissed by Tribunal	7 Years	1950
		5. War Crimes & Crimes Against Humanity: Atrocities & Offenses Committed Against Civilian Populations	Acquitted		
		6. War Crimes & Crimes Against Humanity: Plunder	Convicted		
		7. War Crimes & Crimes Against Humanity: Slave Labor	Acquitted		
		8. Membership in a Criminal Organization: SS	Convicted		
Paul Koerner	Permanent Deputy of Goering as Plenipotentiary of the Four Year Plan; Chief of the Office of the Four Year Plan	1. Crimes Against Peace	Convicted	15 Years	1951
		2. Conspiracy to Commit Crimes Against Peace	Acquitted	10 Years	
		6. War Crimes & Crimes Against Humanity: Plunder	Convicted		
		7. War Crimes & Crimes Against Humanity: Slave Labor	Convicted		
		8. Membership in a Criminal Organization: SS	Convicted		
Paul Pleiger	Chairman of the Reich Association Coal; Reich	1. Crimes Against Peace	Acquitted	15 Years	1951
		2. Conspiracy to Commit Crimes Against Peace	Acquitted	9 Years	

continued

Defendant	Position	Indictment	Verdict	Sentence	McCloy Revision	Released
	Commissioner for Coal in the Occupied Territories	6. War Crimes & Crimes Against Humanity: Plunder	Convicted			
		7. War Crimes & Crimes Against Humanity: Slave Labor	Convicted			
Hans Kehrl	Chief of the Planning Office of the Central Planning Board; Chief of the Planning Office of the Reich Ministry for Armament and War Production	5. War Crimes & Crimes Against Humanity: Atrocities & Offenses Committed Against Civilian Populations	Convicted	15 Years	Time Served	1951
		6. War Crimes & Crimes Against Humanity: Plunder	Convicted			
		7. War Crimes & Crimes Against Humanity: Slave Labor	Convicted			
		8. Membership in a Criminal Organization: SS	Convicted			

United States of America vs. Wilhelm von Leeb, et al. *(High Command)*

Defendant	Position	Indictment	Verdict	Sentence	McCloy Revision	Released
Wilhelm von Leeb	General of the Army; Commander in Chief Army Group Command; Commander in Chief 12th Army; Commander in Chief Army Group C; Commander in Chief Army Group North	1. Crimes Against Peace	Acquitted	3 Years		1948
		2. War Crimes and Crimes Against Humanity: Atrocities and Offenses Against POWs	Acquitted			
		3. War Crimes and Crimes Against Humanity: Atrocities and Offenses Against Civilians	Convicted			
		4. Conspiracy to Commit Crimes Against Peace	Acquitted			
Hugo Sperrle		1. Crimes Against Peace	Acquitted			

Name	Position	Charge	Verdict	Sentence	Year
	General of the Army; Commander of Air Fleet 3; Deputy Commander in Chief West (During Absences of Field Marshal von Rundstedt)	2. War Crimes and Crimes Against Humanity: Atrocities and Offenses Against POWs	Acquitted		
		3. War Crimes and Crimes Against Humanity: Atrocities and Offenses Against Civilians	Acquitted		
		4. Conspiracy to Commit Crimes Against Peace	Acquitted		
Georg Karl Friedrich-Wilhelm von Kuechler	General of the Army; Commander of East Prussian Defense Zone; Commander in Chief 18th Army; Commander in Chief Army Group North	1. Crimes Against Peace	Acquitted		
		2. War Crimes and Crimes Against Humanity: Atrocities and Offenses Against POWs	Convicted	20 Years	
		3. War Crimes and Crimes Against Humanity: Atrocities and Offenses Against Civilians	Convicted	12 Years	1953
		4. Conspiracy to Commit Crimes Against Peace	Acquitted		
Johannes Blaskowitz	General; Commander in Chief Army Group Command; Commander in Chief East; Military Commander Northern France; Commander in Chief Netherlands and 25th Army	1. Crimes Against Peace	Committed Suicide During Trial		
		2. War Crimes and Crimes Against Humanity: Atrocities and Offenses Against POWs			
		3. War Crimes and Crimes Against Humanity: Atrocities and Offenses Against Civilians			
		4. Conspiracy to Commit Crimes Against Peace			
Hermann Hoth		1. Crimes Against Peace	Acquitted	15 Years	1954

continued

Defendant	Position	Indictment	Verdict	Sentence	McCloy Revision	Released
	General; Commander Panzer Group 3; Commander in Chief 4th Panzer Army	2. War Crimes and Crimes Against Humanity: Atrocities and Offenses Against POWs	Convicted		No Modification	
		3. War Crimes and Crimes Against Humanity: Atrocities and Offenses Against Civilians	Convicted			
		4. Conspiracy to Commit Crimes Against Peace	Acquitted			
Hans Reinhardt	General; Commander Panzer Group 3, Acting Commander in Chief Army Group Center	1. Crimes Against Peace	Acquitted	15 Years	No Modification	1952
		2. War Crimes and Crimes Against Humanity: Atrocities and Offenses Against POWs	Convicted			
		3. War Crimes and Crimes Against Humanity: Atrocities and Offenses Against Civilians	Convicted			
		4. Conspiracy to Commit Crimes Against Peace	Acquitted			
Hans von Salmuth	General; Chief of Staff Army Group Command; Chief of Staff Army Group North; Commander in Chief 15th Army	1. Crimes Against Peace	Acquitted	20 Years	12 Years	1953
		2. War Crimes and Crimes Against Humanity: Atrocities and Offenses Against POWs	Convicted			
		3. War Crimes and Crimes Against Humanity: Atrocities and Offenses Against Civilians	Convicted			
		4. Conspiracy to Commit Crimes Against Peace	Acquitted			
Karl Hollidt		1. Crimes Against Peace	Acquitted	5 Years		1949

Name	Position	Charge	Verdict	Sentence	Modification	
	General; Commander of Infantry in District 9; Chief of Staff to the Commander in Chief East; Commander Army Hollidt	2. War Crimes and Crimes Against Humanity: Atrocities and Offenses Against POWs	Convicted			
		3. War Crimes and Crimes Against Humanity: Atrocities and Offenses Against Civilians	Convicted			
		4. Conspiracy to Commit Crimes Against Peace	Acquitted			
Otto Schniewind	Admiral Commander of the Fleet; Commander of Naval Battle Forces in Norway; Commander of Naval Group North	1. Crimes Against Peace	Acquitted			
		2. War Crimes and Crimes Against Humanity: Atrocities and Offenses Against POWs	Acquitted			
		3. War Crimes and Crimes Against Humanity: Atrocities and Offenses Against Civilians	Acquitted			
		4. Conspiracy to Commit Crimes Against Peace	Acquitted			
Karl von Roques	Lieutenant General, Infantry; Commander of a Division in the Zone of the Interior; Commanding General of Group von Roques, Commander Rear Area, Army Group A	1. Crimes Against Peace	Acquitted	20 Years		Died in Prison, 1949
		2. War Crimes and Crimes Against Humanity: Atrocities and Offenses Against POWs	Convicted			
		3. War Crimes and Crimes Against Humanity: Atrocities and Offenses Against Civilians	Convicted			
		4. Conspiracy to Commit Crimes Against Peace	Acquitted			
Hermann Reinecke	Lieutenant General, Infantry; Chief of the Department "Armed Forces General Affairs" in the OKW; Chief of the National Socialist Guidance Staff of the OKW	1. Crimes Against Peace	Acquitted	Life	No Modification	1954
		2. War Crimes and Crimes Against Humanity: Atrocities and Offenses Against POWs	Convicted			
		3. War Crimes and Crimes Against Humanity: Atrocities and Offenses Against Civilians	Convicted			

continued

Defendant	Position	Indictment	Verdict	Sentence	McCloy Revision	Released
		and Offenses Against Civilians				
		4. Conspiracy to Commit Crimes Against Peace	Acquitted			
Walter Warlimont	Lieutenant General, Artillery; Military Envoy to General Franco in Spain and Leader of the German Volunteer Corps; Chief of Department National Defense in the Armed Forces Operations Staff	1. Crimes Against Peace	Acquitted	Life	18 Years	1954
		2. War Crimes and Crimes Against Humanity: Atrocities and Offenses Against POW's	Convicted			
		3. War Crimes and Crimes Against Humanity: Atrocities and Offenses Against Civilians	Convicted			
		4. Conspiracy to Commit Crimes Against Peace	Acquitted			
Otto Woehler	Lieutenant General, Infantry; Chief of Staff Army Group Centre; Commander in Chief Army Group South	1. Crimes Against Peace	Acquitted	8 Years		1951
		2. War Crimes and Crimes Against Humanity: Atrocities and Offenses Against POW's	Convicted			
		3. War Crimes and Crimes Against Humanity: Atrocities and Offenses Against Civilians	Convicted			
		4. Conspiracy to Commit Crimes Against Peace	Acquitted			
Rudolf Lehmann	Lieutenant General, Judge Advocate; Ministerial Director in the OKW and Chief of the Legal Division; Judge Advocate General of the OKW	1. Crimes Against Peace	Acquitted	7 Years		1950
		2. War Crimes and Crimes Against Humanity: Atrocities and Offenses Against POW's	Convicted			
		3. War Crimes and Crimes Against Humanity: Atrocities and Offenses Against Civilians	Convicted			
		4. Conspiracy to Commit Crimes Against Peace	Acquitted			

Charter of the International Military Tribunal

I. Constitution of the International Military Tribunal

Article 1

In pursuance of the Agreement signed on the 8th day of August 1945 by the Government of the United States of America, the Provisional Government of the French Republic, the Government of the United Kingdom of Great Britain and Northern Ireland and the Government of the Union of Soviet Socialist Republics, there shall be established an International Military Tribunal (hereinafter called "the Tribunal") for the just and prompt trial and punishment of the major war criminals of the European Axis.

Article 2

The Tribunal shall consist of four members, each with an alternate. One member and one alternate shall be appointed by each of the Signatories. The alternates shall, so far as they are able, be present at all sessions of the Tribunal. In case of illness of any member of the Tribunal or his incapacity for some other reason to fulfill his functions, his alternate shall take his place.

Article 3

Neither the Tribunal, its members nor their alternates can be challenged by the prosecution, or by the Defendants or their Counsel. Each Signatory may replace its members of the Tribunal or his alternate for reasons of health or for other good reasons, except that no replacement may take place during a Trial, other than by an alternate.

Article 4

(a) The presence of all four members of the Tribunal or the alternate for any absent member shall be necessary to constitute the quorum.

(b) The members of the Tribunal shall, before any trial begins, agree among themselves upon the selection from their number of a President, and the President shall hold office during the trial, or as may otherwise be agreed by a vote of not less than three members. The principle of rotation of presidency for successive trials is agreed. If, however, a session of the Tribunal takes place on the territory of one of the four Signatories, the representative of that Signatory on the Tribunal shall preside.

(c) Save as aforesaid the Tribunal shall take decisions by a majority vote and in case the votes are evenly divided, the vote of the President shall be decisive: provided always that convictions and sentences shall only be imposed by affirmative votes of at least three members of the Tribunal.

Article 5

In case of need and depending on the number of the matters to be tried, other Tribunals may be set up; and the establishment, functions, and procedure of each Tribunal shall be identical, and shall be governed by this Charter.

II. Jurisdiction and General Principles

Article 6

The Tribunal established by the Agreement referred to in Article 1 hereof for the trial and punishment of the major war criminals of the European Axis countries shall have the power to try and punish persons who, acting in the interests of the European Axis countries, whether as individuals or as members of organizations, committed any of the following crimes.

The following acts, or any of them, are crimes coming within the jurisdiction of the Tribunal for which there shall be individual responsibility:

(a) **Crimes Against Peace:** namely, planning, preparation, initiation or waging of a war of aggression, or a war in violation of international treaties, agreements or assurances, or participation in a common plan or conspiracy for the accomplishment of any of the foregoing;

(b) **War Crimes:** namely, violations of the laws or customs of war. Such violations shall include, but not be limited to, murder, ill-treatment or deportation to slave labor or for any other purpose of civilian population of or in occupied territory, murder or ill-treatment of prisoners of war or persons on the seas, killing of hostages, plunder of public or private property, wanton destruction of cities, towns or villages, or devastation not justified by military necessity;

(c) **Crimes Against Humanity:** namely, murder, extermination, enslavement, deportation, and other inhumane acts committed against any civilian population, before or during the war; or persecutions on political, racial or religious grounds in execution of or in connection with any crime within the jurisdiction of the Tribunal, whether or not in violation of the domestic law of the country where perpetrated.

Leaders, organizers, instigators and accomplices participating in the formulation or execution of a common plan or conspiracy to commit any of the foregoing crimes are responsible for all acts performed by any persons in execution of such plan.

Article 7

The official position of defendants, whether as Heads of State or responsible officials in Government Departments, shall not be considered as freeing them from responsibility or mitigating punishment.

Article 8

The fact that the Defendant acted pursuant to order of his Government or of a superior shall not free him from responsibility, but may be considered in mitigation of punishment if the Tribunal determines that justice so requires.

Article 9

At the trial of any individual member of any group or organization the Tribunal may declare (in connection with any act of which the individual may be convicted) that the group or organization of which the individual was a member was a criminal organization.

After the receipt of the Indictment the Tribunal shall give such notice as it thinks fit that the prosecution intends to ask the Tribunal to make such declaration and any member of the organization will be entitled to apply to the Tribunal for leave to be heard by the Tribunal upon the question of the criminal character of the organization. The Tribunal shall have power to allow or reject the application. If the application is allowed, the Tribunal may direct in what manner the applicants shall be represented and heard.

Article 10

In cases where a group or organization is declared criminal by the Tribunal, the competent national authority of any Signatory shall have the right to bring an individual to trial for membership therein before national, military or occupation courts. In any such case the criminal nature of the group or organization is considered proved and shall not be questioned.

Article 11

Any person convicted by the Tribunal may be charged before a national, military or occupation court, referred to in Article 10 of this Charter, with a crime other than of membership in a criminal group or organization and such court may, after convicting him, impose upon him punishment independent of and additional to the punishment imposed by the Tribunal for participation in the criminal activities of such group or organization.

Article 12

The Tribunal shall have the right to take proceedings against a person charged with crimes set out in Article 6 of this Charter in his absence, if he has not been found or if the Tribunal, for any reason, finds it necessary, in the interests of justice, to conduct the hearing in his absence.

Article 13

The Tribunal shall draw up rules for its procedure. These rules shall not be inconsistent with the provisions of this Charter.

III. Committee for the Investigation and Prosecution of Major War Criminals

Article 14

Each Signatory shall appoint a Chief Prosecutor for the investigation of the charges against and the prosecution of major war criminals.

The Chief Prosecutors shall act as a committee for the following purposes:

(a) to agree upon a plan of the individual work of each of the Chief Prosecutors and his staff,

(b) to settle the final designation of major war criminals to be tried by the Tribunal,

(c) to approve the Indictment and the documents to be submitted therewith,

(d) to lodge the Indictment and the accompany documents with the Tribunal,

(e) to draw up and recommend to the Tribunal for its approval draft rules of procedure, contemplated by Article 13 of this Charter. The Tribunal shall have the power to accept, with or without amendments, or to reject, the rules so recommended.

The Committee shall act in all the above matters by a majority vote and shall appoint a Chairman as may be convenient and in accordance with the principle of rotation: provided that if there is an equal division of vote concerning the designation of a Defendant to be tried by the Tribunal, or the crimes with which he shall be charged, that proposal will be adopted which was made by the party which proposed that the particular Defendant be tried, or the particular charges be preferred against him.

Article 15

The Chief Prosecutors shall individually, and acting in collaboration with one another, also undertake the following duties:

(a) investigation, collection and production before or at the Trial of all necessary evidence,

(b) the preparation of the Indictment for approval by the Committee in accordance with paragraph (c) of Article 14 hereof,

(c) the preliminary examination of all necessary witnesses and of all Defendants,

(d) to act as prosecutor at the Trial,

(e) to appoint representatives to carry out such duties as may be assigned them,

(f) to undertake such other matters as may appear necessary to them for the purposes of the preparation for and conduct of the Trial.

It is understood that no witness or Defendant detained by the Signatory shall be taken out of the possession of that Signatory without its assent.

IV. Fair Trial for Defendants

Article 16

In order to ensure fair trial for the Defendants, the following procedure shall be followed:

(a) The Indictment shall include full particulars specifying in detail the charges against the Defendants. A copy of the Indictment and of all the documents lodged with the Indictment, translated into a language which he understands, shall be furnished to the Defendant at reasonable time before the Trial.

(b) During any preliminary examination or trial of a Defendant he will have the right to give any explanation relevant to the charges made against him.

(c) A preliminary examination of a Defendant and his Trial shall be conducted in, or translated into, a language which the Defendant understands.

(d) A Defendant shall have the right to conduct his own defense before the Tribunal or to have the assistance of Counsel.

(e) A Defendant shall have the right through himself or through his Counsel to present evidence at the Trial in support of his defense, and to cross-examine any witness called by the Prosecution.

V. Powers of the Tribunal and Conduct of the Trial

Article 17

The Tribunal shall have the power

(a) to summon witnesses to the Trial and to require their attendance and testimony and to put questions to them,

(b) to interrogate any Defendant,

(c) to require the production of documents and other evidentiary material,

(d) to administer oaths to witnesses,

(e) to appoint officers for the carrying out of any task designated by the Tribunal including the power to have evidence taken on commission.

Article 18

The Tribunal shall

(a) confine the Trial strictly to an expeditious hearing of the cases raised by the charges,

(b) take strict measures to prevent any action which will cause reasonable delay, and rule out irrelevant issues and statements of any kind whatsoever,

(c) deal summarily with any contumacy, imposing appropriate punishment, including exclusion of any Defendant or his Counsel from some or all further proceedings, but without prejudice to the determination of the charges.

Article 19

The Tribunal shall not be bound by technical rules of evidence. It shall adopt and apply to the greatest possible extent expeditious and nontechnical procedure, and shall admit any evidence which it deems to be of probative value.

Article 20

The Tribunal may require to be informed of the nature of any evidence before it is entered so that it may rule upon the relevance thereof.

Article 21

The Tribunal shall not require proof of facts of common knowledge but shall take judicial notice thereof. It shall also take judicial notice of official governmental documents and reports of the United Nations, including the acts and documents of the committees set up in the various allied countries for the investigation of war crimes, and of records and findings of military or other Tribunals of any of the United Nations.

Article 22

The permanent seat of the Tribunal shall be in Berlin. The first meetings of the members of the Tribunal and of the Chief Prosecutors shall be held at Berlin in a place to be designated by the Control Council for Germany. The first trial shall be held at Nuremberg, and any subsequent trials shall be held at such places as the Tribunal may decide.

Article 23

One or more of the Chief Prosecutors may take part in the prosecution at each Trial. The function of any Chief Prosecutor may be discharged by him personally, or by any person or persons authorized by him.

The function of Counsel for a Defendant may be discharged at the Defendant's request by any Counsel professionally qualified to conduct cases before the Courts of his own country, or by any other person who may be specially authorized thereto by the Tribunal.

Article 24

The proceedings at the Trial shall take the following course:

(a) The Indictment shall be read in court.

(b) The Tribunal shall ask each Defendant whether he pleads "guilty" or "not guilty."

(c) The prosecution shall make an opening statement.

(d) The Tribunal shall ask the prosecution and the defense what evidence (if any) they wish to submit to the Tribunal, and the Tribunal shall rule upon the admissibility of any such evidence.

(e) The witnesses for the Prosecution shall be examined and after that the witnesses for the Defense. Thereafter such rebutting evidence as may be held by the Tribunal to be admissible shall be called by either the Prosecution or the Defense.

(f) The Tribunal may put any question to any witness and to any defendant, at any time.

(g) The Prosecution and the Defense shall interrogate and may crossexamine any witnesses and any Defendant who gives testimony.

(h) The Defense shall address the court.

(i) The Prosecution shall address the court.

(j) Each Defendant may make a statement to the Tribunal.

(k) The Tribunal shall deliver judgment and pronounce sentence.

Article 25

All official documents shall be produced, and all court proceedings conducted, in English, French and Russian, and in the language of the Defendant. So much of the record and of the proceedings may also be translated into the language of any country in which the Tribunal is sitting, as the Tribunal is sitting, as the Tribunal considers desirable in the interests of the justice and public opinion.

VI. Judgment and Sentence

Article 26

The judgment of the Tribunal as to the guilt or the innocence of any Defendant shall give the reasons on which it is based, and shall be final and not subject to review.

Article 27

The Tribunal shall have the right to impose upon a Defendant, on conviction, death or such other punishment as shall be determined by it to be just.

Article 28

In addition to any punishment imposed by it, the Tribunal shall have the right to deprive the convicted person of any stolen property and order its delivery to the Control Council for Germany.

Article 29

In case of guilt, sentences shall be carried out in accordance with the orders of the Control Council for Germany, which may at any time reduce or otherwise alter the sentences, but may not increase the severity thereof. If the Control Council for Germany, after any Defendant has been convicted and sentenced, discovers fresh evidence which, in its opinion, would found a fresh charge against him, the Council shall report accordingly to the Committee established under Article 14 hereof, for such action as they may consider proper, having regard to the interests of justice.

VII. Expenses

Article 30

The expenses of the Tribunal and of the Trials, shall be charged by the Signatories against the funds allotted for maintenance of the Control Council of Germany.

Control Council Law No. 10

Punishment of Persons Guilty of War Crimes, Crimes Against Peace and Against Humanity

In order to give effect to the terms of the Moscow Declaration of 30 October 1943 and the London Agreement of 8 August 1945, and the Charter issued pursuant thereto and in order to establish a uniform legal basis in Glermany for the prosecution of war criminals and other similar offenders, other than those dealt with by the International Military Tribunal, the Control Council enacts as follows:

Article I

The Moscow Declaration of 30 October 1943 "Concerning Responsibility of Hitlerites for Committed Atrocities" and the London Agreement of 8 August 1945 "Concerning Prosecution and Punishment of Major War Criminals of European Axis" are made integral parts of this Law. Adherence to the provisions of the London Agreement by any of the United Nations, as provided for in Article V of that Agreement, shall not entitle such Nation to participate or interfere in the operation of this Law within the Control Council area of authority in Germany.

Article II

1. Each of the following acts is recognized as a crime:
   (a) **Crimes against Peace.** Initiation of invasions of other countries and wars of aggression in violation of international laws and treaties, including but not limited to planning, preparation, initiation or waging a war of aggression, or a war of violation of international treaties, agreements or assurances, or participation in a common plan or conspiracy for the accomplishment of any of the foregoing.
   (b) **War Crimes.** Atrocities or offenses against persons or property constituting violations of the laws or customs of war, including but not limited to, murder, ill treatment or deportation to slave labour or for any other purpose, of civilian population from occupied territory, murder or ill treatment of prisoners of war or persons on the seas, killing of hostages, plunder of public or private property, wanton destruction of cities, towns or villages, or devastation not justified by military necessity.
   (a) **Crimes Against Humanity.** Atrocities and offenses, including but not limited to murder, extermination, enslavement, deportation, imprisonment, torture, rape, or other inhumane acts committed against any civilian population, or persecutions on political, racial or religious grounds whether or not in violation of the domestic laws of the country where perpetrated.

    (d) Membership in categories of a criminal group or organization declared criminal by the International Military Tribunal.

2. Any person without regard to nationality or the capacity in which he acted, is deemed to have committed a crime as defined in paragraph 1 of this Article, if he was (a) a principal or (b) was an accessory to the commission of any such crime or ordered or abetted the same or (c) took a consenting part therein or (d) was connected with plans or enterprises involving its commission or (e) was a member of any organization or group connected with the commission of any such crime or (f) with reference to paragraph 1 (a) if he held a high political, civil or military (including General Staff) position in Germany or in one of its Allies, co-belligerents or satellites or held high position in the financial, industrial or economic life of any such country.

3. Any persons found guilty of any of the crimes above mentioned may upon conviction be punished as shall be determined by the Tribunal to be just. Such punishment may consist of one or more of the following:
    (a) Death.
    (b) Imprisonment for life or a term of years, with or without hard labor.
    (c) Fine, and imprisonment with or without hard labour, in lieu thereof.
    (d) Forfeiture of property.
    (e) Restitution of property wrongfully acquired.
    (f) Deprivation of some or all civil rights.

Any property declared to be forfeited or the restitution of which is ordered by the Tribunal shall be delivered to the Control Council for Germany, which shall decide on its disposal.

4. (a) The official position of any person, whether as Head of State or as a responsible official in a Government Department, does not free him from responsibility for a crime or entitle him to mitigation of punishment.

    (b) The fact that any person acted pursuant to the order of his Government or of a superior does not free him from responsibility for a crime, but may be considered in mitigation.

5. In any trial or prosecution for a crime herein referred to, the accused shall not be entitled to the benefits of any statute of limitation in respect to the period from 30 January 1933 to 1 July 1945, nor shall any immunity, pardon or amnesty granted under the Nazi regime be admitted as a bar to trial or punishment.

Article III

1. Each occupying authority, within its Zone of Occupation,

    (a) shall have the right to cause persons within such Zone suspected of having committed a crime, including those charged with crime by one of the United Nations, to be arrested and shall take under control the property, real and personal, owned or controlled by the said persons, pending decisions as to its eventual disposition.

    (b) shall report to the Legal Directorate the name of all suspected criminals, the reasons for and the places of their detention, if they are detained, and the names and location of witnesses.

(c) shall take appropriate measures to see that witnesses and evidence will be available when required.

(d) shall have the right to cause all persons so arrested and charged, and not delivered to another authority as herein provided, or released, to be brought to trial before an appropriate tribunal. Such tribunal may, in the case of crimes committed by persons of German citizenship or nationality against other persons of German citizenship or nationality, or stateless persons, be a German Court, if authorized by the occupying authorities.

2. The tribunal by which persons charged with offenses hereunder shall be tried and the rules and procedure thereof shall be determined or designated by each Zone Commander for his respective Zone. Nothing herein is intended to, or shall impair or limit the jurisdiction or power of any court or tribunal now or hereafter established in any Zone by the Commander thereof, or of the International Military Tribunal established by the London Agreement of 8 August 1945.

3. Persons wanted for trial by an International Military Tribunal will not be tried without the consent of the Committee of Chief Prosecutors. Each Zone Commander will deliver such persons who are within his Zone to that committee upon request and will make witnesses and evidence available to it.

4. Persons known to be wanted for trial in another Zone or outside Germany will not be tried prior to decision under Article IV unless the fact of their apprehension has been reported in accordance with Section 1 (b) of this Article, three months have elapsed thereafter, and no request for delivery of the type contemplated by Article IV has been received by the Zone Commander concerned.

5. The execution of death sentences may be deferred by not to exceed one month after the sentence has become final when the Zone Commander concerned has reason to believe that the testimony of those under sentence would be of value in the investigation and trial of crimes within or without his zone.

6. Each Zone Commander will cause such effect to be given to the judgments of courts of competent jurisdiction, with respect to the property taken under his control pursuant thereto, as he may deem proper in the interest of Justice.

Article IV

1. When any person in a Zone in Germany is alleged to have committed a crime, as defined in Article II, in a country other than Germany or in another Zone, the government of that nation or the Commander of the latter Zone, as the case may be, may request the Commander of the Zone which the person is located for his arrest and delivery for trial to the country or Zone in which the crime was committed. Such request for delivery shall be granted by the Commander receiving it unless he believes such person is wanted for trial or as a witness by an International Military Tribunal, or in Germany, or in a nation other than the one making the request, or the Commander is not satisfied that delivery should be made, in any of which cases he shall have the right to forward the said request to the Legal Directorate of the Allied Control Authority. A similar procedure shall apply to witnesses, material exhibits and other forms of evidence.

2. The Legal Directorate shall consider all requests referred to it, and shall determine the same in accordance with the following principles, its determination to be communicated to the Zone Commander.

   (a) A person wanted for trial or as a witness by an International Military Tribunal shall not be delivered for trial or required to give evidence outside Germany, as the case may be, except upon approval by the Committee of Chief Prosecutors acting under the London Agreement of 8 August 1945.

   (b) A person wanted for trial by several authorities (other than an International Military Tribunal) shall be disposed of in accordance with the following priorities:

(1) If wanted for trial in the Zone in which he is, he should not be delivered unless arrangements are made for his return after trial elsewhere;

(2) If wanted for trial in a Zone other than that in which he is, he should be delivered to that Zone in preference to delivery outside Germany unless arrangements are made for his return to that Zone after trial elsewhere;

(3) If wanted for trial outside Germany by two or more of the United Nations, of one of which he is a citizen, that one should have priority;

(4) If wanted for trial outside Germany by several countries, not all of which are United Nations, United Nations should have priority;

(5) If wanted for trial outside Germany by two or more of the United Nations, then, subject to Article IV 2 (b) (3) above, that which has the most serious charges against him, which are moreover supported by evidence, should have priority.

Article V

The delivery, under Article IV of this law, of persons for trial shall be mades on demands of the Governments or Zone Commanders in such a manner that the delivery of criminals to one jurisdiction will not become the means of defeating or unnecessarily delaying the carrying out of justice in another place. If within six months the delivered person has not been convicted by the Court of the Zone or country to which he has been delivered, then such person shall be returned upon demand of the Commander of the Zone where the person was located prior to delivery

Done at Berlin, 20 December 1945. (Signed) Joseph T. McNarney JOSEPH T. MCNARNEY General, U. S. Army (Signed) Bernard B. Montgomery BERNARD B. MONTGOMERY Field Marshall (Signed) Louis Koeltz, General de Corps d'Armee for PIERRE KOENIG General d'Armee (Signed) Georgi Zhukov GEORGI ZHUKOV Marshall of the Soviet Union

Ordinance No. 7

Organization and Power of Certain Military Tribunals

Article I

The purpose of this Ordinance is to provide for the establishment of military tribunals which shall have power to try and punish persons charged with offenses recognized as crimes in Article II of Control Council Law No. 10, including conspiracies to commit any such crimes. Nothing herein shall prejudice the jurisdiction or the powers of other courts established or which may be established for the trial of any such offenses.

Article II

a) Pursuant to the powers of the Military Governor for the United States Zone of Occupation within Germany and further pursuant to the powers conferred upon the Zone Commander by Control Council Law No. 10 and Articles 10 and 11 of the Charter of the International Military Tribunal annexed to the London Agreement of 8 August 1945 certain tribunals to be known as "Military Tribunals" shall be established hereunder.

b) Each such tribunal shall consist of three or more members to be designated by the Military Governor. One alternate member may be designated to any tribunal if deemed advisable by the Military Governor. Except as provided in subsection (c) of this Article, all members and alternates shall be lawyers who have been admitted to practice, for at least five years, in the highest courts of one of the United States or its territories or of the District of Columbia, or who have been admitted to practice in the United States Supreme Court.

c) The Military Governor may in his discretion enter into an agreement with one or more other zone commanders of the member nations of the Allied Control Authority providing for the joint trial of any case or cases. In such cases the tribunals shall consist of three or more members us may be provided in the agreement. In such cases the tribunals may include properly qualified lawyers designated by the other member nations.

d) The Military Governor shall designate one of the members of the tribunal to serve as the presiding judge.

e) Neither the tribunals nor the members of the tribunals or the alternates may be challenged by the prosecution or by the defendants or their counsel.

f) In case of illness of any member of a tribunal or his incapacity for some other reason, the alternate, if one has been designated, shall take his place as a member in the pending trial. Members may be replaced for reasons of health or for other good reasons, except that no replacement of a member may take place, during a trial, other than by the alternate. If no alternate has been designated, the trial shall be continued to conclusion by the remaining members.

g) The presence of three members of the tribunal or of two members when authorized pursuant to subsection (f) supra shall be necessary to constitute a quorum. In the case of tribunals designated under (c) above the agreement shall determine the requirements for a quorum.

h) Decisions and judgments, including convictions and sentences, shall be by majority vote of the members. If the votes of the members are equally divided, the presiding member shall declare a mistrial.

Article III

a) Charges against persons to be tried in the tribunals established hereunder shall originate in the Office of the Chief of Counsel for War Crimes, appointed by the Military Governor pursuant to Paragraph 3 of Executive Order Numbered 9679 of the President of the United States dated 16 January 1946. The Chief of Counsel for War Crimes shall determine the persons to be tried by the tribunals and he or his designated representative shall file the indictments with the Secretary General of the tribunals (See Article XIV, *infra*) and shall conduct the prosecution.

b) The Chief of Counsel for War Crimes, when in his judgment it is advisable, may invite one or more United Nations to designate representatives to participate in the prosecution of any case.

Article IV

In order to ensure fair trial for the defendants, the following procedure shall be followed:

a) A defendant shall be furnished, at a reasonable time before his trial, a copy of the indictment and of all documents lodged with the indictment, translated into a language which he understands. The indictment shall state the charges plainly, concisely and with sufficient particulars to inform defendant of the offenses charged.

b) The trial shall be conducted in, or translated into, a language which the defendant understands.

c) A defendant shall have the right to be represented by counsel of his own selection, provided such counsel shall be a person qualified under existing regulations to conduct cases before the courts of defendant's country, or any other person who may be specially authorized by the tribunal. The tribunal shall appoint qualified counsel to represent a defendant who is not represented by counsel of his own selection.

d) Every defendant shall be entitled to be present at his trial except that a defendant may be proceeded against during temporary absences if in the opinion of the tribunal defendant's interests will not thereby be impaired, and except further as provided in Article VI (c). The tribunal may also proceed in the absence of any defendant who has applied for and has been granted permission to be absent.

e) A defendant shall have the right through his counsel to present evidence at the trial in support of his defense, and to cross-examine any witness called by the prosecution.

f) A defendant may apply in writing to the tribunal for the production of witnesses or of documents. The application shall state where the witness or document is thought to be located and shall also state the facts to be proved by the witness or the document and the relevancy of such facts to the defense. If the tribunal grants the application, the defendant shall be given such aid in obtaining production of evidence as the tribunal may order.

Article V

The tribunals shall have the power—

a) to summon witnesses to the trial, to require their attendance and testimony and to put questions to them;

b) to interrogate any defendant who takes the stand to testify in his own behalf, or who is called to testify regarding another defendant;

c) to require the production of documents and other evidentiary material;

d) to administer oaths;

e) to appoint officers for the carrying out of any task designated by the tribunals including the taking of evidence on commission;

f) to adopt rules of procedure not inconsistent with this Ordinance. Such rules shall be adopted, and from time to time as necessary, revised by the members of the tribunals or by the committee of presiding judges as provided in Article XIII.

Article VI

The tribunals shall—

a) confine the trial strictly to an expeditious hearing of the issues raised by of the charges;

b) take strict measures to prevent any action which will cause unreasonable delay, and rule out irrelevant issues and statements of any kind whatsoever;

c) deal summarily with any contumacy, imposing appropriate punishment, including the exclusion of any defendant or his counsel from some or all further proceedings, but without prejudice to the determination of the charges.

Article VII

The tribunals shall not be bound by technical rules of evidence. They shall adopt and apply to the greatest possible extent expeditious and nontechnical procedure, and shall admit any evidence which they deem to have probative value. Without limiting the foregoing general rules, the following shall be deemed admissible if they appear to the tribunal to contain information of probative value relating to the charges: affidavits, depositions, interrogations and other statements, diaries, letters, the records, findings, statements and judgments of the military tribunals and the reviewing and conffrming authorities of any of the United Nations, and copies of any document or other secondary evidence of the contents of any document, if the original is not readily available or cannot be produced without delay. The tribunal shall afford the opposing party such opportunity to question the authenticity or probative value of such evidence as in the opinion of the tribunal the ends of justice require.

Article VIII

The tribunals may require that they be informed of the nature of any evidence before it is offered so that they may rule upon the relevance thereof.

Article IX

The tribunals shall not require proof of facts of common knowledge but shall take judicial notice thereof. They shall also take judicial notice of official governmental documents and reports of any of the United Nations, including the acts and documents of the committees set up in the various Allied countries for the investigation of war crimes, and the records and findings of military or or other tribunals of any of the United Nations.

Article X

The determinations of the International Military Tribunal in the judgments In Case No. 1 that invasions, aggressive acts, aggressive wars, crimes, atrocities or inhumane acts were planned or occurred, shall be binding on the tribunals established hereunder and shall not be questioned except insofar as the participation therein or knowledge thereof by any particular person may be concerned. Statements of the International Military Tribunal in the judgment in Case No. 1 constitute proof of the facts stated, in the absence of substantial new evidence to the contrary.

Article XI

The proceedings at the trial shall take the following course:

a) The tribunal shall inquire of each defendant whether he has received and had an opportunity to read the indictment against him and whether he pleads "guilty" or "not guilty."

b) The prosecution may make an opening statement.

c) The prosecution shall produce its evidence subject to the cross examination of its witnesses.

d) The defense may make an opening statement.

e) The defense shall produce its evidence subject to the cross examination of lts witnesses.

f) Such rebutting evidence as may be held by the tribunal to be material may be, produced by either the prosecution or the defense.

g) The defense shall address the court.

h) The prosecution shall address the court.

i) Each defendant may make a statement to the tribunal.

j) The tribunal shall deliver judgment and pronounce sentence.

Article XII

A Central Secretariat to assist the tribunals to be appointed hereunder shall be established as soon as practicable. The main office of the Secretariat shall be located in Nuernberg. The Secretariat shall consist of a Secretary General and such assistant secretaries, military officers, clerks, interpreters and other personnel as may be necessary.

Article XIII

The Secretary General shall be appointed by the Military Governor and shall organize and direct the work of the Secretariat. He shall be subject to the supervision of the members of the tribunals, except that when at least three tribunals shall be functioning, the presiding judges of the several tribunals may form the supervisory committee.

Article XIV

The Secretariat shall:

a) Be responsible for the administrative and supply needs of the Secretariat and of the several tribunals.

b) Receive all documents addressed to tribunals.

c) Prepare and recommend uniform rules of procedure, not inconsistent with the provisions of this Ordinance.

d) Secure such information for the tribunals as may be needed for the approval or appointment of defense counsel.

e) Serve as liaison between the prosecution and defense counsel.

f) Arrange for aid to be given defendants and the prosecution in obtaining production of witnesses or evidence as authorized by the tribunals.

g) Be responsible for the preparation of the records of the proceedings before the tribunals.

h) Provide the necessary clerical, reporting and interpretative services to the tribunals and its members, and perform such other duties as may be required for the efficient conduct of the proceedings before the tribunals, or as may be requested by any of the tribunals.

Article XV

The judgments of the tribunals as to the guilt or the innocence of any defendant shall give the reasons on which they are based and shall be final and not subject to review. The sentences imposed may be subject to review as provided in Article XVII, *infra*.

Article XVI

The tribunal shall have the right to impose upon the defendant, upon conviction, such punishment as shall be determined by the tribunal to be just, which may consist of one or more of the penalties provided in Article II, Section 3 of Control Council Law No. 10.

Article XVII

a) Except as provided in (b) infra, the record of each case shall be forwarded to the Military Governor who shall have the power to mitigate, reduce or otherwise alter the sentence imposed by the tribunal, but may not increase the severity thereof.

b) In cases tried before tribunals authorized by Article II (c) the sentence shall be reviewed jointly by the zone commanders of the nations involved, who may mitigate, reduce or otherwise alter the sentence, by majority vote, but may not increase the severity thereof. If only two nations are represented, the sentence may be altered only by the consent of both zone commanders.

Article XVIII

No sentence of death shall be carried into execution unless and until confirmed in writing by the Military Governor. In accordance with Article III, Section 5 of Law No. 10, execution of the death sentence may be deferred by not to exceed one month after such confirmation if there is reason to believe that the testimony of the convicted person may be of value in the investigation and trial of other crimes.

Article XIX

Upon the pronouncement of a death sentence by a tribunal established thereunder and pending confirmation thereof, the condemned will be remanded to the prison or place where he was confined and there be segregated from the other inmates, or be transferred to a more appropriate place of confinement.

Article XX

Upon the confirmation of a sentence of death the Military Governor will issue the necessary orders for carrying out the execution.

Article XXI

Where sentence of confinement for a term of years has been imposed the condemned shall be confined in the manner directed by the tribunal imposing sentence. The place of confinement may be changed from time to time by the Military Governor.

Article XXII

Any property declared to be forfeited or the restitution of which is ordered by a tribunal shall be delivered to the Military Governor, for disposal in accordance with Control Council Law No. 10, Article II (3).

Article XXIII

Any of the duties and functions of the Military Governor provided for herein may be delegated to the Deputy Military Governor. Any of the duties and functions of the Zone Commander provided for herein may be exercised by and in the name of the Military Governor and may be delegated to the Deputy Military Governor.

This Ordinance becomes effective 18 October 1946.
BY ORDER OF MILITARY GOVERMENT

Uniform Rules of Procedure

Rule 1. Authority to Promulgate Rules

The present rules of procedure of the Military Tribunal constituted by General Order No. 68 of the Office of Military Government for Germany (US) (hereinafter called "Military Tribunal I" or "the Tribunal") are hereby promulgated by the Tribunal in accordance with the provisions of Article V (f) of Military Government Ordinance No. 7 issued pursuant to the powers conferred by Control Council Law No. 10.

Rule 2. Languages in Which Pleadings, Documents, and Rules Shall Be Transcribed

When any rule of procedure adopted by Military Tribunal I directs or requires that a defendant in any prosecution before the Tribunal shall be furnished with a copy of any pleading, document, rule, or other instrument in writing, such rule shall be understood to mean that such defendant shall receive a true and correct copy of such pleading, document, rule, or other instrument, written in the English language, and also a written translation thereof in a language which the defendant understands.

Rule 3. Notice to Defendants

(a) The Marshal of Military Tribunals, or his duly authorized deputy, shall make service of the indictment upon a defendant in any prosecution before the Tribunal by delivering to and leaving with him (1) a true and correct copy of the indictment and of all documents lodged with the indictment, (2) a copy of Military Government Ordinance No. 7, (3) a copy of Control Council Law No. 10, and (4) a copy of these Rules of Procedure.

(b) When such service has been made as aforesaid, the Marshal shall make a written certificate of such fact, showing the day and place of service, and shall file the same with the Secretary General of Military Tribunal.

(c) The certificate, when filed with the Secretary General, shall constitute a part of the record of the cause.

Rule 4. Time Intervening Between Service and Trial

A period of not less than 30 days shall intervene between the service of the indictment upon a defendant and the day of his trial pursuant to the indictment.

Rule 5. Notice of Amendments or Additions to Original Indictment

(a) If before the trial of any defendant the Chief of Counsel for War Crimes offers amendments or additions to the indictment, such amendments or additions, including any accompanying documents, shall be filed with the Secretary General of Military Tribunals and served upon such defendant in like manner as the original indictment.

Rule 6. Defendant to Receive Certain Additional Documents on Request.

(a) A defendant shall receive a copy of such Rules of Procedure or amendments thereto as may be adopted by the Tribunal from time to time.

(b) Upon written application by a defendant or his counsel lodged with the Secretary General for a copy of (1) the Charter of the International Military Tribunal annexed to the London Agreement of 8 August 1945, or (2) the judgment of the International Military Tribunal of 30 September and 1 October 1946, the same shall be furnished to such defendant, without delay.

Rule 7. Right to Representation by Counsel

(a) A defendant shall have the right to conduct his own defense or to be represented by counsel of his own selection, provided such counsel is a person qualified under existing regulations to conduct cases before the courts of defendant's country, or is specially authorized by the Tribunal.

(b) Application for particular counsel shall be filed with the Secretary General promptly after service of the indictment upon the defendant.

(c) The Tribunal will designate counsel for any defendant who fails to apply for particular counsel, unless the defendant elects in writing to conduct his own defense.

(d) Where particular counsel is requested by a defendant but is not available or cannot be found within 10 days after application therefor has been filed with the Secretary General, the Tribunal will designate counsel for such defendant, unless the defendant elects in writing to conduct his own defense. If thereafter, before trial, such particular counsel is found and is available, or if in the meanwhile a defendant selects a substitute counsel who is found to be available, such particular counsel, or substitute, may associated with or substituted for counsel designated by the Tribunal; provided that (1) only one counsel shall be permitted to appear at the trial for any defendant, except by special permission of the Tribunal, and (2) no delay will be allowed for making such substitution or association.

Rule 8. Order at the Trial

In conformity with and pursuant to the provisions of Articles IV and VI of Military Government Ordinance No. 7, the Tribunal will provide for maintenance of order at the trial.

Rule 9. Oath; Witnesses

(a) Before testifying before the Tribunal each witness shall take such oath or affirmation or make such declaration as is customary and lawful in his own country.

(b) When not testifying, the witnesses shall be excluded from the courtroom. During the course of any trial, witnesses shall not confer among themselves before or after testifying.

Rule 10. Applications and Motions, Before Trial

(a) All motions, applications, or other requests addressed to the Tribunal shall be made in writing and filed, together with a copy thereof, with the Secretary General of Military Tribunals, at the Palace of Justice, Nuernberg, Germany.

(b) When any motion, application, or other request has been filed, the Secretary General shall deliver a copy thereof to the adverse party and note the fact of delivery, specifying date and place, upon the original. The adverse party shall have 2 days after delivery within which to file with the Secretary General his objections to the granting of such motion, application, or other request. If no objection is filed within the time allowed, the presiding judge of the Tribunal will make the appropriate order on behalf of the Tribunal. If objections are filed the Tribunal will consider the objections and determine the questions raised.

(c) Delivery of a copy of any such motion, application, or other request to counsel of record for the adverse party, shall constitute delivery to such adverse party.

Rule 11. Rulings During the Trial

The Tribunal will rule upon all questions arising during the course of the trial. If such course is deemed expedient, the Tribunal will order the clearing or closing of the courtroom while considering such questions.

Rule 12. Production of Evidence for a Defendant

(a) A defendant may apply to the Tribunal for the production of witnesses, or of documents on his behalf, by filing his application therefor with the Secretary General of Military Tribunals. Such application shall state where the witness or document is thought to be located, together with a statement of the last known location thereof. Such application shall also state the general nature of the evidence sought to be adduced thereby, and the reason such evidence is deemed relevant to the defendant's case.

(b) The Secretary General shall promptly submit any such application to the Tribunal, and the Tribunal will determine whether or not the application shall be granted.

(c) If the application is granted by the Tribunal, the Secretary General shall promptly issue a summons for the attendance of such witness or the production of such documents, and inform the Tribunal of the action taken. Such summons shall be served in such manner as may be provided by the appropriate occupation authorities to ensure its enforcement, and the Secretary General shall inform the Tribunal of the steps taken.

(d) If the witness or the document is not within the area controlled by the United States Office of Military Government for Germany, the Tribunal will request through proper channels that the Allied Control Council arrange for the production of any such witness or document as the Tribunal may deem necessary to the proper presentation of the defense.

Rule 13. Records, Exhibits, and Documents

(a) An accurate stenographic record of all oral proceedings shall be maintained. Exhibits shall be suitably identified and marked as the Tribunal may direct. All exhibits and transcripts of the proceedings, and such other material as the Tribunal may direct, shall be filed with the Secretary General and shall constitute a part of the record of the cause.

(b) Documentary evidence or exhibits may be received in the language of the document, but a translation thereof into a language understood by the adverse party shall be furnished to such part:

(c) Upon proper request, and approval by the Tribunal, copies of all exhibits and transcripts of proceedings, and such other matter as the Tribunal may direct to be filed with the Secretary General, and all official acts and documents of the Tribunal, may be certified by said Secretary General to any government, to and other tribunal, or to any agency or person as to whom it is appropriate that copies of such documents or representations as to such acts be supplied.

Rule 14. Withdrawal of Exhibits and Documents, and Substitution of Photostatic Copies Therefor

If it be made to appear to the Tribunal by written application that one of the government signatories to the Four Power Agreement of 8 August 1945, or any other government having received the consent of the said four Signators Powers, desires to withdraw from the records of any cause, and preserve, any original document of file with the Tribunal, and that no substantial injury will result thereby, the Tribunal may order any such original document to be delivered to the applicant, and a photostatic copy thereof, certified by the Secretary General, to be substituted in the record therefor.

Rule 15. Effective Date and Powers of Amendment and Addition

These rules shall take effect upon their approval by the Tribunal. Nothing herein contained shall be construed to prevent the Tribunal at any time in the interest of fair and expeditious procedure, from departing from, amending, or adding to these rules, either by general rules or special orders for particular cases, in such form and on such notice as the Tribunal may prescribe.

Promulgated and adopted by Military Tribunal I, this 2d day of November, A.D. 1946, at the Palace of Justice, Nuernberg, Germany.

[Signed] WALTER B. BEALS, Presiding Judge
[Signed] HAROLD L. SEBRING, Judge
[Signed] JOHNSON T. CRAWFORD, Judge
[Signed] VICTOR C. SWEARINGEN, Alternate Judge
ATTEST: [Signed] CHARLES E. SANDS
Acting Secretary General for
Military Tribunals

Bibliography

BOOKS

Appleman, John Alan, *Military Tribunals and International Crimes* (Bobbs-Merrill Company, 1954)

Barton, Charles K.B., *Getting Even: Revenge as a Form of Justice* (Open Court, 1999)

Bassiouni, M. Cherif, *Crimes Against Humanity in International Criminal Law* (Springer, 2nd rev. edn, 1999)

—— *The Legislative History of the International Criminal Court: Introduction, Analysis, and Integrated Text* (Transnational Publishers, 2005)

Benvenisti, Eyal, *The International Law of Occupation* (Princeton University Press, 2004)

Bird, Kai, *The Chairman: John J. McCloy and the Making of the American Establishment* (Simon & Schuster, 1992)

Bloxham, Donald, *Genocide on Trial* (Oxford University Press, 2001)

Boister, Neil & Cryer, Robert, *The Tokyo International Military Tribunal: A Reappraisal* (Oxford University Press, 2008)

Bower, Tom, *Blind Eye to Murder* (William Collins & Sons Co., 1981)

Buscher, Frank M., *The U.S. War Crimes Trial Program in Germany, 1946–1955* (Greenwood Press, 1989)

Cryer, Robert, et al., *An Introduction to International Criminal Law and Procedure* (Cambridge University Press, 2nd edn, 2010)

Dinstein, Yoram, *War, Aggression, and Self-defense* (Cambridge University Press, 2001)

Drumbl, Mark A., *Atrocity, Punishment, and International Law* (Cambridge University Press, 2007)

Dubois, Josiah, *The Devil's Chemists: 24 Conspirators of the International Farben Cartel Who Manufacture Wars* (Beacon Press, 1952)

—— *Generals in Grey Suits* (Bodley Head, 1953)

Earl, Hilary, *The Nuremberg SS-Einsatzgruppen Trial, 1945–1958* (Cambridge University Press, 2010)

Frei, Norbert, *Adenauer's Germany and the Nazi Past* (Columbia University Press, Joel Golb trans., 2002)

Freyhofer, Horst H., *The Nuremberg Medical Trial: The Holocaust and the Origin of the Nuremberg Medical Code* (Peter Lang, 2004)

Gross, Leo, *Selected Essays on International Law and Organization* (Transnational Publishers, 1993)

Haensel, Carl, *Das Organisationsverbrechen: Nürnberger Betrachtungen zum Kontrollratsgesetz nr. 10* (Biederstein Verlag, 1947)

Hagan, John, *Justice in the Balkans* (University of Chicago Press, 2003)

Hébert, Valerie, *Hitler's Generals on Trial* (University Press of Kansas, 2010)

Jeffreys, Diarmuid, *Hell's Cartel: IG Farben and the Making of Hitler's War Machine* (Metropolitan Books, 2008)

Jescheck, Hans-Heinrich, *Die Verantwortlichkeit der Staatsorgane nach Völkerstrafrecht* (Röhrscheid, 1952)

Lael, Richard L., *The Yamashita Precedent: War Crimes and Command Responsibility* (Senior Books, 1982)

Maguire, Peter, *Law and War: An American Story* (Columbia University Press, 2001)

Mendelsohn, John, *Trial by Document: The Use of Seized Records in the United States Proceedings at Nurnberg* (Garland Publishing, 1988)

Merritt, Anna J. & Merritt, Richard L., *Public Opinion in Occupied Germany: The OMGUS Surveys, 1945–49* (University of Illinois Press, 1980)

Persico, Joseph E., *Nuremberg: Infamy on Trial* (Penguin, 2000)

Pictet, Jean S., *Commentary on the Geneva Convention Relative to the Protection of Civilian Persons in Time of War* (International Committee of the Red Cross, 1958)

——*Commentary on the Geneva Convention Relative to the Protection of Prisoners of War* (International Committee of the Red Cross, 1960)

Salter, Michael, *Nazi War Crimes, U.S. Intelligence and Selective Prosecution at Nuremberg* (Cavendish, 2007)

Sandoz, Yves, et al., *Commentary on the Additional Protocols* (International Committee of the Red Cross, 1987)

Schabas, William, *The International Criminal Court: A Commentary on the Rome Statute* (Oxford University Press, 2010)

Schwartz, Thomas Alan, *America's Germany: John J. McCloy and the Federal Republic of Germany* (Harvard University Press, 1991)

Sellars, Kirsten, *The Rise and Rise of Human Rights* (Sutton Publishing, 2002)

Silverglate, Jesse Joseph, *The Role of the Conspiracy Doctrine in the Nuremberg War Crimes Trials* (University Microfilm Library Services, 1969)

Solis, Gary D., *The Law of Armed Conflict* (Cambridge University Press, 2010)

Stave, Bruce M., et al., *Witnesses to Nuremberg: An Oral History of American Participants at the War Crimes Trials* (Prentice-Hall International, 1998)

Szanajda, Andrew, *The Restoration of Justice in Postwar Hesse, 1945–1949* (Lexington Books, 2007)

Taylor, Telford, *The Anatomy of the Nuremberg Trials: A Personal Memoir* (Little, Brown & Co., 1992)

——*Final Report to the Secretary of the Army on the Nuernberg War Crimes Trials Under Control Council Law No. 10* (William S. Hein & Co., 1949)

Turley, Mark, *From Nuremberg to Nineveh* (Vandal Publications, 2008)

United Nations War Crimes Commission, *History of the United Nations War Crimes Commission and the Development of the Laws of War* (William S. Hein & Co., 1948)

Von Knieriem, August, *The Nuremberg Trials* (Regnery, 1959)

Weingartner, James J., *Crossroads of Death: The Story of the Malmedy Massacre and Trial* (University of California Press, 1979)

Wilkins, William John, *The Sword and the Gavel* (The Writing Works, 1981)

Woetzel, Robert K., *The Nuremberg Trials in International Law* (Stevens & Sons, Ltd., 1962)

ARTICLES

Albrecht, A.R., "War Reprisals in the War Crimes Trials and in the Geneva Conventions of 1949," 47 *Am. J. Int'l L.* 590 (1953)

April, Nathan, "An Inquiry into the Juridical Basis for the Nuernberg War Crimes Trial," 30 *Minn. L. Rev.* 311 (1945–46)

Amann, Diane Marie, "Portraits of Women at Nuremberg," in *Proceedings of the Third Int'l Humanitarian L. Dialogs* 31 (Elizabeth Andersen & David M. Crane eds, 2010)

Arens, Richard, "Nuremberg and Group Prosecution," 1951 *Wash. U. L. Q.* 329

Askin, Kelly D., "Prosecuting Wartime Rape and Other Gender-Related Crimes Under International Law: Extraordinary Advances, Enduring Obstacles," 21 *Berkeley J. Int'l L.* 288 (2003)

Barrett, John Q., "Henry T. King, Jr., at Case, and on the Nuremberg Case," 60 *Case W. Res. L. Rev.* 1 (2010)

Bass, Gary Jonathan, "War Crimes and the Limits of Legalism," 97 *Mich. L. Rev.* 2103 (1999)

Baxter, Richard R., "So-Called "Unprivileged Belligerency: Spies, Guerillas, and Saboteurs," 28 *Brit. Y.B. Int'l L.* 323 (1951)

Bendersky, Joseph W., "The Expendable Kronjurist: Carl Schmitt and National Socialism, 1933–1936," 14 *J. Contemp. Hist.* 309 (1979)

——"Carl Schmitt's Path to Nuremberg: A Sixty-Year Reassessment," 139 *Telos* 6 (2007)

Bing Bing, Jia, "The Doctrine of Command Responsibility Revisited," 3 *Chinese J. Int'l L.* 1 (2004)

Bohlander, Michael, "International Criminal Tribunals and Their Power to Punish Contempt and False Testimony," 12 *Crim. L. Forum* 91 (2001)

Brand, G., "The War Crimes Trials and the Laws of War," 26 *Brit. Y.B. Int'l L.* 414 (1949)

Bush, Jonathan A., "The Prehistory of Corporations and Conspiracy in International Criminal Law: What Nuremberg Really Said," 109 *Colum. L. Rev.* 1094 (2009)

——"Soldiers Find Wars: A Life of Telford Taylor," 37 *Colum. J. Transnat'l L.* 675 (1999)

Carnegie, A.R., "Jurisdiction Over Violations of the Laws and Customs of War," 39 *Brit. Y.B. Int'l L.* 402 (1963)

Carter, Edward F., "The Nurnberg Trials: A Turning Point in the Enforcement of International Law," 28 *Neb. L. Rev.* 370 (1949)

Clark, Roger S., "Crimes Against Humanity," in *The Nuremberg Trial and International Law* 177 (Kluwer Academic Publishers, G. Ginsburgs & V. N. Kudriavtsev eds., 1990)

Clapham, Andrew, "The Question of Juridsdiction Under International Criminal Law Over Legal Persons," in *Liability of Multinational Corporations under International Law* 139 (Kluwer Academic Publishers, Menno T. Kamminga & Saman Zia-Zarifi eds, 2000)

Cogan, Jacob Katz, "International Criminal Courts and Fair Trials: Difficulties and Prospects," 27 *Yale J. Int'l L.* 111 (2002)

Colby, Elbridge, "Occupation Under the Laws of War," 25 *Colum. L. Rev.* 904 (1925)

——"War Crimes," 23 *Mich. L. Rev.* 482 (1924–25)

Cowles, Willard B., "Trials of War Criminals (Non-Nuremberg)," 42 *Am. J. Int'l L.* 299 (1948)

——"Universality of Jurisdiction Over War Crimes," 33 *Cal. L. Rev.* 177 (1945)

Cryer, Robert, "General Principles of Liability in International Criminal Law," in *The Permanent International Criminal Court: Legal and Policy Issues* 242 (Oxford University Press, McGoldrick et al. eds, 2004)

Damaška, Mirjan, "Free Proof and Its Detractors," 43 *Am. J. Comp. L.* 343 (1995)

Danner, Allison M., "Constructing a Hierarchy of Crimes in International Criminal Law Sentencing," 87 *Va. L. Rev.* 415 (2001)

——"The Nuremberg Industrialist Prosecutions and Aggressive War," 46 *Va. J. Int'l L.* 651 (2006)

Dautricort, Joseph Y., "Crimes Against Humanity: European Views on Its Conception and Future," 40 *J. Crim. L. & Criminology* 170 (1949–50)

Dillon, J.V., "The Genesis of the 1949 Convention Relative to the Treatment of Prisoners of War," 5 *Miami L.Q.* 40 (1950–51)

Doman, Nicholas R., "The Nuremberg Trials Revisited," 47 *A.B.A. J.* 261 (1961)

Dörmann, Knut, "Preparatory Commission for the International Criminal Court: The Elements of War Crimes," 82 *Int'l Rev. Red Cross* 461 (2001)

Douglas, Lawrence, "History and Memory in the Courtroom: Reflections on Perpetrator Trials," in *The Nuremberg Trials: International Criminal Law Since 1945*, 96 (K.G. Sauer Verlag, Herbert R. Reginbogin & Cristoph J. Safferling eds, 2006)

Douglass, John J., "*High Command* Case: A Study in Staff and Command Responsibility," 6 *Int'l Lawyer* 686 (1972)

Downey, William Gerald, Jr., "The Law of War and Military Necessity," 47 *Am. J. Int'l L.* 251 (1953)

Freeman, Alwyn V., "War Crimes by Enemy Nationals Administering Justice in Occupied Territory," 41 *Am. J. Int'l L.* 579 (1947)

Fried, John H.E., "Transfer of Civilian Manpower From Occupied Territory," 40 *Am. J. Int'l L.* 303 (1946)

Friedmann, W., "The Legal and Constitutional Position of Germany Under Allied Military Government," 3 *Res Judicatae* 133 (1947)

Glaser, Stefan, "The Charter of the Nuremberg Tribunal and New Principles of International Law," in *Perspectives on the Nuremberg Trial* 55 (Oxford University Press, Guénaël Mettraux ed., 2008)

Glueck, Sheldon, "By What Tribunal Shall War Offenders Be Tried?," 56 *Harv. L. Rev.* 1059 (1943)

Goetz, Cecelia, "Impressions of Telford Taylor at Nuremberg," 37 *Colum. J. Transnat'l L.* 669 (1999)

Gross, Leo, "The Criminality of Aggressive War," 41 *Am. Pol. Sci. Rev.* 205 (1947)

Hale, Winfield B., "Nurenberg War Crimes Tribunals," 21 *Tenn. L. Rev.* 8 (1949–51)

Harvard Research, "Jurisdiction with Respect to Crime," 29 *Am. J. Int'l L. Supp.* 439 (1935)

Hebert, Paul M., "The Nurnberg Subsequent Trials," 16 *Ins. Counsel J.* 226 (1949)

Heller, Kevin Jon, "Retreat from Nuremberg: The Leadership Requirement in the Crime of Aggression," 18 *Eur. J. Int'l L.* 477 (2007)

——"Situational Gravity Under the Rome Statute," in *Future Perspectives on International Criminal Justice* 227 (T.M.C Asser Press, Carsten Stahn & Larissa van den Herik eds, 2010)

Jessberger, Florian & Geneuss, Julian, "On the Application of a Theory of Indirect Perpetration in *Al Bashir*: German Doctrine at the Hague?," 6 *J. Int'l Crim. Just.* 853 (2008)

Jochnick, Chris & Normand, Roger, "The Legitimation of Violence: A Critical History of the Laws of War," 35 *Harv. Int'l L. J.* 49 (1994)

Kelsen, Hans, "The Legal Status of Germany According to the Declaration of Berlin," 39 *Am. J. Int'l L.* 518 (1945)

——"Will the Judgment in the Nuremberg Trial Constitute a Precedent in International Law?," in *Perspectives on the Nuremberg Trial* 274 (Oxford University Press, Guénaël Mettraux ed., 2008)

Kopelmans, L., "The Problem of Aggression and the Prevention of War," 31 *Am. J. Int'l L.* 244 (1937)

Kranzbuehler, Otto, "Nuremberg Eighteen Years Afterwards," 14 *Depaul L. Rev.* 333 (1964–65)

Kress, Claus, "*Erdemović*," in *Oxford Companion to International Criminal Justice* 661 (Oxford University Press, Antonio Cassese ed., 2009)

Kunz, Josef L., "The Laws of War," 50 *Am. J. Int'l L.* 313 (1956)

Laternser, Hans, "Looking Back at the Nuremberg Trials with Special Consideration of the Processes Against Military Leaders," in *Perspectives on the Nuremberg Trial* 473 (Oxford University Press, Guénaël Mettraux ed., 2008)

Lauterpacht, Hersh, "The Law of Nations and the Punishment of War Crimes," 21 *Brit. Y.B. Int'l L.* 58 (1944)

——"The Problem of the Revision of the Law of War," 29 *Brit. Y.B. Int'l L.* 360 (1952)

——"The Limits of the Operation of the Law of War," 30 *Brit. Y.B. Int'l L.* 206 (1953)

Lawrence, Jessica C. & Heller, Kevin Jon, "The First Ecocentric Environmental War Crime: The Limits of Article 8(2)(b)(iv) of the Rome Statute," 20 *Geo. Int'l Env. L. Rev.* 61 (2007)

Lippman, Matthew, "The Other Nuremberg: American Prosecutions of Nazi War Criminals in Occupied Germany," 3 *Ind. Int'l & Comp. L. Rev.* 1 (1992)

Llewellyn, Karl N., "Remarks on the Theory of Appellate Decision and the Rules or Canons About How Statutes are to be Construed," 3 *Vand. L. Rev.* 395 (1950)

Lozier, Marion E., "Nuremberg: A Reappraisal," 1 & 2 *Colum J. Transnat'l L.* 64 (1961–63)

Marrus, Michael R., "The Nuremberg Doctors' Trial in Historical Context," 73 *Bull. Hist. Med.* 106 (1999)

Morgenstern, Felice, "Validity of the Acts of the Belligerent Occupant," 28 *Brit. Y.B. Int'l L.* 291 (1951)

Morris, James, "Major War Crimes Trials in Nurnberg," 25 *N.D. B. Br.* 97 (1949)

Murphy, Peter, "No Free Lunch, No Free Proof," 8 *J. Int'l Crim. Just.* 539 (2010)

Musmanno, Michael A., "Are Subordinate Officials Penally Responsible for Obeying Superior Orders Which Direct the Commission of a Crime?," 67 *Dick. L. Rev.* 221 (1962–63)

Nurick, Lester, "The Distinction Between Combatant and Noncombatant in the Law of War," 39 *Am. J. Int'l L.* 680 (1945)

Nurick, Lester & Barrett, Roger W., "Legality of Guerrilla Forces Under the Laws of War," 40 *Am. J. Int'l L.* 563 (1946)

Ohlin, Jens D., "The Co-Perpetrator Model of Joint Criminal Enterprise," 14 *Annotated Leading Cases of the Int'l Crim. Tribs.* 739 (2008)

Perlman, Philip B., "The Genocide Convention," 30 *Neb. L. Rev.* 1 (1950–51)

Philips, C.P., "Air Warfare and Law: An Analysis of the Legal Doctrines, Practices and Policies," 21 *Geo. Wash. L. Rev.* 311 (1953)

Ramasastry, Anita, "Corporate Complicity: From Nuremberg to Rangoon," 20 *Berkeley J. Int'l L.* 91 (2002)

Rheinstein, Max, "The Legal Status of Occupied Germany," 47 *Mich. L. Rev.* 23 (1948)

Roberts, Adam, "Land Warfare: From Hague to Nuremberg," in *The Laws of War* 116 (Yale University Press, Michael Howard et al. eds, 1994)

Robinson, Darryl, "The Identity Crisis of International Criminal Law," 21 *Leiden J. Int'l L.* 925 (2008)

Rogers, A.P.V., "War Crimes Trials Under the Royal Warrant: British Practice 1945–49," 39 *I.C.L.Q.* 780 (1990)

Sack, Alexander N., "War Criminals and the Defense of Act of State In International Law," 5 *Law. Guild Rev.* 288 (1945)

Schabas, William A., "Sentencing by International Tribunals: A Human Rights Approach," 7 *Duke J. of Comp. & Int'l L.* 461 (1997)

——"State Policy as an Element of International Crimes," 98 *J. Crim. L. & Criminology* 953 (2008)

Schick, F.B., "Crimes Against Peace," 38 *J. Crim. L. & Criminology* 445 (1947–48)

——"The Nuremberg Trial and the International Law of the Future," 41 *Am. J. Int'l L.* 770 (1947)

——"International Criminal Law—Facts and Illusions," 11 *Mod. L. Rev.* 290 (1948)

Schmidt, Ulf, "'The Scars of Ravensbrück': Medical Experiments and British War Crimes Policy, 1945–1950," 23 *German Hist.* 20 (2005)

Schwartz, Thomas Alan, "John J. McCloy and the Landsberg Cases," in *American Policy and the Reconstruction of West Germany* 433 (German Historical Institute, Hartmut Lehmann ed., 1993)

Schwarzenberger, Georg, "The Judgment of Nuremberg," in *Perspectives on the Nuremberg Trial* 473 (Oxford University Press, Guénaël Mettraux ed., 2008)

Spicka, Mark E., "The Devil's Chemists on Trial," 61 *The Historian* 865 (1999)

Sprecher, Drexel A., "The Central Role of Telford Taylor as U.S. Chief of Counsel in The Subsequent Proceedings," 37 *Colum. J. Transnat'L L.* 673 (1999)

Taylor, Telford, "Arms and the Germans," *Harper's* 23 (Mar. 1950)

——"The Nazis Go Free," *The Nation* 170 (24 Feb. 1951)

——"The Krupp Trial: Fact v. Fiction," 53 *Colum. L. Rev.* 197 (1953)

——"The Nuremberg Trials," in *Perspectives on the Nuremberg Trial* 372 (Oxford University Press, Guénaël Mettraux ed., 2008)

Von Laun, Kurt, "The Legal Status of Germany," 45 *Am. J. Int'l L.* 267 (1951)

Wagner, Wienczyslaw J., "Conspiracy in Civil Law Countries," 42 *J. Crim. L. Criminology & Police Sci.* 171 (1951)

Weindling, Paul, "From International to Zonal Trials: The Origins of the Nuremberg Medical Trial," 14 *Holocaust & Genocide Studies* 367 (2000)

Wolfe, Robert, "Flaws in the Nuremberg Legacy: An Impediment to International War Crimes Tribunal's Prosecution of Crimes Against Humanity," 12 *Holocaust & Genocide Studies* 434 (1998)

Wright, Lord, "The Killing of Hostages as a War Crime," 25 *Brit. Y.B. Int'l L.* 296 (1948)

Wright Quincy, "The Concept of Aggression in International Law," 29 *Am. J. Int'l L.* 373 (1935)

——"The Outlawry of War," 19 *Am. J. Int'l L.* 76 (1925)

——"The Outlawry of War and the Law of War," 47 *Am. J. Int'l L.* 365 (1953)

——"The Prevention of Aggression," 50 *Am. J. Int'l L.* 514 (1956)

——"The Law of the Nuremberg Trial," in *Perspectives on the Nuremberg Trial* 320 (Guénaël Mettraux ed., 2008)

Yee, Sienho, "The Tu Quoque Argument as a Defence to International Crimes, Prosecution or Punishment," 3 *Chinese J. Int'l L.* 87 (2004)

Zeck, William Allen, "Nuremberg: Proceedings Subsequent to Goering et al.," 26 *N.C. L. Rev.* 350 (1948)

Zuppi, Alberto L., "Slave Labor in Nuremberg's I.G. Farben Case: The Lonely Voice of Paul M. Hebert," 66 *La. L. Rev.* 495 (2006)

Index